COMPREHENSIVE

Computer Confluence
exploring tomorrow's technology

COMPREHENSIVE

Computer Confluence

exploring tomorrow's technology

SIXTH EDITION

George Beekman

OREGON STATE UNIVERSITY

PEARSON

Prentice
Hall

Upper Saddle River, New Jersey 07458

Computer Confluence, **Sixth Edition**
Comprehensive edition / George Beekman

Publisher and Vice President: Natalie E. Anderson
Executive Acquisitions Editor: Jodi McPherson
Senior Sponsoring Editor: Maureen Allaire Spada
Senior Project Manager, Editorial: Mike Ruel
Assistant Editor: Melissa Edwards
Editorial Assistants: Jodi Bolognese, Alana Myers and Jasmine Slowik
Senior Media Project Manager: Cathi Profitko
Manager, Production: Gail Steier de Acevedo
Project Manager, Production: Lynne Breitfeller
Marketing Manager: Emily Knight
Associate Director, Manufacturing: Vincent Scelta
Manufacturing Buyer: Lynne Breitfeller
Manager Print Production: Christy Mahon
Design Manager: Maria Lange
Art Director: Kevin Kall
Cover Design: George Beekman and Kevin Kall
Back Cover Photo: Scobel Wiggins
Interior Design: Kevin Kall
Composition: Pre-Press Company, Inc.
Photo Research: Abby Reip and Pre-Press Company, Inc
Printer/Binder: Von Hoffmann
Cover Printer: Phoenix Color

10 9 8 7 6 5 4 3 2 1
ISBN 0-13-143567-1

To

Dr. Jack Dymond (1939-2003)

Friend, neighbor, mentor, and visionary.

You envisioned a future world where decisions are made based on long-term sustainability rather than short-term greed, and you worked to turn that vision into a reality.

—G.B.

Brief Contents

Contents

PART 1   Approaching Computers
Hardware and Software Fundamentals

Chapter 2   Hardware Basics: Inside the Box   62

Chapter 3   Hardware Basics: Peripherals   88

Chapter 4   Software Basics: The Ghost in the Machine   124

PART 2   Using Software
Essential Applications

Chapter 5   Basic Office Applications   156

Chapter 6   Graphics, Digital Media, and Multimedia   200

Chapter 7   Database Applications and Implications   236

PART 3   Exploring with Computers:
Networking and the Internet

Chapter 8   Networking and Telecommunication   272

Chapter 9   Inside the Internet and the World Wide Web   306

PART 4   Living with Computers:
Issues and Implications

Chapter 10   Computer Security and Risks   346

Chapter 11   Computers at Work, School, and Home   384

Part 5 Managing Computers
Information Systems at Work

Part 6   Mastering Computers
From Algorithms to Intelligence

Chapter 14   Systems Design and Development   490

Chapter 15   Is Artificial Intelligence Real?   530

About this Book

Confluence

1: a **coming or flowing together**, meeting, or gathering at one point (a happy confluence of weather and scenery);

2a: the flowing together of **two or more streams**;

b: the **place of meeting** of two streams;

c: the **combined stream** formed by conjunction

—Merriam Webster's Collegiate Dictionary, Electronic Edition

When powerful forces come together, change is inevitable. Today we're standing at the confluence of three powerful technological forces: computers, telecommunications, and electronic entertainment. The computer's digital technology is showing up in everything from telephones to televisions, and the lines that separate these machines are eroding. This digital convergence is rapidly—and radically—altering the world's economic landscape. Start-up companies and industries are emerging to ride the waves of change. Some thrive; others dive into oblivion. Meanwhile, older organizations reorganize, regroup, and redefine themselves to keep from being washed away.

Smaller computers, faster processors, smarter software, larger networks, new communication media—in the world of information technology, it seems like change is the only constant. In less than a human lifetime, this technological cascade has transformed virtually every facet of our society—and the transformation is just beginning. As old technologies merge and new technologies emerge, far-fetched predictions routinely come true. This headlong rush into the high-tech future poses a challenge for all of us: How can we extract the knowledge we need from the deluge of information? What must we understand about information technology to successfully navigate the waters of change that carry us into the future? *Computer Confluence: Exploring Tomorrow's Technology* is designed to aid travelers on their journey into that future.

What Is Computer Confluence?

Computer Confluence presents computers and information technology on three levels:

- Explanations: *Computer Confluence* clearly explains what a computer is and what it can (and can't) do; it clearly explains the basics of information technology, from multimedia PCs to the Internet and beyond.
- Applications: *Computer Confluence* illustrates how computers and networks are—and will be—used as practical tools to solve a wide variety of problems.
- Implications: *Computer Confluence* puts computers in a human context, illustrating how information technology affects our lives, our world, and our future.

The sixth edition of *Computer Confluence* has been reorganized to reflect changes in the technology, changes in the way instructors teach about the technology, and feedback from readers and reviewers.

The book consists of book consists of 16 chapters numbered 0–15 in the grand tradition of computer science. Chapter 0, "Basics," new to this edition, provides an introduction for

students who have little or no experience with PCs and the Internet. The chapter also includes an orientation to the *Computer Confluence* book, CD-ROM, and Web site.

The remaining chapters are organized into six broad sections:

1. Approaching Computers: Hardware and Software Fundamentals
2. Using Computers: Essential Applications
3. Exploring with Computers: Networks and Gateways
4. Living with Computers: Issues and Implications
5. Managing Computers: Information Systems at Work
6. Mastering Computers: From Algorithms to Intelligence

In general, the book's focus flows from the concrete to the controversial and from the present to the future. Individual chapters have a similarly expanding focus. After a brief introduction, each chapter flows from basic concepts toward abstract, future-oriented questions and ideas.

About the Author

George Beekman is an Honorary Instructor in the School of Electrical Engineering and Computer Science at Oregon State University. For more than two decades he designed and taught courses in computer literacy, interactive multimedia, computer ethics, and computer programming at OSU. An innovative computer literacy course he created more than a decade ago served as the inspiration for *Computer Confluence*. George Beekman has taught workshops in computer literacy and multimedia for students, educators, and economically disadvantaged families from the Atlantic to Alaska. He has written more than 20 books on computers, information technology, and multimedia, as well as more than 100 articles and reviews for *Macworld* and other popular publications. In his spare time he runs with his dog in the woods and plays music with his band, Oyaya.

About this Edition

Even if you're **on the right track**, you'll get **run over** if you **just sit** on it.
—Pat Koppman

The pace of change threatens to make even the most successful introductory computer classes irrelevant. *Computer Confluence*, Sixth Edition, helps students and instructors deal with rapid changes by emphasizing big ideas, broad trends, and the human aspects of technology—critical concepts that tend to remain constant even while hardware and software change. Every edition of *Computer Confluence* is rewritten to reflect changes in the technological landscape. This edition is, in the jargon of the computer industry, a major upgrade. In response to massive reviews and feedback from readers and reviewers, the book has been significantly reorganized to better meet the needs of students and instructors. There are new features, new artwork, and a new design. The CD-ROM has been completely redesigned, too, and packed with new material to enhance and expand on material presented in the book.

The User's View boxes of previous editions have been replaced by streamlined Screen Tests—three-screen sequences that test-drive software applications, offering students glimpses of programs they might not otherwise experience. The Inventing the Future chapter has been eliminated in favor of Inventing the Future boxes that provide futuristic perspectives at the ends of most chapters. Throughout the book there's less coverage of familiar applications and more emphasis on emerging technologies and the ethical and social impact of those technologies.

WinInfo's Paul Thurrott, expert on all things Microsoft, worked with us on this edition, providing an industry insider's insights into important software and hardware trends. He also provided many of the Screen Tests and made other contributions throughout the book.

Here's a chapter-by-chapter list of highlights new to this edition:

Chapter 0, "Basics," addresses the most commonly reported problem of introductory computer concepts classes—the diverse backgrounds of students in those classes. Many instructors report that the majority of their new students have some PC and Internet experience. These students don't need to be told about keyboarding, using a CD-ROM, or navigating a Web site. But if these topics aren't covered, the inexperienced students are at a distinct disadvantage. The Basics Chapter, revised and expanded in this edition, is designed for those beginners, so they can fill in the gaps in their knowledge before launching into the rest of the book, the CD-ROM, and the Web site. In response to reviewer suggestions, we added coverage on file management and Internet security. The chapter also includes an orientation to all three components of *Computer Confluence* that includes time-saving tips for everyone.

Chapter 1, "Computer Currents: From Calculation to Connection," now includes an important introduction to the Information Age that previously appeared much later in the book. The chapter provides a necessary perspective for understanding the future by emphasizing broad trends rather than historical details. The Inventing the Future box that closes the chapter provides an overview of strategies for predicting the future—strategies that are applied in later chapters.

Chapter 2, "Hardware Basics: Inside the Box," and Chapter 3, "Hardware Basics: Peripherals," have been updated with coverage of state-of-the-market hardware. The popular "Green Computing" Rules of Thumb box has been relocated in Chapter 2.

Chapter 3 now includes "Computer Consumer Concepts," a Rules of Thumb box that illuminates the concepts behind PC buyers' guides. Both Chapter 2 and Chapter 3 end with Inventing the Future boxes that describe emerging and experimental hardware technologies.

Chapter 4, "Software Basics: The Ghost in the Machine," has been updated and streamlined. Chapter 4 includes examples and explanations of Linux, UNIX, and other operating systems to provide a broader perspective for students familiar with PCs. The chapter also includes a new section on file management.

Chapter 5 In response to users' requests, "Basic Office Applications" combines two chapters from the previous edition. The chapter offers a brief overview of software tools used for writing, publishing, calculating, and simulating, from Microsoft Office to powerful professional modeling tools.

Chapter 6, "Graphics, Digital Media, and Multimedia," includes new desktop video material, with updated coverage of nonlinear video editing and desktop DVD authoring. There's also a revised and expanded section on emerging sound and music applications. A new Rules of Thumb box provides helpful tips for working with digital music files. An Inventing the Future box describes cutting-edge work in virtual reality and telepresence.

Chapter 7, "Database Applications and Implications," includes an Inventing the Future box on ubiquitous computing.

Chapter 8, "Networking and Telecommunication," has been completely reorganized, streamlined, and updated to present a clear, concise introduction to networking technology today and tomorrow. This chapter and the next include detailed coverage of Wi-Fi (802.11), the networking phenomenon that's revolutionizing the way people connect to networks.

Chapter 9, "Inside the Internet and the World Wide Web," combines two chapters from the previous edition. This chapter looks "under the hood" of the Internet with clear explanations of basic Internet technology, including protocols, addresses, connections, and the rapidly changing world of Web technology. It also deals with important questions about the future of the Net.

Chapter 10, "Computer Security and Risks," has been updated with the latest data on computer crime and security, from software piracy and viruses to sabotage and beyond. The Chapter now winds down with "Human Questions for a Computer Age," a thought-provoking section that puts the computer revolution in perspective. The Inventing the Future box takes a hard look at microtechnology and nanotechnology—technologies that will force us to confront many of the questions raised in the previous section.

Chapter 11, "Computers at Work, School, and Home." This chapter combines two chapters from the previous edition, streamlining the material so it's easy to cover it in a typical class. The chapter looks at the social, rather than technological, impact of information technology on our personal lives.

Chapters 12 and **13** are condensed from three chapters in the previous IT edition. These chapters are written specifically for students and faculty who want more of a business orientation.

Chapters 14 and **15** cover programming, systems design, the nature of computer science, and the fascinating branch of computer science known as artificial intelligence. The AI chapter provides a thought-provoking conclusion to this book about tomorrow's technology and its impact on our future.

Crosscurrents articles that close each chapter are, with a few exceptions, new to this edition. They include some of the best short essays on our relationship to technology that have been published in the past year. Topics include the erosion of personal privacy, the abuse of intellectual property laws, software reliability, and machine intelligence.

For the Student

If you're like most students, you aren't taking this course to read about computers—you want to use them. That's sensible. You can't really understand computers without some hands-on experience, and you'll be able to apply your computer skills to a wide variety of future projects. But it's a mistake to think that you're computer savvy just because you can use a PC to write term papers and surf the Internet. It's important to understand how people use and abuse computer technology, because that technology has a powerful and growing impact on your life. (If you can't imagine how your life would be different without computers, read the vignette called "Living without Computers" in Chapter 1.)

Even if you have lots of computer experience, future trends are almost certain to make much of that experience obsolete—probably sooner than you think. In the next few years, computers are likely to take on entirely new forms and roles because of breakthroughs in artificial intelligence, voice recognition, virtual reality, interactive multimedia, networking, and cross-breeding with telephone and home entertainment technologies. If your knowledge of computers stops with a handful of PC and Internet applications, you may be standing still while the world changes around you.

When you're cascading through white water, you need to be able to use a paddle, but it's also important to know how to read a map, a compass, and the river. *Computer Confluence: Exploring Tomorrow's Technology* is designed to serve as a map, compass, and book of river lore to help you ride the information waves into the future.

Computer Confluence will help you understand the important trends that will change the way you work with computers and the way computers work for you. This book discusses the promise and the problems of computer technology without overwhelming you with technobabble.

Computer Confluence is intentionally nontechnical and down to earth. Occasional ministories bring concepts and speculations to life. Illustrations and photos make abstract concepts concrete. Quotes add thought-provoking and humorous seasoning.

Whether you're a hard-core hacker or a confirmed computerphobe, there's something for you in *Computer Confluence*. Dive in!

Student CD-ROM

For the first time, this edition includes links to TechTV videos on the CD-ROM and the Web. These fascinating videos are carefully selected from the wealth of material aired on the TechTV channel.

The CD-ROM has been completely revised and updated, with a more powerful engine, a streamlined user interface, and a wealth of new multimedia material, from provocative TechTV video clips to interactive tutorials and tests. The material on the CD is clearly keyed to corresponding sections in the book. The Web site (**www.computerconfluence.com**) is continually updated to reflect changes in the Web and the subject matter.

Companion Web Site
www.computerconfluence.com

This text is accompanied by a Companion Web site at **www.computerconfluence.com**. This redesigned site brings you and your students a richer, more interactive Web experience than ever before. Features of this new site include an interactive study guide, downloadable supplements, online end-of-chapter materials, additional Internet exercises, Tech TV videos, Web resource links such as Careers in IT, and crossword puzzles, plus Technology Updates and Bonus Chapters on the latest trends and hottest topics in information technology. All links to Web exercises will be constantly updated to ensure accuracy for students.

For the Instructor

Computer Confluence is designed to help you to provide students with the background they need to survive and prosper in a world transformed by information technology. The new edition comes in two forms, the Introductory Edition and the Comprehensive Edition. The Introductory Edition covers all of the essentials in eleven chapters. It is similar to the previous Concise Edition, but with more thorough coverage of critical topics. The Comprehensive Edition includes five additional chapters for classes where additional coverage is important. It incorporates material from the previous Standard and IT editions into one volume that's well suited for courses in business, CIS, CS, and other subjects.

Both books include a variety of supplements and ancillary materials designed to help you enhance your students' learning experience.

OneKey

OneKey lets you in to the best teaching and learning resources all in one place. OneKey for *Computer Confluence* is all your students need for anywhere–anytime access to your course materials, conveniently organized by textbook chapter to reinforce and apply what they've learned in class. OneKey is all you need to plan and administer your course. All your instructor resources are in one place to maximize your effectiveness and minimize your time and effort. OneKey for convenience, simplicity, and success . . . for you and your students.

Instructor's Resource CD-ROM

The new and improved Prentice Hall Instructor's Resource CD-ROM includes the tools you expect from a Prentice Hall Computer Concepts text like:

- The Instructor's Manual in Word and PDF formats
- Test Bank with TestGen & QuizMaster Software
- Solutions to all questions and exercises from the book and Web site
- Multiple, customizable PowerPoint Slide Presentations for each chapter
- Tech TV Videos
- Image Library of all of the figures from the text

This CD-ROM is an interactive library of assets and links. This CD writes custom "index" pages that can be used as the foundation of a class presentation or online lecture. By navigating through this CD, you can collect the materials that are most relevant to your interests, edit them to create powerful class lectures, copy them to your own computer's hard drive, and/or upload them to an online course management system.

Companion Web Site
www.computerconfluence.com

This text is accompanied by a Companion Web site at **www.computerconfluence.com**. This redesigned site brings you and your students a richer, more interactive Web experience than ever before. Features of this new site include an interactive study guide, downloadable supplements, online end-of-chapter materials, additional Internet exercises, Tech TV videos, Web resource links such as Careers in IT, and crossword puzzles, plus Technology Updates and Bonus Chapters on the latest trends and hottest topics in information technology. All links to Web exercises will be constantly updated to ensure accuracy for students.

TestGen Software

TestGen is a test generator program that lets you view and easily edit testbank questions, transfer them to tests, and print in a variety of formats suitable to your teaching situation. The program also offers many options for organizing and displaying testbanks and tests. Powerful search and sort functions let you easily locate questions and arrange them in the order you prefer.

QuizMaster, also included in this package, allows students to take tests created with TestGen on a local area network. The QuizMaster Utility built into TestGen lets instructors view student records and print a variety of reports. Building tests is easy with TestGen and exams can be easily uploaded into WebCT, Blackboard and CourseCompass.

Training and Assessment
www2.phgenit.com/support

Prentice Hall offers Performance Based Training and Assessment in one product—Train & Assess IT. The training component offers computer-based training that a student can use to preview, learn, and review Microsoft Office application skills. Web or CD-ROM delivered, Train IT offers interactive, multimedia, computer-based training to augment classroom learning. Built-in prescriptive testing suggests a study path based not only on student test results but also on the specific textbook chosen for the course.

The assessment component offers computer-based testing that shares the same user interface as Train IT and is used to evaluate a student's knowledge about specific topics in Word, Excel, Access, PowerPoint, Outlook, the Internet Windows Computer Concepts, and much more. It does this in a task-oriented environment to demonstrate proficiency as well as comprehension of the topics by the students. More extensive than the testing in Train IT, Assess IT offers more administrative features for the instructor and additional questions for the student.

Assess IT also allows professors to test students out of a course, place students in appropriate courses, and evaluate skill sets.

TechTV

TechTV is the San Francisco–based cable network that showcases the smart, edgy, and unexpected side of technology. By telling stories through the prism of technology, TechTV provides programming that celebrates its viewers' passion, creativity, and lifestyle.

TechTV's programming falls into three categories:

1. Help and Information, with shows like The Screen Savers, TechTV's daily live variety show featuring everything from guest interviews and celebrities to product advice and demos; Tech Live, featuring the latest news on the industry's most important people, companies, products and issues; and Call for Help, a live help and how-to show providing computing tips and live viewer questions.

2. Cool Docs, with shows like The Tech Of . . . , a series that goes behind the scenes of modern life and shows you the technology that makes things tick; Performance, an investigation into how technology and science are molding the perfect athlete; and Future Fighting Machines, a fascinating look at the technology and tactics of warfare.

3. Outrageous Fun, with shows like X-Play, exploring the latest and greatest in videogaming, and Unscrewed with Martin Sargent, a new late-night series showcasing the darker, funnier world of technology.

For more information, log onto **www.techtv.com** or contact your local cable or satellite provider to get TechTV in your area.

Tools for Online Learning

Online Courseware for Blackboard, WebCT, and CourseCompass

Now you have the freedom to personalize your own online course materials!

Prentice Hall provides the content and support you need to create and manage your own online course in WebCT, Blackboard, or Prentice Hall's own CourseCompass. Content includes lecture material, interactive exercises, e-commerce case videos, additional testing questions, and projects and animations.

CourseCompass
www.coursecompass.com

CourseCompass is a dynamic, interactive online course-management tool powered exclusively for Pearson Education by Blackboard. This exciting product allows you to teach market-leading Pearson Education content in an easy-to-use, customizable format.

Blackboard
www.prenhall.com/blackboard

Prentice Hall's abundant online content combined with Blackboard's popular tools and interface result in robust Web-based courses that are easy to implement, manage, and use—taking your courses to new heights in student interaction and learning.

WebCT
www.prenhall.com/webct

Course management tools within WebCT include page tracking, progress tracking, class and student management, a grade book, communication tools, a calendar, reporting tools, and more. GOLD LEVEL CUSTOMER SUPPORT, available exclusively to adopters of Prentice Hall courses, is provided free of charge upon adoption and provides you with priority assistance, training discounts, and dedicated technical support.

Throughout **Computer Confluence,** special focus boxes complement the text:

Inventing the Future

Inventing the Future boxes provide futuristic perspectives at the end of every chapter. Inventing the Future boxes cover a range of topics including: *Tomorrow Never Knows* (Chapter 1), *Shared Virtual Spaces* (shown here from Chapter 6), *Truly Intelligent Agents* in Chapter 5, *Microtechnology & Nanotechnology* in Chapter 10.

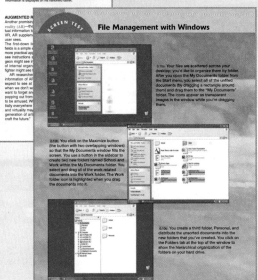

Screen Test

Screen Test boxes test drive software applications, offering students glimpses of programs and software uses they might not otherwise experience. The one-page boxes replace the User's View of previous editions. We've included commonly used software like Microsoft Word and common tasks like *File Management* shown here from Chapter 0. We've also included more creative applications such as *Creating a CD Cover with Adobe Photoshop.*

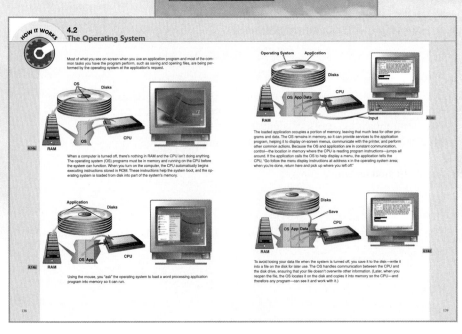

How it Works

How it Works boxes provide additional technical material on more complex topics. This example is a graphic representation of how the operating system works. Other How It Works boxes include coverage on *Representing the World's Languages, Executing a Program, Font Technology, Data Compression, The World Wide Web,* and *Cryptogaphy.*

For classes where this kind of technical detail isn't necessary, students can skip these boxes. How It Works boxes are numbered so that instructors can create customized reading assignments by specifying which are required and which are optional.

Crosscurrents

Crosscurrents boxes at the end of each chapter provide thought-provoking, timely, and sometimes controversial essays and articles by respected writers, analysts, and industry insiders. In Chapter 7 Michael J. Miller considers *Privacy and Security: Finding a Balance*. In Chapter 8 David Brooks tells us that he has *Time to Do Everything Except Think*. In Chapter 5 spreadsheet inventor Dan Bricklin tells students that *Copy Protection Robs the Future Labor of Love*.

Rules of Thumb

Rules of Thumb boxes provide practical, nontechnical tips for avoiding the pitfalls and problems created by computer technology. In Chapter 6, *Digital Audio Do's and Don'ts* gives guidance on digitizing a CD collection and downloading music. Other Rules of Thumb boxes cover netiquette, privacy protection, creating multimedia, and security issues.

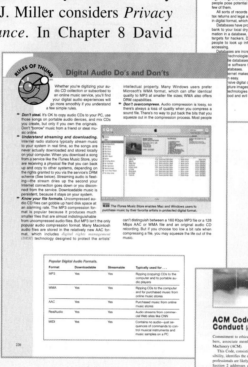

ACM Guidelines

The ACM Guidelines is the most widely known code of conduct for computer professionals. The appendix reprints the code, along with detailed annotations that link specific tenants to related ethics material throughout the text.

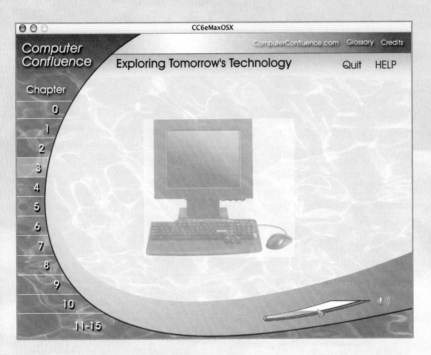

The CD-ROM has been completely revised and updated, with a more powerful engine, a streamlined user interface, and a wealth of new multimedia material, from provocative TechTV video clips to interactive tutorials and tests. The material on the CD is clearly keyed to corresponding sections in the book at the ends of most chapters.

The Web site (www.computerconfluence.com) is continually updated to reflect changes in the Web and the subject matter.

Training and Assessment
www2.phgenit.com/support

Prentice Hall offers Performance Based Training and Assessment in one product—Train & Assess IT. The training component offers computer-based training that a student can use to preview, learn, and review Computer Concepts, Microsoft Office applications, and other software-related skills. Built-in prescriptive testing suggests a study path based not only on student test results but also on the specific textbook chosen for the course. The assessment component offers computer-based testing that shares the same user interface as Train IT and is used to evaluate a student's knowledge about specific topics in Word, Excel, Access, PowerPoint, Outlook, the Internet and Computing Concepts. It does this in a task-oriented environment to demonstrate proficiency as well as comprehension of the topics by the students. Assess IT offers more administrative features for the instructor and additional questions for the student. Assess IT also allows professors to test students out of a course, place students in appropriate courses, and evaluate skill sets.

Acknowledgements

I'm deeply grateful to all of the people who've come together to make *Computer Confluence* a success. Their names may not be on the cover, but their high quality work shows in every detail of this project.

I'm especially thankful to Natalie Anderson, whose clear vision and personal commitment to *Computer Confluence* helped elevate the learning package to a new level of excellence. I'm also grateful to Jodi McPherson, the savvy Executive Editor who worked with Natalie and the rest of the team to ensure that the project stayed on track. Thanks to Editorial Project Manager Mike Ruel, who worked on all aspects of the project, from initial book planning to coordinating the CD and Web efforts. And thanks to Alana Meyers, Jodi Bolognese, and Jasmine Slowik, who quietly toiled behind the scenes, taking care of countless details.

My most heartfelt thanks go to Maureen Allaire Spada, the editor responsible for making the first edition of this book a reality. I was delighted when Maureen agreed to join the team for this new edition. Throughout the project she rose to every challenge, redefining her role to deal with unanticipated circumstances and keep the project on schedule. Her work was consistently professional, timely, and thorough, and she kept her cheerful demeanor even in the most stressful situations. Just as she did with the first edition, Maureen made this book happen.

Paul Thurrott deserves thanks for the countless hours he logged in the early stages of creating this edition. Paul has contributed words, ideas, and technical expertise to several editions of *Computer Confluence*, and his perspectives on the technology and the industry are always valuable. For this edition Paul was intimately involved in the development of the manuscript until the other demands of his busy professional life pulled him off the project. Paul's writing and consulting work are in high demand, and his work on *Computer Confluence* is greatly appreciated.

Thanks also go to Gene Rathswohl, who co-wrote several chapters in the original IT edition. These chapters morphed into chapters 12 and 13 of the current edition. Gene's business perspective made these chapters possible.

Many others brought their considerable talents to *Computer Confluence*. Kevin Kall, designer, is the person most responsible for the design of the book. Lynne Breitfeller and Gail Steier de Acevedo worked on all aspects of production, helping ensure that the project could make all those nearly impossible deadlines. Abby Reip's patient and persistent research uncovered most of the excellent photos in these pages. Gordon Laws and the staff at Pre-Press Company, Inc. produced the final book from all of the raw materials supplied by the others listed here. Von Hoffman Press handled the printing process. Melissa Edwards coordinated the supplements that make *Computer Confluence* a complete educational package.

I'm delighted that Dave Trenkel and Mark Dinsmore, the team of Oregon multimedia wizards who produced the original *Computer Confluence* CD-ROM, are back on the team. Dave headed a dynamite group that included Mark, designer Pat Grimaldi, and content provider Melissa Hartley. Back East the details of the CD-ROM and the Web site were coordinated by Cathleen Profitko, Media Product Manager, and Mike Ruel, Editorial Project Manager.

All of this effort would be wasted if *Computer Confluence* didn't reach its intended audience. Thankfully, Emily Knight is a first-rate marketing manager who thoroughly understands *Computer Confluence* and the academic world it serves. I'm delighted to have Emily on the *Computer Confluence* Team. Of course, Emily's work would be in vain if she didn't have Prentice Hall's amazing team of sales reps. These people work hard to bring books to professors and students, and I can't thank them enough for their efforts.

I owe special thanks to members of my family who temporarily set aside many of their own personal and professional goals to help me with this project. My daughter Johanna helped organize research materials and did all kinds of support work on the project.

My son Ben Beekman served as an indispensable assistant on previous editions of *Computer Confluence*. As a college student, Ben knows our readership from the inside. But Ben also knows the business of writing and the business of multimedia. When we started the sixth edition, Ben was busy with final school projects, a computer consulting job, and several freelance projects. But when we ran the risk of falling behind on *Computer Confluence*, Ben found the time to help with manuscript development, screen shots, research, and other critical tasks. His contributions were invaluable.

It's not so easy to list the contributions of my wife Susan Grace. She was there to help in all kinds of ways, from research and organization to communication and collaboration. She played a critical role in developing the Crosscurrents sections of the book, and helped me wrestle with countless organizational and editorial decisions. Just as importantly, she selflessly maintained the infrastructure of our home, our family, and our business, making it possible for me to meet the difficult deadlines of this project.

There are others who contributed to *Computer Confluence* in all kinds of ways, including critiquing chapters, answering technical questions, tracking down obscure references, guiding me through difficult decisions, and being there when I needed support. There's no room here to detail their contributions, but I want to thank the people who gave time, energy, talent, and support during the years that this book was under development, including Scobel Wiggins, Jim Folts, Jan Dymond, Mike Quinn, Mike Johnson, Margaret Burnett, Michelle Baxter, Sherry Clark, Walter Rudd, Cherie Pancake, Bruce D'Ambrosio, Bernie Feyerham, Rajeev Pandey, Dave Stuve, Clay Cowgill, Keith Vertanen, Nicole Mahan, Gary Brent, Robert Rose, Marion Rose, Megan Slothover, Claudette Hastie-Baehrs, Shjoobedebop, Oyaya, Breitenbush, Oregon Public Broadcasting, KLCC, and all of the editors and others who helped with previous editions of *Computer Confluence*. Thanks also to all the hardware and software companies whose cooperation made my work easier.

Reviewers of the 6th Edition

Thanks to all of the dedicated educators who reviewed the manuscript at various stages of development; *Computer Confluence* and its accompanying CD-ROM are significantly more valuable educational tools as a result of your ideas, suggestions, and constructive criticism.

Nazih Abdallah, University of Central Florida

Lancie Affonso, College of Charleston

Allen Alexander, Delaware Tech, Wilmington Campus

Gary Armstrong, Shippensburg University

Ita Borger-Boglin, San Antonio College

Carol Buse, Amarillo College

Kristen Callahan, Mercer County Community College

Ken Custer, Delaware Tech, Owens Campus

Mimi Duncan, University of Missouri, St. Louis

Beverly Fite, Amarillo College

Timothy Flanagan, Portland Community College, Sylvania Campus

Donna Fremont, University of Calgary

Cherryl Frye, University of Wisconsin, La Crosse

Marta Gonzalez, Hudson County Community College

Mary Hollingsworth, Georgia Perimeter College, Clarkston Campus

Lisa Jamba-Joyner, University of North Florida

Eric Kisling, Indiana University at Bloomington

Barbara G. Korb, Bucks County Community College

John Liefert, Middlesex Community College

Valerie A. Martin, Immaculata University

Charles G. Miri, Delaware Tech, Terry Campus

Ellen Monk, University of Delaware

Rebecca Mundy, University of Southern California

Tim Pelton, University of Victoria

Jennifer Pickle, Amarillo College

Pratap P. Reddy, Raritan Valley Community College

Patricia Rodihan, Union County Community College

Ana R. Soler, Raritan Valley Community College

Mary Ann Zlotow, College of DuPage

COMPREHENSIVE

Computer Confluence

exploring tomorrow's technology

AFTER YOU READ THIS CHAPTER YOU SHOULD BE ABLE TO:

- Describe the basic parts of a PC and how they work together

- Explain the relationship between hardware and software

- Explain how the Internet extends the functionality of a PC

- Describe some of the risks of Internet use and how to minimize them

- Use a Windows PC or Macintosh to explore the *Computer Confluence* CD-ROM

- Use a Windows PC or Macintosh to explore the *Computer Confluence* Web site

 Multimedia extras on the CD-ROM and the Web:

- A **Hitchiker's Guide** to the Future

- **Interactive tutorial** on using a computer keyboard

- **Instant Access** to glossary and key word references

- Interactive **self-study quizzes**

    . . . and more.

 computerconfluence.com

BASICS

HUMAN DREAMS AND DREAM MACHINES

In 1983 Steve Roberts realized he wasn't happy chained to his desk and his debts. He decided to build a new lifestyle that combined his passions—writing, adventure, computers, bicycling, learning, and networking. Six months later he hit the road on Winnebiko, a recumbent bike equipped with a laptop and solar panel. He connected each day to the CompuServe network through pay phones, transmitting magazine articles and book chapters.

Years later Roberts was exploring America on BEHEMOTH (Big Electronic Human-Energized Machine . . . Only Too Heavy), a million-dollar bike with seven networked computers and wireless communication capability. Roberts pedaled 17,000 miles before pursuing a new dream: "life with no hills." His latest project is Microship, a high-tech craft that will allow him to extend his techno-madic lifestyle to the ocean. "There's a *lot* of world to explore out there. Having had a taste of it, how could I spend my life in one place?"

The obvious choices **aren't the only choices**.

—Steve Roberts

0.1 Steve Roberts with BEHEMOTH

0.2 Vaughn Rogers in his own art work

Vaughn Rogers "wasn't into computers." Computers, he thought, were useful for typing papers, but they weren't exciting. *Art* was exciting to Rogers, who had been drawing all his life.

In 1995 he went with a friend to the Computer Clubhouse, a nonprofit educational center at the Museum of Science in Cambridge, Massachusetts. He saw other teens using computers to create art, edit video, and mix music. Before long, Vaughn was doing his art at the Computer Clubhouse after school.

Today, 22-year-old Rogers studies visual communication and animation at Katharine Gibbs College. His goal is to work in computer animation and video, using his drawing talent enhanced with computer technology. He now works as an assistant manager at the Computer Clubhouse, helping others learn to use computers to pursue their passions. ■

When Patricia Walsh lost her sight at 14, she almost lost sight of her dreams. She had already completed the advanced mathematics and science classes at her high school, and she wanted to go further. She learned to read and write Braille, but Braille couldn't help with the equations and formulas she needed to study. Her PC could talk using text-to-speech software, but it had nothing to say about scientific graphs and charts.

Fortunately, Walsh met John Gardner, a blind physics professor at Oregon State University. Gardner was developing tools to make math and science accessible to visually impaired people. His Tiger Tactile Graphics and Braille Embosser printed equations, formulas, and graphs as raised patterns that could be read by touch. Using this technology, Walsh could read class notes emailed by her professors. Once again she could "see" the figures that were critical to her studies.

Walsh started helping Gardner develop accessibility tools. She became a spokesperson for adaptive technology, telling others about tools that can open doors for people with disabilities. Walsh is now a

0.3 Patricia Walsh

computer science major at Oregon State University, where she uses the tools that she helped develop to pursue her dream. "Computers have allowed me to get in the mainstream. Now I can do what I used to love before I became blind." ■

Steve Roberts, Vaughn Rogers, and Patricia Walsh would be living very different lives today if they hadn't connected with computers. Their stories are interesting and inspiring, but they aren't unique. Every day computer technology changes people's lives all around the world.

Sometimes it seems like everybody uses computers. In fact, the great majority of people on our planet have never touched a computer!

Most of the people who *do* use computers have fairly limited experience and ability—typically the basics of word processing, electronic mail, and finding information on the World Wide Web. The percentage of people who can go beyond the basics and harness the power of a modern PC is relatively small.

If you're a member of this tiny community of *power users*, the next few pages aren't for you. But before you move on to Chapter 1, take a look at the *Computer Confluence* Quick Start and Navigating *Computer Confluence* sections later in this chapter. You'll find tips for getting the most out of this book and the companion CD-ROM and Web site. This chapter closes with a Crosscurrents article that will give you something to think about.

If you're a *casual computer user*, comfortable with the basic operation of a PC, a CD-ROM drive, and a Web browser, you may want to look through this chapter quickly and spend more time with the Quick Start, Navigating *Computer Confluence*, and Crosscurrents sections before moving on to Chapter 1, where the real story begins. (If you're not sure about your knowledge level, check out the questions at the end of the chapter. If you have trouble answering them, spend a little more time looking over this chapter before you move on.)

If you're a *beginner*, your experience is limited or out-of-date, you're uncomfortable with PC technology, or you just want to be thorough, this chapter is for you. Here you'll find the basic knowledge you'll need to bring you up to speed, so you're not struggling to catch up as you explore the rest of the book. You'll also learn what you need to know to take full advantage of the *Computer Confluence* CD-ROM and Web site. Along with this book, these resources can provide you with a rich multimedia introduction to the world of computers and information technology.

Whichever path you choose, don't wait until you're sitting in front of a computer to read *Computer Confluence*. Hands-on computer experience is important, but you won't need the computer to take advantage of this book. Wherever you are, just dive in.

> *Key terms in this chapter, and throughout the book, are highlighted in blue boldface. Secondary terms are highlighted in blue italics. In this chapter, the key terms are the ones that are critical for getting started with the Computer Confluence book, CD-ROM, and Web site; secondary terms are terms that are introduced briefly here and covered in more detail later.*

PC Basics

Computers come in all kinds of packages, from massive supercomputers to tiny computers embedded in cell phones, credit cards, and even microscopic machines and "smart"

> The beginning is the **most important part** of the work.
> —Plato

pills. But in this chapter, we'll focus on the typical desktop computer—the personal computer, or PC. We'll start with a look at the physical parts of a PC—the PC's hardware. This whirlwind tour will offer a quick, practical overview; you'll learn more in later chapters.

PC Hardware Basics

Modern desktop PCs don't all look alike, but under the skin, they're more alike than different. Every PC is built around a tiny *microprocessor* that controls the workings

> **Hardware**: the parts of a computer that **can be kicked**.
> —Jeff Pesis

of the system. This central processing unit, or CPU, is usually housed in a box, called the *system unit* (or, more often, just "the computer" or "the PC") that serves as command central for the entire computer system. The CPU is the brains of the computer—it controls the operation of the core computer components, like its memory and ability to perform mathematical operations. Some computer components are housed in the system unit with the *CPU*; others are peripheral devices—or simply peripherals—external devices connected via cables to the system unit.

The system unit includes built-in memory, sometimes called *RAM*, and a hard disk for storage and retrieval of information. The CPU uses memory for instant access to information while it's working. The built-in hard disk serves as a longer-term storage device for large quantities of information.

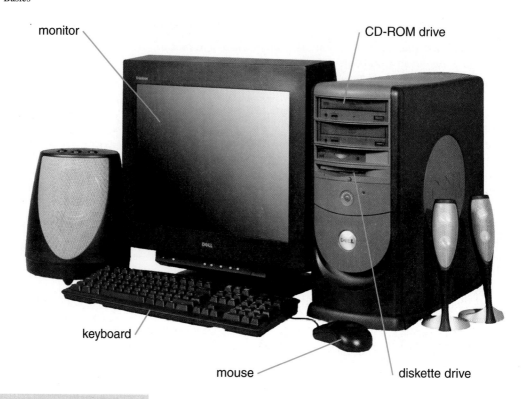

monitor

CD-ROM drive

keyboard

mouse

diskette drive

0.4 A standard desktop PC or Mac is made up of several components, including a system unit, a monitor, a keyboard, and a mouse. The system unit typically includes an internal hard disk and an optical drive such as a CD-ROM or DVD drive.

The PC's main hard disk is a permanent fixture in the system unit. Other types of disk drives work with *removable media*—disks that can be separated from their drives, just as an audio CD can be removed from a stereo system. The most popular types of removable media today are 5-1/4 inch optical discs that look like common audio CDs. A typical PC system unit includes a CD-ROM drive, a CD-RW drive, a DVD drive, or some other kind of optical drive. A CD-ROM drive enables the computer to read audio CDs and CD-ROMs (including the one included with this book). A CD-RW drive can read CDs and also write, or *burn*, information onto CD media. A DVD drive can read (and sometimes burn) DVD movies and high-capacity data DVDs as well as audio and data CDs. In addition to an optical drive, an older PC might also include a *diskette drive* (also known as a *floppy disk drive*), which enables the computer to store small amounts of information on pocket-sized plastic-covered magnetic diskettes.

Disk drives that are included in the system unit are called *internal drives*. *External drives* can be attached to the system unit via cables. For example, a PC system might include an external hard disk for additional storage and a DVD/CD-RW drive for reading and writing CDs and reading DVDs.

Other system unit components, including the video display card, the sound card, the network interface card, and the modem, communicate with external devices, with other computers, and with networks.

But the PC's main purpose isn't to communicate with other machines—it's there to communicate with you. Four common peripherals aid this human–computer interaction:

■ A keyboard enables you to type text and numerical data into the computer's memory.
■ A mouse enables you to point to text, graphical objects, menu commands, and other items on the screen.

Using a Keyboard

Typing letters, numbers, and special characters with a computer keyboard is similar to typing on a standard typewriter keyboard. But unlike a typewriter, the computer responds by displaying the typed characters on the monitor screen at the position of the line or rectangle called the *cursor*. Some keys on the computer keyboard—the *cursor (arrow) keys*, the *Delete key*, the *Enter key*, *function keys (f-keys)*, and others—send special commands to the computer. These keys may have different names or meanings on different computer systems. This figure shows a typical keyboard on a Windows-compatible PC. Keyboards for Macintoshes and other types of systems have a few differences but operate on the same principles.

Function keys (f-keys), labeled F1, F2, and so on, send signals to the computer that have no inherent meaning. The function of these keys depends on the software being used. F1 might mean "Save file" to one program and "Delete file" to another. In other words function keys are programmable.

Backspace on a PC tells the computer to delete the character just typed (or the one to the left of the cursor on the screen, or the currently selected data).

Control and *Alt* are modifier keys that cause nothing to happen by themselves but change the meaning of other keys. When you hold down a modifier key while pressing another key, the combination makes that other key behave differently. For example, typing S while holding down the Control key might send a command to save the current document.

Enter sends a signal telling the computer or terminal to move the cursor to the beginning of the next line on the screen. For many applications this key also "enters" the line just typed, telling the computer to process it.

Cursor (arrow) keys are used to move the cursor up, down, left, or right.

0.5

- A **monitor** (or *display*) displays text, numbers, and pictures from the computer's memory.
- A **printer** generates printed letters, papers, transparencies, labels, and other hard copies. (The printer might be directly connected to the computer, or it might be shared by several computers on a network.)

The next two pages illustrate the fundamentals of a basic PC keyboard and mouse. Chapter 3 explores peripherals in more detail.

Using a Mouse

The mouse enables you to perform many tasks quickly that might be tedious or confusing with a keyboard. As you slide the mouse across your desktop, a pointer echoes your movements on the screen. You can *click* the mouse—press the button while the mouse is stationary—or *drag* it—move it while holding the button down. On a two-button mouse, the left button is usually used for clicking and dragging. You can use these two techniques to perform a variety of operations.

CLICKING THE MOUSE

If the pointer points to an on-screen *button*, clicking the mouse presses the button.

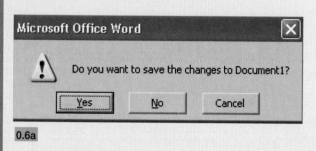

0.6a

If the pointer points to a picture of a tool or object on the screen, clicking the mouse *selects* the tool or object; for example, clicking the pencil tool enables you to draw with the mouse.

If the pointer points to a part of a text document, it turns from an arrow into an *I-beam*; clicking repositions the flashing cursor.

Jack and Jill fell down and I Jill came tumbling after.

0.6f

0.6e

DRAGGING THE MOUSE

If you hold the button down while you drag the mouse with a selected graphic tool (like a paintbrush), you can draw by remote control.

0.6b

If you drag the mouse from one point in a text document to another, you select all the text between those two points so you can modify or move it. For example, you might select this movie title so you could italicize it.

The zany Duck Soup captured the Marx Brothers at their peak.

0.6c

You can drag the mouse to select a command from a *menu* of choices. For example, this command enables you to locate specific documents that are stored on your computer.

0.6g

OTHER MOUSE OPERATIONS

If you *double-click* the mouse—click twice in rapid succession—while pointing to an on-screen object, the computer will probably open the object so you can see inside it. For example, double-clicking this *icon* representing a letter causes the letter to open.

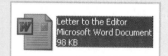

0.6d

If you *right-click*—click the right mouse button—while pointing to an object, the computer will probably display a menu of choices of things you can do to the object. For example, if you right-click the letter icon, a menu appears at the pointer.

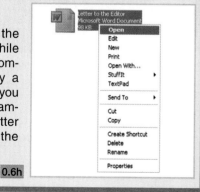

0.6h

PC Software Basics

All of this hardware is controlled, directly or indirectly, by the tiny CPU in the system unit. And the CPU is controlled by software—instructions that tell it what to do.

> Computers can figure out **all kinds of problems**, except the things in the world that **just don't add up**.
>
> —James Magary

System software, including the operating system (OS), continuously takes care of the behind-the-scenes details and (usually) keeps things running smoothly. The operating system also determines what your screen display looks like as you work and how you tell the computer what you want it to do. Most PCs today use some version of the *Microsoft Windows* operating system; Macintosh computers use some version of Apple's *Mac OS*.

Application programs, also called simply applications, are the software tools that enable you to use a computer for specific purposes. Some applications are designed to accomplish well-defined short-term goals. For example, the *Computer Confluence* CD-ROM includes an application that supplements and expands on the material in this book using interactive quizzes, animated demos, video presentations, and other multimedia material. Other applications programs are more general and open-ended in their goals. For example, you can use a word processing program, such as Microsoft Word, to create memos, letters, term papers, novels, textbooks, or World Wide Web pages—just about any kind of text-based document.

In the PC world, a document is something created by an application, regardless of whether it has actually been printed. Applications and documents are two different types of files. A file is a named collection of data stored on a computer disc or some other storage medium. Applications are sometimes called *executable files*, because they contain instructions that can be executed by the computer. Documents are sometimes called *data files* because they contain passive data rather than instructions. When you write a letter with the Microsoft Word application; the computer executes the Word instructions. When you save the letter on the computer's hard disk, the computer creates a Word document—a data file that contains the contents of the letter.

The Screen Test boxes on the following pages show examples of software at work. In these simple examples, we'll use a word processing application to edit and print a term paper we created in an earlier session and stored as a document on the hard disk. In the first example, we'll use Microsoft Word on a PC with the Microsoft Windows XP operating system. In the second example we'll do the same thing using Microsoft Word on a Macintosh with Mac OS X. In both examples we'll perform the following steps:

1. Locate the document on the hard disk.
2. Open the application—copy it from the computer's hard disk into memory so we can use it—and open the document.
3. Type some additional text at the end of the document.
4. Print the document.
5. Close the application.
6. Delete the document file from the hard disk.

Before we begin, a reminder and a disclaimer:

The reminder: The *Screen Test* examples are designed to give you a feel for the software, not to provide how-to instructions. You can learn how to use the software using lab manuals or other books on the subject, some of which are listed in *Sources and Resources* at the end of chapters in this book.

The disclaimer: These examples are intended to compare different types of interfaces—not to establish a favorite. The brand of software in a particular Screen Test box isn't as important as the general concepts built into that software. One of the best things about computers is that they offer lots of different ways to do things. These examples, and others throughout the book, are designed to expose you to possibilities. Even if you have no plans to use the operating systems or applications in the examples—*especially* if you have no plans to use them—you can learn something by looking at them as a curious observer.

Using Microsoft Word with Microsoft Windows

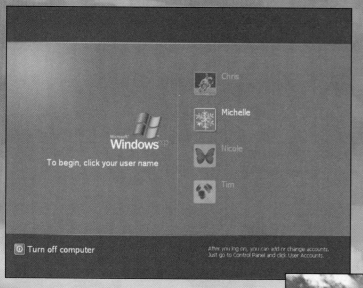

0.7a After your PC completes its startup process, you see a Login screen with a list of users. You click your user name from the list, so Windows will use your personal settings. You enter your password (not shown) and log on to the system.

0.7b The Windows desktop appears—a screen that includes icons representing objects used in your work. You click Start in the lower-left corner of the screen. The Start menu appears, enabling you to select from the applications and documents you use most frequently. You select Microsoft Word, and click to open the program. The PC is now ready to work on any Word document, including your paper.

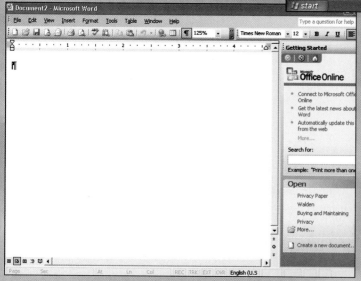

0.7c The Microsoft Word application opens, and you are presented with a blank document and a task pane (right) containing options that represent frequently used commands and files. You use the task pane to open your paper.

0.7d Microsoft Word displays the term paper in a window. You use the mouse to move the pointer to the end of the text; you click the mouse button. A flashing cursor (sometimes called an insertion point) indicates your location in the document. You type additional text to be added at that point. As you type, the cursor moves to the right, leaving a trail of text in its wake. At the same time, those characters are stored in the computer's memory. If you mistype a character or string of characters, you can press Delete or Backspace to eliminate the typos. Every few minutes you select the Save command to save your document in a disk file containing your work so far. This provides insurance against accidental erasure of the text you've entered.

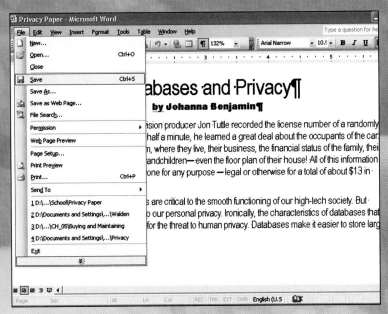

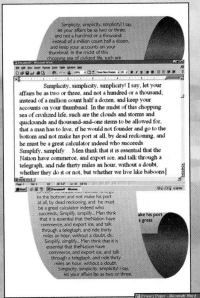

0.7e As you type, the top-most lines scroll out of view to make room on the screen for the new ones. The text you've entered is still in memory, even though you can't see it on the screen. You can retrieve it anytime by scrolling backward through the text. In this respect a word processor document is like a modern version of ancient paper scrolls.

0.7f You choose the Print command to print the paper.

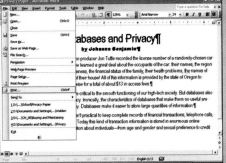

Using Microsoft Word with Mac OS X

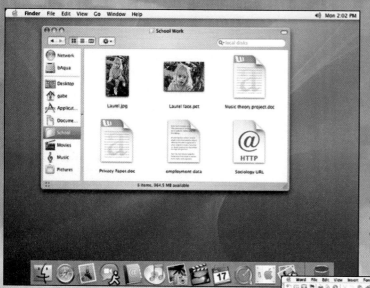

0.8a The Macintosh menu bar spans the top of the screen. At the bottom of the screen is the Dock, which is a holding place for frequently used applications and documents. Like the Windows desktop, the Macintosh desktop, called the Finder, includes icons representing objects used in your work. Many commonly used icons are visible on the left side of every Finder window. An open window shows the contents of the School Work folder on the hard disk. Folders, like their real-world counterparts, enable you to group related documents. You double-click on the Term Paper document to open it.

0.8b The document opens in a window. You edit and print the document; the process is similar for the Macintosh and Windows versions of Word.

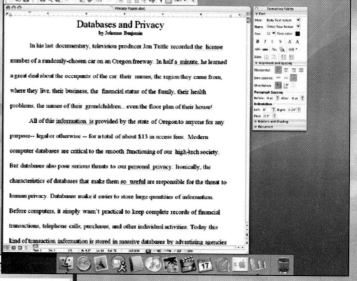

0.8c A Mac OS feature called Exposé enables you, with a single keystroke, to see shrunken images of all of your open windows neatly tiled on the screen so you can quickly find the one you're looking for—in this case, the School Work folder window. You can then click on it to bring it to the foreground so you can drag the Privacy Paper into the trash.

0.9 Software makes it possible for PCs to be put to work in homes, schools, offices, factories, and farms.

File Management with Windows

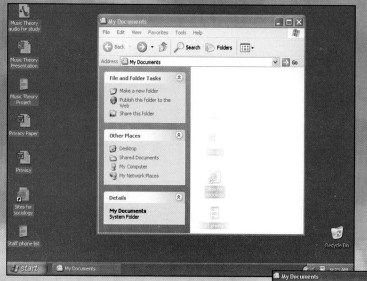

0.10a Your files are scattered across your desktop; you'd like to organize them by folder. After you open the My Documents folder from the Start menu, you select all of the unfiled documents (by dragging a rectangle around them) and drag them to the "My Documents" folder. The icons appear as transparent images in the window while you're dragging them.

0.10b You click on the Maximize button (the button with two overlapping windows) so that the My Documents window fills the screen. You use a button in the sidebar to create two new folders named School and Work within the My Documents folder. You select and drag all of the work related documents into the Work folder. The Work folder icon is highlighted when you drag the documents into it.

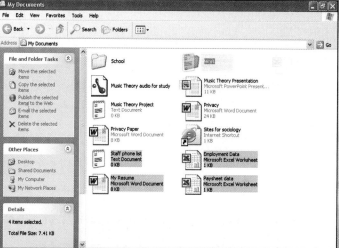

0.10c You create a third folder, Personal, and distribute the unsorted documents into the new folders that you've created. You click on the Folders tab at the top of the window to show the hierarchical organization of the folders on your hard drive.

File Management Basics

In Windows and the Mac OS, a file is represented by a name and an icon. It's not always easy to tell what a file contains based on its name. Most people know that it's a good idea to name files with clearly descriptive names, but some names are difficult to decipher. A file name might include an *extension*—a string of (usually) three characters that follows a period (.) at the end of the file name. The extension gives more information about the file's origin or use. For example, the name of a Windows executable file typically includes the extension *exe*, as in *biggame.exe*. A document created with Microsoft Word may be named with a file name ending in *.doc*, such as *termpaper.doc*. If a file doesn't have a visible extension in its name, you still might be able to tell what it is by looking at its icon. Most popular applications create documents with distinctive icons.

In the physical world, people often use file folders to organize their paper documents into meaningful collections—class documents, financial papers, receipts, and the like. Similarly, computer files can be organized into collections using *folders* (sometimes called directories). The OS allows you to create folders, give them meaningful names, and store documents and other files inside them. When you open a folder, the folder's window opens, revealing the files that it contains. Folders can be organized *hierarchically*—a folder can contain other folders, which in turn can contain still more folders. For example, a folder called "My Documents" might contain folders called "My School Work," "My Financial Papers," "My Letters," and "My Pictures." "My School Work" might contain folders for individual classes, each of which might be subdivided into "Homework," "Projects," and so on. The Windows and Mac OS include a variety of tools for quickly navigating through nested folders to locate particular files.

In the real world, people aren't as organized as computers, and files don't always end up in the appropriate folders. Modern operating systems include *Search* or *Find* commands that can help find files no matter where they might be stored on the system. You can search for file names, but you can also search for words or phrases inside a document. So if you don't know the name of a file but do know some of the text in that file, you can still use the search tool to find your data.

PC Network Basics

Today's PCs are powerful tools that can perform a variety of tasks that go far beyond the basic word processing examples illustrated here. In later chapters we'll explore many of these applications, from money management to multimedia. But a PC becomes even more powerful when it's connected to other computers through a network.

A computer may have a *direct connection* to a network—for example, cables might connect it to other computers, printers, and other devices in an office or student lab. These networked machines can easily and quickly share information with each other. When a computer isn't physically close to the other machines in the network, it can still communicate with those machines through a *remote access* connection. Using a *modem*, the remote computer can connect to the network through an ordinary phone line.

An entire computer network can be connected to other networks through cables, wireless radio transmissions, or other means. The *Internet* is an elaborate network of interconnected networks—a network that is dramatically changing the way people work, play, and communicate.

> Networks aren't made of printed circuits, but of **people . . . My terminal is a door** to countless, intricate pathways, leading to **untold numbers of neighbors.**
>
> —Cliff Stoll, in *The Cuckoo's Egg*

0.11 Networked computers in this lab allow students to share files, send messages, and connect to the Internet.

Internet Basics

> What interests me about it . . . is that it's a form of communication **unlike any other** and yet the second you start doing it **you understand it**.
>
> —Nora Ephron, Director of *You've Got Mail*

There was a time, not too many years ago, when word processing was the most popular computer activity among students. For most students, the computer was little more than a high-powered typewriter. Today, a PC can be a window into the global system of interconnected networks known as the Internet, or just the *Net*.

The Internet is used by mom-and-pop businesses and multinational corporations that want to communicate with their customers, sell products, and track economic conditions; by kindergarteners and college students doing research and exploration; by consumers and commuters who need access to timely information, goods, and services; and by families and friends who just want to stay in touch. Most people connect to the Internet because it gives them the power to do things that they couldn't easily do otherwise.

Using the Internet you can

- Study material designed to supplement this book, including late-breaking news, interactive study aids, and multimedia simulations that can't be printed on paper.
- Send a message to 1 or 1,001 people, around town or around the world, and receive replies almost as quickly as the recipients can read the message and type a response.
- Explore vast libraries of research material, ranging from classic scholarly works to contemporary reference works.
- Find instant answers to time-sensitive questions such as "What's the weather like in Boston right now?" or "What software do I need to make my new computer work with my new printer?" or "Who won this morning's Olympic high-diving competition?" or "What did the United Nations secretary general say on National Public Radio's *All Things Considered* last night?" or "Where in the world is the Federal Express package I sent yesterday?"
- Get medical, legal, or technical advice from a wide variety of experts.
- Listen to live radio broadcasts from around the world.
- Participate in discussions or play games with people all over the globe who share your interests; with the right equipment, you can set aside your keyboard and communicate through live audio-video links.
- Shop for obscure items such as out-of-print books and CDs that you can't find elsewhere.
- Download free software or music clips from servers all over the world onto your computer.

0.12 In Seattle, Washington (top), a mother checks on her four-year-old daughter from work using Internet-link video cameras. In Philadelphia, Pennsylvania (bottom), the press corps at the Republican National Convention used the Internet to conduct and transmit live telecasts.

- Order a custom-built computer, car, or condominium.
- Track hourly changes in the stock markets and buy and sell stocks based on those changes.
- Take a course for college credit from a school thousands of miles away.
- Publish your own writings, drawings, photos, and multimedia works so Internet users all over the world can view them.
- Start your own business and have a worldwide clientele.

Every revolution has a dark side, and the Internet explosion is no exception. The Internet has plenty of worthless information, scams, and questionable activities. People who make the most of the Internet know how to separate the best of the Net from the rest of the Net. Every chapter of this book contains information that will help you to understand and use the Internet wisely. In this chapter we'll focus on the basics of the two most popular Internet applications: finding information on the World Wide Web and communicating with electronic mail.

World Wide Web Basics

The World Wide Web (WWW), makes the Internet accessible to people all over the planet. The *Web* is a huge portion of the Internet that includes a wealth of multimedia content accessible through simple point-and-click programs called Web browsers. Web browsers on PCs and other devices serve as windows into the Web's richly diverse information space.

The World Wide Web is made up of millions of interlinked documents called Web pages. A Web page is typically made up of text and images, like a page in a book. A collection of related pages stored on the same computer is called a Web site; a typical Web site is organized around a home page that serves as an entry page and a stepping off point for other pages in the site. Each Web page has a unique address, technically referred to as a URL (uniform resource locator). For example, the URL for this book's home page is **http://computerconfluence.com**. You can visit the site by typing the exact URL into the address box of your Web browser.

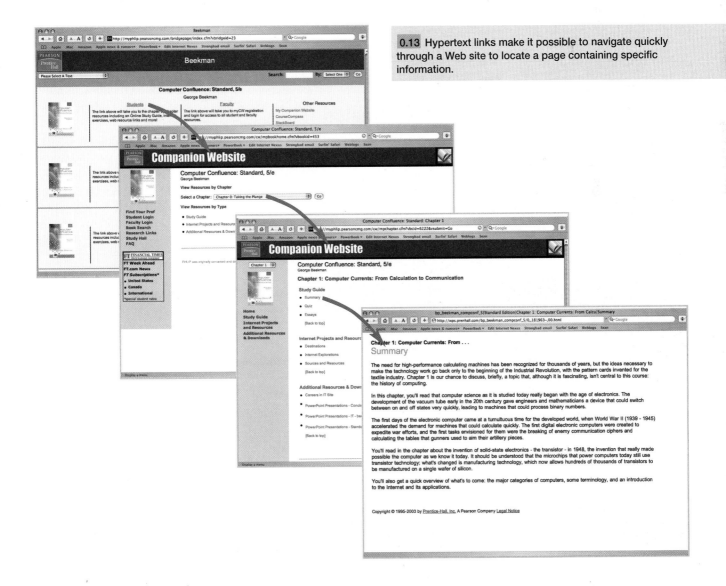

0.13 Hypertext links make it possible to navigate quickly through a Web site to locate a page containing specific information.

At the heart of the Web is the concept of *hypertext*. A Web browser enables you to jump from one Web page to another by clicking **hyperlinks** (often called just *links*)—words, pictures, or menu items that act as buttons. For example, at the *Computer Confluence* Web site you can select a chapter number to jump to pages related to that chapter. Within the chapter, you can click Multiple Choice to jump to a page containing practice quiz questions. Or you can click Chapter Connections to jump to a page full of hyperlinks that can take you to pages on other Web sites. These off-site pages contain articles, illustrations, audio clips, video segments, and other resources created by others. They reside on computers owned by corporations, universities, libraries, institutions, and individuals around the world.

Text links are typically, but not always, underlined and displayed in a different color than standard text on the page. In the example shown on the previous page, the off-site chapter connection hyperlinks are underlined in blue; the Chapter Connection hyperlink is part of a white-on-black menu on the left side of the screen, and the original Chapter link is part of a pop-up menu.

You can explore an amazing variety of Web pages by clicking links. But this kind of random jumping isn't without frustrations. Some links lead to cobwebs—Web pages that haven't been kept up-to-date by their owners—and dead ends—pages that have been removed or moved. Even if a link is current, it may not be reputable or accurate; since anybody can create Web pages, they don't all have the editorial integrity of trusted print media.

It can also be frustrating to try to find your way back to pages you've seen on the Web. That's why browsers have *Back* and *Forward buttons*; you can retrace your steps and re-retrace your steps as often as you like. These buttons won't help, though, if you're trying to find an important page from an earlier session. Most browsers include tools for keeping personal lists of memorable sites, called *bookmarks* or *favorites*. When you run across a page worth revisiting, you can mark it with a Bookmark or Add to Favorites command. Then you can revisit that site anytime by selecting it from the list.

Web Search Basics

The ability to **ask the right question** is more than half the battle of **finding the answer**.

—Thomas J. Watson, founder of IBM

The World Wide Web is like a giant, loosely woven, constantly changing document created by thousands of unrelated authors and scattered about in computers all over the world. The biggest challenge for many Web users is extracting the useful information from the rest. If you're looking for a specific information resource, but you don't know where it is located on the Web, you might be able to find it using a search engine.

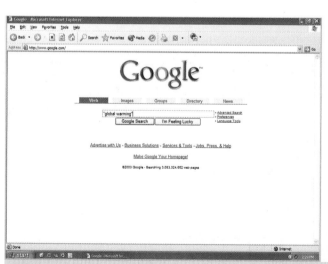
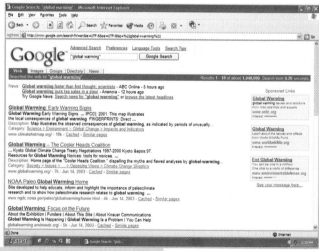

0.14 A search for the phrase *global warming* yields hundreds of hits on the Google search engine.

A search engine is built around a database that catalogs Web locations based on content. (Databases are covered later in the book; for now, you can just think of it as an indexed collection of information stored in a computer.) For some search engines, researchers organize and evaluate Web sites. Other search engines use software to search the Web and catalog information automatically. The usefulness of a search engine depends in part on the information in its database. But it also depends on how easy it is for people to find what they're looking for in the database.

To find information with a typical search engine, you type a key word or key words into a search field, click a button, and wait a few seconds for your Web browser to display a list of *hits*—pages that contain requested key words. A search engine can easily produce a list of hundreds or thousands of hits. Most search engines attempt to list pages in order from best to worst, but these automatic rankings aren't always reliable.

Another popular way to use a search engine is to repeatedly narrow the search using a *directory* or *subject tree*—a hierarchical catalog of Web sites compiled by researchers. The search engine at Yahoo! is probably the best-known example. A screen presents you with a menu of subject choices. When you click a subject—say, Government—you narrow your search to that subject, and you're presented with a menu of subcategories within that subject—Military, Politics, Law, Taxes, and so on. You can continue to narrow your search by proceeding through subject menus until you reach a list of selected Web sites related to the final subject. The sites are usually rank-ordered based on estimated value. The list of Web sites on a given index page is not exhaustive—there may be hundreds of pages related to the subject that aren't included in any directory. It's simply not possible to keep a complete index of all the pages on the ever-changing Web.

Popular search engines are located on Netscape Netcenter, Yahoo!, and other Internet *portals*—Web sites designed as first-stop gateways for Internet explorers. The Windows and Macintosh operating systems include search engines. Internet Explorer, Netscape Communicator, and other Web browsers include Search buttons that connect to popular search engines. And many large Web sites include search engines that enable you to search for site-specific information.

0.15 Yahoo's subject tree enables you to narrow your search by clicking categories within a subject.

Email Basics

Electronic mail (also called email or *e-mail*) is the application that lures many people to the Internet for the first time. Email programs make it possible for even casual

Each person on the **"Internet"** has a unique email **"address"** created by **having a squirrel run** across a computer keyboard . . . .
—Dave Barry, humorist

computer users to easily send messages to family, friends, and colleagues. Because an email message can be written, addressed, sent, delivered, and answered in a matter of minutes—even if the correspondents are on opposite sides of the globe—email has replaced air mail for rapid, routine communication in many organizations. Closer to home, email makes it possible to replace time-consuming phone calls and meetings with more efficient online exchanges.

Details vary, but the basic concepts of email are the same for almost all systems. When you sign up for an email account—through your school, your company, or a private *Internet service provider (ISP)*—you receive a user name (sometimes called a *login*

0.16a Hotmail is a popular email service available through the World Wide Web. When you navigate to www.hotmail.com in a Web browser, you are presented with the Hotmail logon page. Here, you enter your username and password and then click Sign In to continue.

0.16b Once you've signed on, you are presented with the contents of your electronic inbox. This is the folder where incoming mail—email that was sent by others to you—is stored. Here, you can see a list of read and unread mail, navigate to other email folders, and delete email. You can also jump to other email tasks, such as composing a new email message of your own or managing your *Contacts*—those people with which your correspond regularly.

0.16c To open an email message, simply click the sender's name, which is highlighted as a hyperlink. The email message displays. From here, you can respond to the message, forward the message to others, delete the message, or move it to a different email folder.

name or *alias*) and a storage area for messages (sometimes called a *mailbox*). Any user can send a mail message to anyone else, regardless of whether the recipient is currently *logged in*—connected to the network. The message will be waiting in the recipient's *inbox* the next time he launches his email program and logs in. An email message can be addressed to one person or hundreds of people. Most email messages are plain text, without the kinds of formatting and graphic images found in printed documents. Messages can carry documents, pictures, multimedia files, and other computer files as *attachments*.

You can send messages to anyone on your local system or ISP by simply addressing the message to that person's user name. You can also send messages to anyone with access to Internet email, provided you know that person's Internet address. An Internet email address is made up of two parts separated by an at sign (the person's user name and the *host name*—the name of the host computer, network, or ISP address where the user receives mail. Here's the basic form:

```
username@hostname
```

Here are a few examples of typical email addresses:

```
realgeorge999@aol.com
jandumont@engr.ucla.edu
enathab@pop3.ispchannel.com
```

Some organizations use standardized email addresses so it's easy to guess member addresses. For example, every employee at ABCXYZ Company might have an email address of the form *firstname_lastname@abcxyzco.com*. (The underscore character is sometimes used as a substitute for a space because spaces can't be embedded in email addresses). It's important to address email messages with care—they can't be delivered if even a single character is mistyped. Fortunately, most email programs include address books, so users can look up email addresses by name and automatically address messages. Many World Wide Web sites, including Yahoo!, Excite, and search.com, offer free email search services and directories.

Many commercial Web sites offer free email accounts. Sometimes these free email services are subsidized by advertisers; sometimes they're provided to attract Web site visitors. Free email services are popular with users of public computers (for example, in libraries), people who don't receive email from their ISPs, people who want multiple email addresses not associated with their workplace, and travelers who want to check email on the road without lugging a laptop.

The example in the Screen Test shows a simple email session using Hotmail—an email service that's accessible through a standard Web browser. The concepts illustrated in the example apply to all email programs.

Internet Security Basics

Despite its wonders, the Internet can be a dangerous place. In the same way that you should wear a seat belt and observe local laws when driving a car, you should approach the Internet understanding the security risks involved. Once you connect a computer to a network or the Internet, you dramatically increase the risk that your system will be compromised in some way. But that doesn't mean that the Internet should be avoided. Rather, you just need to make sure you're taking the proper precautions.

The most common form of Internet-based security risk is probably spam, or junk mail. This is unwanted email you receive from (usually) unknown senders, such as mass mailers who are attempting to sell goods or even deceive people into paying for nonexistent items. Most email programs now include *spam filters*, which help keep this problem manageable, but even with a filter you're likely to spend plenty of time manually deleting spam messages.

Viruses are a more sinister email problem. Generally delivered as email attachments, viruses are executable programs designed by sinister programmers—sometimes called *hackers*—to infiltrate your system. Some viruses simply duplicate themselves and send themselves to other PCs by harvesting email addresses in your email address book; these types of viruses can slow the performance of your network, making Internet access unbearably slow. Others can delete files and folders on your system. Either way, you shouldn't open unexpected attachments from unknown senders.

Another problem on the Internet is password theft. There are low-tech methods for stealing others' passwords: For example, someone might look over your shoulder and watch as you type a password. Hackers sometimes create applications that can electronically monitor keystrokes and then send the information over the Internet to others. A wider but related issue concerns *identity (ID) theft*, where hackers or other unscrupulous individuals obtain enough information about you to assume your identity. In cases of ID theft, thieves have been known to use victims' credit cards to rack up thousands of dollars in bills. To protect yourself against ID theft, you should keep personal information, including your social security number, credit card numbers, and passwords a secret while online.

Obviously, there's a lot more to Internet security. We look extensively at this issue in Chapter 10.

Applying the Basics

> It is good to have **an end** to journey toward, but it is **the journey** that matters in the end.
>
> —Ursula K. LeGuin, author of *The Dispossessed*

In a few pages, you've learned the bare-bones basic concepts behind the PC and the Internet. Now it's time to apply what you've learned in a practical, hands-on way. The next few pages guide you, step-by-step, through an opening session with the *Computer Confluence* CD-ROM and Web site. They're followed by a few helpful rules of thumb for navigating through the remaining chapters of this book. Once you've completed this quick tour, you'll be ready to dive into the heart of *Computer Confluence*, starting with Chapter 1. So what are you waiting for?

0.17 The Mississippi state official is using software to compare previous and current driver's license photos. The software makes identity theft more difficult by discouraging false driver's license applicants.

RULES OF THUMB

Here are a few pointers for exploring *Computer Confluence*. Take a minute to read these and you'll probably save hours later.

➡ *Know your boxes.* Text chapters include several types of boxes, each of which is designed to be read in a particular way.

    The *Screen Test* boxes show you short sequences of screens from test drives of some of today's most popular software. These boxes can be especially helpful if they cover applications you aren't learning first-hand. The *Computer Confluence* CD-ROM includes multimedia introductions to some of the applications featured in these boxes.

    ***Rules of Thumb* boxes (similar to this one) provide practical tips on everything from designing a publication to protecting your privacy. They bring concepts down to earth with useful suggestions that can save you time, money, and peace of mind.**

    How It Works **boxes are for those readers who want—or need—to know more about what's going on under the hood. These boxes use words and pictures to take you deeper into the inner workings without getting bogged down in technical detail. The *Computer Confluence* CD-ROM includes multimedia versions of many of these boxes as well as bonus How It Works features that aren't in the text. If your course objectives or personal curiosity doesn't motivate you to learn how it works, that's okay; you can skip every How It Works box and still understand the rest of *Computer Confluence*.**

    Inventing the Future **boxes examine today's technological trends and research projects in order to speculate on the future of the technology and its impact on our lives. The *Computer Confluence* CD-ROM includes video clips that supplement and illustrate the ideas in many of these boxes.**

    Crosscurrents **boxes showcase diverse, timely, and often controversial points of view on the technology and its impact on our lives. These short essays, which close each chapter, offer perspectives from some of the most important writers and thinkers on information technology.**

➡ ***Read it and read it again.*** If possible, read each chapter twice: once for the big ideas and the second time for more detailed understanding. You may also find it helpful to survey each chapter's outline in the table of contents before reading the chapter for the first time.

➡ ***Don't try to memorize every term the first time through.*** Throughout the text, key terms are introduced in boldface blue, and secondary terms are *italicized in blue*. Use the Key Terms list at the end of each chapter to review and the glossary to recall any forgotten terms. The CD-ROM contains an interactive cross-referenced version of the glossary to find any term quickly.

➡ ***Don't overanalyze examples.*** *Computer Confluence* is designed to help you understand concepts, not memorize keystrokes. You can learn the nuts and bolts of working with computers in labs or at home. The examples in this text may not match the applications in your lab, but the concepts are similar.

➡ ***Don't get stuck.*** If a concept seems unclear on the first reading, make a note and move on. Sometimes ideas make more sense after you've seen the bigger picture. If you still don't understand the concept the second time through, check the CD-ROM and the Web site for further clarification. When in doubt, ask questions.

➡ ***Remember that there's more than one way to learn.*** Some of us learn best by reading, others learn best by exploring interactive examples, and still others learn best by discussing ideas with others, online or in person. *Computer Confluence* offers you the opportunity to learn in all of these ways. Use the learning tools that work best for you.

➡ ***Get your hands dirty.*** Try the applications while you're reading about them. Your reading and lab work will reinforce each other and help solidify your newfound knowledge.

➡ ***Study together.*** There's plenty to discuss here, and discussion is a great way to learn.

In a hurry? Turn the page. The next page will give you a quick start—just enough information so you can start using the CD-ROM, the Web site, and related computer applications right away.

Computer Confluence Quick Start

The first few chapters of this book provide you with a broad orientation to computers, CD-ROMs, the Internet, and related technology. In the meantime, this Quick Start provides the basics—without detailed explanations—so you can get started with the *Computer Confluence* CD-ROM and Web site right away.

Details vary from computer to computer, but the basics are generally the same. If you're working in a computer lab, you'll probably need a few additional lab instructions to supplement the steps in this Quick Start.

Launching the *Computer Confluence* CD-ROM

1. Turn on the computer. After a minute or so the screen will show icons that represent disks and other computer resources. It may also show open windows that reveal the contents of these resources. A row of menus appears at the top of each window (or, if you're using a Macintosh, at the top of the screen).
2. As you move the mouse around, the pointer on the screen moves in the same motion. (If you run out of space on the mouse pad or desk, you can lift the mouse and reposition it.) Point to an icon and click it by pressing the mouse button. (If there are two or more buttons, use the left button.) You'll click this way to select objects, press on-screen buttons, and navigate around the Web site and CD-ROM.
3. Insert the *Computer Confluence* CD-ROM in the CD-ROM drive. Press the drive's button to make the CD tray slide open. Place the CD, label side up, on the tray, being careful not to handle the other side. Close the CD tray by pressing the button again. (Some CD-ROM drives automatically close.) The *Computer Confluence* CD-ROM application may launch automatically, filling your screen with a Welcome screen. If it does, skip to step 5.
4. The next step depends on your operating system software. If you're not sure, ask.

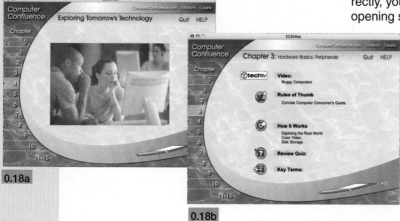

0.18a

0.18b

Windows

a. Point to the icon called "My Computer" and double-click it (click twice in rapid succession with the left mouse button).
b. Double-click the CD-ROM icon in the My Computer window.
c. Double-click the CCWin.EXE icon.

Macintosh

a. Point to the CCCD icon and double-click it (click twice in rapid succession).
b. Double-click the CCMac icon in the CCCD window.

5. The application takes a few seconds to load into the computer's memory. When it does, a new window will open on your screen. On-screen instructions will guide you through the CD's contents.

Exploring the *Computer Confluence* Web Site

To explore the *Computer Confluence* Web site, you'll need a Web browser and an Internet connection. Your computer probably includes one or more of these browsers: Internet Explorer, Netscape Navigator, Netscape Communicator, or America Online's Web browser.

1. Locate the browser and double-click its icon. If you're using a modem to connect to the Internet, this will probably cause the modem to dial the appropriate number.
2. Point to the long rectangle at the top of the browser window. If the text in that window is black on a white background, double-click it to highlight it. Then type **www.computerconfluence.com** to replace the highlighted text. (Depending on your browser, you may be able to get the same results by simply typing **computerconfluence**.) Press Return or Enter.
3. If an error message appears, click the OK button, check your typing carefully, correct any errors, and press Return or Enter again. When you type it correctly, you'll be taken to the *Computer Confluence* opening screen.
4. If you're using your own computer, you can mark this page so you can return by selecting it from a menu rather than re-typing its name. If you're using Internet Explorer, select Add to Favorites from the Favorites menu. If you're using Netscape Navigator or Communicator, select Add Bookmark from the Bookmark menu.
5. At the *Computer Confluence* site you can click on on-screen images and menus to select the edition of the book you're using, select a chapter, and Web site then select activities within that chapter.

The Myth of Generation N   Simson Garfinkel

Every chapter of this book ends with an article that explores issues related to computer technology and its impact on our lives. This essay was first published in August 2003, in MIT Technology Review. *In it Simson Garfinkel, author of* Database Nation, *raises some thought-provoking questions about the "net generation."*

For decades, social scientists and technologists have alternatively predicted the emergence of "computer kids" or a "net generation"—a cohort of children, teenagers, and young adults who have been immersed in digital technology and the digital way of thinking since their conception.

This new generation, the thinking went, would be everything that their parents weren't when it came to technology: They would know how to type, partake in electronic communications, and be able to rapidly figure out how all this stuff worked. They would be so adept at using computers that calling them "computer literate" would be an insult. They would see society as something to be mastered and hacked, not something that they need to fit inside.

Certainly, a lot of evidence supports a "net generation" effect. Although there are no reliable statistics on computer literacy, good figures do exist on Internet usage, thanks to the Pew Internet Project. According to its survey released earlier this year, 74 percent of people in the United States age 18 to 29 have Internet access, compared with 52 percent of those age 50 to 64. Among the over-65 set, Internet access plummets to just 18 percent. And in my own age group, 30 to 49, 52 percent have some kind of Net access. These figures certainly argue for the existence of a "Generation N."

But the more time I spend with the kids who should be members of Generation N—today's high school and college students—the more convinced I am that the notion of universal computer competence among young people is a myth. And the techno-laggards among us risk being relegated to second-class citizenship in a world that revolves around, and often assumes, access to information technology.

People who spend years working with computers learn how to use them; people who lack that experience, don't. I've seen 40- and 50-somethings who burn their own CDs and have phenomenal command of applications like Word, PowerPoint, and Excel. Like Generation N, they've wanted to get something done and invested the time to do it.

The difference between these old fogies and today's teens is that, for many teens today, learning to use a computer is no longer optional. The teachers in my town's high school refuse to accept papers unless they are typed on a computer. Typing itself is taught in the middle school (where they call it "keyboarding"); students who went to a less technologically progressive school system and transferred in are expected to pick up the skill on their own. Not a problem! "We all figured out how to get Napster going and download music," says a friend of mine who recently graduated from Stanford University and now works for a major investment firm. Everybody her age knows how to use a computer, she says, just like "everybody knows how to change their oil."

Experts in human–computer interaction say that the real difference between teenagers and their elders is teens' willingness to experiment with computers, combined with their acceptance of the seemingly arbitrary conventions that are endemic to contemporary computer interfaces. In other words, teens aren't worried about breaking their computers, and they're not wise enough or experienced enough to get angry at and reject poorly written programs. The teens just deal with computers, as they are forced to deal with many other aspects of their lives. These strategies, once learned and internalized, are incredibly effective for working with today's computer technology.

Likewise, today's systems are teaching their users—young and old alike—to multitask as never before. Just as their parents talked on the phone while doing math homework, today's teens browse the Web, send e-mail, and simultaneously engage in multiple chat and Instant Message sessions while allegedly working on an essay. A friend of mine has a daughter who developed a flair for language: she routinely has chat windows going in English, French, and Japanese—and both her parents are native English speakers!

But the point that seems to have escaped my friend is that everybody doesn't know how to change the oil on their car. It's not a generational thing; it's simply the result of 20 years' experience. But when you are surrounded by people who all share the same technological skills, it's easy to forget that there are others who aren't with the program (so to speak). Unfortunately, with the changes overtaking our society, today's kids who don't have tech experience and tech aptitude are going to be left behind much faster than their elders.

And that's the danger in believing that time will give us a population that's completely computer literate. Remember, the Pew study found that 26 percent of young adults do not have Internet access. An even bigger determiner than age is education: only 23 percent of people who did not graduate from high school have Internet access, compared with 82 percent of those who have graduated from college.

Certainly, more kids today are growing up wired—but millions of them are not. Meanwhile, we're rebuilding our society in ways that make things increasingly difficult for people who aren't online. For example, people who don't want to (or can't) buy their airplane tickets on the Web now typically have to wait on hold for 30 minutes with the airline or go through a travel agent and pay an agency fee—sometimes as much as $50. When I needed to renew my passport, the local post office didn't have the form: they told me to download it from the Internet.

This is a problem that won't be solved through more education or federal grants. As a society, we need to come to terms with the fact that a substantial number of people, young and old alike, will never go online. We need to figure out how we will avoid making life unbearable for them.

DISCUSSION QUESTIONS

1. Do you think there is a difference between the way young people approach computers and the way their parents approach computers? If so, what is the difference?

2. Do you agree with the statements in the last paragraph of this essay? Why or why not?

SUMMARY

PCs come in a variety of shapes and sizes, but they're all made up of two things—the physical parts of the computer, called hardware, and the software instructions that tell the hardware what to do. The PC's system unit contains the CPU, which controls the other components, including memory, disk drives, and monitor screens. The keyboard and mouse enable a user to communicate with the computer, which sends information back to the user through displays on the monitor.

The computer's operating system software takes care of details of the computer's operation. Application software provides specific tools for computer users.

PCs can be networked to other computers using cables, radio waves, or other means. A computer can also connect to a network through standard phone lines using a modem.

The Internet is a global network of computer networks used for education, commerce, and communication. The most popular Internet activities are exploring the World Wide Web and communicating with electronic mail.

A Web browser is a PC application that provides easy access to the World Wide Web—a wide-ranging array of multimedia information on the Internet. Web pages are interconnected by hyperlinks that make it easy to follow information trails. Search engines serve as indices for the Web, locating pages with subject matter that matches key words.

Electronic mail is the most popular Internet application. Email enables almost instant communication among Internet users. Some email systems can be accessed through Web browsers.

The Internet is not without risks. Internet users must be prepared to deal with unsolicited (and often unsavory) email, computer viruses, identity theft, and other risks.

The *Computer Confluence* CD-ROM and companion Web site use PC multimedia and Internet technology to enhance and expand the information and ideas presented in this book.

KEY TERMS

(Terms introduced in this chapter will be revisited in later chapters.)

application program (application) (p. 9)
button (p. 8)
CD-ROM drive (p. 6)
CD-RW drive (p. 6)
central processing unit (CPU) (p. 5)
click (p. 8)
diskettes (p. 6)
document (p. 9)
double-click (p. 8)
drag (p. 8)
DVD drive (p. 6)
electronic mail (email) (p. 19)

file (p. 9)
Find (p. 15)
folder (p. 15)
hard disk (p. 5)
hardware (p. 5)
hyperlink (p. 18)
Internet (p. 15)
keyboard (p. 6)
memory (p. 5)
menu (p. 8)
monitor (p. 7)
mouse (p. 6)
Open (p. 9)
operating system (OS) (p. 9)
peripheral (p. 5)

personal computer (PC) (p. 5)
printer (p. 7)
Search (p. 15)
search engine (p. 18)
software (p. 9)
spam (p. 21)
URL (uniform resource locator) (p. 17)
user name (p. 19)
viruses (p. 21)
Web browser (p. 17)
Web page (p. 17)
Web site (p. 17)
World Wide Web (WWW) (p. 17)

INTERACTIVE QUIZ QUESTIONS

1. The *Computer Confluence* CD-ROM contains self-test quiz questions related to this chapter, including multiple-choice, true or false, and matching questions.

2. The *Computer Confluence* Web site, http://www.prenhall.com/beekmancomputerconfluence.com, contains self-test exercises related to this chapter. Follow the instructions for taking a quiz. After you've completed your quiz, you can email the results to your instructor.

3. The Web site also contains open-ended discussion questions called Internet Explorations. Discuss one or more of the Internet Exploration questions at the section for this chapter.

TRUE OR FALSE

1. The majority of people in the world use computers at least occasionally. T

2. A computer keyboard includes some keys that don't respond by displaying characters on the screen, but instead send special commands to the computer. T

3. Windows PCs and Macintoshes use the same operating system (OS). F

4. An entire computer network can be connected to other networks through cables, wireless radio transmissions, or other means. T

5. Hypertext links make it easy to jump between Web pages created by different authors around the world. T

6. A Web search engine is built around a database that catalogs Web locations based on content. T

7. An Internet email address is made up of a user name and a host name separated by an at sign (@). T

8. Web searching and email checking require different application programs on virtually all PCs. T

9. Spam is a type of computer virus that attacks only email documents. F

10. The Internet has become virtually risk-free within the last few years. F

MULTIPLE CHOICE

1. The computer's system unit typically contains the computer's "brain, " the
   a. central processing unit.
   b. memory.
   c. peripheral.
   d. monitor.
   e. modem.

2. All of these are considered removable media except
   a. diskettes.
   b. CD-ROMs.
   c. audio CDs.
   d. hard disks.
   e. DVDs.

3. All of these are peripherals except
   a. a printer.
   b. a mouse.
   c. a CD-ROM drive.
   d. a processor.
   e. These are all peripherals.

4. A software program designed to help you accomplish a specific task is called
   a. an application.
   b. an operating system.
   c. a document.
   d. a desktop.
   e. a browser.

5. Every Web site on the World Wide Web has
   a. hyperlinks to dozens of other Web sites.
   b. multimedia material.
   c. publicly accessible information on a particular subject.
   d. a unique address called a URL.
   e. All of the above.

6. If you want to retrace your steps and return to the screen previously displayed in the browser window, you should use
   a. the left-arrow key.
   b. the R key.
   c. the browser's Back button.
   d. the spacebar.
   e. the Undo key.

7. You can repeatedly narrow your search for information on the Web by using
   a. the down-arrow key.
   b. the right mouse button.
   c. the scroll bar.
   d. an email browser.
   e. a directory or subject tree.

8. An attachment to an email message can carry
   a. a picture.
   b. a multimedia file.
   c. a word processor document.
   d. a computer virus.
   e. All of the above.

9. Which of these is definitely *not* a valid email address?
   a. http://www.computerconfluence.com
   b. beanbag_boxspring@prenhall.com
   c. president@whitehouse.gov
   d. thisisaverylongnameindeed@aol.com
   e. All of the above could be valid email addresses.

10. The most common use of spam is for
    a. transmitting computer viruses.
    b. identity theft.
    c. marketing unsolicited goods and services.
    d. Web searches.
    e. hacking.

REVIEW QUESTIONS

1. Briefly define or describe each of the key terms listed in the Key Terms section.
2. How are hardware and software related?
3. Which computer component is the most critical to the computer's functioning, and why?
4. Which two computer components are most often used by people for getting information into PCs?
5. What is the difference between operating system software and application software?
6. List some ways that a computer might be connected to a network.
7. Give examples of ways email can change the way you communicate with other people.
8. How can you use hyperlinks to explore the World Wide Web? Give an example.
9. How can you find a site on the Web if you don't know the URL?
10. What security procedures should you follow while exploring the *Computer Confluence* Web site?

DISCUSSION QUESTIONS

1. Spend some time exploring the *Computer Confluence* CD-ROM. What features of the software do you think will be most helpful to you? Why?
2. Spend some time exploring the *Computer Confluence* Web site, **www.computerconfluence.com**. What features of the site do you think will be most helpful to you? Why?

PROJECT

1. Keep a log of your progress as you use the *Computer Confluence* book, CD-ROM, and Web site. Make notes on which features are most helpful and which are least helpful. When you finish the book and related material, you may want to send a summary of your log to the author c/o Prentice Hall. Your notes will help make future editions of *Computer Confluence* more useful for others.

SOURCES AND RESOURCES

At the end of every chapter of *Computer Confluence*, you'll find an annotated list of valuable resources for learning more about the subjects covered in the chapter. Some of these resources are magazines, journals, and other periodicals with particularly good coverage of computers, the Internet, and the impact of technology on our lives. Some of the resources are books, both fiction and nonfiction, that provide insights into the world of information technology. Some are films and videos that vividly portray concepts and issues related to the technology. And, of course, some are Web sites that can take you far beyond the basic ideas covered in this book. If you want to learn more, start with these sources and resources.

AFTER YOU READ THIS CHAPTER YOU SHOULD BE ABLE TO:

- Characterize what a computer is and what it does

- Describe several ways computers play a critical role in modern life

- Discuss the circumstances and ideas that led to the development of the modern computer

- Describe several trends in the evolution of modern computers

- Comment on the fundamental difference between computers and other machines

- Explain the relationship between hardware and software

- Outline the four major types of computers in use today and describe their principal uses

- Describe how the explosive growth of the Internet is changing the way people use computers and information technology

- Explain how today's information age differs from other times in history and prehistory

- Discuss the social and ethical impact of information technology on our society

 Multimedia extras on the CD-ROM and the Web:

- Stewart Brand on computers and the **counter-culture**

- Instant access to **glossary** and **key term** references

- Interactive **self-study** quizzes

    . . . and more.

 computerconfluence.com

COMPUTER CURRENTS
From Calculation to Connection

CHARLES BABBAGE, LADY LOVELACE, AND THE MOTHER OF ALL COMPUTERS

The Analytical Engine Lady Lovelace referred to was the mother of all computers, conceived by Charles Babbage, a nineteenth-century mathematics professor at Cambridge University. Babbage was an eccentric genius known by the public for his dislike of street musicians and the efforts he made to illegalize them. But Babbage was much more than an irascible crank; his many inventions included the skeleton key, the speedometer, and . . . the computer.

> The Analytical Engine has **no pretensions whatever** to originate anything. It can do **whatever** we know **how to order it** to perform.
>
> —Augusta Ada King, Countess of Lovelace

Babbage's computer vision grew out of his frustration with the tedious and error-prone process of creating mathematical tables. In 1823, he received a grant from the British government to develop a "difference engine"—a mechanical device for performing repeated numeric additions. Two decades earlier, Joseph-Marie Charles Jacquard, a French textile maker, had developed a loom that could automatically reproduce woven patterns by reading information encoded in patterns of holes punched in stiff paper cards. After learning of Jacquard's programmable loom, Babbage abandoned the difference engine for a more ambitious enterprise: an Analytical Engine that could be programmed with punched cards to carry out any calculation to 20 digits of accuracy. Babbage's design included the four basic components found in every modern computer: components for performing the basic functions of input, output, processing, and storage.

1.1 Analytical Engine
1.2 Charles Babbage (1791–1871)

Augusta Ada King, Countess of Lovelace (sometimes erroneously called "Ada Lovelace"), the daughter of poet Lord Byron, visited Babbage and his Analytical Engine. Ada corresponded regularly with him, and she is often called the first computer programmer because she wrote a plan for using the Analytical Engine to calculate sequences of Bernoulli numbers. But *programmer* is probably the wrong term to describe her actual contribution. She was more of an interpreter and promoter of Babbage's visionary work.

Babbage was obsessed with completing the Analytical Engine. Eventually, the government withdrew financial support; there simply wasn't enough public demand to justify the ever-increasing cost. The technology of the time was not sufficient to turn their ideas into reality. The world wasn't ready for computers, and it wouldn't be for another 100 years.

1.3 Augusta Ada King, Countess of Lovelace (1815–1852)

Computers are so much a part of modern life that we hardly notice them. But computers are everywhere, and we'd certainly notice them if they suddenly stopped working. Imagine …

Living Without Computers

You wake up with the sun well above the horizon and realize your alarm clock hasn't gone off. You wonder if you've overslept. You have a big research project due today. The face of your digital wristwatch stares back at you blankly. The TV and radio are no help; you can't find a station on either one. You can't even get the time by telephone because the phone doesn't work either.

The morning newspaper is missing from your doorstep. You'll have to guess the weather forecast by looking out the window. No music to dress by this morning, as your CD player and your MP3 player refuse your requests. How about some breakfast? Your automatic coffeemaker refuses to be programmed; your microwave oven is on strike too.

You decide to go out for breakfast. Your car won't start. In fact, the only cars moving are at least 15 years old. The lines at the subway are unbelievable. People chatter nervously about the failure of the subway's computer-controlled scheduling device.

You duck into a coffee shop and find long lines of people waiting while cashiers clumsily handle transactions by hand. While you're waiting, you join the conversation that's going on around you. People seem more interested in talking to each other in person since all the usual tools of mass communication have failed.

You're down to a couple of dollars in cash, so you stop after breakfast at an automated teller machine. Why bother?

1.4 Computer screens and television screens populate today's television control rooms.

You return home to wait for the book you ordered online. You're in for a long wait; planes aren't flying because air traffic control facilities aren't working. You head for the local library to see if the book is in stock. Of course, it's going to be tough to find since the book catalog is computerized.

As you walk home, you speculate on the implications of a worldwide computer failure. How will people function in high-tech, high-rise office buildings that depend on computer systems to control everything from elevators to humidity? Will electric power plants be able to function without computer control? What will happen to patients in computerized medical facilities? What about satel-lites that are kept in orbit by computer-run control systems? Will the financial infrastruc-ture collapse without computers to process and communicate transactions? Will the world be a safer place if all computer-controlled weapons are grounded?

1.5 Computers are used to coordinate thousands of Union Pacific trains in this high-tech Omaha control room.

Our story could go on, but the message should be clear enough by now. Computers are everywhere, and our lives are affected in all kinds of ways by their operation—and nonoperation. It's truly amazing that computers have infiltrated our lives so thoroughly in such a short time.

Computers in Perspective: An Evolving Idea

While computers have been with us for only about half a century, the roots of these now commonplace devices go back to a time long before Charles Babbage conceived of the Analytical Engine in 1823. These extraordinary machines are built on centuries of insight and intellectual effort.

1.6 This cart's built-in computer helps golfers navigate the course.

Before Computers

Computers grew out of a human need to quantify. Early humans were content to count with fingers, rocks, or other everyday objects. As cultures be-came more complex, so did their counting tools.

Consider the past and you shall know the future.
—Chinese Proverb

The abacus (a type of counting tool and calculator used by the Babylonians, the Chinese, and others for thousands of years) and the Hindu-Arabic number system are examples of early calculating tools that had an immediate and profound effect on the human race. (Imagine trying to conduct business without a number system that allows for easy addi-tion and subtraction.)

The Analytical Engine had little impact until a century after its invention, when it served as a blueprint for the first real programmable computer. Virtually every computer in use today follows the basic plan laid out by Babbage and Lady Lovelace.

The Information-Processing Machine

Like the Analytical Engine, the computer is a machine that changes information from one form to another. All computers take in information called input and give out information called output, as shown here.

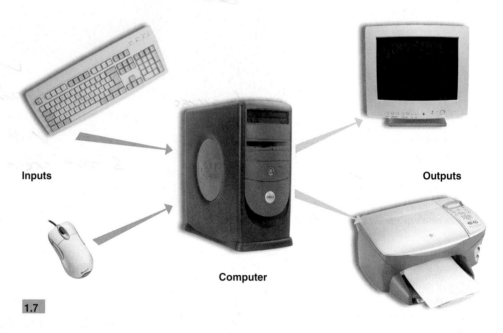

Inputs

Outputs

Computer

1.7

Because information can take many forms, the computer is an incredibly versatile tool, capable of everything from computing federal income taxes to guiding the missiles those taxes buy. For calculating taxes, the input to the computer might be numbers representing wages, other income, deductions, exemptions, and tax tables, and the output might be the number representing the taxes owed or the tax refund due. If the computer is deploying a missile, for example, the input might be satellite signals used to locate the missile and the target, and the output might be electrical signals to control the flight path of the missile. Amazingly enough, the same computer could be used to accomplish both of these tasks.

How can a machine be so versatile? The computer's flexibility isn't hidden in hardware—the physical parts of the computer system. The secret of its functionality is in its software, or programs—the instructions that tell the hardware how to transform the input data (information in a form it can read) into the necessary output.

Whether a computer is performing a simple calculation or producing a complex animation, a software program of some type controls the process from beginning to end. In effect, changing programs can turn the computer into a different tool. Because it can be programmed to perform various tasks, the typical modern computer is a general-purpose tool, not a specialized device with one use.

The First Real Computers

First we shape our tools, thereafter **they shape us**.

—Marshall McLuhan

Although Lady Lovelace predicted that the Analytical Engine might someday compose music, the scientists and mathematicians who designed and built the first working computers a century later had a more modest goal: to create machines capable of doing repetitive calculations. Even so, their stories are rich with drama and irony. Here are a few highlights:

■ In 1939, a young German engineer named Konrad Zuse completed the first programmable, general-purpose digital computer. "I was too lazy to calculate and so I invented the computer," Zuse recalls. In 1941, Zuse and a friend asked the German government for funds to build a faster electronic computer to help crack enemy codes during World War II. The Nazi military establishment turned him down, confident that their aircraft would quickly win the war without the aid of sophisticated calculating devices.

■ At about the same time, the British government was assembling a top-secret team of mathematicians and engineers to crack Nazi military codes. In 1943, the team, led by mathematician Alan Turing and others, completed Colossus, considered by many to be the first electronic digital computer. This special-purpose computer successfully broke secret codes used by the Nazis, allowing British military intelligence to eavesdrop on even the most secret German messages throughout most of the war.

■ In 1939, Iowa State University professor John Atanasoff, seeking a tool to help his students solve differential equations, developed what could have been the first electronic digital computer, the Atanasoff–Berry Computer (ABC). His university neglected to patent the machine, and Atanasoff never managed to turn it into a fully operational product. The International Business Machines Corporation responded to his queries by telling him "IBM will never be interested in an electronic computing machine."

■ Harvard professor Howard Aiken was more successful in financing the automatic general-purpose calculator he was developing. Thanks to a $1 million grant from IBM, he completed the Mark I in 1944. This 51-foot-long, 8-foot-tall monster used noisy electromechanical relays to calculate five or six times faster than a person could, but it was far slower than a modern $5 pocket calculator.

■ After consulting with Atanasoff and studying the ABC, John Mauchly teamed up with J. Presper Eckert to help the U.S. effort in World War II by constructing a machine to calculate trajectory tables for new guns. The machine was the ENIAC (Electronic Numerical Integrator and Computer), a 30-ton behemoth with 18,000 vacuum tubes that broke down, on average, once every seven minutes. When it was running, it could calculate 500 times faster than the existing electromechanical calculators—about as fast as a modern pocket calculator. It wasn't completed until two months after the end of the war, but it convinced its creators that large-scale computers were commercially feasible. After the war, Mauchly and Eckert started a private company called Sperry and created UNIVAC I, the first general-purpose commercial computer. UNIVAC I went to work for the U.S. Census Bureau in 1951.

Evolution and Acceleration

Invention breeds **invention**.

—Ralph Waldo Emerson

Computer hardware evolved rapidly from those early days, with new technologies replacing old every few years. The first computers were big, expensive, and finicky. Only a big institution like a major bank or the U.S. government could afford a computer, not to mention the climate-controlled computing center needed to house it and the staff of technicians needed to program it and keep it running. But with all their faults, computers quickly became indispensable tools for scientists, engineers, and other professionals.

The transistor, invented in 1948, could perform the same function as vacuum tubes used in early computers by transferring electricity across a tiny resistor. Transistors were first used in a computer in 1956. Computers that used transistors were radically smaller, more reliable, and less expensive than tube-based computers. Because of improvements in software at about the same time, these machines were also much easier and faster to program and use. As a result, computers became more widely used in business as well as in science and engineering.

But America's fledgling space program needed computers that were even smaller and more powerful than the transistor-based machines, so researchers developed technology that enabled them to pack hundreds of transistors into a single integrated circuit on a tiny silicon chip. By the mid-1960s, transistor-based computers were replaced by smaller, more powerful machines built around the new integrated circuits.

Integrated circuits rapidly replaced transistors for the same reasons that transistors superseded vacuum tubes:

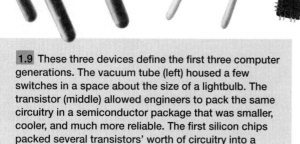

1.9 These three devices define the first three computer generations. The vacuum tube (left) housed a few switches in a space about the size of a lightbulb. The transistor (middle) allowed engineers to pack the same circuitry in a semiconductor package that was smaller, cooler, and much more reliable. The first silicon chips packed several transistors' worth of circuitry into a speck much smaller than a single transistor.

- *Reliability.* Machines built with integrated circuits were less prone to failure than their predecessors, because the chips could be rigorously tested before installation.
- *Size.* Single chips could replace entire circuit boards containing hundreds or thousands of transistors, making it possible to build much smaller machines.
- *Speed.* Because electricity had shorter distances to travel, the smaller machines were markedly faster than their predecessors.
- *Efficiency.* Since chips were so small, they used less electrical power. As a result, they created less heat.
- *Cost.* Mass production techniques made it easy to manufacture inexpensive chips.

Just about every breakthrough in computer technology since the dawn of the computer age has presented similar advantages over the technology it replaced.

The relentless progress of the computer industry is illustrated by Moore's law. In 1965, Gordon Moore, the chairman of chipmaker Intel, predicted half-seriously that the power of a silicon chip of the same price would double about every 18 months for at least two decades. So far, Moore's prediction has been uncannily accurate, over three decades later!

The Microcomputer Revolution

Computer cost-effectiveness has risen **100 millionfold** since the late 1950s—a 100,000-fold rise in **power** times a thousandfold drop in **cost**.

—George Gilder

The inventions of the vacuum tube, the transistor, and the silicon chip had tremendous impact on our society. But none of these had a more profound effect than the invention in 1971 of the first microprocessor—the critical components of a complete computer housed on a tiny silicon chip. The development of the *microprocessor* by Intel engineers caused immediate and radical changes in the appearance, capability, and availability of computers.

The research and development costs for the first microprocessor were awesome. But once the assembly lines were in place, silicon computer chips could be mass-produced cheaply. The raw materials were certainly cheap enough; silicon, the main ingredient in beach sand, is the second most common element (after oxygen) in the Earth's crust.

U.S. companies soon flooded the marketplace with watches and pocket calculators built around inexpensive microprocessors. The economic effect was immediate: Mechanical calculators and slide rules became obsolete overnight, electronic hobbyists became wealthy entrepreneurs, and California's San Jose area gained the nickname Silicon Valley when dozens of microprocessor manufacturing companies sprouted and grew there.

The microcomputer revolution began in the late 1970s when companies such as Apple, Commodore, and Tandy introduced low-cost, typewriter-sized computers as powerful as many of the room-sized computers that had come before. Personal computers, or PCs, as microcomputers have come to be known, are now common in offices, factories, homes, schools, and just about everywhere else. Because chip manufacturers have been so successful at obeying Moore's law, microcomputers have steadily increased in speed and power during the last two decades. At the same time, personal computers have taken over many tasks formerly performed by large computers, and every year people find new, innovative ways to harness these tiny, versatile workhorses.

With the rise of PCs, the era of *institutional computing* came to a close. Indeed, small computers had an even greater impact on society than their room-sized predecessors. Still, desktop computers haven't completely replaced big computers, which have also evolved. Today's world is populated with a variety of computers, each particularly well suited to specific tasks.

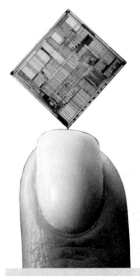

1.10 Today, a single chip the size of your fingernail can contain the equivalent of millions of transistors.

1.11 The microcomputer revolution didn't just increase the number of computers in offices, it opened up entirely new possibilities for computing habitats. This police officer uses a computer to record case notes and track crime information. David Solove uses a portable computer, a digital camera, and a scanner to produce an online diary of circus life for his family and friends. The marine biologist uses a laptop computer to record research notes and analyze data in the field.

Computers Today: A Brief Taxonomy

An IBM electronic calculator speeds through **thousands of intricate computations** so quickly that on many complex problems, it's just like having **150 extra engineers** ...

—IBM ad showing dozens of slide-rule-toting engineers in the February 1952 issue of *National Geographic*

Today, people work with mainframe computers, supercomputers, workstations, notebook computers, handheld computers, embedded computers, and, of course, PCs. Even though they're based on the same technology, these machines have important differences.

1.12 Computer-driven display systems are important fixtures in meeting rooms.

Mainframes and Supercomputers

Before the microcomputer revolution, most information processing was done on mainframe computers—room-sized machines with price tags to match. Today, large organizations, such as banks and airlines, still use mainframes for big computing jobs. But today's mainframes are smaller and cheaper than their ancestors; a typical mainframe today might be the size of a refrigerator and cost around a million U.S. dollars. These industrial-strength computers are largely invisible to the general public, because they're hidden away in climate-controlled rooms.

But the fact that you can't see them doesn't mean you don't use them. When you make an online airline reservation or deposit money in your bank account, a mainframe computer is involved in the transaction, behind the scenes. Your travel agent and your bank teller communicate with a mainframe using a computer terminal—a combination keyboard and screen with little local processing power that transfers information to and from the computer. The computer might be in another room or even in another country halfway around the globe.

1.13 Terminals like the one in the photo on the left make it possible for ticket agents all over the world to send information to a single mainframe computer like the one shown on the right.

A mainframe computer can communicate with several users simultaneously through a technique called timesharing. For example, a timesharing system allows travel agents all over the country to make reservations using the same computer and the same flight information at the same time.

Timesharing also makes it possible for users with diverse computing needs to share expensive computing equipment. Many research scientists and engineers, for example, need more mathematical computing power than they can get from personal computers. Their computing needs might require a powerful mainframe computer. A timesharing machine can simultaneously serve the needs of scientists and engineers in different departments working on a variety of projects.

Many researchers can't get the computing power they need from a mainframe computer; traditional "big iron" simply isn't fast enough for their calculation-intensive work, such as weather forecasting, telephone network design, simulated car crash testing, oil exploration, computer animation, and medical imaging. Power users with these special requirements need access to the fastest, most powerful computers made. These superfast, superpowerful computers are called supercomputers.

1.14 The Blue Mountain supercomputer at the U.S. Department of Energy's Los Alamos National Laboratory can perform 1.6 trillion operations per second. The machine is used to simulate nuclear tests and perform intensive calculations for other research projects.

Servers, Workstations, and PCs

For applications that serve multiple users, a high-end computer called a server—a computer designed to provide software and other resources to other computers over a network—is used. Although just about any computer can be used as a server, some computers are specifically designed with this purpose in mind. (Networks and servers are discussed later in this chapter and in later chapters.)

A workstation—a high-end desktop computer with massive computing power—is used for high-end interactive applications, such as large-scale scientific data analysis. Workstations are widely used by scientists, engineers, financial analysts, designers, and animators whose work involves intensive computations. Of course, like many computer terms, *workstation* means different things to different people. Some people refer to all desktop computers and terminals as workstations. Those who reserve the term for the most powerful desktop machines admit that the line separating workstations and high-end personal computers is fading. As workstations become less expensive and personal computers become more powerful, the line becomes as much a marketing distinction as a technical one.

Most computer users don't need the power of a scientific workstation to do their day-to-day business. A modern PC has plenty of computing power for word processing, accounting, gaming, enjoying digital music and video, and other common applications. A personal computer, as the name implies, is almost always dedicated to serving a single user at a time.

A word about terminology: The terms *personal computer* and *PC* occasionally generate confusion because in 1981 IBM named its desktop computer the IBM Personal Computer. That's why the terms *personal computer* and *PC* often are used to describe only IBM computers or machines compatible with IBM hardware. ("The office has a network of Macs and PCs.") But in another context, PC might describe any general-purpose single-user computer. ("Every student needs a PC to connect to the Internet.") When we refer to PCs generically in this book, we are referring to any PC, not just those that are made by or compatible with IBM's products.

1.15 Workstations are used by scientists, engineers, and others who need more computational power than a standard PC can deliver.

1.16 Personal computers today come in a variety of forms. Apple's iMac houses the CPU, display, and storage devices in an all-in-one design. The Dell Dimension tower on the right is a more traditional design, with the display separate from the CPU and storage.

Portable Computers

Two decades ago, the terms *personal computer* and *desktop computer* were interchangeable because virtually all PCs were desktop computers. Today, however, one of the fastest-growing segments of the PC market involves machines that aren't tied to the desktop. We call these devices portable computers.

Of course, *portability* is a relative term. The first "portable" computers were 20-pound suitcases with foldout keyboards and small, TV-like screens. Today, those "luggable" computers have been replaced by flat-screen, battery-powered notebook computers (sometimes called laptop computers) that are so light you can rest one on your lap while you work or carry it in a briefcase when it's closed.

Today's notebook typically weighs between 3 and 10 pounds, depending on the machine. Many laptops perform as well as desktop PCs; these heavy but powerful devices are called desktop replacements. Extra-light, ultramobile notebooks are sometimes called subnotebooks. To keep size and weight down, manufacturers often leave out some components that would be standard equipment on desktop machines. For example, some laptops don't have built-in optical drives for playing or recording CD-ROM or DVD discs. Some have expansion bays that allow these devices to be inserted one at a time. Most have several ports that allow external drives to be attached with cables. A few models can be expanded with docking stations or port replicators, which enables a user to connect the laptop to an external monitor, keyboard, mouse, and disk drives. Many mobile workers use docking stations to turn their laptops into full-featured desktop PCs when they return to their offices. Even without docking stations, a laptop can be easily connected to peripherals and networks when it's deskbound.

Handheld computers, which are often small enough to tuck into a shirt pocket, serve the needs of users who value mobility over a full-sized keyboard and screen. Docking cradles for handheld computers enable them to share information with desktop and laptop PCs. Handheld computers are sometimes called personal digital assistants (PDAs) or palm-sized computers.

Size notwithstanding, most portable computers in all their variations are general-purpose computers built around microprocessors similar to those that drive desktop models. But portability comes at a price—portable computers generally cost more than comparable desktop machines. They're also more difficult to upgrade when newer harware components become available.

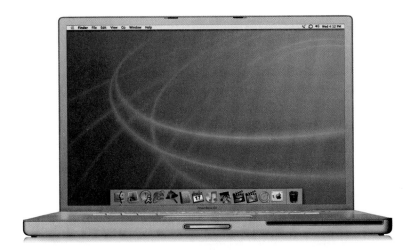

1.17 The portable computers shown here represent just a small sample of the sizes of types available today. Apple's PowerBook G4 (above, left) is a full-featured desktop replacement notebook computer. The IBM ThinkPad T40 (bottom, right) can be converted from a notebook to a desktop system using a docking station (pictured) or port replicator. The Palm Tungsten (above, center) is a handheld computer designed to accept input via a stylus; it can synchronize wirelessly with a PC. The RIM Blackberry (bottom, left) is a handheld computer designed for email communications with a tiny, thumb-operated keyboard. The Hewlett-Packard iPAQ Pocket PC device (above, right) uses a version of Microsoft Windows designed for handheld computers and ships with Pocket versions of popular Office applications.

Embedded Computers and Special-Purpose Computers

Not all computers are general-purpose machines. Many are special-purpose, dedicated computers that perform specific tasks, ranging from controlling the temperature and humidity in a high-rise office building to monitoring your heart rate while you work out. Embedded computers enhance all kinds of consumer goods: wristwatches, toys, game machines, stereos, digital video recorders (DVRs), and ovens. In fact, more than 90 percent of the world's microprocessors are hidden inside common household and electronic devices! Because of embedded computers, a typical new car probably has more computing power than the salesperson's PC.

Most special-purpose computers are, at their core, similar to general-purpose personal computers. But unlike their desktop cousins, these special-purpose machines typically have their programs etched in silicon so they can't be altered. When a program is immortalized on a silicon chip, it becomes known as firmware—a hybrid of hardware and software.

1.18 Embedded computers are so common in today's world that they're all but invisible. This experimental children's doll is really a robot.

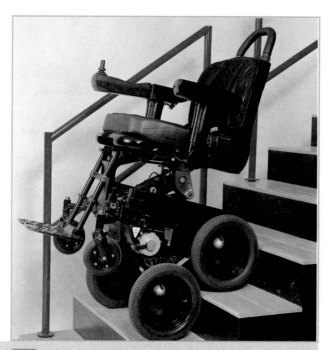

1.19 The Independence 3000 IBOT Transporter is an intelligent wheelchair that allows people to climb up and down stairs, "stand up" on two wheels, and even stroll on the beach.

1.20 The dashboard computer in this car provides maps and navigation information for the driver.

Computer Connections: The Internet Revolution

All persons are caught in an **inescapable network of mutuality**, tied in a single garment of destiny. Whatever affects **one** directly, affects **all** indirectly . . .

—Martin Luther King, Jr.

We've seen how breakthroughs in various technologies have produced new types of computers. Each of these technological advances had an impact on our society as people found new ways to put computers to work. Most historians stopped counting computer generations after the microcomputer became commonplace; it was hard to imagine another breakthrough having as much impact as the tiny microprocessor. But while the world was still reeling from the impact of the microcomputer revolution, another information technology revolution was quietly building up steam: the network revolution. Today we can look back on the late 1990s as the beginning of the era of *interpersonal computing*.

The Emergence of Networks

The invention of timesharing in the 1960s allowed multiple users to connect to a single mainframe computer through individual terminals. When personal computers started replacing terminals, many users found they had all the computing power they needed on their desktops. Still, there were advantages to linking some of these computers in local area networks (LANs), sometimes simply referred to as networks. When clusters of computers were networked, they could share resources such as storage, printers, and even processing power. Using a network, a single high-speed printer could meet the needs of an entire office. As a bonus, people could use computers to send and receive messages electronically through the networks.

The advantages of electronic communication and resource sharing were multiplied when smaller networks were joined to larger networks. Emerging telecommunication tech-

Computer Time Line

These *Time* covers symbolize changes in the way people saw and used computers as they evolved through the last half of the twentieth century. Notice that the beginning of each new "era" doesn't mean the end of the old ways of computing; today we live in a world of institutional, personal, and interpersonal computing.

1950   1975   1995

Institutional Computing Era
(Starting approximately 1950)

Characterized by a few large, expensive mainframe computers in climate-controlled rooms; controlled by experts and specialists; used mainly for data storage and calculation.

Personal Computing Era
(Starting approximately 1975)

Characterized by millions of small, inexpensive micro-computers on desktops in offices, schools, homes, factories, and almost everywhere else; controlled mostly by independent users; used mostly for document creation, data storage, and calculation.

Interpersonal Computing Era
(Starting approximately 1995)

Characterized by networks of interconnected computers in offices, homes, schools, vehicles, and almost everywhere else; controlled by users (clients) and network operators; used mostly for communication, document creation, data storage, and calculation.

1.21

nology eventually allowed wide area networks (WANs) to span continents and oceans. A remote computer could connect to a network through standard telephone lines by using a modem—an electronic device that could translate computer data into signals compatible with the telephone system. Banks, government agencies, and other large, geographically distributed institutions gradually built information-processing systems to take advantage of long-distance networking technology. But for most computer users outside of these organizations, networking was not the norm. People saw computers as tools for doing calculations, storing data, and producing paper documents—not as communication tools. So until the late 1990s, most PCs were stand-alone devices, islands of information.

There were exceptions: A group of visionary computer scientists and engineers, with financial backing from the U.S. government, built an experimental network called ARPANET in 1969. This groundbreaking network would become the Internet—the global collection of networks that radically transformed the way the world uses computers.

The Internet Explosion

In its early years, the Internet was the domain of researchers, academics, and government officials. It wasn't designed for casual visitors; users had to know cryptic commands and codes that only a programmer could love. But in the 1990s, Internet software suddenly took giant leaps forward in usability.

> It is **not proper** to think of networks as connecting computers. Rather, they connect people using computers to **mediate**. The **great success of the Internet** is not technical, but **its human impact**.
>
> —Dave Clark, Internet pioneer, now a senior research scientist at MIT

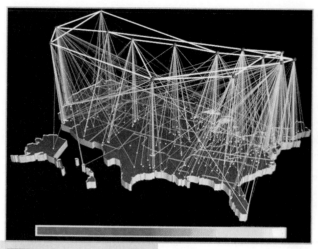

1.22 This computer-generated 3-D map represents major Internet connections in the United States.

Electronic mail programs first attracted nontechnical people to the Internet. **Email** software made it easy to send messages across the office or around the world without learning complex codes.

But the biggest changes came in the early 1990s with the development of the **World Wide Web** (**WWW**, or **Web**), a vast tract of the Internet accessible to just about anyone who could point to buttons on a computer screen. The Web led the Internet's transformation from a text-only environment into a multimedia landscape incorporating pictures, animation, sounds, and video. Millions of people connect to the Web each day through **Web browsers**—programs that, in effect, serve as navigable windows into the Web. **Hypertext links** on Web pages loosely tie together millions of Web pages created by diverse authors, making the Web into a massive, ever-changing global information storehouse.

Widespread email and Web use have led to astounding Internet growth in the last decade. In 1994, three million people were connected; by the end of 2002, over 550 million people had Internet connections. Over 54 percent of all American households are connected to the Internet; before the first decade of the twenty-first century is over, 90 percent of U.S. households will likely be connected, making the Internet almost as universal as the television and the telephone. The United States leads the world in Internet activity, but the rest of the world is catching up. About 34 percent of all Europeans were online in 2001, and their numbers are rising quickly. By 2004, some predict, over 79 percent of Europeans will be online.

1.23 People throughout the world use "Cyber Cafés" as both access points to the Web and places to socialize.

In the late 1990s, Internet users tended to be younger, better educated, and wealthier than the rest of the population. But as the Internet's population grew, it has come to look more like the population at large. According to the U.S. Internet Council, the percentage of African-Americans and Hispanics who use the Internet is rising rapidly. More than half of all active Internet users are now female. And while there are still some areas, even in the United States, with no Internet access, those are becoming harder to find. In just about any city on Earth, you can rent time on a PC to check your email or explore the Web.

The Internet is growing faster than television, radio, or any other communication technology that came before it. This growth is largely fueled by the rapid expansion of commerce on the Web. The U.S. Internet economy generates hundreds of billions of dollars in revenues and millions of jobs each year.

The Internet has become so pervasive that many organizations have rebuilt their entire information-processing systems around Internet technology.

A growing number of companies are replacing their aging mainframe-and-PC-based systems with **intranets**—private intraorganizational networks based on Internet technology. Intranets mimic the Internet in the ways in which they enable people to transmit, share, and store information within an organization.

Some companies, including Sun, Oracle, and Hewlett-Packard (HP), are so taken with the notion of Internet-based computing that they are developing and marketing stripped-down computers designed to function mainly as network terminals. These companies don't all agree on exactly what these boxes should include, how much they should be able to do without the aid of a server, or even what they should be called. You might hear people referring to these machines as **network computers**, *NCs*, or *thin clients* when they talk about network-centric machines.

Whatever they're called, all these machines share two common characteristics: They typically cost less than most PCs, because they contain less hardware, and they are easier to maintain, because much of the software can be stored on a central server. Like a TV, a network computer is designed to receive information from elsewhere. But unlike a TV, an NC allows you to send and receive information; it's a two-way connection to the wired world. However, network computers are unlikely to outsell PCs any time soon, and it's likely that they may simply replace terminals in certain situations.

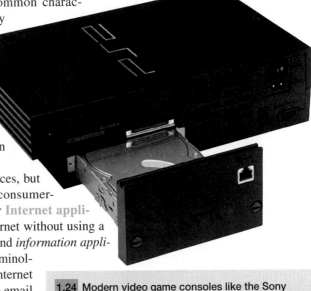

Network computers make economic sense in many workplaces, but most of them are not designed for use in homes. But some consumer-oriented manufacturers now sell **information appliances** (or **Internet appliances**) that enable home and office users to connect to the Internet without using a full-blown PC. (Some people use the terms *Internet appliance* and *information appliance* to refer to network computers in offices and homes; the terminology is, at this point, as fluid as the technology.) For example, Internet telephones have screens and keyboards to enable easy access to email and the Web. **Set-top boxes**, including modern video game consoles like the Sony PlayStation 2 and Microsoft Xbox, provide Internet access through television sets. Many new handheld computers provide wireless access to the Internet. And many cellular phones can display Internet data on their tiny screens. Who knows? Future homes and businesses may have dozens of devices—computers, telephones, televisions, stereos, security systems, and even kitchen appliances—continually connected to the Internet, monitoring all kinds of data that can have an impact on our lives and our livelihoods. Whatever happens, it's clear that the Internet is going to play an increasing role in our future.

1.24 Modern video game consoles like the Sony PlayStation 2 allow users to connect to the Internet and play games against their friends and other people from around the globe.

1.25 Millions of homes may soon be connecting to the Internet using televisions through set-top boxes such as this one.

Into the Information Age

Every so often civilization dramatically changes course. Events and ideas come together to transform radically the way people live, work, and think. Traditions go by the wayside, common sense is turned upside down, and lives are thrown into turmoil until a new order takes hold. Humankind experiences a **paradigm shift**—a change in thinking that results in a new way of seeing the world. Major paradigm shifts take generations because individuals have trouble changing their assumptions about the way the world works.

> It is the **business of the future** to be dangerous. . . . The **major advances** in civilization are processes that all but **wreck** the societies in which they occur.
>
> —Alfred North Whitehead

Roughly ten thousand years ago people learned to domesticate animals and grow their own food using plows and other agricultural tools. Over the next few centuries, a paradigm shift occurred as people gave up nomadic hunter–gatherer lives to live and work on farms, exchanging goods and services in nearby towns. The **agricultural age** lasted until about a century ago, when advances in machine technology triggered what has come to be known as an **industrial revolution**.

About a century ago, another paradigm shift moved masses of people from farms to factories, ushering in the **industrial age**. Factory work promised a higher material standard of living for a growing population, but not without a price. Families who had worked the land on sustainable farms for generations found it necessary to take low-wage factory jobs for survival. As work life became separate from home life, fathers were removed from day-to-day

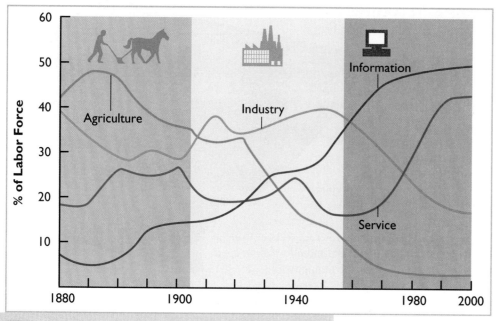

1.26 In a single century, the workforce moved from the farm to the factory, and then finally to the office. Where will tomorrow's workforce end up?

family life, and those mothers who didn't have to work in factories assumed the bulk of domestic responsibilities. As towns grew into cities, crime, pollution, and other urban problems grew with them.

The convergence of computer and communication technology is at the heart of another paradigm shift—the shift from an industrial economy to an information economy. In the information age, most people earn their living working with words, numbers, and ideas. Instead of planting corn or making shoes, most of us shuffle bits in one form or another. As we roar through the information age, we're riding a wave of social change that rivals any that came before.

Living with Computers

> Just as Michelangelo's contemporaries couldn't have foreseen **abstract expressionism**, we **can't foresee** how people will use the computing medium in the future.
>
> —Clement Mok, in *Designing Business*

In less than a human lifetime, computers have evolved from massive, expensive, error-prone calculators like the Mark I and ENIAC into (mostly) dependable, versatile machines that have worked their way into just about every nook and cranny of modern society. The pioneers who created and marketed the first computers did not foresee these spectacular advances in computer technology. Thomas Watson, Sr., the founding father of IBM, declared in 1953 that the world would not need more than five computers! And the early pioneers certainly couldn't have predicted the extraordinary social changes that resulted from the computer's rapid evolution. In the time of UNIVAC, who could have imagined Apple's iMac, Sony PlayStations, handheld Palm devices, smart bombs, or online shopping?

Technological breakthroughs encourage further technological change, so we can expect the rate of change to continue to increase in coming decades. In other words, the technological and social transformations of the past five decades may be dwarfed by the changes that occur over the next half-century! It's just a matter of time, and not very much time, before today's state-of-the-art PCs and Palms look as primitive as ENIAC looks to us today. Similarly, today's high-tech society just hints at a future world that we haven't yet begun to imagine.

1.27 Smart bombs, such as those employed in both Gulf wars, helped the U.S. armed forces target enemy installations with greater accuracy than was possible in earlier wars.

What do you really need to know about computers today? The remaining chapters of this book, along with the accompanying CD-ROM and Web site, provide answers to that question by looking at the technology on three levels: explanations, applications, and implications.

Explanations: Clarifying Technology

You don't need to be a computer scientist to coexist with computers. But your encounters with technology will make more sense if you understand a few basic computer concepts. Computers are evolving at an incredible pace and many hardware and software details change every few years. And the Internet is evolving even faster; some suggest that one normal year is equal to several "Internet years," a phrase coined by Intel cofounder Andy Grove. But most of the underlying concepts remain constant as computers and networks evolve. If you understand the basics, you'll find that it's a lot easier to keep up with the changes.

Applications: Computers in Action

Many people define *computer literacy* as the ability to use computers. But because computers are so versatile, you can learn no single set of skills to become computer literate in every situation. Application programs, also known simply as applications, are the software tools that enable you to use a computer for specific purposes. Many computer applications in science, government, business, and the arts are far too specialized and technical to be of use or of interest to people outside the field. On the other hand, some applications are so flexible that nearly anyone can use them.

Regardless of your background or aspirations, you can almost certainly benefit from knowing a little about the following applications:

- *Word processing and desktop publishing.* Word processing is a critical skill for anyone who communicates in writing—on paper, via documents, or on the Web. Desktop-publishing software can transform written words into polished, visually exciting publications.
- *Spreadsheets and other number-crunching applications.* In business, the electronic spreadsheet is the personal computer application that pays the rent—or at least calculates it. If you work with numbers of any kind, spreadsheets and statistical software can help you turn those numbers into insights.
- *Databases.* Word processors may be the most popular stand-alone-PC productivity applications, but databases reign supreme in the world of mainframes and servers. Of course, databases are widely used on PCs, too. Even if you don't have database software on a PC, you can apply database-searching skills to find books in your library—or just about anything on the Internet.
- *Computer graphics and digital photos.* Computers make it possible to produce and manipulate all kinds of graphics, including charts, drawings, digital photographs—even realistic 3-D animation. As graphics tools become more accessible, visual communication skills become more important for all of us.
- *Digital audio, digital video, and multimedia.* Modern desktop computers make it easy to edit and manipulate audio and video, opening up creative possibilities for all kinds of people, including potential artists. Multimedia software can combine audio and video with traditional text and graphics, adding new dimensions to computer communications. Interac-tive multimedia documents, including those found on many Web sites, enable users to explore a variety of paths through media-rich information sources.

1.28 Digital media applications such as Apple iMovie blur the line between entertainment and utility, giving computer users the power to capture, edit, and produce home movies with effects that rival those available to movie companies.

15th century
Gutenberg's printing press

16th century
algebraic symbols, lead pencil

17th century
typewriter, three-color printing, industrial revolution

18th century
calculus, Pascal's calculator, probability, binary arithmetic, newspapers, mailboxes

19th century
automated loom, Analytical Engine, telegraph, vacuum tube, cathode ray tube, telephone, color photograph, Hollerith's data processing machine, radio, sound recordings

Early 20th century
assembly-line automated production, analog computer, television, motion pictures

1930's
first digital computer created in U.S., first programmable general-purpose computer created in Germany

1940's
Turing's Colossus computer breaks Nazi codes, Mark 1 completed, ENIAC designed, Von Neumann proposes storing programs as data transistor invented, Orwell writes 1984

1950's
computerized banking begins, IBM creates first mass-marketed computer, Sony introduces first transistor radio, Bell Labs builds first transistorized computer, USSR launches Sputnik, U.S. forms ARPA, integrated circuit created

1960's
laser invented, DEC introduces first minicomputer, Doug Engelbart patents computer mouse, first computer crime prosecuted, software sold separately from hardware for the first time, ARPANET created, Bell Labs develops UNIX, first person on the moon, first microprocessor

1970's
First ROM developed, first home computer game created, first email message sent, first microcomputer created, Cray-1 supercomputer introduced, Xerox pioneers graphical user interface, Apple II introduced, first spreadsheet created, Pac-Man appears

1.29 The floodgates are open, and information technology ideas are flowing faster all the time.

11th century
movable type,
decimal number
system, musical notation

12th century
modern abacus

1980's
IBM PC released, Apple Macintosh released, desktop publishing takes off, first trans-Atlantic fiber-optic
cable completed, Connection Machine massively parallel supercomputer introduced, first major
Internet worm cripples thousands of computers, Apple's HyperCard pioneers multimedia software

1990's
Microsoft creates de facto computing standard with Windows, handheld computers take off,
computers become multimedia machines, World Wide Web introduced, U.S. completes GPS
system, dot-com boom is followed by dot-bomb bust, Linux open-source operating system
introduced, Apple iMac heralds age of innovative PC designs, first full-length computer-animated
feature film is released, Internet email outpaces post office volume, computer programs beats
world chess champion, Y2K bug captures public attention and costs businesses billions

2000's
Denial of service attacks cripple commercial Web sites, Arizona holds first Internet primary election,
email viruses afflict millions of users, Microsoft is found guilty of monopolistic practices but later settles
with U.S. government, U.S. videogame receipts eclipse movie box office receipts, 9/11 terrorist attacks
result in bolstered security and compromised civil liberties, U.S. high-tech weapons demolish Iraqi
defenses, Internet file sharing frenzy fuels music industry downturn

- *Telecommunication and networking.* A network connection is a door into a world of email, online discussion groups, Web-publishing ventures, and information sharing.
- *Artificial intelligence.* Artificial intelligence is the branch of computer science that explores the use of computers in tasks that require intelligence, imagination, and insight—tasks that have traditionally been performed by people rather than machines. Until recently, artificial intelligence was mostly an academic discipline—a field of study reserved for researchers and philosophers. But that research is paying off today with commercial applications that exhibit intelligence, from basic speech recognition to sophisticated expert systems.
- *Entertainment.* With fast processors, advanced graphics capabilities, and huge displays, computers make excellent video game systems, and because they are often connected to the Internet, it's possible for gamers to compete online with people they've never met in person. But PCs aren't just good for games; they are also used to watch DVD movies and downloaded digital video, listen to audio CDs and digital sound files, read electronic books, and perform other tasks that help users pass time when they're not working
- *General problem solving.* People often use computers to solve problems. Most people use software applications written by professional programmers. But some kinds of problems can't easily be solved with off-the-shelf applications; they require at least some custom programming. Programming languages aren't applications; they're tools that enable you to build and customize applications. Many computer users find their machines become more versatile and valuable when they learn a little about programming.

Implications: Social and Ethical Issues

> True **computer literacy** is not just **knowing how** to make use of computers and **computational ideas**. It is knowing **when it is appropriate** to do so.
>
> —Seymour Papert, in *Mindstorms*

Computers and networks are transforming the world rapidly and irreversibly. Jobs that existed for hundreds of years are eliminated by automation while new careers are built on emerging technology. Start-up businesses create new markets overnight while older companies struggle to keep pace with "Internet time." Instant worldwide communication changes the way businesses work and challenges the role of governments. Computers routinely save lives in hospitals, keep space flights on course, and predict the weekend weather.

More than any other recent technology, the computer is responsible for profound changes in our society; we just need to imagine a world without computers to recognize their impact. Of course, computer scientists and computer engineers are not responsible for all the technological turbulence. Developments in fields as diverse as telecommunications, genetic engineering, medicine, and atomic physics contribute to the ever-increasing rate of social change. But researchers in all these fields depend on computers to produce their work.

While it's exciting to consider the opportunities arising from advances in artificial intelligence, multimedia, robotics, and other cutting-edge technologies of the electronic revolution, it's just as important to pay attention to the potential risks. Here's a sampling of the kinds of social and ethical issues we'll confront in this book:

- *The threat to personal privacy posed by large databases and computer networks.* When you use a credit card, buy an airline ticket, place a phone call, visit your doctor, send an email message, or explore the Web, you are leaving a trail of personal information in one or more computers. Who owns that information? Is it okay for the business or organization that collected the information to share it with others or make it public? Do you have the right to check its accuracy and change it if it's wrong? Do laws protecting individual privacy rights place undue burdens on businesses and governments?
- *The hazards of high-tech crime and the difficulty of keeping data secure.* Even if you trust the institutions and businesses that collect data about you, you can't be sure that data will remain secure in their computer systems. Computer crime is at an all-time high, and law enforcement officials are having a difficult time keeping it under control.

1.30 This robot security guard protects a museum from vandals and thieves. But does it threaten the jobs of human security guards?

How can society protect itself from information thieves and high-tech vandals? How can lawmakers write laws about technology that they are just beginning to understand? What kinds of personal risk do you face as a result of computer crime?

■ *The difficulty of defining and protecting intellectual property in an all-digital age.* Software programs, musical recordings, videos, and books can be difficult and expensive to create. But in our digital age, all of these can easily be copied. What rights do the creators of intellectual property have? Is a teenager who copies music files from the Web a computer criminal? What about a shopkeeper who sells pirated copies of Microsoft Office for $10? Or a student who posts a clip from *The Matrix* on his Web site? Or a musician who uses a two-second sample from a Beatles song in an electronic composition?

■ *The risks of failure of computer systems.* Computer software is difficult to write, because it is incredibly complex. As a result, no computer system is completely fail-safe. Computer failures routinely cause communication problems, billing errors, lost data, and other inconveniences. But they also occasionally result in power blackouts, telephone system meltdowns, weapons failure, and other potentially deadly problems. Who is responsible for loss of income—or loss of life—caused by software errors? What rights do we have when buying and using software? How can we, as a society, protect ourselves from software disasters?

■ *The threat of automation and the dehumanization of work.* Computers and the Internet fueled unprecedented economic growth in the last decade of the twentieth century, producing plenty of new jobs for workers with the right skills. But the new information-based economy has cost many workers—especially older workers—their jobs and their dignity. And many workers today find that their jobs involve little more than tending to machines—and being monitored by bosses with high-tech surveillance devices. As machines replace people in the workplace, what rights do the displaced workers have? Does a worker's right to privacy outweigh an employer's right to read employee email or monitor worker actions? What is the government's role in the protection of worker rights in the high-tech workplace?

1.31 What impact will computer technology have on traditional cultures that evolved for thousands of years without computers?

- *The abuse of information as a tool of political and economic power.* The computer age has produced an explosion of information, and most of that information is concentrated in corporate and government computers. The emergence of low-cost personal computers and the Inter-net makes it possible for more people to access information and the power that comes with that information. But the majority of the people on the planet have never made a phone call, let alone used a computer. Will the information revolution leave them behind? Do information-rich people and countries have a responsibility to share technology and information with the information-poor?

- *The dangers of dependence on complex technology.* One of the biggest news stories of 1999 was the impending threat of massive problems caused by the so-called Y2K bug—the failure of some computer programs on January 1, 2000, because those systems represented the year with only two digits. People stockpiled food and fuel, hid cash and jewels, and prepared for the possibility that the power grid would fail, leaving much of the world's population helpless and hungry. Businesses and governments spent billions of dollars repairing and replacing computer systems, and the Y2K crisis never materialized. But the Y2K scare reminded us how much we have come to depend on this far-from-foolproof technology. Are we, as a society, addicted to computer technology? Should we question new technological innovations before we embrace them? Can we build a future in which technology never takes precedence over humanity?

Today's technology raises fascinating and difficult questions. But these questions pale in comparison to the ones we'll have to deal with as the technology evolves in the coming years:

- *The death of privacy.* Governments and private companies alike are installing extensive video surveillance networks to monitor security and track lawbreakers. Computer databases are accumulating more information about you all the time, and networks are making it easier to transmit, share, and merge that information. Will these converging technologies destroy the last of our personal privacy, as some experts have suggested? Is there anything we can do about it?

- *The blurring of reality.* Virtual reality (VR) is widely used by scientific researchers and computer gamers alike. But if VR doesn't live up to its name, it does suggest a future technology in which artificial environments look and feel real. Rapid developments in Internet technology are likely to lead us to shared virtual environments ranging from shopping malls to gaming centers. Already some people are suffering from computer and Internet addictions. Will these diseases become epidemics when VR feels like real life, only better? Will unscrupulous con artists abuse VR technology? Should governments limit what's legal when just about anything is possible?

- *The evolution of intelligence.* Artificial intelligence research is responsible for many products, including software that can read books to the blind, understand spoken words, and play world-class chess. But tomorrow's machine intelligence will make today's smartest machines look stupid. What rights will human workers have when software can do their jobs better, faster, and smarter? What rights will smart machines have in a world run by humans? Will there come a time when humans aren't smart enough to maintain control of their creations?

- *The emergence of bio-digital technology.* Today, thousands of people walk around with computer chips embedded in their bodies, helping them to overcome disabilities and lead normal lives. At the same time, researchers are attempting to develop computers that use biology, rather than electronics, as their underlying technology. As the line between organism and machine blurs, what happens to our vision of ourselves? What are the limits of our creative powers, and what are our responsibilities in using those powers?

For better and for worse, we will be coexisting with computers until death do us part. As with any relationship, a little understanding can go a long way. The remaining chapters of this book will help you gain the understanding you need to survive and prosper in a world of computers.

1.32 Though somewhat controversial, cochlear implants use modern technology to help the profoundly deaf hear.

Tomorrow Never Knows

It is **the unexpected** that always happens.

—Old English proverb

There is no denying the importance of the future. In the words of scientist Charles F. Kettering, "We should be concerned about the future because we will have to spend the rest of our lives there." However, important or not, the future isn't easy to see.

In 1877, when Thomas Edison invented the phonograph, he thought of it as an office dictating machine and lost interest in it; recorded music did not become popular until 21 years later. When the Wright brothers offered their invention to the U.S. government and the British Royal Navy, they were told airplanes had no future in the military. A 1900 Mercedes-Benz study estimated that worldwide demand for cars would not exceed 1 million, primarily because of the limited number of available chauffeurs. In 1899, Charles B. Duell, the director of the U.S. Patent Office, said, "Everything that can be invented has been invented."

History is full of stories of people who couldn't imagine the impact of new technology. Technology is hard to foresee, and it is even harder to predict the impact that technology will have on society. Who could have predicted in 1950 the profound effects, both positive and negative, television would have on our world?

Computer Scientist Alan Kay has said, "The best way to predict the future is to invent it." Kay's visionary research at XEROX more than three decades ago defined many of the essential qualities of today's PCs. Of course, we can't all invent world-changing tools. But Kay says there are other ways to predict the future. For example, we can look in the research labs today to see the commercial products of the next few years. Of course, many researchers work behind carefully guarded doors, and research often takes surprising turns.

A third way is to look at products from the past and see what made them succeed. According to Kay, "There are certain things about human beings that if you remove, they wouldn't be human any more. For instance, we have to communicate with others or we're not humans. So every time someone has come up with a communications amplifier, it has succeeded the previous technology." The pen, the printing press, the telephone, the television, the PC, and the Internet are all successful communication amplifiers. What's next?

Kay says we can also predict the future by recognizing the four phases of any technology or media business: hardware, software, service, and way of life.

➡ **Hardware.** Inventors and engineers start the process by developing new hardware. But whether it's a television set, a PC, or a global communication network, the hardware is of little use without software.

➡ **Software.** The next step is software development. Television programs, sound recordings, video games, databases, and Web pages are examples of software that give value to hardware products.

➡ **Service.** Innovative hardware and clever software aren't likely to take hold unless they serve human needs. The PC industry is now in the service phase, and the companies that focus on serving their customers are generally the most successful.

1.33 The 1930 movie *Just Imagine* presented a bold, if not quite accurate, vision of the future; here Maureen O'Sullivan sits in her personal flying machine.

➡ **Way of life.** The final phase happens when the technology becomes so entrenched that people don't think about it any more; they only notice if it isn't there. We seldom think of pencils as technological tools. They're part of our way of life, so much so that we'd have trouble getting along without them. Similarly, the electric motor, which was once a major technological breakthrough, is now all but invisible; we use dozens of motors every day without thinking about them. Computers are clearly headed in that direction.

Kay's four ways of predicting the future don't provide a foolproof crystal ball, but they can serve as a framework for thinking about tomorrow's technology. In the remaining chapters of this book we'll examine trends and innovations that will shape future computer hardware and software. Then we look at how this technology will serve users as it eventually disappears into our way of life.

Silicon Hogs Katharine Mieszkowski

When we consider how computers are changing the world, we don't often think about its environmental impact. In this article, which first appeared in the online magazine Salon *on Nov. 13, 2002, senior writer Katharine Mieszkowski discusses a hidden cost of our digital devices.*

If we all had to lug around the true environmental weights of the microchips in our iPods, cellphones or laptops, most of those portable gadgets would never make it off their docking stations, much less out the front door.

It takes 3.7 pounds of fossil fuels and other chemicals and 70.5 pounds of water to produce a single two-gram microchip, according to a study in the Dec. 15 [2002] issue of *Environmental Science & Technology,* a publication of the American Chemical Society.

"The technology is not free," says Eric Williams of the United Nations University in Tokyo, one of the co-authors of the study. "The environmental footprint of the device is much more substantial than its small physical size would suggest."

The technology industry has been heralded as a clean alternative to smoke-belching industrial factories of yore, but in recent years, its squeaky-clean image has eroded with news reports about high cancer rates among clean-room workers, and old CPUs and monitors piling up in landfills.

This study suggests that not only is chip manufacturing toxic, it's just plain wasteful. And the waste starts not when last year's cast-off model ends up at the dump, but when a chip is born.

Sixty-nine billion integrated-circuits were produced last year, according to the Semiconductor Industry Association. The production of a silicon wafer—"the purest product manufactured on a commercial scale," according to the study, is a complex, energy intensive procedure. The six-stage process consumes 2130 kilowatt-hours of electricity for every kilogram of silicon. When multiplied against billion of chips, the consequent consumption of fossil fuels necessary just to provide the power is enormous. Then the wafers are repeatedly doped with chemicals, rinsed with ultra-pure water to remove impurities, etched, rinsed again and doped with more chemicals.

Not everyone agrees with the critical analysis: Some scientists point out that the study only looks at one-half of the equation—what goes into the chips, not what they're used for. Chip use could potentially save as much energy and resources as their manufacture consumes. Still, the new data is raising eyebrows.

"We've certainly known about the significant problems that happen at the end of the computer's life cycle as e-waste," says Joel Makower, editor of the Green Business Letter. "But this is as pointed a reference as has been made yet as to the extraordinary amount of waste that is created at the front end."

Hard data about the resources that go into producing chips is scarce. "We have been trying for 10 years to find ways to get the semiconductor industry to report their inputs and outputs on a per unit basis," says Ted Smith, executive director of the Silicon Valley Toxics Coalition. For this study, Williams, Heller and co-author Robert U. Ayeres of INSEAD used data provided by an anonymous plant.

Among the study's conclusions: It's 160 times more energy-intensive to create a silicon wafer out of quartz than to produce regular silicon. That's because chips are extremely highly organized forms of matter, or "low-entropy."

The findings fly in the face of the high-tech theory of "dematerialization," which holds that technological progress should lead to the use of increasingly fewer resources. "The smaller you make it, the less forgiving you are of defects," Heller explains. "In this case, dematerialization may lead to increased energy intensity to achieve a high level of purity and low defect levels."

Just how energy-demanding is this process? Consider that it takes 3,300 pounds of fossil fuel and other chemicals to fabricate a whole car, and just 3.7 pounds to create a chip. But if you compare the resources used to create a car to the weight of the vehicle, the ratio is 2-1. For a chip, that same ratio is 630-1.

But not everyone concerned with the impact of chips on the environment is convinced that such a car and chip comparison is meaningful.

"The weight of a product is not a logical basis for normalizing the environmental impact," says Farhang Shadman, director of the NSF/SRC Engineering Re-search Center for Environmentally Benign Semiconductor Manufacturing at the University of Arizona, which receives some of its funding from the chip industry.

And even the scientists behind the study caution against tarring chips for environmental malfeasance based on what it takes to produce them, since the study considers the chip's creation, but not the impact of its use. "What is the chip replacing?" Heller asks. "Should you compare it to a vacuum tube? Should we be comparing e-mail to surface mail?"

How a chip is used could make up for its consumptive beginnings. "That little tiny chip may actually save vast amounts of electricity," says Jonathan Koomey, a staff scientist and leader of the end-use forecasting group at Lawrence Berkeley National Laboratory. Chips are deployed to make everything from industrial production to household appliances more energy-efficient. For example, the chip-powered sensor in a dishwasher that tells the machine the dishes are clean and to stop sloshing the water around. "So what if the chip uses a lot of power relative to its mass, if it saves vastly more than that in the system?" says Koomey.

But this argument doesn't impress environmental critics. Makower argues that chip manufacturing can be made more resource-efficient. His example: Intel reduced water consumption at a number of plants in water-starved areas such as Albuquerque, N. M., when local communities demanded it. Since 1994, Intel's water usage in Albuquerque has decreased by 47 percent.

"Now that the bubble has burst, it gives us all a chance to look a little less bleary-eyed at these industries that we've spawned, and what their genuine impacts are," says Makower.

DISCUSSION QUESTIONS

1. Do you think that silicon chips save more energy and resources than they consume? Explain.

2. Do you favor laws requiring computer manufacturers to minimize their negative environmental impact? Why or why not?

SUMMARY

While the basic idea behind a computer goes back to Charles Babbage's nineteenth-century plan for an Analytical Engine, the first real computers were developed during the 1940s. Computers have evolved at an incredible pace since those early years, becoming consistently smaller, faster, more efficient, more reliable, and less expensive. At the same time, people have devised all kinds of interesting and useful ways to put computers to use in both work and play.

Computers today, like their ancestors, are data processing machines designed to transform information from one form to another. When a computer operates, the hardware accepts input data from some outside source, transforms the data by following instructions called software, and produces output that can be read by a human or by another machine.

Computers today come in all shapes and sizes, with specific types being well suited for particular jobs. Mainframe computers and supercomputers provide more power and speed than smaller desktop machines, but they are expensive to purchase and operate. Timesharing makes it possible for many users to work simultaneously at terminals connected to these large computers. At the other end of the spectrum, servers, workstations, personal computers, and a variety of portable devices provide computing power for those of us who don't need a mainframe's capabilities. Microprocessors aren't just used in general-purpose computers; they're embedded in appliances, automobiles, and a rapidly growing list of other products.

Connecting to a network enhances the value and power of a computer—it can share resources with other computers and facilitate electronic communication with other computer users. Some networks are local to a particular building or business; others connect users at remote geographic locations. The Internet is a collection of networks that connects the computers of businesses, public institutions, and individuals around the globe. Email provides hundreds of millions of people with near-instant worldwide communication capabilities. With Web browsing software, those same Internet users have access to millions of Web pages on the World Wide Web. The Web is a distributed network of interlinked multimedia documents. Although it started out as a tool for scientists, researchers, and scholars, the Web has quickly become a vital center for entertainment and commerce as well.

Computers and information technology have changed the world rapidly and irreversibly. Our civilization is in a transition from an industrial economy to what we might call the information age, and this paradigm shift is having an impact on the way we live and work. Computers and information technology are central to this change, and we can easily list dozens of ways in which computers now make our lives easier and more productive. Personal computer applications, such as word processing, spreadsheets, graphics, multimedia, and databases, continue to grow in popularity. Emerging technologies, such as artificial intelligence, offer promise for future applications. At the same time, computers threaten our privacy, our security, and perhaps our way of life. As we rush into the information age, our future depends on computers and on our ability to understand and use them in productive, positive ways.

KEY TERMS

agricultural age (p. 45)
Analytical Engine (p. 31)
application program (application)
    (p. 47)
data (p. 34)
desktop replacements (p. 40)
docking station (p. 40)
electronic mail (email) (p. 44)
embedded computer (p. 41)
firmware (p. 41)
handheld computer (p. 40)
hardware (p. 34)
hypertext link (p. 44)
industrial age (p. 45)
Industrial Revolution (p. 45)
information age (p. 46)
information appliance (p. 45)
input (p. 34)

integrated circuit (p. 36)
Internet (p. 43)
Internet appliance (p. 45)
intranet (p. 44)
laptop computer (p. 40)
local area network (LAN) (p. 42)
mainframe computer (p. 38)
modem (p. 43)
Moore's law (p. 36)
network (p. 42)
network computer (NC) (p. 44)
notebook computer (p. 40)
output (p. 34)
palm-sized computer (p. 40)
paradigm shift (p. 45)
personal computer (PC) (p. 37)
personal digital assistant (PDA)
    (p. 40)

portable computers (p. 40)
port replicator (p. 40)
program (p. 34)
server (p. 39)
set-top box (p. 45)
silicon chip (p. 36)
Silicon Valley (p. 37)
software (p. 34)
subnotebooks (p. 40)
supercomputer (p. 39)
terminal (p. 38)
timesharing (p. 39)
transistor (p. 36)
Web browsers (p. 44)
wide area network (WAN) (p. 43)
workstation (p. 39)
World Wide Web (WWW) (p. 44)

INTERACTIVE QUIZ QUESTIONS

1. The *Computer Confluence* CD-ROM contains self-test quiz questions related to this chapter, including multiple-choice, true or false, and matching questions.

2. The *Computer Confluence* Web site, http://www.computerconfluence.com, contains self-test exercises related to this chapter. Follow the instruc-tions for taking a quiz. After you've completed your quiz, you can email the results to your instructor.

3. The Web site also contains open-ended discussion questions called Internet Explorations. Discuss one or more of the Internet exploration questions at the section for this chapter.

TRUE OR FALSE

1. The information age began when Charles Babbage invented the Analytic Engine.

2. Because it can be programmed to perform various tasks, the typical modern computer is a general-purpose tool, not a specialized device with one use.

3. One of the first computers helped the Allies crack Nazi codes during World War II.

4. According to Moore's law, the power of a silicon chip of the same price would double about every 10 years for at least 50 years.

5. A mainframe computer is, by definition, the main computer on a network.

6. Timesharing technology allows one person to use several computers at the same time.

7. Workstations are typically more powerful than standard desktop PCs.

8. More than 90 percent of the world's microprocessors are hidden inside common household and electronic devices.

9. A local area network (LAN) is usually the best way to connect houses in a neighborhood to the Internet and to each other.

10. Computer technology, like any technology, carries significant risks to individuals and society.

MULTIPLE CHOICE

1. Charles Babbage and Lady Augusta Lovelace conceived of and designed
   a. the first fully functional computer.
   b. the first commercially produced programmable digital computer.
   c. a computerlike device about a century before the first working computer was built.
   d. the first personal computer.
   e. the Internet.

2. We depend on computer technology for
   a. controlling our money and banking systems.
   b. keeping our transportation systems running smoothly.
   c. making many of our household appliances and gadgets work properly.
   d. All of the above.
   e. None of the above.

3. PCs are extremely versatile tools because they can accept instructions from a wide variety of
   a. hardware.
   b. software.
   c. firmware.
   d. networks.
   e. programmers.

4. Many of the most important developments in the earliest days of the computer were motivated by what world event?
   a. World War I.
   b. The Great Depression.
   c. World War II.
   d. The Vietnam War.
   e. The Cold War.

5. Which represents the order in which computer circuitry evolved through three generations of technology?
   a. silicon chip, vacuum tube, transistor.
   b. vacuum tube, silicon chip, transistor.
   c. transistor, vacuum tube, silicon chip.
   d. vacuum tube, transistor, silicon chip.
   e. transistor, silicon chip, vacuum tube.

6. As computers evolved, they
   a. grew in size.
   b. became faster.
   c. consumed more electricity.
   d. became less reliable.
   e. cost more.

7. When a bank clerk transfers money into your account, the actual transaction is probably being stored in
   a. a supercomputer.
   b. a mainframe computer.
   c. a workstation.
   d. an embedded computer.
   e. a Web page.

8. A personal digital assistant (PDA) is a handheld device that
   a. serves as a limited input device to a PC.
   b. contains thousands of tiny transistors.
   c. is a fully functional computer designed with portability in mind.
   d. cannot be programmed to do anything more than simple calendar and address book functions.
   e. costs thousands of dollars because of its expensive circuitry.

9. Several people in an office can share a printer by using a
   a. local area network (LAN).
   b. wide area network (WAN).
   c. building area network (BAN).
   d. circuit area network (CAN).
   e. None of the above.

10. An intranet is
    a. a network that connects the Internet to a LAN.
    b. a network that uses Internet technology for communication within an organization.
    c. a network that uses LAN technology for Internet communication.
    d. a wireless communication technology used mainly with handheld computers.
    e. None of the above.

REVIEW QUESTIONS

1. List several ways you interact with computers in your daily life.

2. Why was the Analytical Engine never completed during Charles Babbage's lifetime?

3. How are computers today similar to those from World War II? How are they different?

4. How are hardware and software related?

5. What is the most important difference between a computer and a calculator?

6. What is the difference between a mainframe and a microcomputer? What are the advantages and disadvantages of each?

7. What kinds of computer applications require the speed and power of a supercomputer? Give some examples.

8. What types of computers typically employ timesharing?

9. List several common personal computer applications.

10. Why is it important for people to know about and understand computers?

11. Describe some of the benefits and drawbacks of the information age.

DISCUSSION QUESTIONS

1. What do people mean when they talk about the information age? Why is it a societal paradigm-shift?

2. How do you feel about computers? Examine your positive and negative feelings.

3. What major events before the twentieth century influenced the development of the computer?

4. Suppose Charles Babbage and Lady Lovelace had been able to construct a working Analytical Engine and develop a factory for mass-producing it. How do you think the world would have reacted? How would the history of the twentieth century have been different as a result?

5. How would the world be different today if a wrinkle in time transported a state-of-the-art notebook computer, complete with software, peripherals, and manuals, onto the desk of Herbert Hoover? Adolf Hitler? Albert Einstein?

6. The automobile and the television set are two examples of technological inventions that changed our society drastically in ways that were not anticipated by their inventors. Outline several positive and negative effects of each of these two inventions. Do you think, on balance, that we are better off as a result of these machines? Why or why not? Now repeat this exercise for the computer.

7. Should all students be required to take at least one computer course? Why or why not? If so, what should that course cover?

8. Computerphobia—fear or anxiety related to computers—is a common malady among people today. What do you think causes it? What, if anything, should be done about it?

9. In your opinion what computer applications offer the most promise for making the world a better place? Which computer applications pose the most significant threats to our future well-being?

PROJECTS www

1. Start a collection of news articles, cartoons, or television segments that deal with computers. Does your collection say anything about popular attitudes toward computers?

2. Trace computer-related articles through several years in the same magazine. Do you see any changes or trends?

3. Develop a questionnaire to try to determine people's attitudes about computers. Once you have people's answers to your questions, summarize your results.

4. Take an inventory of all the computers you encounter in a single day. Be sure to include embedded computers such as those in cars, appliances, entertainment equipment, and other machines.

SOURCES AND RESOURCES

Books

The Difference Engine: Charles Babbage and the Quest to Build the First Computer, by Doron Swade and Charles Babbage (New York: Viking Press, 2001). This book tells the story of the design of Babbage's visionary computing machine. It also reveals the problems Babbage faced getting funding for the ill-fated project. Swade led a team that built a working model of a Difference Engine for the 1991 Babbage bicentenary.

The Difference Engine, by William Gibson and Bruce Sterling (New York: Spectra, 1992). How would the world of the nineteenth century be different if Charles and Ada had succeeded in constructing the Analytical Engine 150 years ago? This imaginative mystery novel takes place in a world where the computer revolution arrived a century early. Like other books by these two pioneers of the "cyberpunk" school of science fiction, *The Difference Engine* is dark, dense, detailed, and thought-provoking.

A History of Modern Computing, by Paul E. Ceruzzi (Cambridge, MA: MIT Press, 2000). This book traces the first 50 years of computer history, from ENIAC to Internetworked PCs. The social context of the technology is clear throughout the book.

Accidental Empires: How the Boys of Silicon Valley Make Their Millions, Battle Foreign Competition, and Still Can't Get a Date, Revised Edition, by Robert X. Cringely (New York: Harper Business, 1996). Robert X. Cringely is the pen name for *InfoWorld*'s computer-industry gossip columnist. In this opinionated, irreverent, and highly entertaining book Cringely discusses the past, present, and future of the volatile personal computer industry. When you read the humorous, colorful characterizations of the people who run this industry, you'll understand why Cringely didn't use his real name. *Triumph of the Nerds*, a 1996 PBS TV show and video based loosely on this book, lacks much of the humor and insight of the book but includes some fascinating footage of the pioneers reminiscing about the early days.

Crystal Fire: The Birth of the Information Age, by Michael Riordan and Lillian Hoddeson (New York: Norton, 1997). One of the defining moments of the information age occurred in 1947 when William Shockley and his colleagues invented the transistor. *Crystal Fire* tells the story of that earthshaking invention, clearly describing the technical and human dimensions of the story.

ENIAC: The Triumphs and Tragedies of the World's First Computer, by Scott McCartney (New York: Walker and Co., 1999). This engaging book tells the human story of two pioneers and their struggles to be recognized for their monumental achievements in those early days of computing.

Fire in the Valley: The Making of the Personal Computer, Second Edition, by Paul Freiberger and Michael Swaine (Berkeley, CA: Osborne/McGraw-Hill, 1999). This book chronicles the early years of the personal computer revolution. The text occasionally gets bogged down in details, but the photos and quotes from the early days are fascinating. The 1999 film *Pirates of Silicon Valley* is based loosely on this book.

Dave Barry in Cyberspace, by Dave Barry (New York: Fawcett Columnbine, 1996). Dave Barry, the irreverent humor columnist, turns his wit loose on the information revolution in this hilarious little book. Here's a typical chapter title: "A Brief History of Computing from Cave Walls to Windows 95—Not That This Is Necessarily Progress." Whether you think computers are frustrating or funny, you'll probably find a few good laughs here.

Dictionary of Computer and Internet Words: An A to Z Guide to Hardware, Software, and Cyberspace, edited by American Heritage Dictionaries (New York: Houghton Mifflin, 2001). It sometimes seems like the computer industry makes three things: hardware, software, and jargon. Many computer terms are too new, too obscure, or too technical to appear in standard dictionaries. Fortunately, several good dictionaries specialize in computer terminology. This is one of the most comprehensive and up-to-date. It covers PC, Macintosh, and Internet terms.

In the Beginning Was the Command Line, by Neal Stephenson (New York: Avon Books, 1999). Stephenson, one of today's leading science fiction and cyberspace novelists, and "the hacker Hemingway," discusses his take on cyberculture past and present with a look at the pros and cons of the major computing platforms of the early twenty-first century. A funny and insightful read, and highly recommended to anyone pondering the role of computers in the meaning of life.

Periodicals

PC World (http://www.pcworld.com). Because the world of personal computers changes so rapidly, computer users depend on magazines to keep them up-to-date on hardware and software developments. This periodical is one of the most popular sources for keeping up with developments in the PC world. The companion Web site offers up-to-the-minute information along with archives from past issues.

PC Magazine (http://www.pcmag.com). *PC Magazine* is a popular PC periodical, containing news, reviews, and feature articles for a variety of interests.

Macworld (http://www.macworld.com). This is the premiere periodical for Mac users, covering hardware, software, and Internet issues with clear, easy-to-read articles and reviews.

MacAddict (http://www.macaddict.com). This magazine for Macintosh true believers tends to be slightly more technical—and more partisan—than the more mainstream *Macworld*.

Mobile Computing & Communication ([http://www.mobile computing.com](http://www.mobilecomputing.com)). This is a good source of news and information on portable computing devices, from laptops to palmtops, as well as mobile phones and other traveling companions.

Pen Computing (http://www.pencomputing.com). This magazine covers pen-based computers, from tiny Palm devices to full-sized Tablet PCs.

Windows & .NET Magazine (http://www.winnetmag.com). Dedicated to IT professionals and systems administrators working with Microsoft's platforms, this magazine is the premier resource for Windows and the .NET. technologies.

InfoWorld (http://www.infoworld.com). This magazine covers business computing, including applications for mainframes, servers, and other behind-the-scenes machines that aren't typically covered in PC-centric publications.

Wired (http://www.wired.com). This highly stylized monthly started out as "the first consumer magazine for the digital generation to track technology's impact on all facets of the human condition." Today, *Wired* devotes more pages to the business of technology and less to the impact of technology, but it's still a thought-provoking, influential magazine.

Technology Review (http://www.technologyreview.com). This relatively new periodical from MIT provides excellent coverage of technology in the labs today that will change our lives tomorrow.

Scientific American (http://www.scientificamerican.com). This old standby still provides some of the best writing on science and technology, including emerging information technologies.

Web Pages

Some of the best sources and resources on computers and information technology are on the World Wide Web. But the Web is changing quickly, and new sites are appearing every day. The *Computer Confluence* Web pages include up-to-date links to many of the best computer-related resources on the Web. To find them, open your Web browsing software, enter the address **http://computerconfluence.com**, follow the on-screen buttons to the table of contents, select a chapter, and click the links that interest you.

**AFTER YOU READ THIS CHAPTER YOU
SHOULD BE ABLE TO:**

■ Explain in general terms how computers store and
manipulate information

■ Describe the basic structure and organization of a
computer

■ Discuss the functions and interactions of a
computer system's principal internal components

■ Explain why a computer typically has different
types of memory and storage devices

 **Multimedia extras on the
CD-ROM and the Web:**

■ Videos on computer **recycling** and energy
efficient office equipment

■ A binary number **counting game**

■ **Animated** tutorials explaining how **CPU** and
memory work

■ **Instant** access to glossary and key word
references

■ **Interactive** self-study quizzes

. . . and more.

 **computerconfluence.com**

HARDWARE BASICS
Inside the Box

THOMAS J. WATSON, SR., AND THE EMPEROR'S NEW MACHINES

As president or, as he has been called, the "emperor" of IBM, Thomas J. Watson, Sr., created a corporate culture that fostered both invention and discovery. In 1914, he joined the ailing Computing-Tabulating-Recording Company (C-T-R) as a salesperson. The company specialized in counting devices that used punched cards to read and store information. Ten years later, Watson took it over, renamed it International Business Machines (IBM), and turned it into the dominant force in the information industry.

Thomas Watson has been called autocratic. He demanded unquestioning allegiance from his employees and enforced a legendary dress code that forbade even a hint of color in a shirt. But in many ways Watson ran his company like a family, rewarding loyal employees with uncommon favors. During the Depression he refused to lay off workers, choosing instead to stockpile surplus machines. As if to prove that good deeds don't go unrewarded, the director of the newly formed Social Security Administration bought Watson's excess stock.

One of Watson's most enduring contributions to the IBM legacy was his creation of the company's unofficial slogan "THINK." In 1911, while Watson was managing sales and advertising for the National Cash Register Company (NCR), he reportedly told co-workers, "The trouble with every one of us is that we don't think enough. Thought has been the father of every advance since time began. 'I didn't think' has cost the world millions of dollars." He then wrote the letters "THINK" on the easel behind him. Watson brought the THINK concept with him when he joined IBM forerunner C-T-R in 1914, eventually making it IBM's one-word company slogan. When IBM entered the portable computing market in the early 1990s, it

> There is no invention—**only discovery**.
>
> —Thomas J. Watson, Sr.

2.1 Thomas J. Watson, Sr. (1874–1956)

2.2 Though he developed the concept in 1914 before joining IBM, Watson's THINK slogan eventually became the unofficial slogan for all of IBM, appearing on signs at company offices worldwide.

used the name ThinkPad. Today, the company uses the word to brand many of its other products.

Watson provided financial backing for Howard Aiken's Mark I, the pioneering electromechanical computer developed in the early 1940s at Harvard. But he stubbornly refused to develop a commercial computer, even as UNIVAC I achieved fame and commercial contracts for the fledgling Sperry company.

Shortly after Watson retired from the helm of IBM in 1949, his son, Thomas Watson, Jr., took over. When Watson Senior died of a heart attack in 1956 he still held the title of chairman of IBM. The younger Watson led IBM into the computing field with a vengeance, eventually building a computing empire that dwarfed all competitors for decades to come.

After establishing its first microcomputer as the de facto business computing standard in 1981, the conservative giant was slow to adjust to the rapid-fire changes of the 1980s and 1990s, making it possible for smaller, more nimble companies such as Compaq, Dell, Sun, and Microsoft to seize emerging markets. Massive revenue losses forced IBM to reorganize, replace many of its leaders, and abandon the company's longstanding no-layoffs policy. Eventually, IBM even abandoned its legendary dress code, opting for a more casual image. But today, in spite of stiff competition (or perhaps because of it), IBM is again a major source of innovation in the industry, with major research projects in everything from massive supercomputers to microscopic storage devices. Thomas Watson is long gone, but invention and discovery—and even the THINK motto—are alive and well at IBM today.

Computers schedule airline flights, predict the weather, play and even create music, control space stations, and keep the world's economic wheels spinning. How can one kind of machine do so many things?

To understand what really makes computers tick, you would need to devote considerable time and effort to studying computer science and computer engineering. Most of us don't need to understand every detail of a computer's inner workings, any more than a parent needs to explain wave and particle physics when a child asks why the sky is blue. We can be satisfied with simpler answers, even if those answers are only approximations of the technical truth. We'll spend the next three chapters exploring answers to the question, "How do computers do what they do?"

The main text of each of these chapters provides simple, nontechnical answers and basic information. How It Works boxes use text and graphics to dig deeper into the inner workings of the computer. Depending on your course, learning style, and level of curiosity, you may read these boxes as they appear in the text, read them after you've completed the basic material in the chapter, or (if you don't need the technical details) bypass some or all of them. You'll find interactive multimedia versions of many of these How It Works boxes on the *Computer Confluence* CD-ROM and the *Computer Confluence* Web site, **http://www.computerconfluence.com**. Use the Sources and Resources section at each chapter's end for further explorations.

2.3 PCs are assembled in factories such as this one owned by Dell Computer. In this chapter and the next, we'll examine the hardware components that make up a modern computer.

What Computers Do

The simple truth is that computers perform only four basic functions:

> Stripped of its interfaces, **a bare computer** boils down to little more than a pocket calculator that can **push its own buttons** and **remember** what it has done.
>
> —Arnold Penzias, in *Ideas and Information*

- *Receive input.* Computers accept information from the outside world.
- *Process information.* Computers perform arithmetic or logical (decision-making) operations on information.
- *Produce output.* Computers communicate information to the outside world.
- *Store information.* Computers move and store information in memory.

Every computer system contains hardware components—physical parts—that specialize in each of these four functions:

- Input devices accept input from the outside world. The most common input devices today, of course, are keyboards and pointing devices such as mice.
- Output devices send information to the outside world. Most computers use a TV-like display, or video monitor, as their main output device, a printer to produce paper printouts, and speakers to output sounds.
- A microprocessor, also called the processor or central processing unit (CPU), is, in effect, the computer's "brain." The CPU processes information, performs arithmetic calculations, and makes basic decisions by comparing information values.
- Memory and storage devices both store information, but they serve different purposes. The computer's memory (sometimes called *primary storage* or RAM, for random access memory) is used to store programs and data (information) that need to be instantly accessible to the CPU. Storage devices (sometimes called *secondary storage*), including hard disk drives, recordable CD and DVD drives, and tape drives, serve as long-term repositories for data. You can think of a storage device, such as a hard disk drive, as a combination input and output device because the computer sends information to the storage device (output) and later retrieves that information from it (input).

These four types of components, when combined, make up the hardware part of a computer system. Of course, the system isn't complete without software—the instructions that tell the hardware what to do. But for now we can concentrate on hardware. In this chapter, we take a look at the central processing unit and the computer's memory; these components are at the center of all computing operations. In the next chapter, we look at the input, output, and storage devices—that is, the peripherals of the computer system. Because every computer hardware component is designed either to transport or to transform information, we start with a little bit of information about information.

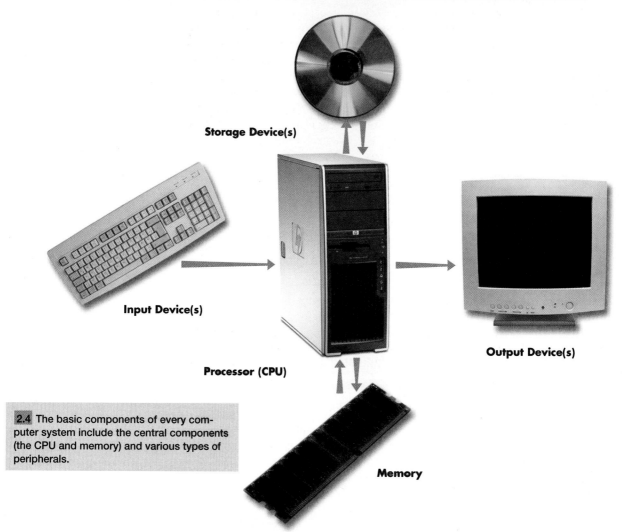

Storage Device(s)

Input Device(s)

Processor (CPU)

Output Device(s)

Memory

2.4 The basic components of every computer system include the central components (the CPU and memory) and various types of peripherals.

A Bit About Bits

The great Information Age is really an **explosion of non-information**; it is an **explosion of data**. To deal with the increasing **onslaught of data**, it is imperative to distinguish between the two; information is **that which leads to understanding.**

—Richard Saul Wurman, in *Information Anxiety*

The term information is difficult to define because it has many meanings. According to one popular definition, information is communication that has value because it *informs*. This distinction can be helpful for dealing with data from television, magazines, computers, and other sources. But it's not always clear and it's not absolute. As educator and author Richard Saul Wurman points out, "Everyone needs a personal measure with which to define information. What constitutes information to one person may be data to another. If it doesn't make sense to you, it doesn't qualify."

At the opposite extreme, one communication theory defines information as anything that can be communicated, whether it has value or not. By this definition, information comes in many forms. The words, numbers, and pictures on these pages are symbols representing information. If you underline or highlight this sentence, you're adding new information to the page. Even the sounds and pictures that emanate from a television commercial are packed with information, though it's debatable whether most of that information is useful.

Some people attempt to strictly apply the first definition to computers, claiming that computers turn raw data, which has no value in its current form, into information, which is valuable. This approach emphasizes the computer's role as a business data processing machine. But in our modern interconnected world, one computer's output is often another's input. If a computer receives a message from another computer, is the message worthless data or valuable information? And whose personal measure of value applies?

For our purposes, describing the mechanics of computers in these chapters, we lean toward the second, more subjective, approach and use the terms *data* and *information* more or less interchangeably. In later chapters, we present plenty of evidence to suggest that not all computer output has value. In the end, it is up to you to decide what the real information is.

Bit Basics

Whatever you call it, in the world of computers information is digital: This means it's made up of discrete, countable units—digits—so it can be subdivided. In many situations, people need to reduce information to simpler units to use it effectively. For example, a child trying to pronounce an unfamiliar word can sound out each letter or syllable individually before tackling the whole word.

A computer doesn't understand words, numbers, pictures, musical notes, or even letters of the alphabet. Like a young reader, a computer can't process information without dividing it into smaller units. In fact, computers can only digest information that has been broken into bits. A bit, or binary digit, is the smallest unit of information a computer can process. A bit can have one of two values, 0 and 1. You can also think of these two values as yes and no, on and off, black and white, or high and low.

If you think of the innards of a computer as a collection of microscopic on/off switches, it's easy to understand why computers process information bit by bit. Each switch stores a tiny amount of information: a signal to turn on a light, for example, or the answer to a yes/no question. (In modern integrated circuits, high and low electrical charges represent bits, but these circuits work the same as if they were really made up of tiny switches.)

Remember Paul Revere's famous midnight ride to warn the American colonists of the British invasion? His co-conspirators used a pair of lanterns to convey a choice between two messages, "One if by land, two if by sea"—a binary choice. It's theoretically possible to send a message like this with just one lantern. But "One if by land, zero if by sea" wouldn't have worked very well unless there was some way to know exactly when the message was being sent. With two lanterns, the first lantern could say "Here is the message" when it was turned on. The second lantern communicated the critical bit's worth of information: land or sea. If the revolutionaries had wanted to send a more complex message, they could have used more lanterns ("Three if by subway!").

In much the same way, a computer can process larger chunks of information by treating groups of bits as logical units. For example, a collection of 8 bits, called a byte, can represent 256 different messages ($256 = 2^8$). If you think of each bit as a light that can be either on or off, you can make different combinations of lights represent different messages. (Computer scientists usually speak in terms of 0 and 1 instead of on and off, but the concept is the same either way.) The computer has an advantage over Paul Revere in that it sees not just the number of lights turned on but also their order, so 01 (off–on) is different from 10 (on–off).

2.1
Binary Numbers

In a computer, all information—program instructions, pictures, text, sounds, or mathematical values—is represented by patterns of microscopic switches. In most cases, these groups of switches represent numbers or numerical codes.

The easiest kind of switch to manufacture is an on/off toggle switch: It has just two settings, on and off, like an ordinary light switch. That's the kind of switch that's used in every modern computer.

2.5 The MITS Altair, the first personal computer, came with no keyboard or monitor. It could only be programmed by manipulating a bank of binary switches on the front panel for input. Binary patterns of lights provided the output.

Binary arithmetic follows the same rules as ordinary decimal arithmetic. But with only two digits available for each position, you have to borrow and carry (manipulate digits in other positions) more often. Even adding 1 and 1 results in a two-digit number. Multiplication, division, negative numbers, and fractions can also be represented in binary, but most people find them messy and complicated compared with the decimal arithmetic commonly used by human beings.

1. In our decimal number system the position of a digit is important: In the number 7,357, the 7 on the left stands for seven thousands, the other 7 for seven ones. The use of switches to represent numbers would be easy to understand if the switches each had 10 settings (0 through 9). The decimal number 67 might look like this:

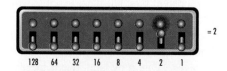

2.6

2. In the binary system the positional values are powers of 2, not 10. They start at 1 (the unit's place) and double in value for each additional place. Each switch represents a bit, and the collection of eight switches is a byte.

2.7

3. A byte (8 bits) can represent any number between 0 and 255. If all switches are off, the represented value is 0; if all eight switches are on, the value is 255 (1 + 2 + 4 + 8 + 16 + 32 + 64 + 128).

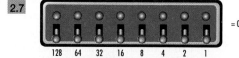

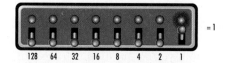

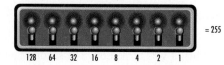

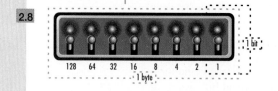

2.8

4. Numbers larger than 255 are represented by using multiple bytes, called *words*. For example, a 2-byte word can represent numbers from 0 to 65,535.

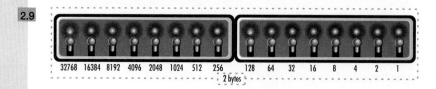

2.9

Building with Bits

What does a bit combination like 01100110 mean to the computer? There's no single answer to that question; it depends on context and convention. A string of bits can be interpreted as a number, a letter of the alphabet, or almost anything else.

> There's a **runaway market** for bits.
> —Russell Schweickart, astronaut

Bits as Numbers

Because computers are built from switching devices that reduce all information to 0s and 1s, they represent numbers using the *binary number system* a system that denotes all numbers with combinations of two digits. Like the 10-digit decimal system you use every day, the binary number system has clear, consistent rules for every arithmetic operation.

The people who worked with early computers had to use binary arithmetic. But today's computers include software that converts decimal numbers into binary numbers automatically, and vice versa. As a result, the computer's binary number processing is completely hidden from the user.

Bits as Codes

Today's computers work as much with text as with numbers. To make words, sentences, and paragraphs fit into the computer's binary-only circuitry, programmers have devised codes that represent each letter, digit, and special character as a unique string of bits.

The most widely used code, ASCII (an abbreviation of American Standard Code for Information Interchange, pronounced "as-kee"), represents each character as a unique 8-bit code. Out of a string of 8 bits, 256 unique ordered patterns can be made—enough to make unique codes for 26 letters (upper- and lowercase), 10 digits, and a variety of special characters.

As the world shrinks and our information needs grow, ASCII's 256 unique characters simply aren't enough. ASCII is too limited to accommodate Chinese, Greek, Hebrew, Japanese, and other languages. To facilitate multilingual computing, the computer industry is embracing Unicode, a coding scheme that supports 65,000 unique characters—more than enough for all major world languages.

Of course, today's computers work with more than characters. A group of bits can also represent colors, sounds, quantitative measurements from the environment, or just about any other kind of information that we need to process. We explore other types of information in later chapters.

Bits as Instructions in Programs

So far we've dealt with the ways bits represent data. But another kind of information is just as important to the computer: the programs that tell the computer what to do with the data you give it. The computer stores programs as collections of bits, just as it stores data.

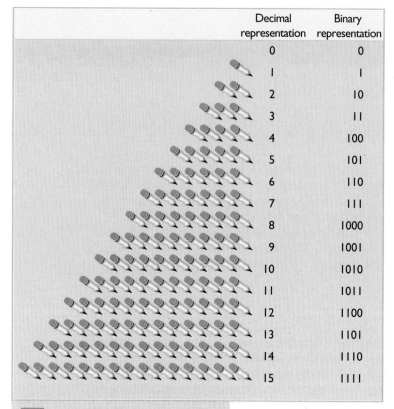

	Decimal representation	Binary representation
	0	0
	1	1
	2	10
	3	11
	4	100
	5	101
	6	110
	7	111
	8	1000
	9	1001
	10	1010
	11	1011
	12	1100
	13	1101
	14	1110
	15	1111

2.10 In the binary number system, every number is represented by a unique pattern of 0s and 1s.

Character	ASCII binary code
A	01000001
B	01000010
C	01000011
D	01000100
E	01000101
F	01000110
G	01000111
H	01001000
I	01001001
J	01001010
K	01001011
L	01001100
M	01001101
N	01001110
O	01001111
P	01010000
Q	01010001
R	01010010
S	01010011
T	01010100
U	01010101
V	01010110
W	01010111
X	01011000
Y	01011001
Z	01011010
0	00110000
1	00110001
2	00110010
3	00110011
4	00110100
5	00110101
6	00110110
7	00110111
8	00111000
9	00111001

2.11 The capital letters and numeric digits are represented in the ASCII character set by 36 unique patterns of 8 bits each. (The remaining 92 ASCII bit patterns represent lower-case letters, punctuation characters, and special characters.

Program instructions, like characters, are represented in binary notation through the use of codes. For example, the code 01101010 might tell the computer to add two numbers. Other groups of bits—instructions in the program—contain codes that tell the computer where to find those numbers and where to store the result. You learn more about how these computer instructions work in later chapters.

Bits, Bytes, and Buzzwords

> Even the most **sophisticated** computer is really only a large, well-organized **volume of bits**.
>
> —David Harel, in *Algorithmics: The Spirit of Computing*

Trying to learn about computers by examining their operation at the bit level is a little like trying to learn about how people look or act by studying individual human cells; there's plenty of information there, but it's not the most efficient way to find out what you need to know. Fortunately, people can use computers without thinking about bits. Some bit-related terminology does come up in day-to-day computer work, though. Most computer users need to have at least a basic understanding of the following terms for quantifying data:

■ **Byte**: A logical group of 8 bits. If you work mostly with words, you can think of a byte as one character of ASCII-encoded text.

2.2
Representing the World's Languages

The United States has long been at the center of the computer revolution; that's why the ASCII character set was originally designed to include only English-language characters. ASCII code numbers range from 0 to 127, but this isn't enough to handle all of the characters used in the languages of Western Europe, including accents and other diacritical marks.

The Latin I character set appends 128 additional codes onto the original ASCII 128 to accommodate additional characters.

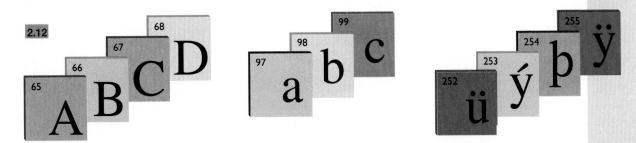

Both the ASCII and the Latin 1 character sets can use 8 bits—1 byte—to represent each character, but there's no room left for the characters used in languages such as Arabic, Greek, Hebrew, and Hindi, each of which has its own 50- to 150-character alphabet or syllabary. East Asian languages such as Chinese, Korean, and Japanese present bigger challenges for computer users. Chinese alone has nearly 50,000 distinct characters, of which about 13,000 are in current use.

A character set that uses 2 bytes, or 16 bits, per character allows for 256 × 256, or 65,536 distinct codes—more than enough for all modern languages. The international standard double-byte character set called Unicode is designed to facilitate multilingual computing. In Unicode, the first 256 codes (0 through 255) are identical to the codes of the Latin I character set. The remaining codes are distributed among the writing systems of the world's other languages.

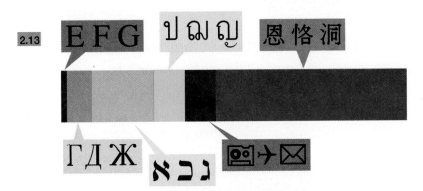

Most major new software applications and operating systems are designed to be transported to different languages. Making a software application work in different languages involves much more than translating the words. For example, some languages write from right to left or top to bottom. Pronunciation, currency symbols, dialects, and other variations often make it necessary to produce customized software for different regions even where the same language is spoken.

Computer keyboards for East Asian languages don't have one key for each character. Using phonetic input, a user types a pronunciation for a character using a Western-style keyboard and then chooses the character needed from a menu of characters that appears on the screen. The software can make some menu choices automatically based on common language-usage patterns.

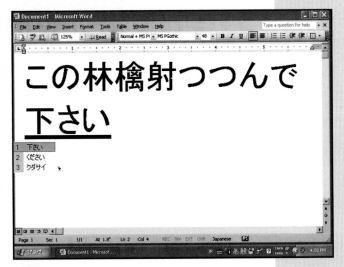

- KB (kilobyte or K): About 1,000 bytes of information. For example, about 5K of storage is necessary to hold 5,000 characters of ASCII text. (Technically, 1K is 1,024 bytes because 1,024 is 210, which makes the arithmetic easier for binary-based computers. For those of us who don't think in binary, 1,000 is often close enough.)
- MB (megabyte or meg): Approximately 1,000KB, or 1 million bytes.
- GB (gigabyte or gig): Approximately 1,000MB.
- TB (terabyte): Approximately 1 million MB or 1 trillion bytes. This massive unit of measurement applies to the largest storage devices commonly available today.
- PB (petabyte): This astronomical value is the equivalent of 1,024 terabytes, or 1 quadrillion bytes. While it's unlikely that anyone will be able to store 1PB of data on their home PC any time soon, we're definitely heading in that direction.

The abbreviations K, MB, GB, and PB describe the capacity of memory and storage components. You could, for example, describe a computer as having 512MB of memory (RAM) and a hard disk as having a 120GB storage capacity. The same terms are used to quantify sizes of computer files as well. A file is an organized collection of information, such as a term paper or a set of names and addresses, stored in a computer-readable form. For example, the text for this chapter is stored in a file that occupies about 132KB of space on a hard disk drive.

To add to the confusion, people often measure data transfer speed or memory size in *megabits (Mb)* rather than megabytes (MB). A megabit, as you might expect, is approximately 1,000 bits—one-eighth the size of a megabyte. When you're talking in bits and bytes, a little detail like capitalization can make a significant difference.

The Computer's Core: CPU and Memory

The **microprocessor** that makes up your personal computer's central processing unit, or CPU, is the **ultimate computer brain, messenger, ringmaster,** and **boss**. All the other components—RAM, disk drives, the monitor—exist only to bridge the gap between you and the processor.

—Ron White, in *How Computers Work*

It may seem strange to think of automated teller machines, video game consoles, and supercomputers as bit processors. But whatever it looks like to the user, a digital computer is at its core a collection of on/off switches designed to transform information from one form to another. The user provides the computer with patterns of bits—input—and the computer follows instructions to transform that input into a different pattern of bits—output—to return to the user.

The CPU: The Real Computer

The CPU, often called just the *processor*, performs the transformations of input into output. Every computer has at least one CPU to interpret and execute the instructions in each program, to do arithmetic and logical data manipulations, and to communicate with all the other parts of the computer system indirectly through memory.

A modern *microprocessor*, or CPU, is an extraordinarily complex collection of electronic circuits. In a desktop computer, the CPU is housed along with other chips and electronic components on a circuit board. The circuit board that contains a computer's CPU is called the motherboard.

Many different kinds of CPUs are in use today; when you choose a computer, the type of CPU in the computer is an important part of the decision. Although there are many variations in design among these chips, only two factors are important to a casual computer user: compatibility and performance.

Compatibility

Not all software is compatible with every CPU; that is, software written for one processor will usually not work with another. Every processor has a built-in instruction set—a vocabulary of instructions the processor can execute. CPUs in the same product family are generally designed so newer processors can process all of the instructions handled by earlier models. For example, chips in Intel's Pentium 4 microprocessor family are backward compatible with the Celeron, Pentium III, Pentium II, Pentium Pro, Pentium, 486, 386, and 286 chips that preceded it, so they can run most software written for those older CPUs. (Likewise, many of the processors designed by Advanced Micro Devices—AMD—are purposefully made to be compatible with those made by Intel.) But software written for the PowerPC family of processors used in Macintosh computers won't run on the Intel processors found in most IBM-compatible computers; the Intel processors can't understand programs written for the PowerPC CPUs. Similarly, the Macintosh PowerPC processor can't generally run Windows software.

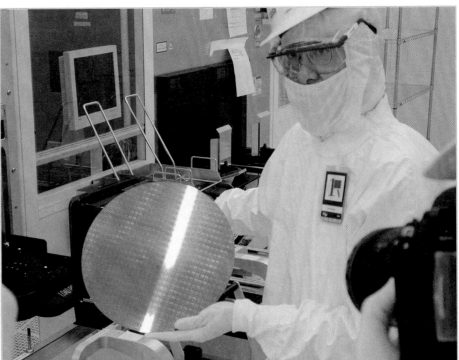

2.15 The motherboard of a typical PC contains the CPU, memory, and several other important chips and components.

A related issue involves the software systems that run on these hardware platforms. Programs written for Linux, a popular UNIX-like operating system, can't run on Windows, even though both systems run on PCs powered by Intel's microprocessor. In Chapter 4, you will learn more about these issues and see how virtual machine software can often overcome incompatibility problems by translating instructions written for one CPU or software system into instructions that another can execute.

Performance

There's a tremendous variation in how fast different processors can handle information. Most computer applications, such as word processing, are more convenient to use on a faster machine. Many applications that use graphics or do computations, such as statistical programs, graphic design programs, and many computer games, require faster machines to produce satisfactory results.

A computer's overall performance is determined in part by the speed of its microprocessor's internal *clock*—the timing device that produces electrical pulses to synchronize the computer's operations. A computer's clock speed is measured in units called *gigahertz (GHz)*, for billions of clock cycles per second. Ads for new computer systems often emphasize gigahertz ratings as a measure of speed. But these numbers can be somewhat misleading; judging a computer's speed by its gigahertz rating alone is like measuring a car's speed by the engine's RPM (revolutions per minute).

2.16 This chip specialist is examining a silicon wafer before it is sliced into many silicon chips.

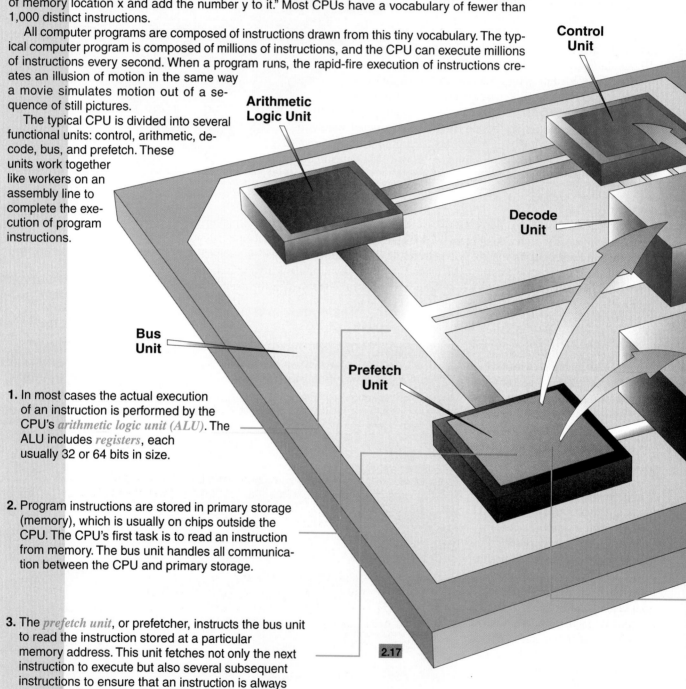

The central processing unit (CPU) is the hardware component that executes the steps in a software program, performing math and moving data from one part of the system to another. The CPU contains the circuitry to perform a variety of simple tasks, called *instructions*. An individual instruction does only a tiny amount of work. A typical instruction might be "Read the contents of memory location x and add the number y to it." Most CPUs have a vocabulary of fewer than 1,000 distinct instructions.

All computer programs are composed of instructions drawn from this tiny vocabulary. The typical computer program is composed of millions of instructions, and the CPU can execute millions of instructions every second. When a program runs, the rapid-fire execution of instructions creates an illusion of motion in the same way a movie simulates motion out of a sequence of still pictures.

The typical CPU is divided into several functional units: control, arithmetic, decode, bus, and prefetch. These units work together like workers on an assembly line to complete the execution of program instructions.

Control Unit

Arithmetic Logic Unit

Decode Unit

Bus Unit

Prefetch Unit

1. In most cases the actual execution of an instruction is performed by the CPU's *arithmetic logic unit (ALU)*. The ALU includes *registers*, each usually 32 or 64 bits in size.

2. Program instructions are stored in primary storage (memory), which is usually on chips outside the CPU. The CPU's first task is to read an instruction from memory. The bus unit handles all communication between the CPU and primary storage.

3. The *prefetch unit*, or prefetcher, instructs the bus unit to read the instruction stored at a particular memory address. This unit fetches not only the next instruction to execute but also several subsequent instructions to ensure that an instruction is always ready to be executed.

2.17

4. The *decode unit* takes the instruction read by the prefetcher and translates it into a form suitable for the CPU's internal processing. It does this by looking up the steps required to complete an instruction in the control unit.

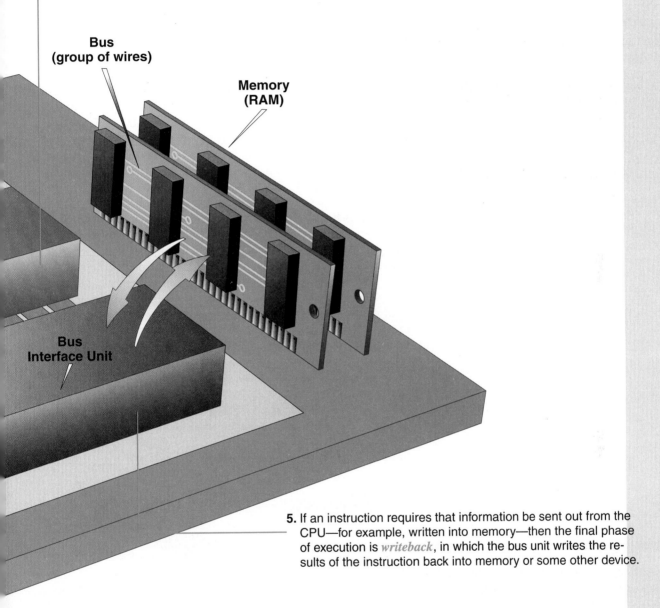

Bus (group of wires)

Memory (RAM)

Bus Interface Unit

5. If an instruction requires that information be sent out from the CPU—for example, written into memory—then the final phase of execution is *writeback*, in which the bus unit writes the results of the instruction back into memory or some other device.

6. Microprocessor manufacturers use many techniques to eliminate bottlenecks and speed up processing. For example, in the same way it prefetches the next likely instructions to be read, the CPU prereads the next likely data to be used into a cache in memory (called a *Level 2 cache (L2 cache)* or, for faster access, in the CPU itself (a *Level 1 cache*).

2.18 The Intel Pentium-M (left) and Pentium 4 chips contain circuitry that looks like geometric patterns when magnified.

The PC notebook powered by a 2.4-GHz Pentium 4-M chip isn't necessarily faster than a 1.42-GHz Power Mac G4 or a 2-GHz Pentium 4 chip; in fact, for some tasks, it's actually slower. That's because much of the notebook's circuitry isn't as advanced, or speedy, as the circuitry in the other systems.

PC performance can also be limited by the **architecture** of the processor—the design that determines how individual components of the CPU are put together on the chip. For example, newer chips can manipulate more bits simultaneously than older chips, which makes them more efficient, and therefore faster, at performing most operations. The number of bits a CPU can process at one time—typically 32 or 64—is sometimes called the CPU's *word size*. More often, though, people use the number without a label, as in "The Itanium is Intel's first mainstream 64-bit processor." Today, only high-end workstations and servers use 64-bit processors, while most PCs and Macintoshes use 32-bit processors. Some embedded and special-purpose computers still use 8- and 16-bit processors because their performance needs are smaller.

Because performance is so important, engineers and computer scientists are constantly developing techniques for speeding up a computer's ability to manipulate and move bits. One common technique for improving a computer's performance is to put more than one processor in the computer. Many personal computers, for example, have specialized subsidiary processors that take care of mathematical calculations or graphics displays, and many Macs and some PCs now employ two microprocessors to improve overall performance. This capability, **parallel processing** (sometimes called **symmetric multiprocessing** or just **multiprocessing** in the PC world) has been used in high-end servers and workstations for some time. Indeed, some of the largest servers in the world now include up to 64 or 128 processors!

Another way to improve performance on high-end server systems is to simply add more machines to the mix. This way, the processing resources of multiple servers can be grouped together in a **cluster** to improve rendering speeds in lifelike computer graphics or calculate the sums of complex financial trading computations more quickly. Server clusters are also used for reliability reasons: If one machine in a cluster shuts down because of errors, or to be serviced, the other servers can pick up the slack.

The Computer's Memory

"**What's one** and **one** and **one** and **one** and **one** and **one** and **one** and **one** and **one** and **one**?" "**I don't know**," said Alice. "I lost count." "**She can't do addition**," said the Red Queen.

—Lewis Carroll, in *Through the Looking Glass*

The CPU's main job is to follow the instructions encoded in programs. But like Alice in *Through the Looking Glass*, the CPU can handle only one instruction and a few pieces of data at a time. The computer needs a place to store the rest of the program and data until the processor is ready for them. That's what RAM is for.

RAM (*random access memory*) is the most common type of primary storage, or computer memory. RAM chips contain circuits that store program instructions and data temporarily. The computer divides each RAM chip into many equal-sized memory locations. Memory locations, like houses, have unique addresses so the computer can tell them apart when it is instructed to save or retrieve information. You can store a piece of information in any RAM location—you can pick one at random—and the computer can, if so instructed, quickly retrieve it. Hence the name random access memory.

2.19 POPULAR CPU FAMILIES AND WHERE TO FIND THEM

	CPU Family	Word Size	Developer/ Manufacturer	Where They Are Used
	Itanium family	64-bit	Intel Corporation	High-end servers and workstations.
	Pentium family (including Celeron and Xeon)	32-bit	Intel Corporation	PCs, notebooks, workstations, and servers. Celeron is designed for low-end systems; Xeon is designed for workstations and servers.
	Opteron family (compatible with Intel Pentium family)	32/64-bit	Advanced Micro Devices (AMD)	High-end PCs, workstations, and servers.
	Athlon family (compatible with Intel Pentium family)	32-bit	AMD	PCs and notebooks.
	Crusoe family (compatible with Intel Pentium family)	32-bit	Transmeta	Ultramobile notebook PCs and embedded devices.
	PowerPC family (including G3, G4, and G5)	64-bit (G5) and 32-bit (G3, G4)	IBM and Motorola	Macintosh computers, notebooks, and servers.
	SPARC	64-bit	Sun Microsystems	High-end UNIX servers and workstations.
	Xscale	32-bit	Intel Corporation	PDAs and handheld computers.

The information stored in RAM is nothing more than a pattern of electrical current flowing through microscopic circuits in silicon chips. This means that when the power goes off the computer instantly forgets everything it was remembering in RAM. RAM is sometimes referred to as volatile memory because information stored there is not held permanently.

This could be a serious problem if the computer didn't have another type of memory to store information that you don't want to lose. This nonvolatile memory is called ROM

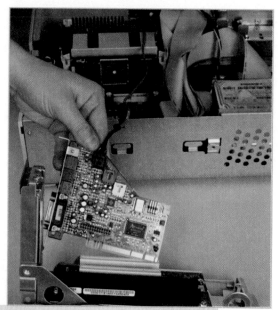

2.20 Slots and ports enable the CPU to communicate with the outside world via peripheral devices. Here an add-on card is being inserted into an internal slot in the PC.

(*read-only memory*) because the computer can only read information from it; it can never write any new information on it. All modern computers include ROM that contains start-up instructions and other critical information. The information in ROM was etched in when the chip was manufactured, so it is available whenever the computer is operating, but it can't be changed except by replacing the ROM chip.

Other types of memory are available; most are seldom used outside of engineering laboratories. There are two notable exceptions:

- *CMOS (complementary metal oxide semiconductor)* is a special low-energy kind of RAM that can store small amounts of data for long periods of time on battery power. CMOS RAM stores the date, time, and calendar in a PC. (CMOS RAM is called *parameter RAM* in Macintoshes.)
- *Flash memory* chips, like RAM chips, can be written and erased rapidly and repeatedly. But unlike RAM, flash memory is nonvolatile; it can keep its contents without a flow of electricity. Digital cameras, cell phones, pagers, portable computers, handheld computers, PDAs, and other digital devices use flash memory to store data that needs to be changed from time to time. Data flight recorders also use it. Flash memory is still too expensive to replace RAM and other common storage media, but it may in the future replace disk drives as well as memory chips.

It takes time for the processor to retrieve data from memory—but not very much time. The *access time* for most memory is measured in *nanoseconds (ns)*—billionths of a second. Compare this to hard disk access time, which is measured in *milliseconds (ms)*—thousandths of a second. Memory speed (access time) is another factor that affects the computer's overall speed.

Buses, Ports, and Peripherals

In a desktop computer, the CPU, memory chips, and other key components are attached to the motherboard. Information travels between components on the motherboard through groups of wires called *system buses*, or just *buses*. Buses typically have 32 or 64 wires, or data paths; a bus with 32 wires is called a *32-bit bus* because it can transmit 32 bits of information at a time, twice as many as an older 16-bit bus. Just as multilane freeways allow masses of automobiles to move faster than they could on single-lane roads, wider buses can transmit information faster than narrower buses. Newer, more powerful computers have wider buses so they can process information faster.

Buses connect to storage devices in *bays*—open areas in the system box for disk drives and other devices. Buses also connect to *expansion slots* (sometimes just called *slots*) inside the computer's housing. Users can customize their computers by inserting special-purpose circuit boards (called *expansion cards*, or just *cards*) into these slots. Buses also connect to external buses and *ports*—sockets on the outside of the computer chassis. The back of a computer typically has a variety of ports to meet a variety of needs. Some of these ports—where you might plug in the keyboard and mouse, for example—are connected directly to the system board. Others, such as the monitor port, are generally attached to an expansion card. In fact, many expansion cards do little more than provide convenient ports for attaching particular types of peripherals.

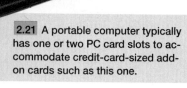

2.21 A portable computer typically has one or two PC card slots to accommodate credit-card-sized add-on cards such as this one.

2.4
Memory

Memory is the work area for the CPU. Think of memory as millions of tiny storage cells, each of which can contain a single byte of information. A typical personal computer has from 256 to 512 megabytes (million bytes) of memory. The information in memory includes program instructions, numbers for arithmetic, codes representing text characters, digital codes representing pictures, and other kinds of data.

Memory chips are usually grouped on small circuit boards called *SIMMs (single in-line memory modules)* and *DIMMs (dual in-line memory modules)* and are plugged into the motherboard.

2.22 Two SIMMs plugged into a circuit board.

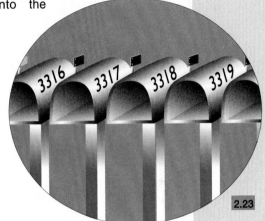

2.23

Like mailboxes in a row, bytes of memory have unique addresses that identify them and help the CPU keep track of where things are stored.

The CPU can only see into and access memory. Memory addresses make up the CPU's entire world, so any program that needs to be executed or data that needs to be modified must make its way into memory.

1. When you turn on the computer, the CPU automatically begins executing instructions stored in read-only memory (ROM). On most computer systems, ROM also contains parts of the operating system. The firmware programs in ROM are sometimes called the *BIOS (basic input/output system)*.

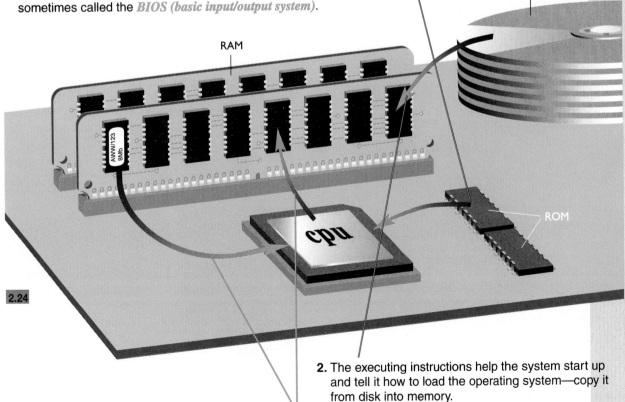

HARD DISK

RAM

cpu

ROM

2.24

2. The executing instructions help the system start up and tell it how to load the operating system—copy it from disk into memory.

3. Once executing instructions are loaded into memory, the CPU is able to execute them.

79

When compared with heavy industries such as automobiles and energy, the computer industry is relatively easy on the environment. But the manufacture and use of computer hardware and software does have a significant environmental impact, especially now that so many of us are using the technology. Fortunately, you have some control over the environmental impact of your computing activities. Here are a few tips to help minimize your impact:

➡ *Buy green equipment*. Today's computer equipment uses relatively little energy, but as world energy resources dwindle, less is always better. Many modern computers and peripherals are specifically designed to consume less energy. Look for the Environmental Protection Agency's Energy Star certification on the package.

➡ *Use a notebook*. Portable computers use far less energy than desktop computers. They're engineered to preserve precious battery power. But if you use a laptop, keep it plugged in when you have easy access to an electrical outlet. Batteries wear out from repeated usage, and their disposal can cause environmental problems of a different sort. (If you're the kind of person who always needs to have the latest and greatest technology, a notebook isn't the best choice because notebooks are difficult or impossible to upgrade.)

➡ *Take advantage of energy-saving features*. Most modern systems can be set up to go to sleep (a sort of suspended animation state that uses just enough power to preserve RAM) and turn off the monitor or printer when idle for more than an hour or so. If your equipment has automatic energy-saving features, use them. You'll save energy and money.

➡ *Turn it off when you're away*. If you're just leaving your computer for an hour or two, you won't save much energy by turning the CPU off. But if you're leaving it for more than a few hours and it's not on duty receiving faxes and email, you'll do the environment a favor by turning it off or putting it to sleep.

➡ *Save energy, not screens*. Your monitor is probably the biggest power guzzler in your system. A screen saver can be fun to watch, but it doesn't save your screen, and it doesn't save energy, either. As long as your monitor is displaying an image, it's consuming power. Use sleep.

➡ *Print only once*. Don't print out a rough draft just to proofread; try to get it clean on-screen. (Most people find this one hard to follow 100% of the time; some errors just don't seem to show up until you print.)

➡ *Recycle your waste products*. When you do have to reprint that 20-page report because of a missing paragraph on page 1, recycle the flawed printout. When your laser printer's toner cartridge runs dry, ship or deliver it to one of the many companies that recycle cartridges. They may even pay you a few dollars for the empty cartridge. When your portable's battery dies, follow the manufacturer's instructions for recycling it. While you're in recycling mode, don't forget all those computer magazines and catalogs.

➡ *Pass it on*. When you outgrow a piece of hardware or software, don't throw it away. Donate it to a school, civic organization, family member, or friend who can put it to good use.

➡ *Send bits, not atoms*. It takes far more resources to send a letter by truck, train, or plane than to send an electronic message through the Internet. Whenever possible, use your modem instead of your printer.

2.25 Windows and Mac OS X systems have advanced energy-saver control panels that can be used to automatically switch the monitor, hard drive, and CPU to lower-power sleep modes after specified periods of inactivity.

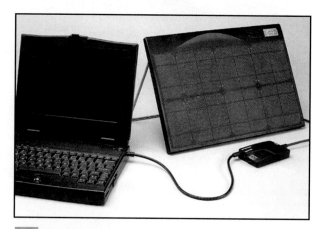

2.26 Portable computers consume far less energy than desktop models. This one is powered by the sun using a Neptune Solar Panel.

In portable computers, where size is critical, most common ports go directly to the system board. Because portable computers don't have room for full-sized cards, many have slots for **PC cards**—credit-card-sized cards that contain memory, miniature peripherals, and additional ports. (When these cards were first released, they were known as *PCMCIA cards*. One writer humorously suggested that this stood for "People Can't Memorize Computer Industry Acronyms" though the unfortunate acronym actually means "Personal Computer Memory Card International Association." Thankfully, the name was shortened to the simpler PC card.)

Slots and ports make it easy to add external devices, called **peripherals**, to the computer system so the CPU can communicate with the outside world and store information for later use. Without peripherals, CPU and memory together are like a brain without a body. Some peripherals such as keyboards and printers serve as communication links between people and computers. Other peripherals link the computer to other machines. Still others provide long-term storage media. In the next chapter, we explore a variety of input, output, and storage peripherals and then revisit the buses, slots, and ports that connect those peripherals to the CPU and memory.

Tomorrow's Processors

The only thing that has consistently **grown faster** than hardware in the last 40 years is **human expectation**.

—Bjarne Stroustrup, AT&T Bell Labs, designer of the C++ programming language

Many research labs are experimenting with alternatives to today's silicon chips. For example, IBM researchers have developed plastic chips that are more durable and energy efficient than silicon chips. Intel, Motorola, and AMD are working with the U.S. government to develop new laser etching technology called *extreme ultraviolet lithography* (EUVL) that could reduce chip size and increase performance radically. Motorola researchers have created chips that combine silicon with gallium arsenide, a semiconductor that conducts electricity faster than silicon and emits light that can be used for information applications; the research should soon produce chips that are much faster than any currently available. IBM and Motorola researchers are making progress producing chips based on carbon rather than silicon.

Other researchers are working on more radical research technologies. Superconductors that transmit electricity without heat could increase computer speed a hundredfold. Unfortunately, superconductor technology generally requires a supercooled environment, which isn't

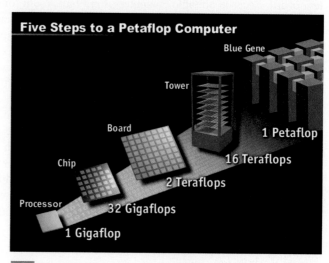

Five Steps to a Petaflop Computer

Blue Gene

Tower

Board

1 Petaflop

16 Teraflops

Chip

2 Teraflops

Processor

32 Gigaflops

1 Gigaflop

2.28 This illustration shows how IBM researchers envision the evolution of high performance computers from simple processors to Blue Gene, IBM's next-generation supercomputer.

practical for most applications. A more realistic alternative is the optical computer, which transmits information in light waves rather than electrical pulses. Optical computers outside research labs are currently limited to a few narrow applications such as robot vision. But when the technology is refined, general-purpose optical computers may process information hundreds of times faster than silicon computers.

Some of the most revolutionary work in computer design involves not what's inside the processors, but how they're put together. One example is IBM's Blue Gene, a supercomputer being developed to help scientists crack the secrets of proteins in the human body. Blue Gene will have 1 million small, simple processors, each capable of handling eight threads of instructions simultaneously. The processors won't have power-hungry embedded caches, but they will have built-in memory to improve speed. The network of processors will be self-healing—it will detect failed components, seal them off, and direct work elsewhere. If it works as planned, Blue Gene will be the first *petaflop* computer, capable of handling 1 quadrillion (1,000,000,000,000,000) instructions per second—2 million times more than today's PC! (The fastest computers have reached *teraflop* speeds—trillions of operations per second.)

2.27 Researchers are exploring ways to apply fiber optic technology to circuit board and chip design to produce faster processors.

Bit Literacy

Mark Hurst

In Information Anxiety 2, *Richard Saul Wurman explores a problem faced by many of us: too much information. In this edited article from that book, Consultant Mark Hurst of Creative Good www.goodexperience.com discusses the problem and a solution: bit literacy.*

Information anxiety is more important today than ever, thanks to the arrival of the bit. The tiniest one- or zero-pulse of digital data, the bit will affect our lives as much as the atom. Ten years ago, Americans may have felt some anxiety over the magazines and newspapers piling up at home, but today the anxiety is increasing as bits appear in all areas of our lives. Email, Web sites, e-newsletters, chat rooms, email, instant messages, and more email—all of these streams of bits can interrupt us, and keep us engaged, anywhere and anytime. Devices made to hold these bits are springing up, too: PDAs and cell phones bring us the bits when we're away from our PC.

For those who own a PC or a PDA, there is little escape from the bits. Even when we turn off the device, the bits pile up quietly, ready to flood us with anxiety when we return to the device. If anything, an escape from the bits can be dangerous. Take a week-long vacation without email, and upon return, a bloated inbox welcomes us back to work with seven times more bits.

And this is still early in the current explosion of digital information. One research study recently predicted that, within a few years, the number of emails we receive every day will increase to forty times its current volume. That's a lot of bits demanding our attention—just from email. It's likely that still other devices and other bitstreams will threaten the typical American with exponentially more information anxiety.

The problem of near-infinite bits, however, does have a solution. The solution is what I call "bit literacy." Bit literacy is an awareness of bits: what bits are, how they affect our lives, and how we can survive in a society permeated by bits. With that awareness, bit literate people are able to control the bits, and not be controlled by the bits, that are becoming central to our lives and jobs.

All of bit literacy can be distilled into a simple philosophy that allows people to regain their life, free from information anxiety, while still living in the bits. Here is the four-word philosophy:

Let the bits go.

That's right, let the bits go. Don't acquire them. Don't try to acquire them, and don't worry about acquiring them, since the bits will come to you. The bits touch our lives at so many points that it's impossible to escape them, and it's insane to try to acquire all of them. Instead, being bit literate means constantly working on letting go of as many of the bits as we can. Bit literacy allows us to clear a path of emptiness through the jungle of bits that surround and distract us; the emptiness allows us to see.

Here's a real-life example. Recently I visited a Web site where visitors can sign up to receive email newsletters, published by respected companies, on any number of topics. Internet news, sports commentary, entertainment gossip—all of these were available to me at the click of a button. I could get all of this information, delivered to my email in-box weekly . . . for free! And unlike subscriptions to paper magazines, these bits wouldn't clutter my apartment or need recycling. (I didn't sign up; I was there to unsubscribe from a newsletter.) So, one might reasonably ask, what's the problem with getting some potentially valuable or entertaining bits, if they don't clutter my living space, don't weigh me down, and don't cost a penny?

The problem is that the bits are different from paper-based information. Bits are more engaging, more immediate, more personal, and more abundant than other types of information. In the middle of lunch with a friend, we're interrupted by bits—perhaps a stock quote—and we instinctively reach for our PDAs to see what it is. Or we sit down to "read through some email" and blow through two hours like it was twenty minutes. Like the magazines and other anxiety-producing information, the bits call for our attention—but the bits call more loudly, more sweetly, more frequently, and in more areas of our lives.

These radically different qualities of bits mean that we must engage bits in a radically different way. Bit literacy is radical about letting the bits go. We can't let all the bits go—we must engage them first, and inevitably save the few most important bits—but our default behavior must be to let the bits go, rather than acquire and save them.

Here are some ways you can let the bits go: Keep your email inbox empty, by deleting your emails after saving the few that you must retain for later reference. Restrict the interruptions you allow on your cell phone and PDA, so that the interruptions that do come through are the important ones. And certainly don't open up any new bitstream—a newsletter, a ticker, or any other ongoing feed—unless it's vitally important. Instead, concentrate on letting go of the bits that find their way to you; the few remaining bits will be all the more valuable to you as a result.

I'd like to emphasize that last sentence: When a person becomes bit literate, what remains after all the letting go is valuable. I equate that with meaningful. Because—and here's the kicker—the bits by themselves aren't meaningful. Bits are just pointers to meaning, just containers of thoughts, just phantom images of the real item. The meaning is what lies behind the bits, what *drives* the bits. In their super-abundant quantities, swarming and overwhelming our consciousness, bits obscure the very meaning that created them. It's only after clearing out a path of emptiness that we can arrive at the meaning *behind* the bits.

DISCUSSION QUESTIONS

1. Do you think information anxiety is a serious problem for many people? Explain your answer.

2. Do you think "bit literacy," as described by the author, makes sense? Explain your answer.

SUMMARY

Whether it's working with words, numbers, pictures, or sounds, a computer is manipulating patterns of bits—binary digits of information that it can store in switching circuitry and that are represented by two symbols. Groups of bits can be treated as numbers for calculations using the binary number system. Bits can be grouped into coded messages that represent alphabetic characters, pictures, colors, sounds, or just about any other kind of information. Even the instructions computers follow—the software programs that tell the computer what to do—must be reduced to strings of bits before the computer accepts them. Byte, kilobyte, megabyte, and other common units for measuring bit quantities are used in descriptions of memory, storage, and file size.

The microprocessor, or central processing unit (CPU), follows software instructions to perform the calculations and logical manipulations that transform input data into output. Not all CPUs are compatible with each other; each is capable of processing a particular set of instructions, so a software program written for one family of processors can't necessarily be understood by a processor from another family. Engineers are constantly improving the clock speed and architecture of CPUs, making computers capable of processing information faster.

The CPU uses RAM (random access memory) as a temporary storage area—a scratch pad—for instructions and data. Another type of memory, ROM (read-only memory), contains unchangeable information that serves as reference material for the CPU as it executes program instructions.

The CPU and main memory are housed in silicon chips on the motherboard and other circuit boards inside the computer. Buses connect to slots and ports that enable the computer to communicate with internal devices and external peripherals.

KEY TERMS

architecture (p. 76)
ASCII (p. 69)
backward compatible (p. 73)
bay (p. 78)
binary (p. 67)
bit (p. 67)
bus (p. 78)
byte (p. 67)
central processing unit (CPU) (p. 65)
cluster (p. 76)
compatible (p. 73)
data (p. 65)
digit (p. 67)
digital (p. 67)

expansion slot (p. 78)
file (p. 72)
GB (gigabyte) (p. 72)
information (p. 66)
input device (p. 65)
KB (kilobyte) (p. 72)
MB (megabyte) (p. 72)
memory (p. 65)
microprocessor (p. 65)
motherboard (p. 72)
multiprocessing (p. 76)
nonvolatile memory (p. 77)
output device (p. 65)
parallel processing (p. 76)

PB (petabyte) (p. 72)
PC card (p. 78)
peripheral (p. 66)
port (p. 78)
processor (p. 65)
RAM (random access memory) (p. 65)
ROM (read-only memory) (p. 77)
storage device (p. 65)
symmetric multiprocessing (p. 76)
system bus (p. 78)
TB (terabyte) (p. 72)
Unicode (p. 69)

INTERACTIVE QUIZ QUESTIONS

1. The *Computer Confluence* CD-ROM contains self-test quiz questions related to this chapter, including multiple-choice, true or false, and matching questions.

2. The *Computer Confluence* Web site, **http://www.computerconfluence.com**, contains self-test exercises related to this chapter. Follow the instruc-

tions for taking a quiz. After you've completed your quiz, you can email the results to your instructor.

3. The Web site also contains open-ended discussion questions called Internet Explorations. Discuss one or more of the Internet Exploration questions at the section for this chapter.

TRUE OR FALSE

1. The term "information" is always defined in terms of value.

2. The data processed by digital computers is made up of discrete units, or digits.

3. A simple on/off switch can store exactly one bit of information.

4. There are more than enough characters in standard ASCII codes to represent all of the major world languages.

5. A kilobyte (KB) is twice as big as a kilobit (Kb).

6. If a processor is backward compatible with another, older processor, it can run older programs written for that processor.

7. A CPU with a clock speed of 3.2 gigahertz can perform all tasks at least twice as fast as a processor that runs at 1.5 gigahertz.

8. The information stored in RAM is nothing more than a pattern of electrical current flowing through microscopic circuits in silicon chips.

9. The access time for most memory is slower than the access time for a typical hard disk.

10. Slots and ports make it possible for the CPU to communicate with the outside world through peripherals.

MULTIPLE CHOICE

1. A binary choice offers how many options?
   a. none.
   b. one.
   c. two.
   d. It depends on the amount of memory in the computer.
   e. It depends on the speed of the computer's processor.

2. A collection of bits in the computer's memory might be treated as
   a. binary numbers that can be added and subtracted.
   b. ASCII codes representing letters and other characters.
   c. program instructions that tell the computer what to do.
   d. Any of the above.
   e. None of the above.

3. One megabyte equals approximately
   a. 1,000 bits.
   b. 1,000 bytes.
   c. 1 million bytes.
   d. 1 million bits.
   e. 2,000 megabits.

4. Transformation of input into output is performed by
   a. peripherals.
   b. memory.
   c. storage.
   d. the CPU.
   e. the ALU.

5. The speed of a computer depends on
   a. the architecture of the processor.
   b. the clock speed of the processor.
   c. the word size of the processor
   d. the number of processors.
   e. All of the above.

6. Software written for the Pentium III CPU will generally run on the Pentium 4 CPU because
   a. Microsoft uses special encoding techniques that only work with Pentium CPUs.
   b. the Pentium 4 has special compatibility registers in RAM.
   c. the Pentium 4 is designed to be backward compatible with earlier Pentium chips.
   d. every CPU is, by definition, compatible with the Pentium III.
   e. all software written for the Pentium 4 is compiled on Pentium III processors.

7. When you are working on a document on a PC, the document is temporarily stored in
   a. RAM.
   b. ROM.
   c. the CPU.
   d. flash memory.
   e. the CD-ROM.

8. Information travels between components on the motherboard through
   a. flash memory.
   b. CMOS.
   c. bays.
   d. buses.
   e. peripherals.

9. PC cards (formerly called PCMCIA cards) are
   a. cards that are designed to be inserted into slots on desktop PCs.
   b. high-speed cards that are designed to work with workstations.
   c. compact cards that are designed to work with notebook computers.
   d. cards that attach directly to the PC motherboard.
   e. None of the above.

10. Storage devices can be connected to the CPU and memory via
    a. expansion slots.
    b. ports.
    c. bays.
    d. All of the above.
    e. None of the above.

REVIEW QUESTIONS

1. Provide a working definition of each of the key words listed in the "Key Terms" section. Check your answers in the glossary.

2. Draw a block diagram showing the major components of a computer and their relationship. Briefly describe the function of each component.

3. Think of this as computer input: *123.4*. The computer might read this as a number or as a set of ASCII codes. Explain how these concepts differ.

4. Why is information stored in some kind of binary format in computers?

5. Why can't you normally run Macintosh software on a PC with an Intel Pentium 4 CPU?

6. Clock speed is only one factor in determining a CPU's processing speed. What is another?

7. Why is it important that computers support both internal and external expansion?

8. Explain how symmetrical multiprocessing can increase a computer's performance; use an example or a comparison with the way people work if you like.

9. What is the difference between RAM and ROM? What is the purpose of each?

10. What is the difference between primary and secondary storage?

DISCUSSION QUESTIONS

1. Why are computer manufacturers constantly releasing faster computers? How do computer users benefit from the increased speed?

2. How is human memory similar to computer memory? How is it different?

PROJECTS

1. Collect computer advertisements from newspapers, magazines, and other sources. Compare how the ads handle discussions of speed. Evaluate the usefulness of the information in the ads from a consumer's point of view.

2. Interview a salesperson in a computer store. Find out what kinds of questions people ask when buying a computer. Develop profiles for the most common types of computer buyers. What kinds of computers do these customers buy, and why?

SOURCES AND RESOURCES

Books

Building IBM: Shaping an Industry and Its Technology, by Emerson W. Pugh (Cambridge, MA: MIT Press, 1995). This book traces IBM's history from Herman Hollerith's invention of the punch card machine more than a century ago. This thoroughly researched and clearly written book is a valuable resource for anyone interested in understanding IBM's history.

Who Says Elephants Can't Dance? Inside IBM's Historic Turnaround, by Louis V. Gerstner, Jr. (New York: Harper Business, 2002). Written by the ex-CEO of IBM, this fascinating look at IBM's late-1990s comeback, the IBM culture, and why IBM still matters in a world seemingly dominated by Microsoft. Famous for his quote "the last thing IBM needs right now is a vision," Gerstner is credited with changing IBM into a highly successful and profitable services company.

Information Anxiety 2, by Richard Saul Wurman (Indianapolis: Que, 2001). This is a revised and updated version of Wurman's popular 1989 book, which foresaw the data clutter problem we now face. The style and organization are sometimes quirky, but the content is useful and thought-provoking. Wurman discusses the nature and value of information and offers advice about how to cope with the explosion of non-information—"stuff that doesn't inform."

The Soul of a New Machine, by Tracy Kidder (New York: Back Bay Books, 2000). This Pulitzer Prize–winning book provides a journalist's inside look at the making of a new computer in the late 1970s, including lots of insights into what makes computers (and computer people) tick. It's still a good read—and highly relevant—more than two decades later.

How Computers Work, Sixth Edition, by Ron White (Indianapolis: Que, 2001). The first edition of *How Computers Work* launched a successful series that inspired many imitators. Like its predecessor, this revised and expanded edition clearly illustrates with beautiful pictures and accessible prose how each component of a modern personal computer system works. If you're interested in looking under the hood, this is a great place to start. The explanations and illustrations are based on IBM-compatible computers, but most of the concepts apply to computers in general. A Windows-only CD-ROM includes a multimedia tour of a computer.

How the Mac Works, by John Rizzo and K. Daniel Clark (Indianapolis: Que, 2000). This book covers the basics of Macintosh anatomy in the same style as *How Computers Work* and includes Mac-related technologies such as Firewire, networks, and printing.

Personal Computers for Technology Students, by Charles Raymond (Upper Saddle River, NJ: Prentice Hall, 2001). This is a technical but readable text on the PC, from CPU to peripherals. It includes a useful glossary of acronyms, in case you ever need to know what SRAM or SVGA stands for.

Peter Norton's New Inside the PC, by Scott Clark, Peter Norton, and Scott H. A. Clark (Indianapolis: Sams, 2002). Norton's name is almost a household word among PC enthusiasts, many of whom consider Norton Utilities to be indispensable software. This book offers clear, detailed explanations of the inner workings of the PC, from CPU to peripherals, from hardware to software. You don't need to be a technical wizard to understand and learn from this book.

The Essential Guide to Computing: The Story of Information Technology, by E. Garrison Walters (Upper Saddle River, NJ: Prentice Hall, 2001). This is a highly readable and surprisingly broad overview of computer technology, with coverage of hardware, software, and networks. The book provides historical and industry perspectives along with solid technical information that goes beyond the usual introductory books.

World Wide Web Pages

Most computer hardware manufacturers have Web pages on the Internet. Use a Web browser to visit some of these sites for information about the latest hardware from these companies. It's not hard to guess the Web addresses of computer companies; most follow the pattern suggested by these examples:

http://www.apple.com

http://www.dell.com

http://www.ibm.com

The *Computer Confluence* Web site, http://www.computerconfluence.com, will guide you to these and other hardware pages of interest.

**AFTER YOU READ THIS CHAPTER YOU
SHOULD BE ABLE TO:**

- List several examples of input devices and explain
  how they can make it easier to get different types
  of information into the computer

- List several examples of output devices and
  explain how they make computers more useful

- Explain why a typical computer has different types
  of storage devices

- Diagram how the components of a computer
  system fit together

 **Multimedia extras on the
CD-ROM and the Web:**

- **Interactive** Computer buyer's Guide

- An **interactive demonstration** showing how
  monitors create color images

- Instant access to **glossary** and **key word**
  references

- Interactive **demonstrations** showing how
  scanners and audio digitizers work

  . . . and more.

 computerconfluence.com

HARDWARE BASICS:
Peripherals

STEVE WOZNIAK, STEVE JOBS, AND THE GARAGE THAT GREW APPLES

What Steve Wozniak and all those other people failed to foresee was the personal computer revolution—a revolution that he helped start. Wozniak, a brilliant engineer called Woz by his friends, worked days as a calculator technician at Hewlett-Packard; he was refused an engineer's job because he lacked a college degree. At night he designed and constructed a scaled-down computer system that would fit the home hobbyist's budget. When he completed it in 1975, he offered it to HP, but they turned it down.

Wozniak took his invention to the Homebrew Computer Club in Palo Alto, where it caught the imagination of another college dropout, Steve Jobs. A free-thinking visionary, Jobs persuaded Wozniak to quit his job in 1976 to form a company born in Job's garage. They marketed the machine as the Apple I.

With the help and financial backing of businessman A. C. Markkula, the two Steves turned Apple into a thriving business. Wozniak created the Apple II, a more refined machine, and in the process invented the first personal computer disk operating system. Because it put computing power within the reach of individuals, the Apple II became popular in businesses, homes, and especially schools. Apple became the first company in American history to join the Fortune 500 in less than five years. Still in his mid-twenties, Jobs was running a corporate giant. But troubled times were ahead for Apple.

> It's **not** like we were all **smart enough** to see a **revolution coming**. Back then I thought there might be a revolution in **opening** your garage door, **balancing** your checkbook, **keeping** your recipes, that sort of thing. There are a **million people** who study markets and analyze economic trends, people who are **more brilliant than I am**, people who worked for companies like Digital Equipment and IBM and Hewlett-Packard. **None of them foresaw** what was going to happen either.
>
> —Steve Wozniak

When IBM introduced its PC in 1982, it overshadowed Apple's presence in the business world, where people were accustomed to working with IBM mainframes. Other companies developed PC

3.1 Steve Wozniak and Steve Jobs in the early days.

3.2 Today, Steve Wozniak runs a wireless product design company called Wheels of Zeus.

clones, treating the IBM PC as a standard—a standard that Apple refused to accept. Inspired by a visit to Xerox's Palo Alto Research Center (PARC), Jobs worked with a team of Apple engineers to develop the Macintosh, a futuristic computer Jobs hoped would leapfrog IBM's advantage. When Jobs insisted on focusing most of Apple's resources on the Macintosh, Wozniak resigned to pursue other interests.

Businesses failed to embrace the Mac, and Apple stockholders grew uneasy with Jobs' controversial management style. In 1985, a year and a half after the Macintosh was introduced, Jobs was ousted. He went on to form NeXT, a company that produced expensive workstations and software. He also bought Pixar, the computer animation company that later captured the public's attention with *Toy Story*, the first computer-generated full-length motion picture.

After Apple's fortunes declined under a string of CEOs, the company bought NeXT in 1997 and invited an older and wiser Jobs to retake the helm. He agreed to share his time between Pixar and Apple. Under his leadership, Apple has regained its innovative edge, releasing a flurry of elegant and trend-setting products.

3.3 Steve Jobs eventually returned to the helm at Apple, where he introduced the best-selling iMac.

Though its share of the PC market is small, Apple retains a fanatically loyal customer base and now focuses mainly on the consumer, creative, and education markets. While Jobs continues to lead Apple and Pixar, Woz runs a wireless product design company called Wheels of Zeus (WOZ).

The Apple II's phenomenal success wasn't due to a powerful processor or massive memory; the machine had at its core a relatively primitive processor and only 16K of memory. But the Apple II was more than a processor and memory; it included a keyboard, a monitor, and disk and tape drives for storage. While other companies sold computer kits to technical tinkerers, the two Steves delivered complete computer systems to hobbyists, schools, and businesses. They recognized that a computer wasn't complete without peripherals.

In this chapter we'll complete the tour of hardware we started in the last chapter. We've seen the CPU and memory at the heart of the system unit; now we'll explore the peripherals that radiate out from those central components. We'll start with input devices, then move on to output devices, and finish with a look at external storage devices. As usual, the main text provides the basic overview; if you want or need to know more about the inner workings, consult the How It Works boxes scattered throughout the chapter.

Input: From Person to Processor

The nuts and bolts of information processing are usually hidden from the user, who sees only the input and output, or as the pros say, *I/O*. This wasn't always the case. Users of the first computers communicated one bit at a time by flipping switches on massive consoles or plugging wires into switchboards; they had to be intimately familiar with the inner workings of the machines before they could successfully communicate with them. In contrast, today's users have a choice of hundreds of input devices, which make it easy to enter data and commands into their machines. Of these input devices, the most familiar is the computer keyboard.

> A computer terminal is **not** some **clunky old** television with a typewriter in front of it. It is an **interface** where the **mind** and **body** can **connect** with the **universe** and **move bits** of it about.
>
> —Douglas Adams, author of *The Hitchhiker's Guide to the Galaxy*

The Keyboard

In spite of nearly universal acceptance as an input device, the QWERTY keyboard (named for the middle row of letter keys) seems strangely out of place in a modern computer system. The original arrangement of the keys was chosen to reduce the likelihood of mechanical jams on early typewriters. Technological traditions die hard, and the QWERTY keyboard became standard equipment on typewriters and later on virtually all PCs.

3.4 A standard computer keyboard (above) has a straight row of keys. An ergonomic keyboard (below) puts the keys at an angle to allow your wrists to assume a more natural position while you type.

Some modern computer keyboards stray from the traditional typewriter design, however. Typing on a standard keyboard, with keys lined up in straight rows, forces you to hold your arms and wrists at unnatural angles. Evidence suggests that long hours of typing this way may lead to medical problems, including repetitive-stress injuries such as tendonitis and carpal tunnel syndrome. Ergonomic keyboards place the keys at angles that are easier on your arms and hands without changing the ordering of the keys.

Whether it's straight or ergonomic, a typical keyboard sends signals to the computer through a cable of some sort. A *wireless keyboard* can send wireless signals (similar to those of a TV remote control, though modern keyboards use newer technology), so it isn't tethered to the rest of the system by a cable.

Other variations on keyboard design include folding keyboards for use with palm-sized computers, miniature keyboards built into pocket-sized devices, one-handed keyboards for people who need to (or prefer to) keep one hand free for other work, and keyboards printed on membranes that can be rolled or folded like paper. Innovative ideas are still emerging from that ancient typewriter technology.

3.6 Some pocket computers have QWERTY keyboards even though they're too small for touch typing.

3.5 This portable keyboard, designed for various Palm and Pocket PC handhelds, folds so that it can easily fit in your pocket.

Pointing Devices

Computer users today use their keyboards mostly to enter text and numeric data. For other traditional keyboard functions, such as sending commands and positioning the cursor, they typically use a mouse. The mouse is designed to move a pointer around the screen and point to specific characters or objects. Until recently, the most common type of mouse had a ball on its underside that allowed it to roll around on the desktop. But a newer type of mouse uses reflected light to detect movement. Either way, most mice have one or more buttons that can be used to send signals to the computer, conveying messages such as "Perform this command," "Activate the selected tool," and "Select all the text between these two points." Many mice also include a scrolling wheel between the two standard buttons.

3.7 The most common type of computer mouse has two or more buttons. The Microsoft mouse (right) has multiple buttons and a scroll wheel to streamline the process of scrolling through documents or graphical windows. The Apple mouse has only a single button; in this mouse (left) the entire top surface of the mouse acts as a button.

It's virtually impossible to find a new computer today that doesn't come with a mouse as standard equipment, but there is one exception: The mouse is impractical as a pointing device on portable computers because these machines are often used where there's no room for a mouse to roam across a desktop. Portable computer manufacturers provide a variety of alternatives to the mouse as a general-purpose pointing device, and some of these devices are becoming popular as desktop solutions as well:

■ The touchpad (sometimes called *trackpad*) is a small flat panel that's sensitive to light applications of pressure. The user moves the pointer by dragging a finger across the pad.

■ The pointing stick (often called TrackPoint, IBM's brand name for the device) is a tiny handle that sits in the center of the keyboard, responding to finger pressure by moving the pointer in the direction in which it's pushed. It's like a miniature embedded joystick.

■ The trackball resembles an upside-down mouse. It remains stationary while the user moves the large protruding ball to control the pointer on the screen. Trackballs are also available as an ergonomic mouse alternative for desktop machines.

Other pointing devices offer advantages for specific types of computer work (and play). Here are some examples:

■ The joystick is a gearshift-like device that's a favorite controller for arcade-style computer games. Other gaming devices, like a game pad, racing wheel, and multifunction devices with multiple programmable buttons, help gamers become more immersed in different game types.

■ The graphics tablet is popular with artists and designers. Most touch tablets are pressure sensitive, so they can send different signals depending on how hard the user presses on the tablet with a stylus. The *stylus* performs the same point-and-click functions as a mouse. A similar screen used on Tablet PC devices uses a screen with an active digitizer to track a specially made stylus, letting users input data in their own handwriting.

■ The touch screen responds when the user points to or touches different screen regions. Computers with touch screens are frequently used in public libraries, airports, and shopping malls, where many users are unfamiliar with computers. Touch screens are also used in many handheld computers, PDAs, and smart displays; a stylus can be used for pointing or writing on these small screens.

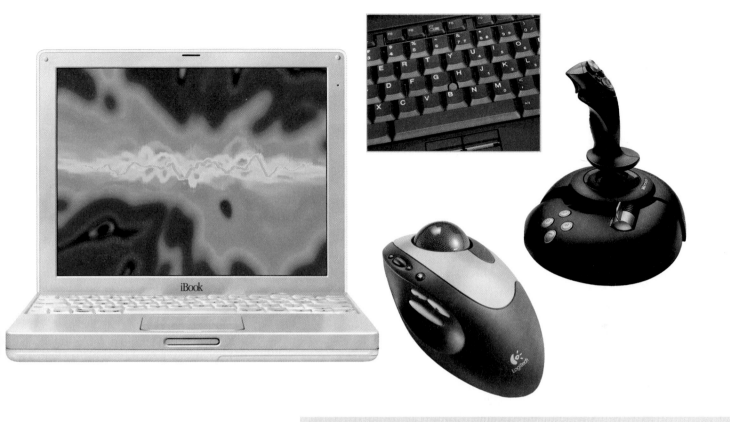

3.8 The Apple iBook (above left), like many portable computers, includes a built-in touchpad as a pointing device. The IBM ThinkPad (above center top) has a tiny pointing stick, called a TrackPoint, embedded in the center of its keyboard for moving the cursor on the screen. Some computer users choose to use a trackball (above center bottom) as a pointing device. Joysticks (above right) and game pads are often used by computer gamers. Some portable computers, like the Tablet PC (below left), use a stylus as the pointing device. Touch-screen monitors are often used in kiosks, ATM machines, self-serve checkout stands in stores, and in home automation stations (below right).

Reading Tools

In spite of their versatility, pointing devices are woefully inefficient for the input of large quantities of text into computers, which is why the mouse hasn't replaced the keyboard on the standard personal computer. Still, there are alternatives to typing for entering numbers and words into computers. Some types of devices allow computers to rapidly read marks, representing codes, specifically designed for computer input:

- **Optical mark readers** use reflected light to determine the location of pencil marks on standardized test answer sheets and similar forms.
- **Magnetic ink character readers** read those odd-shaped numbers printed with magnetic ink on checks.
- **Bar code readers** use light to read *universal product codes (UPCs)*, inventory codes, and other codes created from patterns of variable-width bars. In many stores, bar code readers are attached to **point-of-sale (POS) terminals**. These terminals send scanned information to a mainframe computer. The computer determines the item's price, calculates taxes and totals, and records the transaction for future use in inventory, accounting, and other areas.

Because test forms, magnetic ink characters, and bar codes were designed to be read by computers, the devices that read them are extremely accurate. Reading text from books, magazines, and other printed documents is more challenging because of the great variety of printed text. **Optical character recognition (OCR)** is the technology of recognizing individual characters on a printed page, so they can be stored and edited as text.

Before a computer can recognize handwriting or printed text, it must first create a digital image of the page that it can store in memory. This is usually done with an input device known as a *scanner*. There are many types of scanners, as you'll see in the next section. A scanner doesn't actually read or recognize letters and numbers on a page—it just makes a digital "picture" of the page available to the computer. The computer can then use OCR software to interpret the black-and-white scanned patterns as letters and numbers.

Actually, a few special-purpose scanners take care of the OCR work themselves. *Pen scanners* look like highlighters, but they're actually wireless scanners that can perform character recognition on the fly. When you drag a pen scanner across a line of printed text, it creates a text file in its built-in memory, where it's stored until you transfer it into your computer's memory through a cable or infrared beam. A wireless pen scanner actually contains a small

3.9 Computers use specialized input devices to read information stored as optical marks, bar codes, and specially designed characters.

3.10 This self-service POS terminal uses two input devices for gathering information about a purchase: A touch screen for entering commands and answering questions and a bar code reader for scanning product information. Before the transaction is completed, another input device reads information encoded in the magnetic strip on the customer's credit card.

3.11 A pen scanner can capture text from a printed document and transfer it to a PC.

computer programmed to recognize printed text. This kind of optical character recognition isn't 100 percent accurate, but it's getting better all the time.

Handwriting recognition is far more difficult and error-prone than printed character recognition. But handwriting recognition has many practical applications today, especially in **pen-based computers** such as the Tablet PC. A pen-based computer can work without a keyboard and can accept input from a stylus applied directly to a flat-panel screen. The computer electronically simulates the effect of using a pen and pad of paper. **Handwriting recognition software** translates the user's handwritten forms into ASCII characters. In the past, such systems required users to modify their handwriting so that it was consistent and unambiguous enough for the software to decipher reliably, but Tablet PCs have dramatically increased the accuracy and efficiency of this machine type.

Personal digital assistants (PDAs) are handheld pen computers that serve as pocket-sized organizers, notebooks, appointment books, and communication devices. These popular, versatile devices can also be programmed for specialized work, ranging from sports scorekeeping to medical analysis. Newer models feature multimedia functionality such as music playback and video and photo viewing.

Handwriting recognition software can even be applied to notes scrawled on a whiteboard in a meeting room or classroom. A *smart whiteboard* can serve as an input device for a PC, so each board full of information is stored as a digital image on the computer's disk. If the writing is clear enough, handwriting recognition software can turn the whiteboard notes into a text file that can be emailed to meeting or class participants. (OCR and handwriting recognition are covered in more detail in later chapters.)

3.12 The Palm OS software uses the Graffiti system (above left) to let users input single-stroke characters using a stylus. This type of input is used in devices like the Sony CLIE (left). The larger Tablet PC (above) is a full-fledged Windows XP notebook computer with stylus input capabilities.

3.13 A smart whiteboard can send its contents to a PC, simplifying and streamlining the note-taking process for meetings and classes.

Digitizing the Real World

> ## The . . . **number-one peripheral device**
> is not a drive. It's not a printer, scanner, hub, or
> network. It's you, the user.
> —John K. Rizzo and K. Daniel Clark, in *How the Mac Works*

Before a computer can recognize handwriting or printed text, a scanner or other input device must digitize the information—convert it into a digital form. Because real-world information comes in so many forms, a variety of input devices have been designed for capturing and digitizing information. In this section we'll examine several of these devices, from common scanners to exotic sensors.

A scanner is an input device that can create a digital representation of a printed image. The most common models today are *flatbed scanners*, which look and work like photocopy machines, except that they create computer files instead of paper copies. Inexpensive flatbed scanners are designed for home and small business use. More expensive models used by graphics professionals are capable of producing higher-quality reproductions and, with attachments, scan photographic negatives and slides. Some scanners, called *slide scanners*, can scan only slides and negatives, but generally produce higher-quality results than flatbed scanners when scanning transparencies. *Drum scanners* are larger and more expensive than flatbeds; they're used in publishing applications where image quality is critical. At the other end of the spectrum, *sheetfed scanners* are small, portable, and inexpensive. Regardless of its type or capabilities, however, a scanner converts photographs, drawings, charts, and other printed information into bit patterns that can be stored and manipulated in a computer's memory, usually using graphics software.

In the same way, a digital camera can capture snapshots of the real world as digital images. Unlike a scanner, a digital camera isn't limited to capturing flat printed images; it can record anything that a normal camera can. A digital camera often looks like a normal camera. But instead of capturing images on film, a digital camera stores bit patterns on disks or other digital storage media.

A *video digitizer* is a collection of circuits that can capture input from a video camera, videocassette recorder, television, or other video source and convert it to a digital signal that can be stored in memory and displayed on computer screens. A *digital video camera* can send video signals directly into a computer without a video digitizer, because its video images are digitized when they're captured by the camera. Digital video input makes it possible for professionals and hobbyists and even consumers to edit videos with a computer. Digital video is also used for multimedia applications such as Web page and CD-ROM development. And a growing number of businesses use video cameras and PCs for

3.14 Flatbed scanners (left) capture and digitize images from external paper sources, while slide and photo scanners (right) can reproduce photographs from slides and negatives. A slide scanner can produce high-quality digital reproductions from photographic negatives and slides.

3.15 Consumer cameras like the one shown in the top-right photo sell for a few hundred dollars or less; professional models like the one in the top-left photo cost much more. Many cell phones like the one in the center include picture and movie-taking capabilities and can send these images to other phone users. Digital video cameras like the one in the bottom-left photo can deliver video directly to a PC or Macintosh. A Web cam like the one shown in the above right photo can continuously feed still pictures or video directly to an attached PC or Mac.

desktop *videoconferencing*. With videoconferencing software and hardware, people in diverse locations can see and hear each other while they conduct long-distance meetings; their video images are transmitted through networks. These video applications are discussed in more detail in later chapters.

Audio digitizers contain circuitry to digitize sounds from microphones and other audio devices. Digitized sounds can be stored in a computer's or PDA's memory and modified with software. Of course, audio digitizers can capture spoken words as well as music and sound effects. But digitizing spoken input isn't the same thing as converting speech into text. Like scanned text input, digitized *voice input* is just data to the computer. Speech recognition software, a type of artificial intelligence software, can convert voice data into words that can be edited and printed. *Speech recognition* software has been available for years, but until recently it wasn't reliable enough to be of much practical use. The latest products are still too limited to replace keyboards for most people. They generally must be trained to recognize individual voices, they typically require the speaker to carefully articulate each word, and they often work with only a limited vocabulary. Still, they're invaluable for people with disabilities and others who can't use their hands while they work. The promise and problems of automated speech recognition will be explored in later chapters.

3.16 Speech recognition software allows this officer to record spoken notes without using a keyboard.

3.1
Digitizing the Real World

We live in an analog world, where we can perceive smooth, continuous changes in color and sound. Modern digital computers store all information as discrete binary numbers. To store analog information, such as an analog sound or image, in a computer we must digitize it—convert it from analog to digital form.

Digitizing involves using an input device, such as a desktop scanner or audio board, to take millions of tiny samples of the original. A sample of an image might be one pinpoint-sized area of the image; each sample from an audio source is like a brief recording of the sound at a particular instant.

The value of a sample can be represented numerically and therefore stored on a computer. A representation of the original image or sound can be reconstructed by assembling all the samples in sequence.

SCANNERS

A typical desktop scanner contains a camera similar to the kind found in many video camcorders. The scanner camera moves back and forth across an original image, recording for each sample the intensities of red, green, and blue light at that point. (Human eyes have receptors for red, green, and blue light; all colors are perceived as combinations of these three.) A single byte commonly represents the intensity of each color component; a 3-byte (24-bit) code represents the color for each sample. The scanner sends each digital code to the computer, where it can be stored and manipulated.

3.17a

AUDIO DIGITIZERS

Digital audio is commonplace today; the CD player is really a computer system designed to translate digital information on a compact disc into analog signals that can be amplified and sent to speakers. In digital audio recording using a PC, sound waves vibrate the diaphragm of a microphone connected to the computer, usually through a sound card. The position of the microphone diaphragm is sampled frequently—as much as 44,000 times each second—and its level is stored as a number. The faster the sampling frequency is, the better the sound recording. Using more storage to represent finer gradations of the sound level also offers better sound. An 8-bit sample can represent 256 distinct levels; a 16-bit sample can represent 65,536 levels. Whether digitizing sounds or images, attempts to increase fidelity to the original usually increases storage requirements.

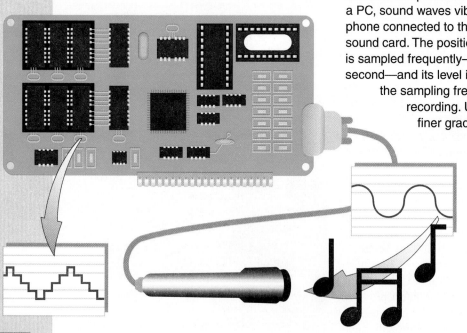

3.17b

Sensors designed to monitor temperature, humidity, pressure, and other physical quantities provide data used in robotics, environmental climate control, weather forecasting, medical monitoring, biofeedback, scientific research, and hundreds of other applications. Even our sense of smell can be simulated with sensors. Such sensors might soon be used to detect spoiled foods, land mines, chemical spills, or halitosis.

Computers can accept input from a variety of other sources, including manufacturing equipment, telephones, communication networks, and other computers. New input devices are being developed all the time as technologies evolve and human needs change. By stretching the computer's capabilities, these devices stretch our imaginations to develop new ways of using computers. We'll consider some of the more interesting and exotic technologies later; for now we turn our attention to the output end of the process.

Output: From Pulses to People

A computer can do all kinds of things, but none of them is worth anything to us unless we have a way to get the results out of the box. Output devices convert the computer's internal bit patterns into a form that humans can understand. The first computers were limited to flashing lights, teletypewriters, and other primitive communication devices.

3.18 Sensors in this LifeShirt monitored life signs of this Indy Racing League driver when he crashed in the 2001 Indy 500.

Most computers today produce output through two main types of devices: display screens for immediate visual output and printers for permanent paper output.

> As a rule, men **worry more** about **what they can't see** than about what they can.
>
> —Julius Caesar

Screen Output

The display, also called a monitor, or video display terminal (VDT), serves as a one-way window between the computer user and the machine. Early computer displays were designed to display characters—text, numbers, and tiny graphic symbols. Today's displays are as likely to present graphics, photographic images, animation, and video as they are to display text and numbers. Because of the display's ever-expanding role as a graphical output device, computer users need to know a bit about the factors that control image size and quality.

Display size, like television size, is measured as the length of a diagonal line across the screen; a typical desktop display today measures from 15 to 21 inches diagonally, but the actual viewable area is often smaller. Images on a display are composed of tiny dots, called *pixels* (for picture elements). A square inch of an image on a display is typically a grid of dots about 96 pixels on each side. Such a monitor has a resolution of 96 dots per inch (dpi). The higher the resolution is, the closer together the dots and the clearer the image. Another way to describe resolution is to refer to the total number of pixels displayed on the screen. Assuming that two displays are the same size, the one that places the dots closest together displays more pixels—and creates a sharper, clearer image. When describing resolution in this way, people usually indicate the number of columns and rows of pixels rather than the total number of pixels. For example, a 1,024 × 768 image is composed of 1,024 columns by 768 rows of pixels, for a total of 786,432 pixels.

Resolution isn't the only factor that determines image quality. Computer displays are limited by *color depth*—the number of different colors they can display at the same time. Color depth is sometimes called *bit depth*, because a wider range of colors per pixel takes up more bits of space in video memory. If each pixel is allotted 8 bits of memory, the resulting image can have up to 256 different colors on screen at a time. (There are 256 unique combinations of 8 bits to use as color codes.) In other words, 8-bit color, common in older PCs, has a color depth of 256. Most graphics professionals use 24-bit color, or *true color*, because it allows more than 16 million color choices per pixel—more than enough for photorealistic images. Older *monochrome monitors* can display only monochrome

3.19 These four images show the same photograph displayed in four different bit depths: 1, 4, 8, and 16 bits.

images. *Gray-scale monitors* (which can display black, white, and shades of gray but no other colors) and *color monitors* (which can display a range of colors) have greater color depth. A modern PC or Macintosh can portray different combinations of resolution and color depth on the same display.

The monitor is connected to the computer by way of the *video adapter*, which is typically a circuit board installed in a slot inside the main system unit. An image on the monitor exists inside the computer in video memory, or *VRAM*, a special portion of RAM on the video adapter dedicated to holding video images. The amount of VRAM determines the maximum resolution and color depth that a computer system can display. The more video memory a computer has, the more detail it can present in a picture.

Most displays fall into one of two classes: television-style **CRT (cathode-ray tube) monitors** and flat-panel **LCD (liquid crystal display) displays**. Once used primarily in portable computers, LCDs are dropping in price and they are turning up on more and more desktops. LCD displays are now more popular than the older, bulky, CRT monitors. *Overhead projection panels* and *video projectors* also use LCDs to project computer screen images for meetings and classes.

3.20 Most desktop computers have historically used CRT monitors because they're inexpensive and they produce high-quality images at a variety of resolutions. However, sales of flat-panel LCD monitors are starting to surpass CRTs as their prices drop and image quality improves (left). LCDs are also used in projectors that allow computer screen images to be projected for large viewing audiences (right).

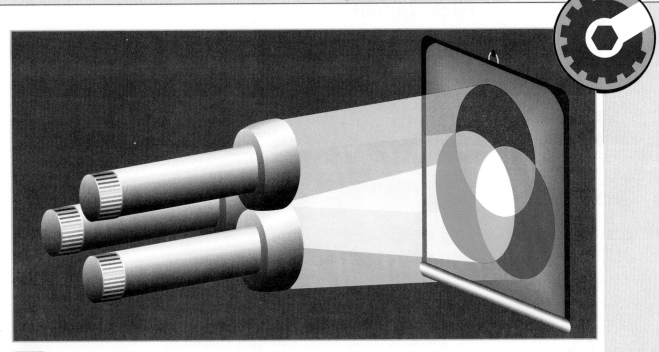

3.21a The colors in some CRT video images glow because the monitor is a luminous source of light using additive color synthesis—colors are formed by adding different amounts of red, green, and blue light.

Like television sets, computer displays refresh or update their images many times per second. If a CRT monitor refreshes its image fewer than 70 times per second (70 hertz), the flicker may be enough to cause eyestrain, headaches, and nausea. Many CRT monitors slow down their refresh rates if the resolution is increased, so if you're shopping for a CRT monitor, buy one with a refresh rate of more than 70 hertz at the maximum resolution you expect to be using. Because flat-panel LCD displays don't refresh their images in the same way as these CRT monitors, this is not an issue with devices; most LCDs refresh at 60 hertz, and have no flickering at all.

Another factor that should figure into your purchasing decision is the monitor's dot pitch—the measurement of how close the holes in the grid are to each other. The smaller the dot pitch, the closer the holes and the sharper the image.

3.21b When viewed from a distance of more than a few inches, the three dots visually merge; the color created by this mixing depends on the strength of each of the color electron beams.

Paper Output

Output displayed on a monitor is immediate but temporary. A printer can produce a hard copy on paper of any static information that can be displayed on the computer's screen. Printers come in several varieties, but they all fit into two basic groups: *impact printers* and *nonimpact printers*.

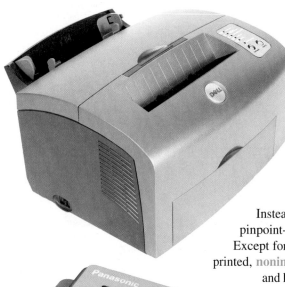

Older impact printers include line printers and dot matrix printers. Printers of this type share one common characteristic: They form images by physically striking paper, ribbon, and print hammer together, the way a typewriter does. Mainframes use line printers to produce massive printouts; these speedy, noisy beasts hammer out thousands of lines of text per minute. You might have seen form letters from banks and stores, bills from utility companies, and report cards from schools that were printed with line printers. Because they're limited to printing characters, line printers are inadequate for applications such as desktop publishing, where graphics are essential.

Dot matrix printers print text and graphics with equal ease. Instead of printing each character as a solid object, a dot matrix printer uses pinpoint-sized hammers to transfer ink to the page.

Except for those applications, such as billing, where multipart forms need to be printed, nonimpact printers have replaced impact printers in most offices, schools, and homes. The two main types of nonimpact printers are laser printers and inkjet printers. Laser printers can quickly print numerous pages per minute of high-quality text and graphical output. Because of their speed, durability, and reliability, they're often shared between PCs in office environments. Laser printers use the same technology as photocopy machines: A laser beam creates patterns of electrical charges on a rotating drum; those charged patterns attract black toner and transfer it to paper as the drum rotates. Color laser printers can print multicolor images by mixing different toner shades.

People who work in color tend to use less-expensive inkjet printers, which spray ink directly onto paper to produce printed text and graphic images. Inkjets generally print fewer pages per minute than laser printers. But high-quality color inkjet printers cost far less than color laser printers, and many are less expensive than the cheapest black-and-white laser printers. Inkjet printers are also smaller and lighter than laser printers. Portable inkjet printers designed to travel with laptops weigh only a couple of pounds each. Newer inkjet printers, often called photo printers, are specially optimized to print high-quality photos captured with digital cameras and scanners; these printouts are often indistinguishable from the photos you might order from a professional photo-printing service.

Both laser and inkjet printers produce output with much higher resolution—usually 600 or more dots per inch—than is possible with older dot matrix models. At these resolutions it's hard to tell with the naked eye that characters are, in fact, composed of dots. Because of their ability to print high-resolution text and pictures, nonimpact printers dominate the printer market today.

Multifunction printers (MFP, also called *all-in-one devices*) take advantage of the fact that different tools can use similar technologies. A multifunction printer usually combines a scanner, a laser or inkjet printer, and a fax modem (described in the next section). Such a device can serve as a printer, a scanner, a color photocopy machine, and a fax machine.

3.22 An inkjet printer (top), a portable photo printer (center), and a laser printer (bottom) all provide different types of hard copy output.

Printed colors can't be as vivid as video colors because printed images don't produce light like a monitor does; they only reflect light. Most color printers use subtractive synthesis to produce colors: They mix together various amounts of cyan (light blue), magenta (reddish purple), yellow, and black pigments to create a color.

Most printers, like monitors, are raster devices—they form images from little dots. The resolution of raster printers is normally measured in dots per inch (dpi). Printers have resolutions of hundreds—or even thousands—of dpi.

Matching on-screen color with printed color is difficult because monitors use additive color synthesis to obtain the color, whereas printers use subtractive synthesis. Monitors are able to display more colors than printers, though printers can display a few colors that monitors can't. But the range of colors that humans can perceive extends beyond either technology.

You can demonstrate subtractive synthesis by painting overlapping areas of cyan, magenta, and yellow ink. The combination of all three is black; combinations of pairs produce red, green, and blue, which are secondary colors of the subtractive system.

3.23

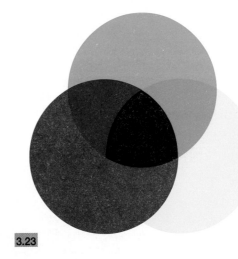

For certain scientific and engineering applications, a plotter is more appropriate than a printer for producing hard copy. A plotter is an automated drawing tool that can produce large, finely scaled drawings, engineering blue prints, and maps by moving the pen and/or the paper in response to computer commands.

Fax Machines and Fax Modems

A facsimile (fax) machine is a fast and convenient tool for transmission of information stored on paper. When you send a fax of a paper document, the sending fax machine scans each page, converting the scanned image into a series of electronic pulses and sending those signals over phone lines to another fax machine. The receiving fax machine uses the signals to construct and print black-and-white facsimiles or copies of the original pages. In a sense, the two fax machines and the telephone line serve as a long-distance photocopy machine.

A computer can send on-screen documents through a fax modem to a receiving fax machine. The fax modem translates the document into signals that can be sent over phone wires and decoded by the receiving fax machine. In effect, the receiving fax machine acts like a remote printer for the document. A computer can also use a fax modem to receive transmissions from fax machines, treating the sending fax machine as a kind of remote scanner. A faxed letter can be displayed on screen or printed to paper, but it can't immediately be edited with a word processor the way an email message can. Like a scanned document, a digital facsimile is nothing more than a collection of black-and-white dots to the computer. Before a faxed document can be edited, it must be processed by optical character recognition (OCR) software.

3.24 A multifunction printer combines a printer with a scanner and a fax modem so that it can print, scan, fax, and photocopy.

Output You Can Hear

Most modern PCs include sound cards. A sound card enables the PC to accept microphone input, play music and other sound through speakers or headphones, and process sound in a variety of ways. (All Macintoshes and some PCs have audio circuitry integrated with the rest of the system, so they don't need separate sound cards.) With a sound card, a PC can play digital recordings of all kinds of sounds, from personal recordings made with the PC and a microphone to music downloaded from the Internet.

Most sound cards also include synthesizers—specialized circuitry designed to generate sounds electronically. These *synthesizers* can be used to produce music, noise, or anything in between. A computer also can be connected to a stand-alone music synthesizer so that the computer has complete control of the instrument. Computers can also generate synthesized speech with the right software. Of course, to produce any kind of sound, the computer needs to include or be attached to speakers or headphones.

3.25a Moby, like many modern musicians, uses computers and electronic synthesizers for composing and performing music.

Controlling Other Machines

In the same way that many input devices convert real-world sights and sounds into digital pulses, many output devices work in the other direction, taking bit patterns and turning them into nondigital movements or measurements. Robot arms, telephone switchboards, transportation devices, automated factory equipment, spacecraft, and a host of other machines and systems accept their orders from computers.

In one example familiar to computer gamers, an enhanced input device delivers output. The *force feedback joystick* can receive signals from a computer and give tactile feedback—jolts, scrapes, and bumps—that matches the visual output of the game or simulation. Many video arcades take the concept further by having the computer shake, rattle, and roll the gamer's chair while displaying on-screen movements that match the action. Output devices that generate synthetic smells are also beginning to appear. If these devices catch on, Web sites might commonly include smells as well as sights and sound. While you're virtually visiting your favorite beach resort you might smell synthetic surf, sand, and sunblock.

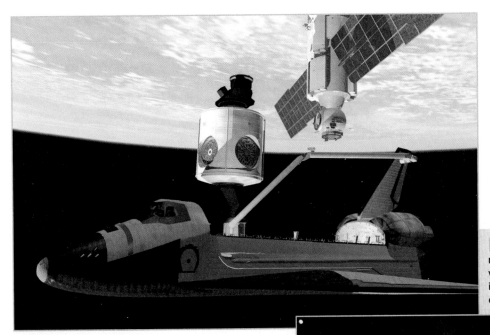

3.25b Computers control the movements of spacecraft and virtual reality arcade games using output devices that operate on similar principles.

Of course, computers can send information directly to other computers, bypassing human interaction altogether. The possibilities for computer output are limited only by the technology and the human imagination, both of which are stretching further all the time.

Storage Devices: Input Meets Output

Some computer peripherals are capable of performing both input and output functions. These devices, which include tape and disk drives, are the computer's storage devices. They're sometimes referred to as *secondary* storage devices, because the computer's memory is its *primary storage*. Unlike RAM, which forgets everything when the computer is turned off, and ROM, which can't learn anything new, storage devices enable the computer to record information semipermanently so it can be read later by the same computer or by another computer.

A **retentive memory** may be a good thing, but **the ability to forget** is the true token of greatness.

—Elbert Hubbard

Magnetic Tape

Tape drives are common storage devices on most mainframe computers and some PCs. A tape drive can write data onto, and read data off of, a magnetically coated ribbon of tape. The reason for the widespread use of magnetic tape as a storage medium is clear: A magnetic tape can store massive amounts of information in a small space at a relatively low cost. The spinning tape reels that symbolized computers in so many old science fiction movies have for the most part been replaced by tape cartridges based on similar technology.

Along with the benefits of computer technology comes the potential for unwelcome side effects. For people who work long hours with computers, the side effects include risks to health and safety due to radiation emissions, repetitive-stress injuries, or other computer-related health problems. Inconclusive evidence suggests that low-level radiation emitted by video display terminals (VDTs) and other equipment might cause health problems, including miscarriages in pregnant women and leukemia. The scientific jury is still out, but the mixed research results so far have led many computer users and manufacturers to err on the side of caution.

More concrete evidence relates keyboarding to occurrences of *repetitive-stress injuries* such as *carpal tunnel syndrome*, a painful affliction of the wrist and hand that results from repeating the same movements over long periods. Prolonged computer use also increases the likelihood of headaches, eyestrain, fatigue, and other symptoms of "techno-stress."

Ergonomics, (sometimes called *human engineering*) is the science of designing work environments that enable people and things to interact efficiently and safely. Ergonomic studies suggest preventative measures you can take to protect your health as you work with computers:

➡ **Choose equipment that's ergonomically designed.** When you're buying computer equipment, look beyond functionality. Use Web site and magazine reviews, manufacturer's information, and personal research to check on health-related factors, such as monitor radiation and glare, disk-drive noise levels, and keyboard layout. A growing number of computer products, such as split, angled ergonomic keyboards, are specifically designed to reduce the risk of equipment-related injuries.

➡ **Create a healthy workspace.** Keep the paper copy of your work at close to the same height as your screen. Position your monitor and lights to minimize glare. Sit at arm's length from your monitor to minimize radiation risks.

➡ **Build flexibility into your work environment.** Whenever possible work with an adjustable chair, an adjustable table, an adjustable monitor, and a removable keyboard. Change your work position frequently.

➡ **Rest your eyes.** Look up from the screen periodically and focus on a faraway object or scene. Blink frequently. Take a 15-minute break from using a VDT every 2 hours.

➡ **Stretch.** While you're taking your rest break, do some simple stretches to loosen tight muscles. Occasional stretching of the muscles in your arms, hands, wrists, back, shoulders, and lower body can make hours of computer work more comfortable and less harmful.

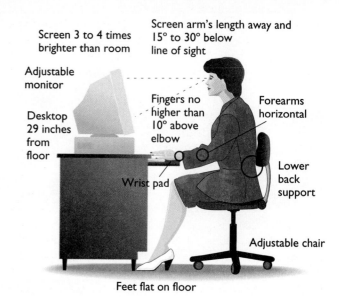

Screen 3 to 4 times brighter than room

Screen arm's length away and 15° to 30° below line of sight

Adjustable monitor

Desktop 29 inches from floor

Fingers no higher than 10° above elbow

Forearms horizontal

Wrist pad

Lower back support

Adjustable chair

Feet flat on floor

3.26a

➡ **Listen to your body.** If you feel uncomfortable, your body is telling you to change something or take a break. Don't ignore it. Ergonomic keyboards like the split, angled keyboard allow computer users to hold their hands and arms in more natural positions while typing to reduce the risk of repetitive-stress injuries.

➡ **Seek help when you need it.** If your wrists start hurting when you work, or you have persistent headaches, or you're feeling some other problem that may be related to excessive computer work, talk to a professional. A medical doctor, chiropractor, physical therapist, or naturopath may be able to help you to head off the problem before it becomes chronic.

3.26b Microsoft's line of ergonomic keyboards offers the typing angle and spread key layout that's recommended by ergonomic experts.

Magnetic tape has one clear limitation: Tape is a sequential access medium. Whether a tape holds music or computer data, the computer must zip through information in the order in which it was recorded. Retrieving information from the middle of a tape is far too time-consuming for most modern computer applications, because people expect immediate response to their commands. As a result, magnetic tape is used today primarily for backup of data and a few other operations that aren't time-sensitive.

Magnetic Disks

Like magnetic tape, a magnetic disk has a magnetically coated surface that can store encoded information; a *disk drive* writes data onto the disk's surface and reads data from the surface. But unlike a tape drive, a disk drive can rapidly retrieve information from any part of a magnetic disk without regard for the order in which the information was recorded, in the same way you can quickly select any track on an audio compact disc. Because of their random-access capability, disks are the most popular media for everyday storage needs.

3.27 Tape backup devices have replaced spinning tape reels as backup storage devices.

Many computer users are familiar with the 3.5-inch diskette (also called floppy disk)—a small, magnetically sensitive, flexible plastic wafer housed in a plastic case. The diskette was once routinely used for transferring data files between machines, though their limited capacity—typically just 1.44MB—and slow speed make them less useful today. Today, Macintoshes and some PCs no longer include diskette drives as standard equipment.

Virtually all PCs include hard disks as their main storage devices. A hard disk is a rigid, magnetically sensitive disk that spins rapidly and continuously inside the computer chassis or in a separate box connected to the computer housing. This type of hard disk is usually not removed by the user. Information can be transferred to and from a hard disk much faster than from a diskette. A hard disk might hold hundreds of gigabytes (thousands of megabytes) of information—more than enough room for every word and picture in this book, an entire music collection, several movie-length video clips, and years of photographs.

To fill the gap between low-capacity, slow diskettes and nonremovable, fast hard disks, manufacturers have developed high-capacity transportable storage solutions. There are many choices beyond diskettes in removable cartridge media. The most popular is the *Zip disk*, developed by Iomega. A Zip disk looks like a thicker version of a standard diskette. The most common Zip disks can hold up to 100MB of data; a newer variety can hold up to 750MB. Zip drives cannot read or write standard floppy disks, even though they use a similar technology. Zip disks, like floppy disks, are declining in popularity today because of advances in optical disc storage technology.

Optical Discs

An optical disc drive uses laser beams rather than magnets to read and write bits of data on a reflective layer of the disk. A transparent plastic disc surface protects the reflective layer from routine physical damage while letting laser light through. Access speeds are slower for optical discs than for magnetic hard disks. But optical storage is generally highly reliable, especially for long-term storage.

3.28 Internal hard drives and smaller microdrives are based on very similar technologies, despite the differences in size.

3.4
Disk Storage

MAGNETIC DISKS

Both hard disks and floppy disks are coated with a magnetic oxide similar to the material used to coat cassette tapes and videotapes. The read/write head of a disk drive is similar to the record/play head on a tape recorder; it magnetizes parts of the surface to record information. The difference is that a disk is a digital medium—binary numbers are read and written. The typical hard disk consists of several *platters*, each accessed via a read/write head on a movable *armature*. The magnetic signals on the disk are organized into concentric tracks; the tracks in turn are divided into sectors. This is the traditional scheme used to construct addresses for data on the disk.

Hard disks spin much faster than floppy disks and have a higher storage density (number of bytes per square inch). The *read/write head* of a hard disk glides on a thin cushion of air above the disk and never actually touches the disk.

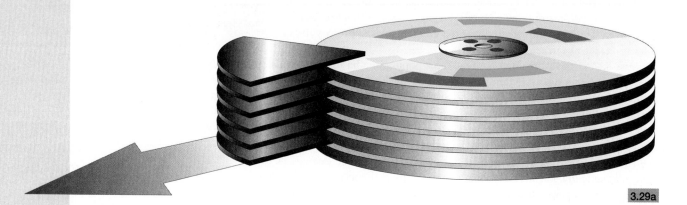

3.29a

CD-ROM

A CD-ROM drive contains a small laser that shines on the surface of the disk, "reading" the reflections. Audio CDs and computer CD-ROMs have similar formats; that's why you can play an audio CD with a CD-ROM drive. Information is represented optically—the bottom surface of the CD, under a protective layer of plastic, is coated with a reflective metal film. A laser burns unreflective pits into the film to record data bits. After a pit is burned, it can't be smoothed over and made shiny again; that's why CD-ROMs are read-only.

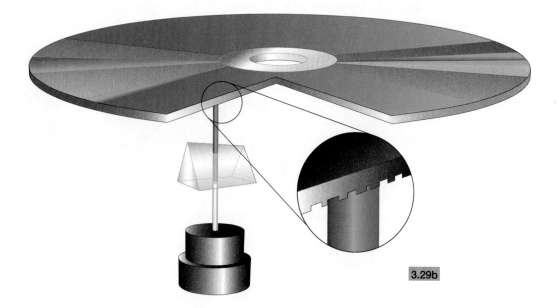

3.29b

DVD-ROM

A DVD-ROM drive works on the same principle as a CD-ROM drive; the main difference is that the pits are packed much closer together on a DVD, so about seven times as many can fit on the disk surface. (To read these tightly packed bits, the DVD-ROM uses a narrower laser beam.) A DVD can hold even more data—up to 8.5GB—if it has a second layer of data. On a layered DVD, the top layer is semireflective, allowing a second readback

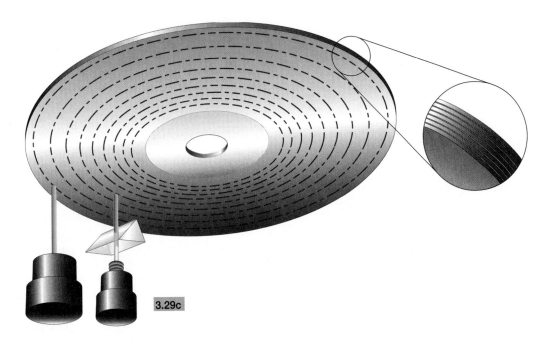

3.29c

laser to penetrate to the layer below. The laser can "see through" the top layer, just as you can see through a picket fence when you look at it from exactly the right angle. For truly massive storage jobs, a DVD can have data on both sides—up to 17GB. Two-sided DVDs usually have to be turned over for the reader to read both sides; future drives may use additional readback lasers to read the second side without flipping the disk.

RECORDABLE CD AND DVD DRIVES

Recordable CD and DVD drives use laser beams to write data on recordable disks. But recordable optical media have layers with chemical structures that react to different temperatures created by different types of lasers. To write data, a high-intensity laser beam produces high temperatures that break down the crystalline structure of the original surface. The resulting pits dissipate, rather than reflect, low-level lasers during the process of reading recorded data. To erase data, a laser heats the pits to about 400 degrees, causing them to revert to their original reflectivecrystalline state.

3.29d

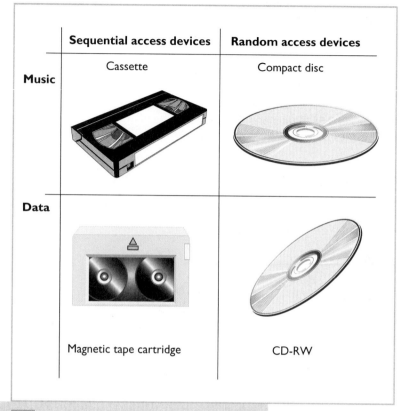

	Sequential access devices	Random access devices
Music	Cassette	Compact disc
Data	Magnetic tape cartridge	CD-RW

3.30 Home theater systems include sequential-access devices—VHS tape decks—and random-access devices—DVD players. The advantages of random access are the same for stereos as for computers.

From CD-ROM to DVD-R/CD-RW, there's an alphabet soup of choices in optical disc drives for PCs today. The names can be especially confusing because they aren't consistent. Does R stand for Read, Recordable, Rewriteable, or Random? It depends on the context. Many of these drive types will undoubtedly go by the wayside as the cost of the expensive all-purpose drives comes down. But until then, it's helpful to know something about these oddly named devices.

The most common optical drive in computers is the CD-ROM drive. A CD-ROM drive can read data from CD-ROM (compact disc—read-only memory) discs—data disks that are physically identical to music compact discs. The similarity of audio and data CDs is no accident; it makes it possible for CD-ROM drives to play music CDs under computer control. A CD-ROM can hold up to about 800MB of data—more raw text than you could type in your lifetime. But because CD-ROM drives are read-only devices, they can't be used as storage devices. Instead, they're mostly used to read commercially pressed CD-ROMs containing everything from business applications to multimedia games and reference libraries.

Many PCs now include CD-RW drives (sometimes referred to as *CD-R/RW drives*) instead of CD-ROM drives. Like a CD-ROM drive, a CD-RW drive can read data from CD-ROMs and play music from audio CDs. But a CD-RW drive can also *burn*, or record, data onto CD-R and CD-RW disks.

CD-R (compact disc—recordable) disks are *WORM* (write-once, read-many) media. That is, a drive can write onto a blank (or partially filled) CD-R disk, but it can't erase the data once it's burned in. CD-Rs are commonly used to make archival copies of large data files, backup copies of software CDs, and personal music CDs. They're also useful for creating master copies of CD-ROMs and audio CDs for professional duplication.

CD-RW (compact disc—rewritable) discs are more expensive than CD-R media, but they have the advantage of being erasable. A drive can write, erase, and rewrite a CD-RW disk repeatedly. Some people use CD-RW disks instead of removable cartridge media for storing, transporting, and backing up large quantities of data.

CD-RW drives are advertised with three different speeds: a speed for *burning* (writing) CD-Rs, a speed for writing CD-RWs, and a much faster speed for reading CD-ROMs. All three *data transfer rates* are expressed as multiples of 150K per second, the speed of the original CD-ROM drives. A typical drive might have maximum speeds specified as 52X/24X/52X. Actual drives speeds don't always measure up to these values, and even the fastest CD-RW drives are pokey compared to a magnetic hard drive.

Several types of DVD drives are also used as replacements for CD-ROM drives in PCs. The DVD is the same size as a standard CD-ROM, but can hold between

3.31 A CD-RW drive can read CD-ROMs, play audio CDs, and burn audio and data CDs using recordable and re-recordable discs.

4.7 and 17GB of information, depending on how the information is stored. DVD originally stood for *digital video disc*, because the discs were designed to replace VHS tapes in video stores. Today, many people say DVD stands for *digital versatile disks*, because these high-capacity disks are used to store and distribute all kinds of data.

DVD-ROM drives can play DVD movies, read DVD data disks, read standard CD-ROMs, and play audio CDs. But because they're read-only, they can't record data, music, or movies.

A combination *DVD/CD-RW drive* offers the advantages of a DVD-ROM drive and a CD-RW drive in a single unit that can play DVD movies, play audio CDs, record and erase data on CD-RW disks, and burn audio CDs and CD-ROMs. But this type of drive can't record movies or other large files on blank DVDs; it can only record on CD-R and CD-RW media. For that functionality, you will need a recordable DVD drive. Unfortunately, manufacturers haven't yet agreed on a single standard for these drives, so choosing a drive can be confusing.

DVD-RAM drives can read, erase, and write data (but not DVD video) on multigigabyte *DVD-R* (but not CD-R or CD-RW) media. A *DVD-RW drive* can read all the standard CD and DVD disc types and record on CD-R, CD-RW, DVD-R (recordable) and *DVD-RW* (rewritable) media. (Apple refers to its DVD-R drive as the SuperDrive.) A competing standard, the *DVD+RW drive*, can read all the standard CD and DVD disc types and record on CD-R, CD-RW, *DVD+R* (recordable) and *DVD+RW* (rewritable) media. And an emerging new standard, *DVD+MRW* (also called *Mt. Rainier*), offers similar functionality. Some companies, including Sony, have released combination drives that support both DVD-RW and DVD+RW media. With the right software, most of these recordable DVD drives can be used to create DVD videos that you can play on DVD movie players.

Common Optical Drives: What They Can Do

Drive type	Read CD-ROM data	Play Audio CDs	Write CD-R data	Record Audio CDs	Write/rewrite CD-RW data	Read DVD-ROM data	Play DVD Movie	Write DVD data	Write/rewrite DVD-RAM data	Record DVD Video
CD-ROM	✓	✓								
CD-RW	✓	✓	✓	✓	✓					
DVD-ROM	✓	✓				✓	✓			
DVD/CD-RW	✓	✓	✓	✓	✓	✓	✓			
DVD-RAM	✓	✓				✓	✓	✓	✓	
DVD-R CD-RW	✓	✓	✓	✓	✓	✓	✓	✓		✓

3.32

Solid-State Storage Devices

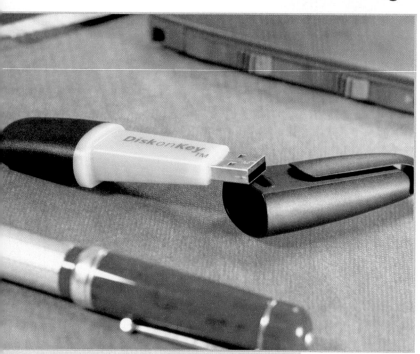

3.33 Keychain USB storage devices can store up to hundreds of megabytes of data; they plug into a computer's USB port.

Until recently, disk drives were the only realistic random-access storage devices for most computer applications. In spite of their popularity, disk drives present problems for today's computer users. The moving parts in disk drives are more likely to fail than other computer components. For airline travelers and others who must depend on battery power for long periods of time, spinning disk drives consume too much energy. Disk drives can be noisy—a problem for musicians and others who use computers for audio applications. And disk drives are bulky when compared with computer memory; they're often not practical for palm-sized computers and other applications where space is tight and battery life is at a premium.

Flash memory is a type of erasable memory chip that can serve as a reliable, low-energy, quiet, compact alternative to disk storage. Until recently, flash memory was too expensive for most storage applications. But flash memory today has many practical applications. Some flash memory devices are designed for specific applications, such as storing pictures in digital cameras and transferring them to PCs for editing. Sony's Memory Stick is an all-purpose digital storage card about the size of a stick of gum. *Keychain USB flash memory devices* are becoming popular for storing and transporting data files. These tiny devices typically hold less data than a CD-ROM disc and plug directly into the computer's USB port (discussed later in this chapter.) Most experts believe that flash memory or some other type of solid-state storage technology—storage with no moving parts—will eventually replace disk and tape storage in computers and other digital devices. Today, most flash memory devices ship in sizes ranging from 16MB all the way up to 1GB.

3.34 Memory Stick media is a solid-state storage device that is often used in digital cameras, portable audio players, video equipment, computers, and PDAs, making it easy for these devices to share information.

3.35 This flash memory card is small enough to wear on a wristband and contains enough information to potentially save a life in an emergency.

The Computer System: The Sum of Its Parts

Most personal computers fall into one of four basic design classes:

> The computer is by all odds the most **extraordinary** of the **technological clothing** ever devised by man, since it is an **extension** of our **central nervous system**. Beside it **the wheel is a mere hula hoop** . . .
>
> —Marshall McLuhan, in *War and Peace in the Global Village*

- *Tower systems*—tall, narrow boxes that generally have more expansion slots and bays than other designs
- Flat *desktop systems* (sometimes called "pizza box" systems) designed to sit under the monitor like a platform
- *All-in-one systems* (like the iMac) that combine monitor and system unit into a single housing
- *Portable computers*, which include all the essential components, including keyboard and pointing device, in one compact box

Whatever the design, a PC must allow for attachment of input, output, and storage peripherals. That's where slots, ports, and bays figure in. Now that we've explored the peripherals landscape, we can look again at the ways of hooking those peripherals into the system.

Ports and Slots Revisited

The system board, or motherboard, of a computer system generally includes several ports, some of which are now considered *legacy ports* because the most common ports on system boards have been standard on PCs for years. They include the following:

- A *serial port* for attaching a modem or other device that can send and receive messages one bit at a time
- A *parallel port* for attaching a printer or other device that communicates by sending or receiving bits in groups, rather than sequentially
- *Keyboard/mouse ports* for attaching a keyboard and a mouse

Other ports are typically included on expansion boards rather than the system board:

- A *video port* for plugging a color monitor into the video board
- *Microphone, speaker, headphone, and MIDI* (musical instrument digital interface) ports for attaching sound equipment to the sound card

All of these ports follow interface standards agreed on by the hardware industry so that devices made by one manufacturer can be attached to systems made by other companies. The downside of industry standards is that they can sometimes hold back progress. For example, today's color printers are often kept waiting by the pokey parallel port.

Computer manufacturers and owners use expansion cards to get around the limitations of these standard ports. For example, many modern computers include an internal *modem* in an expansion slot; this modem card adds a standard phone jack as a communication port. For faster connection to a local-area network (LAN), most modern PCs include a *network card* that adds a LAN port. For faster communication with external drives, scanners, and other peripherals, a PC might include a *SCSI* (small computer systems interface, pronounced "scuzzy") card that adds a SCSI port to the back of the system box. SCSI is becoming less common, however, as standard hard drive technology improves.

Internal and External Drives

Disk drives generally reside in *bays* inside the system unit. A new PC will often include a floppy disk drive in one bay, a hard drive in another, and some kind of CD or DVD drive in a third bay. Some PCs have extra bays for additional internal hard drives or removable media. Tall tower models generally have more expansion bays than flat desktop systems designed to sit under monitors. But even if there's no room in the system unit for additional internal drives, external drives can be connected to the system through ports.

Most portable computers are too small to include three drive bays. But some models have bays that enable you to swap drives. For example, you might remove the CD-ROM drive from a laptop and insert a floppy disk drive or extra battery. Some models enable you to hot swap devices—remove and replace them without powering down. All portables enable you to attach external peripherals through ports. Some portables can be plugged into docking stations that contain, or are attached to, all the necessary peripherals. When docked, a portable can function like a desktop computer, complete with large-screen monitor, full-sized keyboard, mouse, sound system, and a variety of other peripherals.

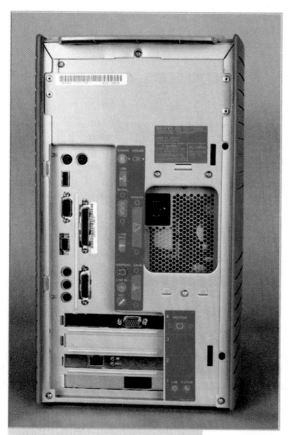

3.36a This rear view of a tower system unit shows several ports, including some (below) that are included in add-on-boards in slots.

3.36b This tower system has its side panel removed so you can see the storage bays containing disk drives (top right) and the extension boards inserted into slots (top left).

RULES OF THUMB

The **best computer** for your specific needs is the one that will come on the market **immediately after** you actually purchase some other model.

—Dave Barry, humorist

This book's appendix, CD-ROM, and Internet Web site contain specific information about the nuts and bolts of buying hardware and software to make your own computer system. Of course, any brand-specific advice on choosing computer equipment is likely to be outdated within a few months of publication. Still, some general principles remain constant while the technology races forward. Here are some consumer criteria worth considering, even if you have no intention of buying your own computer:

➡ **Cost.** Buy what you can afford, but be sure to allow for extra memory, extended warranties, peripherals (printer, extra storage devices, modem, cables, speakers, and so on), and software. If you join a user group or connect to an online shareware site, you'll be able to meet some of your software needs at low (or no) cost. But you'll almost certainly need some commercial software too. Don't be tempted to copy copyrighted software from your friends or public labs; software piracy is theft, prosecutable under federal laws. (Choosing software isn't easy, but many periodicals and Web sites publish regular reviews to help you sort out the best programs.)

➡ **Capability.** Is it the right tool for the job? Buy a computer that's powerful enough to meet your needs. Make sure the processor is fast enough to handle your demands. If you want to take advantage of state-of-the-art multimedia programs, consider only machines that meet the latest standards. If you want to create state-of-the-art multimedia programs, you'll need a powerful computer that can handle audio and video input as well as output—FireWire (IEEE 1394) if you'll be using a digital video camera. Be sure the machine you buy can do the job you need it to do, now and in the foreseeable future.

➡ **Capacity.** If you plan to do graphic design, publishing, or multimedia authoring, make sure your machine has enough memory and disk storage to support the resource-intensive applications you'll need. Consider adding removable media drives for backup and transport of large files.

➡ **Customizability.** Computers are versatile, but they don't all handle all jobs with equal ease. If you'll be using word processors, spreadsheets, and other mainstream software packages, just about any computer will do. If you have off-the-beaten-path needs (advanced video editing, instrument monitoring, and so on), choose a system with enough slots and ports to enable it to be extended for your work.

➡ **Compatibility.** Will the software you plan to use run on the computer you're considering? Most popular computers have a good selection of compatible software, but if you have specific needs, such as being able to take your software home to run on Mom's computer, study the compatibility issue carefully. Total compatibility isn't always possible or necessary. A typical Windows-compatible computer, for example, will probably not run every "Windows-compatible" program. Many people don't care if all their programs will run on another kind of computer; they just need data compatibility—the ability to move documents back and forth between systems on disk or through a network connection. It's common, for example, for Windows users and Macintosh users to share documents over a network.

➡ **Connectivity.** In today's networked world, it's shortsighted to see your computer as a self-contained information appliance. Make sure you include a high-speed modem and/or network connection in your system so you can take full advantage of the communication capabilities of your computer.

➡ **Convenience.** Just about any computer can do most common jobs, but which is the most convenient for you? Do you value portability over having all the peripherals permanently connected? Is it important to you to have a machine that's easy to install and maintain so you can take care of it yourself? Or do you want to choose the same kind of machine as the people around you so you can get help easily when you need it? Which user interface makes the kind of work you'll be doing easiest?

➡ **Company.** If you try to save money by buying an off-brand computer, you may find yourself the owner of an orphan computer. High-tech companies can vanish overnight. Make sure you'll be able to get service and parts down the road.

➡ **Curve.** Most models of personal computers seem to have a useful life span of just a few years—if they survive the first year or two. If you want to minimize financial risk, avoid buying a computer during the first year of a model's life, when it hasn't been tested on the open market. Also avoid buying a computer that's over the hill; you'll know it because most software developers will have abandoned this model for greener CPUs. In the words of eighteenth-century British poet Alexander Pope, "Be not the first by whom the new are tried, nor yet the last to lay the old aside."

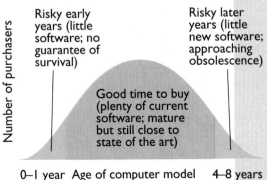

Computer consumer's curve

Number of purchasers

Risky early years (little software; no guarantee of survival)

Risky later years (little new software; approaching obsolescence)

Good time to buy (plenty of current software; mature but still close to state of the art)

0–1 year   Age of computer model   4–8 years

3.37

115

Expansion Made Easy

It's clear that the *open architecture* of the PC—the design that enables you to add expansion cards and peripherals—gives it flexibility and longevity that it wouldn't have otherwise. Many hobbyists have been using the same computer system for years; they just swap in new cards, drives, and even CPUs and motherboards to keep their systems up to current standards. But most computer users today prefer to use their computers, not take them apart. Fortunately, new interface standards are emerging that will enable casual computer users to add the latest and greatest devices to their systems without cracking the box.

A USB, or *universal serial bus*, can transmit data at approximately 11 megabits per second (Mbps)—roughly 100 times faster than the PC serial port—and a newer, faster version called *USB 2.0* is even faster, offering transfer rates of 480Mbps. Theoretically, up to 126 devices, including keyboards, mice, digital cameras, scanners, and storage devices, can be chained together from a single USB port. USB devices can be hot swapped, so the system instantly recognizes the presence of a new device when it is plugged in. And USB is *platform independent*, so USB devices can often work on both PCs and Macintoshes. In fact, this paragraph is being typed on a keyboard that's shared by a PC and a Mac through a USB hub. All new PCs and Macintoshes include several USB or USB 2.0 ports. In time, computer manufacturers may phase out other ports made unnecessary by USB's presence. Some produce *legacy-free PCs* that cost less because they use USB ports instead of older serial, parallel, keyboard, mouse, and SCSI ports.

Another interface standard that shows promise is FireWire, a high-speed connection standard developed by Apple. Some PC makers refer to FireWire by the less friendly designation, *IEEE 1394*, assigned by the Institute of Electrical and Electronic Engineers when they approved it as a standard. (Sony calls their version iLink.) FireWire can move data between devices at 400Mbps—far faster than most peripheral devices can handle it. This high speed makes it ideal for data-intensive work like digital video. Most modern digital video cameras have FireWire ports, so they can be connected directly to 1394-equipped PCs. Like USB, FireWire allows multiple devices to be connected to the same port and to be hot swapped. FireWire can also supply power to peripherals so they don't need an external power supply. Because of its speed and versatility, FireWire is expected to be standard equipment on all new PCs soon. A new version, *FireWire 800*, was recently introduced on Macintosh systems. This new version of FireWire offers 800Mbps transfer speeds. (Apple now refers to the comparatively pokey FireWire as FireWire 400).

Putting It All Together

A typical computer system might have several different input, output, and storage peripherals. From the computer's point of view, it doesn't matter which of these devices is used at any given time. Each input device is just another source of electrical signals; each output device is just another place to send signals; each storage device is one or the other, depending on what the program calls for. Read from here, write to there—the CPU doesn't care; it dutifully follows instructions. Like a stereo receiver, the computer is oblivious to which input and output devices are attached and operational, as long as they're compatible.

3.38 A typical desktop computer system includes a computer, a display, and several peripheral devices.

Networks: Systems without Boundaries

Unlike a stereo system, which has clearly defined boundaries, a computer system can be part of a network that blurs the boundaries between computers. When computers are connected in a network, one computer can, in effect, serve as an input device for another computer, which serves as an output device for the first computer. Networks can include hundreds of different computers, each of which might have access to all peripherals on the system. Many public and private networks span the globe by taking advantage of satellites, fiber-optic cables, and other communication technologies. Using a modem, a computer can connect to a network through an ordinary phone line. The rise in computer networks is making it more difficult to draw lines between individual computer systems. If you're connected to the Internet, your computer is, in effect, just a tiny part of a global system of interconnected networks. We'll take a closer look at networks in Chapter 8.

Software: The Missing Piece

In the span of a few pages we've surveyed a mind-boggling array of computer hardware, but, in truth, we've barely scratched the surface. Nonetheless, all this hardware is worthless without software to drive it. In the next few chapters we'll take a look at the software that makes a computer system come to life.

Tomorrow's Peripherals

You can count how many **seeds are in the apple**, but not how many **apples are in the seed**.

—Ken Kesey, author of
One Flew over the Cuckoo's Nest

Silicon chips aren't the only parts of computers that are evolving. Here's a sampler of peripheral technologies that are making their way from research labs into products.

TOMORROW'S STORAGE

Smaller disks that hold more—the trend will continue, producing tiny hard disks that can store astronomical quantities of data. But solid-state storage breakthroughs will threaten the dominance of disks in a few years. For example, Cambridge University researchers funded by Hitachi have developed a single-electron memory chip the size of a thumbnail that can store all the sounds and images of a full-length feature film. This experimental chip consumes very little power and retains memory for up to 10 years when the power is switched off.

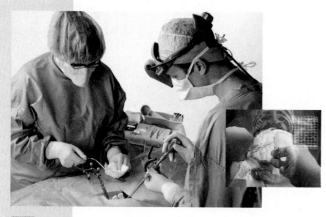

3.39 This surgeon's retinal scanner display makes video images and the patient's vital signs continually visible throughout the surgical procedure.

TOMORROW'S OUTPUT

Flat-panel screens are replacing desktop CRTs at an ever-increasing rate. Soon we'll be using ultra-high-resolution displays that are thin enough to hang on walls like pictures and efficient enough to run on batteries for days. LCD goggle displays—the visual equivalent to headphones—may soon be common for portable PC users who want to shut the rest of the world out. Those who need to see what's going on around them and inside their computer can wear eyeglasses with built-in transparent heads-up displays. Researchers at the University of Washington have developed a *retinal display* that works without a screen; it shines a focused beam of light through the wearer's pupil, moving across the field of vision to draw pixels directly on the retina. Fighterpilots,

neurosurgeons, and people with limited vision are using these displays to see critical computer data without taking their eyes off of their work. We may eventually see these displays attached to PDAs and mobile phones.

3.40 This page of electronic paper is being reloaded with a fresh image.

TOMORROWS INPUT: SENSORS

Technology forecaster Paul Saffo predicts that the next major breakthroughs will occur as researchers develop—and companies market—inexpensive sensors that enable digital devices to monitor the analog world. Temperature sensors, optical sensors, motion sensors, and other types of sensors already make it possible for computers to track a variety of real-world activities and conditions. But as these technologies mature, more sophisticated devices will serve as eyes, ears, and other types of sense organs for computer networks. Saffo wrote in a special anniversary issue of the *Communications* of the ACM:

Two parallel universes currently exist—an everyday analog universe that we inhabit, and a newer digital universe created by humans, but inhabited by digital machines. We visit this digital world by peering through the portholes of our computer screens, and we manipulate with keyboard and mouse much as a nuclear technician works with radioactive material via glovebox and manipulator arms. . . . Now we are handing sensory organs and manipulators to the machines and inviting them to enter into analog reality. The scale of possible surprise this may generate over the next several decades as sensors, lasers, and microprocessors co-evolve is breathtakingly uncertain.

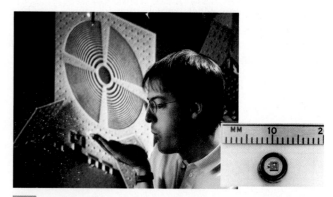

3.41 "Smart dust" computers at the University of California at Berkeley help monitor and control heating and cooling systems using environmental sensors and wireless communication links.

Shifting Into Overdrive By J. Bradford DeLong

Computer journalists and sales people tend to focus on the CPU when discussing PC evolution. In this article, first published in the May, 2003 issue of Wired, *Bradford DeLong discusses the rapid changes in computer storage capacity and the impact those changes will have on our lives.*

Those of us with one foot far enough in the grave to have been using computers in the mid-1980s remember our extraordinary liberation from the floppy disk. We were freed from the requirement that all our programs and operating systems and files come in 360-kilobyte, 5½-inch chunks. It was a marvelous advance, the revolution in hard disk technology that gave us 10-megabyte mass storage devices for $1,000.

But it is the advances since then—and those we can firmly see our future promising—that are even more marvelous. Right now I am sitting in front of a whirring 60-gigabyte hard disk that cost less than $100. Do the math: If back then 10 megabytes cost $1,000, then 60 gigabytes would have cost x, where x = $6,000,000 and "back then" = 18 years ago. I'm sitting in front of $6,000,000 worth of mass storage, measured at mid-1980s prices. Happy me!

We have Moore's law for microprocessors. But who's coined a law for hard disks? In mass storage we have seen a 60,000-fold fall in price—more than a dozen times the force of Moore's law, with less than one-hundredth the press excitement.

My entire music library—1,803 tracks, 128.8 hours of relatively high-quality MP3 files—now sits in what seems like a small 8-gigabyte corner of my hard disk. *San Jose Mercury News* columnist Dan Gillmor carries the entire *Encyclopaedia Britannica* on his laptop—the thing that fills 6½ linear feet on my family room bookshelf takes up 4 percent of his disk space. Today, a $350 investment in mass storage can buy enough space to hold approximately 250 hours—one and a half 24-hour-a-day weeks—of moderate-quality digital video. And tomorrow? I'm willing to guess that by 2012 the $100 mass storage option for PCs should hold a full terabyte.

Computing power and connectivity hogged the headlines in the past decade, but mass storage will take the lead for three reasons. The first is regulatory: It does not look as though we in the United States will get the capital and regulatory structures of telecommunications right fast enough to see the bandwidth explosion that we know is technically possible during the next several years. The second is that keeping up with Moore's law in silicon is becoming more and more expensive. Intel, IBM, et al. are designing the next generations of microprocessors right now. But the cost of a semiconductor fab is now $3 billion and rising—few companies can afford one. The third is that mass storage is very simple: You write marks, you read marks, whether on modern magneto-optical or Babylonian clay-tablet media. What matters is the size and precision of your chisel, and our engineers' technical creativity makes it a favorable bet that the next five or ten years will see connectivity and Moore's law lagging behind the explosion of mass storage.

So, what will the world look like if mass storage is not a limiting factor?

First, the cheaper the disk space, the more dead the traditional business models of the entertainment industry. Money will come from new content for which a premium price based on must-haveness can still be justified, much like the hardcover-softcover distinction in bookselling. Substantial money will also come from special big-screen, live, and other experiences that cannot be duplicated at home. It's not that information—in the multimedia content sense—wants to be free. Deep in people's minds is a powerful human drive to exchange, to reciprocate, to not just take but also give. But reciprocity works only if the terms of the exchange are seen as fair.

Second, the overwhelming cheapness of storage will lead to the apotheosis of librarianship—or, rather, of search. Overwhelmingly cheap storage means that we will save copies of everything. But saved copies of everything are useful only when you can find what you are looking for. I already find it much, much easier to locate things on the publicly accessible part of my hard disk that is www.j-bradford-delong.net than in my private directories. Why? Google. Other people have omnivorously plowed through the directories opened up to the world, and Google has aggregated the Web traces they have made. Intelligence—artificial or otherwise—at assessing the value of documents and their relevance to you may well become the truly scarce factor. And one of the basic principles of economics is that the truly scarce factor is highly rewarded. Google's children will be a big part of the picture. Tomorrow's movie studio profits may well accrue to the studio that can write the best algorithms to download copies of the 50 films you'd most enjoy to your hard disk overnight.

Finally, and most important, your memory will improve. There will be space to store whatever you wish to recall from your day—pictures of people you saw (grabbed from the Internet), words you heard (recorded via laptop microphone and then translated into text), not to mention whatever thoughts you found time to write down. Your life is your archive, and your archive is your life. Forgetting will be much more difficult—unless, of course, you want to. Then you can always edit it.

DISCUSSION QUESTIONS

1. Do you agree that mass storage, not CPUs, will "hog the headlines" in the coming decade? Why or why not?

2. Do you agree that advancements in storage technology will help your memory to improve? Why or why not?

SUMMARY

A computer with just a CPU and internal memory is of limited value; peripherals allow that computer to communicate with the outside world and store information for later use. Some peripherals are strictly input devices. Others are output devices. Some are external storage devices that accept information from and send information to the CPU.

The most common input devices today are the keyboard and the mouse, but a variety of other input devices can be connected to the computer. Trackballs, touch-sensitive pads, touch screens, and joysticks provide alternatives to the mouse as a pointing device. Bar code readers, optical mark readers, and magnetic ink readers are designed to recognize and translate specially printed patterns and characters. Scanners and digital cameras convert photographs, drawings, and other analog images into digital files that the computer can process. Sound digitizers do the same thing to audio information. All input devices are designed to do one thing: convert information signals from an outside source into a pattern of bits that the computer can process.

Output devices perform the opposite function: They accept strings of bits from the computer and transform them into a form that is useful or meaningful outside the computer. Video displays, including CRT monitors and LCDs, are almost universally used to display information continually as the computer functions. A variety of printers are used for producing paper output. Fax machines and fax modems let you share printed information using standard phone lines. Sound output from the computer, including music and synthesized speech, is delivered through audio speakers. Output devices also allow computers to control other machines.

Unlike most input and output peripherals, storage devices such as disk drives and tape drives are capable of two-way communication with the computer. Because of their high-speed random access capability, magnetic disks—high-capacity hard disks, inexpensive diskettes, and a variety of removable media—are the most common forms of storage on modern computers. Sequential access tape devices are generally used only to archive information that doesn't need to be accessed often. Optical discs are used mostly as high-capacity, read-only media, but newer types of optical drives can both read and write data. In the future, solid-state storage technology will probably replace disks and tapes for most applications.

The hardware for a complete computer system generally includes at least one processor, memory, storage devices, and several I/O peripherals for communicating with the outside world. Network connections make it possible for computers to communicate with one another directly. Networks blur the boundaries between individual computer systems. With the hardware components in place, a computer system is ready to receive and follow instructions encoded in software.

KEY TERMS

bar code reader (p. 94)
CD-R (p. 110)
CD-ROM (p. 110)
CD-ROM drive (p. 110)
CD-RW (p. 110)
CD-RW drive (p. 110)
CRT (cathode-ray tube) monitor (p. 100)
digital camera (p. 96)
digitize (p. 96)
disk drive (p. 107)
diskette (floppy disk) (p. 107)
display (p. 99)
dot matrix printer (p. 102)
DVD (p. 110)
DVD-ROM drive (p. 111)
ergonomics (p. 106)
ergonomic keyboard (p. 91)
facsimile (fax) machine (p. 103)
fax modem (p. 103)
FireWire (IEEE 1394, FireWire 400, FireWire 800) (p. 116)
flash memory (p. 112)

graphics tablet (p. 92)
handwriting recognition software (p. 95)
hard disk (p. 107)
hot swap (p. 114)
impact printer (p. 102)
inkjet printer (p. 102)
interface standards (p. 113)
joystick (p. 92)
keyboard (p. 91)
laser printer (p. 102)
LCD (liquid crystal display) (p. 100)
line printer (p. 102)
magnetic disk (p. 107)
magnetic ink character reader (p. 94)
magnetic tape (p. 105)
monitor (p. 99)
mouse (p. 92)
multifunction printer (MFP) (p. 102)
nonimpact printer (p. 102)
optical character recognition (OCR) (p. 94)
optical disk drive (p. 107)

optical mark reader (p. 94)
pen-based computer (p. 95)
photo printer (p. 102)
plotter (p. 103)
pointing stick (TrackPoint) (p. 92)
point-of-sale (POS) terminal (p. 94)
printer (p. 102)
random access (p. 107)
removable cartridge media (p. 107)
repetitive-stress injuries (p. 91)
resolution (p. 99)
scanner (p. 96)
sensor (p. 99)
sequential access (p. 107)
solid-state storage (p. 112)
sound card (p. 104)
storage device (p. 105)
tape drive (p. 105)
touchpad (trackpad) (p. 92)
touch screen (p. 92)
trackball (p. 92)
USB (universal serial bus) (p. 116)
video display terminal (VDT) (p. 99)

INTERACTIVE QUIZ QUESTIONS

 1. The Computer Confluence CD-ROM contains self-test quiz questions related to this chapter, including multiple choice, true or false, and matching questions.

 2. The Computer Confluence Web site, http://www.computerconfluence.com, contains self-test exercises related to this chapter. Follow the instructions for taking a quiz. After you've completed your quiz, you can email the results to your instructor.

TRUE OR FALSE

1. The disk drive was invented at about the same time the first computers came into existence.

2. Palm-sized computers can't have keyboards because the stylus is the only input device they can recognize.

3. The touchpad on a notebook computer serves the same function as a QWERTY keyboard on a desktop PC.

4. Because bar codes were designed to be read by computers, the devices that read them are extremely accurate.

5. A scanner creates an analog representation of a printed digital image.

6. The display quality of a monitor is determined in large part by the monitor's resolution and color depth.

7. Most PC printers today are laser printers, because color laser printers are far less expensive to buy than color inkjet printers.

8. A CD-RW drive can be used to store and back up data files.

9. Several years ago the computer industry agreed on a universal standard for rewriteable DVD storage, so today virtually all drives are based on the same standard.

10. Legacy-free computers don't include early PC standards, such as the serial port, that are inefficient when compared to more recent technologies like USB.

MULTIPLE CHOICE

1. The mouse is standard equipment on virtually all modern PCs except
   a. PCs without USB or FireWire ports.
   b. IBM PCs.
   c. iMacs.
   d. portable PCs.
   e. workstation PCs.

2. Which of these is both an input and an output device?
   a. a bar-code reader.
   b. a flatbed scanner.
   c. a touch screen.
   d. a sensor.
   e. a plotter.

3. Optical character recognition can be used to extract text from writing on
   a. smart whiteboards.
   b. tablet PCs.
   c. PDAs.
   d. scanned letters.
   e. All of the above.

4. LCD technology is used in
   a. notebook computer displays.
   b. many desktop computer displays.
   c. video projectors.
   d. All of the above.
   e. None of the above.

5. A multifunction printer generally includes several devices, including
   a. a scanner.
   b. a CRT monitor.
   c. a QWERTY keyboard.
   d. a mouse.
   e. All of the above.

6. Magnetic tape is not practical for applications where data must be quickly recalled because tape is
   a. a random access medium.
   b. a sequential access medium.
   c. a read-only medium.
   d. fragile—easily damaged.
   e. an expensive storage medium.

7. The diskette is considered obsolete by many professionals because
   a. it is strictly read-only.
   b. it is especially vulnerable to hacker attacks.
   c. it doesn't have enough storage capacity for today's large data files.
   d. it isn't as reliable as a modern floppy disk.
   e. All of the above.

8. Most digital cameras today store images using
   a. DVD-RAM.
   b. CD-ROM.
   c. flash memory.
   d. digital ink.
   e. None of the above.

9. Which of these technologies is being phased out on modern PCs?
   a. USB 2.0.
   b. FireWire 800.
   c. the parallel printer port.
   d. expansion slots.
   e. hot-swappable devices.

10. Which of these is most like the open architecture of the modern PC?
    a. a modern car with a computer-controlled emissions system that can be adjusted by factory-authorized mechanics.
    b. a "smart" microwave with an embedded computer that allows for complex recipes and scheduling.
    c. a stereo system that allows speakers, disc players, and other components to be replaced by the owner.
    d. a handheld computer with built-in firmware for all of the most common PDA tasks.
    e. a music keyboard that includes a built-in synthesizer and an LCD display.

REVIEW QUESTIONS

1. Provide a working definition for each of the key terms listed in the Key Terms section. Check your answers in the glossary.

2. List five input devices and three output devices that might be attached to a PC. Describe a typical use for each.

3. Name and describe three special-purpose input devices people commonly use in public places, such as stores, banks, and libraries.

4. Many people find that the mouse is impractical for use as a pointing device on a laptop computer. Describe at least three alternatives that are more appropriate.

5. What are the advantages of CRT monitors over LCDs?

6. Name at least two hardware devices that use LCDs because using a CRT would be impractical.

7. What are the advantages of nonimpact printers such as laser printers over impact printers? Are there any disadvantages?

8. Some commonly used peripherals can be described as both input and output devices. Explain.

9. What is the difference between sequential access and random access storage devices? What are the major uses of each?

DISCUSSION QUESTIONS

1. If we think of the human brain as a computer, what are the input devices? What are the output devices? What are the storage devices?

2. What kinds of new input and output devices do you think future computers might have? Why?

PROJECTS

1. The keyboard is the main input device for computers today. If you don't know how to touch-type, you're effectively handicapped in a world of computers. Fortunately, many personal computer software programs are designed to teach keyboarding. If you need to learn to type, try to find one of these programs and use it regularly until you are a fluent typist.

2. Using the inventory of computers you developed in Project 4 in Chapter 1, determine the major components of each (input devices, output devices, storage, and so on).

3. Visit a bank, store, office, or laboratory. List all the computer peripherals you see, categorizing them as input, output, or storage devices.

4. Using computer advertisements in magazines, newspapers, and catalogs, try to break down the cost of a computer to determine, on the average, what percentage of the cost is for the system unit (including CPU, memory, and disk drives), what percentage is for input and output devices, and what percentage is for software. How do the percentages change as the price of the system goes up?

SOURCES AND RESOURCES

Books

Infinite Loop: How the World's Most Insanely Great Computer Company Went Insane, by Michael S. Malone (New York: Doubleday, 1999). Malone's book tells the Apple story from the early days of the Apple I through the roller-coaster years of the Macintosh.

Insanely Great: The Life and Times of Macintosh, the Computer That Changed Everything, Reissue Edition, by Steven Levy (New York: Penguin, 2000). Apple fan and *Newsweek* columnist Steven Levy recounts the first 10 years of the Macintosh's history in breathless detail.

The Second Coming of Steve Jobs, by Alan Deutschman (New York: Broadway Books, 2000). This book focuses on Apple's controversial CEO in the years at Next and his return to Apple. Jobs is a controversial, complex, and private person who has achieved fame that rivals rock stars. His story makes good reading.

Disclosure, by Michael Crichton (New York: Ballantine Books, 1994). This book-turned-movie provides an inside look at a fictional Seattle corporation that manufactures computer peripherals. Even though the author has clearly tampered with credibility for the sake of a suspenseful plot, the story provides insights into the roles money and power play in today's high-stakes computer industry. It also features some cool and realistic computer technology of the near future.

Real World Scanning and Halftones, Second Edition, by David Blatner and Steve Roth (Berkeley, CA: Peachpit Press, 1998). It's easy to use a scanner, but it isn't always easy to get high-quality scans. This illustrated book covers scanner use from the basics to advanced tips and techniques.

Digital Photographer's Handbook, by Tom Ang (London, UK: DK Publishing, 2002). This heavily illustrated book from renowned photographic lecturer Ang covers everything from the basics to the advanced image manipulation and editing.

The Essential Guide to Computer Data Storage: From Floppy to DVD, by Dr. Andrei Khurshudov (Upper Saddle River, NJ: Prentice Hall, 2001). This book provides in-depth explanations of a variety of PC peripherals and interface standards, including magnetic disks, optical discs, and storage for cameras and MP3 music players.

Direct from Dell: Strategies That Revolutionized an Industry, by Michael Dell with Catherine Fredman (New York: HarperBusiness, 1999). The inside story of how a college student from Texas turned his dorm room into the start of America's most successful computer company. Dell brought the "direct model" to the PC industry, forever changing how PC makers do business, and his company was the first lasting Internet success story, as he successfully transitioned from print ad sales to e-commerce.

Desktop Yoga, by Julie T. Lusk (New York: Perigee, 1998). Like any activity, computer work can be hazardous to your health if you don't exercise care and common sense. This book describes stretching and relaxation exercises for deskbound workers and students. If you spend hours a day in front of a computer screen, these activities can help you to take care of your body and mind.

Periodicals

E-media. This monthly magazine, aimed at multimedia professionals, includes extensive coverage of input, output, and storage technologies.

Computer Shopper. This monthly typically includes a few consumer-oriented articles, but it has evolved over time from an ad-based reference to a print version of CNET's popular shopper.com Web site, with reprints of reviews and editorials by the site's leading writers.

World Wide Web Pages

Most computer peripheral manufacturers have Web pages. The Computer Confluence Web site will guide you to many of the most interesting pages.

AFTER YOU READ THIS CHAPTER YOU SHOULD BE ABLE TO:

- Describe three fundamental categories of software and their relationship

- Explain the relationship of algorithms to software

- Discuss the factors that make a computer application a useful tool

- Describe the role of the operating system in a modern computer system

- Outline the evolution of user interfaces from early machine-language programming to futuristic virtual reality interfaces

Multimedia extras on the CD-ROM and the Web:

- Activities on how **operating systems** work and how programs are executed

- Video explaining what **Linux** is and why you might want to use it

- A **Program** is **executed** in an animated demo

- **Instant** access to glossary and key word references

- **Interactive** self-study quizzes

- **Free** software sources

    . . . *and more.*

 computerconfluence.com

SOFTWARE BASICS
The Ghost in the Machine

LINUS TORVALDS AND THE SOFTWARE NOBODY OWNS

When Linus Torvalds bought his first PC in 1991, he never dreamed it would be a critical weapon in a software liberation war. He just wanted to avoid waiting in line to get a terminal to connect to his university's mainframe. Torvalds, a 21-year-old student at the University of Helsinki in Finland, had avoided buying a PC because he didn't like the standard PC's "crummy architecture with this crummy MS-DOS operating system." But Torvalds had been studying operating systems, and he decided to try to build something on his own.

He based his work on Minix, a scaled-down textbook version of the powerful UNIX operating system designed to run on PC hardware. Little by little, he cobbled together pieces of a kernel, the part of the system where the real processing and control work is done.

When he mentioned his project on an Internet discussion group, a member offered him space to post it on a university server. Others copied it, tinkered with it, and sent the changes back to Torvalds. The communal work-in-progress eventually became known as Linux (pronounced "Linn-uks" by its creator). Within a couple of years, it was good enough to release as a product.

Instead of copyrighting and selling Linux, Torvalds made it freely available under the General Public License (GPL) developed by the Free Software Foundation. According to the GPL, anyone can give away, modify, or even sell Linux, as long as the source code—the program instructions—remain freely available for others to improve. Linux is the best-known

> I had **no idea** what I was doing. I knew I was the **best programmer in the world**. Every 21-year-old programmer knows that. "**How hard can it be**, it's just **an operating system?**"
>
> —Linus Torvalds

example of open source software, and now it spearheads the popular open source software movement.

Thousands of programmers around the world have worked on Linux, with Torvalds still at the center of the activity. Some do it because they believe there should be alternatives to expensive corporate products; others do it because they can customize the software; still others do

4.1 Linus Torvalds

it just for fun. As a result of all their efforts, Linux has matured into a powerful, versatile product with millions of users.

Today, Linux powers Web servers, film and animation workstations, scientific supercomputers, a handful of handheld computers, some general-use PCs, and even Internet-savvy appliances like refrigerators. Linux is especially popular among people who do computing on a tight budget—particularly in debt-ridden Third World countries.

The success of Linux has inspired Apple, Sun, Hewlett-Packard, and other software companies to release products with open source code. Even the mighty Microsoft is paying attention as this upstart operating system grows in popularity, and the company has responded with a pseudo-open source strategy covering its embedded products that compete directly with Linux.

Today, Torvalds is an Internet folk hero. Web pages pay homage to him, his creation, and the stuffed penguin, Tux, that has become the Linux mascot. In 1996, he completed his master's degree in computer science and went to work for Transmeta Corp., a chip design company in Silicon Valley. But he still spends hours every week online with the Linux legions, improving the operating system that belongs to everybody—and nobody.

4.2 Torvalds talking to Linux fans

Chapters 2 and 3 told only part of the story of how computers do what they do. Here's a synopsis of our story so far:

On one side we have a person—you, me, or somebody else—it hardly matters. We all have problems to solve—problems involving work, communication, transportation, finances, and more. Many of these problems cry out for computer solutions.

On the other side we have a computer—an incredibly sophisticated bundle of hardware capable of performing all kinds of technological wizardry. Unfortunately, the computer *recognizes only zeros and ones*.

A great chasm separates the person who has a collection of vague problems from the stark, rigidly bounded world of the computer. How can humans bridge the gap to communicate with the computer?

That's where software comes in. Software enables people to communicate certain kinds of problems to computers and makes it possible for computers to communicate solutions back to those people.

Modern computer software didn't just materialize out of the atmosphere; it evolved from the plug boards and patch cords and other hardware devices that were used to program early computers like the ENIAC. Mathematician John von Neumann, working with ENIAC's creators, J. Presper Eckert and John Mauchly, wrote a 1945 paper suggesting that program instructions could be stored with the data in memory. Every computer created since has been based on the *stored-program concept* described in that paper. That idea established the software industry.

Instead of flipping switches and patching wires, today's programmers write *programs*—sets of computer instructions designed to solve problems—and feed them into the computer's memory through keyboards and other input devices. These programs are the computer's software. Because software is stored in memory, a computer can switch from one task to another and then back to the first without a single hardware modification.

4.3 The communications gap . . .

For instance, the computer that serves as a word processor for writing this book can, at the click of a mouse, turn into an email terminal, a browser into the World Wide Web, a reference library, an accounting spreadsheet, a drawing table, a video editing workstation, a musical instrument, or a game machine.

What is software, and how can it transform a mass of circuits into an electronic chameleon? This chapter provides some general answers to that question along with details about each of the three major categories of software:

■ Compilers and other translator programs, which enable programmers to create other software

■ Software applications, which serve as productivity tools to help computer users solve problems

■ System software, which coordinates hardware operations and does behind-the-scenes work the computer user seldom sees.

Processing with Programs

Software is invisible and complex. To make the basic concepts clear, we start our exploration of software with a down-to-earth analogy.

> **Leonardo da Vinci** called music "**the shaping of the invisible**" and his phrase is **even more apt** as a description of **software**.
> —Alan Kay, conceiver of the notebook computer, user interface architect

Food for Thought

Think of the hardware in a computer system as the kitchen in a short-order restaurant: It's equipped to produce whatever output a customer (user) requests, but it sits idle until an order (command) is placed. Robert, the computerized chef in our imaginary kitchen, serves as the CPU, waiting for requests from the users/customers. When somebody provides an input command—say, an order for a plate of French toast—Robert responds by following the instructions in the appropriate recipe.

As you may have guessed, the recipe is the software. It provides instructions telling the hardware what to do to produce the output the user desires. If the recipe is correct, clear, and precise, the chef turns the input data—eggs, bread, and other ingredients—into the desired output—French toast. If the instructions are unclear or if the software has bugs, or errors, the output may not be what the user wanted.

For example, suppose Robert has this recipe for "Suzanne's French Toast Fantastique."

4.4 SUZANNE'S FRENCH TOAST FANTASTIQUE

1. Combine 2 slightly beaten eggs with 1 teaspoon vanilla extract, ½ teaspoon cinnamon, and ⅔ cup milk
2. Dip 6 slices of bread in mixture.
3. Fry in small amount of butter until golden brown.
4. Serve bread with maple syrup, sugar, or tart jelly.

This seemingly foolproof recipe has several trouble spots. Since step 1 doesn't say otherwise, Robert might include the shells in the "slightly beaten eggs." Step 2 says nothing about separating the six slices of bread before dipping them in the batter; Robert would be within the letter of the instruction if he dipped all six at once. Step 3 has at least two potential bugs. Since it doesn't specify what to fry in butter, Robert might conclude that the mixture, not the bread, should be fried. Even if Robert decides to fry the bread, he may let it overcook waiting for the butter to turn golden brown, or he may wait patiently for the top of the toast to brown while the bottom quietly blackens. Robert, like any good computer, just follows the instructions he's given.

A Fast, Stupid Machine

The **most useful** word in any computer language is **"oops."**

—David Lubar, in *It's Not a Bug, It's a Feature*

Our imaginary automated chef may not seem very bright, but he's considerably more intelligent than a typical computer's CPU. Computers are commonly called "smart machines" or "intelligent machines." In truth, a typical computer is incredibly limited, capable of doing only the most basic arithmetic operations (such as $7 + 3$ and $15 - 8$) and a few simple logical comparisons ("Is this number less than that number?" "Are these two values identical?").

Computers *seem* smart because they can perform these arithmetic operations and comparisons quickly and accurately. A typical desktop computer can do thousands of calculations in the time it takes you to pull your pen out of your pocket. A well-crafted program can tell the computer to perform a sequence of simple operations that, when taken as a whole, print a term paper, organize the student records for your school, or simulate a space flight. Amazingly, everything you've ever seen a computer do is the result of a sequence of extremely simple arithmetic and logical operations done very quickly. The challenge for software developers is to devise instructions that put those simple operations together in ways that are useful and appropriate.

Suzanne's recipe for French toast isn't a computer program; it's not written in a language that a computer can understand. But it could be considered an algorithm—a set of step-by-step procedures for accomplishing a task. A computer program generally starts as an algorithm written in English or some other human language. Like Suzanne's recipe, the initial algorithm is likely to contain generalities, ambiguities, and errors.

4.5 SUZANNE'S FRENCH TOAST FANTASTIQUE: THE ALGORITHM

1. Prepare the batter by following these instructions.
   1a. Crack 2 eggs so whites and yolks drop in bowl; discard shells.
   1b. Beat eggs slightly with wire whip, fork, or mixer.
   1c. Mix in 1 teaspoon vanilla extract, ½ teaspoon cinnamon, and ⅔ cup milk.
2. Place small amount of butter in frying pan and place on medium heat.
3. For each of 6 pieces of bread, follow these steps:
   3a. Dip slice of bread in mixture.
   3b. For each of the two sides of the bread do the following steps:
      3b1. Place the slice of bread in the frying pan with this (uncooked) side down.
      3b2. Wait 1 minute and then peek at underside of break; if lighter than golden brown, repeat this step.
   3c. Remove bread from fry pan and place on plate.
4. Serve bread with maple syrup, sugar, or tart jelly.

The programmer's job is to turn the algorithm into a program by adding details, hammering out rough spots, testing procedures, and debugging—correcting errors. For example, if we were turning Suzanne's recipe into a program for our electronic-brained short-order cook, we might start by rewriting it like the recipe shown here.

We've eliminated much of the ambiguity from the original recipe. Ambiguity, while tolerable (and sometimes useful) in conversations between humans, is a source of errors for computers. In its current form the recipe contains far more detail than any human chef would want but not nearly enough for a computer. If we were programming a computer (assuming we had one with input hardware capable of recognizing golden brown French toast and output devices capable of flipping the bread), we'd need to go into excruciating detail, translating every step of the process into a series of absolutely unambiguous instructions that could be interpreted and executed by a machine with a vocabulary smaller than that of a 2-year-old child!

The Language of Computers

Every computer processes instructions in a native machine language. Machine language uses numeric codes to represent the most basic computer operations—adding numbers, subtracting numbers, comparing numbers, moving numbers, repeating instructions, and so on. Early programmers were forced to write every program in a machine

> The programmer, **like the poet**, works only slightly removed from **pure thought-stuff**. He builds **castles in the air**, creating by exertion of the **imagination**. Yet the program construct, unlike the poet's words, is **real** in the sense that **it moves and works**, producing visible outputs **separate from the construct itself**.
>
> —Frederick P. Brooks, Jr., in *The Mythical Man Month*

language, tediously translating each instruction into binary code. This process was an invitation to insanity; imagine trying to find a single mistyped character in a page full of zeros and ones!

Today, most programmers use programming languages such as C++, C#, Java, and Visual Basic.NET that fall somewhere between natural human languages and precise machine languages. These languages, referred to as high-level languages, make it possible for scientists, engineers, and businesspeople to solve problems using familiar terminology and notation rather than cryptic machine instructions. For a computer to understand a program written in one of these languages, it must use a translator program to convert the English-like instructions to the zeros and ones of machine language.

To clarify the translation process, let's go back to the kitchen. Imagine a recipe translator that enables our computer chef to look up phrases like "fry until golden brown." Like a reference book for beginning cooks, this translator fills in all of the details of testing and flipping foods in the frying pan, so Robert understands what to do whenever he encounters "fry until golden brown" in any recipe. As long as our computer cook is equipped with the translator, we don't need to include so many details in each recipe. We can communicate at a higher level. The more sophisticated the translator, the easier the job of the programmer. The most common type of translator program is called a compiler because it compiles a complete translation of the program in a high-level computer language (such as C#) before the program runs for the first time. The compiled program can run again and again; it doesn't need to be recompiled unless instructions need to be changed.

Programming languages have steadily evolved during the last few decades. Each new generation of languages makes the programming process easier by taking on, and hiding from the programmer, more of the detail-oriented work. The computer's unrelenting demands for technical details haven't gone away; they're just handled automatically by translation software. As a result, programming is easier and less error prone. As translators become more sophisticated, programmers can communicate in computer languages that more closely resemble natural languages— the languages people speak and write every day.

Even with state-of-the-art computer languages, programming requires a considerable investment of time and brainpower. Fortunately, many tasks that required programming two decades ago can now be accomplished with spreadsheets, and graphics programs, and other easy-to-use software applications.

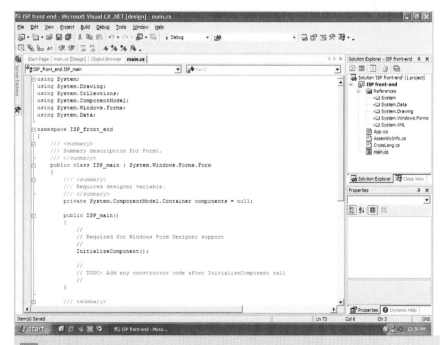

4.6 Compilers enable programmers to write in high-level languages such as C# (shown), C++, or Java.

4.1
Executing a Program

Most programs are composed of millions of simple machine language instructions. Here we'll observe the execution of a tiny part of a running program: a series of instructions that performs some arithmetic. The machine instructions are similar to those in actual programs, but the details have been omitted. The computer has already loaded (copied) the program from disk into memory so that the CPU can see it.

The CPU automatically fetches and executes instructions in sequence—from a series of consecutive memory addresses—unless it's told to "jump" somewhere else. The CPU is about to read the next instruction from memory location 100. This instruction and the ones that follow (in locations 101, 102, and 103) tell the CPU to read a couple of numbers from memory (locations 2000 and 2001), add them, and store the result back into memory (location 2002). Translated into English, the instructions look like this:

(100) Get (read) the number stored in memory address 2000 (not the number 2000, but the number stored in that location) and place it in register A.

(101) Get the number at memory address 2001 and place it in register B.

(102) Add the contents of registers A and B, placing the result in register C.

(103) Write (copy) the number in register C to memory address 2002.

For this example, let's suppose that memory location 2000 contains the number 7 and memory location 2001 contains 9.

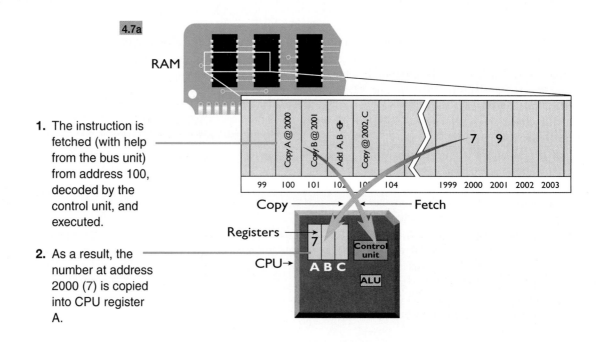

1. The instruction is fetched (with help from the bus unit) from address 100, decoded by the control unit, and executed.

2. As a result, the number at address 2000 (7) is copied into CPU register A.

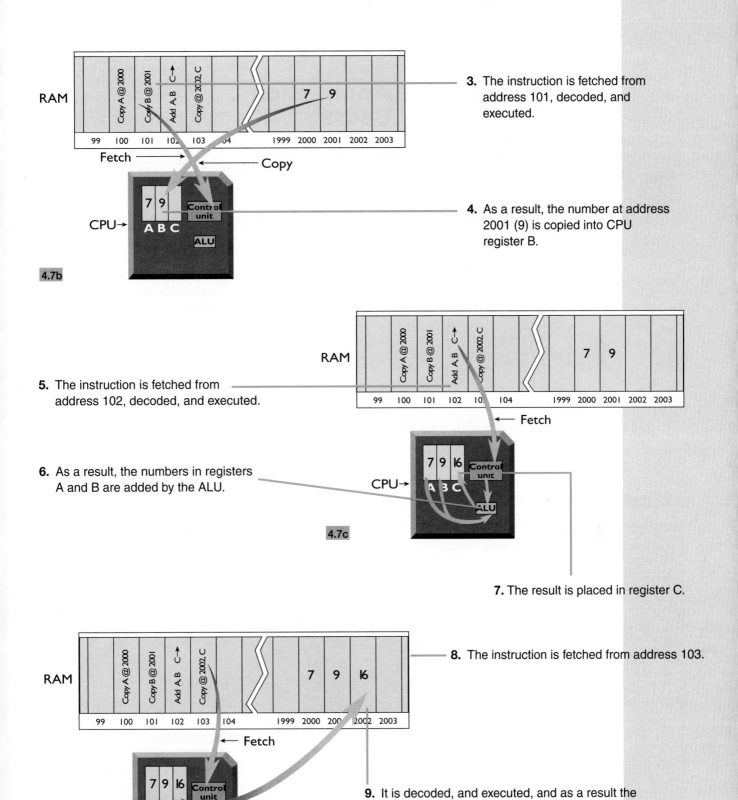

3. The instruction is fetched from address 101, decoded, and executed.

4. As a result, the number at address 2001 (9) is copied into CPU register B.

4.7b

5. The instruction is fetched from address 102, decoded, and executed.

6. As a result, the numbers in registers A and B are added by the ALU.

4.7c

7. The result is placed in register C.

8. The instruction is fetched from address 103.

9. It is decoded, and executed, and as a result the number in register C (16) is copied into memory location 2002.

4.7d

Programming languages are still used to solve problems that can't be handled with off-the-shelf software, but virtually all computer users manage to do their work without programming. Programming today is done mainly by professional software developers, who use programming languages to create and refine the applications and other programs the rest of us use.

Software Applications: Tools for Users

The computer is only a **fast idiot**, it has **no imagination**; it **cannot originate** action. It is, and will remain, **only a tool to man**.
—American Library Association reaction to the UNIVAC computer exhibit at the 1964 New York World's Fair

Software applications enable users to control computers without thinking like programmers. We now turn our attention to applications.

Consumer Applications

Computer and software stores, consumer electronics stores, and mail-order houses sell thousands of software titles: publishing programs, accounting software, personal-information managers, graphics programs, multimedia tools, educational titles, games, and more. The process of buying computer software is similar to the process of buying music software (audio CDs) to play on a stereo system. But there are some important differences; we'll touch on a few here.

Documentation

A computer software package generally includes printed documentation with instructions for installing the software on a computer's hard disk. Some software packages also include tutorial manuals and reference manuals that explain how to use the software. Many software companies have replaced these printed documents with tutorials, reference materials, and *help files* that appear on-screen at the user's request. Most help files are supplemented and updated with *online help* that can be accessed through the local help files or at the company's Web site. Many programs are so easy to use that it's possible to put them to work without reading the documentation. But many programs include advanced features that aren't obvious through trial-and-error experimentation.

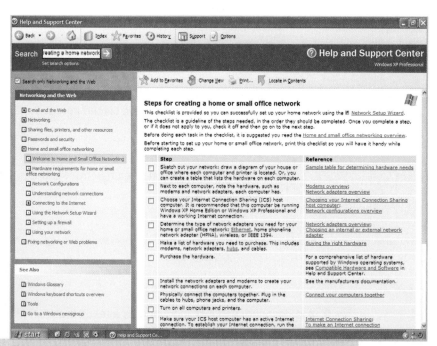

4.8 Most modern computer software provides some kind of online help on demand. Microsoft Windows provides context-sensitive help—help windows whose contents depend on what else is currently on the screen. Many software companies, including Microsoft, use Web databases to augment the help included with the system.

Upgrading

Most software companies continually work to improve their products by removing bugs and adding new features. As a result, new versions of many popular programs are released every year or two. To distinguish between versions, program names are generally followed by version numbers, such as 7.0 in Photoshop 7.0. Most companies use decimals to indicate minor revisions and whole numbers to indicate major revisions. For example, one can assume that Adobe Premiere 5.1, a video editing program, includes only a few more features than Premiere

5.0, while Premiere 6.0 should be significantly different from version 5.1. Not all software follows this logical convention. For example, the last several versions of Microsoft's consumer operating system have been marketed as Microsoft Windows 95 (version 4.0), Windows 98 (4.1), Windows Millennium Edition (Windows Me, version 4.9), and Windows XP Home Edition (5.1). When you buy a software program, you generally buy the current version. When a new version is released, you can upgrade your program to the new version by paying an upgrade fee to the software manufacturer.

Compatibility

A computer software buyer must be concerned with compatibility. When you buy an audio CD you don't need to specify the brand of your CD player, because all manufacturers adhere to common industry standards. But no complete, universal software standards exist in the computer world, so a program written for one type of computer system may not work on another. Software packages contain labels with statements such as "Requires Windows 9x, Me, or XP with 128MB of RAM." (An x in a version specification generally means "substitute any number" so "Windows 9x" means "Windows ninety-*something*.") These demands should not be taken lightly; without compatible hardware and software, most software programs are worthless.

Disclaimers

According to the little-read warranties included with many software packages, some applications might technically be worthless even if you have compatible hardware and software. Here's the first paragraph from a typical software warranty, which is part of a longer end-user license agreement (*EULA*, pronounced "yoo-la"):

> *This program is provided "as is" without warranty of any kind. The entire risk as to the result and performance of the program is assumed by you. Should the program prove defective, you—and not the manufacturer or its dealers—assume the entire cost of all necessary servicing, repair, or correction. Further, the manufacturer does not warranty, guarantee, or make any representations regarding the use of, or the result of the use of, the program in terms of correctness, accuracy, reliability, for being current, or otherwise, and you rely on the program and its results solely at your own risk.*

Software companies hide behind disclaimers because nobody's figured out how to write error-free software. Remember our problems providing Robert with a foolproof set of instructions for producing French toast? Programmers who write applications such as word processing programs must try to anticipate and respond to all combinations of commands and actions performed by users under any conditions. Given the difficulty of this task, most programs work amazingly well—but not perfectly.

Licensing

When you buy a typical computer software package, you're not actually buying the software. Instead, you're buying a software license to use the program, typically on a single machine. While end-user licensing agreements vary from company to company, most include limitations on your right to copy disks, install software on hard drives, and transfer information to other users. Many companies offer *volume licenses*—special licenses for entire companies, schools, or government institutions. Some companies even rent software to corporate and government clients.

Virtually all commercially marketed software is copyrighted so it can't be legally duplicated for distribution to others. Some software CDs and DVDs (mostly entertainment products) are physically *copy protected* so they can't be copied *at all*. A milder, more common form of copy protection is to require the user to type in his or her name and a product serial number before a newly installed program will work. Between these two extremes, some software doesn't work properly until the owner registers the software purchase via the Internet.

Because programming is so difficult, software development is expensive. Software developers use copyrights and copy protection to ensure that they sell enough copies of their products to recover their investments and stay in business to write programs.

Distribution

Software is distributed through direct sales forces to corporations and other institutions. Software is sold to consumers in computer stores, software specialty stores, book and record stores, and other retail outlets. Much software is sold through mail-order catalogs and Web sites. Web distribution makes it possible for some companies to offer software without packaging or disks. For example, you might download (copy) a demo version of a commercial program from a company's Web site or some other source; the demo program is identical to the commercial version, but with some key features disabled or a time limit placed on its usage. After you try the program and decide you want to buy it, you can often contact the company (by phone or through its Web site), pay (by credit card) for the full version of the program, and receive (by email) a code that you can type in to unlock the disabled features of the program.

Not all software is copyrighted and sold through commercial channels. Web sites, user groups, and other sources commonly offer public domain software (free for the taking) and shareware (free for the trying, with a send-payment-if-you-keep-it honor system) along with demonstration versions of commercial programs. Unlike copyrighted commercial software, public domain software, shareware, and demo software can be legally copied and shared freely.

Why We Use Applications

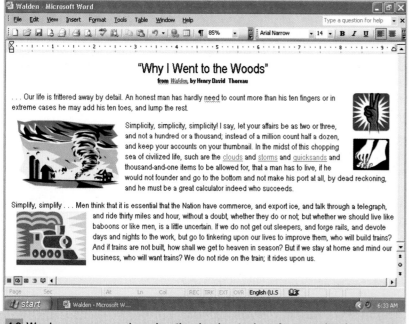

4.9 Word processors are based on the visual metaphor of a typewriter, but a modern word processor makes it easy to add graphics, video, and even Web links to an on-screen document.

It may seem strange that anyone would pay several hundred dollars for a product that comes with no warranty and dozens of legal restrictions about how you can use it. In fact, the rapidly growing software industry has spawned dozens of programs that have sold millions of copies. Why do so many people buy and use these hit programs? Of course, the answer varies from person to person and from product to product. But in general most successful software products share these two important characteristics:

■ *They are built around visual metaphors of real-world tools.* A drawing program turns the screen into a sheet of drawing paper and a collection of drawing tools. Spreadsheets resemble an accountant's ledger sheets. Video editing software puts familiar VCR controls on the screen. But if these programs merely mimicked their real-world counterparts, people would have no compelling reason to use them.

■ *They extend human capabilities in some way.* Popular programs enable people to do things that can't be done easily, or at all, with conventional tools. An artist using a graphics program can easily add an eye-catching distortion effect to a drawing and just as easily remove it if it doesn't look right. Spreadsheet programs enable managers to project future revenues based on best guesses and then instantly recalculate the bottom line with a different set of assumptions. And the possibilities opened up by computer video editing are mind-boggling. All kinds of software applications that extend human capabilities are the driving force behind the computer revolution.

Integrated Applications and Suites: Software Bundles

Although most software packages specialize in a particular application, such as word processing or photographic editing, low-priced integrated software packages include several applications designed to work well together. Popular integrated packages, such as AppleWorks and Microsoft Works, generally include simple word processing, database, spreadsheet, graphics, telecommunication, and personal-information management (PIM) modules.

The parts of an integrated package may not have all the features of their separately packaged counterparts, but integrated packages still offer advantages. They apply a similar look and feel to all of their applications so users don't need to memorize different commands and techniques for doing different tasks. The best integrated programs blur the lines between applications so, for example, you can create a table full of calculations right in the middle of a typed letter without explicitly switching from a word processor to a spreadsheet. Interapplication communication enables automatic transfer of data among applications, so, for example, changes in a financial spreadsheet are automatically reflected in a graphic table embedded in a word-processed memo.

These advantages aren't unique to integrated packages. Many software companies offer application suites—bundles containing several full application programs that are also sold as separate programs. The best-selling application suite, Microsoft Office System, comes in several different versions designed for different types of users. The core programs in Microsoft Office include Microsoft Word (a word processor), Excel (a spreadsheet program), PowerPoint (a presentation graphics program), Access (a database program), and Outlook (an email/personal-information management program). Microsoft has designed these applications so that they have similar command structures and easy interapplication communication. The price of a suite such as Microsoft Office is generally less than the total price of its applications purchased separately, but more than the cost of an integrated package such as Microsoft Works. Suites have more features than integrated programs but also make greater demands on system memory, disk storage, and the CPU. Many older computers simply aren't powerful enough to run a modern application suite. Still, Microsoft Office is the most widely used application package on newer PCs and Macintoshes.

4.10 AppleWorks is an integrated application program that combines several popular applications in an easy-to-use package.

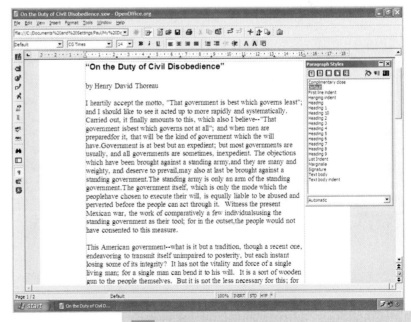

4.11 The open source application suite OpenOffice.org provides compatibility with Microsoft Office documents but runs on a variety of platforms, including Windows, Linux, and the Mac OS.

4.12 Vertical-market software helps this researcher track geographic information.

Vertical-Market and Custom Software

Because of their flexibility, word processors, spreadsheets, databases, and graphics programs are used in homes, schools, government offices, and all kinds of businesses. But many computer applications are so job specific that they're of little interest or use to anybody outside a given profession. Medical billing software, library cataloging software, legal reference software, restaurant management software, and other applications designed specifically for a particular business or industry are called vertical-market or custom applications.

Vertical-market applications tend to cost far more than mass-market applications, because companies that develop the software have very few potential customers through which to recover their development costs. In fact, some custom applications are programmed specifically for single clients. For example, the software used to control the space shuttle was developed with a single customer—NASA—in mind.

System Software: The Hardware–Software Connection

Originally, **operating systems** were envisioned as a way to handle one of the **most complex** input/output operations: **communicating** with a variety of **disk drives**. But, the operating system quickly **evolved** into **an all-encompassing bridge** between your PC and the software you run on it.

—Ron White, in *How Computers Work*

When you're typing a paper or writing a program, you don't need to concern yourself with low-level details, like which parts of the computer's memory hold your document, the segments of the word processing software currently in the computer's memory, or the output instructions sent by the computer to the printer. System software, a class of software that includes the *operating system* and *utility programs*, handles these details and hundreds of other tasks behind the scenes.

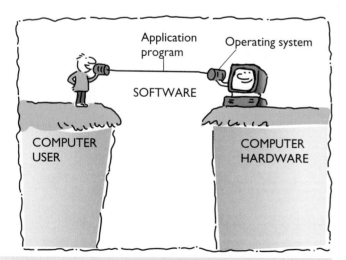

4.13 The user's view: When a person uses an application, whether a game or an accounting program, the person doesn't communicate directly with the computer hardware. Instead, the user interacts with the application, which depends on the operating system to manage and control hardware.

What the Operating System Does

Virtually every general-purpose computer today, whether it's a timesharing supercomputer or laptop PC, depends on an operating system (OS) to keep hardware running efficiently and to make the process of communication with that hardware easier. Operating system software runs continuously whenever the computer is on, providing an additional layer of insulation between you and the bits-and-bytes world of computer hardware. Because the operating system stands between the software application and the hardware, application compatibility is usually defined by the operating system as well as the hardware.

The operating system, as the name implies, is a system of programs that performs a variety of technical operations, from basic communication with peripherals to complex networking and security tasks.

Communicating with Peripherals

Some of the most complex tasks performed by a computer involve communicating with screens, printers, disk drives, and other peripheral devices. A computer's operating system includes programs that transparently communicate with peripherals.

Coordinating Concurrent Processing of Jobs

Large, multiuser computers often work on several jobs, or tasks, at the same time—a technique known as concurrent processing. State-of-the-art parallel-processing machines use multiple CPUs to process jobs simultaneously. But a typical computer has only one CPU, so it must work on several tasks by rapidly switching back and forth between them. The computer takes advantage of idle time in one process (for example, waiting for input) by working on another program. (Our computerized chef, Robert, might practice concurrent processing by slicing fruit while he waits for the toast to brown.) A timesharing computer practices concurrent processing whenever multiple users are connected to the system. The computer quickly moves from terminal to terminal, checking for input and processing each user's data in turn. If a PC has multitasking capabilities, the user can issue a command that initiates a process (for example, to print this chapter) and continue working with other applications while the computer executes the command.

Memory Management

When several jobs are being processed concurrently, the operating system must keep track of how the computer's memory is being used and make sure that no job encroaches on another's territory.

Memory management is accomplished in a variety of ways, from simple routines that subdivide the available memory between jobs to elaborate schemes that temporarily swap information between the computer's memory and external storage devices. One common technique for dealing with memory shortages is to set aside part of a hard disk as virtual memory. Thanks to the operating system, this chunk of disk space looks just like internal memory to the CPU, even though access time is considerably slower than with internal memory.

Resource Monitoring, Accounting, and Security

Many multiuser computer systems are designed to charge users for the resources they consume. These systems keep track of each user's time, storage demands, and pages printed so accounting programs can calculate and print accurate bills. Each user generally has a unique identification name and password, so the system can track and bill for individual resource usage. Even in environments where billing isn't an issue, the operating system should monitor resources to ensure the privacy and security of each user's data.

Program and Data Management

In addition to serving as a traffic cop, a security guard, and an accountant, the operating system acts as a librarian, locating and accessing files and programs requested by the user and by other programs.

Coordinating Network Communications

Until recently, network communications weren't handled by typical desktop operating systems used by consumers; instead, they were handled by specialized network operating systems. But modern operating systems are designed to serve as gateways to networks, from the inner office to the Internet, so networking is now a central feature of all modern operating systems. These network communication functions are described in detail in later chapters.

4.2
The Operating System

Most of what you see on-screen when you use an application program and most of the common tasks you have the program perform, such as saving and opening files, are being performed by the operating system at the application's request.

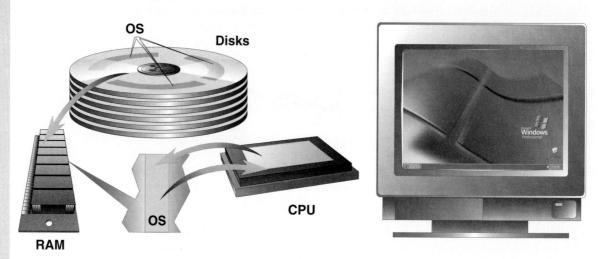

4.14a

When a computer is turned off, there's nothing in RAM and the CPU isn't doing anything. The operating system (OS) programs must be in memory and running on the CPU before the system can function. When you turn on the computer, the CPU automatically begins executing instructions stored in ROM. These instructions help the system boot, and the operating system is loaded from disk into part of the system's memory.

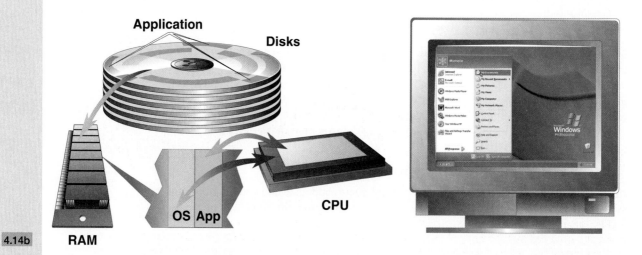

4.14b

Using the mouse, you "ask" the operating system to load a word processing application program into memory so it can run.

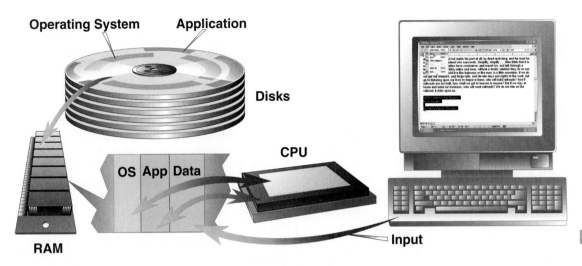

Operating System Application

Disks

CPU

OS | App | Data

RAM

Input

4.14c

The loaded application occupies a portion of memory, leaving that much less for other programs and data. The OS remains in memory, so it can provide services to the application program, helping it to display on-screen menus, communicate with the printer, and perform other common actions. Because the OS and application are in constant communication, control—the location in memory where the CPU is reading program instructions—jumps all around. If the application calls the OS to help display a menu, the application tells the CPU, "Go follow the menu display instructions at address x in the operating system area; when you're done, return here and pick up where you left off."

Disks

Save

CPU

OS | App | Data

RAM

4.14d

To avoid losing your data file when the system is turned off, you save it to the disk—write it into a file on the disk for later use. The OS handles communication between the CPU and the disk drive, ensuring that your file doesn't overwrite other information. (Later, when you reopen the file, the OS locates it on the disk and copies it into memory so the CPU—and therefore any program—can see it and work with it.)

Utility Programs and Device Drivers

Even the best operating systems leave some housekeeping tasks to other programs and to the user. Utility programs serve as tools for doing system maintenance and repairs that aren't automatically handled by the operating system. Utilities make it easier for users to copy files between storage devices, to repair damaged data files, to translate files so that different programs can read them, to guard against viruses and other potentially harmful programs (as described in the chapter on computer security and risks), to compress files so they take up less disk space, and to perform other important, if unexciting, tasks.

The operating system can directly invoke many utility programs, so they appear to the user to be part of the operating system. For example, device drivers are small programs that enable I/O devices—keyboard, mouse, printer, and others—to communicate with the computer. Once a device driver—say, for a new printer—is installed, the printer driver functions as a behind-the-scenes intermediary whenever the user requests that a document be printed on that printer. Some utility programs are included with the operating system. Others, including many device drivers, are bundled with peripherals. Still others are sold or given away as separate products.

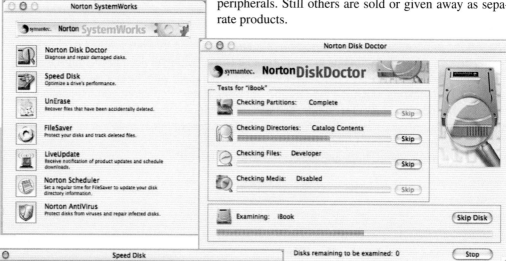

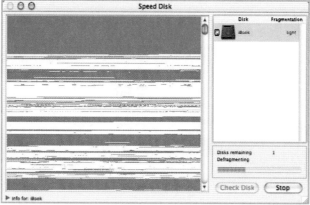

4.15 Symantec Norton Utilities is a popular utility package that includes software tools for recovering damaged files, repairing damaged disks, and improving disk performance.

Where the Operating System Lives

Some computers—mostly game machines, handheld computers, and special-purpose computers—store their operating systems permanently in ROM (read-only memory) so they can begin working immediately when turned on. But since ROM is unchangeable, these machines can't have their operating systems modified or upgraded without hardware transplants. Some computers, including many handheld devices, store their operating system in flash memory so they can be upgraded. But most computers, including all modern PCs, include only a very small portion of the operating system in ROM. The remainder of the operating system is loaded into memory in a process called booting, which occurs when you turn on the computer. (The term *booting* is used because the computer seems to pull itself up by its own bootstraps.)

Most of the time the operating system works behind the scenes, taking care of business without the knowledge or intervention of the user. But occasionally it's necessary for a user to communicate directly with the operating system. For example, when you boot a PC, the operating system takes over the screen, waiting until you tell it—with the mouse, the keyboard, or some other input device—what to do. If you tell it to open a graphics application, the operating system locates the program, copies it from disk into memory, turns the screen over to the application, and then accepts commands from the application while you draw pictures on the screen.

Interacting with the operating system, like interacting with an application, can be intuitive or challenging. It depends on something called the *user interface*. Because of its profound impact on the computing experience, the user interface is a critically important component of almost every piece of software.

The User Interface: The Human–Machine Connection

Early computer users had to spend tedious hours writing and debugging machine language instructions. Later users programmed in languages that were easier to understand but still technically challenging. Today, users spend much of their time working with preprogrammed applications, such as

> The anthropologist Claude Levi-Strauss has called human beings **tool makers** and **symbol makers**. The user interface is potentially **the most sophisticated** of these constructions, one in which the **distinction between tool and symbol is blurred**.
> —Aaron Marcus and Andries van Dam, user interface experts

word processors, that simulate and amplify the capabilities of real-world tools. As software evolves, so does the user interface—the look and feel of the computing experience from a human point of view.

Desktop Operating Systems

The earliest PC operating systems, created for the Apple II, the original IBM PC, and other machines, looked nothing like today's Macintosh and Windows operating systems. When IBM introduced its first personal computer in 1981, a typical computer monitor displayed 24 80-column lines of text, numbers, and/or symbols. The computer sent messages to the monitor telling it which character to display in each location on the screen. To comply with this hardware arrangement, the PC's dominant operating system, MS-DOS, was designed with a character-based interface—a user interface based on characters rather than graphics.

MS-DOS (Microsoft Disk Operating System, often simply called just DOS) became the standard operating system on IBM-compatible computers—computers functionally identical to an IBM personal computer and therefore capable of running IBM-compatible software. Unlike the Windows desktop, MS-DOS used a command-line interface

4.16 The user's view revisited: The user interface is the part of the computer system that the user sees. A well-designed user interface hides the bothersome details of computing from the user.

where the user typed commands and the computer responded. Some MS-DOS-compatible applications had a command-line interface, but it was more common for applications to have a menu-driven interface that enabled users to choose commands from on-screen lists called menus.

In the years since the introduction of the original IBM PC, graphic displays have become the norm. A computer with a graphic display is not limited to displaying rows and columns of characters; it can individually control every dot on the screen. When the Apple Macintosh was introduced in 1984, it was the first low-cost computer whose operating system was designed with a graphic display in mind. The Mac OS sports a graphical user interface—abbreviated GUI, and pronounced "gooey."

Instead of reading typed commands and file names from a command line, the Macintosh operating system determines what the user wants by monitoring movements of

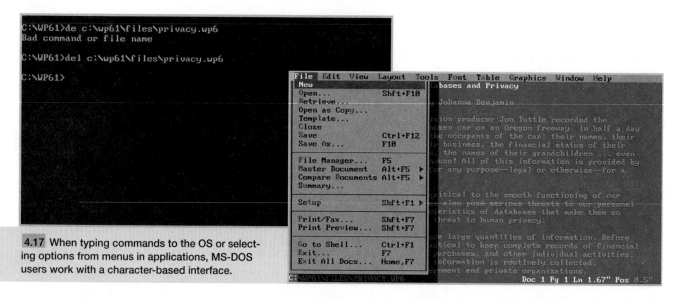

4.17 When typing commands to the OS or selecting options from menus in applications, MS-DOS users work with a character-based interface.

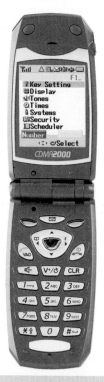

4.18 Many consumer devices today, including VCRs, cell phones, and pagers, use character-based user interfaces.

the mouse. With the mouse the user points to **icons** (pictures) that represent applications, **documents** (files, such as term papers and charts created with applications), **folders** (collections of files, sometimes called *directories*), and disks. These pictures are arranged on a metaphorical **desktop**—a virtual workspace designed to resemble in some ways the physical desktops we use in day-to-day work. Documents are displayed in **windows**—framed areas that can be opened, closed, and rearranged with the mouse. The user selects commands from **pull-down menus** at the top of the screen. **Dialog boxes** enable users to specify preferences by simply filling in on-screen blanks and clicking check boxes and buttons.

Though it was first to market, the Macintosh was eclipsed in the GUI operating system market by a product from Microsoft, the company that produces MS-DOS. Originally,

4.19 Mac OS X refines the traditional graphical user interface with a modern take on windows, icons, and pull-down menus.

Microsoft Windows (commonly called *Windows*) was a type of program, known as a shell, which put a graphical face on MS-DOS. The Windows shell stood between the user and the operating system, translating mouse movements and other user input into commands that could be recognized by MS-DOS. With the introduction of Windows 95 in 1995, Microsoft began transitioning Windows from an operating system shell into a full operating system that seldom showed its MS-DOS roots. Today, the latest Windows version, Windows XP, has no ties at all to the DOS past.

Windows and the Mac OS have evolved over the years, adding new features to their GUIs to make them easier to use. The Windows *task bar* provides one-click access to open applications and other windows, making it easy to switch back and forth between different tasks. Hierarchical menus in both Windows and Mac OS organize frequently needed commands into compact, efficient submenus, and pop-up menus can appear anywhere on the screen. Many of these menus are context-sensitive; that is, the choices they offer depend on what on-screen object is currently selected.

While there are many differences between Windows and Mac OS, the two now have user interfaces that are more alike than different. Many applications, including Adobe Photoshop and Microsoft Office, are almost identical on Windows and the Mac OS. Many users effortlessly switch back and forth between the two operating systems every day. (For a more thorough introduction to Windows and Mac OS, see Chapter 0: "The Basics.")

4.20 Windows replaced MS-DOS as the standard operating system for PCs years ago, and Windows XP, the latest Windows version, features and innovative task-based user interface that adapts to the type of data the user is viewing, making this system easier to use and more operating systems (OS); Microsoft Windows.

File Management: Where's My Stuff?

An operating system acts as an interface layer between the computer user and the user's data. Windows and the Mac OS employ a user interface that represents computer data as files inside folders on a virtual desktop. As with a typical desk in the real world, these files can be scattered all over the system, making data management difficult.

> The first principle of human interface design, whether for a **doorknob** or a **computer**, is to keep in mind the **human being** who wants to use it. **The technology is subservient to that goal**.
> —Donald Norman, in *The Art of Human–Computer Interface Design*

One solution to this problem is to organize data files logically. To this end, both Windows and the Mac support the notion of common system folders with self-explanatory names. For example, your documents might be stored in a folder called *My Documents* (*Documents* in Mac OS X). Likewise, digital photos can be stored in *My Pictures* (*Pictures*) and digital music files can be stored in *My Music* (*Music*). These folders are specific to each user, so multiple users on a single PC will each have unique data in their system folders.

Modern operating systems include search tools that can help find files wherever they're stored. In Windows you can search for file names, but you can also search for words or phrases inside a file. So if you don't know the name of a file—a fairly common occurrence—but do know some of the text that might be contained in that file, you can still use the search tool to find your data. In Mac OS X you can find information on your local hard drive using the integrated Find tool, which is similar to the Windows Search. Mac OS X also includes a special tool called Sherlock for finding information online.

The search and find commands are designed to help answer the common computer user's question, "Where's my stuff? Windows and the Mac were originally designed when today's massive hard disks seemed like a distant fantasy and low-capacity floppy disk drives seemed spacious. As our PCs grow to store more and more vital data, Apple and Microsoft are developing innovative techniques for helping people keep track of their data files.

In recent years, Apple has emphasized the Macintosh's role as a digital media hub with applications such as iTunes, iMovie, and iPhoto. (We cover these applications in Chapter 6). But the proliferation of digital media files on a typical Mac's hard drive makes the folders-and-windows GUI less effective than ever for finding particular songs, photos, or movies. Apple has included a view-based interface in many of its digital media applications; this innovative interface presents a simpler way of organizing and finding the files you want.

For example, iTunes supports the notion of playlists, which divide a complete music library into more digestible chunks. Some playlists are made manually by the user. Others are created automatically by iTunes. These automatic playlists include such things as *Top 25 Most Played* and *60's Music*. Apple iTunes also supports smart playlists, which can be automatically populated with songs based on database-like criteria. For example, you might rate the songs in your music library and then create a smart playlist that displays only those songs that received your highest ratings. This smart playlist is a *live* list of your favorite songs—one that changes automatically as you rate newly imported or purchased music.

The next major Windows version will include database capabilities in the file system so that you can more easily locate information stored anywhere in your PC. Like the smart playlist feature in Apple iTunes, this feature will help users find their stuff more quickly and easily, while shielding them from the intricacies of the underlying system. And as we move toward distributed computing environments, where data might be stored on different systems on a network or across the Internet, these technologies will become even more valuable.

Multiple-User Operating Systems: UNIX and Linux

Because of its historical ties to academic and government research sites, the Internet is still heavily populated with computers running the UNIX operating system. UNIX, developed at Bell Labs over a decade before the first PCs, enables a timesharing computer to communicate with several other computers or terminals at one time. UNIX has long been the operating system of choice for workstations and mainframes in research and academic settings. In recent years it has taken root in many business environments. In spite of competition from Microsoft, UNIX is still the most widely available multiuser operating system today. Some form of UNIX is available for personal computers, workstations, servers, mainframes, and supercomputers.

Because of widespread licensing, commercial brands of UNIX are available from many companies, including Sun (Solaris), Hewlett Packard (HP-UX), and IBM (AIX). Most Mac users don't know it, but Mac OS X is built around a version of UNIX. Linux, a UNIX clone described at the beginning of this chapter, is widely distributed for free and supported without cost by a devoted, technically savvy group of users.

At its heart, in all its versions, UNIX is a command-line, character-based operating system. The command-line interface is similar to that of MS-DOS, although the commands aren't the same. For most tasks the UNIX command-line interface feels like a single-user system, even when many users are *logged in*—connected to and using the system. But today's UNIX systems don't just work with typed commands. Several companies, including Apple, Sun, and IBM, market UNIX variations and shells with graphical interfaces.

```
UNIX(r) System V Release 4.0


login: sanchez
Password:
AFS (R) 3.4 Login

=================================================================

=Welcome to node ai.asu.edu - Sparc 20 1000 running Solaris 2.3=
      =This system is only for use authorized by ASU=

=================================================================


You have mail.
Terminal type is vt100
Erase is Backspace
type 'menu' without quotes and press the enter key for our menu


ai > ls
AppleVolumes      Mail            dead.letter
Backup            Work            mbox
School            Reports         News
booklist          saved.notes     readme
ai > pine
```

4.21 In its basic form, UNIX is a character based operating system. This screen shows the beginning of a session on a school's multi-user Unix mainframe. After the user (sanchez) types her login name and password, the system responds with some introductory messages and a prompt (in this case, ai>). Sanchez types the "ls" command to view the names of files in her home directory. The system lists the files and then displays a new prompt. Sanchez types "pine" to run the pine email program. The session continues this way until sanchez responds to a prompt with a command to log off the system.

4.22a GNOME is a graphical Linux shell with a customizable user interface; here it's configured with familiar features of Windows and the Macintosh OS. You select the document you wish to open using the GUI in a manner similar to that used in Windows and Mac OS X.

4.22b Alternatively, you could simply launch OpenOffice.org Writer and use the standard Open dialog to locate the file you want.

4.22c When the document opens, you can edit it as you would with Microsoft Word on Windows or the Mac. In fact, OpenOffice.org lets you open and save Word documents so you can interoperate with Mac and Windows users.

Hardware and Software Platforms

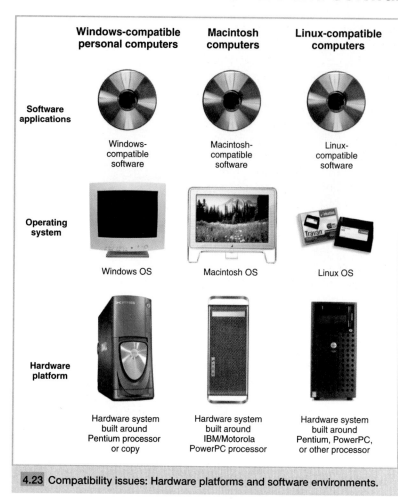

4.23 Compatibility issues: Hardware platforms and software environments.

In most electronic devices the operating system operates invisibly and anonymously. But some operating systems, especially those in PCs, are recognized by name and reputation. The most well-known operating systems include:

- *Microsoft Windows XP.* This is Microsoft's flagship product introduced in 2001. Microsoft sells different versions of Windows XP, including Windows XP Home Edition, for home users; Windows XP Professional, for business users; Windows XP Tablet PC Edition, for Tablet PC-style notebooks; and Windows XP Media Center Edition, for a new generation of multimedia-enabled PCs that are typically used in a den instead of the home office. All of these products are based on the same core operating system code. Windows XP is a more recent and enhanced version of Windows 2000 Professional, which was aimed solely at business users. Both Windows XP and Windows 2000 are technically successors to Windows NT, not Windows 9x/DOS.

- *Windows Server 2003.* Essentially the server-based counterpart to Windows XP and the successor to the Windows 2000 Server product family, this version of Windows runs on everything from small Web servers up to the mightiest hardware on the planet. This product competes directly with many server versions of UNIX and LINUX.

- *Microsoft Windows Millennium Edition (Windows Me)/Windows 9x.* This is Microsoft's last "consumer" operating system before XP Home Edition and the end of the DOS-based Windows versions. Previous versions of this OS include Windows 98, Windows 95, and Windows 3.1; Windows 98 is still widely used.

- *Microsoft Windows CE.NET.* This stripped-down Windows variant is designed mostly for embedded, connected devices, and a special version of the OS, targeted at handheld computers like the Pocket PC and smart cell phones, competes directly with Palm's operating system (see following).

- *Palm OS.* This OS, originally developed for the Palm Pilot, is now used in handheld devices manufactured by many companies, including Palm, Handspring, and Sony. Its pen-based user interface is simple and convenient to use. The Palm OS has communication capabilities that make it easy to transfer data between a handheld device and another computer. Palm OS is now also available in phones and other communication devices.

- *Mac OS X (10).* Introduced in 2001, OS X is the latest operating system for the Mac. It sports a stylish, animated user interface that looks strikingly different from previous Mac operating systems. Underneath its friendly exterior, OS X is built on UNIX, the powerful OS known for security and stability rather than simplicity. OS X runs only on Macintosh hardware.

- *Mac OS 9.* This is the last in a long line of Macintosh operating systems that started with the original Mac system in 1984. OS 9 and its predecessors run only on Macs.

- *Linux, Sun Solaris, and other UNIX variations.* Some form of UNIX or Linux can be found on PCs, Macs, workstations, supercomputers, mainframes, and a variety of other devices. Linux is especially popular because it is free—and freely supported by its partisans. Since Linux doesn't offer as many applications programs as Windows, some people use *dual-boot PCs* that can switch back and forth between Windows and Linux by simply rebooting.

Operating systems by themselves aren't very helpful to people. They need application software so they can do useful work. But application software can't exist by itself; it needs to be built on some kind of platform. People often use the term *platform* to describe the combination of hardware and operating system software on which application software is built. *Cross-platform applications*, such as Microsoft Office and Adobe Photoshop, are programs that are available in similar versions for multiple platforms.

The trends are unmistakable. In the early days of the personal computer revolution, there were dozens of different platforms—machines from Apple, Atari, Coleco, Commodore, Tandy, Texas Instruments, and other companies. All of these products have vanished from the marketplace, sometimes taking their parent companies with them. Today's market for new PC hardware and software is dominated by three general platforms: Windows in all its variations, the Mac OS, and various versions of UNIX/Linux. UNIX isn't often found in desktop PCs; it's mostly used in servers and high-end workstations. While the Mac commands a decent share of specialized markets like graphic design, publishing, music, video, and multimedia, it runs far behind Windows in the massive corporate and home markets.

Most personal computers today are built on what's sometimes called the "Wintel" platform: some form of the Windows OS running on an Intel (or compatible) CPU. The Macintosh platform—Mac OS software running on PowerPC processors—makes up a much smaller segment of the market. The Linux OS can run on many hardware platforms, including Intel and PowerPC processors, but different versions of Linux aren't necessarily compatible.

To interoperate with the Windows-dominated world, Mac users can buy software programs that create a simulated Windows machine in the Mac, translating all Windows-related instructions into signals the Mac's operating system and CPU can understand. Translation takes time, however, so software *emulation* often isn't adequate when speed is critical. But emulation blurs the lines between platforms and enables users to avoid having to choose a single operating system and user interface.

With the growing importance of the Internet and other networks, future applications may be more tied to networks than to desktop computer platforms. Computer users are spending less time dealing with information stored locally on their desktop computers and more time on the Web. Microsoft has responded to that trend with .NET, a strategy that blurs the line between the Web and Microsoft's operating systems and applications. As .NET evolves, more and more software components will be delivered by the network rather than residing on the desktop.

4.24 Virtual machine software such as Virtual PC, available on both Mac and Windows platforms, lets users run Windows and Linux environments inside of a window on the host OS and move data back and forth between the virtual machine and the host OS.

Microsoft's .NET strategy is a response to the popularity of Java, a platform-neutral computer language developed by Sun Microsystems for use on multiplatform networks. Programs written in Java can run on computers running Windows, Macintosh, UNIX, and other operating systems, provided those computers have *Java virtual machine* software installed. However, like emulation software, Java applications run more slowly than applications targeted to a specific OS platform. Small Java *applets*—miniature application pieces designed to work with other applications or applets—are often included in World Wide Web pages today to add animation and interactivity. As this technology matures, it may make it possible for computer users to do their work without knowing—or caring—where in the world their software is.

Tomorrow's User Interfaces

I **hate** computers. **Telepathy** would be better.

—John Perry Barlow, writer and cofounder of the Electronic Frontier Foundation

Twenty years ago the typical computer could be operated only by a highly trained professional, and using a computer was pretty much synonymous with programming a computer. Today, computers are so easy to use that they're sold at shopping malls and operated by preschoolers.

The graphical user interface pioneered by Xerox and popularized by Apple and Microsoft has become an industry standard, making it possible for users to move back and forth between computer types almost as easily as drivers can adjust to different brands of cars. But experts expect user interfaces to continue to evolve before they settle down into the kind of long-lasting standard we're used to in automobiles. Today's WIMP (windows, icons, menus, and pointing devices) interface is easier to learn and use than earlier character-based interfaces, but it's not the end of the user interface evolution.

Researcher Raj Reddy uses another acronym to describe emerging user interface technologies: SILK, for speech, image, language, and knowledge capabilities. SILK incorporates many important software technologies:

➡ **Speech and language.** Although we still don't have a language-translating telephone or a foolproof dictation-taking "talkwriter," speech technology is maturing into a practical alternative to keyboard and mouse input. Voice recognition systems are used for security systems, automated voicemail systems, hands-free Web navigation, and other applications. New applications are being developed and marketed every day. With or without speech, natural language processing will be part of future user interfaces. It's just a matter of time before we'll be able to communicate with computers in English, Spanish, Japanese, or some other natural language. Today, many computers can reliably read subsets of these languages or can be trained to understand spoken commands and text. Tomorrow's machines should be able to handle much day-to-day work through a natural-language interface, written or spoken. Researchers expect that we'll soon be using programs that read documents as we create them, edit them according to our instructions, and file them based on their content.

➡ **Image.** In the last decade computer graphics have become an integral part of the computing experience. Tomorrow's graphics won't just be still, flat images; they'll include three-dimensional models, animation, and video clips. Today's two-dimensional desktop interfaces will give way to three-dimensional workspace metaphors complete with 3-D animated objects—

4.25 Virtual reality user interfaces can enhance research and recreation. In Argonne's CAVE (top), a scientist can interactively study the relationships between the nucleic acids of the molecule. In a similar CAVE (bottom) at the Center for Supercomputer Applications at the University of Illinois, a student plays a CAVE version of Quake II, a 3-D video game.

virtual workspaces unlike anything we use today. Virtual reality (VR) user interfaces will create the illusion that the user is immersed in a world inside the computer—an environment that contains both scenes and the controls to change those scenes. (Virtual reality is discussed in more detail in the Chapter 6 *Inventing the Future*.)

➡ **Knowledge.** Many experts predict that knowledge will be the most important enhancement to the user interface of the future. Advances in the technology of knowledge will enable engineers to design self-maintaining systems that can diagnose and correct common problems without human intervention. Advances in knowledge will make user interfaces more friendly and forgiving. Intelligent applications will be able to decipher many ambiguous commands and correct common errors as they happen. But more important, knowledge will enable software agents to really be of service to users. Software agents are discussed in next chapter's *Inventing the Future*.

The Bugs in the Machine

Brendan I. Koerner

Computer software is plagued by bugs—errors in the instructions that create incorrect results, system failures, or worse. In this article from the August, 2002 issue of Wired, *writer Brendan I. Koerner explores the implications of buggy software that's burned into firmware. Are bugs making our tools and toys unsafe?*

Ed Yourdon was on a tarmac in Pittsburgh when he got a glimpse of the coming software hell. His New York shuttle had been cleared for takeoff when the pilot pulled a U-turn and headed back to the gate. The flaps were stuck. "We're going to have to power down and reboot," the pilot announced. It was the aeronautical equivalent of Ctrl+Alt+Delete. "Makes you think," says Yourdon, author of *Byte Wars*. "Maybe they had Windows 95 underneath the hood."

He's not necessarily joking. The so-called embedded systems crammed into jets, cars, and "smart" appliances increasingly rely on the same bug-ridden code that corrupts PowerPoint slides, freezes *Ultima* games midquest, and costs corporate America $293 billion a year in lost productivity. "They're starting to put Windows CE into automobile dashboards," says Philip Koopman, a computer engineer at Carnegie Mellon University. "What used to be some gears and springs is now a sophisticated computing complex. Think about it."

Or don't, if you scare easily. The software industry's nasty secret is that—surprise!—off-the-shelf code doesn't magically turn trustworthy once it's jammed behind a steering wheel. This sleight of hand wouldn't be so alarming if lives weren't at stake. But imagine the blue screen of death at highway speed.

The problem is built into the software industry. There are 5 to 15 flaws in every 1,000 lines of code, the Software Engineering Institute estimates. Mindful of cost-benefit ratios, vendors have little incentive to boost quality; it's cheaper to write postrelease patches than to spend months triple-checking every string of code. Even if they wanted to churn out more reliable products, most programmers lack the skills. Point-and-click development aids like Visual C++ have turned software creation into a *For Dummies* exercise.

That reality is now making its way into embedded systems. Code-imbued hardware, once built as a cohesive whole by in-house designers, is more and more likely to incorporate off-the-shelf software. Only 40 percent of embedded operating systems are made from scratch, a figure sure to drop as Microsoft and its Linux rivals push their cheaper options. Why assemble a novel OS when you can shoehorn in Windows 2005 Embedded?

So laptops crash, government servers botch Medicaid requests, and the occasional NASA robot goes haywire on Mars—c'est la vie digitale, right? Except that buggy software is creeping into systems where failure can't be dismissed with curses and a sigh. Consider: Darpa is using wearable computers designed to beam tactical information to the "data visors" of combat troops. The devices run Windows 2000, an OS so flawed that its bug-cleansing "service packs" run to 100 Mbytes. A sniper-filled valley near Mazar-i-Sharif would be a particularly lousy spot to encounter a Runtime Error pop-up. Or take mobile phones. They worked fine when telephony was their sole task. Now that they're equipped with Web browsers and GPS chips, software glitches are routine. If you're one of the 200,000 Americans a day who dial 911 on a cell, shabby code could be a real downer. And the problem will only get worse as the tech industry's weakness for bloatware infects all those code-enriched gizmos now on the drawing board—refrigerators that email repairmen, alarms that sniff chemical leaks, cars with drive-by-wire setups.

Yet the shoddiness of these products is hardly inevitable. With a bit more elbow grease, software designers can write increasingly reliable code. One smart move would be to use mutation testing, a quality-control technique that flushes out errors by analyzing the behavior of software that's deliberately infested with bugs. Though effective, it's rarely used by commercial coders because it adds to development costs. But if software jockeys are going to be responsible for lives as well as spreadsheets, their fixation on the bottom line must change.

ONE SOLUTION IS TO UNLEASH THE LAWYERS

If it doesn't, there's always the American way: Unleash the lawyers. At the moment, shrink-wrap licenses and clickthrough agreements shield software makers from damage claims—even if they broke it, you bought it. Just as the legal fallout from exploding Pintos shamed Detroit, exposing software to class-action lawsuits might induce Silicon Valley to code more cautiously.

Of course, there will be bobsledding in Hades before the software industry willingly accepts such an arrangement. Software is intrinsically complex, lobbyists might aver, and bugs are an ineradicable part of the bargain. Let them think that—at least until the day they find themselves aloft in a plane that needs to reboot.

DISCUSSION QUESTIONS

1. Are you troubled by the idea of a car or airplane running on Windows, Linux, or some other commercial operating system? Why or why not?

2. *What do you think can be done to make products with embedded code safer?*

SUMMARY

Software provides the communication link between humans and their computers. Because software is soft—stored in memory rather than hard-wired into the circuitry—it can easily be modified to meet the needs of the computer user. By changing software, you can change a computer from one kind of tool into another.

Most software falls into one of three broad categories: compilers and other translator programs, software applications, and system software. A compiler is a software tool that enables programs written in Englishlike languages such as Visual Basic, .NET, and C# to be translated into the zeros and ones of the machine language the computer understands. A compiler frees the programmer from the tedium of machine language programming, making it easier to write quality programs with fewer bugs. But even with the best translators, programming is a little like communicating with an alien species. It's a demanding process that requires more time and mental energy than most people are willing or able to invest.

Fortunately, software applications make it easy for most computer users today to communicate their needs to the computer without learning programming. Applications simulate and extend the properties of familiar real-world tools like typewriters, paintbrushes, and file cabinets, making it possible for people to do things with computers that would be difficult or impossible otherwise. Integrated software packages combine several applications in a single unified package, making it easy to switch between tools. For situations when a general commercial program won't do the job, programmers for businesses and public institutions develop vertical-market and custom packages.

Whether you're writing programs or simply using them, the computer's operating system is functioning behind the scenes, translating your software's instructions into messages that the hardware can understand. An operating system serves as the computer's business manager, taking care of the hundreds of details that need to be handled to keep the computer functioning. A timesharing operating system has the particularly challenging job of serving multiple users concurrently, monitoring the machine's resources, keeping track of each user's account, and protecting the security of the system and each user's data. Many of those system-related problems that the operating system can't solve directly can be handled by utility programs. Popular operating systems today include several versions of Microsoft Windows, the Mac OS, and several versions of UNIX.

Applications, utilities, programming languages, and operating systems all must, to varying degrees, communicate with the user. A program's user interface is a critical factor in that communication. User interfaces have evolved over the years to the point where sophisticated software packages can be operated by people who know little about the inner workings of the computer. A well-designed user interface shields the user from the bits and bytes, creating an on-screen façade or shell that makes sense to the user. Today, the computer industry has moved away from the tried-and-true command-line interfaces toward a friendlier graphical user interface that uses windows, icons, mice, and pull-down menus in an intuitive, consistent environment. Tomorrow's user interfaces are likely to depend more on voice, three-dimensional graphics, and animation to create an artificial reality.

KEY TERMS

.NET (p. 147)
agents (p. 148)
algorithm (p. 128)
application suite (p. 135)
booting (p. 140)
bug (p. 127)
character-based interface (p. 141)
command-line interface (p. 141)
compatibility (p. 133)
compiler (p. 129)
concurrent processing (p. 137)
context-sensitive menus (p. 143)
copyrighted software (p. 133)
custom application (p. 136)
debugging (p. 128)
desktop (p. 142)
device drivers (p. 140)
dialog box (p. 142)
document (p. 142)

documentation (p. 132)
End-User License Agreement
    (EULA) (p. 133)
Folder (p. 142)
graphical user interface (GUI)
    (p. 141)
hierarchical menus (p. 143)
high-level language (p. 129)
icon (p. 142)
integrated software (p. 135)
Java (p. 147)
Linux (p. 125)
machine language (p. 129)
Mac OS (p. 141)
Menu (p. 141)
menu-driven interface (p. 141)
Microsoft Windows (p. 143)
MS-DOS (p. 141)
Multitasking (p. 137)

natural language (p. 129)
open source software (p. 125)
operating system (OS) (p. 136)
platform (p. 147)
pop-up menus (p. 143)
public domain software (p. 134)
pull-down menu (p. 142)
shareware (p. 134)
shell (p. 143)
software license (p. 133)
system software (p. 136)
UNIX (p. 144)
upgrade (p. 133)
user interface (p. 141)
utility program (p. 140)
vertical-market application (p. 136)
virtual memory (p. 137)
virtual reality (p. 148)
window (p. 142)

INTERACTIVE QUIZ QUESTIONS

1. The *Computer Confluence* CD-ROM contains self-test multiple-choice quiz questions related to this chapter.

2. The *Computer Confluence* Web site, **http://www.computerconfluence.com**, contains self-test exercises related to this chapter. Follow the instruc-

tions for taking a quiz. After you've completed your quiz, you can email the results to your instructor.

3. The Web site also contains open-ended discussion questions called Internet Explorations. Discuss one or more of the Internet Exploration questions at the section for this chapter.

TRUE OR FALSE

1. Linux is the original Microsoft operating system with a command-line interface.

2. An algorithm is a computer program written in machine language.

3. When you buy a software program, you're really buying a license to use the program according to rules specified by the software company.

4. Shareware is a type of software application used for sharing files over a network or the Internet.

5. Operating system software runs continuously whenever a PC is on.

6. Your computer can't print documents unless it has a device driver that allows it to communicate with your printer.

7. The first low-cost operating system with a graphical user interface was an early version of Microsoft Windows.

8. It is impossible to run Windows applications on a Macintosh computer.

9. A PC can have only one operating system installed on its hard disk at a time.

10. The PC's user interface isn't likely to change significantly in the next decade.

MULTIPLE CHOICE

1. The most famous example of open source software is
   a. Microsoft Windows.
   b. Mac OS X.
   c. UNIX.
   d. Linux.
   e. Palm OS.

2. A compiler translates a program written in a high-level language into
   a. machine language.
   b. an algorithm.
   c. debugged program.
   d. C#.
   e. natural language.

3. A program's end-user license agreement (EULA) typically includes
   a. rules specifying how the software may be used.
   b. warranty disclaimers.
   c. rules concerning the copying of the software.
   d. All of the above.
   e. None of the above.

4. Microsoft Office is
   a. shareware.
   b. public domain software.
   c. open source software.
   d. a vertical-market application.
   e. an application suite.

5. The computer's operating system
   a. communicates with peripherals.
   b. coordinates concurrent processing of jobs.
   c. monitors resources and handles basic security.
   d. All of the above.
   e. None of the above.

6. Most system functions that aren't handled directly by the operating system can be handled by
   a. vertical-market applications.
   b. utilities.
   c. algorithms.
   d. integrated software
   e. compilers.

7. The operating system is stored in ROM or flash memory in most
   a. Windows and Macintosh computers.
   b. mainframes and supercomputers.
   c. handheld and special-purpose computers.
   d. open source and public domain computers.
   e. workstations and servers.

8. When you boot up a PC,
   a. portions of the operating system are copied from disk into memory.
   b. portions of the operating system are copied from memory onto disk.
   c. portions of the operating system are compiled.
   d. portions of the operating system are emulated.
   e. None of the above.

9. UNIX is
   a. a multiuser operating system designed more than three decades ago.
   b. at the heart of Mac OS X.
   c. the operating system that is widely used for Internet servers.
   d. All of the above.
   e. None of the above.

10. Future PC user interfaces will almost certainly involve more use of
    a. machine language.
    b. natural language.
    c. high-level language.
    d. assembly language.
    e. algorithmic language.

REVIEW QUESTIONS

1. What is the relationship between a program and an algorithm?

2. Most computer software falls into one of three categories: compilers and other translator programs, software applications, and system software. Describe and give examples of each.

3. Which must be loaded first into the computer's memory, the operating system or software applications? Why?

4. Write an algorithm for changing a flat tire. Check your algorithm carefully for errors and ambiguities. Then have a classmate or your instructor check it. How did your results compare?

5. Describe several functions of a single-user operating system. Describe several additional functions of a multiuser operating system.

6. What does it mean when software is called IBM-compatible or Macintosh-compatible? What does this have to do with the operating system?

7. Why is the user interface such an important part of software?

8. What is a graphical user interface? How does it differ from a character-based interface? What are the advantages of each?

9. What are the three main platforms for desktop computers today? Briefly describe each of them.

DISCUSSION QUESTIONS

1. In what way is writing instructions for a computer more difficult than writing instructions for a person? In what way is it easier?

2. How would using a computer be different if it had no operating system? How would programming be different?

3. Speculate about the user interface of a typical computer in the year 2010. How would this user interface differ from those used in today's computers?

4. If you had the resources to design a computer with a brand-new user interface, what would your priorities be? Make a rank-ordered list of the qualities you'd like to have in your user interface.

5. How do you feel about the open software movement? Would you be willing to volunteer your time to write software or help users for free?

PROJECTS

1. Write a report about available computer applications in your field of study or in your chosen profession.

2. Take an inventory of computer applications available in your computer lab. Describe the major uses for each application.

SOURCES AND RESOURCES

Books

Just for Fun: The Story of an Accidental Revolutionary, by Linus Torvalds and David Diamond (New York: Harperbusiness, 2001). Red Herring Executive Editor convinced Linus Torvalds to tell his story. The result is this book, a quirky collection of tidbits from the life of the creator of Linux.

Rebel Code: Linux and the Open Source Revolution, by Glyn Moody (New York: Perseus, 2001). This book tells the Linux story in a style that's more conventional, and for many readers, more readable, than the Torvalds/Diamond book.

The Cathedral and the Bazaar: Musings on Linux and Open Source by an Accidental Revolutionary, Revised Edition, by Eric S. Raymond (Sebastapol, CA: O'Reilly, 2001). This widely praised book is an expanded version of the original manifesto for the open source software movement—the movement that threatens to revolutionize the software industry. Tom Peters calls it "wonderful, witty, and, ultimately, wise."

Windows XP for Dummies, by Andy Rothbone (Indianapolis, IN: Hungry Minds, 2001). The Dummies series that started with *DOS for Dummies* has expanded to cover everything from antiquing to yoga. Unlike Microsoft, this book series isn't a monopoly. There are hundreds of books on Windows for dummies and nondummies alike.

Mac OS X 10.3 Panther: Visual QuickStart Guide by Maria Langer (Berkeley, CA: Peachpit Press, 2004). Peachpit's VQS series is popular with people who want to learn software with illustrated step-by-step instructions and minimal verbage. This particular volume introduces the Mac OS using the VQS formula.

Switching to the Mac: The Missing Manual, by David Pogue (Sebastapol, CA: O'Reilly, 2003). Windows and Macintosh computers are just different enough to be confusing to people who occasionally have to switch platforms. Example: An alias on the Macintosh is, roughly speaking, the equivalent of a Windows shortcut, but what are the differences? This book is written in a clear, concise, and clever style and, like most Pogue books, is highly recommended.

UNIX: Visual QuickStart Guide, Second Edition, by Deborah S. Ray and Eric J. Ray (Berkeley, CA: Peachpit Press, 2003). Many UNIX books assume that you speak fluent technojargon and that you want to know all about the operating system and how it works. This book is designed for people who want to (or need to) use UNIX but don't particularly want to read a massive volume of UNIX lore. No book can make mastering UNIX simple, but this one at least makes getting started with UNIX simpler.

Palm Organizers Visual QuickStart Guide, Third Edition, by Jeff Carlson (Berkeley, CA: Peachpit Press, 2004). Palm organizers are essential tools for many busy people. This book can help you tap the power of a Palm.

Piloting Palm: The Inside Story of Palm, Handspring and the Birth of the Billion Dollar Handheld Industry, by Andrea Butter and David Pogue (New York: John Wiley & Sons, 2002). In this fascinating behind-the-scenes look at the making of the original Palm Pilot, we learn how a new industry was created in the aftermath of previous technological failures.

StarOffice 6.0 Office Suite Companion and **OpenOffice.org 1.0 Resource Kit**, by Solveig Haugland, Floyd Jones (Upper Saddle River, NJ: Prentice Hall, 2002–2003). There are dozens of books on Microsoft Office and other commercial PC applications, but very few on freeware apps. These book can serve as an introduction and a valuable reference for anyone wanting to use the powerful, free StarOffice and OpenOffice.org suites on Windows or Linux.

Things That Make Us Smart: Defending Human Attributes in the Age of the Machine, by Donald A. Norman (Reading, MA: Addison-Wesley, 1993). Norman left his position as the founding Chairman of the Department of Cognitive Science at the University of California, San Diego, to work in the computer industry. His research on the relationship between technology and the human cognitive system is especially relevant in an industry where user interface decisions affect millions of users every day. This book, like Norman's others, is informative, thought provoking, and enjoyable. His argument for a more human-centered technology should be required reading for all software designers.

World Wide Web Pages

Software companies, like hardware companies, have established their presence on the Net. Most of the companies use addresses that follow the formula http://www.companyname.com. Examples include http://www.microsoft.com, http://www. apple.com, and http://www.adobe.com. Content varies from company to company; you might find technical support, product descriptions, demo software, software updates, and user tips on a typical software home page. For more software information check the home pages of publishers that specialize in computer books. For example, Peachpit Press (http://www.peachpit.com), McGraw-Hill (http://www.books.mcgraw-hill.com), and other publishers include sample chapters from software books on their Web sites. As usual, http://www.computerconfluence .com provides up-to-date links to a variety of valuable Web resources.

AFTER YOU READ THIS CHAPTER YOU SHOULD BE ABLE TO:

- Describe how word processing and desktop publishing software have revolutionized writing and publishing

- Discuss the potential impact of desktop publishing and Web publishing on the concept of freedom of the press

- Speculate about future developments in word processing and digital publishing

- Describe the basic functions and applications of spreadsheets and other types of statistical and simulation programs

- Explain how computers can be used to answer "what if?" questions

- Explain how computers are used as tools for simulating mechanical, biological, and social systems.

 Multimedia extras on the CD-ROM and the Web:

- Historic video of Douglas Engelbart's **"Augment" demonstration**

- Animated interactive demonstration of **font technology**

- **Simulation** and **visualization** tools

- A **scientific computing gam**e

- **Instant access** to glossary and key word references

- Interactive **self-study quizzes**

- Free software sources

    . . . *and more.*

 **computerconfluence.com**

BASIC OFFICE APPLICATIONS

DOUG ENGELBART EXPLORES HYPERSPACE

On a December day in 1950, Doug Engelbart looked into the future and saw what no one had seen before. Engelbart had been thinking about the growing complexity and urgency of the world's problems and wondering how he could help solve those problems. In his vision of the future Engelbart saw computer technology augmenting and magnifying human mental abilities, providing people with new powers to cope with the urgency and complexity of life.

Engelbart decided to dedicate his life to turning his vision into reality. Unfortunately, the rest of the world wasn't ready for Engelbart's vision. His far-sighted approach didn't match the prevailing ideas of the time, and most of the research community denounced or ignored Engelbart's work. In 1951, there were only about a dozen computers in the world, and those spent most of their time doing military calculations. It was hard to imagine ordinary people using computers to boost their personal productivity. So Engelbart put together the Augmentation Research Center at the Stanford Research Institute to create working models of his visionary tools.

In 1968, he demonstrated his Augment system to an auditorium full of astonished computer professionals and changed forever the way people think about computers. A large screen showed a cascade of computer graphics, text, and video images, controlled by

Engelbart and a co-worker several miles away. "It was like magic," recalls Alan Kay, one of the young computer scientists in the audience. Augment introduced

> If you **look out in the future**, you can see how best to **make right choices**.
>
> —Doug Engelbart

the mouse, video display editing (the forerunner to word processing), mixed text and graphics, windowing, outlining, shared-screen video conferencing, computer conferencing, groupware, and hypermedia. Although Engelbart used a large computer, he was really demonstrating a futuristic "personal" computer—an interactive multimedia workstation for enhancing individual abilities.

5.1 Doug Engelbart

Today, many of Engelbart's inventions and ideas are commonplace. He is widely recognized for one small part of his vision: the mouse. But Engelbart hasn't stopped looking into the future. He now heads the Bootstrap Institute at Stanford University, a non-profit think tank dedicated to helping organizations make decisions with the future in mind. In a world where automation can dehumanize and eliminate jobs, Engelbart is still committed to replacing automation with augmentation. But now he focuses more on the human side of the equation, helping people chart a course into the future guided by intelligent, positive vision. He talks about turning organizations into "networked improvement communities" and demonstrates ways to "improve the improvement

5.2 Doug Engelbart's visionary 1968 presentation showed the world how computers could be used as collaborative tools.

process." If anyone understands how to build the future from a vision, Doug Engelbart does.

Doug Engelbart was one of the first people to recognize that computer technology could be used to augment human capabilities. Thanks in large part to his visionary work, people all over the world use computer applications to enhance their abilities to write papers and articles, publish periodicals and books, perform complex calculations, conduct scientific research, and even predict the future.

In this chapter we survey a variety of applications that people use to manipulate words and numbers. We consider software tools for working with words, from outliners to sophisticated reference tools, and numbers, from spreadsheets to statistical packages and money managers. We look at how desktop publishing technology has transformed the publishing process and provided more people with the power to communicate in print. We examine how scientific visualization software can help us understand relationships that are invisible to the naked eye and how computer simulations simulate reality for work and pleasure.

Word Processors and Other Word Tools

I . . . cannot imagine now that I **ever** wrote with a typewriter.
—Arthur C. Clarke, author and scientist

The way in which we write has forever been transformed by software. Instead of suffering through the painful process of typing and retyping in pursuit of a "clean" draft, a writer can focus on developing ideas and let the machine take care of the details of laying out the words neatly on the page. Word processing technology makes it possible for just about any literate person to communicate effectively in writing.

Working with a word processor involves several steps:

- Entering text
- Editing text
- Formatting the document

- Proofreading the document
- Saving the document on disk
- Printing the document.

Early word processing systems generally forced users to follow these steps in a strict order. Some systems still in use today—mainly on mainframes and other timesharing systems—segregate these processes into steps that can't easily be mixed. Most writers today use word processors that allow them to switch freely between editing and formatting, in some cases doing both at the same time.

Entering, Editing, and Formatting Text

With virtually all modern word processors, words appear on the screen almost exactly like they will appear on a printed page. This feature is often referred to as WYSIWYG—short for "what you see is what you get" and pronounced "wizzy-wig." As you type, your text is displayed on the screen and stored in RAM. Because of a feature called word wrap, the word processor automatically transports any words that won't fit on the current line to the next line along with the cursor.

Most word processors contain powerful text editing tools for changing and rearranging the words on the screen. Most computer users are familiar with the Clipboard, which can temporarily store chunks of text and other data, making it possible to cut or copy words from one part of a document and paste them into another part of the same document or a different document. In many programs you can achieve similar results using drag-and-drop technology that allows a selected block of text to be dragged from one location to another. Find-and-replace (search and replace) tools make it possible to make repetitive changes throughout a document.

Text formatting commands enable you to control the *format* of the document—how the words will look on the page. Most modern word processors include commands for controlling the formats of individual characters and paragraphs as well as complete documents.

Formatting Characters

Most printers can print text in a variety of point sizes, typefaces, and styles that aren't possible with typewriters. Characters are measured by point size, with one point equal to 1/72 inch. Most documents, including this book, use smaller point sizes for text to fit more information on each page and larger point sizes to make titles and headings stand out.

In the language of typesetters, a font is a size and style of typeface. For example, the Helvetica typeface includes many fonts, one of which is 12-point Helvetica bold. In the PC world, many people use the terms *font* and *typeface* interchangeably.

Whatever you call them, you have hundreds of choices of typefaces. Serif fonts, like those in the Times family, are embellished with serifs—fine lines at the ends of the main strokes of each character. Sans-serif fonts, like those in the Helvetica family, have plainer, cleaner lines. Monospaced fonts that mimic

Examples of	12-point size	24-point size
Serif fonts	Georgia Courier	Georgia Courier
Sans-serif fonts	Helvetica Verdana	Helvetica Verdana
Script fonts	Zapf Chancery Kuenstler Script	Zapf Chancery Kuenstler Script
Display fonts	Comic Sans Birch Remedy	Comic Sans Birch Remedy
Symbol fonts (Symbol and Zapf Dingbats)	Σψμβολ ✳❀☐❄ ✤✱■	Σψμβολ ✳❀☐❄ ✤✱■

5.3 These fonts represent just a few of the hundreds of typefaces available for personal computers and printers today. The two symbol fonts given, Symbol and Zapf Dingbats, provide special characters not available with other fonts.

typewriters, like those in the Courier family, produce characters that always take up the same amount of space, no matter how skinny or fat the characters are. In contrast, proportionally spaced fonts enable more room for wide characters, like w's, than for narrow characters, like i's. (See the font table on the previous page for examples.)

Formatting Paragraphs

Many formatting commands apply to paragraphs rather than characters: those commands that control margins, space between lines, indents, tab stops, and justification. Justification refers to the alignment of text on a line. Four justification choices are commonly available: left justification (with a smooth left margin and ragged right margin), right justification, full justification (both margins are smooth), and centered justification.

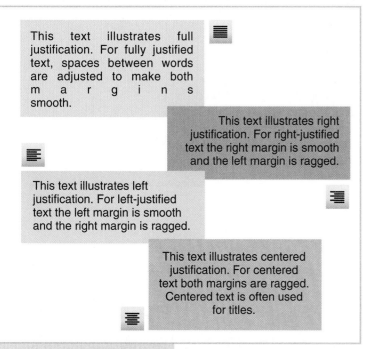

This text illustrates full justification. For fully justified text, spaces between words are adjusted to make both m a r g i n s smooth.

This text illustrates right justification. For right-justified text the right margin is smooth and the left margin is ragged.

This text illustrates left justification. For left-justified text the left margin is smooth and the right margin is ragged.

This text illustrates centered justification. For centered text both margins are ragged. Centered text is often used for titles.

5.4 Word processors and other applications typically provide these four options for justifying text.

Formatting the Document

Some formatting commands apply to entire documents. For example, Microsoft Word's Page Setup command enables you to control the margins that apply throughout the document. Other commands enable you to specify the content, size, and style of headers and footers—blocks that appear at the top and bottom of every page, displaying repetitive information, such as chapter titles, author names, and automatically calculated page numbers.

Most word processing programs provide a great deal of formatting flexibility. Advanced formatting features enable you to:

- Define style sheets containing custom styles for each of the common elements in a document. (For example, you can define a style called "subhead" as a paragraph that's left-justified in a boldface, 12-point Helvetica font with standard margins and then apply that style to every subhead in the document without reselecting all three of these commands for each new subhead. If you decide later to change the subheads to 14-point Futura, your changes in the subhead style are automatically reflected throughout the document.)
- Define alternate headers, footers, and margins so that left- and right-facing pages can have different margins, headers, and footers.
- Create documents with multiple variable-width columns.
- Create, edit, and format multicolumn tables.
- Incorporate graphics created with other applications.
- Use automatic footnoting to save you from having to place footnotes and endnotes; the program automatically places them where they belong on the page.
- Use automatic hyphenation to divide long words that fall at the ends of lines.
- Use automatic formatting (autoformat) to automatically apply formatting to your text; for example, to automatically number lists (like the exercises at the end of this chapter) and apply proper indentation to those lists.
- Use automatic correction (autocorrect) to catch and correct common typing errors. For example, if you type *THe* or *Teh*, the software will automatically change it to *The*.
- Generate tables of contents and indexes for books and other long works (with human help for making judgments about which words belong in the index and how they should be arranged).
- Attach hidden comments that can be seen without showing up in the final printed document.
- Use coaching or help features (sometimes called wizards) to walk you through complex document formatting procedures.
- Convert formatted documents to *HTML (hypertext markup language)* so they can be easily published on the Web.

5.1
Font Technology

When a computer displays a character on a monitor or prints it on a laser, inkjet, or dot matrix printer, the character is nothing more than a collection of dots in an invisible grid. Bit-mapped fonts store characters in this way, with each pixel represented as a black or white bit in a matrix. A bit-mapped font usually looks fine on screen in the intended point size but doesn't look smooth when printed on a high-resolution printer or enlarged on screen.

5.5a A bit-mapped font becomes pixelated when enlarged.

Most computer systems now use scalable outline fonts to represent type in memory until it is displayed or printed. A scalable font represents each character as an outline that can be scaled—increased or decreased in size without distortion. Curves and lines are smooth and don't have stair-stepped, jagged edges when they're resized. The outline is stored inside the computer or printer as a series of mathematical statements about the position of points and the shape of the lines connecting those points.

Downloadable fonts (soft fonts) are stored in the computer system (not the printer) and downloaded to the printer only when needed. These fonts usually have matching screen fonts and are easily moved to different computer systems. Most important, you can use the same downloadable font on many printer models.

5.5b This outline for a lowercase "a" retains its original shape at any size or resolution.

Laser printers are really dedicated computer systems that contain their own CPU, RAM, ROM, and specialized operating system. Printer fonts are stored in the printer's ROM and are always available for use with that printer, but you may not be able to achieve WYSIWYG if your computer doesn't have a screen font to match your printer font. And if you move your document to a different computer and printer, the same printer font may not be available on the new system.

Fonts are most commonly available in two scalable outline forms: Adobe PostScript and Apple/Microsoft TrueType. Because Apple and Microsoft supply TrueType downloadable fonts with their operating systems, TrueType fonts are more popular among general computer users. PostScript fonts usually require additional software but are the standard among many graphics professionals. PostScript is actually a complete page description language particularly well suited to the demands of professional publishers.

For the past few years, Adobe and Microsoft have been codeveloping OpenType, a universal font format that combines TrueType and PostScript technology. OpenType enables character shapes to travel with documents in compressed forms so that a document transmitted electronically or displayed on the World Wide Web will look like the original even if the viewer's system doesn't include the original document's fonts.

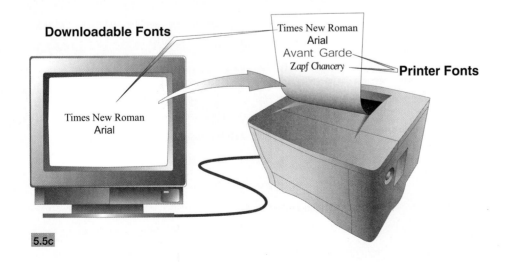

Downloadable Fonts

Times New Roman
Arial
Avant Garde
Zapf Chancery

Printer Fonts

Times New Roman
Arial

5.5c

Editing a Document with Microsoft Word

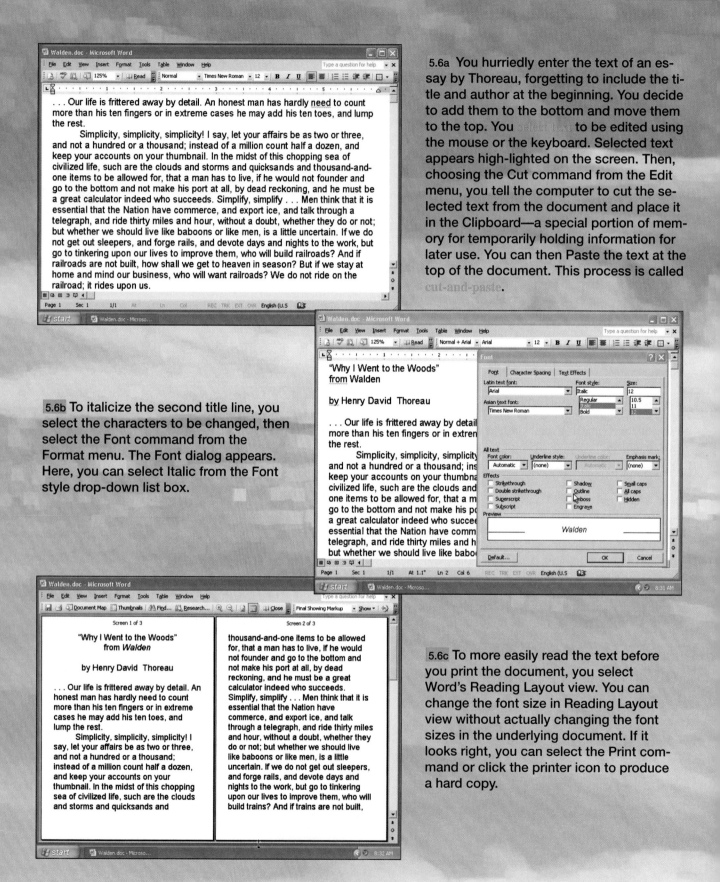

5.6a You hurriedly enter the text of an essay by Thoreau, forgetting to include the title and author at the beginning. You decide to add them to the bottom and move them to the top. You select text to be edited using the mouse or the keyboard. Selected text appears high-lighted on the screen. Then, choosing the Cut command from the Edit menu, you tell the computer to cut the selected text from the document and place it in the Clipboard—a special portion of memory for temporarily holding information for later use. You can then Paste the text at the top of the document. This process is called cut-and-paste.

5.6b To italicize the second title line, you select the characters to be changed, then select the Font command from the Format menu. The Font dialog appears. Here, you can select Italic from the Font style drop-down list box.

5.6c To more easily read the text before you print the document, you select Word's Reading Layout view. You can change the font size in Reading Layout view without actually changing the font sizes in the underlying document. If it looks right, you can select the Print command or click the printer icon to produce a hard copy.

If you're already a touch typist, your typing skills will help you become proficient at word processing quickly. Unfortunately, a few typing skills are counterproductive on a modern word processor. Here's a short list of new word processing habits that should replace your outmoded typing habits:

➡ **Use the Return or Enter key only when you must**. Let the computer's automatic word wrap handle routine end-of-line business.

➡ **Use tabs and margin guides, not the spacebar, to align columns**. WYSIWYG is a matter of degree, and text that looks perfectly aligned on-screen may not line up on paper if you depend on your eyes and the spacebar.

➡ **Don't underline**. Use italics and boldface for emphasis. Italicize book and journal titles.

➡ **Use only one space after a period**. Most type experts agree that proportionally spaced fonts look better if you avoid double spaces.

➡ **Take advantage of special characters**. Bullets (•), em dashes (—), curly quotes (" "), and other nontypewriter characters make your work look more professional, and they don't cost a thing.

The Wordsmith's Toolbox

In addition to basic editing and formatting functions, a typical word processor might include a built-in outliner, spelling checker, and thesaurus. But even word processors that don't include those features can be enhanced with stand-alone programs specifically designed to accomplish the same things. We examine a few of these tools next.

When you had to carve things in **stone**, you got the **Ten Commandments**. When things had to be written with a **goose quill** and you had to **boil blood** or whatever to make ink, you got **Shakespeare**. When you went over to the **steel pen** and manufactured inks, you got **Henry James**. You get to the **typewriter**, you get **Jack Kerouac**. When you get down to the **word processor**—you get **me**. So improvement in **the technology** of writing hasn't improved **writing itself**, as far as I can tell.

—P. J. O'Rourke, Humorist

Outliners and Idea Processors

For many of us the hardest part of the writing process is collecting and organizing our thoughts. Tradi-tional English-class techniques, including outlines and 3-by-5 note cards, involve additional work. But when computer technology is

If any man wishes to **write** in a **clear style**, let him first **be clear** in his **thoughts**.

—Johann W. von Goethe

applied to these time-honored techniques, they're transformed into high-powered tools for extending our minds and streamlining the process of turning vague thoughts into solid prose.

Outliners, such as the *Outline View* option built into Microsoft Word are, in effect, idea processors. Outliners are particularly effective at performing three functions:

1. Arranging information into hierarchies or levels so that each heading can be fleshed out with more detailed subheads, which can then be broken into smaller pieces

2. Rearranging ideas and levels so that subideas are automatically moved with their parent ideas

3. Hiding and revealing levels of detail as needed so that you can examine the forest, the trees, or an individual leaf of your project.

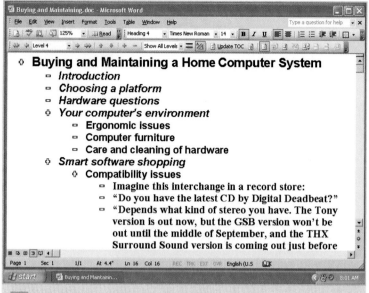

5.7 Microsoft Word's Outline view enables you to examine and restructure the overall organization of a document, while showing each topic in as much detail as you need. When you move headlines, the attached subheads and paragraphs follow automatically.

> The difference between the **right word** and the **almost-right word** is the difference between the **lightning** and the **lightning bug**.
>
> —Mark Twain

For a project that requires research, an outliner can be used as a replacement for note cards. Ideas can be collected, composed, refined, rearranged, and reorganized much more efficiently when they're stored in an outline. When the time comes to turn research into a research paper, the notes don't need to be retyped; they can be polished with standard text-editing techniques. If the outliner is built into the word processor, the line between notes and finished product blurs to the point where it almost disappears.

Synonym Finders

The classic synonym finder, or *thesaurus*, is an invaluable tool for finding just the right word, but it's not particularly user-friendly. A computerized thesaurus is another matter altogether. With a good thesaurus, it's a simple matter to select a word and issue a command for a synonym search. The computerized thesaurus provides almost instant gratification, displaying all kinds of possible replacements for the word in question. If you find a good substitute in the list, you can indicate your preference with a click or a keystroke; the software even makes the substitution for you.

Digital References

Writers rely on dictionaries, quotation books, encyclopedias, atlases, almanacs, and other references. Just about all of these resources are now available in digital form, on CD-ROM, DVD, and the Web.

Searching for subjects or words by computer is usually faster than thumbing through a book. Well-designed electronic references make it easy to jump between related topics in search of elusive facts. In addition, copying quotes electronically takes a fraction of the time it takes to retype information from a book. Of course, this kind of quick copying makes plagiarism easier than ever and may tempt more writers to violate copyright laws and ethical standards.

Because pictures, maps, and drawings take up so much disk space (and Internet

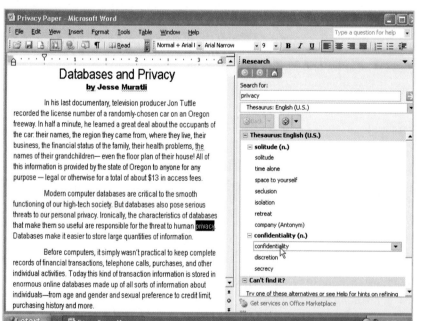

5.8 Microsoft Word's Thesaurus feature puts synonyms at your fingertips. In this case, the computer is providing synonyms for the word *privacy*.

transmission time), they're sometimes removed or modified in computerized references. On the other hand, many digital references include sounds, animation, video, and other forms of information that aren't possible to include in books.

Reference materials are everywhere on the Web. Unfortunately, not all of those sources are useful or reliable. Still, the Web offers a combination of currency and cross-referencing that can't be found in any other reference source. We'll revisit Web references in later chapters.

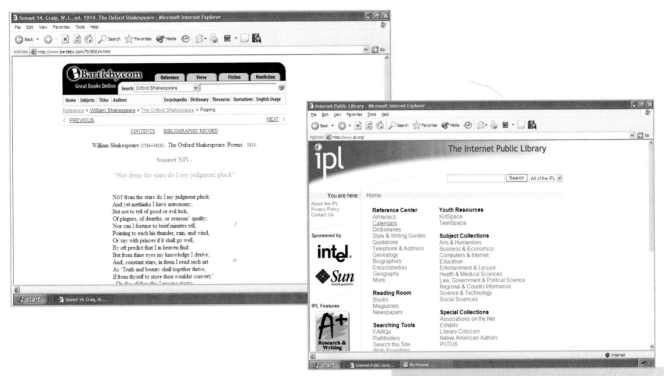

5.9 Students and other researchers can save time searching for facts, quotes, ideas, or inspiration using specially designed reference sites on the Web.

Spelling Checkers

Although many of us sympathize with Jackson's point of view, the fact remains that correct spelling is an important part of most written communication. That's why a word processor typically includes a built-in spelling checker. A spelling checker compares the words in your document with words in a disk-based dictionary. Every word that's not in the dictionary is flagged as a suspect word—a

> It's a **darn poor mind** that can only think of **one way** to spell a word.
>
> —Andrew Jackson

potential misspelling. In many cases, the spelling checker suggests the corrected spelling and offers to replace the suspect word. Ultimately, though, it's up to you to decide whether the flagged word is, in fact, spelled incorrectly.

Spelling checkers are wonderful aids, but they can't replace careful proofreading by alert human eyes. When you're using a spelling checker, it's important to keep two potential problems in mind:

1. *Dictionary limitations and errors.* No dictionary includes every word, so you have to know what to do with unlisted words—proper names, obscure words, technical terms, foreign terms, colloquialisms, and other oddities. If you add words to your spelling checker's dictionary, you run the risk of adding an incorrectly spelled word, making future occurrences of that misspelling invisible to the spelling checker and to you.

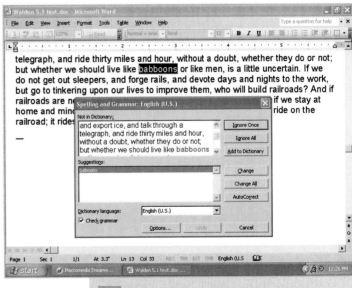

5.10 Most spell checkers, including the one in Microsoft Word, offer the user several choices for handling words that aren't in the dictionary.

2. *Errors of context.* The fact that a word appears in a dictionary does not guarantee that it is correctly spelled in the context of the sentence. The following passage, for example, contains eight spelling errors, none of which would be detected by a spelling checker:

> *I wood never have guest that my spelling checker would super seed my editor as my mane source of feed back. I no longer prophet from the presents of an editor while I right.*

Grammar and Style Checkers

The errors in the preceding quote would have slipped by a spelling checker; but many of them would have been detected by a grammar and style checker. In addition to checking spelling, grammar-and-style-checking software analyzes each word in context, checking for errors of context ("I wood never have guest"), common grammatical errors ("Ben and me went to Boston"), and stylistic foibles ("Suddenly the door was opened by Bethany"). In addition to pointing out possible errors and suggesting improvements, it can analyze prose complexity using measurements such as sentence length and paragraph length. This kind of analysis is useful for determining whether your writing style is appropriate for your target audience.

Grammar-and-style-checking software is, at best, imperfect. A typical program misses many true errors, while flagging correct passages. Still, it can be a valuable writing aid, especially for students who are mastering the complexities of a language for the first time. But software is no substitute for practice, revision, editing, and a good English teacher.

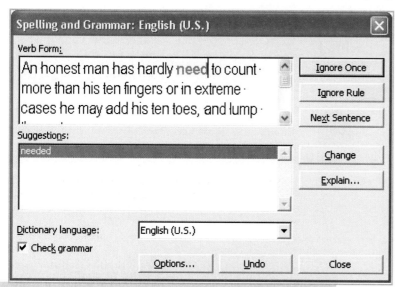

5.11 Grammar-and-style-checking software flags possible errors and makes suggestions about how they might be fixed. Here, Microsoft Word suggests a way to change a particular sentence.

Form Letter Generators

Congratulations, Mr. <lastname>. You may already have won!
—Junk mail greeting

Most word processors today have mail merge capabilities for producing personalized form letters. When used with a database containing a list of names and addresses, a word processor can quickly generate individually addressed letters and mailing labels. Many programs can incorporate custom paragraphs based on the recipient's personal data, making each letter look as if it were individually written. Direct-mail marketing companies exploited this kind of technology for years before it became available in inexpensive PC software.

Collaborative Writing Tools

Writing only leads to **more writing.**
—Colette

Most large writing projects, including this one, involve groups of people working together. Computer networks make it easy for writers and editors to share documents; but it's not always easy for one person to know how a document has been changed by others. Groupware—software designed to be used by a workgroup—can keep track of a document's history as it's passed among group members and make sure that all changes are incorporated into a single master document. Using groupware, each writer can monitor and make suggestions concerning the work of any other writer on the team. Editors can "blue pencil" corrections and attach notes directly to the electronic manuscript. The notes can be read by any or all of the writers—even those who are on the other side of the continent. This kind of collaborative writing and editing doesn't require specialized software anymore; it can be done with many word processing and publishing programs. For example, Microsoft Word's Track Changes option can record and display contributions of several writers and editors; it can also compare document versions and highlight differences between versions.

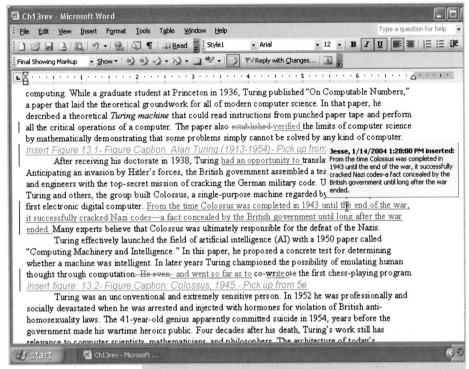

5.12 The Track Changes feature in Microsoft Word enables writers, editors, and other collaborative document creators to contribute to the same document and see each other's changes.

Emerging Word Tools

Word processing software has evolved rapidly in the last few years. The evolution isn't over; current trends suggest big changes are coming in word processing technology.

> The **real technology**—behind all of our other technologies—is **language**. It actually creates **the world our consciousness lives in**.
> —Norman Fischer, Abbot, Green Gulch Farm Zen Center

Processing Handwritten Words

For a small but growing population, pen-based systems provide an alternative tool for entering text. Handwriting recognition doesn't come easy to computers; it requires sophisticated software that can interpret pen movements as characters and words. The diversity in handwriting makes it difficult for today's software to translate all of our scribbles into text. Powerful pen-based systems like the Tablet PC work reliably because they use all of the processing punch of modern notebook PCs and advanced handwriting recognition algorithms. Simpler pen-based systems like those based on the Palm OS require users to print characters using a carefully defined system that minimizes errors.

Processing Words with Speech

Ultimately, most writers long for a computer that can accept and reliably process *speech* input—a *talkwriter*. With such a system, a user can tell the computer what to type—and how to type it—by simply talking into a micro-

> I think that the **primary means of communication** with computers in the next millennium will be **speech**.
> —Nicholas Negroponte, director of MIT's Media Lab

phone. The user's speech enters the computer as a digital audio signal. Speech-recognition software looks for patterns in the sound waves and interprets sounds by locating familiar patterns, segmenting input sound patterns into words, separating commands from the text, and passing those commands on to the word processing software.

5.13 Speech recognition software enables this doctor to dictate notes and other documents into her computer.

Speech-recognition software systems have been around for many years, but until recently, most were severely limited. It takes a great deal of intelligence to understand the complexities of human speech. Most current commercial systems need to be trained to recognize a particular person's voice before they can function reliably. Even then, many systems require that the user speak slowly in a quiet environment and use a small, predefined vocabulary. Otherwise the machine might interpret, say, "recognize speech" as "wreck a nice beach." Research in speech recognition today focuses on overcoming these limitations and producing systems that can accomplish the following tasks:

- Recognize words without being trained to an individual speaker, an ability known as *speaker independence*
- Handle speech without limiting vocabulary
- Handle continuous speech—natural speech in which words run together at normal speed

Researchers are making great strides toward these goals. Several companies have developed programs that can achieve two of them. No one has yet developed a system that consistently achieves all three goals, the human body excepted.

Although it's not yet trouble-free or error-free, PC speech recognition software is growing in popularity, especially for people who can't use keyboards because of physical disabilities or job restrictions. As the technology improves, the microphone may become the preferred input device for PC users. Future pocket-sized personal digital assistants may become digital dictation machines.

Intelligent Word Processors

Speech recognition is just one aspect of artificial intelligence research that's likely to end up in future word processors. Many experts foresee word processors that are able to anticipate the writer's needs, acting as an electronic editor or coauthor. Today's grammar and style checkers are primitive forerunners of the kinds of electronic writing consultants that might appear in a few years. Here are some possibilities:

- As you're typing a story, your word processor reminds you (via a pop-up notification message on the screen or an auditory message) that you've used the word *delicious* three times in the last two paragraphs and suggests that you choose an alternative from the list shown on the screen.
- Your word processor continuously analyzes your style as you type, determines your writing habits and patterns, and learns from its analysis. If your writing tends to be technical and formal, the software modifies its thesaurus, dictionary, and other tools so they're more appropriate for that style.
- You're writing a manual for a large organization whose documentation has specific style guidelines. Your word processor modifies your writing as you type so that it conforms to the organizational style.
- You need some current figures to support your argument on the depletion of the ozone layer. You issue a command, and the computer does a quick search of the literature on the Web and quickly reports back to you with several relevant facts.

All of these examples are technically possible now. The trend toward intelligent word processors is clear. Nevertheless, you're in for a long wait if you're eager to buy a system with commands such as Clever Quote, Humorous Anecdote, and Term Paper.

The Desktop Publishing Story

Freedom of the press belongs to the person who **owns** one.
—A. J. Liebling, the late media critic for *The New Yorker*

Just as word processing changed the writer's craft in the 1970s, the world of publishing was radically transformed in the 1980s when Apple introduced its first LaserWriter printer and a new company named Aldus introduced PageMaker, a Macintosh program that could take advantage of that printer's high-resolution output capabilities. Publishing—traditionally an expensive, time-consuming, error-prone process—instantly became an enterprise that just about anyone with a computer and a little cash could undertake.

What Is Desktop Publishing?

The process of producing a book, magazine, or other publication includes several steps:

- Writing text
- Editing text
- Producing drawings, photographs, and other graphics to accompany the text
- Designing a basic format for the publication
- Typesetting text
- Arranging text and graphics on pages
- Typesetting and printing pages
- Binding pages into a finished publication

In traditional publishing, many of these steps required expensive equipment, highly trained specialists to operate the equipment, and lots of time. With **desktop publishing (DTP)** technology, the bulk of the production process can be accomplished with tools that are small, affordable, and easy to use. A desktop publishing system generally includes one or more Macs or PCs, a scanner, a high-resolution printer, and software. It's now possible for a single person with a modest equipment investment to do all the writing, editing, graphic production, design, page layout, and typesetting for a desktop publication. Of course, few individuals have the skills to handle all of these tasks, so most publications are still the work of teams that include writers, editors, designers, artists, and supervisors. But even if the titles remain the same, each of these jobs is changing because of desktop publishing technology.

The first steps in the publishing process involve producing **source documents**—articles, chapters, drawings, maps, charts, and photographs that are to appear in the publication. Desktop publishers generally use standard word processors and graphics programs to produce most source documents. Scanners with image editing software are used to transform photographs and hand-drawn images into computer-readable documents. **Page-layout software**, such as QuarkXPress, Adobe PageMaker, or Adobe InDesign, is used to combine the various source documents into a coherent, visually appealing publication. Pages are generally laid out one at a time on-screen, although most programs have options for automating multiple-page document layout.

5.14 A typical desktop publishing system includes a personal computer, a high-resolution printer, a scanner and other imaging hardware, and a variety of graphical software programs.

Page-layout software provides graphic designers with control over virtually every element of the design, right down to the spacing between each pair of letters (*kerning*) and the spacing between lines of text (*leading*). Today's word processing programs include basic page-layout capabilities, too; they're sufficient for creating many types of publications. But to produce more complex layouts for newspapers, newsletters, magazines, and flyers, publishers need the kind of advanced formatting capabilities found only in dedicated desktop publishing applications. (Word processors and desktop publishers often work hand-in-hand: For example, writers usually use word processors to create the text that is poured into a desktop publishing layout.)

For users without background in layout and design, most page-layout and word processing programs include **templates**—professionally designed "empty" documents that

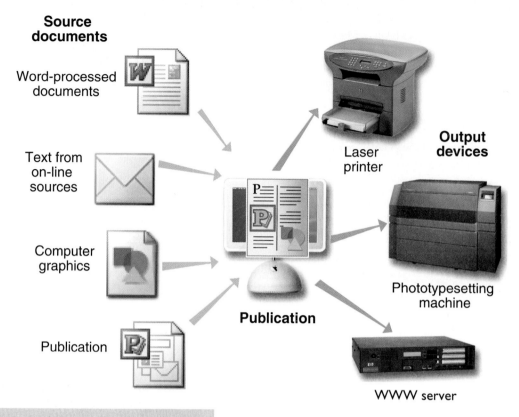

Source documents

Word-processed documents

Text from on-line sources

Computer graphics

Publication

Publication

Laser printer

Output devices

Phototypesetting machine

WWW server

5.15 Source documents are merged in a publication document, which can be printed on a laser or inkjet printer, printed on high-resolution phototypesetter, or published on the Web.

can easily be adapted to specific user needs. Even without templates, it's possible for beginners to create professional-quality publications with a modest investment of money and time.

Desktop publishing becomes more complicated when color is introduced. *Spot color*—the use of a single color (or sometimes two) to add interest—is relatively easy. But *full-color* desktop publishing, including color photos, drawings, and paintings, must deal with the inconsistencies of different color output devices. Because printers and monitors use different types of color-mixing technologies (as described in the *How It Works* boxes in Chapter 3), what you see on the screen isn't always what you get when you print it. It's even difficult to get two monitors (or two printers) to produce images with exactly the same color balance. Still, color desktop publishing is big business, and advances in *color-matching* technology are making it easier all the time.

Most desktop publications are printed on ink-jet and laser printers capable of producing output with a resolution of at least 600 dots per inch (dpi). The number of dots per inch influences the resolution and clarity of the image. Output of 600 dpi is sufficiently sharp for most applications, but it's less than the 1,200 dpi that is the traditional minimum for professional typesetting. High-priced devices, called *phototypesetting machines* or *imagesetters*, enable desktop publications to be printed at 1,200 dpi or higher. Many desktop publishers rely on outside *service bureaus* with phototypesetting machines to print their final *camera-ready* pages—pages that are ready to be photographed and printed.

Why Desktop Publishing?

Desktop publishing offers several advantages for businesses. Desktop publishing saves money. Publications that used to cost hundreds or thousands of dollars to produce through outside publishing services can now be produced in-house for a fraction of their former cost. Desktop publishing also saves time. The turnaround time for a publication done on the desktop can be a few days instead of the weeks or months it might take to publish the

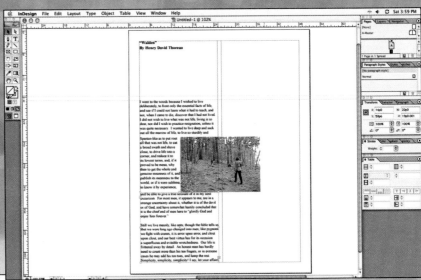

5.16a You decide to create an illustrated publication featuring excerpts from Thoreau's works. Your source documents—word processor files and pictures imported from a digital camera—are ready to go. You create a new InDesign document and specify the size of the pages, the margin sizes, and the number of columns per page. You use the text box tool to draw boxes to contain text from a Word document.

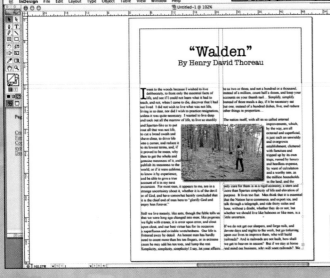

5.16b After placing the photograph on the page, you pour the document text into the text boxes. You add a drop shadow to the photograph. You modify the font, size, and justification of the title text and add a drop cap to the beginning of the first paragraph of the body text.

5.16c After adding a color background to the title area, you save the document in Adobe PDF format and preview it before sending it off to production for printing and distribution.

BEYOND Desktop Tacky!

Many first-time users of WYSIWYG word processors and desktop publishing systems become intoxicated with the power at their fingertips. It's easy to get carried away with all those fonts, styles, and sizes and to create a document that makes supermarket tabloids look tasteful. Although there's no substitute for a good education in the principles of design, it's easy to avoid tacky-looking documents if you follow a few simple guidelines:

➡ **Plan before you publish.** Design (or select) a simple, visually pleasing format for your document, and use that format throughout the document.

➡ **Use appropriate fonts.** Limit your choices to one or two fonts and sizes per page, and be consistent throughout your document. Serif fonts like the one used in the main text of this book generally are good choices for paragraphs of text; the serifs gently guide the reader's eye from letter to letter. Sans-serif fonts, like the one used in the box you are reading, work well for boxed text, tables, headings, and titles. It's generally better to use only one sans-serif font in a document. Make sure all your chosen fonts work properly with your printer.

➡ **Don't go style-crazy.** Avoid overusing *italics*, **boldface**, ALL CAPS, underlines, and other styles for emphasis. When in doubt, leave it out.

➡ **Look at your document through your readers' eyes.** Make every picture say something. Don't try to cram too much information on a page. Don't be afraid of white space. Use a format that speaks clearly to your readers. Make sure the main points of your document stand out. Whatever you do, do it for the reader.

➡ **Learn from the masters.** Study the designs of successful publications. What makes them work? Use design books, articles, and classes to develop your aesthetic skills along with your technical skills. With or without a computer, publishing is an art.

➡ **Know your limitations.** Desktop publishing technology makes it possible for anyone to produce high-quality documents with a minimal investment of time and money. But your equipment and skills may not be up to the job at hand. For many applications, personal desktop publishing is no match for a professional design artist or typesetter. If you need the best, work with a pro.

➡ **Remember the message.** Fancy fonts, tasteful graphics, and meticulous design can't turn shoddy ideas into words of wisdom, or lies into the truth. The purpose of publishing is communication; don't try to use technology to disguise the lack of something to communicate.

same thing using traditional channels. Finally, desktop publishing can reduce the quantity of publication errors. Quality control is easier to maintain when documents are produced in-house.

The real winners in the desktop publishing revolution might turn out to be not big businesses but everyday people with something to say. With commercial TV networks, newspapers, magazines, and book publishers increasingly controlled by a few giant corporations, many media experts worry that the free press guaranteed by our First Amendment is seriously threatened by de facto media monopolies. Desktop publishing technology offers new hope for every individual's right to publish. Writers, artists, and editors whose work is shunned or ignored by large publishers and mainstream media now have affordable publishing alternatives. The number of small presses and alternative, low-circulation periodicals is steadily increasing as publishing costs go down. If, as media critic A. J. Liebling suggested, freedom of the press belongs to the person who owns one, that precious freedom is now accessible to more people than ever before.

Beyond the Printed Page

The first books were so difficult to produce that they were considered priceless. They were kept in cabinets with multiple locks so that they couldn't be removed without the knowledge and permission of at least two monks. Today, we can print professional-quality publications in short order using equipment that costs less than a used car. But the publishing revolution isn't over yet.

> **Paper**, often underrated as a communication medium, **will not be eliminated** by the growth of electronic media. It remains **inexpensive**, extremely **portable**, and **capable** of carrying very high-resolution images.
>
> —Mark Duchesne, Vice President, AM Multigraphics

Paperless Publishing and the Web

A common prediction is that desktop publishing—and paper publishing in general—will be replaced by paperless electronic media. Paper still offers advantages for countless communication tasks. Reading printed words on pages is easier on the eyes than reading from a screen. Paper documents can be read and scribbled on almost anywhere, with or without electricity. And there's no electronic equivalent for the aesthetics of a beautifully designed, finely crafted book. Predictions aside, the printed word isn't likely to go away anytime soon.

Still, digital media *are* likely to eclipse paper for many applications. Email messages now outnumber post office deliveries of letters. CD-ROM encyclopedias briskly outsell

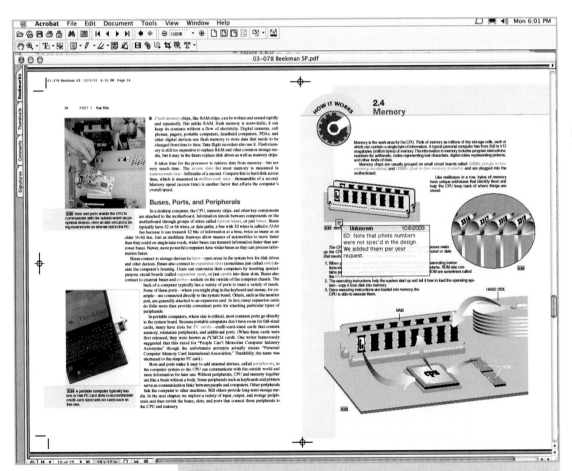

5.17 Adobe Acrobat is a cross-platform software program that enables the electronic sharing of PDF documents, eliminating the need for paper in many publishing projects. People who worked on *Computer Confluence* attached their comments to PDF pages and shared them electronically using Acrobat.

5.18 Mountains of waste paper like this one should become less common as paperless publishing grows in popularity. That's the theory, anyway.

their overweight paper counterparts. Adobe's *PDF (Portable Document Format)* enables documents of all types to be stored, viewed, or modified on any Windows or Macintosh computer, making it possible for organizations to reduce paper flow.

The Web offers unprecedented mass publishing possibilities to millions of Internet users. Programs as diverse as Microsoft Word, AppleWorks, and PageMaker can save documents in HTML formats, so they can be published on the Web. Other programs, specifically designed for Web publishing, offer advanced capabilities for graphics, animation, and multimedia publishing. (We'll explore some of these tools in later chapters when we discuss multimedia and the Web in greater depth.)

Never before has a communication medium made it so easy or inexpensive for an individual to reach such a wide audience. For a few dollars a month an Internet service provider can provide you with space to publish your essays, stories, reviews, and musings. It doesn't matter whether you're a student, a poet, an artist, a government official, a labor organizer, or a corporate president—on the Web all URLs are created equal.

Of course, the most popular commercial Web sites cost their owners more than a few dollars a month. A typical Web storefront costs a million dollars just to build. And one of the biggest challenges in Web publishing

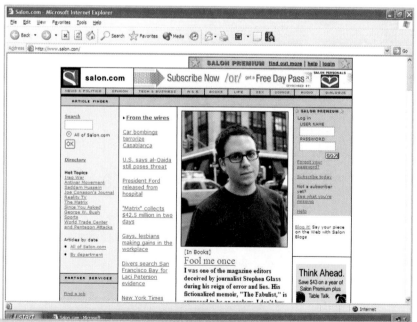

5.19 Many popular periodicals, from *Newsweek* to *Rolling Stone*, are published electronically on the Web as well. *Salon* is an example of a high-quality, popular magazine that is only available on the Web.

is attracting people to your site once it's online. Copyright protection is another problem for Web publishers; anything that's published on the Web for the world to see is also available for all of the world to copy. How can writers and editors be paid fairly for their labors if their works are so easy to duplicate?

Still, the Web is far more accessible to small-budget writers and publishers than any other mass medium. And many experts predict that Web technology will eventually include some kind of mechanism for automatic payment to authors whose works are downloaded. In any case, the free flow of ideas may be more significant than the flow of money. In the words of writer Howard Rheingold, the World Wide Web "might be important in the same way that the printing press was important. By expanding the number of people who have the power to transmit knowledge, the Web might trigger a power shift that changes everything."

Electronic Books and Digital Paper

Science fiction writers have long predicted the electronic book, or ebook—a handheld device that can contain anything from today's top news stories to an annotated edition of *War and Peace*. Until recently, these types of devices have been commercial failures for two reasons: First, the screens were hard to read and second, content for them was not easily accessible.

LCD technology has made great strides in recent years, and screens are brighter and easier to read than ever before. Recent advances in font technologies from Microsoft and Adobe should help, too. Microsoft's ClearType enhances the clarity of text on flat-panel LCD screens, reducing pixel "blockiness." Adobe has developed a similar technology called Precision Graphics. Easy-on-the-eyes ebooks are likely to take advantage of these technologies soon.

5.20 A Tablet PC like this one can replace a stack of textbooks, novels, and other reading material thanks to its pervasive ebook features.

To make it easier for ebook owners to find content—books, periodicals, and other software to download into their devices—several companies are cooperating to develop an open ebook standard. Once industry-wide standards are in place, electronic book publishing will be more practical—and popular. Future students may download texts rather than carry them out of bookstores. Everybook CEO Daniel Munyan predicts that college freshmen will load their ebooks with their notes and texts for the next four years and receive future updates via the Internet.

Ebooks today are mostly read on devices with rigid LCD screens—laptop computers, handheld computers, and special-purpose ebook readers that resemble tables. But researchers may soon perfect a form of digital paper that will enable ebooks (as well as emagazines and enewspapers) to look and feel more like their paper counterparts. Electronic paper, or epaper, is a flexible, portable, paperlike material that can dynamically display black-and-white text and images on its surface. Unlike traditional paper, digital paper can erase itself and display new text and images as the reader "turns" the page. A busy commuter might soon be able to carry a complete morning newspaper and several important business documents in a sheet of digital paper stuffed in his pocket!

5.21 Electronic paper is currently under development by several companies: this demo suggests that practical products aren't too far into the future.

The Spreadsheet: Software for Simulation and Speculation

Compare the **expansion of business** today to the **conquering of the continent** in the nineteenth century. The spreadsheet in that comparison is like **the transcontinental railroad**. It **accelerated the movement**, made it possible, and **changed the course** of the nation.

—Mitch Kapor, creator of the Lotus 1-2-3 spreadsheet software

More than any other type of standalone PC software, the spreadsheet has changed the way people do business. In the same way a word processor can give a computer user control over words, spreadsheet software enables the user to take control of numbers, manipulating them in ways that would be difficult or impossible otherwise. A spreadsheet program can make short work of tasks that involve repetitive calculations: budgeting, investment management, business projections, grade books, scientific simulations, checkbooks, and so on. A spreadsheet can also reveal hidden relationships between numbers, taking much of the guesswork out of financial planning and speculation.

The Malleable Matrix

The goal was that it had to be better than the **back of an envelope**.

—Dan Bricklin, inventor of the first spreadsheet program

Almost all spreadsheet programs are based on a simple concept: the malleable matrix. A spreadsheet document, called a worksheet, typically appears on the screen as a grid of numbered rows and alphabetically lettered columns. The box representing the intersection of a row and a column is called a cell. Every cell in this grid has a unique address made up of a row number and column letter. For example, the cell in the upper-left corner of the grid is called cell A1 (column A, row 1) in most spreadsheet applications. All the cells are empty in a new worksheet; it's up to the user to fill them. Each cell can contain a numeric value, an alphabetic label, or a formula representing a relationship with numbers in other cells.

Values (numbers) are the raw material the spreadsheet software uses to perform calculations. Numbers in worksheet cells can represent wages, test scores, weather data, polling results, or just about anything that can be quantified.

To make it easier for people to understand the numbers, most worksheets include labels at the tops of columns and at the edges of rows, such as "Monthly Wages," "Midterm Exam 1," "Average Wind Speed," or "Final Approval Rating." To the computer, these labels are meaningless strings of characters. The label "Total Points" doesn't tell the computer to calculate the total and display it in an adjacent cell; it's just a road sign for human readers.

To calculate the total points (or the average wind speed or the final approval rating), the worksheet must include a formula—a step-by-step procedure for calculating the desired number. The simplest spreadsheet formulas are arithmetic expressions using symbols such as + (addition), – (subtraction), * (multiplication), and / (division). For example, cell B5 might contain the formula =(B2+B3)/2. This formula tells the computer to add the numbers in cells B2 and B3, divide the result by 2, and display the final result in the cell containing the formula, cell B5.

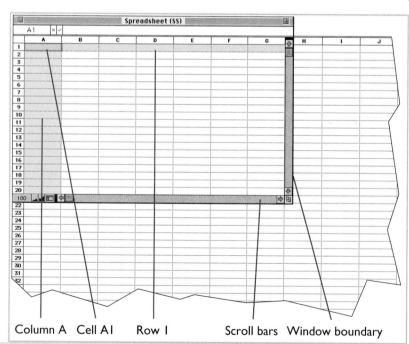

Column A   Cell A1   Row 1   Scroll bars   Window boundary

5.22 The worksheet may be bigger than what appears on your screen. The program enables you to scroll horizontally and vertically to view the larger matrix. (After column Z, columns are labeled with double letters: AA, BB, and so on.)

Creating a Worksheet with Microsoft Excel

5.23a You decide to create a simple budget worksheet showing monthly expenses. The first step in creating this worksheet is to type descriptive labels for the title, rows, and columns. You widen the first column by dragging its border to the right. After typing the labels, you type numeric values to represent dollar values for each category in each month. You choose the Cells command from the Format menu to format cells so numbers are displayed with dollar signs.

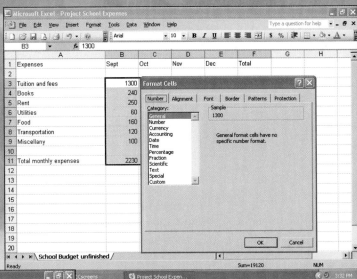

5.23b You enter a formula to calculate the total expenses for September in cell B11: 5sum(B3:B9). You then replicate this formula in cells C11 through F11 with the Fill Right command. You also change numbers in two of December's cells to allow for holiday gifts and travel. A similar process (using the Fill Down command) calculates the totals in column F.

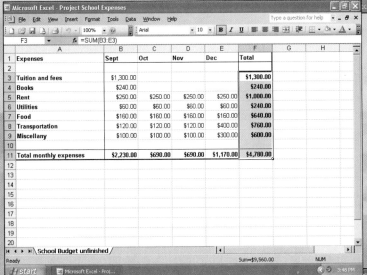

5.23c You use the Chart Wizard to tell Excel to create a pie chart from the data in your spreadsheet.

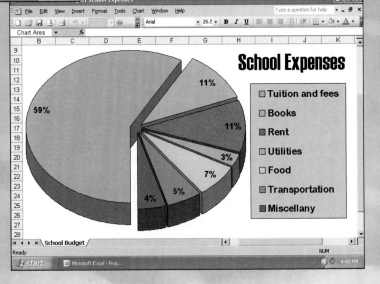

You don't see the formula in cell B5; you just see its effect. It doesn't matter whether the numbers represent test scores, dollars, or nothing at all; the computer obediently calculates their average and displays the results. If either number in cell B2 or B3 changes, the number displayed in B5 automatically changes, too: In many ways, this is the most powerful feature of a spreadsheet.

Different brands of spreadsheets, such as those included in Microsoft Office, StarOffice, OpenOffice.org, and AppleWorks, are distinguished by their features, their user interfaces, and which operating system platforms they support. In spite of their differences, all popular spreadsheet programs work in much the same way and share most of these features:

- *Lists*. Despite the availability of powerful and advanced features in virtually all spreadsheets, most individuals still use these applications for fairly mundane tasks like making and managing lists of grocery items, to-do tasks, phone numbers, and other related information. For most of these lists, the spreadsheet's calculation capabilities will go untapped; however, because spreadsheets have sophisticated data formatting capabilities, they are often used like this.

- *Automatic replication of values, labels, and formulas*. Most worksheets contain repetition: Budgetary amounts remain constant from month to month; exam scores are calculated the same way for every student in the class; a scheduling program refers to the same seven days each week. Many spreadsheet commands streamline entry of repetitive data, labels, and formulas. Replication commands are, in essence, flexible extensions of the basic copy-and-paste functions found in other software. The most commonly used replication commands are the Fill Down and Fill Right commands. Formulas can be constructed with *relative references* to other cells, as in the example, so they refer to different cells when replicated in other locations, or as *absolute references* that don't change when copied elsewhere.

- *Automatic recalculation*. Automatic recalculation is one of the spreadsheet's most important capabilities. It not only makes possible the easy correction of errors but also makes it easy to try out different values while searching for solutions. For large, complicated worksheets, recalculation can be painfully slow, so most spreadsheets enable you to turn off the automatic recalculation feature and recalculate the worksheet only when necessary.

- *Predefined functions*. The first calculators made computing a square root a tedious and error-prone series of steps. On today's calculators a single press of the square-root button tells the calculator to do all the necessary calculations to produce the square root. Spreadsheet programs contain built-in functions that work like the calculator's square-root button. A function in a formula instructs the computer to perform some predefined set of calculations. For example, the formula =SQRT(C5) calculates the square root of the number in cell C5. Modern spreadsheet applications have large libraries of predefined functions. Many, such as SUM, AVERAGE (or AVG), MIN, and MAX, represent simple calculations that are performed often in all kinds of worksheets. Others automate complex financial, mathematical, and statistical calculations that would be extremely difficult to calculate manually. The IF function enables the worksheet to decide what to do based on the contents of other cells, giving the worksheet logical decision-making capability. (For example: If the number of hours worked is greater than 40, calculate pay using the overtime schedule.) Like the calculator's square-root button, these functions can save time and reduce the likelihood of errors.

- *Macros*. A spreadsheet's menu of functions, like the menu in a fast-food restaurant, is limited to the most popular selections. For situations in which the built-in functions don't fill the bill, most spreadsheets enable you to capture sequences of steps as reusable macros—custom-designed procedures that you can add to the existing menu of options. Some programs insist that you type macros using a special macro language; others enable you to turn on a macro recorder that captures every move you make with the keyboard and mouse, recording those actions in a macro transcript. Later you can ask the computer to carry out the instructions in that macro. Suppose, for example, you use the same set of calculations every month when preparing a statistical analysis of environmental data. Without macros you'd have to repeat the same sequence of keystrokes, mouse clicks, and commands each time you created the monthly report. But by creating a macro called, for instance, Monthstats, you can effectively say, "Do it again" by issuing the Monthstats command.

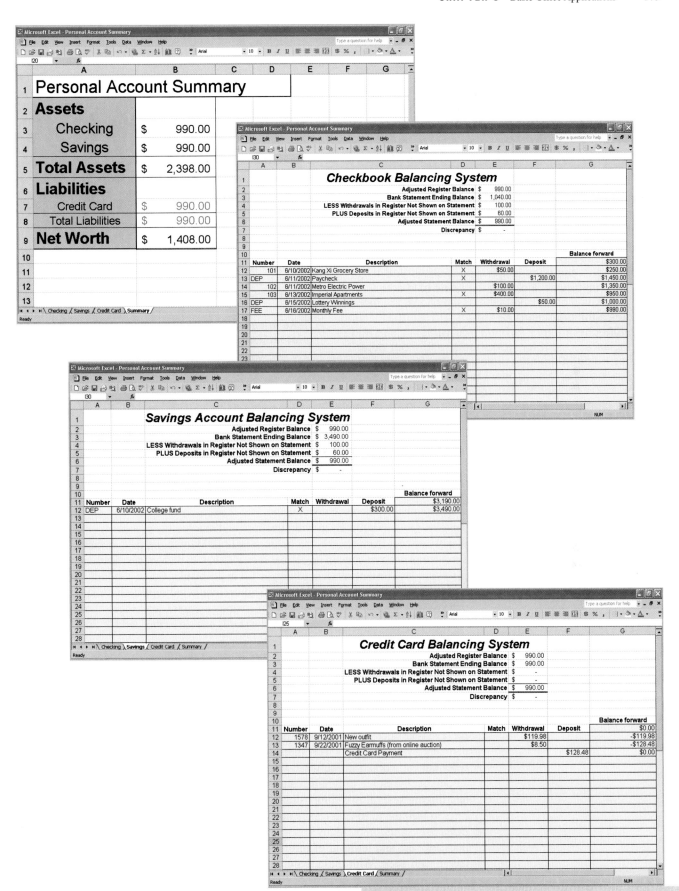

5.24 All of these worksheets are linked together into a single 3-D worksheet.

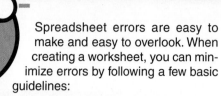

Avoiding Spreadsheet Pitfalls

Spreadsheet errors are easy to make and easy to overlook. When creating a worksheet, you can minimize errors by following a few basic guidelines:

➡ **Plan the worksheet before you start entering values and formulas.** Think about your goals, and design the worksheet to meet those goals.

➡ **Make your assumptions as accurate as possible.** Answers produced by a worksheet are only as good as the assumptions built into the data values and formulas. A worksheet that compares the operating costs of a gas guzzler and a gas miser must make assumptions about future trips, repair costs, and, above all, gasoline prices. The accuracy of the worksheet is tied to all kinds of unknowns, including the future of Middle East politics. The more accurate the assumptions, the more accurate the predictions.

➡ **Double-check every formula and value.** Values and formulas are input for worksheets, and input determines output. Computer professionals often describe the dark side of this important relationship with the letters GIGO—garbage in, garbage out. One highly publicized spreadsheet transcription error for Fidelity Investments resulted in a $2.6 billion miscalculation because of a single missing minus sign! You may not be working with values this big, but it's still important to proofread your work carefully.

➡ **Make formulas readable.** If your software can attach names to cell ranges, use meaningful names in formulas. It's easier to create and debug formulas when you can use readily understandable language like payrate*40+1.5*payrate* (hours worked–40) instead of a string of characters like C2*40+1.5*C2*(D2-40).

➡ **Check your output against other systems.** Use another program, a calculator, or pencil and paper to verify the accuracy of a sampling of your calculations.

➡ **Build in cross-checks.** Compare the sum of row totals with the sum of column totals. Does everything add up?

➡ **Change the input data values and study the results.** If small input adjustments produce massive output changes, or if major input adjustments result in little or no output changes, something may be wrong.

➡ **Take advantage of preprogrammed functions, templates, and macros.** Why reinvent the wheel when you can buy a professionally designed vehicle?

➡ **Use a spreadsheet as a decision-making aid, not as a decision maker.** Some errors aren't obvious; others don't show up immediately. Stay alert and skeptical.

■ *Formatting.* Most modern spreadsheets enable you to control typefaces, text styles, cell dimensions, and cell borders. They also enable you to include pictures and other graphic embellishments in documents.

■ *Templates and wizards.* Even with functions and macros, the process of creating a complex worksheet from scratch can be intimidating. Many users take advantage of worksheet templates that contain labels and formulas but no data values. These reusable templates produce instant answers when you fill in the blanks. Some common templates are packaged with spreadsheet software; others are marketed separately. A similar feature, called a *wizard*, automates the process of creating complex worksheets that meet particular needs. Well-designed templates and wizards can save considerable time, effort, and anguish.

■ *Validation.* Some spreadsheets incorporate artificial intelligence to guide users through complex procedures. To help users check complex worksheets for consistency of entries and formula logic, future spreadsheets are likely to include *validators*—the equivalent of spelling and grammar checkers for calculations.

■ *Linking.* Sometimes a change in one worksheet produces changes in another. For example, a master sales summary worksheet for a business should reflect changes in each department's sales summary worksheet. Most spreadsheet programs can create automatic links among worksheets so when values change in one, all linked worksheets update automatically. Some programs can create three-dimensional worksheets by stacking and linking several two-dimensional sheets. Some spreadsheet programs can create links to Web pages so data can be downloaded and updated automatically.

■ *Database capabilities.* Many spreadsheet programs can perform basic database functions: storage and retrieval of information, searching, sorting, report generation, mail merge, and such. With these features, a spreadsheet can serve users whose database needs are modest. For those who require a full-featured database management system, spreadsheet software might still be helpful; many spreadsheet programs support automatic two-way communication with database software.

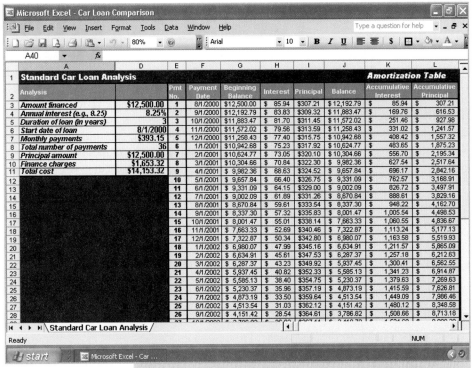

5.25 Using an Excel template, it's easy to calculate the true cost of a car. After you enter the interest rate, amount financed, and other loan information, Excel calculates and displays the total cost. You can compare car costs entering new numbers for each car.

"What If?" Questions

A spreadsheet program is a versatile tool, but it's especially valuable for answering "what if?" questions: "What if I don't complete the third assignment? How will that affect my

> The purpose of computation is not **numbers** but **insight**.
> —R. W. Hamming

chances for getting an A?" "What if I put my savings in a high-yield, tax-sheltered IRA account with a withdrawal penalty? Will I be better off than if I leave it in a low-yield passbook account with no penalty?" "What if I buy a car that gets only 15 miles per gallon instead of a car that gets 40? How much more will I pay altogether for fuel over the next four years?" Because it enables you to change numbers and instantly see the effects of those changes, spreadsheet software streamlines the process of searching for answers to these questions.

Some spreadsheet programs include equation solvers that turn "what if?" questions around. Instead of forcing you to manipulate data values until formulas give you the numbers you're looking for, an equation solver enables you to define an equation, enter your target value, and watch while the computer determines the necessary data values. For example, an investor might use an equation solver to answer the question "What is the best mix of these three stocks for minimizing risk while producing a 10 percent return on my investment?"

Spreadsheet Graphics: From Digits to Drawings

Most spreadsheet programs include charting and graphing functionality that can turn worksheet numbers into charts and graphs automatically. The process of creating a chart

> **Our work** . . . is to present things that are **as they are**.
> —Frederick II (1194–1250), King of Sicily

is usually as simple as filling in a few blanks in a dialog box.

The growth in election campaign spending seems more real as a line shooting toward the top of a graph than as a collection of big numbers on a page. The federal budget makes more (or less?) sense as a sliced-up dollar pie than as a list of percentages. The correct chart can make a set of stale figures come to life, awakening our eyes and brains to trends and relationships that we might not have otherwise seen. The charting and graphing functionality in spreadsheet programs offers a variety of basic chart types and options for embellishing charts. The differences among these chart types are more than aesthetic; each chart type is well suited for communicating particular types of information.

Pie charts show the relative proportions of the parts to a whole. Line charts are most often used to show trends or relationships over time or to show relative distribution of one variable through another. (The classic bell-shaped normal curve is a line chart.) Bar charts are similar to line charts, but they're more appropriate when data falls into a few categories. Bars can be stacked in a stack chart that shows how proportions of a whole change over time; the effect is similar to a series of pie charts. Scatter charts are used to discover, rather than display, a relationship between two variables. A well-designed chart can convey a wealth of information, just as a poorly designed chart can confuse or mislead.

A DECADE OF BANK FAILURES

5.26 Line and bar charts show trends over time or distribution over categories. Scatter charts show relationships between variables.

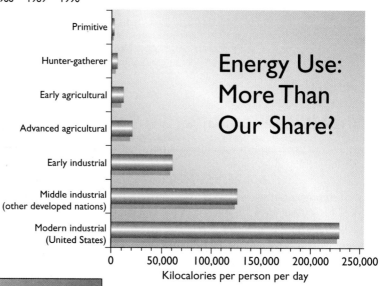

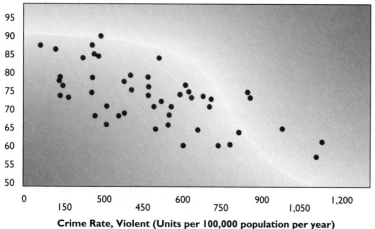

A chart can be a powerful communication tool if it's designed intelligently. If it's not, the message may miss the mark. Here are some guidelines for creating charts that are easy to read and understand.

➡ **Choose the right chart for the job.** Think about the message you're trying to convey. Pie charts, bar charts, line charts, and scatter charts are not interchangeable.

➡ **Keep it simple, familiar, and understandable.** Use charts in magazines, books, and newspapers as models.

➡ **Strive to reveal the truth, not hide it.** Whether accidentally or intentionally, many computer users create charts that convey misinformation. Changes in the scale or dimensions of a chart can completely transform the message, turning information into propaganda.

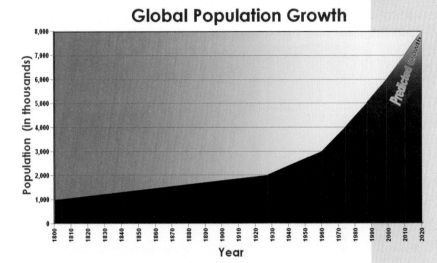

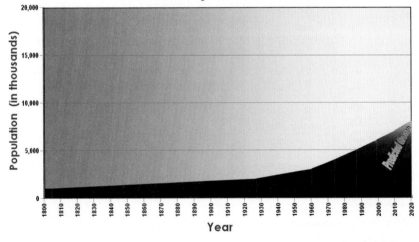

5.27 These charts are based on identical data, but only the first one clearly illustrates the data relationships. The second chart distorts the relationship by changing the vertical axis. The third chart hides the relationship with an inappropriately chosen pie chart.

Statistical Software: Beyond Spreadsheets

Science is what we understand well enough to **explain to a computer; art** is **everything else**.

—Donald Knuth, author of *The Art of Computer Programming*

Spreadsheet software is remarkably versatile, but no program is perfect for every task. Other types of number-manipulation software are available for those situations in which spreadsheets don't quite fit the job.

Money Managers

Spreadsheet software has its roots in the accountant's ledger sheets, but spreadsheets are seldom used for business accounting and bookkeeping. Accounting is a complex concoction of rules, formulas, laws, and traditions, and creating a worksheet to handle the details of the process is difficult and time-consuming. Instead of relying on general-purpose spreadsheets for accounting, most businesses (and many households) use professionally designed accounting and financial management software.

Whether practiced at home or at the office, accounting involves setting up accounts—monetary categories to represent various types of income, expenses, assets, and liabilities—and keeping track of the flow of money among those accounts. An accountant routinely records *transactions*—checks, cash payments, charges, and other activities—that move money from one account to another. Accounting software, such as Intuit's popular Quicken, automatically adjusts the balance in every account after each transaction. What's more, it records every transaction so that you can retrace the history of each account step-by-step. This *audit trail* is a necessary part of business financial records, and it is one reason accountants use special-purpose accounting packages rather than spreadsheet programs.

In addition to keeping records, financial management software can automate check writing, bill paying, budgeting, and other routine money matters. Periodic reports and charts can provide detailed answers to questions such as "Where does the money go?" and "How are we doing compared to last year?"

Through an Internet connection, a home accounting program can recommend investments based on up-to-the-hour performance statistics, track investment portfolios, comparison shop for insurance and mortgages, and link to specialized online calculators and advisors. Hundreds of financial institutions offer online banking services, making it possible to pay bills, check account balances, and transfer funds using software.

5.28 Inexpensive personal financial management programs make the accounting process easier to understand by simulating the look of checks and other familiar documents on the screen. Portable versions of these applications run on devices running Palm OS and the Pocket PC.

Most accounting and financial management programs don't calculate income taxes, but they can export records to programs that do. Tax preparation software works like a prefabricated worksheet. As you enter numbers into the blanks in on-screen forms, the program automatically fills in other blanks. Every time you enter or change a number, the bottom line is recalculated automatically. When the forms are completed, they're ready to print, sign, and mail to the Internal Revenue Service. Many taxpayers now bypass paper forms altogether by sending the completed forms electronically to the IRS.

Automatic Mathematics

Most of us seldom do math more complicated than filling out our tax forms. But higher mathematics is an essential part of the work of many scientists, researchers, engineers, architects, economists, financial analysts, teachers, and other professionals. Mathematics is a universal language for defining and understanding natural phenomena as well as a tool used to create all kinds of products and structures. Whether or not we work with it directly, our lives are constantly being shaped by mathematics.

Many professionals and students whose mathematical needs go beyond the capabilities of spreadsheets depend on symbolic mathematics processing software to grapple with complex equations and calculations. Mathematics processors make it easier for mathematicians to create, manipulate, and solve equations in

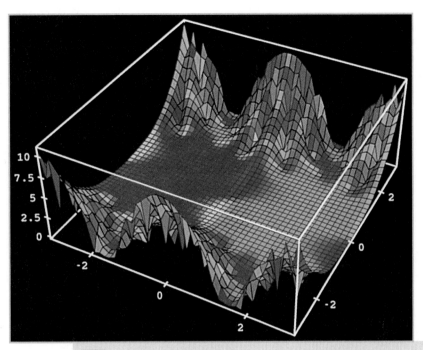

5.29 An abstract mathematical relationship is easier to understand when it is turned into a visible object with software such as Mathematica.

much the same way word processors help writers. Features vary from program to program, but a typical mathematics processor can do polynomial factoring, symbolic and numeric calculus, real and complex trigonometry, matrix and linear algebra, and three-dimensional graphics.

Mathematics processors generally include an interactive, wizardlike question-and-answer mode, a programming language, and tools for creating interactive documents that combine text, numerical expressions, and graphics. Although mathematics processors have only been available for a few years, they've already changed the way professionals use mathematics and the way students learn it. By handling the mechanics of mathematics, these programs enable people to concentrate on the content and implications of their work.

Statistics and Data Analysis

One branch of applied mathematics that has become more important in the computer age is statistics—the science of collecting and analyzing data. Modern computer technology provides us with mountains of data—census data, political

> Yet **to calculate** is not in itself **to analyze**.
> —Edgar Allan Poe, 1841

data, consumer data, economic data, sports data, weather data, scientific data, and more. We often refer to the data as statistics. ("The government released unemployment statistics today.") But the numbers by themselves tell only part of the story. The analysis of those numbers—the search for patterns and relationships among them—can provide meaning for the data. ("Analysts note that the rise in unemployment is confined to cities most heavily impacted by the freeze on government contracts.") Statisticians in government, business, and science depend on computers to make sense of raw data.

Do people who live near nuclear power plants run a higher cancer risk? Does the current weather pattern suggest the formation of a tropical storm? Are rural voters more likely to support small-town candidates? These questions can't be answered with absolute certainty; the element of chance is at the heart of statistical analysis.

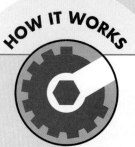

5.2
Scientific Computing

Computers have long been used to analyze and visualize scientific data collected through experiments and observation. A computer can also serve as a virtual laboratory that simulates a physical process without real-world experiments. Of course, an inaccurate simulation can give incorrect results. The problem of accurate simulation helped initiate the study of chaos and fractals. Chaos is now a vast field of study with applications in many disciplines.

The "Chaos Game" illustrates how computers can quickly complete repetitive tasks in experiments that would otherwise be impractical or impossible. You could perform the first few steps of such an experiment with pencil, paper, and ruler, like this:

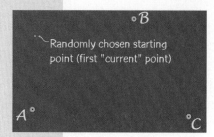

5.30a

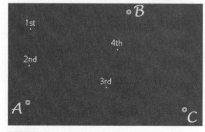

5.30b

5.30c

1. Draw three widely separated points on the paper to form a triangle; label the points A, B, and C. Draw a random starting point anywhere on the paper. This will be the first "current" point.

2. Repeat the following process four times: randomly choose from among points A, B, and C, and draw a new point halfway (on an imaginary straight line) between the current point and the chosen point. The newly drawn point then becomes >the new current point.

3. If you use a simple computer program to plot 100,000 repeats of step 2 (excluding the first few points from the drawing), you'll see a pattern emerge rather than a solid mass of dots. This pattern, called a Sierpinski gasket, is a fractal—an object in which pieces are miniatures of the whole figure. You will see a pattern like this.

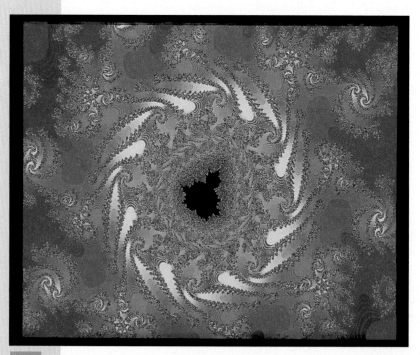

5.30d

Because some fractal formulas mimic the patterns of natural objects, such as coastlines and mountains, chaos has found applications in computer-generated scenery and special effects for movies and television shows.

The Mandelbrot set, discovered by the mathematician Benoit Mandelbrot (who coined the term fractal) while he was working at IBM's Thomas J. Watson Research Facility, is one of the most famous fractals to emerge from the theory of chaos.

But statistical analysis software can suggest answers to questions such as these by testing the strength of data relationships. Statistical software can also produce graphs showing how two or more variables relate to each other. Statisticians can often uncover trends by browsing through two- and three-dimensional graphs of their data, looking for unusual patterns in the dots and lines that appear on the screen. This kind of visual exploration of data is an example of a type of application known as *scientific visualization*.

Scientific Visualization

Scientific visualization software uses shape, location in space, color, brightness, and motion to help us understand relationships that are invisible to us. Like mathematical and

> The **wind blows** over the lake and **stirs the surface** of the water. Thus, **visible effects** of the **invisible** are manifested.
>
> —The *I Ching*

statistical software, scientific visualization software is no longer confined to mainframes and supercomputers; some of the most innovative programs have been developed for use on high-end personal computers and workstations, working alone or in conjunction with more powerful computers.

Scientific visualization takes many forms, all of which involve graphical representation of numerical data. The numbers can be the result of abstract equations, or they can be data gleaned from the real world. Either way, turning the numbers into pictures enables researchers and students to see the unseeable and sometimes, as a result, to know what was previously unknowable. Here are two examples:

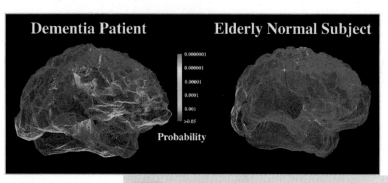

■ Astronomer Margaret Geller of Harvard University created a 3-D map of the cosmos from data on the locations of known galaxies. While using her computer to "fly through" this three-dimensional model, she saw something that no one had seen before: the mysterious clustering of galaxies along the edges of invisible bubbles.

■ Dr. Mark Ellisman of the University of California, San Diego, School of Medicine used a 30-foot electron microscope to collect data from cells of the brain and enter it into a supercomputer, which rendered a

5.31a These two visualizations, created at the Laboratory of Neuro Imaging (LONI), map physical differences between a normal human brain and one with a form of dementia.

3-D representation of the brain cell. When Ellisman's team displayed the data on a graphic workstation, they saw several previously undiscovered aberrations in brains of patients who had Alzheimer's disease—aberrations that may turn out to be clues for discovering the cause and cure for this disease.

In these examples and hundreds of others like them, visualization helps researchers see relationships that might have been obscure or even impossible to grasp without computer-aided visualization tools.

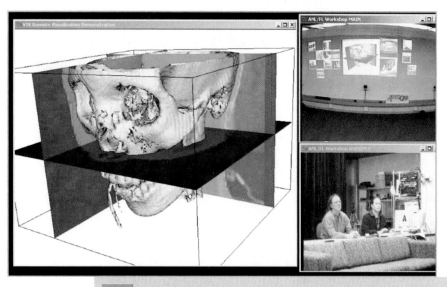

5.31b Using a tool called Access Grid, researchers work with a shared visualization called the Visible Human.

Calculated Risks:
Computer Modeling and Simulation

We have the ability to **model**—to prototype—**faster, better, and cheaper** than ever before. The old back-of-the-envelope is becoming **supercomputer driven** louver!

—Michael Schrage, author of *Serious Play*

Whether part of a simple worksheet or a complex set of equations, numbers often symbolize real-world phenomena. Computer modeling—the use of computers to create abstract models of objects, organisms, organizations, and processes—can be done with spreadsheets, mathematical applications, or standard programming languages. A business executive who creates a worksheet to project quarterly profits and losses is trying to model the economic world that affects the company. An engineer who uses a mathematics processor to test the stress capacity of a bridge is modeling the bridge mathematically. Even a statistician who starts by examining data collected in the real world creates statistical models to describe the data.

Computer models aren't always serious; most computer games are models. Chess-boards, pinball games, battlefields, sports arenas, ant colonies, cities, medieval dungeons, interplanetary cultures, and mythological societies have all been modeled in computer games. Students use computer models to travel the Oregon Trail, explore nuclear power plants, invest in the stock market, and dissect digital frogs.

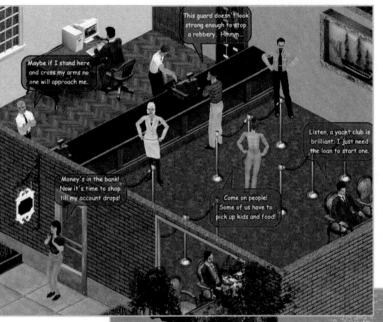

5.32 Consumer-oriented simulations enable people to experience and view artificial life. The Sims is a popular video game title in which users control and observe simulated people, or "Sims," in a virtual world. The Marine Aquarium screen saver offers a stunningly realistic artificial fish tank in which the occupants move and act naturally.

5.33 Flight simulators for home computers and video game consoles are based on the same simulation tehcnology that's used in military flight trainers that pilots use to train for war.

Whether it's created for work, education, or play, a computer model is an *abstraction*—a set of concepts and ideas designed to mimic some kind of system. But a computer model isn't static; you can put it to work in a computer simulation to see how the model operates under certain conditions. A well-designed model should behave like the system it imitates.

Suppose, for example, an engineer constructs a computer model of a new type of airplane to test how the plane will respond to human commands. In a typical flight simulation, the "pilot" controls the plane's thrust and elevator angle by feeding input data to the model plane. The model responds by adjusting air speed and angle of ascent or descent, just as a real plane would. The pilot responds to the new state of the aircraft by adjusting one or more of the controls, which causes the system to respond by revising the aircraft's state again. This **feedback loop**, where plane and pilot react to data from each other, continues throughout the simulation.

A flight simulator might have a graphical user interface that makes the computer screen look and act like the instrument panel of a real plane so that human pilots can run it intuitively. Or it might display nothing more than numbers representing input and output values, and the input values might be generated by a simulated pilot—another computer model! Either way, it can deliver a wealth of information about the behavior of the plane, provided the model is accurate.

Computer Simulations: The Rewards

> We are reaching the stage where **problems** that we **must solve** are going to become **insolvable** without computers. **I do not fear computers**; I fear the **lack of them**.
>
> —Isaac Asimov, scientist and science fiction writer

Computer simulations are widely used for research in the physical, biological, and social sciences and in engineering. Schools, businesses, and the military also use simulations for training. There are many reasons:

- *Safety*. Although it's safer to learn piloting skills sitting in front of a computer than actually flying in the air, it's still possible to learn to fly without a computer simulation. Some activities, however, are so dangerous that they aren't ethically possible without computer simulations. How, for example, can scientists study the effects of a nuclear power plant meltdown on the surrounding environment? Unless a meltdown occurs, there's only one practical answer: computer simulation.
- *Economy*. It's far less expensive for an automobile manufacturer to produce a digital model of a nonexistent car than to build a prototype out of steel. The company can test the computer model for strength, handling, and efficiency in a series of simulations before it builds and tests a physical prototype. The cost of the computer model is small when compared with the possible expense of producing a defective car.
- *Projection*. Without computers, it could take decades for biologists to determine whether the rising deer population on an island threatens other species, and by the time they discover the answer, it would be too late to do anything about it. A computer model of the island's ecosystem could speed up natural biological processes so scientists could measure their effects over several generations in a matter of minutes. A computer simulation can, in effect, serve as a time machine for exploring one or more possible futures.
- *Visualization*. Computer models make visualization possible, and visualization enables researchers and students to see and understand relationships that might otherwise go unnoticed. Computer models can speed time up or slow it down; they can make subatomic particles big and the universe small.
- *Replication*. In the real world, it can be difficult or impossible to repeat a research project with slightly different conditions. But this kind of repetition is an important part of serious research. An engineer needs to fine-tune dimensions and angles to achieve peak performance. A scientist studies the results of one experiment and develops a new hypothesis that calls for further testing. An executive needs to test a business plan under a variety of economic scenarios. If the research is conducted on a computer model, replication is just a matter of changing input values and running a new simulation.

Computer Simulations: The Risks

> All information is **imperfect**.
>
> —Jacob Bronowski

The downside of computer simulation can be summed up in three words: Simulation isn't reality. The real world is a subtle and complex place, and capturing even a fraction of that subtlety and complexity in a computer simulation is a tremendous challenge.

GIGO Revisited

The accuracy of a simulation depends on how closely its mathematical model corresponds to the system being simulated. Mathematical models are built on assumptions, many of which are difficult or impossible to verify. Some models suffer from faulty assumptions; others contain hidden assumptions that may not even be obvious to their creators; still others go astray simply because of clerical or human errors.

The daily weather report is the result of a complex computer model. Our atmosphere is far too complex to capture exactly in a computer model; that's why the weather forecast is sometimes wrong. Occasionally simulation errors produce disastrous results. Faulty computer models have been responsible for deadly flooding of the Colorado River, the collapse of the roof of a Salt Lake City shopping mall, and the crash of a test plane on its first flight. These kinds of disasters are rare. It's much more common for computer models to help avert tragedies by pointing out design flaws. In fact, sometimes things go wrong because people *ignore* the results of accurate simulations. Still, *garbage in, garbage out* is a basic rule of simulation.

Making Reality Fit the Machine

Simulations are computation intensive. Some simulations are so complex that researchers need to simplify models and streamline calculations to get them to run on the best hardware available. Even when there's plenty of computing power available, researchers face a constant temptation to reshape reality for the convenience of the simulation. In one classic example, a U.S. Forest Service computer model reduced complex old-growth forests to "accumulated capital." Aesthetics, ecological diversity, and other hard-to-quantify factors didn't exist in this model.

Sometimes this simplification of reality is deliberate; more often it's unconscious. Either way, information can be lost, and the loss may compromise the integrity of the simulation and call the results into question.

The Illusion of Infallibility

Risks can be magnified because people take computers seriously. People tend to emphasize computer-generated reports, often at the expense of other sources of knowledge. Executives use worksheets to make decisions involving thousands of jobs and millions of dollars. Politicians decide the fate of military weapons and endangered species based on summaries of computer simulations. Doctors use computer models to make life-and-death decisions involving new drugs and treatments. All of these people, in some sense, are placing their trust in computer simulations. Many of them trust the data precisely because a computer produced it.

A computer simulation, whether generated by a PC spreadsheet or churned out by a supercomputer, can be an invaluable decision-making aid. The risk is that the people who make decisions with computers will turn over too much of their decision-making power to the computer. The Jedi Master in *Star Wars* understood the danger when he encouraged Luke Skywalker in the heat of battle to turn off his computer simulation rather than let it overpower his judgment. His admonition was simple: "Trust your feelings."

Truly Intelligent Agents

I don't want to sit and move stuff around on my screen all day and look at figures and have it recognize my **gestures** and listen to my **voice**. I want to tell it what to do and then go away; I don't want to babysit this computer. I want it to act **for me, not with me**.

—Esther Dyson, computer industry analyst and publisher

At Xerox PARC Alan Kay and his colleagues developed the first user interface based on icons—images that represent tools to be manipulated by users. Their pioneering work helped turn the computer into a productivity tool for millions of people. According to Kay, future user interfaces will be based on agents rather than tools.

Agents are software programs designed to be managed rather than manipulated. An intelligent software agent can ask questions as well as respond to commands, pay attention to its user's work patterns, serve as a guide and a coach, take on its owner's goals, and use reasoning to fabricate goals of its own.

Many PC applications include *wizards* and other agent-like software entities to guide users through complex tasks and answer questions when problems arise. The Internet is home to a rapidly growing population of *bots*—software robots that crawl around the Web collecting information, helping consumers make decisions, answering email, and even playing games. But today's wizards, bots, and agents aren't smart enough to manage the many details that a human assistant might juggle.

Tomorrow's agents will be better able to compete with human assistants, though. A well-trained software agent in the future might accomplish these tasks:

➡ Remind you that it's time to get the tires rotated on your car, and make an appointment for the rotation.
➡ Distribute notes to the other members of your study group or work group, and tell you which members opened those notes.
➡ Keep you posted on new articles on subjects that interest you, and know enough about those subjects to be selective without being rigid.
➡ Manage your appointments and keep track of your communications.
➡ Teach you new applications and answer reference questions.
➡ Defend your system and your home from viruses, intruders, and other security breaches.
➡ Help protect your privacy on and off the Net.

Agents are often portrayed with human characteristics; *2001's* Hal and the computers on TV's *Star Trek* are famous examples. Of course, agents don't need to look or sound human—they just need to possess considerable knowledge and intelligence.

Future agents may possess a degree of sensitivity, too. Researchers at MIT and IBM are developing *affective computers* that can detect the emotional states of their users and respond accordingly. Affective computers use sensors to determine a person's emotional state. Sensors range from simple audiovisual devices to mouse-embedded sensors that work like lie detectors, monitoring pulse or skin resistance. Early research has shown limited success at identifying emotions, but the machines still have much to learn. They can't, for example, tell the difference between love and hate, because, from a physiological point of view, they look pretty much the same!

Copy Protection Robs
The Future Labor of Love **Dan Bricklin**

CROSSCURRENTS

Dan Bricklin, inventor of the first spreadsheet program, argues here that copy protection may make today's computer documents indecipherable tomorrow. This thought-provoking piece is an edited version of an article on his Web site, www.danbricklin.com.

The other day I wanted to listen to a song from my youth. I took the record out of its sleeve and put it on my aging turntable. I dropped the needle onto the track, and out came the music, but it was way too fast. My turntable now plays everything at 45 rpm instead of 33. Bummer!

This got me to thinking about preserving old works of composers, musicians, authors, and other creative individuals. How does that preserving come about and will today's works produced on digital media last into the future?

As human beings, we benefit greatly from the works of others. Artists, thinkers, scholars, and performers create works that we all enjoy, learn from, and are inspired by. Many works are timeless. We often hear of authors, artists, or composers who have their greatest impact after their death, sometimes many years later.

How are these works passed down through the generations? Other people make it their job to preserve the works and pass them on. These jobs are either formal, like librarians, or informal, like hobbyists.

How are the works preserved? Sometimes just storing the work is sufficient, but in most cases a change in environment is needed. The artist's original location may be sold for another use. The work may be created in a material that is affected by air and water, and must be kept in a temperature- and humidity-controlled room.

For some works, it's enough to just preserve the words themselves. For others, copies are what we preserve, such as recordings of performances, or microfilm copies of newspapers. We produce the copies in more stable media, or ones that are easier from which to reproduce.

With every changing technology, in order to preserve many works we will need to move them ahead, copying them to each new media form before the previous one becomes obsolete. Also, we need to preserve the knowledge of the methods of converting from one media to another, so we can access the old works that have not yet been moved ahead. This is crucial. Without this information, even preserved works could be unreadable.

The most famous example of that type of translation information was an inscribed slab of rock from 196 BC found in 1799. It contained a decree written in Greek that was also written in two forms of Egyptian. It's called the Rosetta Stone. It let scholars finally read ancient works in hieroglyphics that they had physical possession of but whose language had been a mystery for 1,400 years.

There are things happening that make me worry that the future may not be bright for preserving many of the works we create today. For example: Companies are preparing to produce music CDs that cannot be copied into many other formats (something allowed by law as "fair use"). Most ebooks are copy protected. A new law requires all digital devices to enforce copy protection schemes for copyrightable material. An existing law makes it a crime to tell people how to make copies of protected works.

I believe copy protection will break the chain necessary to preserve creative works. It will make them readable for a limited time and not be able to be moved ahead as media deteriorates or technologies change. Only those works that are thought to be profitable at any given time will be preserved by their "owners" (if they are still in business). We know from history that what's popular at any given time is no certain indication of what will be valuable in the future. Without not-copy protected "originals", archivists, collectors, and preservers will be unable to maintain them the way they would if they weren't protected. We won't even be able to read media in obsolete formats, because the specifications of those formats will not be available. To create a "Rosetta Stone" of today's new formats will be asking to go to jail and having your work banned.

This is different than encryption or patent protection. With encryption, as long as the keys survive, and a description of the method of decryption, you can recreate the unprotected original. It's even better—you can prove authenticity. Patent protection just keeps you from creating and using your unlicensed reader for a limited period of time. For long-term preservation of works patented techniques are good because they discourage secrets and eventually put things in the public domain.

One of the most popular parts of this web site is a copy of the original IBM PC version of VisiCalc. It's not the same exact program you could buy. The original VisiCalc was only shipped on 5¼" copy protected diskettes. I received permission from the copyright holder to distribute the copies, but VisiCalc hadn't been produced for years and they lost track of any original masters they had owned. Luckily for me, an employee of Software Arts kept a "test" copy that was created without the copy protection code. Thanks to those not-copy protected copies it is much more likely that future generations will be able to learn about early PC programs by running VisiCalc.

Copy protection, like poor environment and chemical instability before it for books and works of art, looks to be a major impediment to preserving our cultural heritage.

Artists and authors need to create their works and still make a living. Copy protection is arising as a "simple fix" to preserve business models based upon the physical properties of old media and distribution. Our new media and distribution techniques need new business models that don't shortchange the future. Trying to keep those old business models in place is as inappropriate as continuing to produce only 33 rpm vinyl records.

DISCUSSION QUESTIONS

1. Do you agree that copy protection will break the chain necessary to preserve creative works? Explain your answer.

2. What kind of "new business model" do you think the author is suggesting in the last paragraph?.

SUMMARY

Even though the computer was originally designed to work with numbers, it quickly became an important tool for processing text as well.

Word processing software enables the writer to use commands to edit text on the screen, eliminating the chore of retyping pages until the message is right. With a word processor, you can control the typefaces, spacing, justification, margins, columns, headers, footers, and other visual components of your documents. Most professional word processing programs automate footnoting, hyphenation, and other processes that are particularly troublesome to traditional typists.

Outlining software turns the familiar outline into a powerful, dynamic organizational tool. Spelling checkers and grammar and style checkers partially automate the proofreading process, although they leave the more difficult parts of the job to literate humans. Online thesauruses, dictionaries, and other computer-based references automate reference work.

As word processors become more powerful, they take on many of the features previously found only in desktop publishing software. Still, many publishers use word processors and graphics programs to create source documents that can be used as input for page-layout programs. Desktop publishing has revolutionized the publishing process by enabling publishers and would-be publishers to produce professional-quality text-and-graphics documents at a reasonable cost. Amateur and professional publishers everywhere use desktop publishing technology to produce everything from comic books to reference books.

The near-overnight success of desktop publishing may foreshadow other changes in the way we communicate with words as new technologies emerge. Computer networks in general and the World Wide Web in particular have made it possible for potential publishers to reach mass audiences without the problems associated with printing and distributing paper documents. Typing may no longer be a necessary part of the writing process as handwriting and speech-recognition technologies improve, and word processing software

that incorporates other artificial intelligence technologies may become as much a coach as a tool for future writers.

Spreadsheet programs, first developed to simulate and automate the accountant's ledger, can be used for tracking financial transactions, calculating grades, forecasting economic conditions, recording scientific data—just about any task that involves repetitive numeric calculations. Spreadsheet documents, called worksheets, are grids with individual cells containing alphabetic labels, numbers, and formulas. Changes in numeric values can cause the spreadsheet to update any related formulas automatically. The responsiveness and flexibility of spreadsheet software make it particularly well suited for providing answers to "what if?" questions. Most spreadsheet programs include charting commands to turn worksheet numbers into a variety of graphs and charts. The process of creating a chart from a spreadsheet is automated to the point where human drawing isn't necessary; the user simply provides instructions concerning the type of chart and the details to be included in the chart, and the computer does the rest.

Number crunching often goes beyond spreadsheets. Specialized accounting and tax preparation software packages perform specific business functions without the aid of spreadsheets. Symbolic mathematics processors can handle a variety of higher mathematics functions involving numbers, symbols, equations, and graphics. Statistical analysis software is used for data collection and analysis. Scientific visualization can be done with math processors, statistical packages, graphics programs, or specialized programs designed for visualization.

Modeling and simulation are at the heart of most applications involving numbers. When people create computer models, they use numbers to represent real-world objects and phenomena. Simulations built on these models can provide insights that might be difficult or impossible to obtain otherwise, provided that the models reflect reality accurately. If used wisely, computer simulation can be a powerful tool to help people understand their world and make better decisions.

KEY TERMS

account (p. 184)
accounting and financial
    management software (p. 184)
address (p. 176)
agents (p. 160)
automatic correction (autocorrect)
    (p. 160)
automatic footnoting (p. 160)
automatic formatting (p. 160)
automatic hyphenation (p. 160)

automatic link (p. 180)
automatic recalculation (p. 178)
bar chart (p. 182)
bot (p. 192)
camera-ready (p. 170)
cell (p. 176)
clipboard (p. 159)
column (p. 176)
copy (p. 159)
cut (p. 159)

cut-and-paste (p. 162)
desktop publishing (DTP) (p. 169)
drag-and-drop (p. 159)
electronic book (ebook) (p. 175)
electronic paper (epaper) (p. 175)
equation solvers (p. 181)
feedback loop (p. 189)
find-and-replace (search and replace)
    (p. 159)
font (p. 159)

footer (p. 160)
formatting (p. 159)
formula (p. 176)
function (p. 178)
garbage in garbage out (GIGO)
   (p. 180)
grammar and style checker (p. 166)
groupware (p. 166)
header (p. 160)
justification (p. 160)
label (p. 176)
line chart (p. 182)
macro (p. 178)
mail merge (p. 166)
mathematics processing software
   (p. 185)
modeling (p. 188)

monospaced font (p. 159)
online banking services (p. 184)
outliner (p. 163)
page-layout software (p. 169)
paste (p. 159)
pie chart (p. 182)
point size (p. 159)
proportionally spaced font (p. 160)
replication (p. 178)
sans-serif font (p. 159)
scatter chart (p. 182)
scientific visualization software
   (p. 187)
select text (p. 162)
serif font (p. 159)
source document (p. 169)
speech-recognition software (p. 167)

spelling checker (p. 165)
spreadsheet software (p. 176)
stack chart (p. 182)
statistical analysis software (p. 187)
statistics (p. 185)
style sheet (p. 160)
tax preparation software
   (p. 184)
templates (p. 169)
thesaurus (p. 164)
typeface (p. 159)
value (p. 176)
"what if?" question (p. 181)
wizard (p. 160)
word wrap (p. 159)
worksheet (p. 176)
WYSIWYG (p. 159)

INTERACTIVE QUIZ QUESTIONS

1. The *Computer Confluence* CD-ROM contains self-test multiple-choice quiz questions related to this chapter.

2. The *Computer Confluence* Web site, http://www.computerconfluence.com, contains self-test exercises related to this chapter. Follow the instruc-tions for taking a quiz. After you've completed your quiz, you can email the results to your instructor.

3. The Web site also contains open-ended discussion questions called Internet Explorations. Discuss one or more of the Internet Exploration questions at the section for this chapter.

TRUE OR FALSE

1. WYSIWYG stands for "What you see is what you get."

2. With most word processing programs, text editing must be completed before text formatting is started.

3. A monospaced font assigns equal horizontal space to all characters of the same point size.

4. Desktop publishing software does essentially the same thing as word processing software, but it can process larger documents.

5. One of the biggest problems with desktop publishing technology is that its high cost makes it impractical for small businesses and individuals.

6. Electronic publishing is replacing some forms of print publishing, but paper documents aren't likely to go away anytime soon.

7. Charting software, such as the chart tools built into spreadsheet software, generally contains safeguards that prevent the misrepresentation of information.

8. Most accounting and financial management programs don't calculate income taxes, but they can export records to programs that do.

9. Statistical analysis software can suggest answers to scientific questions by testing the strength of data relationships.

10. People tend to emphasize computer-generated reports, often at the expense of other sources of knowledge.

MULTIPLE CHOICE

1. Which of these is a text formatting feature of a word processing program?
   a. drag-and-drop.
   b. cut-and-paste.
   c. word wrap.
   d. style sheets.
   e. None of the above.

2. Which of these is a text editing feature of a word processing program?
   a. drag-and-drop.
   b. font choice.
   c. justification tools.
   d. style sheets.
   e. None of the above.

3. Justification generally applies to
   a. individual characters.
   b. words.
   c. paragraphs.
   d. fonts.
   e. All of the above.

4. In order to accurately represent full-color images, desktop publishing systems must use
   a. laser printers.
   b. service bureaus.
   c. color-matching technology.
   d. spot color.
   e. phototypesetting machines.

5. A document created with a desktop publishing system can be
   a. printed on a color printer.
   b. converted into a PDF document for electronic distribution.
   c. displayed on the Web.
   d. printed on a phototypesetting machine at a service bureau.
   e. All of the above.

6. If you change the value of numbers in a spreadsheet, changes may occur in cells containing
   a. values.
   b. macros.
   c. formulas.
   d. labels.
   e. templates.

7. Which type of chart is most appropriate for showing the percentages of the U.S. federal budget that go to domestic spending, military spending, other spending, and interest on the national debt?
   a. bar chart.
   b. line chart.
   c. scatter chart.
   d. pie chart.
   e. bullet chart.

8. Which of these types of software is used for creating models?
   a. spreadsheet software.
   b. accounting software.
   c. mathematics processing software.
   d. All of the above.
   e. None of the above.

9. Scientific visualization software
   a. requires visual input devices to work properly.
   b. is the scientific equivalent of desktop publishing software.
   c. creates pictures from numbers.
   d. requires supercomputer power to run.
   e. doesn't exist yet, but it will be a reality before the end of the decade.

10. Simulation software offers many advantages, including all of these EXCEPT:
    a. it can save money.
    b. it can be much safer than "real-world" experience.
    c. it is generally more accurate than standard experimental research.
    d. it can save time.
    e. it makes experimental replication easier.

REVIEW QUESTIONS

1. How is word processing different from typing?

2. How many different ways can a paragraph or line of text be justified? When might each be appropriate?

3. How is working with an outliner (or idea processor) different from working with a word processor?

4. Describe three different ways a spelling checker might be fooled.

5. How does desktop publishing differ from word processing?

6. Is it possible to have a computer publishing system that is not WYSIWYG? Explain.

7. An automated speech-recognition system might have trouble telling the difference between a "common denominator" and a "comedy nominator." What must the speaker do to avoid confusion? What other limitations plague automated speech-recognition systems today?

8. In what ways are word processors and spreadsheet programs similar?

9. What are some advantages of using a spreadsheet over using a calculator to maintain a budget? Are there any disadvantages?

10. If you enter 5B21C2 in cell B1 of a worksheet, the formula is replaced by the number 125 when you press the Enter key. What happened?

11. Explain the difference between a numeric value and a formula.

12. Describe or draw examples of several different types of charts, and explain how they're typically used.

13. Describe several software tools used for numeric applications too complex to be handled by spreadsheets. Give an example of an application of each.

14. List several advantages and disadvantages of using computer simulations for decision making.

DISCUSSION QUESTIONS

1. What do you think of the arguments that word processing reduces the quality of writing because (1) it makes it easy to write hurriedly and carelessly and (2) it puts the emphasis on the way a document looks rather than on what it says?

2. Like Gutenberg's development of the movable-type printing press more than 500 years ago, the development of desktop publishing puts powerful communication tools in the hands of more people. What impact will desktop publishing technology have on the free press and the free exchange of ideas guaranteed in the United States Constitution? What impact will the same technology have on free expression in other countries?

3. Spreadsheets are sometimes credited with legitimizing the personal computer as a business tool. Why do you think they had such an impact?

4. The statement "Computers don't make mistakes, people do" is often used to support the reliability of computer output. Is the statement true? Is it relevant?

5. Before spreadsheets, people who wanted to use computers for financial modeling had to write programs in complex computer languages to do the job. Today, spreadsheets have replaced those programs for many financial applications. Do you think spreadsheets will be replaced by some easier-to-use software tool in the future? If so, try to imagine what it will be like.

PROJECTS

1. Use a word processing system or a desktop publishing system to produce a newsletter, brochure, or flyer in support of an organization or cause that is important to you.

2. Use a spreadsheet or a financial management program to develop a personal budget. Try to keep track of all your income and outgo for the next month or two, and record the transactions with your program. At the end of that time, evaluate the accuracy of your budget, and discuss your reactions to the process.

3. Use a spreadsheet to search for answers to a "what if" question that's important to you. Possible questions: What if I lease a car instead of buying it—am I better off? What if I borrow money for school—how much does it cost me in the long run?

4. Use a spreadsheet to track your grades in this (or another) class. Apply weightings from the course syllabus to your individual scores, calculating a point total based on those weightings.

SOURCES AND RESOURCES

Books

Bootstrapping: Douglas Engelbart, Coevolution, and the Origins of Personal Computing, by Thierry Bardini (Stanford, CA: Stanford University Press, 2000). This long-overdue book shines a spotlight on the visionary, revolutionary work of Douglas Engelbart at SRI.

The Handbook of Digital Publishing, Volumes I & II, by Michael L. Kleper (Upper Saddle River, NJ: Prentice Hall, 2001). These two books, which are available in a box set, cover every aspect of digital publishing, including typography, design, imaging, page layout, color management, workflow, multimedia, Web publishing, and careers.

The Non-Designer's Design Book, by Robin Williams (Berkeley, CA: Peachpit Press, 1994). In this popular book, Robin Williams provides a friendly introduction to the basics of design and page layout in her popular, down-to-earth style. The first half of the book illustrates the four basic design principles (proximity, alignment, repetition, and contrast). The second half focuses on using type as a design element. This book is highly recommended for anyone new to graphic design.

Looking Good in Print, Fourth Edition, by Roger C. Parker and Patrick Berry (Scottsdale, AZ: Paraglyph Publishing, 2003). This book covers the nontechnical side of desktop publishing. Now that you know the mechanics, how can you make your work look good? Parker and Berry clearly describe the basic design tools and techniques and then apply them in sample documents ranging from brochures to books.

Designing for Print: An In-depth Guide to Planning, Creating, and Producing Successful Design Projects, by Charles Conover (New York: Wiley, 2003). This book clearly explains—and shows—how to design successful publications using type, photos, illustrations, and other elements in creative ways.

Bugs in Writing: A Guide to Debugging Your Prose, by Lyn Dupre (Reading, MA: Addison-Wesley, 1998). This entertaining little book is designed to help computer science and computer information systems students—who presumably already know how to debug their programs—debug their prose. It's a friendly, readable tutorial that can help almost anybody to be a better writer.

The Elements of Style, Fourth Edition, by William Strunk, Jr., and E. B. White (Needham Heights, MA: Allyn & Bacon, 2000). If you want to improve your writing, this book is a classic.

The Microsoft Manual of Style for Technical Publications, Third Edition (Redmond, WA: Microsoft Press, 2003). This style guide is a useful alphabetical reference when you need to write about computer hardware and software. Especially useful is its appendix listing industry acronyms and abbreviations.

Scrolling Forward: Making Sense of Documents in the Digital Age, by David M. Levy (Arcade Publishing, 2001). How are computers, the Internet, and digital technology in general changing the notion of documents? The future of books, paper, copyrights, and libraries are discussed in this thought-provoking book.

How to Lie with Statistics, by Darrell Huff (New York: W. W. Norton, 1993). This classic book—first published in 1954—has more relevance in today's computer age than it did when it was written.

The Sum of Our Discontent: Why Numbers Make Us Irrational, by David Boyle (Texere, 2001). Computers, television, and other media bombard us with more numbers than most of us can digest. Boyle argues that all those numbers make it harder, not easier, to understand what's going on around us.

Designing Infographics, by Eric K. Meyer (Indianapolis, IN: Hayden Books, 1997). This book provides an excellent overview of the theory and the practice of designing the modern graphs, charts, and other informative illustrations found in such publications as *USA Today*. It covers tools, techniques, forms, and applications of quantitative and informative graphics; there's even a section on statistical ethics.

Serious Play: How the World's Best Companies Simulate to Innovate, by Michael Schrage (Cambridge, MA: Harvard Business School Press, 1999). "When talented innovators innovate, you don't listen to the specs they quote. You look at the models they've created," says Michael Schrage, MIT Media Lab fellow and *Fortune* magazine columnist. In this book, Schrage looks at the kind of "serious play" being done at innovative companies such as Disney, 3M, Sony, and Hewlett Packard.

World Wide Web Pages

Created as a tool for scientific researchers and engineers, the Web is full of fascinating sites about mathematics, statistics, scientific visualization, and simulation and is an endless resource for publishers, writers, and page designers. Some, like **http://www.adobe.com**, are obvious; others are harder to find but no less useful. Check the *Computer Confluence* Web site at **http://www.computerconfluence.com** for links to the best pages.

AFTER YOU READ THIS CHAPTER YOU SHOULD BE ABLE TO:

- Video Demonstration of a leading 3D software package

- Interactive tutorial on making presentations

- Interactive activities explaining pixel and vector graphics

- How data compression works

- Describe several present and future applications for multimedia technology

 Multimedia extras on the CD-ROM and the Web:

- **Video demonstration** of a leading 3D software package

- Interactive **tutorial** on making presentations

- Interactive **activities** explaining pixel and vector graphics

- How **data compression** works

- Interactive **self-study** quizzes

- **Free** software sources

    . . . and more.

 computerconfluence.com

6

GRAPHICS, DIGITAL MEDIA, AND MULTIMEDIA

TIM BERNERS-LEE WEAVES THE WEB FOR EVERYBODY

The Internet has long been a powerful communication medium and a storehouse of valuable information. But until recently, few people mastered the cryptic codes and challenging languages that were required to unlock the Internet's treasures. The Net was effectively off-limits to most of the world's people. Tim Berners-Lee changed all that when he single-handedly invented the World Wide Web and gave it to all of us.

Tim Berners-Lee was born in London in 1955. His parents met while programming the Ferranti Mark I, the first commercial computer. They encouraged their son to think unconventionally. He developed a love for electronics and even built a computer out of spare parts and a TV set when he was a physics student at Oxford.

Berners-Lee took a software engineering job at CERN, the European Particle Physics Laboratory in Geneva, Switzerland. While he was there, he developed a program to help him track all of his random notes. He tried to make the program, called Enquire, deal with information in a "brainlike way." Enquire was a primitive hypertext system that allowed related documents on his computer to be linked with numbers rather than mouse clicks. (In 1980 PCs didn't have mice.)

Berners-Lee wanted to expand the concept of Enquire so he could link documents on other computers to his own. His idea was to create an open-ended, distributed hypertext system with no boundaries so scientists everywhere could link their work together.

Over the next few years, he single-handedly built a complete system to realize his dream. He designed

> The whole idea you can have some idea and **make it happen** means that **dreamers** all over the world should **take heart** and **not stop**.
>
> —Tim Berners-Lee, creator of the World Wide Web

the URL scheme for giving every Internet document a unique address. He developed HTML, the language for encoding and displaying hypertext documents on the Web. He created HTTP, the set of rules that allows hypertext documents to be linked across the Internet. And he built the first software browser for viewing those documents from remote locations.

When he submitted the first paper describing the Web to a conference in 1991, the conference organizers rejected it because the Web seemed too simple to them. They

6.1 Tim Berners-Lee, the inventor of the World Wide Web.

thought that Berners-Lee's ideas would be a step backward when compared to hypertext systems that had been developed by Ted Nelson, Doug Engelbart, and others over the previous 25 years. It's easy to see now that the simplicity of the Web was a strength, not a weakness.

Rather than trying to own his suite of inventions, Berners-Lee made them freely available to the public. Suddenly, vast tracts of the Internet were open to just about anyone who could point and click a mouse. Other programmers added multimedia capabilities to the Web, and its popularity spread like a virus. In a few short years, the Internet was transformed from a forbidding fortress of cryptic commands and codes into an inviting multimedia milieu for the masses.

When he created the Web, Tim Berners-Lee created a new medium of communication. Few people in history have had so great an impact on the way we communicate. In the words of writer Joshua Quittner, Tim Berners-Lee's accomplishments are "almost Gutenbergian."

Tim Berners-Lee now works in an unassuming office at MIT, where he heads the World Wide Web Consortium (W3C). The W3C is a standards-setting organization dedicated to helping the Web evolve in positive directions rather than disintegrating into incompatible factions. The work of Tim Berners-Lee and the W3C will help ensure that the World Wide Web continues to belong to everyone.

6.2 The multimedia interface to the Internet—called the Web—was born at CERN in Geneva, Switzerland.

The work of Tim Berners-Lee brought multimedia to millions of people all around the world. Today, the Web is a source of images, sounds, animations, video clips, and rich interactive documents that merge multiple media types. Even without the Web, though, today's PC can serve as a digital hub for a network of creative media tools, from digital cameras and graphics tablets to musical instruments and video systems. In this chapter we look into these cutting-edge technologies and see how they're changing the ways we create and communicate.

Focus on Computer Graphics

Mastering technology is only part of what it means **to be an artist** in the twenty-first century. The other hurdle is **mastering creative expression**, so that art has **something substantial** to say. **Expression** has been **the one constant** among artists **from the Stone Age** until now. The only thing that has changed is the **technology**.

—Steven Holtzman, author of *Digital Mantras*

The last chapter explored a variety of computer applications, from basic word processing programs to powerful mathematical software packages that can analyze data and generate quantitative charts and graphs from numbers. But computer graphics today go far beyond page layouts and pie charts. In this section, we explore a variety of graphical applications, from simple drawing and painting tools to complex programs used by professional artists and designers.

Painting: Bitmapped Graphics

An image on a computer screen is made up of a matrix of pixels—tiny dots of white, black, or color arranged in rows. The words, numbers, and pictures we see on the computer display are nothing more than patterns of pixels created by software. Most of the time, the user doesn't directly control those pixel patterns; software creates the patterns automatically in response to commands. For example, when you press the *e* key while word processing, software constructs a pattern that appears on the screen as an *e*. Similarly, when you issue a command to create a bar chart from a spreadsheet, software automatically constructs a pixel pattern that looks like a bar chart. Automatic graphics are convenient, but they can also be restrictive. When you need more control over the details of the screen display, another type of graphics software might be more appropriate.

> **Everything** you **imagine** is real.
>
> —Pablo Picasso

Painting software enables you to "paint" pixels on the screen with a pointing device. A typical painting program accepts input from a mouse, joystick, trackball, touch pad, or stylus, translating the pointer movements into lines and patterns on-screen. A professional artist might prefer to work with a stylus on a pressure-sensitive tablet because it can, with the right software, simulate a traditional pen or paintbrush more accurately than other pointing devices can. A painting program typically offers a palette of tools on-screen. Some tools mimic real-world painting tools, while others can do things that are difficult, even impossible, on paper or canvas.

Painting programs create bitmapped graphics (or, as they're sometimes called, raster graphics)—pictures that are, to the computer, simple maps showing how the pixels on the screen should be represented. For the simplest bitmapped graphics, a single bit of computer memory represents each pixel. Since a bit can contain one of two possible values, 0 or 1, each pixel can display one of two possible colors, usually black or white. Allocating more memory per pixel, so each pixel can display more possible colors or shades, produces even higher-quality graphics. Gray-scale graphics allow each pixel to appear as black, white, or one of several shades of gray. A program that assigns 8 bits per pixel allows up to 256 different shades of gray to appear on the screen—more than the human eye can distinguish.

6.3 When it's used with compatible software, a stylus on a pressure-sensitive tablet can simulate the feel of a paintbrush on paper. As the artist presses harder on the stylus, the line becomes thicker and denser on the screen.

Realistic color graphics require more memory. Many older computers have hardware to support 8-bit color, allowing 256 possible colors to be displayed on the screen at a time—enough to display rich images, but not enough to exactly reproduce photographs. Photorealistic color requires hardware that can display millions of colors at a time—24 or 32 bits of memory for each pixel on the screen. Modern personal computers are equal to this task.

The number of bits devoted to each pixel—called color depth or bit depth—is one of two technological factors limiting an artist's ability to create realistic on-screen images with a bitmapped graphics program. The other factor is resolution—the density of the pixels, usually described in *dots per inch*, or *dpi*. Not surprisingly, these are also the two main factors controlling image quality in monitors, as described in Chapter 3. But some graphics images are destined for the printer after being displayed on-screen, so the printer's resolution comes into play, too. When displayed on a 96-dpi computer screen—on a Web page, for example—a 96-dpi picture looks fine. But when printed on paper, that same image lacks the fine-grain clarity of a photograph. Diagonal lines, curves, and text characters have tiny "jaggies"—jagged, stair-step-like bumps that advertise the image's identity as a collection of pixels.

6.4 Natural painting programs such as Corel Painter allow artists and nonartists to create digital paintings that simulate real-world tools like watercolors, oil paints, and charcoal.

Painting programs get around the jaggies by allowing you to store an image at 300 dots per inch or higher, even though the computer screen can't display every pixel at that resolution and normal magnification. Of course, these high-resolution pictures demand more memory and disk space. But for printed images, the results are worth the added cost. The higher the resolution, the harder it is for the human eye to detect individual pixels on the printed page.

Practically speaking, resolution and bit-depth limitations are easy to overcome with today's hardware and software. Artists can use paint programs to produce works that convincingly simulate watercolors, oils, and other natural media, and transcend the limits of those media. Similarly, bitmapped image-editing software can be used to edit photographic images.

Image Processing: Photographic Editing by Computer

The aim of every artist is to **arrest motion**, which is **life**, by artificial means and **hold it fixed** so that **a hundred years later**, when a stranger looks at it, **it moves again** since it is life.

—William Faulkner

Like a picture created with a high-resolution paint program, a digitized photograph or a photograph captured with a digital camera—often simply referred to as a *digital photo*—is a bitmapped image. Image processing software enables the photographer to manipulate digital photos and other high-resolution images with tools similar to those found in paint programs. Image processing software, such as Adobe Photoshop, is in many ways similar to paint software—both are tools for editing high-resolution bitmapped images.

Digital image processing software makes it easier for photographers to remove unwanted reflections, eliminate "red eye," and brush away facial blemishes—to perform the kinds of editing tasks that were routinely done with magnifying glasses and tiny brushes before photographs were digitized. But digital photographic editing is far more powerful than traditional photo-retouching techniques. With image processing software, it's possible to distort photos,

Creating a CD Cover with Adobe Photoshop

6.5a You select a print of the band and a digital camera photo of a conga drum; your final cover will combine these images. You scan the print, transfer the band image from your camera to your computer, and save each of them as Photoshop documents.

6.5b You create a mask which hides everything except the selected drum. You drag the drum photo into the window with the band photo, which pastes it into a new layer so it can be moved and modified independently.

6.5c To create uniform lighting you flip the drum image horizontally and adjust the brightness on some faces. You resize the canvas to the dimensions of a standard CD booklet. You also resize the drum, distort it, and partially blur it. You add a title, resize it, and bend it so that it matches the perspective of the drum head. You're ready to print.

6.6 This painting served as the cover art for a Herbie Hancock CD called *Dis is de Drum*. Photographer Sanjay Kothari created the image through the process of digital photographic manipulation. Several of the photos used in the final collage are shown along the side of the main image. On the bottom of the image are three small images that show how the photos were merged to create the final image.

6.7 Apple's iPhoto, like many PC photo applications, makes it easy to import, edit, and organize photos. iPhoto also automates the creation of custom photo albums that can be turned into professionally bound books via an online store.

apply special effects, and fabricate images that range from artistic to other-worldly. It's also possible to combine photographs into composite scenes that show no obvious evidence of tampering. Supermarket gossip tabloids routinely use these tools to create sensationalistic cover photos. Many experts question whether photographs should be allowed as evidence in the courtroom now that they can be doctored so convincingly.

A digital camera typically stores images in a small amount of onboard RAM or on a flash memory card; images are typically downloaded from camera to computer via a USB connection. Digital *photo management software* programs such as Apple iPhoto and Microsoft PictureIt! simplify and automate common tasks associated with capturing, organizing, editing, and sharing digital images. Most consumer-oriented digital photo managers make it easy to import photos from digital cameras, remove red eye, adjust color and contrast, fix small errors, print photos on a color printer, upload images to a Web site, email copies to friends and family, store photo libraries on CD or DVD, and order paper prints or hardbound photo albums online.

Modern graphics software isn't just for professional artists. Just about anybody can create pictures and presentations. Here are some guidelines to help you make the most of the computer as a graphic tool:

→ **Reprogram yourself . . . relax.** For many of us the hardest part is getting started. We are all programmed by messages we received in our childhood, which for many of us included "You aren't creative" and "You can't draw." Fortunately, a computer can help us overcome this early programming and find the artist that's locked within us. Most drawing and painting programs are flexible, forgiving, and fun. Allow yourself to experiment; you'll be surprised at what you can create if you're patient and playful.

→ **Choose the right tool for the job.** Will your artwork be displayed on the computer screen or printed? Does your output device support color? Would color enhance the finished work? Your answers to these questions will help you determine which software and hardware tools are most appropriate. As you're thinking about options, don't rule out low-tech tools. The best approach may not involve a computer, or it may involve some combination of computer and nonelectronic tools.

→ **Borrow from the best.** Art supply stores sell *clip art*— predrawn images that artists can legally cut out and paste into their own pictures or posters. Computer artists have hundreds of digital clip art collections to choose from, with a difference: Computer clip art images can be cut, pasted, and edited electronically. Some computer clip art collections are in the public domain (that is, they are free); others can be licensed for a small fee. Computer clip art comes in a variety of formats, and it ranges from simple line drawings to scanned color photographs. If you have access to a scanner, you can create your own digitized clip art from traditional photos and drawings.

→ **Don't borrow without permission.** Computers, scanners, and digital cameras make it all too easy to create unauthorized copies of copyrighted photographs, drawings, and other images. There's a clear legal and ethical line between using public domain or licensed clip art and pirating copyrighted material. If you use somebody else's creative work, make sure you have written permission from the owner.

→ **Protect your own work.** Copyright laws aren't just to protect other people's work. If you've created something that's marketable, consider copyrighting it. The process is easy and inexpensive, and it might help you to get credit (and payment) where credit is due. For more information, go to the U.S. Copyright Office Web Site: http://lcweb.loc .gov/copyright/

Drawing: Object-Oriented Graphics

Because high-resolution paint images and photographs are stored as bitmaps, they can make heavy storage and memory demands. Another type of graphics program can economically store pictures with virtually *infinite* resolution, limited only by the capabilities of the output device. Drawing software stores a picture not as a collection of dots, but as a collection of lines and shapes. When you draw a line with a drawing program, the software doesn't record changes in the underlying pixels. Instead, it calculates and remembers a mathematical formula for the line. A drawing program stores shapes as shape formulas and text as text. Because pictures are collections of lines, shapes, and other objects, this approach is often called object-oriented graphics or vector graphics. In effect, the computer is remembering "a blue line segment goes here and a red circle goes here and a chunk of text goes here" instead of "this pixel is blue and this one is red and this one is white . . . ."

Many drawing tools—line, shape, and text tools—are similar to painting tools in bitmapped programs. But the user can manipulate objects and

> Actually, a root word of technology, **techne**, originally meant **"art."** The ancient Greeks never separated **art** from **manufacture** in their minds, and so never developed **separate words** for them.
> —Robert Pirsig, in *Zen and the Art of Motorcycle Maintenance*

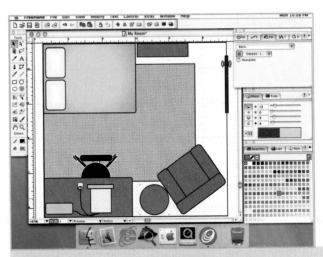

6.8 This room floor plan was created in minutes with Macromedia Freehand, a professional drawing and illustration program. Each piece of furniture can be moved as an independent object in the drawing.

edit text without affecting neighboring objects, even if the neighboring objects overlap. On the screen, an object-oriented drawing looks similar to a bitmapped painting. But when it's printed, a drawing appears as smooth as the printer's resolution allows. (Of course, not all drawings are designed to be printed. You may, for example, use a drawing program to create images for publication on a Web page. Because many Web browsers recognize only bitmapped images, you'll probably convert the drawings to bit maps before displaying them.)

Many professional drawing programs, including Adobe Illustrator and Macromedia Freehand, store images using PostScript—a standard page-description language for describing text fonts, illustrations, and other elements of the printed page. PostScript is built into many laser printers and other high-end output devices, so those devices can understand and follow PostScript instructions. PostScript-based drawing software constructs a PostScript program as the user draws. This program provides a complete set of instructions for reconstructing the picture at the printer. When the user issues a Print command, the computer sends PostScript instructions to the printer, which uses those instructions to construct the grid of microscopic pixels that will be printed on each page. Most desktop publishing software uses PostScript in the same way. Mac OS X uses PostScript to display on-screen graphics.

Object-oriented drawing and bitmapped painting each offer advantages for certain applications. Bitmapped image-editing programs give artists and photo editors unsurpassed control over textures, shading, and fine detail; they're widely used for creating screen displays (for example, in video games, multimedia presentations, and Web pages), for simulating natural paint media, and for embellishing photographic images. Object-oriented drawing and illustration programs are a better choice for creating printed graphs, charts, and illustrations with clean lines and smooth shapes. Some integrated programs, including Corel Draw and AppleWorks, contain both drawing and painting modules, allowing you to choose the right tool for each job. Some programs merge features of both in a single application, blurring the distinction and offering new possibilities for amateur and professional illustrators.

6.9 Pixels versus Objects

How do you edit a picture? It depends on what you're doing and how the picture is stored.

The task . . .	Using bit-mapped graphics	Using object-oriented graphics
Moving and removing parts of pictures	Easier to work with regions rather than objects (note), especially if those objects overlap	Easier to work with individual objects or groups of objects, even if they overlap
Working with shapes	Shapes stored as pixel patterns can be edited with eraser and drawing tools	Shapes stored as math formulas can be transformed mathematically
Magnification	Magnifies pixels for fine detail editing	Magnifies objects, not pixels
Text handling	Text "dries" and can't be edited, but can be moved as a block of pixels — When paint text "dries" it can't be edited like other text	Text can always be edited — Draw text always can be changed
Printing	Resolution of printout can't exceed the pixel resolution of the stored picture	Resolution is limited only by the output device
Working within the limits of the hardware	Photographic quality is possible but requires considerable memory and disk storage	Complex drawings require considerable computational power for reasonable speed

3-D Modeling Software

Working with a pencil, an artist can draw a representation of a three-dimensional scene on a two-dimensional page. Similarly, an artist can use a drawing or painting program to create

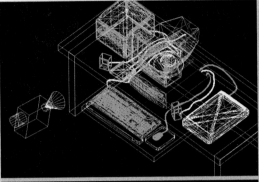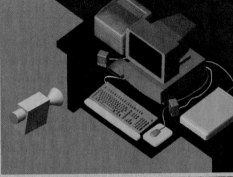

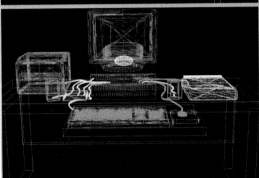

a scene that appears to have depth on a two-dimensional computer screen. But in either case, the drawing lacks true depth; it's just a flat representation of a scene. With **3-D modeling software** graphic designers can create 3-D objects with tools similar to those found in conventional drawing software. You can't touch a 3-D computer model; it's no more real than a square, a circle, or a letter created with a drawing program. But a 3-D computer model can be rotated, stretched, and combined with other model objects to create complex 3-D scenes.

Illustrators who use 3-D software appreciate its flexibility. A designer can create a 3-D model of an object, rotate it, view it from a variety of angles, and take two-dimensional "snapshots" of the best views for inclusion in final printouts. Similarly, it's possible to "walk through" a 3-D environment that exists only in the computer's memory, printing snapshots that show the simulated space from many points of view. For many applications, the goal is not a printout but an animated presentation on a computer screen or videotape. Animation software, presentation graphics software, and multimedia authoring software (all described later in this chapter) can display sequences of screens showing 3-D objects being rotated, explored, and transformed. Many modern television and movie special effects involve combinations of live action and simulated 3-D animation. Techniques pioneered in *The Matrix*, *Jurassic Park*, *Finding Nemo*, and other films continually push computer graphics to new levels of realism.

6.10 This personal computer system is a 3-D model created using Strata Studio Pro 3-D modeling software. These images depict wireframe view and various stages of rendering. The final image is in the lower right.

CAD/CAM: Turning Pictures into Products

Three-dimensional graphics also play an important role in the branch of engineering known as **computer-aided design (CAD)**—the use of computers to design products. CAD software allows engineers, designers, and architects to create designs on-screen for products ranging from computer chips to public buildings. Today's software goes far beyond basic drafting and object-oriented graphics. It allows users to create three-dimensional "solid" models with physical characteristics like weight, volume, and center of gravity. These models can be visually rotated and viewed from any angle.

6.11 Animated 3-D figures using technology from LifeFX can simulate human expressions for use in Internet-based video communications.

6.12 Engineers use CAD software running on powerful workstations to design everything from microscopic electronic circuits to massive structures.

The computer can evaluate the structural performance of any part of the model by applying imaginary force to the object. Using CAD, an engineer can crash-test a new model of an automobile before it ever leaves the computer screen. CAD tends to be cheaper, faster, and more accurate than traditional design-by-hand techniques. What's more, the forgiving nature of the computer makes it easy to alter a design to meet project goals.

Computer-aided design is often linked to **computer-aided manufacturing (CAM)**. When the design of a product is completed, the numbers are fed to a program that controls the manufacturing of parts. For electronic parts, the design translates directly into a template for etching circuits onto chips. The emergence of CAD/CAM has streamlined many design and manufacturing processes. The combination of CAD and CAM is often called **computer-integrated manufacturing (CIM)**; it's a major step toward a fully automated factory.

Presentation Graphics: Bringing Lectures to Life

One common application for computer graphics today is the creation of visual aids—slides, transparencies, graphics displays, and handouts—to enhance presentations. Although drawing and painting programs can create these aids, they aren't as useful as programs designed with presentations in mind.

Presentation graphics software helps to automate the creation of visual aids for lectures, training sessions, sales demonstrations, and other presentations. Presentation graphics programs are most commonly used for creating and displaying a series of on-screen "slides" to serve as visual aids for presentations. Slides might include photographs, drawings, spreadsheet-style charts, or tables. These different graphical elements are usually integrated into a series of **bullet charts** that list the main points of a presentation. Slides can be output as 35-mm color slides, overhead transparencies, or handouts. Presentation graphics programs can also display "slide shows" directly on computer monitors or LCD projectors, including animation and video clips along with still images. Some can convert presentations into Web pages automatically.

Because they can be used to create and display on-screen presentations with animated visual effects and video clips, presentation graphics programs, such as Microsoft's PowerPoint, are sometimes called *multimedia presentation tools*. These programs make it easy for nonartists to combine text, graphics, and other media in simple multimedia presentations. But more dramatic effects are possible. A free add-on for PowerPoint called Producer, makes it possible for users to publish video presentations to the Web or CD/DVD. Producer presentations can include a video of the presenter speaking, a revolving slide show, and a navigable chapter listing.

We now turn our attention to several types of media that go beyond the limitations of the printed page or the static screen; then we look at how *multimedia authoring* software can combine these diverse media types to produce dynamic, interactive documents.

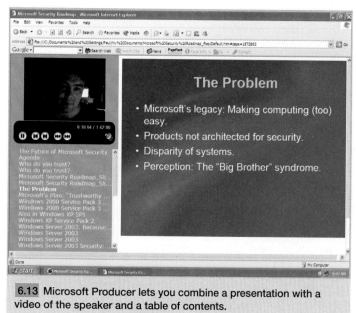

6.13 Microsoft Producer lets you combine a presentation with a video of the speaker and a table of contents.

Creating a Presentation with Microsoft PowerPoint

SCREEN TEST

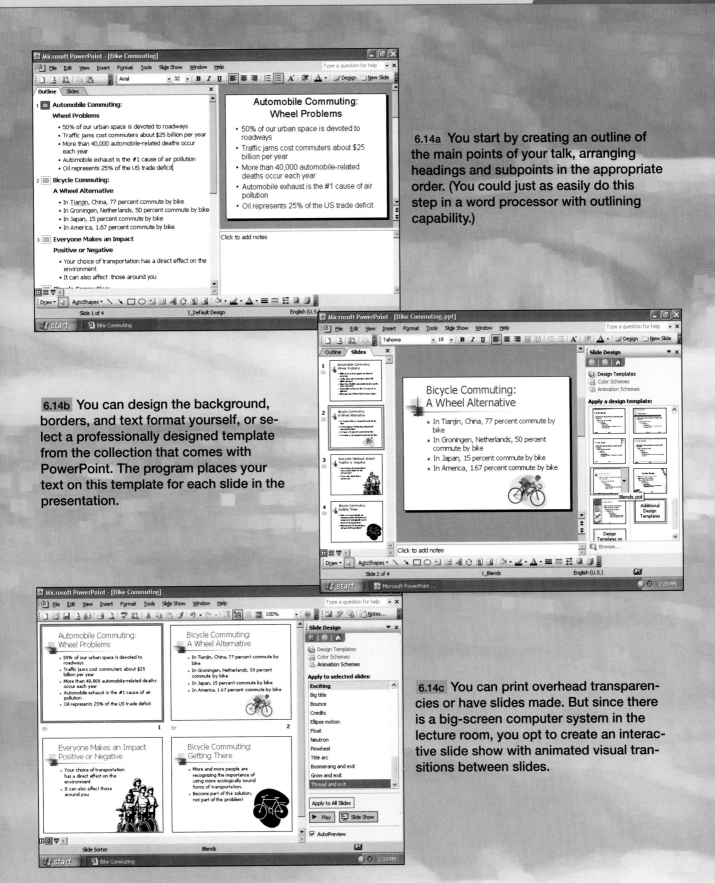

6.14a You start by creating an outline of the main points of your talk, arranging headings and subpoints in the appropriate order. (You could just as easily do this step in a word processor with outlining capability.)

6.14b You can design the background, borders, and text format yourself, or select a professionally designed template from the collection that comes with PowerPoint. The program places your text on this template for each slide in the presentation.

6.14c You can print overhead transparencies or have slides made. But since there is a big-screen computer system in the lecture room, you opt to create an interactive slide show with animated visual transitions between slides.

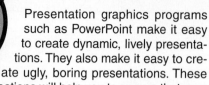

Presentation graphics programs such as PowerPoint make it easy to create dynamic, lively presentations. They also make it easy to create ugly, boring presentations. These suggestions will help you to ensure that your presentations aren't snoozers.

➡ *Remember your goal.* Know what you're trying to communicate. Keep your goal in mind throughout the process of creating the presentation.

➡ *Remember your audience.* How much do they know about your topic? How much do they need to know? Do key terms need to be defined?

➡ *Outline your ideas.* If you can't express your plan in a clear, concise outline, you probably won't be able to create a clear, concise presentation. Once your outline is done, you can import it into your presentation graphics software and massage it into a presentation.

➡ *Be stingy with words.* Avoid big words, long sentences, complex lists, and tiny type. Keep your prose lively and to the point.

➡ *Keep it simple.* Avoid useless decorations and distractions. Avoid fancy borders and backgrounds. Don't use a different transition on every slide.

➡ *Use a consistent design.* Make sure all of your slides look like they belong together. Use the same fonts, backgrounds, and colors throughout your presentation. If you don't trust your design skills, use predesigned templates.

➡ *Be smart with art.* Don't clutter your presentation with random clip art. Make sure each illustration contributes to your message. Use simple data graphs if they can support your main points. When you do use clip art or illustrations, make sure they coordinate with the colors and design of the rest of the presentation.

➡ *Keep each slide focused.* Each screen should convey one idea clearly, possibly with a few concise supporting points.

➡ *Tell them what you're going to tell them, then tell them, then tell them what you told them.* It's the speechmaker's fundamental rule, and it applies to presentations, too.

Dynamic Media: Beyond the Printed Page

The world is **complex, dynamic, multidimensional;** the paper is **static, flat**. How are we to represent the **rich visual world** of experience and measurement on mere **flatland**?

—Edward R. Tufte, in *Envisioning Information*

Most PC applications—painting and drawing programs, word processors, desktop publishers, and so on—are designed to produce paper documents. But many types of modern media can't be reduced to pixels on printouts because they contain dynamic information—information that changes over time or in response to user input. Today's multimedia computers enable us to create and edit animated sequences, video clips, sound, and music along with text and graphics. Just as words and pictures serve as the raw materials for desktop publishing, dynamic media like animation, video, audio, and hypertext are important components of interactive multimedia projects.

Animation: Graphics in Time

We're on the threshold of a moment in cinematic history that is unparalleled. **Anything** you can **imagine** can be done. If you can **draw it**, if you can **describe it**, we can **do it**. It's just a matter of cost.

—James Cameron, filmmaker

Creating motion from still pictures—this illusion is at the heart of all animation. Before computers, animated films were hand-drawn, one still picture, or frame, at a time. Modern computer graphics technology has transformed both amateur and professional animation by automating many of the most tedious aspects of the animation process.

In its simplest form, computer-based animation is similar to traditional frame-by-frame animation techniques; each frame is a computer-drawn picture, and the computer displays those frames in rapid succession. With an animation program, an animator can create key frames and objects and use software to help fill in the movement of the objects in the in-between frames—a process known as *tweening*. The most powerful animation programs include tools for working with animated objects in three dimensions, adding depth to the scene on the screen.

Animation on the Web ranges from simple GIF animation, which works like a children's flip-book, to complex cartoon animations created with programs like Macromedia Flash MX and Director MX. Computer animation has become commonplace in everything from television commercials to feature films. Sometimes computer animation is combined with live-action film; James Cameron's *Terminator* films and George Lucas's recent *Star Wars* episodes rely heavily on computer animation to enhance live action. Other films, including *Toy Story*, *Shrek*, and *Finding Nemo* use computer animation to create every character, scene, and event, leaving only the soundtrack for live actors and musicians to create.

6.15 Macromedia Director MX is a popular multimedia program with powerful animation capabilities. The frames in the Cast window show several different views of an object as it moves through the timeline shown in the Score window.

6.16 The animated films *Shrek* and *Shrek 2* feature computer-generated characters with amazingly emotive faces.

Desktop Video: Computers, Film, and TV

Digital technology is the **same revolution** as adding **sound** to pictures and the same **revolution** as adding **color** to pictures. **Nothing more** and **nothing less**.

—George Lucas, filmmaker

There's more to the digital video revolution than computer animation. Computers can be used to edit video, splice scenes, add transitions, create titles, and do other tasks in a fraction of the time—and at a fraction of the cost—of precomputer techniques. The only requirement is that the video be in a digital form so the computer can treat it as data.

Analog and Digital Video

Conventional television and video images are stored and broadcast as analog (smooth) electronic waves. A video digitizer can convert analog video signals from a television broadcast or videotape into digital data. Most video digitizers must be installed as add-on cards or external devices that plug into serial or USB ports. Broadcast-quality digitizers are relatively expensive; low-cost models are available for consumers who can settle for less-than-perfect images.

Many video digitizers can import signals from televisions, videotapes, video cameras, and other sources and display them on the computer's screen in *real time*—at the same time they're created or imported. The computer screen can serve as a television screen or, with a network connection, a viewing screen for a live video teleconference. For many applications, it's not important to display digitized images in real time; the goal is to capture entire video sequences and convert them into digital "movies" that can be stored, edited, and played on computer screens without external video equipment.

Video professionals and hobbyists who use *digital video cameras* don't need to digitize their video footage before working with it in a computer, because it's already in digital form. Digital video cameras capture and store all video footage as digital data. Most digital video cameras have FireWire (IEEE 1394) ports (see Chapter 3) that can be used to copy raw video footage from tape to a computer and later copy the edited video back from computer to tape. Because digital video can be reduced to a series of numbers, it can be copied, edited, stored, and played back without any loss of quality. Digital video will soon replace analog video for most applications.

Video Production Goes Digital

A typical video project starts with an outline and a simple *storyboard* describing the action, dialog, and music in each scene. The storyboard serves as a guide for shooting and editing scenes.

Digital video image

Video camera

6.17 Video can be easily transferred from a variety of video sources to a computer's hard drive. Separate interfaces are required for digital and analog video sources: Typically, digital video is transferred via FireWire, while analog video can be transferred via USB or proprietary AV converter hardware.

Today, most video editing is done using *nonlinear editing* technology. For nonlinear editing, video and audio clips are stored in digital form on a computer's hard disk. These digital clips can be organized, rearranged, enhanced, and combined using on-screen tools and commands. Nonlinear editing is faster and easier than older editing techniques, and it allows filmmakers to do things that aren't possible without computers. Video editing makes massive storage and memory demands on a computer. Until recently, nonlinear editing technology was only available to professionals. But falling hardware prices and technological advances make it possible for hobbyists to edit video with inexpensive desktop machines.

Video editing software such as Adobe Premiere, Apple iMovie, and Microsoft Windows Movie Maker 2 makes it easy to eliminate extraneous footage, combine clips from multiple takes into coherent scenes, splice together scenes, insert visual transitions, superimpose titles, synchronize a soundtrack, and create special effects. High-end editing software can combine live action with computer animation. Software can also create **morphs**—video clips in which one image metamorphoses into another. Photoshop-style tools allow artists to, for example, paint one or two frames with a green polka-dotted sky and then have those painting effects automatically applied to the other frames.

After it's edited, the video clip can be output to a videotape. The process is simplest and most effective in an all-digital system using FireWire and a digital camcorder. With a DVD-R drive and software such as Apple's iDVD or Sonic MyDVD, video footage can be pressed onto a DVD, complete with menus and navigational features not available on tape.

6.18 Software can turn a desktop or notebook computer into a video editing and production station. Programs like Apple's iMovie and iDVD (above) make it easy for non-professionals to capture and edit video footage, add special effects and audio, and publish the finished movie on a DVD, tape, CD-ROM, or Web site. Professional programs such as Apple's Final Cut Pro and DVD Studio Pro (below) perform the same functions to the exacting standards of industry professionals.

6.19 Many CD-ROMs combine digital video with animation and interactivity. In Steven Spielberg's *Survivors: Testimonies of the Holocaust,* four Holocaust survivors tell their stories in illustrated video presentations that emphasize the importance of tolerance in everyday life.

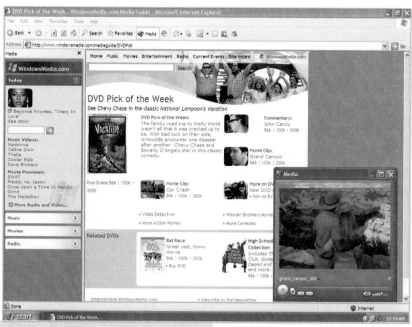

6.20 Many Web sites deliver streaming video content to viewers with fast broadband Internet connections.

Edited video doesn't need to be exported to tape or DVD. Many digital clips end up in multimedia presentations. On-screen digital movies can add realism and excitement to educational, training, presentation, and entertainment software. Video clips are also common on the Web. Media players such as Apple's cross-platform QuickTime, Microsoft Windows Player, and RealNetworks RealONE make it possible for any multimedia-capable computer to display digital video clips without additional hardware.

Data Compression

Digital movies can make heavy hardware demands; even a short full-screen video clip can quickly fill a large hard disk or CD-ROM. To save storage space and allow the processor to keep up with the quickly changing frames, digital movies designed for the Web or CD-ROM are often displayed in small windows with fewer than the standard video rate of 30 frames per second. In addition, data compression software and hardware squeezes data out of movies so they can be stored in smaller spaces, often with a slight loss of image quality, though newer formats like MPEG-4 and Windows Media Video 9 lessen this problem. General data compression software can be used to reduce the size of almost any kind of data file; specialized *image compression software* is generally used to compress graphics and video files. Modern media players, such as QuickTime and Windows Media Player, include several common software compression schemes. Some compression schemes involve specialized hardware as well as software.

Even highly compressed video clips gobble up storage space quickly. As compression and storage technologies continue to improve, digital movies will become larger, longer, smoother, and more common in everyday computing applications.

Professionals in the motion picture, television, and video industries create their products using graphics workstations that cost hundreds of thousands of dollars. Today, it's possible to put together a Windows- or Macintosh-based system that can perform most of the same functions for a fraction of the cost. Low-cost desktop video systems are transforming the film and video industry in the same way that desktop publishing has revolutionized the world of the printed word. They're also making it possible for individuals, schools, and small businesses to create near-professional quality videos.

The Synthetic Musician: Computers and Audio

Sound and music can turn a visual presentation into an activity that involves the ears, the eyes, and the whole brain. For many applications, sound puts the *multi* in *multimedia*. Computer sounds can be digitized—digitally recorded—or

> It's **easy to play** any musical instrument: all you have to do is **touch the right key** at the right time and **the instrument will play itself**.
>
> —J. S. Bach

synthesized—synthetically generated. Windows PCs (using sound cards; see Chapter 3, "Hardware Basics: Peripherals") and Macintoshes (which have sound hardware already built in) can produce sounds that go far beyond the basic beeps of early computers; most of them can also digitize sounds.

Digital Audio Basics

Any sound that can be recorded can be captured with an audio digitizer and stored as a data file on a disk. Digitized sound data, like other computer data, can be loaded into the computer's memory and manipulated by software. Sound-editing software can change a sound's volume and pitch, add special effects such as echoes, remove extraneous noises, and even rearrange musical passages. Sound data is sometimes called *waveform audio* because this kind of editing often involves manipulating a visual image of the sound's waveform. To play a digitized sound, the computer must load the data file into memory, convert it to an analog sound, and play it through a speaker.

Recorded sound can consume massive amounts of space on disk and in memory. As you might expect, higher-quality sound reproduction generally requires more memory. The difference is due in part to differences in *sampling rate*—the number of sound "snapshots" the recording equipment takes each second. A higher sampling rate produces more realistic digital sounds in the same way that higher resolution produces more realistic digital photographs—it allows for more accurate modeling of the analog source. The number of bits per sample, usually 8 or 16, also affects the quality of the sound; this is similar to a digital photograph's bit depth.

Music is digitized on audio CDs at a high sampling rate and bit depth—high enough that it's hard to tell the difference between the original analog sound and the final digital recording. But CD audio is memory intensive; a 3-minute song takes about 30 megabytes of space on a compact disc. Files that large are expensive to store and slow to transmit through networks. That's why most computer sound files are recorded at a lower sampling rate and bit depth—and therefore don't have the sound quality of an audio CD recording. Sound data compression, like image compression, can make a file even smaller. Since computers can read standard audio CDs, it's easy to *rip*, or copy, songs from a CD to the computer's hard drive, and *burn*, or copy, audio CDs that contain ripped songs. Until recently, high-quality sounds required large files, and compact files compromised quality. But relatively new methods of compression, including MP3 (for MPEG Audio Layer 3), AAC (Advanced Audio Codec), and WMA (Windows Media Audio) can squeeze music files to a fraction of their original CD-file sizes, often with an imperceptible loss of quality. MP3, AAC, and WMA make it practical to transmit songs and other recordings through the Internet, store them on hard disks, and play them on pocket-sized devices without disk or tape. Audio files are available for free on hundreds of Web sites. Many are contributed by undiscovered musicians who want exposure; others are copied from copyrighted CDs and distributed illegally.

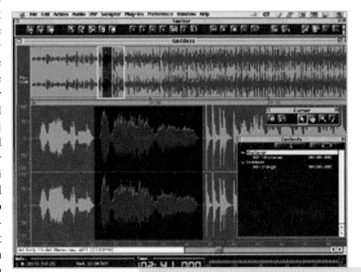

6.21 You can edit waveform audio files in a variety of ways using software tools such as Peak, from Bias, Inc.

6.1
Data Compression

A full-screen 256-color photograph or painting takes about a megabyte of storage—the same as the complete text from a typical paperback book! Graphic images, digital video, and sound files can consume massive amounts of storage space on disk and in memory; they can also be slow to transmit over computer networks. Data compression technology allows large files to be temporarily squeezed so they take less storage space and network transmission time. Before they can be used, compressed files must be decompressed. (In the physical world, many companies "compress" goods to save storage and transportation costs: When you "just add water" to a can of concentrated orange juice, you're "decompressing" the juice.)

All forms of compression involve removing bits; the trick is to remove bits that can be replaced when the file can be restored. Different compression techniques work best for different types of data.

Suppose you want to store or transmit a large text file. Your text compression software might follow steps similar to those shown here:

1. Each character in the uncompressed ASCII file occupies 8 bits; a seven-character word—*invoice*, for example—requires 56 bits of storage.

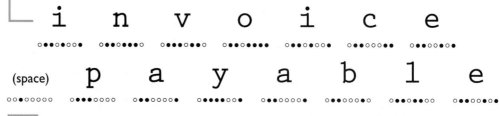

6.22a

2. A 2-byte binary number can contain code values ranging from 0 to 65,535—enough codes to stand for every commonly used word in English. This partial code dictionary shows the code values for a few words, including *invoice* and *payable*.

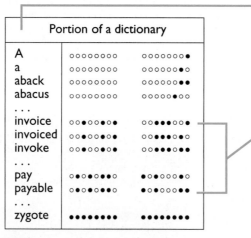

6.22b

3. To compress a file using a code dictionary, the computer looks up every word in the original file; in this example, *invoice* and *payable*. It replaces each word with its 2-byte code value. In this example, they are % 9 and V ú. The seven-character word now takes up only 16 bits—less than one-third of its original size.

%   9   V   ú

6.22c

4. In a compressed file, these 2-byte code values would be used to store or transmit the information for *invoice* and *payable*, using fewer bits of information either to increase storage capacity or to decrease transmission time.

5. To reverse the process of compression, the same dictionary (or an identical one on another computer) is used to decompress the file, creating an exact copy of the original. All the tedious dictionary lookup is performed quickly by a computer program.

6.22d

Compression programs usually work on patterns of bits rather than English words. One type of digital video compression stores values for pixels that change from one frame to the next; there's no need to repeatedly store values for pixels that are the same in every frame. For example, the only pixels that change in these two pictures are the ones that represent the unicycle and the shadows.

In general, compression works because most raw data files contain redundancy that can be "squeezed out." *Lossless compression* systems allow a file to be compressed and later decompressed without any loss of data; the decompressed file will be an identical copy of the original file. Popular lossless compression systems include ZIP/PKZIP (DOS/Windows), StuffIt (Macintosh), tar (UNIX), and GIF (general graphics). A *lossy compression* system can usually achieve better compression than a lossless one but may lose some information in the process; the decompressed file isn't always identical to the original. This is tolerable in many types of sound, graphics, and video files but not for most program and data files. JPEG is a popular lossy compression system for graphics files.

MPEG is a popular compression system for digital video. An MPEG file takes just a fraction of the space of an uncompressed video file. Because decompression programs demand time and processing power, playback of compressed video files can sometimes be jerky or slow. Some computers get around the problem with MPEG hardware boards that specialize in compression and decompression, leaving the CPU free for other tasks. *Hardware compression* is likely to be built into most computers as multimedia becomes more commonplace.

6.22e The original photographic image (above) is clear with an uncompressed size of 725 KB. The image on the right shows the visible lossy effect of agressive JPEG compression. But the size of the compressed file is only 19 KB.

Digital Audio Do's and Don'ts

RULES OF THUMB

Whether you're digitizing your audio CD collection or subscribed to an online music service, you'll find your digital audio experiences will go more smoothly if you understand a few simple rules.

➡ **Don't steal.** It's OK to copy audio CDs to your PC, use those songs on portable audio devices, and mix CDs you create, but only if you own the originals. Don't "borrow" music from a friend or steal music online.

➡ **Understand streaming and downloading.** Internet radio stations typically *stream* music to your system in real time, so the songs are never actually downloaded and stored locally on your computer. When you download a song from a service like the iTunes Music Store, you are receiving a physical file that you can back up and copy to other systems, depending on the rights granted to you via the service's DRM scheme (See below). Streaming audio is fleeting—the stream dries up the second your Internet connection goes down or you disconnect from the service. Downloadable music is persistent, because it stays on your system.

➡ **Know your file formats.** Uncompressed audio CD files can gobble up hard disk space at an alarming rate. The MP3 compression format is popular because it produces much smaller files that are almost indistinguishable from uncompressed audio files. But MP3 isn't the only popular audio compression format. Many Macintosh audio files are stored in the relatively new AAC format, which includes *digital rights management (DRM)* technology designed to protect the artists'

intellectual property. Many Windows users prefer Microsoft's WMA format, which can offer identical quality to MP3 at smaller file sizes; WMA also offers DRM capabilities.

➡ **Don't overcompress.** Audio compression is lossy, so there's always a loss of quality when you compress a sound file. There's no way to put back the bits that you squeeze out in the compression process. Most people

6.23 The iTunes Music Store enables Mac and Windows users to purchase music by their favorite artists in protected digital format.

can't distinguish between a 160 Kbps MP3 file or a 128 Mbps AAC or WMA file and an original audio CD recording. But if you choose too low a bit rate when compressing a file, you may squeeze the life out of the music.

Popular Digital Audio Formats.

Format	Downloadable	Streamable	Typically used for . . .
MP3	Yes	Yes	Ripping (copying) CDs to the computer and to portable audio players
WMA	Yes	Yes	Ripping CDs to the computer and for purchased music from online music stores
AAC	Yes	Yes	Purchased music from online music stores
RealAudio	Yes	Yes	Audio streams from commercial Web sites like CNN
MIDI	Yes	Yes	Contains no audio—just sequences of commands to control musical instruments and music samples on a PC

A few years ago, online *peer-to-peer (P2P) file sharing services* such as Napster popularized the illegal sharing of stolen music. Napster is no longer the center of illegal file trading, but music piracy thrives in other Internet venues. Still, there are many online sources for legally downloading music files using AAC and WMA formats. One of the first commercial online music services, Apple's iTunes Music Store, pioneered the concept of selling individual songs rather than entire albums. The iTunes Music Store and others that followed offer convenience for customers without robbing musicians and others who work in the music industry. Customers can play their purchases on their computers, burn them to CDs, or download them into iPods and other portable music players.

Ethical and legal issues raised by digital audio files will be discussed in more detail in Chapter 9 and Chapter 10.

Samplers, Synthesizers, and Sequencers: Digital Audio and MIDI

Multimedia computers can control a variety of electronic musical instruments and sound sources using **MIDI** (Musical Instrument Digital Interface)—a standard interface used to send commands to instruments and sound sources. MIDI commands can be interpreted by a variety of music *synthesizers* (electronic instruments that synthesize sounds using mathematical formulas), *samplers* (instruments that can digitize, or sample, audio sounds, turn them into notes, and play them back at any pitch), and hybrid instruments that play sounds that are part sampled and part synthesized. But most multimedia PCs can also interpret and execute MIDI commands using sounds built into their sound cards or stored in software form. Whether the sounds are played back on external instruments or internal devices, the computer doesn't need to store the entire recording in memory or on disk; it just has to store commands to play the notes in the proper sequence. A MIDI file containing the MIDI messages for a song or soundtrack requires only a few kilobytes of memory.

Anyone with even marginal piano-playing skills can create MIDI music files. A piano-style keyboard sends MIDI signals to the computer, which interprets the sequence of MIDI commands using **sequencing software**. (While the keyboard is the most common MIDI controller for sequencing, MIDI communication capabilities are built into other types of instruments, including drums, guitars, and horns.) Sequencing software turns a computer into a musical composition, recording, and editing machine. The computer records MIDI signals as a musician plays each part on a keyboard. The musician can use the computer to layer instrumental tracks, substitute instrument sounds, edit notes, cut and paste passages, transpose keys, and change tempos, listening to each change as it's made. The finished composition can be played by the sequencing software or exported to any other MIDI-compatible software, including a variety of multimedia applications.

6.24 In the modern music studio, computer keyboards and music keyboards often sit side-by-side.

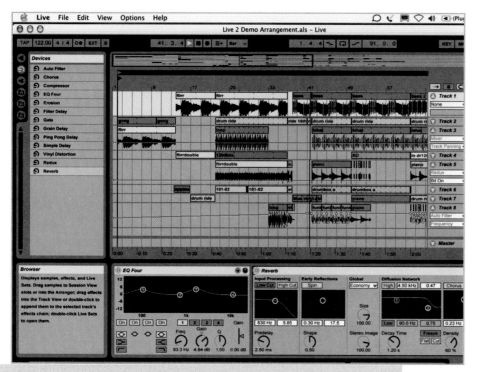

6.25 A growing number of musicians depend on sequencers to play along with live musicians in performances. Abelon's Live is a sequencer with special features for bridging the communication gap between human players and computer in concert.

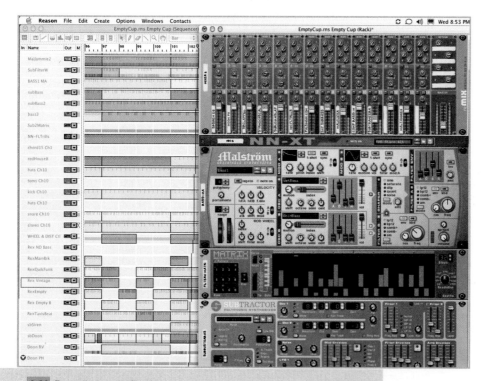

6.26 Propellerhead's Reason is a powerful electronic music program that includes a sequencer and a rack full of virtual electronic instruments.

Sequencing software can be used to imitate (with varying degrees of success) anything from a Bach fugue to a rock jam. Some of the most interesting sequenced music is *electronica*—music that is designed from the ground up with digital technology. Today's sequencers aren't limited to sequencing MIDI commands; most can record digital audio tracks as well as MIDI tracks, making it possible to include voices and nonelectronic instruments in the mix. The audio and MIDI data is recorded directly onto the computer's hard disk, making tape unnecessary.

A typical electronic music studio includes a variety of synthesizers, samplers, and other instruments. But the trend today is to replace many bulky, expensive hardware devices with virtual instruments—instruments that exist only in software. With today's powerful CPUs and massive storage devices, it's possible to have a professional-level multitrack recording and editing studio that fits in a suitcase.

Professional musicians use computers for composing, recording, performing, music publishing, and music education. Just as computer graphics technology has changed the way many artists work, electronic music technology has transformed the world of the musician. What's more, computer music technology has the power to unleash the musician in the rest of us.

Hypertext and Hypermedia

Word processors, drawing programs, and most other applications today are WYSIWYG—what you see (on the screen) is what you get (on the printed page). But WYSIWYG isn't always necessary or desirable. If a document doesn't need to be printed, it doesn't need to be

> Human Beings are naturally predisposed **to hear, to remember, and to tell stories.** The **problem**—for teachers, parents, government leaders, friends, and **computers**—is to have **more interesting stories** to tell.
>
> —Roger Schank et al., in *Tell Me a Story: Narrative and Intelligence*

structured like a paper document. If we want to focus on the relationship of ideas rather than the layout of the page, we may be better off with another kind of document—a dynamic, cross-referenced super document that takes full advantage of the computer's interactive capabilities.

Since 1945 when President Roosevelt's science advisor, Vannevar Bush, first wrote about such an interactive cross-referenced system, computer pioneers like Doug Engelbart and Ted Nelson (who coined the term *hypertext*) pushed the technology toward that vision. Early efforts were called hypertext because they allowed textual information to be linked in *nonsequential* ways. Conventional text media like books are linear, or *sequential*: They are designed to be read from beginning to end. A hypertext document contains *links* that can lead readers quickly to other parts of the document or to other related documents. Hypertext invites readers to cut their own personal trails through information.

Hypertext first gained widespread public attention in 1987, when Apple introduced HyperCard, a hypermedia system that could combine text, numbers, graphics, animation, sound effects, music, and other media in hyperlinked documents. (Depending on how it's used, the term *hypermedia* might be synonymous with *interactive multimedia*.) Today, millions of Windows and Macintosh users routinely use hypertext whenever they consult online Help files, and handheld computer and Tablet PC users navigate hypermedia-enabled ebooks. But the biggest hotbed of hypertext/hypermedia activity is the World Wide Web, where hypertext links connect documents all over the Internet.

But in spite of its popularity, hypertext isn't likely to replace paper books any time soon. Web users and others who use hypertext have several legitimate complaints:

- Hypermedia documents can be disorienting and leave readers wondering what they've missed. When you're reading a book, you always know where you are and where you've been in the text. That's not necessarily true in hypermedia.
- Hypermedia documents don't always have the links readers want. Hypermedia authors can't build every possible connection into their documents, so some readers are frustrated because they can't easily get "there" from "here."
- Hypermedia documents sometimes contain "lost" links, especially on the Web, where even a popular page can disappear without a trace anytime.
- Hypermedia documents don't encourage scribbled margin notes, highlighting, or turned page corners for marking key passages. Some hypermedia documents provide controls for making "bookmarks" and text fields for adding personal notes, but they aren't as friendly and flexible as traditional paper markup tools.
- Hypermedia hardware can be hard on humans. Most people find that reading a computer screen is more tiring than reading printed pages, though modern screen technology like Microsoft ClearType seeks to reduce this problem. Many people complain that extended periods of screen-gazing cause eyestrain, headache, backache, and other ailments. It's not always easy to stretch out under a tree or curl up in an easy chair with a Web-linked computer, though notebooks and Tablet PCs are making anywhere–everywhere computing more viable.

The art of hypermedia is still in its infancy. Every new art form takes time to develop. How can writers develop effective plot lines if they don't know what path their readers will choose through their stories? This is just one of the hundreds of questions with which hypermedia authors are struggling. Still, hypermedia is not all hype. As the art matures, advances in software and hardware design will take care of many of these problems. Even today hypermedia documents provide extensive cross-referencing, flexibility, and instant keyword searches that simply aren't possible with paper media.

Interactive Multimedia: Eye, Ear, Hand, and Mind

> The hybrid or the meeting of two media is a **moment of truth and revelation** from which a **new form** is born.
>
> —Marshall McLuhan, in *Understanding Media; The Extensions of Man*

We live in a world rich in sensory experience. Information comes to us in a variety of forms: pictures, text, moving images, music, voice, and more. As information processing machines, computers are capable of delivering information to our senses in many forms. Until recently, computer users could work with only one or two forms of information at a time. Today's multimedia computers allow users to work with information-rich documents that intermix a variety of audiovisual media.

Interactive Multimedia: What Is It?

The term multimedia generally means using some combination of text, graphics, animation, video, music, voice, and sound effects to communicate. By this definition an episode of *Sesame Street* or the evening news might be considered multimedia. In fact, computer-based multimedia tools are used heavily in the production of *Sesame Street*, the evening news, and hundreds of other television programs. Entertainment-industry professionals use computers to create animated sequences, display titles, construct special video effects, synthesize music, edit sound tracks, coordinate communication, and perform dozens of other tasks crucial to the production of modern television programs and motion pictures.

So when you watch a typical TV program, you're experiencing a multimedia product. With each second that passes, you are bombarded with millions of bits of information. But television and video are *passive media*—they pour information into our eyes and ears while we sit and take it all in. We have no control over the information flow. Modern computer technology allows information to move in both directions, turning multimedia into interactive multimedia. Unlike TV, radio, and video, interactive multimedia allow the viewer/listener to take an active part in the experience. The best interactive multimedia software puts the user in charge, allowing that person to control the information flow.

6.27 Interactive multimedia CD-ROMs and DVDs often combine education with entertainment. Sierra's Starry Night Sky turns your computer into a virtual planetarium.

Interactive multimedia software is delivered to consumers on a variety of platforms. Today, multimedia computers equipped with fast processors, large memories, CD-ROM or DVD-ROM drives, speakers, and sound cards are everywhere. Thousands of education and entertainment multimedia programs are available on CD-ROM and DVD-ROM for these machines. Many more multimedia software titles are designed to be used with television sets and controlled by game machines and other *set-top boxes* from Sony, Microsoft, Nintendo, and other companies. Many multimedia documents are created for use in kiosks in stores, museums, and other public places. A typical multimedia kiosk is a PC-in-a-box with a touch screen instead of a keyboard and mouse for input.

Interactive multimedia materials are all over the Web, too. But multimedia on the Web today is full of compromises, because many of today's Web pipelines can't deliver large media files quickly enough. Still, Web technology is improving rapidly, and more people are connecting to the Net with faster broadband technology, making many experts wonder whether disk-based multimedia will eventually be unnecessary. In the meantime, cable, telephone, and other companies are rushing to provide multimedia services, including video on demand.

Multimedia Authoring: Making Mixed Media

Multimedia authoring software is used to create and edit multimedia documents. Like desktop publishing, interactive multimedia authoring involves combining source documents—including graphics, text files, video clips, and sounds—in

> **Style** used to be an interaction between **the human soul** and **tools** that were **limiting**. In the digital era, it will have to come from **the soul alone**.
>
> —Jaron Lanier, virtual reality pioneer

an aesthetically pleasing format that communicates with the user. Multimedia authoring software, like page layout software, serves as glue that binds documents created and captured with other applications. But since a multimedia document can change in response to user input, authoring involves specifying not just *what?* and *where?* but also *when?* and *why?* Some authoring programs are designed for professionals. Others are designed for children. Many are used by both.

Some authoring programs, including HyperStudio and MetaCard, use the card-and-stack user interface originally introduced with Apple's HyperCard. According to this metaphor, a multimedia document is a stack of cards. Each screen, called a card, can contain graphics, text, and **buttons**—"hot spots" that respond to mouse clicks. Buttons can be programmed to transport the user to another card, play music, open dialog boxes, launch other applications, rearrange information, perform menu operations, send messages to hardware devices, or do other things. Some authoring programs, including ToolBook, use a similar user interface with a book-and-page metaphor: A book replaces the stack and a page replaces the card. The World Wide Web uses metaphorical pages to represent screens of information; many authoring tools are designed specifically to create Web pages. The most widely used professional multimedia authoring tool, Macromedia's Director, has a different kind of user interface. A Director document is a *movie* rather than a stack of cards or a book of pages. A button can transport a user to another frame of a movie rather than another card or page. Macromedia Flash, a popular tool for adding multimedia to the Web, is based on an interface similar to Director's. Some authoring tools, such as Authorware, use flowcharts as tools for constructing documents.

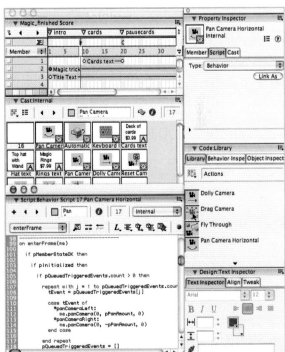

6.28 Multimedia authoring involves programming objects on the screen to react, or behave, in particular ways under particular circumstances. Macromedia Director MX, one of the most popular of such packages, includes prewritten behaviors that can be attached to on-screen buttons, images, and other objects.

The authoring tool's interface metaphor is important to the person creating the multimedia document, but not to the person viewing the finished document, who sees only the user interface that was built into the document by the author. When you're using a well-designed multimedia document, you can't tell whether it was created by Director, Authorware, ToolBook, or another authoring tool.

With the growing interest in the Internet, many people expect the Web to replace CD-ROMs for most multimedia delivery. Most multimedia authoring tools

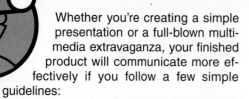
RULES OF THUMB

Whether you're creating a simple presentation or a full-blown multimedia extravaganza, your finished product will communicate more effectively if you follow a few simple guidelines:

➡️ **Be consistent.** Group similar controls together, and keep a consistent visual appearance throughout the presentation.

➡️ **Make it intuitive.** Use graphical metaphors to guide viewers, and make your controls do what they look like they should do.

➡️ **Strive for simplicity.** A clean, uncluttered screen is more inviting than a crowded one—and easier to understand, too.

➡️ **Keep it lively.** If your presentation doesn't include motion, sound, and user interaction, it probably should be printed and distributed as a paper.

➡️ **The message is more important than the media.** Your goal is to communicate information, not saturate the senses. Don't let the bells and whistles get in the way of your message.

➡️ **Put the user in the driver's seat.** Include controls for turning down sound, bypassing repetitive animation, and turning off annoying features. Provide navigation aids, search tools, bookmarks, online help, and "Where am I?" feedback. Never tell the user, "You can't get there from here."

➡️ **Let real people test your presentation.** The best way to find out if your presentation works is to test it on people who aren't familiar with the subject. If they get lost or bored, find out why, fix the problem, and test it again.

can create Web-ready multimedia documents. For example, documents created by Authorware and Director can be converted into Web documents using Macromedia's Shockwave technology. Shockwave software compresses multimedia documents so they can appear and respond more quickly on the Web. But even with compression, the Internet isn't fast enough to deliver the high-quality audio and video that's possible with CD-ROM and DVD-ROM. On the other hand, the contents of a disk are static; they can't be continually updated like a Web site. And CD-ROMs don't offer opportunities for communication with other people the way a Web site can. Many multimedia manufacturers today produce *hybrid disks*—media-rich CD-ROMs and DVD-ROMs that automatically draw content and communication from the Web. Hybrid discs hint at the types of multimedia experiences that will be possible without discs through tomorrow's faster Internet.

Multimedia authoring software today puts a great deal of power into the hands of computer users, but it doesn't solve all of the technical problems in this new art form. Many of the problems with hypertext and hypermedia outlined earlier are even more serious when multiple media are involved. Still, the best multimedia productions transcend these problems and show the promise of this emerging technology.

Interactive Media: Visions of the Future

For most of recorded history, the **interactions of humans with their media** have been **primarily passive** in the sense that marks on paper, paint on walls, even motion pictures and television, **do not change** in response to the viewer's wishes. [But computers can] **respond to queries and experiments**—so that the message may involve the learner in a **two-way conversation**.

—Alan Kay

For hundreds of thousands of years, two-way interactive communication was the norm: One person talked, another responded. Today television, radio, newspapers, magazines, and books pour information into billions of passive people every day. For many people one-way passive communication has become more common than interactive discourse.

According to many experts, interactive multimedia technology offers new hope for turning communication back into a participatory sport. With interactive multimedia software the audience is a part of the show.

Interactive multimedia tools can give people control over the media—control traditionally reserved for professional artists, filmmakers, and musicians. The possibilities are far-reaching, especially when telecommunication enters the picture. Consider these snapshots from a not-too-distant future:

- Instead of watching your history professor flip through overhead transparencies, you control a self-paced interactive presentation complete with video footage illustrating key concepts.

- Using an electronic whiteboard, a professor's writings are automatically transmitted to your wireless-equipped notebook or Tablet PC, allowing you to take notes on what he says, and not what he writes. Students can present questions in real time, using an electronic ballot.

- In your electronic mailbox you find a "letter" from your sister. The letter shows her performing all of the instrumental parts for a song she composed, followed by a request for you to add a vocal line.

- Your favorite TV show is an interactive thriller that allows you to control the plot twists and work with the main characters to solve mysteries.

- While working on a biology project in the field, you come across an unusual bird with a song you don't recognize. Using a pocket-sized digital device, you record some audio/video footage of the bird as it sings. Using the same device, you dial your project partner's phone number and send the footage directly to her computer for editing and analysis.

- You share your concerns about a proposed factory in your hometown at the televised electronic town meeting. Thousands of others respond to questions from the mayor by pressing buttons on their remote control panels. The overwhelming citizen response forces the city council to reconsider the proposal.

6.29 Animators at Pixar Studios work on film projects, including *Toy Story* and *Finding Nemo*. Many of these projects spawn games, educational software programs, and other interactive multimedia products.

Of course, the future of interactive multimedia may not be all sunshine and roses. Many experts fear that these exciting new media possibilities will further remove us from books, other people, and the natural world around us. If television today can mesmerize so many people, will tomorrow's interactive multimedia TVs cause even more serious addiction problems? Or will interactive communication breathe new life into the media and the people who use them? Will interactive electronic media make it easier for abusers of power to influence and control unwary citizens, or will the power of the push button create a new kind of digital democracy? Will interactive digital technology just turn "sound bites" into "sound bytes," or will it unleash the creative potential in the people who use it? For answers, stay tuned.

Shared Virtual Spaces

> What I'm hoping is that **inside virtual worlds**, eventually, people can both have the **power and excitement of imagination** while also **being connected** with other people because the virtual world is really **shared with the real world**, even though you make it up.
>
> —Jaron Lanier, virtual reality pioneer

Tomorrow's multimedia is likely to extend beyond the flat screen, creating immersive experiences that challenge our notion of reality.

VIRTUAL REALITY

Since the 1960s researchers have experimented with *virtual worlds*—computer-generated worlds that created the illusion of immersion. Virtual worlds typically involve special hardware—for input, a glove or body suit equipped with motion sensors, and for output, a head-mounted display—a helmet with eye-sized screens whose views change as the helmet moves. This equipment, when coupled with appropriate software, enables the user to explore an artificial world of data as if it were three-dimensional physical space. *Virtual reality* combines virtual worlds with networking, placing multiple participants in a virtual space. People see representations of each other, sometimes called *avatars*. Most avatars today are cartoonish, but they convey a sense of presence and emotion.

TELE-IMMERSION

Jaron Lanier, who coined the term *virtual reality*, is now the lead scientist in the National Tele-Immersion Initiative. *Tele-immersion* uses multiple cameras and high-speed networks to create an environment in which multiple remote users can interact with each other and with computer-generated objects. (Lanier was a consultant for Spielberg's *Minority Report*, a movie that shows a similar technology.) Tele-immersion combines VR techniques of virtual reality with new vision technologies that allow participants to move around in shared virtual spaces, while maintaining their unique points of view. Today's systems require participants to wear special glasses; future versions may not.

6.30 Virtual reality (VR) pioneer Jaron Lanier.

Tele-immersion systems, when coupled with tomorrow's high-speed Internet2 (see Chapter 9), will allow engineers, archaeologists, and artists, among others, to do long-distance collaboration in shared virtual workspaces. It may allow musicians and actors to give personal interactive performances. Tele-immersion may significantly reduce the need for business travel within a decade.

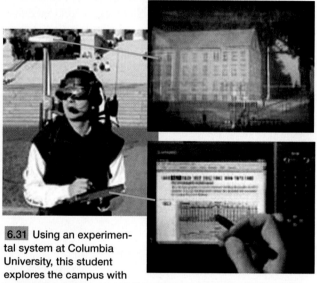

6.31 Using an experimental system at Columbia University, this student explores the campus with a unique historical perspective. He can see and walk around a 3-D image of the Bloomingdale Asylum—the previous occupant of the campus space—in its original location; additional historical information is displayed on his handheld tablet.

AUGMENTED REALITY

Another promising offshoot of VR research is *augmented reality (AR)*—the use of computer displays that add virtual information to a person's sensory perceptions. Unlike VR, AR supplements rather than replaces the world the user sees.

The first-down line that's superimposed on TV football fields is a simple example of AR, but the future offers many more practical applications. With AR, a repair person might see instructions superimposed on a machine part; a surgeon might see inside a patient with live ultrasound scans of internal organs overlaid on the patient's body; a firefighter might see the layout of a burning building.

AR researcher Steven K. Feiner predicts "the overlaid information of AR systems will become part of what we expect to see at work and at play: labels and directions when we don't want to get lost, reminders when we don't want to forget and, perhaps, a favorite cartoon character popping out from the bushes to tell a joke when we want to be amused. When computer user interfaces are potentially everywhere we look, this pervasive mixture of reality and virtuality may become the primary medium for a new generation of artists, designers and storytellers who will craft the future."

Multimedia technology is unleashing the creative potential in budding photographers and video artists. But what will become of all of the digital works created by these amateur archivists? In this essay, first published in the February, 2003 issue of Wired, *writer Jim Lewis suggests that we're storing way too much on our hard drives.*

There's a famous allegory about a map of the world that grows in detail until every point in reality has its counterpoint on paper; the twist being that such a map is at once ideally accurate and entirely useless, since it's the same size as the thing it's meant to represent.

Something very similar is happening in the world around us, though the phenomenon captured is time, not space, and the medium is digital memory rather than paper and ink. Consider, for example, a paradox well known to new parents: Mom and Dad buy a video camera expecting to document Junior's first years, only to find that, while they do indeed shoot anything and everything, they never get around to watching all they recorded. There aren't enough hours in the day for such marathons of consumption.

There was an era when a mechanically captured memory was a rare and precious thing: a formal photo, a faint recording of someone's voice. Nowadays it's all you can do to avoid leaving a recording behind as you go about your day—especially as hard drives get bigger and devices more ubiquitous. The average American is caught at least a dozen times a day on surveillance cameras: at bank machines, above intersections, outside tourist spots, on the dashboards of police cruisers. Businesses log every keystroke made by their employees; help centers store audio of telephone calls, as does 911. DigiMine CEO Usama Fayyad, a computer scientist turned data mining entrepreneur, calculates that the data storage curve is now rocketing upward at a rate of 800 percent per year. "It makes Moore's law look like a flat line," he says. "Companies are collecting so much data they're overwhelmed."

You may know the feeling. Since Kodachrome made way for JPEG, pictures accumulate on hard drives like wet leaves in a gutter. If you wanted to, you could make a fair-quality audio recording of everything that reaches your ears for a month and store it on an iPod that fits in your pocket. Though, of course, you'd need another month to listen to it. Whence the rub: If life gets recorded in real time, it hardly counts as a record at all. It certainly has less impact, and in extreme examples it's self-defeating.

Mechanical memory—to its unexpected advantage—degrades. Colors fade, negatives crack, manuscripts grow brittle, grooves get scratched. What emerges from these depredations is a crucial sense of both the pastness of the past, and its presence. Time takes just enough out of acetate and celluloid to remind us of the distance between now and then, while leaving just enough to remind us of the nearness of our own history.

But digital memory—ubiquitous, fathomless, and literally gratuitous—serves neither idea: The past is always here and always perfect; everything can be represented, no moment need be lost. Moreover, all of it is as good as new, and every copy identical to the original. What's missing is a cadence, a play of values, or a respect for the way loss informs our experience of time. Like the map that's as big as the world itself, it's useless precisely because it's too good.

In a way, we've engineered ourselves back in time. When it was rare and expensive, mechanical memory swamped the real thing; what you most vividly recalled from your vacation wasn't necessarily the most striking part, but what you had the best picture of. Recollecting my own early childhood, I can't tell the experiences from the photographs of them that I've seen since. As recently as 160 years ago, such a phenomenon would have been inconceivable—there simply was no such thing as a photo, film, an audiotape. Now there's a surfeit, to the same effect. Moments are no longer fixed as monuments around which memories accrue—the picture in your wallet, your favorite uncle's Super 8 movies, a single song on a 45. There's just a constant downpour of experience, some of it real and some of it representation, a fluid and uninflected cataract.

Whether this is a boon or a disaster I can't say. Such subtle patterns in the history of human experience tend to escape that kind of judgment. But the result is a telling contradiction: Our culture has become engulfed in its past and can make no use of it at all.

DISCUSSION QUESTIONS

1. When you think about your early childhood, do you have trouble, as the author does, distinguishing memories from photographs? Do you think digital technology will make this phenomenon more or less common? Explain.

2. Do you think the proliferation of recorded experience is a boon or a disaster? Explain your answer.

SUMMARY

Computer graphics today encompass more than quantitative charts and graphs generated by spreadsheets. Bitmapped painting programs enable users to "paint" the screen with a mouse, pen, or other pointing device. The software stores the results in a pixel map, with each pixel having an assigned color. The more possible colors there are and the higher the resolution (pixel density) is, the more the images can approach photorealism. Object-oriented drawing programs also allow users to draw on the screen with a pointing device, with the results stored as collections of geometric objects rather than as maps of computer bits.

Bitmapped graphics and object-oriented graphics each offer advantages in particular situations; trade-offs involve editing and ease of use. Both types of graphics have applications outside the art world. Bitmapped graphics are used in high-resolution image processing software for on-screen photo editing. Object-oriented graphics are at the heart of 3-D modeling software and computer-aided design (CAD) software used by architects, designers, and engineers. Presentation graphics software, which may include either or both graphics types, automates the process of creating slides, transparencies, handouts, and computer-based presentations, making it easy for nonartists to create visually attractive presentations.

Computers today aren't limited to working with static images; they're widely used to create and edit documents in media that change over time or in response to user interaction. For animation and digital video work, PCs mimic many of the features of expensive professional workstations at a fraction of the cost. Similarly, today's personal computers can perform a variety of sound and music editing tasks that used to require expensive equipment and numerous musicians.

The interactive nature of the personal computer makes it possible to create nonlinear documents that enable users to take individual paths through information. Early nonlinear documents were called hypertext because they could contain only text. Today, we can create or explore hypermedia documents—interactive documents that mix text, graphics, sounds, and moving images with on-screen navigation buttons—on disc and on the World Wide Web.

Multimedia computer systems make a new kind of software possible—software that uses text, graphics, animation, video, music, voice, and sound effects to communicate. Interactive multimedia documents are available for desktop computers, video game machines, set-top boxes connected to televisions, and networks. Regardless of the hardware, interactive multimedia software enables the user to control the presentation rather than just watch or listen passively. Only time will tell whether these new media will live up to their potential for enhancing education, training, entertainment, and cultural enrichment.

KEY TERMS

3-D modeling software (p. 209)
animation (p. 212)
audio digitizer (p. 217)
augmented reality (AR) (p. 228)
bit depth (p. 203)
bitmapped graphics (p. 203)
bullet charts (p. 210)
button (p. 225)
color depth (p. 203)
compression (p. 216)
computer-aided design (CAD)
   (p. 209)
computer-aided manufacturing
   (CAM) (p. 210)
computer-integrated manufacturing
   (CIM) (p. 210)
digital video (p. 214)

drawing software (p. 207)
frame (p. 212)
gray-scale graphics (p. 203)
hypermedia (p. 223)
hypertext (p. 223)
image processing software (p. 204)
interactive multimedia (p. 224)
MIDI (p. 221)
morph (p. 215)
MP3 (p. 217)
multimedia (p. 224)
multimedia authoring software
   (p. 225)
object-oriented graphics (p. 207)
page-description language (p. 208)
painting software (p. 203)
palette (p. 203)

pixel (p. 203)
PostScript (p. 208)
presentation graphics software
   (p. 210)
raster graphics (p. 203)
resolution (p. 203)
sequencing software (p. 221)
synthesized (p. 217)
tele-immersion (p. 228)
vector graphics (p. 205)
video digitizer (p. 214)
video editing software (p. 215)
virtual reality (p. 228)
WYSIWYG (p. 223)

INTERACTIVE QUIZ QUESTIONS

1. The *Computer Confluence* CD-ROM contains self-test multiple-choice quiz questions related to this chapter.

2. The *Computer Confluence* Web site, http://www.computerconfluence.com, also contains

self-test exercises related to this chapter. Follow the instructions for taking a quiz. After you've completed your quiz, you can email the results to your instructor.

TRUE OR FALSE

1. Bitmapped graphics represent lines, shapes, and characters as objects with mathematical formulas.

2. Photographic image-editing software calls into question the validity of photographic evidence in the courtroom.

3. 3-D graphics play an important role in the branch of engineering known as computer-aided design (CAD).

4. Presentation graphics programs such as PowerPoint can automatically generate pie charts and bar charts but not bullet charts.

5. Based on trends in animation technology today, it's likely that the first fully computer-animated feature-length film will happen in the second decade of the twenty-first century.

6. Sequencing software allows musicians to record audio and MIDI tracks, edit them, and play them back.

7. Because uncompressed video requires massive amounts of storage, virtually all digital video files are compressed.

8. Hypermedia isn't possible without a PC.

9. Multimedia authoring software today is used almost exclusively for creating animated Web pages.

10. Interactive multimedia on the Web is limited in quality by the bandwidth limitations of many Internet connections.

MULTIPLE CHOICE

1. Photographic image-editing programs are based largely on the technology of
   a. object-oriented graphics.
   b. presentation graphics.
   c. bitmapped graphics.
   d. quantitative graphics.
   e. CAD-CAM graphics.

2. If a photographic image looks fine when displayed on a computer screen but appears jagged and rough when printed, the problem has to do with the image's
   a. bit depth.
   b. dimensions.
   c. vector.
   d. raster.
   e. resolution.

3. 3-D graphics software is based largely on the technology of
   a. object-oriented graphics.
   b. presentation graphics.
   c. bitmapped graphics.
   d. photographic image-editing software.
   e. hypermedia.

4. The process of tweening in animation is similar to which of these video concepts?
   a. averaging.
   b. morphing.
   c. sequencing.
   d. synthesizing.
   e. rasterizing.

5. In order to use a computer to edit footage captured with a digital video camera, you must
   a. install a video digitizer in the PC.
   b. import the video footage using a FireWire cable or the equivalent.
   c. digitize the video footage.
   d. store the video clips on a DVD.
   e. All of the above.

6. For nonlinear video editing, video and audio clips are stored on
   a. tape.
   b. DVD.
   c. CD.
   d. floppy disks.
   e. hard disk(s).

7. Many legal online music stores attempt to prevent piracy by
   a. selling music files with built-in digital rights management technology.
   b. requiring customers to sign antipiracy pledges.
   c. performing background checks on potential customers.
   d. selling only MP3 files, because MP3 is widely known to be secure.
   e. compressing files with lossless compression technology.

8. MP3 is a popular format for music file sharing because
   a. MP3 files typically contain video as well as audio data.
   b. MP3 files work equally well for text and graphics as well as music.
   c. MP3 compression reduces file sizes considerably with minimal loss of music quality.
   d. MP3 compression is lossless.
   e. MP3 files contain DRM technology.

9. A MIDI file of a Beethoven piano concerto is much smaller than a CD audio file of the same piece because
   a. MIDI uses efficient MP3 technology.
   b. MIDI uses MPEG-4 compression.
   c. MIDI uses software rather than hardware for compression.
   d. the MIDI file contains only instructions for playing notes; the note sounds are stored in the computer or musical instrument.
   e. Actually, MIDI files are larger than MP3 files.

10. What is the most important difference between an interactive multimedia version of *Sesame Street* and a *Sesame Street* television program?
   a. The interactive multimedia version allows the viewer to have more control over the experience.
   b. The interactive multimedia version offers a richer mix of media types.
   c. The interactive multimedia version requires a joystick or game controller.
   d. The interactive multimedia version can't be displayed on a standard TV screen.
   e. The interactive multimedia version only exists in theory; it's not technically possible yet.

REVIEW QUESTIONS

1. Define or describe each of the key terms listed in the "Key Terms" section. Check your answers using the glossary.

2. What is the difference between bitmapped graphics and object-oriented graphics? What are the advantages and disadvantages of each?

3. What two technological factors limit the realism of a bitmapped image? How are these related to storage of that image in the computer?

4. How is digital image processing of photographs related to bitmapped painting?

5. Describe several practical applications for 3-D modeling and CAD software.

6. Why is image compression an important part of digital video technology?

7. Describe three different technologies for adding music or other sounds to a multimedia presentation. Describe a practical application of each sound source.

8. How do hypertext and other hypermedia differ from linear media?

9. Describe several practical applications for hypermedia.

10. What are the main disadvantages of hypermedia when compared with conventional media such as books and videos?

11. Is it possible to have hypermedia without multimedia? Is it possible to have multimedia without hypermedia? Explain your answers.

12. How does presentation graphics software differ from multimedia authoring software? Give an example of a practical application of each.

DISCUSSION QUESTIONS

1. How does modern digital image processing technology affect the reliability of photographic evidence? How does digital audio technology affect the reliability of sound recordings as evidence? How should our legal system respond to this technology?

2. Scanners, video digitizers, and audio digitizers make it easier than ever for people to violate copyright laws. What, if anything, should be done to protect intellectual property rights of the people who create pictures, videos, and music? Under what circumstances do you think it's acceptable to copy sounds or images for use in your own work?

3. Do you think hypermedia documents will eclipse certain kinds of books and other media? If so, which ones and why?

4. Thanks to modern electronic music technology, one or two people can make a record that would have required dozens of musicians 20 years ago. What impact will electronic music technology ultimately have on the music profession?

5. Try to answer each of the questions posed at the end of the section called "Interactive Media: Visions of the Future."

PROJECTS

1. Draw a familiar object or scene using a bitmapped painting program. Draw the same object or scene with an object-oriented drawing program. Describe how the process changed using different software.

2. Create visual aids for a speech or lecture using presentation graphics software. In what ways did the software make the job easier? What limitations did you find?

3. Compose some original music using a synthesizer, a computer, and a sequencer. Describe the experience.

4. Review several interactive multimedia titles. Discuss their strengths and weaknesses as communication tools. In what ways did their interactivity enhance their usefulness? (Extra challenge: Make your review interactive.)

SOURCES AND RESOURCES

Books

Most of the best graphics, video, music, and multimedia applications books are software specific. When you decide on a software application, choose books based on your chosen software and on the type of information you need. If you want quick answers with a minimum of verbiage, you'll probably be delighted with a book from Peachpit's Visual Quickstart series. Most of the titles in the following list aren't keyed to specific applications.

Weaving the Web, by Tim Berners-Lee. (San Francisco, CA: Harper San Francisco, 1999). This is the story of the creation of the Web straight from the word processor of the man who did it. Few people in history have had more impact on the way we communicate than this unassuming man.

How the Web Was Born, by James Gillies and Robert Cailliau. (London: Oxford University Press: 2000). This book provides another account of the events leading up to and following the creation of the Web. The authors provide a context that helps explain how Englishman Tim Berners-Lee made critical decisions in shaping the Web.

Computer Graphics Companion, edited by Jeffrey J. McConnell (London, NPG, 2002). This is a collection of articles from the *Computer Science Dictionary* plus some additional material written specifically for this volume. Some of the articles are technical, but there's plenty of useful information here.

Graphic Communications Dictionary, by Daniel J. Lyons (Upper Saddle River, NJ: Prentice Hall, 2000). This is an excellent alphabetic reference for anyone wrestling with the terminology of graphic design.

The New Drawing on the Right Side of the Brain: A Course in Enhancing Creativity and Artistic Confidence, by Betty Edwards (Los Angeles, CA: J. P. Tarcher, 1999). If you're convinced you have no artistic ability, give this book a try; you might surprise yourself.

The Arts and Crafts Computer: Using Your Computer as an Artist's Tool, by Janet Ashford (Berkeley, CA: Peachpit Press, 2001). This lavishly illustrated book covers basic principles of drawing, painting, photography, typography, and design with computers. But unlike other books on computer art, this one goes beyond the computer screen and the printed page as output possibilities. If you want to create original fabric art, greeting cards, labels, decals, bumper stickers, toys, you'll find a wealth of ideas here.

Digital Phtography Top 100 Simplified Tips & Tricks from maranGraphics (Hoboken, NJ: Wiley, 2003). If you want to take pictures that are more than snapshots, this highly graphical book can help. It's packed with useful tips accompanied by clear illustrations.

Visual Quickstart Guide: Photoshop 7 for Windows and Macintosh, by Elaine Weinmann and Peter Lourekas (Berkeley, CA: Peachpit Press, 2002). Peachpit's Visual Quickstart Guides are popular because they provide maximum instruction for a minimal investment of time. This Photoshop guide is one of the best. Using lots of pictures and few words, it unlocks the secrets of the program that is the industry standard for professional photo and bitmap editing software.

Photoshop 7 Artistry: Mastering the Digital Image, by Barry Haynes and Wendy Crumpler (Indianapolis, IN: New Riders, 2002). If the stripped-down Visual Quickstart approach is too sparse for you, this book is an excellent alternative. Combining clear explanations, numerous color screen shots, hands-on tutorials, and a handy CD-ROM, the authors deliver a complete course in Photoshop.

Looking Good in Presentations: Third Edition, by Molly W. Joss and Roger C. Parker (Scottsdale, AZ: Coriolis Group, 1999). Programs like PowerPoint can help nondesigners create stylish presentations, but they're not foolproof. (How many ugly, boring, computer-enhanced presentations have you had to sit through?) This is a great book for anyone creating presentations, from simple slide shows to full-featured multimedia extravaganzas. Starting with "How To Not Be Boring" in Chapter 1, you'll find plenty of tips to make your presentations shine.

The Art of 3D Computer Animation and Effects, Third Edition, by Isaac V. Kerlow (New York: Wiley, 2004). Films like *Shrek* and *Finding Nemo* have turned 3-D graphics into a big business and a popular art form. This book clearly explains the technology that makes it all possible.

Macromedia Flash MX: Training from the Source, by Chrissy Rey (Berkeley, CA: Macromedia Press, 2002). Macromedia's *Training from the Source* books provide clear, easy-to-follow tutorials for using their most popular products. This one covers Flash MX, the premiere tool for creating Web animation and interactivity. Similar books are available for Director MX and Dreamweaver MX.

The Little Digital Video Book, by Michael Rubin (Berkeley, CA: Peachpit Press, 2001). This compact book should be included with every digital camcorder. It's packed with helpful tips for choosing and organizing equipment, preparing a project, shooting quality footage, editing clips, adding soundtracks, and polishing productions.

Real World Digital Video: Industrial Strength Video Production Techniques, by Pete Shaner and Gerald Everett Jones (Berkeley, CA: Peachpit Press, 2003). This book covers the entire video production process, from buying equipment to producing a final video product. You can avoid many of the pitfalls of video production by reading this book before you start.

Essentials of Music Technology, by Mark Ballora (Upper Saddle River, NJ: Prentice Hall, 2003). This book provides a systematic introduction to music technology, from basic acoustics to digital instruments.

The Streaming Media Handbook, by Eyal Menin (Upper Saddle River, NJ: Prentice Hall, 2003). This book, by one of the pros in the field, provides solid information for anyone interested in streaming audio or video on the Web.

Streaming Audio: The FezGuy's Guide, by Jon R. Luini and Allen E. Whitman (Indianapolis, IN: New Riders, 2002). This book gives step-by-step instructions for setting up streaming audio on the Web using all the popular formats and platforms.

MTIV: Process, Inspiration and Practice for the New Media Designer, by Hillman Curtis (Indianapolis, IN: New Riders, 2002). This bold, colorful book presents a successful New Media designer's perspective on creating media that work well. The title stands for "Making the Invisible Visible." If you're interested in graphic design for the Internet age, this book is worth seeking out.

Pause and Effect: The Art of Interactive Narrative, by Mark Stephen Meadows (Indianapolis, IN: New Riders, 2003). One of the biggest challenges in new media is the difficulty of putting the narrative form to nonlinear packages. This beautiful book examines the brave new world at the intersection of storytelling, visual art, and interactivity.

Theoretical Foundations of Multimedia, by Robert S. Tannenbaum (New York: W.H. Freeman, 1998). Multimedia is an ideal profession for a modern Renaissance person. To be truly multimedia literate, a person needs to understand concepts from fields as diverse as computer science, physics, design, law, psychology, and communication. This introductory text/CD-ROM surveys each of these fields from the multimedia perspective, providing valuable conceptual background with practical value.

Understanding Media: The Extensions of Man, by Marshall McLuhan (Cambridge, MA: MIT Press, 1994). This classic, originally published in 1964, explores the relationship of mass media to the masses. The new introduction in this 30th anniversary reissue reevaluates McLuhan's visionary work 30 years later.

net_condition: art and global media (Electronic Culture: History, Theory, and Practice), edited by Peter Weibel and Timothy Druckery (Cambridge, MA: MIT Press, 2001). This bold, colorful book surveys the global landscape of digital art and its impact on our culture.

Multimedia: From Wagner to Virtual Reality, edited by Randall Packer and Ken Jordan (New York: Norton, 2001). This collection of essays by William Burroughs, John Cage, Tim Berners-Lee, and others, offers a broad overview of the historical roots of multimedia.

Periodicals

Artbyte. This stylish magazine explores the world and culture of digital art and design.

Digital Camera. This magazine covers the rapidly changing world of digital photography.

DV. This monthly magazine is aimed at digital video professionals and serious amateurs.

e-Media. This monthly covers the new media landscape, with an emphasis on CDs, DVDs, and other disc-based media.

Keyboard and **Electronic Musician.** These two magazines are among the best sources for up-to-date information on computers and music synthesis.

World Wide Web Pages

The Web is known as the multimedia part of the Internet, and there are plenty of Web sites for learning about—and experiencing first-hand—a variety of mixed media. The *Computer Confluence* Web pages will link you to multimedia hardware and software companies and pages that demonstrate state-of-the-art multimedia on the Web.

AFTER YOU READ THIS CHAPTER YOU SHOULD BE ABLE TO:

■ Explain what a database is and describe its basic structure

■ Identify the kinds of problems that can be best solved with database software

■ Describe different kinds of database software, from simple file managers to complex relational databases

■ Describe database operations for storing, sorting, updating, querying, and summarizing information

■ Explain how databases threaten our privacy

Multimedia extras on the CD-ROM and the Web:

■ Bill Gates talks about **what's wrong** with PCs.

■ An interactive activity for **understanding queries**.

■ **Instant** access to glossary and key word references

■ **Interactive** self-study quizzes

■ **Free** software sources

 . . . *and more.*

 computerconfluence.com

7

DATABASE APPLICATIONS AND IMPLICATIONS

BILL GATES RIDES THE DIGITAL WAVE

In the early days of the personal computer revolution, Bill Gates and Paul Allen formed a company called Microsoft to produce and market a version of the Basic programming language for microcomputers. Microsoft Basic quickly became the standard language installed in virtually every microcomputer.

Microsoft's biggest break came when IBM went shopping for an operating system for its PC. Gates purchased an operating system from a small company, reworked it to meet IBM's specifications, named it MS-DOS (for Microsoft Disk Operating System), and licensed it to IBM, making a royalty on each PC that IBM sold. The IBM PC became an industry standard, and Microsoft found itself owning the operat-ing system that kept most of the PCs in the world running.

Today, Bill Gates and Microsoft dominate the PC software industry, selling operating systems, applica-

> The goal is **information at your fingertips**.
>
> —Bill Gates

7.1 Bill Gates.

tions programs, server software, and software development tools. Software has made Gates the richest man on earth.

Microsoft's desktop dominance was threatened in the mid-1990s by the Internet explosion. For many people, computers became little more than portals into the Internet. Gates responded by making the Internet a critical part of its software strategy. Today, Microsoft's Internet Explorer Web browser is a central component of the Windows OS; Microsoft desktop applications have links to the Internet, and Microsoft has partnerships with dozens of Web-related businesses worldwide.

According to writer Steven Levy, Gates "has the obsessive drive of a hacker working on a tough technical dilemma, yet has an uncanny grasp of the marketplace, as well as a firm conviction of what the future will be like and what he should do about it." The future, says Gates, will be digital. To prepare for this all-digital future, Microsoft is extending its reach beyond software into all kinds of information-related business ventures, from online banking and shopping to the MSNBC cable TV network.

Many competitors and customers insist that Microsoft uses unethical business practices to ruthlessly—and sometimes illegally—stomp out competition and choice. In 1998, 20 states joined the U.S. government in a widely publicized lawsuit against Microsoft's anticompetitive practices. That same year the European Union filed two antitrust lawsuits against the company. Microsoft responded with arrogant denials and a massive P.R. campaign; one state official received pro-Microsoft form letters from hundreds of people, including some who had died years before.

In 2000, a federal judge ruled that Microsoft illegally maintained its desktop operating system monopoly and that Microsoft's crimes had hurt consumers as well as other businesses. The ruling was confirmed by an appeals court in 2001, but the government settled out of court in exchange for minor concessions from the company. Today, Microsoft still faces numerous antitrust-related lawsuits around the world, but the company appears to have escaped from its most dangerous legal challenge.

In recent years, Bill Gates and Microsoft have given billions of dollars to public schools, AIDS research, and other charities. Cynics argue that these gifts are calculated to improve the company's public image in the face of legal troubles. Whatever the motivation, the donations are helping people all over the world.

7.2 Bill Gates and Paul Allen as students.

In early 2000, Gates stepped aside as CEO of Microsoft to become the company's chairman and chief software architect. Today, he spearheads the development of future versions of Windows, moving the OS closer to his "information at your fingertips" vision by making it easier for computer users to find files on their computers and networks. In the future we will have all kinds of information at our fingertips and Bill Gates hopes that Microsoft will provide the tools for delivering that information.

We live in an information age. We're bombarded with information by television, radio, newspapers, magazines, books, and computers. It's easy to be overwhelmed by the sheer quantity of information we're expected to deal with each day. Computer applications such as word processors and spreadsheets can aggravate the problem by making it easier for people to generate more documents full of information.

A *database program* is a data manager that can help alleviate information overload. Databases make it possible for people to store, organize, retrieve, communicate, and manage information in ways that wouldn't be possible without computers. To control the flood of information, people use databases of all sizes and shapes—from massive mainframe database managers that keep airlines filled with passengers to computerized appointment calendars on palmtop computers and public database kiosks in shopping malls.

First the good news: Information at your fingertips can make your life richer and more efficient in a multitude of ways. Ready cash from street-corner ATMs, instant airline reservations from the Web at any time of the day, catalog shopping with overnight mail-order delivery, exhaustive online searches in seconds—none of these conveniences would be possible without databases.

Now the bad news: Some of the information stored in databases is your data, and you have little or no control over who has it and how it is used. Ironically, the database technology that liberates us in our day-to-day lives is, at the same time, chipping away at our privacy. We explore both sides of this important technology in this chapter.

The Electronic File Cabinet: Database Basics

We start by looking at the basics of databases. Like word processors, spreadsheets, and graphics programs, database programs are ap-

> The next best thing to **knowing**, is knowing **where to find it.**
> —Samuel Johnson

plications—programs for turning computers into productive tools. If a word processor is a computerized typewriter and a spreadsheet is a computerized ledger, you can think of a database program as a computerized file cabinet.

While word processors and spreadsheets generally are used to create printed documents, database programs are designed to maintain *databases*—collections of information stored on computer disks. A database can be as simple as a list of names and addresses, or

as complex as an airline reservation system. An electronic version of a phone book, a recipe file, a library's card catalog, an inventory file stored in an office file cabinet, a school's student grade records, a card index containing the names and addresses of business contacts, or a catalog of your compact disc collection—just about any collection of information can be turned into a database.

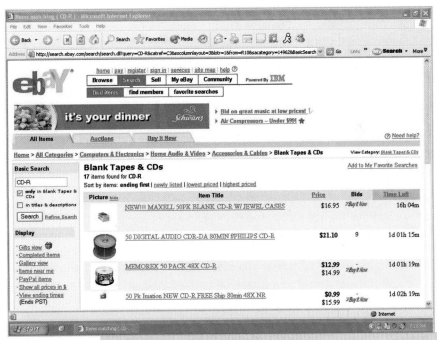

What Good Is a Database?

Why do people use computers for information-handling tasks that can be done with index cards, three-ring binders, or file folders? Computerized databases offer several advantages over their paper-and-pencil counterparts:

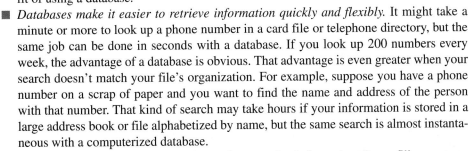

7.3 Internet auction Web sites, such as eBay, wouldn't be possible without database technology.

■ *Databases make it easier to store large quantities of information.* If you have only 20 or 30 compact discs, it may make sense to catalog them in a notebook. But if you have 2,000 or 3,000 CDs, your notebook may become as unwieldy as your CD collection. The larger the mass of information, the bigger the benefit of using a database.

■ *Databases make it easier to retrieve information quickly and flexibly.* It might take a minute or more to look up a phone number in a card file or telephone directory, but the same job can be done in seconds with a database. If you look up 200 numbers every week, the advantage of a database is obvious. That advantage is even greater when your search doesn't match your file's organization. For example, suppose you have a phone number on a scrap of paper and you want to find the name and address of the person with that number. That kind of search may take hours if your information is stored in a large address book or file alphabetized by name, but the same search is almost instantaneous with a computerized database.

■ *Databases make it easy to organize and reorganize information.* Paper filing systems force you to arrange information in one particular way. Should your book catalog be organized by author, by title, by publication date, or by subject? There's a lot riding on your decision, because if you decide to rearrange everything later, you will waste a lot of time. With a database, you can instantly switch between these organizational schemes as often as you like; there's no penalty for flexibility.

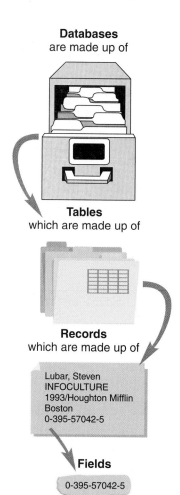

Databases
are made up of

Tables
which are made up of

Records
which are made up of

Lubar, Steven
INFOCULTURE
1993/Houghton Mifflin
Boston
0-395-57042-5

Fields

0-395-57042-5

7.4

■ *Databases make it easy to print and distribute information in a variety of ways.* Suppose you want to send letters to hundreds of friends inviting them to your postgraduation party. You'll need to include directions to your place for out-of-towners but not for home-towners. A database, when used with a word processor, can print personalized form letters, including extra directions for those who need them, and print preaddressed envelopes or mailing labels in a fraction of the time it would take you to do it by hand and with less likelihood of error. You can even print a report listing invitees sorted by zip code so you can suggest possible car pools. (And if you want to bill those who attend the party, your database can help with that, too.)

Database Anatomy

As you might expect, a specialized vocabulary is associated with databases. Unfortunately, some terms take on different meanings depending on their context, and different people use these words in different ways. We'll begin by charting a course through marketing hype and technical terminology to find our way to the definitions most people use today.

For our purposes, a database is a collection of information stored in an organized form in a computer, and a database program is a software tool for organizing storage and retrieval of that information. A variety of programs fit this broad definition, ranging from simple address book programs and other list managers to massive inventory-tracking systems. We explore the differences between types of database programs later in the chapter, but for now we treat them as if they are more or less alike.

Early PC databases were simple file managers; they made it easy for users to store, organize, and retrieve information—names, numbers, prices, whatever—from structured data files. This type of data management is really list management, since these files are just structured lists. Today's spreadsheet software can easily handle this kind of simple list management. Today's database software isn't limited to this kind of simple file management; it can handle complex tasks involving multiple data files.

A database is typically composed of one or more tables. A table is a collection of related information; it keeps that information together the way a folder in a file cabinet does. If a database is used to record sales information for a company, separate tables might contain the relevant sales data for each year. For an address database, separate tables might hold personal and business contacts. It's up to the designer of the database to determine whether information in different categories is stored in separate tables, which are, in turn, stored in files on the computer's disk.

A database table is a collection of records. A record is the information relating to one person, product, or event. In the library's card catalog database a record is equivalent to one card. In an address book database a record contains information about one person. A compact disc catalog database would have one record per CD.

Each discrete chunk of information in a record is called a field. A record in the library's card catalog database would contain fields for author, title, publisher, address, date, and title code number. Your CD database could break records into fields by title, artist, and so on.

The type of information a field can hold is determined by its *field type* or *data type*. For example, the author field in the library database would be defined as a text field, so it could contain text. The field specifying the number of

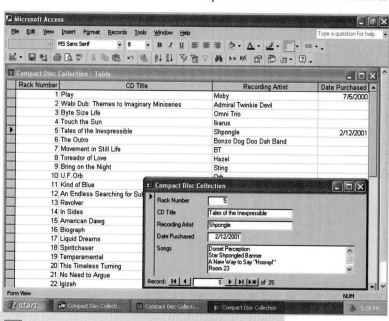

7.5 These two windows show the list and form views of a database.

copies of a book would be defined as a *numeric field*, so it could contain only numbers—numbers that can be used to calculate totals and other arithmetic formulas, if necessary. A date-of-purchase field might be a *date field* that could contain only date values. In addition to these standard field types, many database programs allow fields to contain graphics, digitized photographs, sounds, or video clips. **Computed fields** contain formulas similar to spreadsheet formulas; they display values calculated from values in other numeric fields. For example, a computed field called GPA might contain a formula for calculating a student's grade point average using the grades stored in other fields.

Most database programs provide you with more than one way to view the data, including *form views*, which show one record at a time, and *list views*, which display several records in lists similar to a spreadsheet. In any view, fields can be rearranged without changing the underlying data.

Database Operations

Once the structure of a database is defined, it's easy to get information in; it's just a matter of typing. Typing may not even be necessary

Information has value, but it is as perishable as fresh fruit.
—Nicholas Negroponte, founder and director of the MIT Media Lab

if the data already exists in some computer-readable form. Most database programs can easily **import data** or receive data in the form of text files created with word processors, spreadsheets, or other databases. When information changes or errors are detected, records can be modified, added, or deleted.

Browsing

The challenging part of using a database is retrieving information in a timely and appropriate manner. Information is of little value if it's not accessible. One way to find information is to **browse** through the records of the database just as you would if they were paper forms in a notebook. Most database programs provide keyboard commands, on-screen buttons, and other tools for navigating quickly through records. But this kind of electronic page turning offers no particular advantage over paper, and it's painfully inefficient for large databases. Fortunately, most database programs include a variety of commands and capabilities that make it easy to get the information you need when you need it.

Database Queries

The alternative to browsing is to ask the database for specific information. In database terminology, an information request is called a **query**. A query may be a simple **search** for a specific record (say, one containing information on Abraham Lincoln) or a request to **select** *all* the records that match a set of criteria (for example, records for all U.S. presidents who served more than one term). Once you've selected a group of records, you can browse through it, produce a printout, or do just about anything else you might do with the complete table. Many databases allow you to record, or store, commonly used queries so they can be accessed quickly in the future. The ability to generate a *stored query* is a powerful feature that helps databases blur the line between application programs and development tools.

Sorting Data

Sometimes it's necessary to rearrange records to make the most efficient use of data. For example, a mail-order company's customer file might be arranged alphabetically by name for easy reference, but it must be rearranged in order by zip code to qualify for postal discounts on catalog mailings. A **sort** command allows you to arrange records in alphabetic or numeric order based on values in one or more fields.

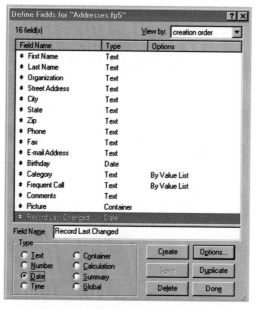

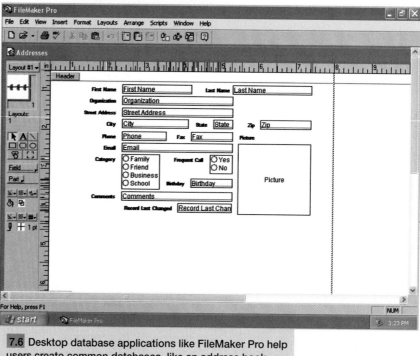

7.6 Desktop database applications like FileMaker Pro help users create common databases, like an address book.

Printing Reports, Labels, and Form Letters

In addition to displaying information on the screen, database programs can produce a variety of printouts. The most common type of database printout is a report—an ordered list of selected records and fields in an easy-to-read format. Most business reports arrange data in tables with rows for individual records and columns for selected fields; they often include summary lines containing calculated totals and averages for groups of records.

Database programs can also be used to produce mailing labels and customized form letters. Many database programs don't actually print letters; they simply export data, or transmit the necessary records and fields, to word processors with mail merge capabilities, which then take on the task of printing the letters.

Creating and Printing a Phone List with FileMaker Pro

Last name	First name	Phone
Row	Mike	804/969-8088
Feyerham	Bernie	413-2879
Parker	Sheryl	821-0719
Knutson	Clara	772-1503
Alvarez	Joe	954-3324
Reigelman	Laurel	818/444-5745
Savage	JoAnn and Jim	754-1212
Westfall	Rosalind	255-2558
Cochrane	Lynn	808-8245
Holmes-Swanson	Anna Marie	322-2877
Dengler	Chelsea	422-7014
Putnam	Matthew	265-1215
Heisner	Philbert	802/433-7348
Cadliz	Asa	314/442-1811

7.7a To create a postable printout of names and phone numbers for frequently called entries, you first create a report or view that selects only the required records.

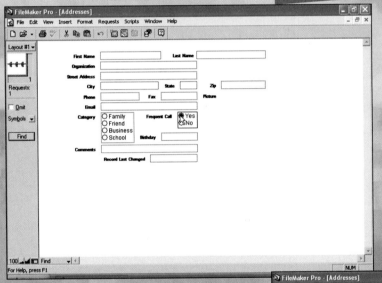

7.7b You select the Find command, and click "Yes" in the Frequently Called field, and click Find. The program then selects all records with "Yes" in the Frequently Called field.

7.7c You create a new layout that will display the name and phone number fields for the selected records in a columnar view. Before printing it out, you preview your report on screen.

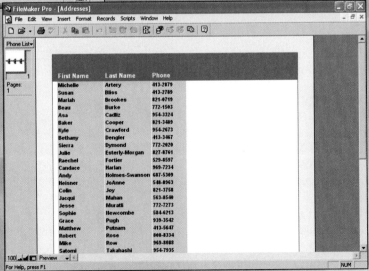

243

Querying a Web Search Database

7.8a You're looking for current news articles about a new method for recycling toner cartridges. You open Northern Lights search engine and select "Newspapers, Wires, and Transcripts".

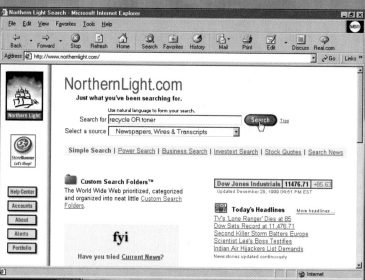

7.8b In a few seconds the search reveals that 12,159 records contain at least one of your two target words in the subject field. Your search strategy was flawed. Most of the articles listed for "recycle" probably have nothing to do with toner cartridges, so you've selected a large collection of mostly irrelevant titles. You replace the OR with AND in the search field and click Search.

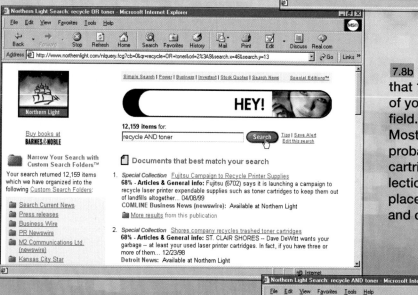

7.8c The search reveals 69 records that contain both words in the subject field, driving home the importance of choosing every word carefully when defining a database query. You can now browse through the abstracts for relevant articles. Of course, there's no guarantee that you've found all the references on these subjects: You can only be sure that you've found all the articles that had both words listed in their subject fields. If you don't find what you're looking for in the list, you might need to try different search strategies or different databases.

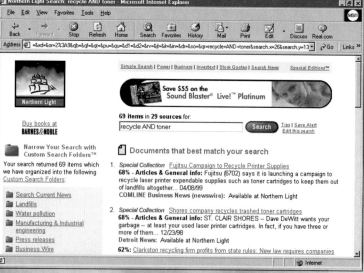

Complex Queries

Queries may be simple or complex, but either way they must be precise and unambiguous. With appropriate databases, queries could be constructed to find the following:

- In a hospital's patient database, the names and locations of all of the patients on the hospital's fifth and sixth floors
- In a database of airline flight schedules, the least expensive way to fly from Boston to San Francisco on Tuesday afternoon
- In a politician's database, all voters who contributed more than $1,000 to last year's legislative campaign and who wrote to express concern over gun control laws since the election

These may be legitimate targets for queries, but they aren't expressed in a form that most database programs can understand. The exact method for performing a query depends on the user interface of the database software. Most programs enable the user to specify the rules of the search by filling in a dialog box or a blank on-screen form. Some require the user to type the request using a special query language that's more precise than English. For example, to view the records for males between 18 and 35, you might type

```
Select * From Population Where
Sex = M and Age >= 18 and Age <= 35
```

Many database programs include programming languages, so queries can be included in programs and performed automatically when the programs are executed. Although the details of the process vary, the underlying logic is consistent from program to program.

Most modern database management programs support a standard language called SQL (from *Structured Query Language*; often pronounced "sequel") for programming complex queries. Because SQL is available for many different database management systems, programmers and sophisticated users don't need to learn new languages when they work with different hardware and software systems. Users are usually insulated from the complexities of the query language by graphical user interfaces that allow point-and-click queries.

Special-Purpose Database Programs

Specialized database software is preprogrammed for specific data storage and retrieval purposes. Users of special-purpose databases don't generally need to define file structures or design forms, because these details have been taken care of by the designers of the software. In fact, some special-purpose database programs are not even sold as databases; they have names that more accurately reflect their purposes.

Directories and Geographic Information Systems

For example, an electronic phone directory can pack millions of names and phone numbers onto a single CD-ROM or Web site. Using an *electronic phone directory* for the United States, you can track down phone numbers of people and businesses all over the country—even if you don't know where they are. You can look up a person's name if you have the phone number or street address. You can generate a list of every dentist in town—any town. Then using another type of specialized database, an *electronic street atlas*, you can pinpoint each of your finds on a freshly printed map. Many street atlases are designed to work with GPS (global positioning system) receivers on laptop, handheld, or automobile-based computers. GPS satellites feed location information to GPS receivers; mapping software uses that information to provide location feedback for travelers and mobile workers.

Geographical information systems (GISs) go beyond simple mapping and tracking programs. A GIS allows a business to combine tables of data such as customer sales lists with demographic information from the U.S. Census Bureau and other sources. The right combination can reveal valuable strategic information. For example, a stock brokerage firm can pinpoint the best locations for branch offices based on average incomes and other neighborhood data; a cable TV company can locate potential customers who live close to existing lines. Because GISs can display geographic and demographic data on maps, they enable users to see data relationships that might be invisible in table form.

Personal Information Managers

One type of specialized database program is often called a personal information manager (PIM). This type of program can automate some or all of the following functions:

- *Address/phone book.* Software address books provide options for quickly displaying specific records and printing mailing labels, address books, and reports. Some include automatic phone-dialing options and fields for recording phone notes.
- *Appointment calendar.* A typical PIM calendar enables you to enter appointments and events and display or print them in a variety of formats, ranging from one day at a time to a monthly overview. Many include built-in alarms for last-minute reminders and ways to share your calendar electronically with other users.
- *To-do list.* Most PIMs enable users to enter and organize ongoing lists of things to do and archive lists of completed tasks.
- *Miscellaneous notes.* Some PIMs accept diary entries, personal notes, and other hard-to-categorize tidbits of information.

PIMs have long been popular among people with busy schedules and countless contacts. They're easier to understand and use than general-purpose database programs, and they're faster and more flexible than their leather-bound paper counterparts. For people on the go, PIMs work especially well with notebook computers or handheld computers. In fact, the market for PIM software has been eclipsed by an even larger market for handheld computers and personal digital assistants (PDAs) with built-in PIM software. For example, software that's built into the Palm OS accepts a pocket-sized device to *hot-sync* with PIM software on a desktop PC or Mac. This instant data linking makes it easy to keep up-to-date personal information both in and out of the office.

In many organizations, PIMs have been replaced by enterprise information systems such as Microsoft Outlook, part of Microsoft Office. These systems enable networked co-workers to easily share calendars and contacts and often include email and other communication tools along with basic PIM features. The Web offers another alternative: Several Web sites provide free PIM software that can be accessed from any Web-accessible computer; many of these applications also permit workgroups to share calendars and other information.

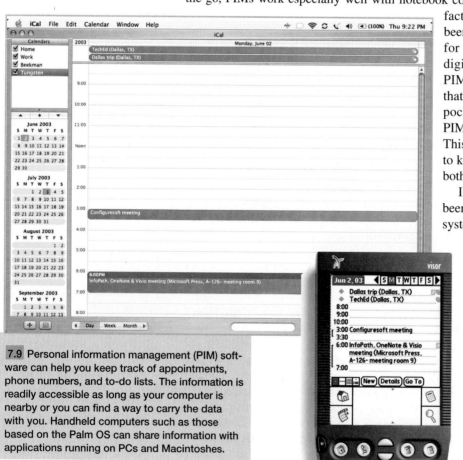

7.9 Personal information management (PIM) software can help you keep track of appointments, phone numbers, and to-do lists. The information is readily accessible as long as your computer is nearby or you can find a way to carry the data with you. Handheld computers such as those based on the Palm OS can share information with applications running on PCs and Macintoshes.

Transporting Data with Outlook and a Palm Device

Export Records to File

Save in: Contact Info

File name: Addresses

Save as type: Comma-Separated Text Files (*.csv)

Save   Cancel

7.10a To move your database-based address book into a Palm handheld computer, you use the Export command to create a file containing the data, with fields separated by commas and records separated by returns.

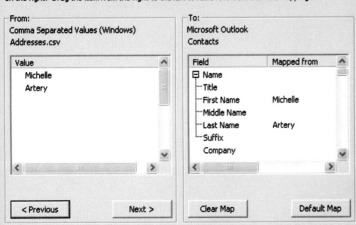

Map Custom Fields

Drag the values from the source file on the left, and drop them on the appropriate destination field on the right. Drag the item from the right to the left to remove it from the field mapping.

From:
Comma Separated Values (Windows)
Addresses.csv

Value
Michelle
Artery

To:
Microsoft Outlook
Contacts

Field	Mapped from
⊟ Name	
├ Title	
├ First Name	Michelle
├ Middle Name	
├ Last Name	Artery
└ Suffix	
Company	

< Previous   Next >   Clear Map   Default Map

OK   Cancel

7.10b Outlook contains a special-pupose database designed to handle personal information such as addresses. Using Outlook's Import command, you import the data from the text file into the Outlook Contacts list.

7.10c To synchronize the address book with a Palm OS device, you use the HotSync application to set up a conduit between Outlook and the Palm.

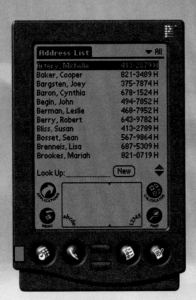

Custom

Nicole Mahan

Conduit	Action
Mail	Synchronize the files
Expense	Synchronize the files
Outlook Calendar	Synchronize the files
Outlook Contacts	Synchronize the files
Outlook Tasks	Synchronize the files
Outlook Notes	Synchronize the files
Install	Enabled
Install Service Templates	Enabled
System	Handheld overwrites Desktop

Done   Change...   Default   Help

Address List ▼ All

Artery, Michelle	413-2879 H
Baker, Cooper	821-3489 H
Bargsten, Joey	375-7874 H
Baron, Cynthia	678-1524 H
Begin, John	494-7852 H
Berman, Leslie	468-7952 H
Berry, Robert	643-9782 H
Bliss, Susan	413-2789 H
Bosset, Sean	567-9864 H
Brenneis, Lisa	687-5309 H
Brookes, Mariah	821-0719 H

Look Up: (New)

7.1
The Language of Database Queries

Years ago the number of incompatible database languages made it difficult for people using different applications to access the same database. In the mid-1970s, IBM's E. F. Codd proposed a standardized Structured English Query Language, which evolved into SQL. With SQL, users and programmers can employ the same language to access databases from a wide variety of vendors.

SQL combines the familiar database concepts of tables, rows (records), and columns (fields) and the mathematical idea of a set. Here we illustrate a simple SQL command using the Rental Vehicles database from Clem's Transportation Rental ("If it moves, we rent it."). Here's a complete listing of the database records:

7.11

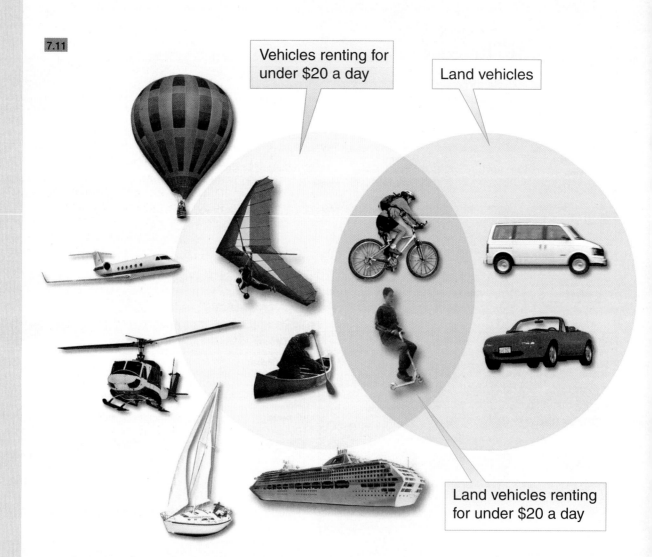

Vehicles renting for under $20 a day

Land vehicles

Land vehicles renting for under $20 a day

Vehicle_ID	Vehicle_Type	Transport_Mode	Num_Passengers	Cargo_Capacity	Rental_Price
1062	Helicopter	Air	6	500	$1,250.00
1955	Canoe	Water	2	30	$5.00
2784	Automobile	Land	4	250	$45.00
0213	Unicycle	Land	1	0	$10.00
0019	Minibus	Land	8	375	$130.00
3747	Balloon	Air	3	120	$340.00
7288	HangGlider	Air	1	5	$17.00
9430	Sailboat	Water	8	200	$275.00
8714	Powerboat	Water	4	175	$210.00
0441	Bicycle	Land	1	10	$12.00
4759	Jet	Air	9	2300	$2,900.00

A typical SQL statement filters the records of a database, capturing only those that meet the specific criteria. For example, suppose you wanted to list the ID numbers and types of the vehicles that travel on land and cost less than $20.00 per day. The SQL statement to perform this task would look like this:

```
SELECT Vehicle_ID, Vehicle_Type FROM Rental_Vehicles
WHERE Transport_Mode = 'Land' AND Rental_Price = 20.00
```

In English, this SQL statement says, "Show me (from the Rental Vehicles database) the vehicle IDs and vehicle types for those vehicles that travel by land and cost less than $20.00 per day to rent."

Two rows in the database meet these criteria, the unicycle and bicycle:

```
0213 Unicycle
0441 Bicycle
```

The selection rules for SQL are consistent and understandable whether queries are simple or complex. This simple example is designed to give you an idea of how they work.

Beyond the Basics: Database Management Systems

When we try to pick out **anything**, we find it hitched to **everything else in the universe**.

—John Muir, first director of the National Park Service

So far we've used simple examples to illustrate concepts common to most database programs. This oversimplification is useful for understanding the basics, but it's not the whole story. In truth, database programs range from simple mailing label programs to massive financial information systems, and it's important to know a little about what makes them different as well as what makes them alike.

From File Managers to Database Management Systems

Technically speaking, many consumer databases and PIM programs aren't really database managers at all; they're file managers. A file manager is a program that enables users to work with one file at a time. A true database management system (DBMS) is a program or system of programs that can manipulate data in a large collection of files—the database—cross-referencing between files as needed. A DBMS can be used interactively, or it can be controlled directly by other programs. A file manager is sufficient for mailing lists and other common data management applications. But for many large, complex jobs there's no substitute for a true database management system.

Consider, for example, the problem of managing student information at a college. It's easy to see how databases might be used to store this information: a table containing one record

Transcript file	Financial info file	Class list file
Student ID	Student ID	Course Number
Name	Name	Department
Local Street Address	Local Street Address	Section Number
Apartment No.	Apartment No.	Instructor
City	City	Time
State	State	Location
Zip	Zip	Number of Students
Permanent Street Address	Permanent Street Address	
Apartment No.	Apartment No.	(Student 1 Information)
City	City	Student ID
State	State	Name
Zip	Zip	Class Standing
Sex	Sex	Major
Citizenship	Citizenship	
Year Admitted	Year Admitted	(Student 2 Information)
Class Standing	Class Standing	Student ID
Major	Major	Name
GPA	GPA	Class Standing
		Major
(Course 1 information)		
Department	Tuition	
Number	Deposits	
Credits	Registration Fees	
Grade	Parking Fees	
Date	Housing Fees	
	Lab Fees	
(Course 2 information)		
Department		

7.12 Student information is duplicated in several different files of this inefficient, error-prone database.

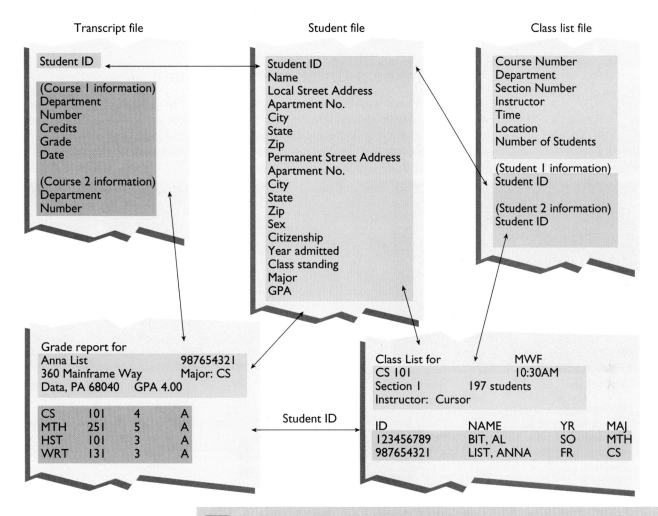

Transcript file

Student ID

(Course 1 information)
Department
Number
Credits
Grade
Date

(Course 2 information)
Department
Number

Student file

Student ID
Name
Local Street Address
Apartment No.
City
State
Zip
Permanent Street Address
Apartment No.
City
State
Zip
Sex
Citizenship
Year admitted
Class standing
Major
GPA

Class list file

Course Number
Department
Section Number
Instructor
Time
Location
Number of Students

(Student 1 information)
Student ID

(Student 2 information)
Student ID

Grade report for
Anna List	987654321
360 Mainframe Way	Major: CS
Data, PA 68040	GPA 4.00

CS	101	4	A
MTH	251	5	A
HST	101	3	A
WRT	131	3	A

Student ID

Class List for   MWF
CS 101   10:30AM
Section 1   197 students
Instructor: Cursor

ID	NAME	YR	MAJ
123456789	BIT, AL	SO	MTH
987654321	LIST, ANNA	FR	CS

7.13 The Student table serves as a reference when grade reports and class lists are created. The Student ID fields in the Transcript table and the Class List table are used as a key for locating the necessary student information in the Student table.

for each student, with fields for name, student ID number, address, phone, and so on. But a typical student generates far too much information to store practically in a single table.

Most schools choose to keep several tables containing student information: one for financial records, one for course enrollment and grade transcripts, and so on. Each of these tables has a single record for each student. In addition, a school must maintain class enrollment tables with one record for each class and fields for information on each student enrolled in the class. Three of these tables might be organized as shown in the accompanying figure.

In this database, each of the three separate tables contains basic information about every student. This redundant data not only occupies expensive storage space but also makes it difficult to ensure that student information is accurate and up-to-date. If a student moves to a different address, several files must be updated to reflect this change. The more changes, the greater the likelihood of a data-entry error.

With a DBMS there's no need to store all of this information in every table. The database can include a basic student table containing demographic information—information that's unique for each student. Because the demographic information is stored in a separate table, it doesn't need to be included in the financial information table, the transcript table, the class list table, or any other table. The student ID number, included in each table, serves as a *key field*; it unlocks the relevant student information in the student table when it's needed elsewhere. The student ID field is, in effect, shared by all tables that use data from this table. If the student moves, the change of address need only be recorded in one place. Databases organized in this way are called *relational databases*.

What Makes a Database Relational?

To most users a relational database program is one that allows tables to be related to each other so that changes in one table are reflected in other tables automatically. To computer scientists, the term *relational database* has a technical definition related to the underlying structure of the data and the rules specifying how that data can be manipulated.

Clerk's view

Video rental view used by clerks to access renter information, scan bar codes on videos, and print rental invoices

Video store database

Manager's view

- Inventory-tracking view used by managers to check on rental history and inventory for individual movies
- Policy view used by managers to change pricing, membership, and other policies

Technician/programmer's view

Technical view used by programmer to create other user interfaces and custom queries

7.14 Clerks, managers, programmers, and customers see different views of a movie rental store's database. Customers can browse through listings and reviews of available movies using a touch-screen kiosk. The clerk's view allows only for simple data-entry and checkout procedures. The manager, working with the same database, has control over pricing, policies, and inventory but can't change the structure or user interface of the database. The programmer can work under the hood to fine-tune and customize the database so it can better meet the needs of other employees and customers.

The structure of a relational database is based on the relational model—a mathematical model that combines data in tables. Other kinds of database management systems are based on different theoretical models, with different technical advantages and disadvantages. But the majority of DBMSs in use today, including virtually all PC-based database management systems, use the relational model. So from the average computer user's point of view, the distinction between the popular and technical definitions of *relational* is academic.

The Many Faces of Databases

Large databases often contain hundreds of interrelated tables. This maze of information could be overwhelming to users if they were forced to deal with it directly. Fortunately, a database management system can shield users from the complex inner workings of the system, providing them with only the information and commands they need to get their jobs done. In fact, a well-designed database puts on different faces for different classes of users.

Retail clerks don't need to be able to access every piece of information in the store's database; they just need to enter sales transactions on point-of-sale terminals. Databases designed for retail outlets generally include simple, straightforward terminal interfaces that give the clerks only the information, and the power, they need to process transactions. Managers, accountants, data processing specialists, and customers see the database from different points of view because they need to work with the data in different ways.

Database Trends

Database technology isn't static. Advances in the last two decades have changed the way most organizations deal with data, and current trends suggest even bigger changes in the near future.

> It is better to ask **some of the questions** than to know **all of the answers**.
>
> —James Thurber, in *Fables for Our Time*

Real-Time Computing

The earliest file management programs could do only batch processing, which required users to accumulate transactions and feed them into computers in large batches. These batch systems weren't able to provide the kind of immediate feedback we expect today. Questions like "What's the balance in my checking account?" or "Are there any open flights to Denver next Tuesday?" were likely to be answered "Those records will be up-dated tonight, so we'll let you know tomorrow."

Today, disk drives, inexpensive memory, and sophisticated software have allowed interactive processing to replace batch processing for most applications. Users can now interact with data through terminals, viewing and changing values online in real time. Batch processing is still used for printing periodic bills, invoices, and reports and for making backup copies of data files—jobs for which it makes sense to do a lot of transactions at once. But for applications that demand immediacy, such as airline reservations, banking transactions, and the like, interactive, multiuser database systems have taken over. These systems are typically run on powerful servers and accessed by users remotely. Companies such as Oracle, IBM, and Microsoft create the *database servers* used by companies of all sizes around the world.

This trend toward real-time computing is accelerated by the Internet, which makes it possible to have almost instant access to information stored in databases from anywhere on Earth, inside or outside the boundaries of the enterprise.

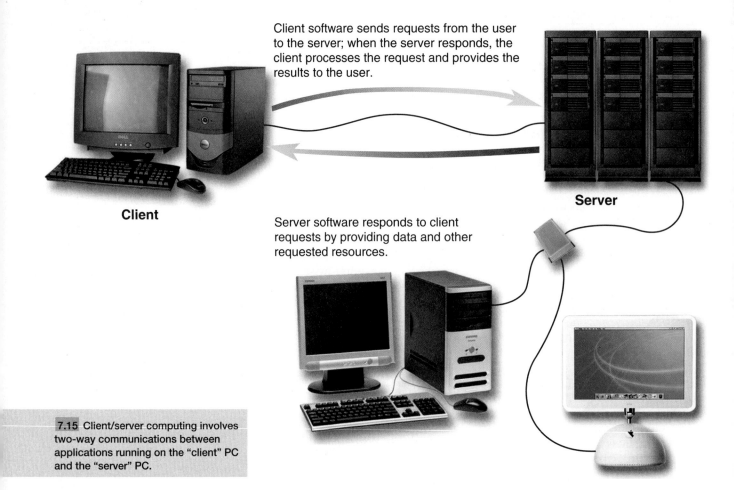

Client software sends requests from the user to the server; when the server responds, the client processes the request and provides the results to the user.

Client

Server

Server software responds to client requests by providing data and other requested resources.

7.15 Client/server computing involves two-way communications between applications running on the "client" PC and the "server" PC.

Downsizing and Decentralizing

In the pre-PC days, most databases were housed in mainframe computers accessible only to information-processing personnel. But the traditional hard-to-access centralized database on a mainframe system is no longer the norm.

Today, many businesses use a client/server approach employing database servers: *Client* programs in desktop computers, notebooks, PDAs, or other devices send information requests through a network or the Internet to database servers or mainframe databases; these *servers* process queries and send the requested data back to the client. A client/server system enables users to take advantage of the PC's simple user interface and convenience, while still having access to data stored on large server systems.

Some corporations keep copies of all corporate data in integrated data warehouses. In some respects, data warehouses are similar to old-style systems: They're large, relatively expensive, and centralized. But unlike older centralized systems, data warehouses give users more direct access to enterprise data. Data warehouses are most commonly found in large corporations and government departments.

Some companies use distributed databases, where data is spread across networks on several different computers rather than stored in one central site. Many organizations have both data warehouses and distributed databases. From the user's point of view, the differences between these approaches may not be apparent. Connectivity software, sometimes called *middleware*, links the client and server machines, hiding the complexity of the interaction between those machines and creating a *three-tier* design that separates the actual data from the programming logic used to access it. However the data is stored, accessed, and retrieved, the goal is to provide quick and easy access to important information.

Whether you're creating an address file with a simple file manager or retrieving data from a full-blown relational database management system, you can save yourself a great deal of time and grief if you follow a few common-sense rules:

➡ **Choose the right tool for the job.** Don't invest time and money in a programmable relational database to computerize your address book, and don't try to run the affairs of your multinational corporation with a spreadsheet list manager.

➡ **Think about how you'll get the information out before you put it in.** What kinds of tables, records, and fields will you need to create to make it easy to find things quickly and print things the way you'll want them? For example, use separate fields for first and last name if you want to sort names alphabetically by last name and print first names first.

➡ **Start with a plan, and be prepared to change your plan.** It's a good idea to do a trial run with a small amount of data to make sure everything works the way you think it should.

➡ **Make your data consistent. Inconsistencies can mess up sorting and make searching difficult.** For example, if a database includes residents of Minnesota, Minn., and MN, it's hard to group people by state.

➡ **Databases are only as good as their data.** When entering data, take advantage of the data-checking capability of your database software. Does the first name field contain nonalphabetic characters? Is the birth date within a reasonable range? Automatic data checking is important, but it's no substitute for human proofreading or for a bit of skepticism when using the database.

➡ **Query with care.** In the words of Aldous Huxley, "People always get what they ask for; the only trouble is that they never know, until they get it, what it actually is that they have asked for." Here's a real example: A student searching a database of classic rock albums requested all records containing the string "Dylan," and the database program obediently displayed the names of several Bob Dylan albums . . . plus one by Jimi Hendrix called Electric Ladyland. Why? Because "dy-lan" is in Ladyland! Unwanted records can go unnoticed in large database selections, so it's important to define selection rules very carefully.

➡ **If at first you don't succeed, try another approach.** If your search doesn't turn up the answers you were looking for, it doesn't mean the answers aren't there; they may just be wearing a disguise. For example, if you search a standard library database for "Vietnam War" references, you might not find any. Why? Because the government officially classifies the Vietnam War as a conflict, so references are stored under the subject "Vietnam Conflict." Technology meets bureaucracy !

Data Mining

Today's technology makes it easy for a business to accumulate masses of information in a database. Many organizations are content to retrieve information using the queries, searches, and reports. But others are finding that there's gold hidden in their large data-bases—gold that can only be extracted using a new technology called *data mining*. **Data mining** is the discovery and extraction of hidden predictive information from large data-bases. It uses statistical methods and artificial intelligence technology to locate trends and patterns in data that would have been overlooked by normal database queries. For example, a grocery chain used data mining to discover differences between male and female shop-ping patterns so they could create gender-specific marketing campaigns. (In an industry ad they announced that some men habitually buy beer and diapers every Friday!) In effect, data-mining technology enables users to "drill down" through masses of data to find valu-able veins of information.

Databases and the Web

Many businesses are retooling to take advantage of Internet technology on their internal networks. These *intranets* enable employees to access corporate databases using the same Web browsers and search engines they use to access information outside the company net-works. As Internet tools rapidly evolve, database access should become easier and more transparent.

HTML, the language used to construct most Web pages, wasn't designed to build database queries. But a newer, more powerful data description language called XML is designed with industrial-strength database access in mind. Database manufacturers are currently retooling their products so they can process data requests in XML. Because XML can serve as both a query language and a Web page construction tool, it's likely to open up all kinds of databases to the Web, making it easy for you to request and receive information online.

For many organizations, Web database strategies revolve around *directories*. Directories were originally little more than repositories for user phone numbers, addresses, and passwords, and they were commonly buried inside network operating systems. But the explosive growth of the Internet and e-commerce has expanded the roles of directories for many organizations. Directories can be used to store basic employee and customer information, along with access policies, identity proof, payment information, and security information. Directories are at the heart of many *customer relationship management (CRM)* systems—software systems for organizing and tracking information on customers.

The Web makes it possible for employees and customers alike to have instant access to databases, opening up all kinds of rapid-response e-commerce possibilities. But this kind of broad real-time database access also increases the probability of data errors—and the importance of eliminating those errors as quickly as possible. High data quality is a critical factor in successful e-commerce. Most large databases use data-checking routines whenever data is entered. But many organizations also depend on data-cleansing tools to correct errors that make it through the entry checks. For errors that aren't corrected by automated cleansing tools, the last wall of defense is typically a human customer service representative who can provide rapid response to customer complaints.

Object-Oriented Databases

Some of the biggest changes in database technology in the next few years may take place under the surface, where they may not be apparent to most users. For example, many computer scientists believe that the relational data model will be supplanted in the next decade by an object-oriented data model and that most future databases will be object-oriented databases rather than relational databases. Instead of storing records in tables and hierarchies, object-oriented databases store software *objects* that contain procedures (or instructions) along with data. Object-oriented databases often are used in conjunction with object-oriented programming languages. Experts suggest that object technology will make construction and manipulation of complex databases easier and less time-consuming. Users will find databases more flexible and responsive as object technology becomes more widespread, even if they aren't aware of the underlying technological reasons for these improvements. Today, many companies are experimenting with databases that combine relational and object concepts into hybrid systems.

Multimedia Databases

Today's databases can efficiently store all kinds of text and numeric data. But today's computers are multimedia machines that routinely deal with pictures, sounds, animation, and video clips. Multimedia databases can handle graphical and dynamic data along with text and numbers. Multimedia professionals use databases to catalog art, photographs, maps, video clips, sound files, and other types of media files. Media files aren't generally stored in databases because they're too large. Instead, a multimedia database serves as an *index* to all of the separately stored files.

Multimedia databases have applications in law enforcement, medicine, entertainment, and other professions where information needs go beyond words and numbers. In one high-profile example, IBM and Sony are transferring 115,000 hours worth of CNN videotape into a digital database. This database enables CNN producers to work more efficiently with archived clips, but it also opens up the possibility of pay-per-view Web access by consumers through the Internet and wireless devices.

Natural Language Databases

Ultimately, database technology will all but disappear from the user's view as interfaces become simpler, more powerful, and more intelligent. Future databases will undoubtedly incorporate more artificial intelligence technology. We're already seeing databases and data-mining software that can respond to simple *natural language* queries—queries in English or some other human language. Many help sites and search engines on the Web can accept queries in English, German, French, Japanese, and several other languages. Today's natural language technology is far from perfect, but it's getting better quickly. It won't be long before you'll be able to ask for data using the same language you use when addressing a human being.

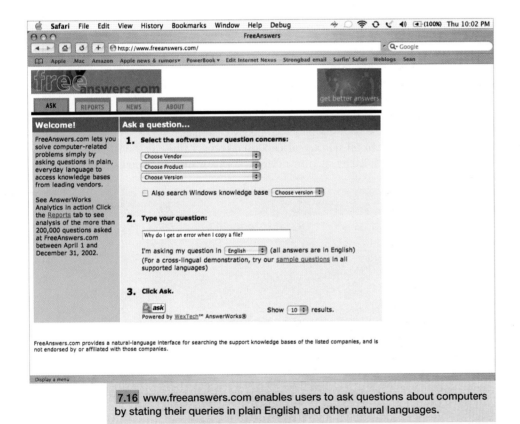

7.16 www.freeanswers.com enables users to ask questions about computers by stating their queries in plain English and other natural languages.

No Secrets: Computers and Privacy

Instant airline reservations, all-night automated banking, overnight mail, instant library searches, Web shopping—databases provide us with conveniences that were unthinkable a generation ago. But convenience isn't free. In the case of databases the price we pay is our privacy.

Advanced technology has created **new opportunities** for America as a nation, but it has also created the possibility for **new abuses** of the individual American citizen. Adequate safeguards must always **stand watch** so that man remains **master** and never the **victim of the computer**.

—Richard Nixon, 37th president of the United States, Feb. 23, 1974

Personal Data: All About You

We live in an information age, and data is one of the currencies of our time. Businesses and government agencies spend billions of dollars every year to collect and exchange information about you and me. More than 15,000 specialized marketing databases contain 2 billion consumer names, along with a surprising amount of personal information. The typical American consumer is on at least 25 marketing lists. Many of these lists are organized by characteristics like age, income, religion, political affiliation, and even sexual preference—and they're bought and sold every day.

Marketing databases are only the tip of the iceberg. Credit and banking information, tax records, health data, insurance records, political contributions, voter registration, credit card purchases, warranty registrations, magazine and newsletter subscriptions, phone calls, passport registration, airline reservations, automobile registrations, arrests, Internet explorations—they're all recorded in computers, and we have little or no control over what happens to most of those records once they're collected.

For most of us this data is out of sight and out of mind. But lives are changed because of these databases. Here are some representative stories:

- When members of Congress investigated ties between President Jimmy Carter's brother Billy and the government of Libya, they produced a report that detailed, among other things, the exact time and location of phone calls placed by Billy Carter in three different states. The phone records, which revealed a great deal about Billy Carter's activities, were obtained from AT&T's massive network of data-collecting computers. Similar information is available on every phone company customer.
- When a credit bureau mistakenly placed a bankruptcy filing in the file of a St. Louis couple, banks responded by shutting off loans for their struggling construction business,

7.17 The Internal Revenue Service workers shown here enter taxpayers' financial information into massive computer databases. When you shop by phone, respond to a survey, or fill out a warranty card, it's likely that a clerk somewhere will enter that data into a computer.

forcing them into real bankruptcy. They sued but lost because credit bureaus are protected by law from financial responsibility for "honest" mistakes!

- A Los Angeles thief stole a wallet and used its contents to establish an artificial identity. When the thief was arrested for a robbery involving murder, the crime was recorded under the wallet owner's name in police databases. The legitimate owner of the wallet was arrested five times in the following 14 months and spent several days in jail before a protracted court battle resulted in the deletion of the record.
- In a more recent, more typical example of identity theft, an imposter had the mail of an innocent individual temporarily forwarded to a post office box so he could easily collect credit card numbers and other personal data. By the time the victim discovered an overdue Visa bill, the thief had racked up $42,000 in bogus charges. The victim wasn't liable for the charges, but it took the better part of a year to correct all of the credit bureau errors.

As these examples indicate, there are many ways that abuse and misuse of databases can take away personal privacy. Sometimes privacy violations are due to government surveillance activities. Sometimes they're the result of the work of private corporations. Privacy breaches may be innocent mistakes, strategic actions, or malicious mischief. The explosive growth of identity theft—which claims millions of victims each year—makes it clear that database technology can be a powerful criminal tool.

7.18 This poster was part of a 2004 campaign to educate the public about identity theft.

Privacy violations aren't new, and they don't always involve computers. The German Nazis, the Chinese Communists, and even Richard Nixon's 1972 campaign committee practiced surveillance without computers. But the privacy problem takes on a whole new dimension in the age of high-speed computers and databases. The same characteristics that make databases more efficient than other information storage methods—storage capacity, retrieval speed, organizational flexibility, and ease of distribution of information—also make them a threat to our privacy.

The Privacy Problem

In George Orwell's *1984*, information about every citizen was stored in a massive database controlled by the ever-vigilant Big Brother. Today's data warehouses in many ways resemble Big Brother's database. Data-mining techniques can be used to extract information about

> What has taken me **a lifetime to build**—my trust, my integrity and my identity—has been **tainted**. I don't know if I'm dealing with **a 14-year-old messing around with a computer** or if I'm dealing with **organized crime**.
>
> —Identity theft victim

individuals and groups without their knowledge or consent. And databases can be easily sold or used for purposes other than those for which they were collected. Most of the time this kind of activity goes unnoticed by the public. Here are some examples where public knowledge changed privacy policy:

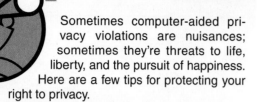

Sometimes computer-aided privacy violations are nuisances; sometimes they're threats to life, liberty, and the pursuit of happiness. Here are a few tips for protecting your right to privacy.

➡ **Your Social Security number is yours—don't give it away.** Since your SSN is a unique identifier, it can be used to gather information about you without your permission or knowledge. For example, you could be denied a job or insurance because of something you once put on a medical form. Never write it (or your driver's license number or phone number, for that matter) on a check or credit card receipt. Don't give your SSN to anyone unless they have a legitimate reason to ask for it.

➡ **Don't give away information about yourself.** Don't answer questions about yourself just because a questionnaire or company representative asks you to. When you fill out any form—coupon, warranty registration card, survey, sweepstakes entry, or whatever—think about whether you want the information stored in somebody else's computer.

➡ **Say no to direct mail, phone, and email solicitations.** Businesses and political organizations pay for your data so they can target you for mail, phone, and email campaigns. You can remove yourself from many lists using forms from the Direct Mail Marketing Association (www.the-dma.org). You can block most telemarketers by enrolling in the U.S. Federal Trade Commission's Opt Out program (www.donotcall.gov). If these calls don't stop the flow, you might want to try a more direct approach. Send back unwanted letters along with "Take me off your list" requests in the postage-paid envelopes that come with them. When you receive an unsolicited phone marketing call, tell the caller, "I never purchase or donate anything as a result of phone solicitations," and ask to be removed from the list. If they call within 12 months of being specifically told not to, you can sue and recover up to $500 per call according to the Telephone Consumer Protection Act of 1991. Unfortunately, there's no comparable federal law to protect you against junk email yet, so you should be especially careful about giving out your email address if you don't like receiving unsolicited email.

➡ **Say no to sharing your personal information.** If you open a private Internet account, tell your Internet service provider that your personal data is not for sale. If you don't want your state's Department of Motor Vehicles selling information about you, notify them. A relatively new federal law gives you more control over DMV use of personal data. If you don't want credit agencies sharing personal information, let them know. The Federal Trade Commission's Privacy Web site (www.ftc.gov/privacy) includes clear guidelines and forms for contacting your DMV and credit agencies. The Financial Modernization Act of 1999 allows you to tell your banks and other financial institutions not to share your personal information with other institutions; check with those institutions for details.

➡ **Say no to pollsters.** Our political system has been radically transformed by polling; most of our "leaders" check the polls before they offer opinions on controversial issues. If you and I don't tell the pollsters what we're thinking, politicians will be more likely to tell us what they're thinking.

➡ **If you think there's incorrect or damaging information about you in a file, find out.** The Freedom of Information Act of 1966 requires that most records of U.S. government agencies be made available to the public on demand. The Privacy Act of 1974 requires federal agencies to provide you with information in your files relating to you and to amend incorrect records. The Fair Credit Reporting Act of 1970 allows you to see your credit ratings—for free if you have been denied credit—and correct any errors. The three big credit bureaus are Equifax (www.equifax.com), Trans Union (www.tuc.com), and Experian (www.experian.com).

➡ **To maximize your privacy, minimize your profile.** If you don't want a financial transaction recorded, use cash. If you don't want your phone number to be public information, use an unlisted number. If you don't want your mailing address known, use a post office box.

➡ **Know your electronic rights.** Privacy protection laws in the United States lag far behind those of other high-tech nations, but they are beginning to appear. For example, the 1986 Electronic Communications Privacy Act provides the same protection that covers mail and telephone communication to some—but not all—electronic communication. The 1988 Computer Matching and Privacy Protection Act regulates the use of government data in determining eligibility for federal benefits.

➡ **Support organizations that fight for privacy rights.** If you value privacy rights, let your representatives know how you feel, and support the American Civil Liberties Union, Computer Professionals for Social Responsibility, the Electronic Frontier Foundation, Electronic Privacy Information Center, Center for Democracy and Technology, Private Citizen, and other organizations that fight for those rights.

- In 1998 CVS drug stores contracted with Elensys, a Massachusetts direct marketing company, to send reminders to customers who had not renewed their prescriptions. While some customers undoubtedly appreciated the reminders, others objected to this commercial use of their private medical records. CVS terminated the practice as a result of protests.

- In many states driver's license information is considered a public record, available to anyone for a fee. In 1998, Florida's legislature voted to make driver's license photographs available on the same basis. But after a public outcry, Florida, along with several other states, ended its practice of selling driver's license photos to private companies.

- In 1999 Amazon.com introduced "Purchase Circles"—a feature that allowed customers to see which books, CDs, tapes, and videos are most popular within particular companies, schools, government organizations, and cities. Amazon didn't make individual purchase information available to the public, but it used that information to create customer profiles for groups. Using these Purchase Circle profiles, Amazon's Web site might tell you the most popular books and videos among Microsoft employees, Stephens College students, or residents of Dedham, Massachusetts, for example. In response to protests, Amazon decided to give customers the option of being excluded from Purchase Circles.

- In 1999, online advertising agency DoubleClick acquired a direct marketing firm along with its database of 90 million households. The company intended to combine supposedly anonymous data on Web user activity with personal information from the massive consumer database, creating data files rich with personal data about consumers. In March, 2000, in response to outcries from consumers and privacy watchdog groups, DoubleClick backed away from the data-matching plan, calling it a "big mistake" to try to match information in that way before government or industry standards could be put into place.

- Prior to February, 2001, N2H2, an Internet filtering software company, sold to other companies "class clicks" marketing research based on Web usage patterns of children. The company insists that its data didn't threaten any individual's privacy. Still, in response to protests, it stopped selling its data.

Centralized data warehouses aren't necessary for producing computerized dossiers of private citizens. With networked computers, it's easy to compile profiles by combining information from different databases. As long as the tables in the databases share a single unique field, such as a Social Security number field, record matching is trivial and quick. And when database information is combined, the whole is often far greater than the sum of its parts.

Sometimes the results are beneficial. Record matching is used by government enforcement agencies to locate criminals ranging from tax evaders to mass murderers. Because credit bureaus collect data about us, we can use credit cards to borrow money wherever we go. But these benefits come with at least three problems:

- *Data errors are common.* A study of 1,500 reports from the three big credit bureaus found errors in 43 percent of the files.
- *Data can become nearly immortal.* Because files are commonly sold and copied, it's impossible to delete or correct erroneous records with absolute certainty.
- *Data isn't secure.* A *Business Week* reporter demonstrated this in 1989 by using his computer to obtain then Vice President Dan Quayle's credit report. Had he been a skilled criminal, he might have been able to change that report.

Protection against invasion of privacy is not explicitly guaranteed by the U.S. Constitution. Legal scholars agree that the right to privacy—freedom from interference in the private sphere of a person's affairs—is implied by other constitutional guarantees, although debates rage about what this means. Federal and state laws provide forms of privacy protection, but most of those laws were written years ago. Most European countries have had strong privacy protection laws for years. The 1998 European Data Protection Directive guarantees a basic set of privacy rights to citizens of all countries in the European

Union—rights that go far beyond those of American citizens. The directive allows citizens to have access to all personal data, to know where that data originated, to have inaccurate data rectified, to seek recourse in the event of unlawful processing, and to withhold permission to use their data for direct marketing. The American legislatures have refused to pass similar laws because of intense lobbying by business interests. When it comes to privacy violation in America, technology is far ahead of the law.

Big Brother and Big Business

> If **all records** told the same tale, then **the lie** passed into history and **became truth**.
>
> —George Orwell, in *1984*

Database technology clearly poses a threat to personal privacy, but other information technologies amplify that threat:

- Networks make it possible for personal data to be transmitted almost anywhere instantly. The Internet is particularly fertile ground for collecting personal information about you. And the Web makes it alarmingly easy for anyone with a connected computer to examine your personal information.
- Microsoft's Passport, part of its .NET technologies, can optionally collect passwords, credit card numbers, and other consumer information in a central database controlled by Microsoft. The company's stated goal is to make it easier for its customers to take advantage of the Web's many services, but the potential for abuse of this technology may outweigh any possible gains in convenience. As a result, few consumers have taken advantage of these Passport features.
- Workplace monitoring technology enables managers to learn more than ever before about the work habits and patterns of workers. Supervisors can (and do) count keystrokes, monitor Web activity, screen email, and remotely view what's on the screens of employees.
- Surveillance cameras, increasingly used for nabbing routine traffic violations and detecting security violators, can be combined with picture databases to locate criminals—and others. Florida law enforcement officials came under fire from privacy groups be-

7.19 Surveillance cameras can be used with facial recognition software to locate criminals, but they may also threaten the privacy of law-abiding citizens.

cause they used cameras, face-recognition software, and criminal databases to find and arrest several attendees of the 2001 Super Bowl. After the terrorist attacks of September 11, 2001, surveillance cameras were installed in hundreds of businesses and government agencies to guard against future attacks.

- Surveillance satellites can provide permanent peepholes into our lives for anyone willing to pay the price.
- Cell phones are now required by law to include technology to determine and transmit their locations to emergency personnel responding to 911 calls. Privacy advocates point out that the same technology can easily be used for less noble purposes.

In George Orwell's *1984* personal privacy was the victim of a centralized Communist police state controlled by Big Brother. Today, our privacy is threatened by many Big Brothers—with new threats emerging almost every day. As Simson Garfinkel says in *Database Nation*, "Over the next 50 years, we will see new kinds of threats to privacy that don't find their roots in totalitarianism, but in capitalism, the free market, advanced technology, and the unbridled exchange of electronic information."

Democracy depends on the free flow of information, but it also depends on the protection of individual rights. Maintaining a balance is not easy, especially when new information technologies are being developed at such a rapid pace. With information at our fingertips it's tempting to think that more information is the answer. But in the timeless words of populist philosopher Will Rogers, "It's not the things we don't know that get us into trouble, it's the things we do know that ain't so."

Embedded Intelligence and Ubiquitous Computing

Computers are disappearing into more of our tools all the time. Information appliances, including cell phones, fax machines, and GPS devices, perform their specialized functions while hiding the technological details from their users. Dozens of household appliances and tools have invisible computers. Even our cars are processing megabytes of information as we drive down the road.

Some car computers are invisible; others are more obvious. Several companies have introduced dashboard computers that can play CDs and DVDs, recognize spoken commands, alert the driver to incoming email messages, read those messages aloud, store and retrieve contacts and appointments, dial phone numbers, recite directions using GPS-based navigation systems, report mechanical problems, and even track stolen vehicles. IBM researchers are developing an in-dash "artificial passenger" to make commuting safer for drivers. This intelligent agent carries on conversations, watching for signs of fatigue in the driver. If it finds them, it might change the radio station, open a window, or even spray the driver with cold water. In 2001, Volkswagen AG became the first automobile company to mass-produce a car with an Internet connection. (Appropriately, the VW eGeneration was initially sold only on the Net.)

7.21 "Smart Dust" computers at the University of California at Berkeley help monitor and control heating and cooling systems using environmental sensors and wireless communication links.

7.20 Sensors in this LifeShirt monitored life signs of this Indy Racing League driver when he crashed in the 2001 Indy 500.

Computers may soon be part of our clothing, too. Most of today's *wearable computers* are strap-on units for active information gatherers. But researchers at MIT and elsewhere are stitching CPUs, keyboards, and touchpads right into the clothes, turning their wearers into wireless Internet nodes. These digital outfits aren't just high-tech fashion statements—when worn with eyeglass monitors (described in Chapter 3's Inventing the Future Box [p. XXX]), they might be invaluable for any number of jobs that require both activity and connectivity.

In Japan computer technology has even found its way into the bathroom. A number of Japanese fixture manufacturers sell computer-controlled smart toilets. Some models automatically collect and store information on blood pressure, pulse, temperature, urine, and weight. The information can be displayed on a LCD display, accumulated for months, and even transmitted by modem to a medical service. Users of these smart toilets get a minicheckup whenever they visit the bathroom. Body-monitoring features give the toilet an entirely new function—a function are that will undoubtedly save lives.

When computers show up in our toilets, we're clearly entering an era of ubiquitous computers—computers everywhere. For several years researchers at Xerox PARC, Cambridge University, Olivetti, and elsewhere have been experimenting with technology that will make computers even more ubiquitous. PARC's Mark Weiser describes an experimental office equipped with intelligent devices, including smart badges described in Chapter 10: "Doors open only to the right badge wearer, rooms greet people by name, telephone calls can be automatically forwarded to wherever the recipient may be, receptionists actually know where people are, computer terminals retrieve the preferences of whoever is sitting at them, and appointment diaries write themselves."

Privacy and Security: Finding a Balance

Michael J. Miller

CROSSCURRENTS

After the terrorist attacks of September 11, 2001, security jumped to the forefront of the political landscape. Many laws quickly passed to strengthen U.S. security reduced the privacy of U.S. citizens and others. This article, first published in the April 29, 2003 Issue of PC Magazine, *clearly describes the delicate balance between security and privacy.*

Over the past year and a half, the tug of war between privacy and security has reached a new level, and I'm not convinced that people are willing to give up their privacy in pursuit of security. Of course, I'm willing to put up with inconveniences at airports and office buildings; I'm now accustomed to removing my shoes before going through airport metal detectors, and I've had my photo taken many times before getting into elevators in office buildings. But I do have a problem with indiscriminate data gathering that invades people's privacy without really improving security.

The mass collection of personal information and subsequent mining of that data will not solve the security problem. Instead, the government ends up with far more information than any person or any computer can analyze. The problem behind the 9/11 attacks was not that the government had too little information. Rather, it had so much information that it couldn't tell what was important.

Data mining is problematic because it results in extensive watch lists of people who share "suspicious" traits, such as an Arabic surname or a fondness for movies about airplanes. But so many people end up on these lists that the lists become an inefficient way of finding the bad guys. Data mining is better for building a case after the fact than for preventing an attack. The massive data collection measures are more effective at trampling our privacy.

Several technology developments for gathering, sorting, mining, and distributing all kinds of information about people pose potential threats to privacy. Here are just a few of them.

All sorts of records are now digitized. Everything from tax returns and legal settlements to sales receipts is now in digital format, which can be easily copied.

Databases have proliferated. Since everyone from your bank to your local dry cleaner is storing customer information in a database, large data repositories are inviting targets for hackers. Databases also make it easier for people to look up information they have no business accessing.

Databases are increasingly linked. New application integration technologies such as Web services are designed to tie databases together easily, allowing business intelligence software to pinpoint specific information in multiple databases.

The Internet makes collecting, sharing, and sending information easy.

Inexpensive digital cameras, particularly Webcams, let people capture images wherever they go.

These technologies are here to stay, and their potential for both good and evil is real. Recently, the NYPD made the right decision to destroy a database it had created of antiwar protesters' prior political activities. But other uses of data-gathering technologies have me concerned.

Under the USA Patriot Act, libraries and bookstores can be required to turn over their patron records. This information used to be considered private. The American Library Association has opposed this legislation, and some libraries have been very public about shredding their records.

Meanwhile, the U.S. Department of Defense's Total Information Awareness research project is looking into surveillance through mass data mining of all sorts of public databases. And the Domestic Security Enhancement Act of 2003, now under discussion, would expand the government's power even more, letting it use a database to collect, analyze, and maintain DNA samples and other identification information from suspected terrorists. It would also enable the government to obtain information from private businesses without a subpoena.

In one camp are those who see these steps as necessary measures in the fight against terrorism. I fall in the opposition camp of those who believe that the security gains aren't worth the intrusion of privacy, which I consider a fundamental freedom. Even more disturbing, most of these new restrictions are being implemented after very little public debate.

So we're left with some difficult problems, and I don't have the answers. But I can suggest some safeguards, such as legislated encryption of identifying data to eliminate or minimize abuse of such data, legislated access to one's own records to correct errors, creation of an oversight panel to put a stop to spurious data collection, and a continuing requirement for judicial oversight and subpoenas for the collection of private information.

Most Americans think they have a right to privacy. But check the Constitution: It's not stated there explicitly. If you want to protect your privacy, you need to get involved in the debate now. Some legislators are pressing for changes to these new laws—some arguing for tighter limitations on the government and some for less, while others are trying to make the USA Patriot Act permanent. (It's currently set to expire at the end of 2005.)

DISCUSSION QUESTIONS

1. Do you think libraries and bookstores should be required to turn over information about their patrons to the government? Why or why not?

2. Do you think increased use of database technology for security purposes is worth the threat to personal privacy? Justify your answer and give specific examples.

SUMMARY

Database programs enable users to quickly and efficiently store, organize, retrieve, communicate, and manage large amounts of information. Each database is made up of tables, which are, in turn, collections of records, and each record is made up of fields containing text strings, numbers, and other chunks of information. Database programs enable users to view data in a variety of ways, sort records in any order, and print reports, mailing labels, and other custom printouts. A user can search for an individual record or select a group of records with a query.

While most database programs are general-purpose tools that can be used to create custom databases for any purpose, some are special-purpose tools programmed to do a particular set of tasks. Geographical information systems, for example, combine maps and demographic information with data tables to provide new ways to look at data. Personal information managers provide automated address books, appointment calendars, to-do lists, and notebooks for busy individuals.

Many database programs are, technically speaking, file managers because they work with only one file at a time. Database management systems (DBMSs) can work with several data sources at once, cross-referencing information among files when appropriate. A DBMS can provide an efficient way to store and manage large quantities of information by eliminating the need for redundant information in different files. A well-designed database provides different views of the data to different classes of users so each user sees and manipulates only the information necessary for the job at hand.

The trend today is clearly away from large, centralized databases accessible only to data processing staff. Instead, most organizations are moving toward a client/server approach that enables users to have access to data stored in servers throughout the organization's network.

The accumulation of data by government agencies and businesses is a growing threat to our right to privacy. Massive amounts of information about private citizens are collected and exchanged for a variety of purposes. Today's technology makes it easy to combine information from different databases, producing detailed profiles of individual citizens. Although there are many legitimate uses for these procedures, there's also a great potential for abuse.

KEY TERMS

batch processing (p. 253)
browse (p. 241)
centralized database (p. 254)
client/server (p. 254)
computed field (p. 241)
data mining (p. 255)
data warehouse (p. 254)
database (p. 240)
database management system
   (DBMS) (p. 250)
database program (p. 240)
distributed database (p. 254)
export data (p. 242)

field (p. 240)
file manager (p. 250)
geographical information system
   (GIS) (p. 245)
identity theft (p. 259)
import data (p. 241)
interactive processing (p. 253)
mail merge (p. 242)
object-oriented database (p. 256)
personal information manager (PIM)
   (p. 246)
query (p. 241)
query language (p. 245)

real time (p. 253)
record (p. 240)
record matching (p. 261)
relational database (p. 252)
report (p. 242)
right to privacy (p. 261)
search (p. 241)
select (records) (p. 241)
sort (p. 241)
SQL (p. 245)
table (p. 240)
XML (p. 256)

INTERACTIVE QUIZ QUESTIONS

 1. The *Computer Confluence* CD-ROM contains self-test quiz questions related to this chapter, including multiple-choice, true or false, and matching questions.

 2. The *Computer Confluence* Web site, http://www.computerconfluence.com, contains self-test exercises related to this chapter. Follow the instruc-

tions for taking a quiz. After you've completed your quiz, you can email the results to your instructor.

3. The Web site also contains open-ended discussion questions called Internet Explorations. Discuss one or more of the Internet Exploration questions at the section for this chapter.

TRUE OR FALSE

1. In a typical database, a record contains the information relating to one person, product, or event.

2. In a database, a numeric field can contain only computed formulas similar to formulas in spreadsheets.

3. Typical database software allows you to view one record at a time in form view or several records at a time in list view.

4. The most common type of database printout is called an export.

5. To query a database you must learn at least some SQL, the universal query language of databases.

6. A database management system (DBMS) can manipulate data in a large collection of files, cross-referencing them as needed.

7. XML is a middleware product designed to link Windows XP databases to HTML Web pages.

8. The right to privacy is explicitly guaranteed by the U.S. Constitution.

9. Democracy depends on the free flow of information and on the protection of individual rights; database technology threatens to upset the balance between these two principles.

10. Middleware is a special class of software designed to link databases in PDAs to databases in PCs.

MULTIPLE CHOICE

1. People use databases rather than paper-based filing systems for information handling tasks because
   a. databases make it easier to store large quantities of information.
   b. databases make it easier to retrieve information quickly and flexibly.
   c. databases make it easy to organize and reorganize information.
   d. databases make it easy to print and distribute information in a variety of ways.
   e. All of the above are true.

2. Early PC databases were simple file managers; today most of the jobs done with these programs can be performed easily and efficiently with
   a. equation-solving software.
   b. financial management software.
   c. spreadsheet software.
   d. word processing software.
   e. authoring software.

3. Which of these is the correct hierarchy for a standard database?
   a. database, field, record, table.
   b. database, record, field, table.
   c. database, record, table, field.
   d. database, table, field, record.
   e. database, table, record, field.

4. Which of these is not a specialized database program?
   a. a geographic information system.
   b. a personal information manager (PIM).
   c. a program for organizing and managing photos.
   d. the software that manages MP3 files in music players like the iPod.
   e. All of these are specialized database programs.

5. By definition, a relational database is
   a. a database that contains several related records.
   b. a database that contains several related fields.
   c. a database that has a relationship with other databases.
   d. a database whose structure combines data in tables based on the relational model.
   e. a database with more than 1,000 records.

6. Because of advances in hardware and software, today's databases perform real-time
   a. batch processing.
   b. interactive processing.
   c. structured processing.
   d. unstructured processing.
   e. file management processing.

7. Data warehouses are similar in some ways to old-style centralized databases; but unlike those older systems, data warehouses
   a. depend on middleware to produce reports.
   b. give users more direct access to enterprise data.
   c. are built on distributed database systems.
   d. are powered by simple file management software.
   e. All of the above.

8. Which of these Web applications depends on database technology?
   a. online auctions like eBay.
   b. search engines like Google.
   c. online stores like Amazon.com.
   d. customer relationship management (CRM) systems.
   e. All of the above.

9. Object-oriented databases
   a. are likely to replace relational databases for many applications in the coming decade.
   b. are likely to be replaced by relational databases for many applications in the coming decade.
   c. are likely to replace most distributed databases for many applications in the coming decade.
   d. are likely to be replaced by file managers for many applications in the coming decade.
   e. are not likely to become practical for the coming decade.

10. Even without centralized data warehouses, government agencies can quickly produce detailed dossiers on millions of private citizens
    a. through the World Wide Web.
    b. by using XML technology.
    c through record matching.
    d. hrough identity theft.
    e. with middleware.

REVIEW QUESTIONS

1. Define or describe each of the key terms listed in the Key Terms section. Check your answers in the glossary.

2. What is the difference between a file manager and a database management system? How are they similar?

3. Describe the structure of a simple database. Use the terms *file*, *record*, and *field* in your description.

4. What is a query? Give examples of the kinds of questions that might be answered with a query.

5. What steps are involved in producing a standard multicolumn business report from a database?

6. What are the advantages of personal information management software over paper notebook organizers? What are the disadvantages?

7. What does it mean to sort a data file?

8. How can a database be designed to reduce the likelihood of data-entry errors?

9. Describe how record matching is used to obtain information about you. Give an example.

10. Do we have a legal right to privacy? On what grounds?

11. Why are computers important in discussions of invasion of privacy?

DISCUSSION QUESTIONS

1. Grade books, checkbooks, and other information collections can be managed with either a database program or a spreadsheet program. How would you decide which type of application is most appropriate for a given job?

2. What have you done this week that directly or indirectly involved a database? How would your week have been different in a world without databases?

3. "The computer is a great humanizing factor because it makes the individual more important. The more information we have on each individual, the more each individual counts." Do you agree with this statement by science fiction writer Isaac Asimov? Why or why not?

4. Suppose you have been incorrectly billed for $100 by a mail-order house. Your protestations are ignored by the company, which is now threatening to report you to a collection agency. What do you do?

5. What advantages and disadvantages does a computerized law enforcement system have for law-abiding citizens?

6. In what ways were George Orwell's "predictions" in the novel *1984* accurate? In what ways were they wrong?

PROJECTS

1. Design a database for your own use. Create several records, sort the data, and print a report.

2. Find out as much as you can about someone (for example, yourself or a public figure) from public records like tax records, court records, voter registration lists, and motor vehicle files. How much of this information were you able to get directly from the Web? How much was available for free?

3. Find out as much as you can about your own credit rating.

4. The next time you order something by mail or phone, try encoding your name with a unique middle initial so you can recognize when the company sells your name and address to other companies. Use several different spellings for different orders if you want to do some comparative research.

5. Determine what information about you is stored in your school computers. What information are you allowed to see? What information are others allowed to see? Exactly who may access your files? Can you find out who sees your files? How long is the information retained after you leave school?

6. Keep track of your purchases for a few weeks. If other people had access to this information, what conclusions might they be able to draw about you?

SOURCES AND RESOURCES

Books

Like word processors, spreadsheet software, and multimedia programs, databases have inspired hundreds of how-to tutorials, user's guides, and reference books. If you're working with a popular program, you should have no trouble finding a book to help you develop your skills.

Database Design for Mere Mortals: A Hands-On Guide to Relational Database Design, Second Edition, by Michael J. Hernandez (Reading, MA: Addison-Wesley Professional, 2003). This book can save time, money, and headaches for anyone who's involved in designing and building a relational database. After defining all of the critical concepts, the author clearly outlines the design process using case studies to illustrate important points.

A Manager's Guide to Database Technology: Building and Purchasing Better Applications, by Michael R. Blaha (Upper Saddle River, NJ: Prentice Hall, 2001). This little book presents clear explanations of database technology and applications from a management perspective. The author does a good job of focusing on strategy rather than getting bogged down in technical details.

The Practical SQL Handbook: Using Structured Query Language, Third Edition, by Judith S. Bowman, Sandra L. Emerson, and Marcy Darnovsky (Reading, MA: Addison-Wesley, 1996). If you want to learn to communicate with relational databases using the standard database query language, this book can help you learn the language.

SQL Fundamentals, Second Edition, by John J. Patrick (Upper Saddle River, NJ: Prentice Hall, 2002). This introduction applies the principles of SQL to Microsoft Access and Oracle, two of the most widely used database products.

Visual Quickpro Guide: PHP and MySQL for Dynamic Web Sites, by Larry Ullman (Berkeley, CA: Peachpit Press, 2003). MySQL is the world's most popular open source database. A combination of PHP and MySQL can turn a static Web site into a dynamic, database-driven site. This book provides an introduction to this dynamic duo.

Data Smog: Surviving the Information Glut, Revised and Updated Edition, by David Shenk (New York: HarperEdge, 1998). It's possible to have too much information at your fingertips. David Shenk's book clearly describes the hazards to individuals and society of all this information.

Surveillance Society: Monitoring Everyday Life (Issues in Society), by David Lyon (Berkshire, UK: Open University Press, 2001). This book intelligently analyzes the deterioration of personal privacy in our information society without getting bogged down in jargon.

Database Nation: The Death of Privacy in the 21st Century, by Simson Garfinkel (Cambridge, MA: O'Reilly, 2001). This is a frightening, sobering account of the erosion of our personal privacy as a result of misuse of technology—databases, on-the-job monitoring, data networks, biometric devices, video surveillance, and more. Simson Garfinkel skillfully mixes chilling true stories and futuristic scenarios with practical advice for reclaiming our individual and collective rights to privacy. Highly recommended.

The Unwanted Gaze: The Destruction of Privacy in America, by Brian Doherty (New York: Knopf, 2001). This book ties together the impeachment of President Clinton with the threat computers present to our control over personal information. The unifying thread is the deterioration of the private space earlier generations of Americans enjoyed.

The Transparent Society: Will Technology Force Us to Choose Between Freedom and Privacy?, by David Brin (Cambridge, MA: Perseus Publishing, 1999). Brin, a mathematician and award-winning science fiction writer, presents a compelling case that personal privacy is doomed by technology. He argues that our best hope is to provide equal access to all information, rather than let the biggest brothers have the only windows into our lives. Compelling reading.

Videos

Many popular films and television shows, from *Clear and Present Danger* to *The X-Files*, deal directly or indirectly with issues related to privacy and technology. One recent action film, *Enemy of the State*, used those issues as central themes. There's plenty of fantasy in this nonstop thriller about a man on the run and a government that can watch his every move. But there's a good deal of truth here, too.

Periodical

The Privacy Journal (**http://www.privacyjournal.net**). This widely quoted monthly newsletter covers all issues related to personal privacy.

Organizations

Privacy Foundation (**http://www.privacyfoundation.org**). The Privacy Foundation isn't an advocacy group; its mission is to report on technology-based privacy threats and circulate alerts.

Computer Professionals for Social Responsibility (**http://www.cpsr.org**). CPSR provides the public and policymakers with realistic assessments of the power, promise, and problems of information technology. Much of their work deals with privacy-related issues. Their newsletter is a good source of information.

The Electronic Frontier Foundation (**http://www.eff.org**). EFF strives to protect civil rights, including the right to privacy, on emerging communication networks.

Electronic Privacy Information Center (**http://www.epic.org**). EPIC serves as a watchdog over government efforts to build surveillance capabilities into the emerging information infrastructure.

American Civil Liberties Union (**http://www.aclu.org**). The ACLU tirelessly defends constitutional rights, including privacy rights.

Private Citizen (**http://www.private-citizen.com**). This organization can help keep you off junk phone lists—for a price.

Web Pages

Check the *Computer Confluence* Web site for links to many of the organizations listed above, along with links to other database and privacy-related sites.

AFTER YOU READ THIS CHAPTER YOU SHOULD BE ABLE TO:

- Describe the basic types of technology that make telecommunication possible

- Describe the nature and function of local area networks and wide area networks

- Discuss the uses and implications of email, instant messaging, teleconferencing, and other forms of online communication

- Explain how wireless network technology is transforming the ways people work and communicate

- Describe current and future trends in telecommunications and networking.

 Multimedia extras on the CD-ROM and the Web:

- **Animated illustrations** of modem and network technology

- A look at the **office of the future**

- How to find **wireless connections**

- **Instant access** to glossary and key word references

- Interactive **self-study quizzes**

    . . . *and more.*

 computerconfluence.com

NETWORKING AND TELECOMMUNICATION

8

ARTHUR C. CLARKE'S MAGICAL PROPHECY

Besides coining Clarke's laws, British writer Arthur C. Clarke has written more than 100 works of science fiction and nonfiction. His most famous work was the monumental 1968 film *2001: A Space Odyssey*, in which he collaborated with movie director Stanley Kubrick. The film's villain, a faceless English-speaking computer with a lust for power, sparked many public debates about the nature and risks of artificial intelligence. These debates continue today.

But Clarke's most visionary work may be a paper published in 1945 in which he predicted the use of *geostationary communications satellites*—satellites that

> If an elderly but distinguished scientist says that something is possible he is almost **certainly right**, but if he says that it is impossible he is **very probably wrong**.
>
> The only way to find the **limits of the possible** is to go beyond them into the impossible.
>
> Any sufficiently advanced technology is **indistinguishable from magic**.
>
> —Clarke's Three Laws

match the Earth's rotation so they can hang in a stationary position relative to the spinning planet below, relaying wireless transmissions between locations. Clarke's paper pinpointed the exact height of the orbit required to match the movement of the satellite with the planetary rotation. He also suggested that these satellites could replace many telephone cables and radio towers, allowing electronic signals to be beamed across oceans, deserts, and mountain ranges, linking the people of the world with a single communications network.

A decade after Clarke's paper appeared, powerful rockets and sensitive radio receiving equipment made communications satellites realistic.

8.1 Arthur C. Clarke

In 1964 the first synchronous TV satellite was launched, marking the beginning of a billion-dollar industry that has changed the way people communicate.

Today Clarke is often referred to as the father of satellite communications. Now in his 80s and largely confined to a wheelchair, Clarke lives in Sri Lanka, where he continues his work as a writer, though he now uses a personal computer and beams his words around the globe to editors using the satellites he envisioned half a century ago.

8.3 Geostationary communications satellites.

8.2 HAL, the rebellious computer in the movie *2001: A Space Odyssey*.

The Battle of New Orleans, the bloodiest battle of the War of 1812, was fought two weeks after the war officially ended; it took that long for the cease-fire message to travel from Washington, D.C., to the front line. In 1991, 179 years later, six hard-line Soviet communists staged a coup to turn back the tide of democratic and economic reforms that were sweeping the U.S.S.R. Within hours, messages zipped between the Soviet Union and Western nations on telephone and computer networks. Cable television and computer conferences provided up-to-the-minute analyses of events—analyses that were beamed to computer bulletin boards inside the Soviet Union. Networks carried messages among the resistors, allowing them to stay steps ahead of the coup leaders and the Soviet military machine. People toppled the coup and ultimately the Soviet Union—not with guns, but with courage, will, and timely information.

Telecommunication technology—the technology of long-distance communication—has come a long way since the War of 1812, and the world has changed dramatically as a result. After Samuel Morse invented the telegraph in 1844, people could, for the first time, send long-distance messages instantaneously. Alexander Bell's invention of the telephone in 1876 extended this capability to the spoken voice. Today, systems of linked computers enable us to send data and software across the room or around the world. The technological transformation has changed the popular definition of the word *telecommunication*, which today means long-distance electronic communication in a variety of forms.

In this chapter we look at the computer as part of a network rather than as a self-contained appliance, and we discuss ways in which such linked computers are used for communication and information gathering. We also consider how networks are changing the way we live and work. In the next chapter we'll delve deeper into the Internet—the global computer network at the heart of the latest telecommunication revolution.

8.4 Students use PCs to connect with online information sources and perform research for a class.

Basic Network Anatomy

A computer network is any system of two or more computers that are linked together. Why is networking important? The answers to this question revolve around the three essential components of every computer system:

> After more than a century of electric technology, we have **extended our central nervous system** itself in a global embrace, **abolishing both space and time** as far as our planet is concerned.
>
> —Marshall McLuhan, in *Understanding Media*

- *Hardware*. Networks enable people to share computer hardware resources, reducing costs and making it possible for more people to take better advantage of powerful computer equipment.
- *Software*. Networks enable people to share data and software programs, increasing efficiency and productivity.
- *People*. Networks enable people to work together, or collaborate, in ways that are otherwise difficult or impossible.

Important information is hidden in these three statements. But before we examine them in more detail, we need to look at the hardware and software that make computer networks possible.

Networks Near and Far

Computer networks come in all shapes and sizes, but most can be categorized as either local area networks or wide area networks.

> Pretty soon you'll have no more idea of **what computer you're using** than you have an idea of **where your electricity comes from**.
>
> —Danny Hillis, computer designer

A local area network (LAN) is a network in which the computers are physically close to each other, usually in the same building. A typical LAN includes a collection of computers and peripherals; each computer and networked peripheral is an individual *node* on the network.

Nodes are connected by cables, which serve as pathways for transporting data between machines. The most common type of LAN cable, known as *twisted pair*, contains copper wires that resemble those in standard telephone cables. Some networks, mostly in homes, use existing household electrical or telephone wiring to transmit data. But the biggest trend in LAN technology today is the explosive growth in wireless networks.

In a wireless network each node has a tiny radio (or, less commonly, infrared) transmitter connected to its network port so it can send and receive data through the air rather than through cables. Wireless network connections are especially convenient for workers who are constantly on the move. They're also used for creating small networks in homes and small businesses because they can be installed without digging or drilling. However, wireless networks are generally slower than wired LANs.

All computers on a LAN do not have to use the same operating system. For example, a single network might include Macintoshes, Windows PCs, and Linux workstations. The computers can be connected in many different ways, and many rules and industry-defined standards dictate what will and won't work. Most organizations depend on *network administrators* to take care of the behind-the-scenes details so others can focus on using the network. For *enterprise network systems*—large, complex networks with hundreds of computers—network administrators depend on *network management system software* to help them track and maintain healthy networks.

A *metropolitan area network (MAN)* is a service that links two or more LANs within a city. MAN service is typically provided by a telephone or telecommunications company. With a MAN, a company can keep employees linked even if they're blocks away from each other.

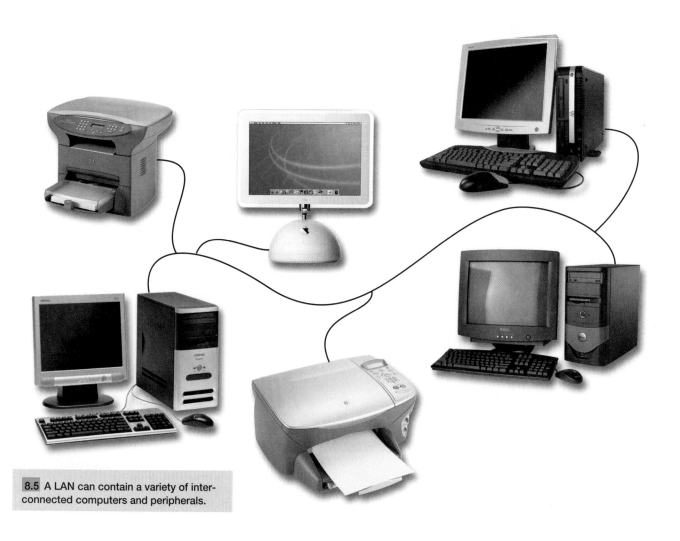

8.5 A LAN can contain a variety of interconnected computers and peripherals.

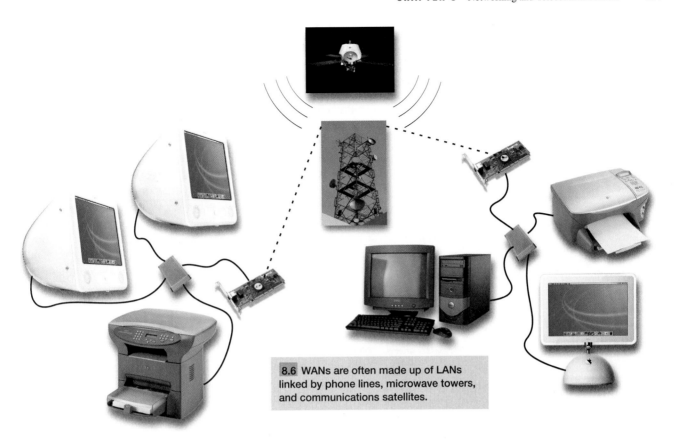

8.6 WANs are often made up of LANs linked by phone lines, microwave towers, and communications satellites.

A wide area network (WAN), as the name implies, is a network that extends over a long distance. In a WAN each network site is a node on the network. Data is transmitted long-distance between networks on a collection of common pathways known as a *backbone*. Large WANs are possible because of the web of telephone lines, microwave relay towers, and satellites that span the globe. Most WANs are private operations designed to link geographically dispersed corporate or government offices.

In today's internetworked world, communication frequently happens between LANs and WANs. Bridges and gateways are hardware devices that can pass messages between networks and, in some cases, translate messages so they can be understood by networks that obey different software protocols. (Software protocols are discussed later in the chapter.) Routers are hardware devices or software programs that route messages as they travel between networks via bridges and gateways. Bridges, gateways, and routers make it possible to connect to the Internet just about anywhere and communicate with computers connected to the Internet through other networks around the planet.

Specialized Networks: From GPS to Financial Systems

It would be a mistake to think of all computer networks as collections of PCs linked to the Internet. Some specialized networks are designed to perform specific functions; these networks may or may not be directly connected to the Internet.

One such specialized network is the U.S. Department of Defense Global Positioning System (GPS). The GPS includes 24 satellites that circle the Earth, carefully spaced so that from any point on the planet, at any time, four satellites will be above the horizon. Each satellite contains a computer, an atomic clock, and a radio. On the ground, a *GPS receiver* can use signals broadcast by three or four visible satellites to determine its position. Handheld GPS receivers can display locations, maps, and directions on small screens; GPS receivers can also be embedded in automobile navigation systems or

8.7 A GPS receiver helps this hiker produce an extremely accurate map of the Colorado trail.

connected to laptop computers. Members of the U.S. military use GPS receivers to keep track of where they are, but so do scientists, engineers, motorists, hikers, boaters, and others. Mobile phones now include GPS receivers so they can be located quickly when used for emergency calls.

Probably the most widely used specialized computer networks are the networks that keep our global financial systems running. When you strip away the emotional trappings, money is just another form of information. Dollars, yen, pounds, and rubles are all just symbols that make it easy for people to exchange goods and services. Money can be just about anything, provided people agree to its value. During the last few centuries, paper replaced metal as the major form of money. Today, paper is being replaced by digital patterns stored in computer media. Money, like other digital information, can be transmitted through computer networks. That's why it's possible to withdraw cash from your checking account using an *automated teller machine (ATM)* at an airport or shopping mall thousands of miles from your home bank. An ATM (not to be confused with the communication protocol with the same initials) is a specialized terminal linked to a bank's main computer through a commercial banking network. Financial networks also make credit card purchases, automatic bill paying, electronic funds transfer, and all kinds of electronic commerce (e-commerce) possible. E-commerce will be discussed in more detail in later chapters.

The Network Interface

In Chapter 2 and Chapter 3 you saw how information travels among the CPU, memory, and other components within a computer as electrical impulses that move along collections of parallel wires called buses. A network extends the range of these information pulses, allowing them to travel to other computers. The Internet is a vast network of interconnected networks that effectively extends the roaming range of those pulses to the entire planet. By connecting to a network that's part of the Internet, a computer can connect to millions of other computers that are connected to the Internet.

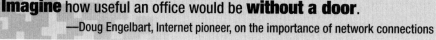

Imagine how useful an office would be **without a door**.
—Doug Engelbart, Internet pioneer, on the importance of network connections

A computer may have a direct connection to a network—for example, it might be one of many machines linked together in an office, or it might be part of a university network. On the other hand, a computer might have remote access to a network through a phone line, a television cable system, or a satellite link.

However it is connected, the computer communicates with the network through a port—a socket that enables information to pass in and out of the system. As described in Chapter 2, *parallel ports*, enable bits to pass through in groups of 8, 16, or 32. They are commonly used to connect older printers to computers. *Serial ports*, on the other hand, require bits to pass through one at a time. The standard serial port is designed to attach peripherals such as modems—not to connect directly to networks. Older PCs (and many newer ones) have at least one serial port and one parallel port. (Older Macintoshes have one or more multipurpose serial ports but no parallel ports.) Standard PC serial and parallel ports—sometimes called *legacy ports*—are being quickly replaced by newer technology. Modern Macs and PCs have multiple *USB* and *FireWire (IEEE 1394)* ports that are much faster and more flexible than traditional serial and parallel ports.

A network interface card (NIC, pronounced "nick") adds a special serial port to the computer—one that's designed for a direct network connection. The network interface card controls the flow of data between the computer's RAM and the network cable. At the same time it converts the computer's internal low-power signals into more powerful signals that can be transmitted through the network. The type of card depends on the type of network connection needed. The most common types of networks today require some kind of Ethernet card or port in each computer. **Ethernet** is a popular networking architecture developed in 1976 at Xerox. Most newer PCs include an *Ethernet port* on the main circuit board, so they don't require NICs to connect to Ethernet networks. Details vary—and there are many details—but the same general principles apply to all common network connections.

In the simplest networks two or more computers are linked by cables. But direct connection is impractical for computers that are miles or oceans apart. For computers to communicate over long distances, they need to transmit information through other paths. To connect directly, the computer needs a *network interface port*—typically an *Ethernet port*. For a remote connection, it generally needs a *modem* or some type of *broadband* connection device.

8.8 Every day, stock traders move billions of dollars in funds electronically through world markets.

Communication á la Modem

An intricate network of cables, radio transmitters, and satellites enables people to talk by telephone between just about any two places on the planet. The telephone network is capable of connecting remote computers, though it was designed to carry sound waves, not streams of bits. Before a **digital signal**—a stream of bits—can be transmitted over a standard phone line, it must be converted to an **analog signal**—a continuous wave. At the receiving end the analog signal first must be converted back into the bits representing the original digital message. Each of these tasks is performed by a **modem** (short for modulator/demodulator)—a hardware device that connects a computer to a telephone line.

An *internal modem* is installed on a circuit board inside the computer's chassis. An *external modem* sits in a box linked to a serial port or USB port. Both types use phone cables to connect to the telephone network through standard modular phone jacks.

A *fax modem* can communicate with *facsimile (fax) machines* as well as computers. With a fax modem, a PC can "print" any document on a remote fax machine by dialing the number of that machine and sending a series of electrical pulses that represent the marks on the pages of the document. When it receives a fax, the PC constructs an on-screen document based on the pulses it receives from the transmitting machine.

Modems differ in their transmission speeds, measured in **bits per second** (bps). Many people use the term *baud rate* instead of bps, but bps is technically more accurate for high-speed modems. Modems today commonly transmit at 28,800 bps to 56.6K (56,600) bps over standard phone lines.

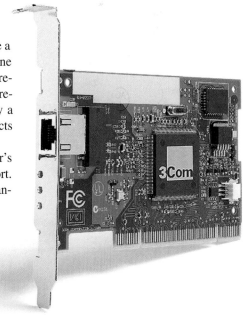

8.9 A network interface card, or NIC, allows a PC to connect to a network.

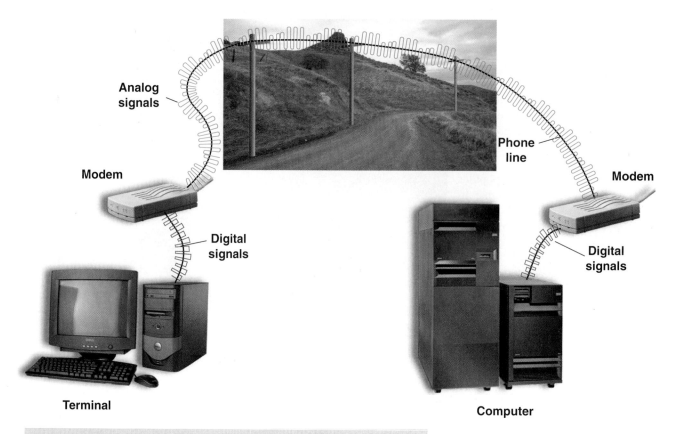

Analog signals

Modem

Digital signals

Phone line

Modem

Digital signals

Terminal

Computer

8.10 A modem converts digital signals from a computer into analog signals that can be transmitted through telephone wires to another modem, which then converts them back into digital signals another PC can understand.

Communication by modem is slower than communication between computers that are directly connected on a network. High-speed transmission isn't usually critical for text messages, but it can make a huge difference when the data being transmitted includes graphics, sound, video, and other multimedia elements—the kinds of data commonly found on the Web.

Broadband Connections

Most people who have explored multimedia on the Web have experienced small, jerky videos, sputtering audio, and (especially) long waits. The cause of most of these problems on the Internet (and other networks) is a lack of *bandwidth* at some point in the path between the sending computer and the receiving computer. The word has a technical definition, but in the world of computer networks bandwidth generally refers to the quantity of information that can be transmitted through a communication medium in a given amount of time. In general, increased bandwidth means faster transmission speeds. Bandwidth is typically measured in kilobits (thousands of bits) or megabits (millions of bits) per second. (Since a byte is 8 bits, a megabit is 1/8 of a megabyte. The text of this chapter is about 100 kilobytes, or 800 kilobits, of information. A physical medium capable of transmitting 100 megabits per second could theoretically transmit this chapter's text more than 100 times in 1 second.) Bandwidth can be affected by many factors, including the physical media that make up the network, the amount of network traffic, the software protocols of the network, and the type of network connection.

Some people find it easier to visualize bandwidth by thinking of a network cable as a highway. One way to increase bandwidth in a cable is to increase the number of parallel

wires in that cable—the equivalent of adding
more lanes to a freeway. Another way is to increase the speed
with which information passes through the cable; this is the same as
increasing the speed of the vehicles on the freeway. Of course, it's
easier and safer to increase highway speed limits if you have a traffic flow system that minimizes the chance of collisions and accidents; in the same way, more efficient, reliable software can increase network bandwidth. But increasing a highway's throughput
doesn't help much if cars pile up at the entry and exit ramps; in the
same way, a high-bandwidth network seems like a low-bandwidth
network if you're connected through a slow modem.

For faster remote connections, many businesses and homes bypass standard modems and use some kind of *broadband connection*—a connection with much greater bandwidth than modems
have. Several competing broadband technologies are available to computer users in many areas: DSL, cable modems, satellite modems, and wireless broadband connections.

8.11 Broadband connections require cable modems or DSL modems. These aren't really modems but are so named because of their similarity, functionally, to modems.

- DSL uses standard phone lines and is provided by phone companies in many areas.
- Cable modems provide fast network connections through cable television networks in many areas.
- High-speed wireless connections can connect computers to networks using radio waves rather than wires.
- Satellite dishes can deliver fast computer network connections as well as television programs.

These broadband technologies are discussed in more detail later in this chapter.

Fiber-optic Connections

Broadband network connections
such as cable modems and DSL are
faster than standard modems because they have greater bandwidth.
But DSL and cable modems have

These are the days of **lasers in the jungle.**
Lasers in the jungle somewhere . . .
—Paul Simon, in "The Boy in the Bubble"

nowhere near the bandwidth of fiber-optic cables that are replacing copper wires in the
worldwide telephone network. Fiber-optic cables use light waves to carry information at
blinding speeds. A single fiber-optic cable can transmit half a gigabit (500 *million* bits) per
second, replacing 10,000 copper telephone cables.

A fiber-optic network can rapidly and reliably transmit masses of multimedia data at the
same time it's handling voice messages. Digital fiber-optic networks now connect major
communication hubs around the world. Many large businesses and government institutions
are connected to the global fiber-optic network. But most small businesses and homes still
depend on copper wires for the "last mile," as it's often referred to in the industry—the link

NETWORKS ARE BUILT ON PHYSICAL MEDIA

Type		Uses	Maximum Operating Distance (without amplification)	Cost
Twisted pair		Small LANS	300 feet	Low
Coaxial cable		Large LANS	600–2,500 feet	Medium
Fiber-optic		Network backbones; WANS	1–25 miles	High
Wireless/infrared		LANS	3–1,000 feet (line of sight)	Medium
Wireless/radio		Connecting things that move	Varies considerably	High

8.12 Different types of networks are built with different physical media, which can play a huge role in the overall performance of the network.

to the closest on-ramp to the fiber-optic freeway. Fiber-optic communication lines will eventually find their way into most homes, radically changing our lives in the process. These cables will provide two-way links to the outside world for our phones, televisions, radios, computers, and a variety of other devices.

Wireless Network Technology

Wireless technology is a **liberating force**. It will make possible **human-centered computers**. This wasn't possible before because we were **anchored to a PC**, and we had to go to it like going to a temple to **pay our respects**.

—Michael Dertouzos, Director, MIT Laboratory for Computer Science

A lightning-fast network connection to your desktop is of little use if you're away from your desk most of the time. When bandwidth is less important than mobility and portability, wireless technology can provide practical solutions.

Infrared wireless technology has been around for many years. Many laptops and handheld computers have infrared ports that can send and receive digital information short distances. Infrared technology isn't widely used in networks because of distance and line-of-sight limitations. Still, infrared technology has practical applications—especially for mobile users. For example, Palm users routinely share programs and data by beaming them through infrared links.

The fastest-growing wireless LAN technology is known as Wi-Fi, or *802.11b*. (Apple refers to its brand of 802.11b as Airport.) Newer, higher-bandwidth, longer-range versions of Wi-Fi are known as *802.11a* and *802.11g* (which Apple called Airport Extreme). These wireless networking technologies allow multiple computers to connect to a LAN through a base station up to 150 feet away. Wi-Fi isn't as fast as a hard-wired Ethernet connection, but it's fast enough for most applications, including multimedia Web downloads. A home Wi-Fi network allows computers to connect from any room without cables. Wi-Fi base stations are showing up in airports, coffee shops, phone booths, and other public places. On many campuses Wi-Fi networks allow students to effortlessly connect their laptops to the Internet from dorm rooms, classrooms, or tree-lined gardens. Free Wi-Fi access points are sprouting everywhere, part of a grassroots movement to provide universal wireless access to the Net.

8.13 This University of Tennessee student can connect to the Internet using the campus wireless network.

Another type of wireless technology is Bluetooth, named for a Danish king who overcame his country's religious differences. Bluetooth technology overcomes differences between mobile phones, handheld computers, and PCs, making it possible for all of these devices to communicate with each other regardless of operating system. Bluetooth uses radio technology similar to Wi-Fi, but its transmissions are limited to about 30 feet. Bluetooth isn't designed to compete with Wi-Fi. It is intended to replace the wires that are often required to connect devices like cell phones, PDAs, and printers. With Bluetooth it's possible to create a *personal area network (PAN)*—a network that links a variety of personal electronic devices so they can communicate with each other. Bluetooth technology is currently limited to simple device connectivity, but in the future it will open up all kinds of possibilities:

- A pacemaker senses a heart attack and notifies the victim's mobile phone to dial 911.
- A car radio communicates with parking-lot video cameras to find out where spaces are available.
- A pen scans business cards and sends the information to a PDA inside a briefcase.
- A medical wristband transmits an accident victim's vital information to a doctor's hand-held computer.
- A cell phone tells you about specials on clothes (available in your size) as you walk past stores in a mall. (Many fear that this technology will usher in a new era of wireless junk mail.)

Wi-Fi and Bluetooth aren't part of mass culture yet, but wireless communication through mobile phones certainly is. In two decades, mobile phones have gone from simple analog systems to powerful digital devices that can handle Internet data, text messages, photos, and other data along with voice traffic.

8.14 Many students living in Japan use their mobile phones regularly for instant messaging and multiplayer games.

Mobile phone Internet connections are more common in Europe and Asia than in the United States. While many Americans enjoy sharing photos with their cell phones, phone users in Europe and Asia are more likely to use their phones as multifunction devices. In Japan, people routinely use their phones to send and receive email, exchange instant messages, check news headlines, shop, play games, share photos, and even do karaoke. The next generation of mobile wireless technology, often called *3G*, promises high-bandwidth connections that will support true multimedia, including real-time video. Some experts believe that Wi-Fi's rapidly growing popularity will force cell phone companies to embrace it rather than 3G. Either way, the boundaries that separate phone networks and computer networks will continue to blur.

The convenience of wireless technology carries a price in security. Wireless networks are far more vulnerable to eavesdropping, data snooping, and hacking than wired networks. Many techniques and tools can help preserve privacy and security, but the most effective ones are expensive and available only to large companies. As a result, most wireless home networks today are extremely insecure. These problems are discussed in more detail in Chapter 10.

8.15 Emerging wireless standards, such as Bluetooth, allow cell phones, PDAs and computer peripherals such as this mouse to announce themselves and describe their capabilities to other devices and PCs in personal area networks.

Communication Software

Whether connected by cables, radio waves, or a combination of modems and telephone lines, computers need some kind of communication software to interact. To communicate with each other, two machines must follow the same protocols—rules for the exchange of data between a terminal and a computer or between two computers. One such protocol is transmission speed: If one

> All the **most promising technologies** making their debut now are chiefly due to communication between computers—that is, to **connections** rather than to **computations**. And since **communication** is the basis of **culture**, fiddling at this level is indeed **momentous**.
>
> —Kevin Kelly, former *Wired* Executive Editor

machine is "talking" at 56,600 bps and the other is "listening" at 28,800 bps, the message doesn't get through. (Most modems can avoid this particular problem by adjusting their speeds to match each other.) Protocols include prearranged codes for messages such as "Are you ready?" "I am about to start sending a data file," and "Did you receive that file?" For two computers to understand each other, the software on both machines must be set to follow the same protocols. Communication software establishes a protocol that is followed by the computer's hardware.

Communication software can take a variety of forms. For users who work exclusively on a local area network, many communication tasks are taken care of by a network operating system (NOS) such as Novell's Netware or Microsoft's Windows Server. Just as a personal computer's operating system shields the user from most of the nuts and bolts of the computer's operation, a NOS shields the user from the hardware and software details of routine communication between machines. But unlike a PC operating system, the NOS must respond to requests from many computers and must coordinate communication throughout the network. Today, many organizations are replacing their specialized PC-based NOSs with intranet systems—systems built around the open standards and protocols of the Internet, as described in more detail in the next chapter.

The function and location of the network operating system depend in part on the LAN model. Some LANs are set up according to the client/server model, a hierarchical model in which one or more computers act as dedicated servers and all the remaining computers act as clients. Each server is a high-speed, high-capacity computer containing data and other resources to be shared with client computers. Using NOS server software, the server

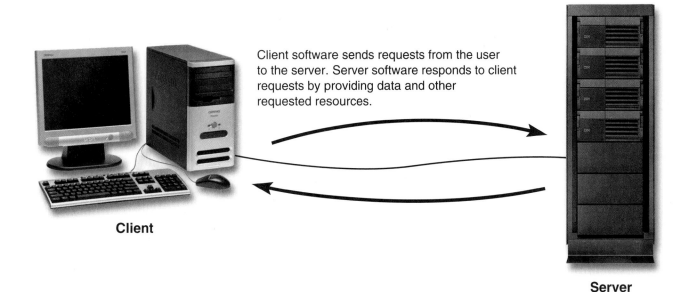

Client software sends requests from the user to the server. Server software responds to client requests by providing data and other requested resources.

Client

Server

8.16 Client/server computing involves two-way communication between so-called client and server programs, each of which runs on a separate PC.

fulfills requests from clients for data and other resources. In a client/server network the bulk of the NOS resides on the server, but each client has NOS client software for sending requests to servers.

Many small networks are designed using the peer-to-peer model (sometimes called *p-to-p* or *P2P*), which enables every computer on the network to be both client and server. In this kind of network every user can make files publicly available to other users on the network. Some desktop operating systems, including many versions of Windows and the Mac OS, include all the software necessary to operate a peer-to-peer network. In practice, many networks are hybrids, combining features of the client/server and peer-to-peer models.

Outside of a LAN, the most basic type of communication software is primitive terminal emulation software, which enables a computer to function as a character-based "dumb" terminal—a simple input/output device for sending messages to and receiving messages from the host computer. A terminal program handles phone dialing, protocol management, and the miscellaneous details necessary for making a PC and a modem work together. With terminal software and a modem, a personal computer can communicate through phone lines with another PC, a network of computers, or, more commonly, a large multiuser computer. The Windows and Macintosh operating system packages include terminal emulation programs.

Basic terminal emulators are fine for bare-bones computer-to-computer connections, but their character-based user interfaces can be confusing to people who are used to point-and-click GUIs. What's more, they can't be used to explore media-rich destinations on and off the World Wide Web. That's why most online explorers today use Web browsers and other specialized graphical client software instead of generic terminal programs. At the other end of the line, communications software is usually built into the multiuser operating system of the host system—the computer that provides service to multiple users. This software enables a timesharing computer to communicate with several other computers or terminals at once. The most widely used host operating system today is UNIX, the 30-year old OS that has many variants, including the noncommercial Linux OS discussed in Chapter 4.

8.17 Servers like these powerful IBM devices can provide software and data for hundreds or thousands of networked computers.

The Network Advantage

A network becomes more valuable as **it reaches more users**.
—Metcalf's Law, by Bob Metcalf, inventor of Ethernet

With this background in mind, let's reconsider the three reasons people use networks:

■ *Networks enable people to share computer hardware resources, reducing costs and making it possible for more people to take better advantage of powerful computer equipment.* When computers and peripherals are connected in a LAN, computer users can share expensive peripherals. Before LANs, the typical office had a printer connected to each computer. Today it's more common to find a small number of high-quality networked printers shared by a larger group of computers and users. In a client/server network, each printer may be connected to a *print server*—a server that accepts, prioritizes, and processes print jobs. Although it may not make much sense for users to try to share a printer on a wide area network, WAN users often share other hardware resources. Many WANs include powerful mainframes and supercomputers that can be accessed by authorized users at remote sites.

■ *Networks enable people to share data and software programs, increasing efficiency and productivity.* In offices without networks people often transmit data and software by sneakernet—that is, by carrying disks between computers. In a LAN one or more computers can be used as file servers—storehouses for software and data that are shared by several users. With client software a user can, without taking a step, download software and data—copy it from a server. Of course, somebody needs to upload the software—copy it to the server—first. A large file server is typically a dedicated computer that does nothing but serve files. But a peer-to-peer approach, allowing any computer to be both client and server, can be an efficient, inexpensive way to share files on small networks. Of course, sharing computer software on a network can violate software licenses (see Chapter 4) if not done with care. Many, but not all, licenses allow the software to be installed on a file server as long as the number of simultaneous users never exceeds the number of licensed copies. Some companies offer site licenses or network licenses, which reduce costs for multiple copies or remove restrictions on software copying and use at a network site. (Software copying is discussed in more detail in the next two chapters.) Networks don't eliminate compatibility differences between different computer operating systems, but they can simplify data communication between machines. Users of Windows-compatible computers, for example, can't run Macintosh applications just because they're available on a file server. But they can, in many cases, use data files and documents created on a Macintosh and stored on the server. For example, a poster created with Adobe Illustrator on a Macintosh could be stored on a file server so it can be opened, edited, and printed by users of Illustrator on Windows PCs. File sharing isn't always that easy. If users of different systems use programs with incompatible file formats, they need to use *data translation software* to read and modify each other's files. On WANs, the transfer of data and software can save more than shoe leather; it can save time. There's no need to send printed documents or discs by overnight mail between two sites if both sites are connected to the same network. Typically, data can be sent electronically between sites in a matter of seconds.

■ *Networks enable people to work together, or collaborate, in ways that are difficult or impossible without network technology.* Some software applications can be classified as groupware—programs designed to enable several networked users to work on the same documents at the same time. Groupware programs include multiuser appointment calendars, project-management software, database-management systems, and software for group editing of text-and-graphics documents. Many groupware programs today, such as Lotus Notes, are built on standard Internet protocols, so group members can communicate and share information using Web browsers and other standard Internet software tools. Workgroups can benefit from networks without groupware packages. Most groupware features—email, message posting, calendars, and the rest—are generally available through Web and PC applications. Still, for large organizations a full-featured groupware package can be easier to manage than a collection of separate programs.

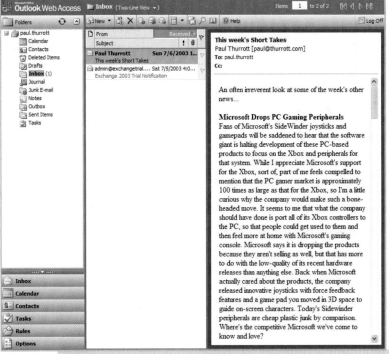

8.18 Microsoft Exchange, the most widely used groupware product, combines email, scheduling, contacts, tasks, and other personal information management features to facilitate information sharing and workgroup collaboration. Exchange Server is the server end of a client/server solution that also includes Microsoft Outlook or its Web-based equivalent, Outlook Web Access (OWA), which is shown here.

Email, Instant Messaging, and Teleconferencing: Interpersonal Computing

New technology gives us two kinds of **newfound freedom**: The ability to **reach each other** 24/7—and the chance to **avoid one another** as never before.

—Lori Gottlieb, Author of *Stick Figure*

For many LAN and WAN users, network communication is limited to sending and receiving messages. A recent study found that the typical Internet user spends about 70 percent of connected time communicating with others. Electronic messaging can profoundly change the way people and organizations work. In the next section we take a close look at the advantages and implications of interpersonal communication with computers.

The Many Faces of Email

Whether you're connected to a LAN, a WAN, a timesharing mainframe, and/or the Internet, you probably have access to an email system that enables you to send and receive messages to others on the network. (Chapter 0 covered the basics of email.) There's no single way to send and receive email. What you see on the screen depends on the type of connection you have and the mail client program you use. If you have a standard modem connection to a UNIX-based Internet host, you might send and receive mail using PINE, the UNIX mail program developed at the University of Washington. Because it's character based, PINE works with almost any kind of Internet connection, but it's less friendly than today's graphical mail applications. Modern GUI mail programs such as Microsoft Outlook Express, Apple OS X Mail, and Qualcomm Eudora Pro are easier to learn and offer more flexibility than most character-based programs. Many email services, including several free ones, are designed to be accessed through Web browsers rather than separate email client programs.

Web-based email systems and many older UNIX-based programs require that read and unread messages be stored in post office boxes or folders on the remote mail servers. Most newer non-Web email clients enable PCs and Macs to download and handle mail locally rather than depending on a remote host as a post office.

Many email messages are plain ASCII text. Plain text messages can be viewed with any mail client program, including those in email-capable PDAs and phones. Many email programs can (optionally) send, receive, edit, and display email messages formatted in HTML, the formatting language used in most Web pages. HTML messages can include text formatting, pictures, and links to Web pages. The email client software hides the HTML source code from the sender and the recipient, displaying only the formatted messages. If the recipient views an HTML-encoded message with a mail program that doesn't recognize HTML, the formatting doesn't appear.

Even if their software can display HTML mail, not all email users *want* it. HTML encoding can slow down an email program. An HTML email message can also carry a *Web bug*—an invisible piece of code that silently notifies the sender about when the message was opened and may report other information about their machine or email software at the same time. Web bugs, which operate through specially encoded one-pixel graphics files, are increasingly common in commercial Web pages as well as HTML email messages. Fortunately, newer email applications can turn off Web bugs, preventing junk mailers and others from getting information about you when you read their messages.

Most email programs can send and receive formatted word processor documents, pictures, and other multimedia files as attachments to messages. Attachments need to be temporarily converted to ASCII text using some kind of encoding scheme before they can be sent through Internet mail. Most modern email programs take care of the encoding and decoding automatically. Of course, attachments aren't practical with many PDAs, cell phones, and other text-only email devices. And attachments can contain viruses and other unwelcome surprises, as described in Chapter 10.

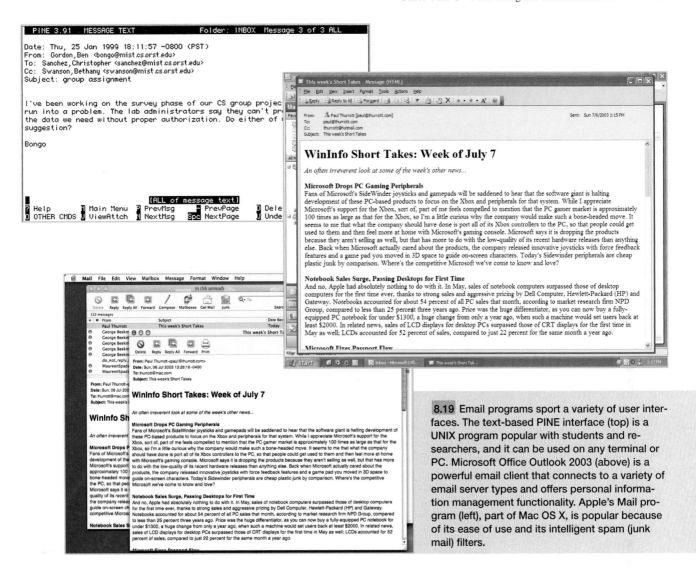

8.19 Email programs sport a variety of user interfaces. The text-based PINE interface (top) is a UNIX program popular with students and researchers, and it can be used on any terminal or PC. Microsoft Office Outlook 2003 (above) is a powerful email client that connects to a variety of email server types and offers personal information management functionality. Apple's Mail program (left), part of Mac OS X, is popular because of its ease of use and its intelligent spam (junk mail) filters.

Mailing Lists

Email is a valuable tool for communicating one-to-one with individuals around the globe, but it's also useful for communicating one-to-many. Mailing lists enable you to participate in email discussion groups on special-interest topics. Lists can be small and local, or large and global. They can be administered by a human being or automatically administered by programs with names like Listserv and Majordomo. Each group has a mailing address that looks like any Internet address.

You might belong to one student group that's set up by your instructor to carry on discussions outside of class, another group that includes people all over the world who use Macromedia Flash to animate Web pages, a third that's dedicated to saving endangered species in your state, and a fourth for customers of an online bookstore. When you send a message to a mailing list address, every subscriber receives a copy. And, of course, you receive a copy of every mail message sent by everyone else to those lists.

Subscribing to a busy list might mean receiving hundreds of messages each day. To avoid being overwhelmed by incoming mail, many list members sign up to receive them in daily digest form; instead of receiving many individual messages each day, they receive one message that includes all postings. But digest messages can still contain lots of repetitive, silly, and annoying messages.

8.20 Wirelessly connected handheld devices let users access their email and the Web without a PC.

Some lists are moderated to ensure that the quality of the discussion remains high. In a *moderated group*, a designated moderator acts as an editor, filtering out irrelevant and inappropriate messages and posting the rest.

Network News

You can participate in special-interest discussions without overloading your mailbox by taking advantage of newsgroups. A newsgroup is a public discussion on a particular subject consisting of notes written to a central Internet site and redistributed through a worldwide newsgroup network called USENET. You can check into and out of a newsgroup discussion whenever you want; all messages are posted on virtual bulletin boards for anyone to read anytime. There are groups for every interest and taste . . . and a few for the tasteless. Newsgroups are organized hierarchically, with dot names like rec.music.makers.percussion and soc.culture.french. You can explore network newsgroups through several Web sites, including Google, or with a newsreader client program.

Many newsgroups contain the same kind of free-flowing discussions you'll find in Internet mailing lists, but there are two important differences:

- Listserv mail messages are delivered automatically to your mailbox, but you have to seek out information in newsgroups.
- Mailing list messages are sent to a specific group of people, whereas newsgroup messages are available for anyone to see . . . for years to come.

Newsgroup discussions can get bogged down by repetitive questions from newcomers, childish rants, off-topic trivia, and other counterproductive messages. *Moderated newsgroups* contain only messages that have been filtered by designated moderators. The moderator discards inappropriate messages, making it easier for others to find the information they're looking for. Yahoo, MSN, AOL, and other portals and information services have discussion groups that are similar to USENET newsgroups; the main difference is that they aren't distributed as widely.

8.21 Google Groups lets users access USENET newsgroup content via friendly Web interface.

When you're online, you're using a relatively new communication medium with new rules. Here are some suggestions for successful online communication:

➡ **Let your system do as much of the work as possible.** If your email program can sort mail, filter mail, or automatically append a signature file to your mail, take advantage of those features. If you find yourself sending messages to the same group of people repeatedly, create an *alias* that includes all of those people—a distribution list that can save you the trouble of typing or selecting all those names each time

➡ **Store names and addresses in an online address book.** Email addresses aren't always easy to remember and type correctly. If you mistype even a single character, your message will probably either go to the wrong person or *bounce*—come back to you with some kind of undeliverable mail message. An online address book enables you to select addresses without typing them each time you use them. Use you email program's backup or export capability to backup your address book.

➡ **Don't share your email address.** It's easy to think of an email address like a physical address, sharing it with roommates, partners, and others who use the same computer. But email works best if each person has a unique address. A personal email address is more secure and private, but it's also more practical; when someone sends a message to you, the sender knows that you are the person who will receive the message.

➡ **Protect your privacy.** Miss Manners said it well in a *Wired* interview: "For email, the old postcard rule applies. Nobody else is supposed to read your postcards, but you'd be a fool if you wrote anything private on one."

➡ **Cross-check online information sources.** Don't assume that every information nugget you see online is valid, accurate, and timely. If you read something online, treat it with the same degree of skepticism that you would if you heard it in a cafeteria or coffee shop.

➡ **Be aware and awake.** It's easy to lose track of yourself and your time online. In his book *Virtual Community*, Howard Rheingold advises, "Rule Number One is to pay attention. Rule Number Two might be: Attention is a limited resource, so pay attention to where you pay attention."

➡ **Avoid information overload.** When it comes to information, more is not necessarily better. Search selectively. Don't waste time and energy trying to process mountains of online information. Information is not knowledge, and knowledge is not wisdom.

Instant Messaging and Teleconferencing: Real-Time Communication

Mailing lists and newsgroups are delayed or asynchronous communication because the sender and the recipients don't have to be logged in at the same time. Computer net-

> **No other medium** gives every participant the capability to communicate **instantly** with thousands and thousands of people.
>
> —Tracy LaQuey, in *The Internet Companion*

works offer many possibilities for real-time communication, too. Instant messaging (IM) has been possible since the days of text-only Internet access. Internet relay chat (IRC) and Talk enable UNIX users to exchange instant messages with their online friends and co-workers. But newer, easier-to-use messaging systems from AOL, Microsoft, Yahoo, Apple, and others have turned instant messaging into one of the most popular Internet activities. Instant messaging programs enable users to create buddy lists, check for "buddies" who are logged in, and exchange typed messages and files with those who are. Most of these programs are available for free. Many businesses now use instant messaging to keep employees connected. IM technology is even built into many mobile phones. Online services also offer chat rooms—public or private virtual conference rooms where people

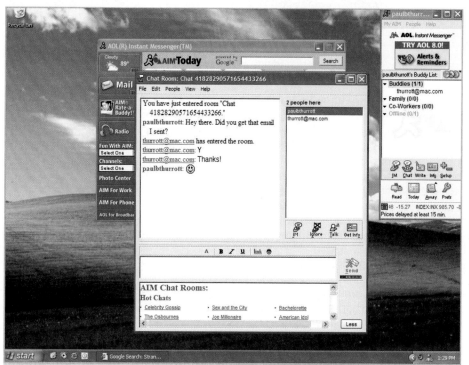

8.22 AOL Instant Messenger (AIM) is the world's most popular instant messaging (IM) client, letting users communicate in real time with friends, family, and other AIM users.

with similar interests or motivations can type messages to each other and receive near-instant responses.

Some IM programs, chat rooms, and multiplayer games on the Web use graphics to simulate real-world environments. Participants can represent themselves with *avatars*—graphical "bodies" that might look like simple cartoon sketches, elaborate 3-D figures, or exotic abstract icons.

Several IM programs make it possible to carry on two-way video teleconferences. A video teleconference enables two or more people to communicate face-to-face over long distances by combining video and computer technology. Until a few years ago, most video teleconferences were conducted in special rooms equipped with video cameras, microphones, television monitors, and other specialized equipment. Today, it's possible to participate in multiperson video teleconferences using a video camera attached to a PC with a high-speed Internet connection. Internet video images don't measure up to the images beamed to professional conference rooms, but they're more than adequate for most applications. With some IM systems, participants can view and edit shared documents while they talk, initiate online games, and collaborate in other ways.

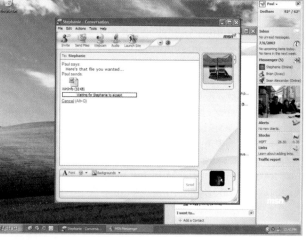

8.23 Apple iChat AV and MSN Messenger allow people to carry on text-, audio-, and video-based conversations, exchange files, and perform other real-time collaborative activities.

Computer Telephony

A voicemail system is a voice messaging system with many of the features of an email system, including the ability to store, organize, and forward messages. Voicemail is a familiar example of a growing trend toward *computer telephony integration (CTI)*—the linking of computers and telephones to gain productivity. Many PCs have telephony software and hardware that allow them to serve as speakerphones, answering machines, and complete voicemail systems. A typical computer telephony system connects to a standard phone line through a modem capable of handling voice conversations.

It's also possible to send voice signals through a LAN, a WAN, or the Internet, bypassing the phone companies (and their charges) altogether. Many programs enable you to use a computer's microphone and speaker to turn the Internet into a toll-free long-distance telephone service. Most Internet telephony (IP telephony) programs work only when both parties are running the same program at the same time, and they're not nearly as trouble-free as traditional long-distance service. Still, many experts predict that this kind of technology will soon pose a serious competitive threat to the current telephone infrastructure.

On the mobile front, the line between computers and telephones is especially fuzzy. Many mobile phones can connect to the Internet, do instant messaging, upload and download short email messages, and display miniature Web pages. Handheld PDAs from Palm, Dell, Hewlett Packard, and other companies can do the same things, but with larger screens and friendlier input devices. These handheld computers use software to integrate the functions of a PDA, a phone, and an Internet terminal. Hybrid PDAs and phones involve trade-offs—do you want to use a boxy PDA as a phone or type email on a tiny phone keypad? But most analysts expect rapid advances in these converging technologies over the next few years—advances such as reliable speech recognition—that will make these devices much more useful for people on the go.

8.24 Modern cell phones are basically miniature portable computers including electronic address books, calendars, image and video viewers, and even onboard digital cameras.

The Advantages of Online Communication

Email, instant messaging, and other types of online communication can replace many memos, letters, phone calls, and face-to-face meetings, making organizations more productive and efficient. Here's why:

Never in history has distance meant less.
—Alvin Toffler, in *Future Shock*

- *Email is fast.* A typical email message takes no more than a few seconds from the time it's sent until it reaches its destination—across the office or across the ocean. That's why email users often refer to traditional mail as "snail mail."
- *Email doesn't depend on location.* If you send someone an electronic message, that person can log in and read it from a computer at home, at the office, or anywhere in the world, at any time of the day.
- *Email facilitates group communication.* In most email systems it's no harder and no more expensive to send a message to several people than to send it to one person. Most systems enable groups to have named distribution lists (sometimes called *aliases*) so a mail message addressed to an alias name (like faculty, office, or sales) is sent automatically to everyone in the group.
- *Email messages are digital data that can be edited and combined with other computer-generated documents.* Because the messages you receive by email are stored in your computer electronically, you can edit text and numbers without having to retype the entire document and without wasting paper. You can easily add text from other documents stored on your computer. When you're finished, you can forward the edited document back to the original sender or to somebody else for further processing.

- *Online communication is less intrusive than the telephone*. A ringing phone can interrupt concentration, disrupt a meeting, and bring just about any kind of activity to a standstill. Instead of shouting "Answer me now!" an email message waits patiently in the mailbox until the recipient has the time to handle it.
- *Online communication allows time shifting*. Email users aren't plagued by busy signals, unanswered rings, and message machines. You can receive email messages when you're busy, away, or asleep, and they'll be waiting for you when you have the time to pick them up. Time zones are largely irrelevant to email users.
- *Online communication enables decisions to evolve over time*. A group can discuss an issue electronically for hours, days, or weeks without the urgency of getting everything settled in a single session. New information can circulate when it's current rather than at the next meeting. Participants have time to think about each statement before responding.
- *Online communication makes long-distance meetings possible*. Email discussions, IM sessions, and video teleconferences can include people from all over the world, and nobody needs to leave home to participate. In fact, a growing number of programmers, writers, and other information workers literally work at home, communicating with colleagues through the Internet.
- *Email and instant messaging emphasize the message over the messenger*. In companies that rely on email and IM for much of their communication, factors like appearance, race, gender, voice, mannerisms, and title tend to carry less weight than they do in other organizations. Status points go to people with good ideas and the ability to express those ideas clearly in writing.

Online Issues: Reliability, Security, Privacy, and Humanity

> Well there's egg and bacon; egg, sausage and bacon; egg and **spam**; bacon and **spam**; egg, bacon, sausage and **spam**; **spam**, bacon, sausage and **spam**; **spam**, egg, **spam**, **spam**, bacon and **spam**; **spam**, **spam**, **spam**, egg and **spam**; **spam**, **spam**, **spam**, **spam**, **spam**, **spam**, baked beans, **spam**, **spam**, **spam** and **spam**; or lobster thermidor aux crevettes with a mornay sauce garnished with truffle paté, brandy, and a fried egg on top of **spam**.
>
> —Waitress in Monty Python's *Flying Circus*

Any new technology introduces new problems, and online communication is no exception. Here are some of the most important:

- *Email and teleconferencing are vulnerable to machine failures, network glitches, human errors, and security breaches*. A system failure can cripple an organization that depends on email for critical communications. Internet users have experienced email blackouts caused by power outages, satellite failures, system overloads, and other technological breakdowns. Email attachment viruses have caused billions of dollars worth of damage worldwide. (See Chapter 10 for more on viruses.)
- *Email can be overwhelming*. Many people receive hundreds of messages every day. Sifting through all those messages can consume hours of time that could have been used in other ways. Email overload has become such a serious problem that some businesses have implemented email-free Fridays to give their employees time to catch up on other work.
- *Email can be unsolicited*. Because it's easy, fast, and free, email is often used to send blanket messages to masses of people without permission. Some of this unsolicited mail is innocent (and not-so-innocent) humor. Some is designed to spread the word for a good cause. (Some "good cause" campaigns are, in fact, fraudulent or misinformed; even so, they continue to circulate.) Most unsolicited email is designed to sell something—weight-loss plans, insurance, vacation homes, cigarettes, pornography, cheap loans, political campaigns, or just about anything that people can pay for with a credit card. Junk email is known as spam because it can be just as annoying and repetitive as the menu in the Monty Python skit quoted above. But spam can also be a security risk,

as you'll see in the next two chapters. Many email clients and Internet service providers offer antispam technology, including filters that recognize and delete obvious spam and challenge-response systems that require unrecognized email senders to reply to questions that can't easily be answered by automated systems. But none of these systems is foolproof, so antispam legislation is probably necessary to curb the problem. The CAN-SPAM Act of 2003 made some types of spam illegal in the U.S., but it also overturned much stricter anti-spam laws in several states. Most experts expect that this law isn't strong enough to stem the tide of spam.

- *Email can pose a threat to privacy.* The U.S. Postal Service has a centuries-old tradition of safeguarding the privacy of first-class mail. Electronic communication is not grounded in that tradition. Although most email messages are secure and private, there's always a potential for eavesdropping by an organization's system administrators and crafty system snoopers. Many businesses routinely monitor email sent by employees. In 1999 an online bookseller was found guilty of intercepting a competitor's email to gain market advantage. That same year users of Microsoft's popular Hotmail service learned that their private email messages and address books could be easily accessed by anyone with a basic knowledge of how Web addresses work. Microsoft corrected the problem, but questions of email security remain.

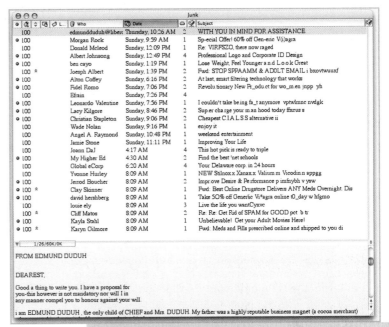

- *Email can be faked.* Email forgery can be a serious threat on a surprising number of email systems. The protocols at the heart of today's email system weren't designed with today's Internet in mind; they don't have mechanisms for ensuring that the sender of a message is who that person claims to be. Some systems have safeguards against sending mail using someone else's ID, but none completely eliminates the threat. In time, it's likely that a digital signature will be encoded into every email message (using cryptography technology described in Chapter 10). Until then, forgery is a problem.

8.25 Many email client programs, including Eudora, include intelligent filters that automatically route spam into junk mailboxes. But it's not always easy to tell whether a message is spam or legitimate email. Many spammers disguise their lowly intentions with subject lines that look like legitimate mail. Other spammers use odd spellings of "hot" words so their messages won't automatically be filtered into the recipient's junk bin.

- *Email works only if everybody plays.* Just as the postal system depends on each of us checking our mailboxes daily, an email system can work only if all subscribers regularly log in and check their mail. Most people develop the habit quickly if they know important information is only available online.

- *Email and instant messaging filter out many "human" components of communication.* When Bell invented the telephone, the public reaction was cool and critical. Businesspeople were reluctant to communicate through a device that didn't allow them to look each other in the eye and shake hands. Although this reaction might seem strange today, it's worth a second look given the even more impersonal nature of email and IM. When people communicate, part of the message is hidden in body language, eye contact, voice inflections, and other nonverbal signals. The telephone strips visual cues out of a message, and this can lead to misunderstandings. Most online communication systems peel away the sounds as well as the sights, leaving only plain words on a screen—words that might be misread if they aren't chosen carefully. What's more, email and teleconferences seldom replace casual "water cooler conversations"—those chance meetings that result in important communications and connections.

Problems notwithstanding, email and electronic messaging have become fixtures in businesses, schools, and government offices everywhere.

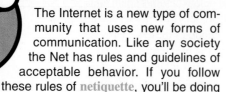
The Internet is a new type of community that uses new forms of communication. Like any society the Net has rules and guidelines of acceptable behavior. If you follow these rules of netiquette, you'll be doing your part to make life on the Net easier for everybody—especially yourself.

➡ **Say what you mean, and say it with care.** Once you send something electronically, there's no way to call it back. Compose each message carefully, and make sure it means what you intend it to mean. If you're replying to a message, double-check the heading to make sure your reply is going only to those people you intend to send it to. Even if you took only a few seconds to write your message, it may be broadcast far and wide and be preserved forever in online archives.

➡ **Keep it short.** Include a descriptive subject line, and limit the body to a screen or two. If you're replying to a long message, include a copy of the relevant part of the message—but not the whole message. Remember that many people receive hundreds of email messages each day, and they're more likely to read and respond to short ones.

➡ **Proofread your messages.** A famous *New Yorker* cartoon by Peter Steiner shows one dog telling another, "On the Internet no one knows you're a dog." You may not be judged by the color of your hair or the clothes you wear when you're posting messages, but that doesn't mean appearances aren't important. Other people will judge your intelligence and education by the spelling, grammar, punctuation, and clarity of your messages. If you want your messages to be taken seriously, present your best face.

➡ **Don't assume you're anonymous.** Your messages can say a lot about you. Those messages might be seen by more than your intended audience, and they won't necessarily go away when you want them to. Researcher Jonathan G. S. Koppell suggests a more contemporary caption for the *New Yorker* cartoon mentioned above: "On the Internet, everyone knows you're an aging, overweight, malamute-retriever mix living in the southwest, and with a preference for rawhide."

➡ **Learn the "nonverbal" language of the Net.** A simple phrase like "Nice job!" can have very different meanings depending on the tone of voice and body language behind it. Since body language and tone of voice can't easily be stuffed into a modem, online communities have developed text-based substitutes, sometimes called *emoticons*. Here are a few:

:-)	These three characters represent a smiling face. (To see why, look at them with this page rotated 90° to the right.) This "smilie" suggests the previous remark should not be taken seriously. (The dash is optional.)
;-)	This winking smile usually means the previous remark was flirtatious or sarcastic.
:-(	This frowning character suggests something is bothering the author—probably the previous statement in the message.
:-I	This character represents indifference.
:-.	This usually follows an extremely biting sarcastic remark.
:-P	This one is sticking its tongue out as if to say, "I'm grossed out!"
<g>	People who don't like smiles use this to say "grin."
ROTFL	This is short for "rolling on the floor laughing"; it's one of hundreds of keystroke-saving acronyms.
LOL	Laughing out loud.
BTW	This one means "by the way."
IMHO	This one says "in my humble opinion."

Digital Communication in Perspective

The lines that separate the telephone industry, the computer industry, and the home entertainment industry are blurring as voices, video, music, and messages flow through a complex web of wires, fiber-optic cables, and wireless connections. Many services we take for granted today—video rentals, cable TV, newspapers, and magazines, for example—will be transformed or replaced by digital, high-bandwidth, interactive delivery systems of the future. At the same time, entirely new forms of communication are likely to emerge. Telecommunications technology is rapidly changing our lives, and the changes will accelerate as the technology improves. We'll explore these changes in the next chapter as we focus on the Internet—the network of networks at the center of the communication revolution.

- **Keep your cool.** Many otherwise timid people turn into raging bulls when they're online. The facelessness of Internet communication makes it all too easy to shoot from the hip, overstate arguments, and get caught up in a digital lynch-mob mentality. There's nothing wrong with expressing your emotions, but broadside attacks and half-truths can do serious damage to your online relationships. Online or off, freedom of speech is a right that carries responsibility.

- **Don't be a source of spam.** It's so easy to send multiple copies of email messages that it's tempting to broadcast too widely. Target your messages carefully; if you're trying to sell tickets to a local concert or advertise your garage sale, don't tell the whole world. If you do send a mass mailing, hide the recipient list to protect the privacy of your recipients. One way is to send the message to yourself and put everyone else in the bcc (blind carbon copy) field. And if you send repeated mass mailings, make sure you always include a message telling people how they can get off your list.

- **Say no to spam.** People send spam because it gets results—mouse clicks to Web links, email replies, purchases, and more. If you want to do your part to wipe out spam, *never* reward spammers with your time or money.

- **Send no-frills mail.** Even if your email program makes it easy to use fancy formatting, embed HTML, and include attachments, it's usually better to err on the side of simplicity. Graphics and fancy formatting make message files bigger and slower to download. Many people turn off the HTML capabilities of their email programs to protect themselves from Web bugs (HTML code that sends messages back to the sender). And many email veterans fear attachments because of the risk of email viruses. If you don't need the extra baggage, why not leave it out?

- **Lurk before you leap.** People who silently monitor mailing lists and newsgroups without posting messages are called *lurkers*. There's no shame in lurking, especially if you're new to a group—it can help you to figure out what's appropriate. After you've learned the culture and conventions of a group, you'll be better able to contribute constructively and wisely.

- **Check your FAQs.** Many newsgroups and mailing lists have FAQs (pronounced "facks")—posted lists of frequently asked questions. These lists keep groups from being cluttered with the same old questions and answers, but only if members take advantage of them.

- **Give something back.** The Internet includes an on-line community of volunteers who answer beginner questions, archive files, moderate newsgroups, maintain public servers, and provide other helpful services. If you appreciate their work, tell them in words and show them in actions—do your part to help others in the Internet community.

Before we do, let's step back and put electronic communication in a larger perspective. As futurist Stewart Brand reminded us in his groundbreaking book, *The Media Lab*:

We can be grateful for the vast dispersed populations of peasant and tribal cultures in the world who have never used a telephone or a TV, who walk where they're going, who live by local subsistence skills honed over millennia. You need to go on foot in Africa, Asia, South America to realize how many of these people there are and how sound they are. If the world city goes smash, they'll pick up the pieces, as they've done before. Whatever happens, they are a reminder that electronic communication may be essential to one kind of living, but it is superfluous to another.

A World Without Wires

We stand at the **brink of a transformation**. It is a moment that echoes the **birth of the Internet** in the mid-'70s. . . . This time it is **not wires but the air** between them that is being transformed.

—Chris Anderson, Editor in Chief, *Wired*

Most of us connect to the Internet through wires—telephone lines, TV cables, or specialized data-only conduits. But there's a wireless revolution afoot, and it's likely to change the game for millions of Internet users before the decade is over. At the heart of this revolution is Wi-Fi, which spent many years in research circles before turning into one of the fastest-growing technologies in history.

Wi-Fi, or 802.11b, is a wireless multiband LAN technology built on Ethernet's data packets and Internet protocols. Newer variations 802.11a and 802.11g are faster and longer-range. Wi-Fi is turning up in home networks, public buildings, and neighborhood freenets. Many Wi-Fi innovations are driven by enthusiastic consumers rather than corporate dictates or research mandates. But developers are responding to consumer demand with a flurry of new technologies.

In a special report on Wi-Fi *Wired* Editor-in-Chief Chris Anderson wrote that "Wi-Fi will become a universal standard, found everywhere in the electronics world. It will show up in consumer electronics devices, from video game consoles to music players. Cell phones will have it, as will PDAs and digital cameras. Any PC bought in a year or so will instantly become the hub of a wireless network, simply by turning it on."

But Wi-Fi isn't the end of the wireless road. Several other promising technologies are being tested and refined in research labs. Here's a sampler:

➡ *Ultrawideband* is a short-range wireless technology that transmits ultra-high-speed signals over a wide spectrum of frequencies. This low-power technology could transform entertainment and communication systems if it can be refined so it doesn't interfere with more critical communication systems.

➡ *Mesh networks* are an alternative to today's networks that rely on centralized routers. In a mesh network, a message hops from wireless device to wireless device until it finds its destination; there's no need to go through a central hub on the way. Mesh networks might offer faster and cheaper connections than today's networks, but they also raise new security issues.

➡ *Adaptive radio* is a technology that enables wireless devices to selectively transmit messages based on other wireless network traffic. By monitoring messages sent by other devices and sending its own messages in unused gaps in the spectrum, an adaptive device will be able to avoid the interference that plagues many other wireless technologies.

➡ *Software-defined radio* is a technology that allows a single wireless hardware device to be reprogrammed on the fly to serve a variety of functions. Just as software can transform a PC from a communication tool to a music workstation to an accountant's ledger, it can be used to change a single wireless tool into a cell phone, a garage door opener, a game machine, a baby monitor, a messaging machine, a Web browser, or a TV remote. Researchers are working on the chip technology to make such a universal device a reality, hopefully eliminating much of the techno-clutter that litters our lives.

It's not clear how all of these emerging technologies will converge. What is clear is that the wireless revolution is far from over.

8.26

Time To Do Everything Except Think

David Brooks

Is there a downside to the digital communication explosion? In this lighthearted article, first published in the April 30, 2001 issue of Newsweek, *David Brooks raises some serious questions about being overconnected. Brooks is the author of* Bobos in Paradise.

Somewhere up in the canopy of society, way above where normal folks live, there will soon be people who live in a state of perfect wirelessness. They'll have mobile phones that download the Internet, check scores and trade stocks. They'll have Palm handhelds that play music, transfer photos and get Global Positioning System readouts. They'll have laptops on which they watch movies, listen to baseball games and check inventory back at the plant. In other words, every gadget they own will perform all the functions of all the other gadgets they own, and they will be able to do it all anywhere, any time.

Wireless Woman will do a full day's work on the beach in her bikini: her personal digital assistant comes with a thong clip so she can wear it on her way to the pina colada stand. Her phones beep, her pagers flash red lights; when they go off, she looks like a video arcade. Wireless Man will be able to put on his performance underwear, hop in his SUV and power himself up to the top of a Colorado mountain peak. He'll be up there with his MP3 device and his carabiners enjoying the view while conference-calling the sales force, and playing MegaDeath with gamers in Tokyo and Sydney. He'll be smart enough to have enough teeny-tiny lithium batteries on hand to last weeks, and if he swallows them they'd cure depression for life. He's waiting for them to develop a laptop filled with helium that would actually weigh less than nothing, and if it could blow up into an inflatable sex doll he'd never have to come down.

So there he sits in total freedom on that Rocky Mountain peak. The sky is blue. The air is crisp. Then the phone rings. His assistant wants to know if he wants to switch the company's overnight carrier. He turns off his phone so he can enjoy a little spiritual bliss. But first, there's his laptop. Maybe somebody sent him an important email. He wrestles with his conscience. His conscience loses. It's so easy to check, after all . . .

Never being out of touch means never being able to get away. But Wireless Man's problem will be worse than that. His brain will have adapted to the tempo of wireless life. Every 15 seconds there is some new thing to respond to. Soon he has this little rhythm machine in his brain. He does everything fast. He answers emails fast and sloppily. He's bought the fastest machines, and now the idea of waiting for something to download is a personal insult. His brain is operating at peak RPMs.

He sits amid nature's grandeur and says, "It's beautiful. But it's not moving. I wonder if I got any new voice mails."

He's addicted to the perpetual flux of the information networks. He craves his next data fix. He's a speed freak, an info junkie. He wants to slow down, but can't.

Today's business people live in an overcommunicated world. There are too many Web sites, too many reports, too many bits of information bidding for their attention. The successful ones are forced to become deft machete wielders in this jungle of communication. They ruthlessly cut away at all the extraneous data that are encroaching upon them. They speed through their tasks so they can cover as much ground as possible, answering dozens of emails at a sitting and scrolling past dozens more. After all, the main scarcity in their life is not money; it's time. They guard every precious second, the way a desert wanderer guards his water.

The problem with all this speed, and the frantic energy that is spent using time efficiently, is that it undermines creativity. After all, creativity is usually something that happens while you're doing something else: when you're in the shower your brain has time to noodle about and create the odd connections that lead to new ideas. But if your brain is always multitasking, or responding to techno-prompts, there is no time or energy for undirected mental play. Furthermore, if you are consumed by the same information loop circulating around everyone else, you don't have anything to stimulate you into thinking differently. You don't have time to read the history book or the science book that may actually prompt you to see your own business in a new light. You don't have access to unexpected knowledge. You're just swept along in the same narrow current as everyone else, which is swift but not deep.

So here's how I'm going to get rich. I'm going to design a placebo machine. It'll be a little gadget with voice recognition and everything. Wireless People will be able to log on and it will tell them they have no messages. After a while, they'll get used to having no messages. They'll be able to experience life instead of information. They'll be able to reflect instead of react. My machine won't even require batteries.

DISCUSSION QUESTIONS

1. Do you think Wireless Woman and Wireless Man are realistic? Explain.

2. Do you agree that speed and efficiency undermine creativity? Explain.

SUMMARY

Networking is one of the most important trends in computing today. Computer networks are growing in popularity because they allow computers to share hardware, allow computers to send software and data back and forth, and enable people to work together in ways that would be difficult or impossible without networks.

LANs are made up of computers that are close enough to be directly connected with cables or wireless radio transmitters/receivers. Most LANs include shared printers and file servers. WANs are made up of computers separated by considerable distance. The computers are connected to each other through the telephone network, which includes cables, microwave transmission towers, and communication satellites. Many computer networks are connected together through the Internet so messages and data can pass back and forth among them. Some specialized networks serve unique functions, including global positioning systems and financial systems.

Most computer networks today use the Ethernet architecture; an Ethernet port is a standard feature on most modern PCs. Computers can be directly connected to networks through Ethernet ports. When high-speed direct connections aren't possible, a PC can transmit and receive signals over standard phone lines with a modem. The modem converts the PC's digital signals to analog so they can travel through standard phone lines. Broadband connections offer much more bandwidth than standard modem connections, so they can transmit large amounts of information more quickly. These include DSL (which uses standard phone lines), cable modem (which uses cable TV lines), satellite (which uses TV satellite dishes), and Wi-Fi (which uses short-range wireless 802.11 transmitters). Wi-Fi is a type of wireless network technology that's exploding in popularity because of its potential for providing universal Internet access. All of these technologies offer connections to Internet backbones, many of which transmit astronomical amounts of data quickly through fiber-optic cables.

Communication software takes care of the details of communication between machines—details like protocols that determine how signals will be sent and received. Network operating systems typically handle the mechanics of LAN communication. Many popular PC operating systems include peer-to-peer networking software, so any PC or Mac on a network can serve as a server as well as a client. Terminal programs enable personal computers to function as character-based terminals when connected to other PCs or to timesharing computers. Other types of specialized client programs have graphical user interfaces and additional functionality. Timesharing operating systems enable multiuser computers to communicate with several terminals at a time.

Email, instant messaging, and teleconferencing are the most common forms of communication between people on computer networks. They offer many advantages over traditional mail and telephone communication and can shorten or eliminate many meetings. But because of several important limitations email and teleconferencing cannot completely replace older communication media. People who communicate with these new media should follow simple rules of netiquette and exercise a degree of caution to avoid many of the most common problems.

KEY TERMS

analog signal (p. 279)

asynchronous communication (p. 291)

attachment (p. 288)

bandwidth (p. 280)

bits per second (bps) (p. 279)

Bluetooth (p. 283)

bounce (p. 291)

bridges (p. 277)

chat room (p. 291)

client/server model (p. 285)

communication software (p. 285)

digital signal (p. 279)

direct connection (p. 278)

download (p. 287)

email (electronic mail) (p. 288)

Ethernet (p. 279)

FAQs (frequently asked questions) (p. 297)

fiber-optic cable (p. 281)

file server (p. 287)

gateway (p. 277)

Global Positioning System (GPS) (p. 277)

groupware (p. 287)

host system (p. 286)

instant messaging (p. 291)

Internet telephony (p. 293)

local area network (LAN) (p. 275)

mailing lists (p. 289)

modem (p. 279)

netiquette (p. 296)

network interface card (NIC) (p. 278)

network license (p. 287)

network operating system (NOS) (p. 285)

newsgroups (p. 290)

peer-to-peer model (p. 286)

port (p. 278)

protocol (p. 285)

real-time communication (p. 291)

remote access (p. 278)

router (p. 277)

server (p. 285)

site license (p. 287)

spam (p. 294)

telecommunication (p. 274)

telephony (p. 293)

terminal emulation software (p. 286)

upload (p. 287)

video teleconference (p. 292)

voicemail (p. 293)

wide area network (WAN) (p. 277)

Wi-Fi (p. 283)

wireless network (p. 276)

INTERACTIVE QUIZ QUESTIONS

1. The *Computer Confluence* CD-ROM contains self-test quiz questions related to this chapter, including multiple-choice, true or false, and matching questions.

2. The *Computer Confluence* Web site, http://computerconfluence.com, contains self-test exercises related to this chapter. Follow the instructions for taking a quiz. After you've completed your quiz, you can email the results to your instructor.

The Web site also contains open-ended discussion questions called Internet Explorations. Discuss one or more of the Internet Exploration questions at the section for this chapter.

TRUE OR FALSE

1. Today virtually all computer networks are general-purpose networks connected to the Internet.

2. The standard PC serial port is being phased out and replaced by a standard parallel port.

3. The most common types of networks today use a standard networking architecture known as Ethernet.

4. A single fiber-optic cable has the bandwidth of thousands of copper telephone cables.

5. Because peer-to-peer networking software is built into the Windows and Macintosh operating systems, a modern desktop computer can act as both client and server on a network.

6. If you want your Windows PC to read a file created on a Macintosh, you must use data translation software.

7. Depending on your email client program and your preferences, your mail might be stored on a remote host or downloaded and stored on your local machine.

8. The line that separates computer communication and telephone communication is being blurred by devices and technologies that operate in both realms.

9. Simple technological solutions can eliminate the spam problem for email users.

10. Email and instant messaging can filter out many human components of communication, increasing the chance of misinterpreted messages.

MULTIPLE CHOICE

1. A service that connects two or more networks within a city is called a
   a. connection area network (CAN).
   b. local area network (LAN).
   c. metropolitan area network (MAN).
   d. remote area network (RAN).
   e. wide area network (WAN).

2. Bandwidth can be affected by all of these except
   a. the amount of network traffic.
   b. the software protocols of the network.
   c. the type of network connection.
   d. the type of information being transmitted.
   e. the physical media that make up the network.

3. The most common reason for installing a Wi-Fi hub in a home is to make it possible
   a. to enable a PC to connect to a cell phone.
   b. to make client/server computing possible.
   c. to make it possible to connect Bluetooth-enabled devices to a network.
   d. to allow PCs to connect to a network without wires.
   e. to create a wireless alternative to hi-fi home entertainment systems.

4. If you want to share a document with other people whose computers are connected to your LAN, you should upload the document to a
   a. file server.
   b. client server.
   c. print server.
   d. document server.
   e. upload server.

5. An important difference between Internet newsgroups and mailing lists is
   a. a mailing list message only goes to a specific group of people, whereas a newsgroup message is available for anyone to see.
   b. a mailing list message is posted via email, whereas a newsgroup message requires special posting software.
   c. a mailing list message is posted to a special Web mailbox, whereas a newsgroup message is delivered directly to group member mailboxes.
   d. All of the above are true.
   e. There are no significant differences between the two.

6. The main difference between instant messaging (IM) and email is
   a. the use of moderated groups for IM.
   b. the ability of email to handle real-time communication.
   c. the GUI of the IM client software.
   d. the asynchronous nature of email communication.
   e. There are no significant differences between the two.

7. The number of email messages delivered each day far exceeds the number of letters delivered by the U.S. postal service. Why?
   a. email is faster than "snail mail."
   b. email is asynchronous communication.
   c. email facilitates group communication.
   d. email can save money.
   e. All of the above.

8. Today's email system is built on protocols that
   a. don't ensure that each sender has a verifiable identity.
   b. automatically filter spam based on objectionable content.
   c. can be modified by anyone with systems administration clearance.
   d. apply directly to instant messaging systems.
   e. All of the above.

9. Which of these is OK according to the generally accepted rules of netiquette?
   a. sending a message to ten thousand members of a worldwide society of birdwatchers inviting them to your local club's weekly outing.
   b. lurking in a hang-glider enthusiasts newsgroup without posting any messages.
   c. quickly posting on a DJ newsgroup 15 "help me" beginner questions about the second-hand turntables you just bought without manuals.
   d. responding to an antiwar group email with a heated message that attacks the personal integrity of the sender.
   e. sending 36 unsolicited high-resolution family photos to everyone on your list of email friends.

10. Many experts say we're at the beginning of a revolution that is creating a vast grassroots network of public and private wireless hubs based on
    a. 3G technology.
    b. mesh network technology.
    c. Wi-Fi technology.
    d. Bluetooth technology.
    e. adaptive radio technology.

REVIEW QUESTIONS

1. Define or describe each of the key terms listed in the Key Terms section. Check your answers using the glossary.

2. Give three general reasons for the importance of computer networking. (*Hint*: Each reason is related to one of the three essential components of every computer system.)

3. How do the three general reasons listed in Question 2 relate specifically to LANs?

4. How do the three general reasons listed in Question 2 relate specifically to WANs?

5. Under what circumstances is a modem necessary for connecting computers in networks? What does the modem do?

6. Describe at least two different kinds of communication software.

7. How could a file server be used in a student computer lab? What software licensing issues would be raised by using a file server in a student lab?

8. What are the differences between email and instant messaging systems?

9. Describe some things you can do with email that can't be done with regular mail.

10. Describe several potential problems associated with email and teleconferencing.

11. "Money is just another form of information." Explain this statement, and describe how it relates to communication technology.

12. Wi-Fi and Bluetooth wireless technologies are designed to serve different purposes than mobile phone technology. Explain this statement.

13. Why is netiquette important? Give some examples of netiquette.

DISCUSSION QUESTIONS

1. Suppose you have an important message to send to a friend in another city, and you can use the telephone, email, real-time teleconference, fax, or overnight mail service. Discuss the advantages and disadvantages of each. See if you can think of a situation for each of the five options in which that particular option is the most appropriate choice.

2. Some people choose to spend several hours every day online. Do you see potential hazards in this kind of heavy modem use? Explain your answer.

3. Should spam be illegal? Explain your answer.

4. In the quote at the end of the chapter, Stewart Brand points out that electronic communication is essential for some of the world's people and irrelevant to others. What distinguishes these two groups? What advantages and disadvantages does each have?

5. Do you think Wi-Fi and other wireless technology put us on the brink of a communication revolution? Why or why not?

PROJECTS

1. Find out about your school's computer networks. Are there many LANs? How are they connected? Who has access to them? What are they used for?

2. Spend a few hours exploring an online service like AOL. Describe the problems you encounter in the process. Which parts of the service are the most useful and interesting?

SOURCES AND RESOURCES

Books

The Communications Miracle: The Telecommunication Pioneers from Morse to the Information Superhighway, by John Bray (New York: Plenum, 1995). This book gives the communication revolution a historical perspective by mixing technical explanations with human stories.

How Networks Work, Sixth Edition, by Frank J. Derfler, Jr., and Les Freed (Indianapolis, IN: Que, 2003). Follows the model popularized with the *How Computers Work* series. It uses a mix of text and graphics to illuminate the nuts and bolts of PC networks.

The Essential Guide to Networking, by James Edward Keogh (Upper Saddle River, NJ: Prentice Hall, 2000). This book is part of a series of technical *Essential* books for nontechnical professionals. This one provides a broad overview of network technology, from LANs and WANs to the Internet and wireless networks.

The Essential Guide to Telecommunications, Third Edition, by Annabel Z. Dodd (Upper Saddle River, NJ: Prentice Hall, 2002). This popular book presents a clear, comprehensive guide to the telecommunications industry and technology, including telephone systems, cable systems, wireless systems, and the Internet. If you want to understand how the pieces of our communication networks fit together, this book is a great place to start.

The Essential Guide to Wireless Communications Applications: From Cellular Systems to Wi-Fi, Second Edition, by Andy Dornan (Upper Saddle River, NJ: Prentice Hall, 2002). Yet another *Essential Guide*, this one focuses on networks without wires. The book includes clear explanations of technical nuts and bolts, plus a chapter on health risks of wireless technology.

Computer Networks and Internets, Third Edition, by Douglas E. Comer, CD-ROM by Ralph Droms (Upper Saddle River, NJ: Prentice Hall, 2001). This text answers the question, "How do computer networks and internets operate?" Coverage includes LANs, WANs, Internet packets, digital telephony, protocols, client/server interaction, network security, and the underpinnings

of the World Wide Web. A CD-ROM and a companion Web site supplement the text.

Wireless Nation: The Frenzied Launch of the Cellular Revolution, by James B. Murray (Perseus Books, 2001). The mobile phone explosion and the PC both burst into our culture in the last decades of the twentieth century, and they came together through the Internet. This book chronicles the rise of mobile communication technology.

Tyranny of the Moment: Fast and Slow Time in the Information Age, by Thomas Hylland (London: Pluto Press, 2001). In an age when instantaneous communication has never been easier, time is one of our scarcest commodities. Hylland explores this paradox and discusses the social and political implications of the evaporation of "slow time."

F2f, by Phillip Finch (New York: Bantam, 1997). As communities form on computer networks, they bring with them many of the problems found in other communities. This suspense thriller captures some of the potential risks of online communities in an exciting, tightly written story.

Periodicals

Network Magazine focuses on networks with a business perspective.

Computer Telephony and **CTI** are two magazines that cover the rapidly changing territory where computers and telephones meet. Both periodicals are aimed at professionals and include a fair amount of technical material.

Web Pages

Computer networking technology is changing faster than publishers can print books and periodicals about it. The *Computer Confluence* Web site can connect you to up-to-date networking information all over the Internet.

AFTER YOU READ THIS CHAPTER YOU SHOULD BE ABLE TO:

■ Explain how and why the Internet was created

■ Describe the technology that's at the heart of the Internet

■ Describe the technology that makes the Web work as a multimedia mass medium

■ Discuss the tools people use to build Web sites

■ Discuss the trends that are changing the Internet and the way people use it

■ Discuss some of the most important social and political issues raised by the growth of the Internet.

 Multimedia extras on the CD-ROM and the Web:

■ **Animated illustrations** of basic Internet and World Wide Web Technologies

■ How **peer-to-peer file sharing** works

■ **Videos** of Kazaa CEO Nikki Hemming and virtual community pioneer Howard Rheingolds

■ Interactive **self-study quizzes**

■ Helpful Web sites

   . . . *and more.*

 **computerconfluence.com**

INSIDE THE INTERNET AND THE WORLD WIDE WEB

ARPANET PIONEERS BUILD AN UNRELIABLE NETWORK . . . ON PURPOSE

In the 1960s, the world of computers was a technological Tower of Babel—most computers couldn't communicate with each other. When people needed to move data from one computer to another, they carried or mailed a magnetic tape or a deck of punch cards. While most of the world viewed computers only as giant number crunchers, J. C. R. Licklider, Robert Taylor, and a small group of visionary computer scientists saw the computer's potential as a communication device. They envisioned a network that would enable researchers to share computing resources and ideas.

U.S. military strategists during those Cold War years had a vision, too: They foresaw an enemy attack crippling the U.S. government's ability to communicate. The Department of Defense wanted a network that could function even if some connections were destroyed. They provided one million dollars to Taylor and other scientists and engineers to build a small experimental network. The groundbreaking result, launched in 1969, was called ARPANET, for Advanced Research Projects Agency NETwork. When a half-dozen researchers sent the first historic message from UCLA to Doug Engelbart's lab at the Stanford Research Institute, no one even thought to take a picture.

ARPANET was built on two unorthodox assumptions: The network itself was unreliable, so it had to be able to overcome its own unreliability, and all computers on the network would be equal in their ability to

> It's a bit like **climbing a mountain**. You don't know how far you've come until you **stop and look back**.
>
> —Vint Cerf, ARPANET pioneer and first president of the Internet Society

communicate with other network computers. In ARPANET there was no central authority because that would make the entire network vulnerable to attack. Messages were contained in software "packets" that could travel independently by any number of different paths, through all kinds of computers, toward their destinations.

ARPANET grew quickly into an international network with hundreds of military and university sites. In addition to carrying research data, ARPANET channeled debates over the Vietnam War and intense discussions about Space War, an early computer game. ARPANET's peer-to-peer networking philosophy and protocols were copied in other networks in the 1980s. Vint Cerf and Bob Kahn, two of the original

9.1 The team that built the predecessor to the Internet included, from front to back: Bob Taylor, Vint Cerf, Frank Heart, Larry Roberts, Len Kleinrock, Bob Kahn, Wes Clark, Doug Engelbart, Barry Wessler, Dave Walden, Severo Ornstein, Truett Thach, Roger Scantlebury, Charlie Herzfeld, Ben Barker, Jon Postel, Steve Crocker, Bill Naylor, and Roland Bryan.

researchers, developed the protocols that became the standard computer communication language, allowing different computer networks to be linked.

In 1990 ARPANET was disbanded, having fulfilled its research mission, but its technology spawned the Internet. In a recent interview, Cerf said about the network he helped create, "It was supposed to be a highly robust technology for supporting military command and control. It did that in the Persian Gulf War. But, along the way, it became a major research support infrastructure and now has become the best example of global information infrastructure that we have."

The ARPANET pioneers have gone on to work on dozens of other significant projects and products. In the words of Bob Kahn, "Those were very exciting days, but there are new frontiers in every direction I can look these days."

The team that designed ARPANET suspected they were building something important. They couldn't have guessed, though, that they were laying the groundwork for a system that would become a universal research tool, a hotbed of business activity, a virtual shopping mall, a popular social hangout, a publisher's clearinghouse of up-to-the-minute information, and one of the most talked about institutions of our time.

The Internet is a technology, a tool, and a culture. Computer scientists originally designed it for computer scientists, and other scientists and engineers are continually adding new features. Consequently, the vocabulary of the Internet often seems like a flurry of technobabble to the rest of us. You don't need to analyze every acronym to make sense of the Internet, but your Net experiences can be far more rewarding if you understand the concepts at the heart of basic netspeak terminology. In this chapter we delve a little deeper into the Internet to make those concepts clearer.

Inside the Internet

It shouldn't be too much of a surprise that the Internet has evolved into a force **strong enough** to reflect the **greatest hopes and fears** of those who use it. After all, it was designed to **withstand nuclear war**, not just the **puny huffs and puffs** of politicians and religious fanatics.

—Denise Caruso, digital commerce columnist, *New York Times*

The Internet includes dozens of national, statewide, and regional networks, hundreds of networks within colleges and research labs, and thousands of commercial sites. Most sites are in the United States, but the Internet has connections in almost every country in the world. More importantly, the Internet is not controlled by any one government, corporation, individual, or legal system. Several international advisory organizations develop standards and protocols for the evolving Internet, but no one has the power to control the Net's operation or evolution. The Internet is, in a sense, a massive anarchy unlike any other organization the world has ever seen.

Counting Connections

In its early days, the Internet connected only a few dozen computers at U.S. universities and government research centers, and the government paid most of the cost of building and operating it. Today, it connects millions of computers in almost every country in the world, and costs are shared by thousands of connected organizations. It's impossible to pin down the exact size of the Internet for several reasons:

> No **LAN** is an **island**.
>
> —Karyl Scott, *InfoWorld* writer

- The Internet is growing too fast to track. Millions of new users connect to the Internet every year in the United States alone, and the rest of the world is adding new connections by the minute.
- The Internet is decentralized. There's no "Internet Central" that keeps track of user activity or network connections. To make matters worse for Internet counters, some parts of the Internet can't be accessed by the general public; they're sealed off to protect private information.
- The Internet doesn't have hard boundaries. There are several ways to connect to the Internet (described later in this chapter); these different types of connections offer different classes of services and different degrees of interactivity. As choices proliferate, it's becoming harder to know exactly what it means to "belong to the Internet."

This last point is worth a closer look. It's easier to understand the different types of Internet access if you know a little bit about the protocols that make the Internet work.

9.2 Cyber-cafes around the world, like this one in China, enable travelers to stay connected to their homes and the rest of the world. Customers often pay by the minute to log into their home servers to keep up on email, favorite Web sites, and IM contacts.

Internet Protocols

The protocols at the heart of the Internet are called **TCP/IP** (Transmission Control Protocol/Internet Protocol). They were developed as an experiment in **internetworking**—connecting different types of networks and computer systems. The TCP/IP specifi-

> The **most important quality** of the Internet is that it lends itself to **radical reinvention**. . . . In another 10 years, the **only part** of the Internet as we know it now that will have survived will be **bits and pieces** of the underlying Internet protocol. . . .
>
> —Paul Saffo, director of the Institute for the Future

cations were published as **open standards**, not owned by any company. As a result, TCP/IP became the "language" of the Internet, allowing cross-network communication for almost every type of computer and network. These protocols are generally invisible to users; they're hidden deep in software that takes care of communication details behind the scenes. They define how information can be transferred between machines and how machines on the network can be identified with unique addresses.

The TCP protocols define a system similar in many ways to the postal system. When a message is sent on the Internet, it is broken into *packets*, in the same way you might pack your belongings in several individually addressed boxes before you ship them to a new location. Each packet has all the information it needs to travel independently from network to network toward its destination. Different packets might take different routes, just as

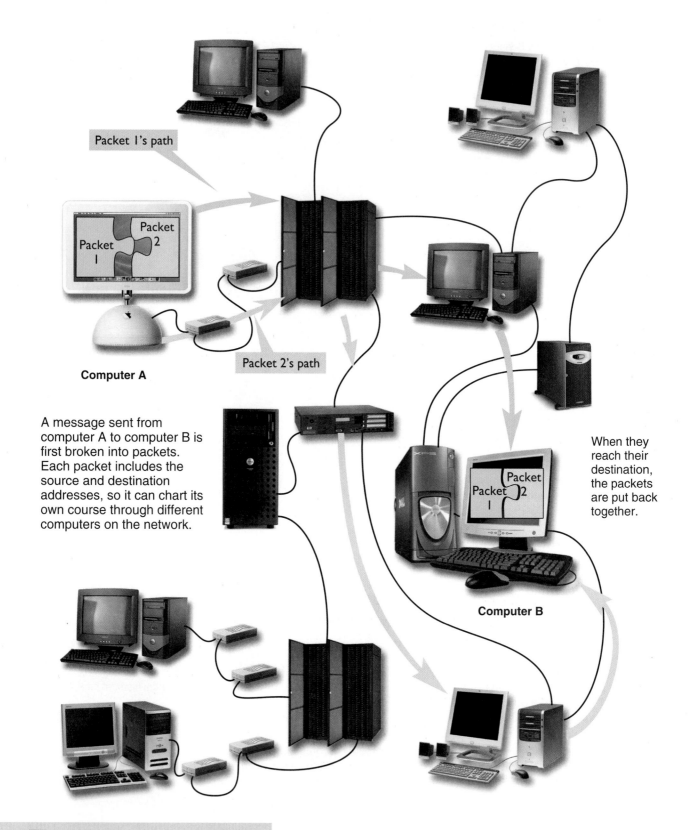

Packet 1's path

Packet 1
Packet 2

Computer A

Packet 2's path

A message sent from computer A to computer B is first broken into packets. Each packet includes the source and destination addresses, so it can chart its own course through different computers on the network.

When they reach their destination, the packets are put back together.

Packet 1
Packet 2

Computer B

9.3 Packet switching gets the message through.

different parcels might be routed through different cities by the postal system. The host systems that use software to decide how to route Internet transmissions are called *routers*, although sometimes less flexible hardware, *switches*, can do the same routing work faster. Regardless of the route they follow, the packets eventually reach their destination, where they are reassembled into the original message. This packet-switching model is flexible and robust, allowing messages to get through even when part of the network is down.

The other part of TCP/IP—the IP part—defines the addressing system of the Internet. Every host computer on the Internet has a unique *IP address*, a string of four numbers separated by periods, or, as they say in Net speak, dots. A typical IP address might look like this: 123.23.168.22 ("123 dot 23 dot 168 dot 22"). Every packet includes the IP address of the sending computer and the receiving computer.

Internet Addresses

In practice, people seldom see or use numerical IP addresses, because the Internet's *domain name system (DNS)* translates the IP address into something that's easier for humans to read and remember. The DNS uses a string of names separated by dots to specify the exact Internet location of the host computer.

Internet addresses are classified by *domains*. In the United States the most widely used top-level domains are general categories that describe types of organizations:

- .edu   Educational sites
- .com   Commercial sites
- .gov   Government sites
- .mil   Military sites
- .net   Network administration sites
- .org   Nonprofit organizations

The Internet Ad Hoc Committee recently created seven additional top-level domain names:

- .aero   Air transport organizations
- .biz   Businesses
- .coop   Cooperative businesses such as credit unions
- .info   Information services
- .museum   Museums
- .name   Personal registration by name
- .pro   Licensed professionals, including lawyers, doctors, and accountants

Some of these domains, including .com, .net, .org, and .info, are open to anyone without restriction. For example, you could have a Web site or an email address in the .net domain whether or not you're part of a nonprofit organization. Other domains, including .edu and .mil, are restricted so only people in the designated organizations can use them. Outside (and occasionally inside) the United States top-level domains are two-letter country codes, such as .jp for Japan, .th for Thailand, .au for Australia, .uk for United Kingdom, and .us for United States.

The top-level domain name is the last part of the address. The other parts of the address, when read in reverse, provide information that narrows down the exact location on the network. The words in the domain name, like the lines in a post office address, are arranged hierarchically from little to big. They might include the name of the organization, the name of the department or network within the organization, and the name of the host computer.

The domain naming system is used in virtually all email addresses and Web URLs. A Web URL specifies the IP address of the Web server that houses the page. In an email address, the domain name system is used to pinpoint the Internet location of the host computer that contains the user's mail server. The email address includes the user name and the host address, as illustrated on the following page:

kelly@cs.allaire.edu

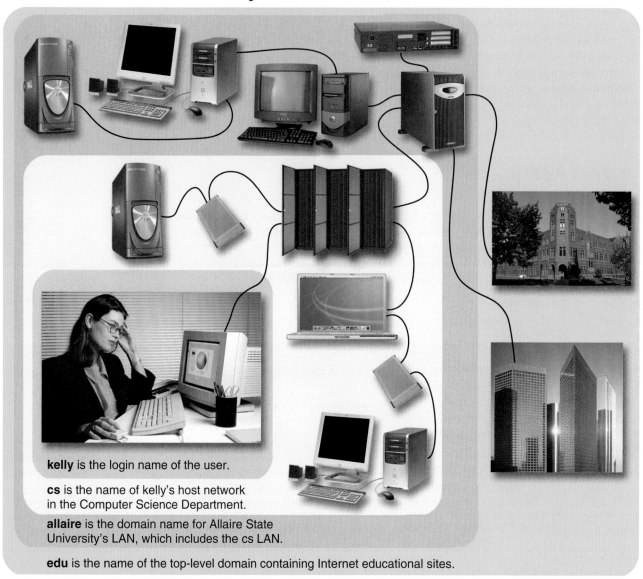

kelly is the login name of the user.

cs is the name of kelly's host network in the Computer Science Department.

allaire is the domain name for Allaire State University's LAN, which includes the cs LAN.

edu is the name of the top-level domain containing Internet educational sites.

9.4 Anatomy of an email address.

Here are some other examples of email addresses using the domain name system:

- president@whitehouse.gov — User *president* whose mail is stored on the host *whitehouse* in the government domain
- crabbyabby@AOL.com — User called *crabbyabby* whose mail is handled by AOL, a commercial service provider
- hazel_filbert@admin.gmcc.ab.ca — User *hazel_filbert* at the *admin* server for Grant MacEwan Community College in Alberta, Canada

Internet Access Options

Computers connect to the Internet through three basic types of connections: direct connections, dial-up connections through modems, and broadband connections through high-speed alternatives to modems.

> The **grand design** keeps getting grander. A **global computer** is taking shape, and we're **all connected** to it.
>
> —Stewart Brand, in *The Media Lab*

Direct Connections

In many schools and businesses the computers have a direct (dedicated) connection to the Internet through a LAN and have their own IP addresses. A direct connection offers several advantages: You can take full advantage of Internet services without dialing in; your files are stored on your computer, not on a remote host; and response time is much faster, making it possible to transfer large files (like multimedia documents) quickly. Direct-connect digital lines come in many varieties, including *T1* connections, which can transmit voice, data, and video at roughly 1.5Mbps, and *T3*, which is even faster. (On some continents a technology called E1 is used instead of T1.)

Dial-up Connections

If your computer isn't directly connected to the Internet, you can temporarily connect to an Internet host through a dial-up connection—a connection using a modem and standard telephone lines.

Software that uses *PPP* (point-to-point protocol) allows a computer connected via modem and phone line to have full Internet access temporarily and a temporary IP address. *Full-access dial-up connections* offer most of the advantages of direct connection, including Web access, but response time is limited by the modem's speed. A typical connection through a modem and *POTS* (plain old telephone service) is much slower (and often less reliable) than a direct Internet connection. Although modern modems are theoretically capable of delivering data at 56Kb or faster, they're often much slower when connected to typical noisy phone lines. Modem connections are sometimes called narrowband connections because they don't offer much bandwidth when compared to other types of connections.

Broadband Connections

Until a few years ago, a slow dial-up connection was the only alternative to direct Internet for homes and small businesses. Today, millions of Internet users connect via DSL, cable modems, and satellites. These modem alternatives are often called broadband connections because they have much higher bandwidth than standard modem connections. In some cases, broadband connections offer data transmission speeds comparable to direct connection speeds. Many broadband services offer another big advantage: They're always on. Users of these services don't need to dial in; the Internet is instantly available anytime, like television or radio. The most common broadband alternatives are based on the following technologies:

■ *DSL.* Many phone companies offer DSL (digital subscriber line), a technology for bringing high-bandwidth always-on connections to homes and small businesses by sharing the copper telephone lines that carry voice calls. DSL is faster and cheaper than *ISDN*, a digital service offered by phone companies in the 1990s. Most experts believe ISDN will soon be obsolete. DSL customers must be geographically close to phone company service hubs. DSL transmission speeds vary considerably. *Downstream traffic*—information from the Internet to the subscriber—sometimes approaches T1 speeds. A graphics-heavy Web page that takes minutes to download through a conventional modem will load in seconds through a DSL connection. *Upstream traffic*—data

INTERNET CONNECTION SPEEDS

Connection type	Downstream		Upstream
	Potential	Typical	Typical
Dial-up modems: connection modem (56K)	56Kbps	42 to 53Kbps	33.6Kbps
T1	1.544Mbps	1.544Mbps	1.544Mbps
T3	44.736Mbps	44.736Mbps	44.736Mbps
ISDN	128Kbps	64 to 128Kbps	64 to 128Kbps
DSL/xDSL	6.1Mbps	512 Kbps to 1.544Mbps	128Kbps
Cable modem	27Mbps	1.5 to 3Mbps	500Kbps to 2.5Mbps
Satellite connection	1.2Mbps	150 to 1,000 Kbps	50 to 150Kbps
Wireless broadband (802.11b)	20Mbps	5.5 or 11Mbps	5.5 or 11Mbps

9.5 Speeds vary widely for different types of Internet connections.

traveling from the home computer to the Internet—typically travels much slower, but still much faster than standard modem transmission. A DSL signal can share a standard telephone line with voice traffic, so it can remain on without interfering with telephone calls. DSL connections are only available in limited areas, and installation can be complicated and expensive.

■ *Cable modem connections.* Some cable TV companies offer ultra-high-speed Internet connections through cable modems. Cable modems allow Internet connections using the same network of coaxial cables that delivers television signals to millions of homes. Like DSL, cable modem service isn't available everywhere. Cable modem speeds often exceed DSL speeds both downstream and upstream. But because a single cable is shared by an entire neighborhood, transmission speeds can go down when the number of users goes up.

9.6 Many airports and other public areas now have Wi-Fi wireless networks that enable travelers to connect to the Internet.

■ *Satellite connections.* Satellite Internet connections are available through many of the same satellite dishes that provide television channels to viewers. Downstream satellite transmission is much faster than conventional modem traffic, although not as fast as DSL or cable modem service. For some satellite services, upstream traffic goes through phone lines at standard modem rates. Some newer services use satellites for both upstream and downstream traffic. For many homes and businesses outside of urban centers, satellites provide the only high-speed Internet access options available.

■ *Wireless broadband connections.* People packing portable computers can, in some places, temporarily connect to the Internet through wireless broadband connections. The wireless broadband technology with the most industry support is commonly called Wi-Fi, but is also referred to by its IEEE certification number, *802.11b*. This technology allows multiple computers to connect to a base station using short-range radio waves. This technology is used in many homes and offices for sharing Internet connections without cables. Newer versions, *802.11a* and *802.11g* offer advantages in both speed and range. Using Wi-Fi technology, students can connect to the Internet while they move around a wireless-equipped campus, travelers can make Web connections while waiting in some airports, and coffee shops can become Internet cafes for people with wireless receivers in their laptops.

Each of these broadband technologies is widely deployed in the United States and each is rapidly expanding its area of coverage. In the future, many homes and small businesses will have direct connection to the Internet via fiber-optic cables. But for now, most Internet users can choose between narrowband modems and various broadband services available in their areas.

Internet Service Providers

Internet service providers (ISPs) generally offer several connection options at different prices. Local ISPs are local businesses with permanent connections to the Internet. They provide connections to their customers, usually through local telephone lines, along with other services. For example, an ISP might provide an email address, a server for customers to post Web pages, and technical help as part of a service package. National ISPs such as EarthLink offer similar services on a nationwide scale. National ISPs have local telephone numbers in most major cities so travelers can dial into the Net on the road without paying long-distance charges. In some cities inexpensive or free access to the Internet is available through a freenet—a local ISP designed to provide community access to online forums, announcements, and services.

My Places

■ Customize My Places
■ Greetings
■ Horoscopes
■ Local News
■ Maps & Directions
■ My Portfolios
■ People Directory
■ Sports Scores
■ Stock Quotes
■ What's New on AOL
■ White Pages

Have You Tried?

■ AOL Anywhere
■ People Directory

■ AOL Help
■ Go to Internet
■ Parental Controls
AOL Keyword: Welcome

9.7 Online services, such as American Online (AOL), offer a variety of services in a privately controlled environment.

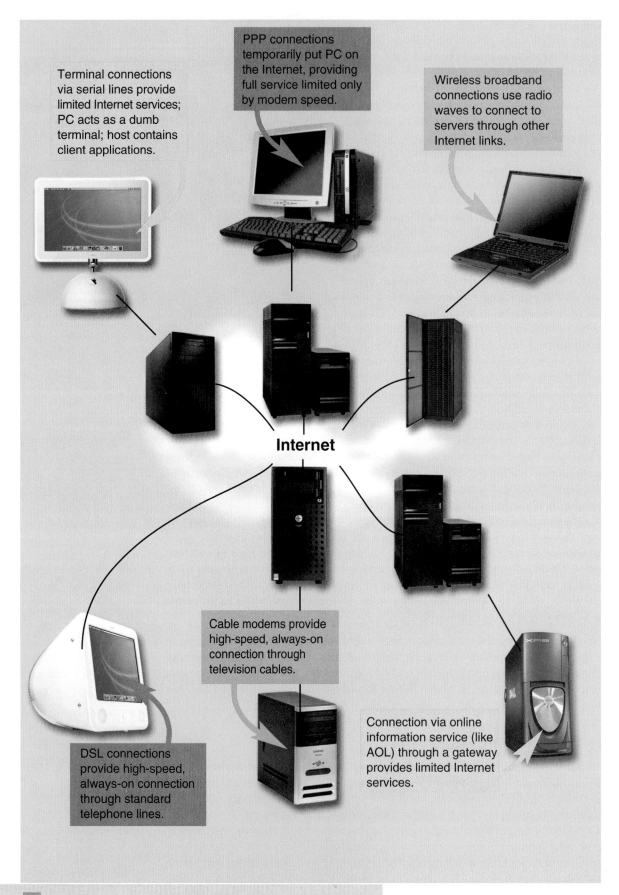

Terminal connections via serial lines provide limited Internet services; PC acts as a dumb terminal; host contains client applications.

PPP connections temporarily put PC on the Internet, providing full service limited only by modem speed.

Wireless broadband connections use radio waves to connect to servers through other Internet links.

Internet

DSL connections provide high-speed, always-on connection through standard telephone lines.

Cable modems provide high-speed, always-on connection through television cables.

Connection via online information service (like AOL) through a gateway provides limited Internet services.

9.8 There are many ways to connect a PC or other device to the Internet.

Many private networks and commercial *online services* (including America Online, CompuServe, and Prodigy) provide Internet access through gateways. A *gateway* is a computer connected to two networks—in this context the Internet and an outside network—that translates communication protocols and transfers information between the two. Some online services, such as MSN, have been rebuilt so they use the same protocols and framework as the Internet; subscribers use standard Web browsers and email programs to access services. Others, such as AOL and CompuServe, use proprietary client software to give subscribers access to their services and to the Internet. These services also enable members to use standard Internet software tools to connect to the Web and check email. Whatever their underlying architecture, online services are essentially ISPs that offer extra services to subscribers, including news, research tools, shopping, banking, games, chat rooms, bulletin boards, email, instant messaging, and software libraries.

Internet Servers

Internet applications, like PC applications, are software tools for users. But working with Internet applications is different from working with word processors or spreadsheets because of the distributed nature of the Internet and the client/server model used by most Internet applications. In the client/server model, a client program asks for information, and a server program fields

> The most desirable interaction with a network is one in which **the network itself is invisible and unnoticeable**. Planners often forget that people **do not want to use systems** at all—easy or not. What people want is to **delegate** a task and **not to worry about how** it is done.
>
> —Nicholas Negroponte, director of MIT's Media Lab

the request and provides the requested information from databases and documents. The client program hides the details of the network and the server from the user.

Different people might access the same server using different client applications with different user interfaces. For example, a user with a direct connection might be using a Web browser with a point-and-click interface to explore a particular server, while another user with a dial-up terminal connection might be typing UNIX commands and seeing only text on screen. A third user might be viewing the same data, a few words at a time, on the tiny screen of a handheld PDA or mobile phone.

Many Internet applications use specialized servers. Some of the most common server types include the following:

- *Email servers*. An email server acts like a local post office for a particular Internet host—a business, an organization, or an ISP. For example, a college might have an email server to handle the mail of all students, faculty, and staff; their email addresses point to that server. The email server receives incoming mail, stores it, and provides it to the email client programs of the addressees when they request it. Similarly, the email server collects mail from its subscribers and sends those messages toward their Internet destinations. Basically, the email server handles local client requests of two types: "Give me my mail," and "Pick up my mail and send it."
- *File servers*. File servers are common within LANs, but they're also used to share programs, media files, and other computer data across the Internet. The Internet's file transfer protocol (FTP) enables users to download files from remote servers (sometimes called FTP servers) to their computers—and to upload files they want to share from their computers to these archives. When you click a Web link that downloads a file, the Web browser's request is probably handled using FTP. A newer technology called *WebDAV* performs the functions of FTP using software with a graphical interface that makes remote servers appear like simple file folders. Wherever they are stored, most files in Net archives are compressed—made smaller using special encoding schemes. File compression saves storage space on disk and saves transmission time when files are transferred through networks. (See Chapter 7 for more on compression.) Once files are downloaded to a PC, they have to be decompressed before they can be used. You don't need to know how compression works to take advantage of it; software makes the process automatic and transparent.

■ *Application servers.* An application server stores applications—PC office applications, databases, or other applications—and makes them available to client programs that request them. An application server might be used within a large company to keep PCs updated with the latest software. Each PC might have a client program that regularly sends requests for updates to the server. The application server might also be housed at an application service provider (ASP)—a company that manages and delivers application services on a contract basis. Users of ASPs don't buy applications; they rent them, along with service contracts. Some application servers supply platform-neutral, Web-centered applications rather than OS-specific PC applications. Many industry watchers believe ASPs will eventually provide most of the software we use. For some companies ASPs are part of larger Web-services strategies, discussed later.

■ *Web servers.* A Web server stores Web pages and sends them to client programs—Web browsers—that request them. It may also store and send Web media, including graphics, audio, video, and animation. In the next section we'll turn our attention to the technology behind the Web.

Inside the Web

> The **dream behind the Web** is of a common information space in which we **communicate by sharing information**.
>
> —Tim Berners-Lee, creator of the World Wide Web

The World Wide Web (WWW) is a distributed browsing and searching system originally developed at CERN (European Laboratory for Particle Physics) by Tim Berners-Lee, a visionary scientist profiled in Chapter 6. He designed a system for giving Internet documents unique addresses, wrote the HTML language for encoding and displaying documents, and built a software browser for viewing those documents from remote locations. Since it was introduced in 1991, the Web has become phenomenally popular as a system for exploring, viewing, and publishing all kinds of information on the Net.

Web Protocols: HTTP and HTML

The Web is built around a naming scheme that allows every information resource on the Internet to be referred to using a uniform resource locator or, as it's more commonly known, URL. Here's a typical URL:

```
http://weatherunderground.com/satellite/vis/1k/US.html/
```

> The Web was built by **millions of people** simply **because they wanted it**, without need, greed, fear, hierarchy, authority figures, ethnic identification, advertising, or any form of manipulation. **Nothing like this ever happened before in history**. We can be blasé about it now, but it is **what we will be remembered for.** We have been made aware of a **new dimension of human potential**.
>
> —Jaron Lanier, virtual reality pioneer

The first part of this URL refers to the protocol that must be used to access information; it might be FTP, news, or something else. It's most commonly *http*, for *hypertext transfer protocol*, the protocol used to transfer Web pages. The second part (the part following the //) is the address of the host containing the resource; it uses the same domain-naming scheme used for email addresses. The third part, following the dot address, describes the *path* to the particular resource on the host—the hierarchical nesting of directories (folders) that contain the resource.

Most Web pages are created using a language called HTML (hypertext markup language). An HTML *source document* is a text file that includes codes that describe the format, layout, and logical structure of a hypermedia document. HTML is not WYSIWYG

http://www.vote-smart.org/help/database.html

| http (hypertext transfer protocol) is the protocol for transporting the resource through the network. | www.vote-smart.org is the domain name of the server containing the resource. | help is the name of the directory (folder) on the server www that contains the file database.html. | database.html is the name of the resource file. |

9.9 Anatomy of a URL.

(What You See Is What You Get); the HTML codes embedded in the document make it look cryptic and nothing like the final page displayed on the screen. But those codes enable a Web browser to translate an HTML source document into that finished page. Because it's a text file, an HTML document can be easily transmitted from a Web server to a client machine anywhere on the Internet.

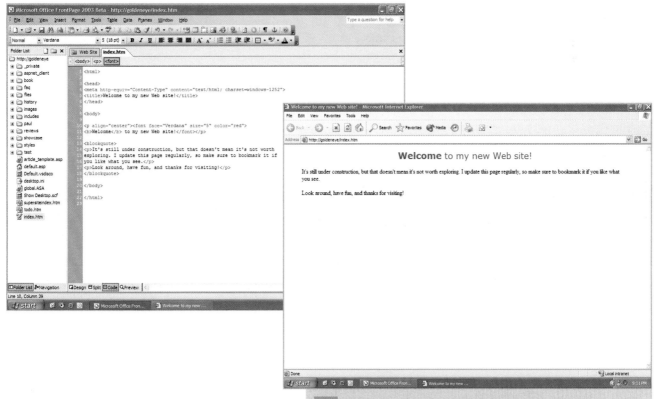

9.10 HTML source code tells the Web browser how to format the text when it's displayed on the screen.

9.1
The World Wide Web

1 When you type a URL into the address box of your Web browser, the browser sends a message through the Internet to the server with the specified domain name www.requestfiles.com.

www.requestfiles.com

2 The server responds by sending the specified file to the client browser. The file is an HTML file containing the text contents of the requested Web page along with HTML codes for formatting and adding other elements to the page. Because HTML files are all text, they're small and easy to transmit through the Internet.

<H1> requestfiles <H1> <IMG>

3 The browser reads the HTML file and interprets the HTML commands, called *tags*, embedded in angle brackets <like this>. It uses the formatting tags to determine the look and layout of the text on the page. For example, <H1> indicates a level-one heading to be displayed in large text; <1> indicates italics, and so on.

Server

4 The HTML file doesn't contain pictures; it's a text file. But it does contain a tag specifying where a picture file is stored and where in the page it is to be displayed. The server responds to this tag by sending the requested graphics files.

Server

5 The HTML file also contains a tag indicating a hyperlink to another document with a URL on another server. When the user clicks that link, a message is sent to the new server; and the process of building a Web page in the bromser window starts anew.

9.11

320

Publishing on the Web

You can create a Web page with any word processor or text editor; you just type the HTML commands along with the rest of the text. But you don't need to write HTML code to create a Web page. Many programs, including Microsoft Word, PowerPoint, and FileMaker Pro, can automatically convert basic formatting features (including character styles, indentation, and justification) into HTML codes. Some Web authoring software, including Macromedia Dreamweaver, Adobe GoLive, and Microsoft FrontPage, work like page layout programs that desktop publishers use. You can lay out text and graphics the way you want them to look, and the authoring program creates an HTML document that looks similar to your original layout when viewed through a Web browser. The best of these Web authoring programs enable you to manage entire Web sites using tools that can automate repetitive edits, apply formatting styles across pages, and check for bad links. Some have tools for connecting large sites to databases containing critical, rapidly changing content.

Once an HTML document is completed, it needs to be uploaded onto a Web server before it's visible on the Web. Many ISPs provide Web server space as part of their subscription service; other companies rent Web server space to individuals and organizations. By default, most Web pages have URLs that include the ISP or Web server domain names—names like **http://hometown.aol.com/shjoobedebop/index.htm**. Many businesses, organizations, and individuals pay an annual fee to a *domain name registry* company for names that match and are easier to remember and use. Many customized domain names resemble company or product names—for example, **http://www.prenhall.com** or **http://www.computerconfluence.com**.

Many individuals post daily diaries, ongoing political commentaries, regularly updated business information, photo journals, and similar documents without using HTML or standard Web authoring software. Instead, they use software that's designed specifically to create Weblog, or blog, documents. Blogs are published to Web servers using simple Web interfaces that shield the user from worrying about technical details like FTP server addresses and URLs. They even provide custom design templates so that users can modify the look of their site without knowing any HTML. Blog software provides a way to post diary-like entries to a blog on an ongoing basis. Some suppliers of blog software, like Google's Blogger.com, will even host your blog for free as long as you don't mind advertising their wares. Today, blogs are revolutionizing Web publishing by bringing the power of personal publishing to individuals who would otherwise be uninterested in learning the technical details of HTML and Web authoring. Using a simple and free Web-based tool, anyone can publish views on any topic, at any time, and reach a worldwide audience instantly. Influential blogs have had an impact on public policy by drawing attention to facts and ideas overlooked by commercial news organizations.

> By expanding the number of people who have **the power to transmit knowledge**, the Web might trigger a **power shift** that **changes everything**.
>
> —Howard Rheingold, author of *Virtual Communities*

From Hypertext to Multimedia

Way back in the early 1990s(!) the first Web pages were straight hypertext. Within a couple of years graphics were common, and a few cutting-edge Web sites enabled browsers to download scratchy video and audio clips to their hard disks. Today, color graphics and animation are everywhere, and a typical Web site can contain any or all of these:

> We are still a **multimedia organism**. If we want to push the envelope of complexity further, we have to use **all of our devices** for accessing information—not all of which are **rational**.
>
> —Psychologist Mihaly Csikszentmihalyi

■ *Tables*—spreadsheet-like grids whose rows and columns contain neatly laid out text and graphical elements. Tables with invisible cell borders are often used as alignment tools to create simple layouts.

9.12a The first step in publishing, whether on paper or on the Web, is to plan the layout for the publication. Since a Web site is a hypertext document, a flowchart can make it easier to plan the links between pages. Once the plan is complete, you collect and edit the source documents—the images, articles, and other elements that will make up the finished publication.

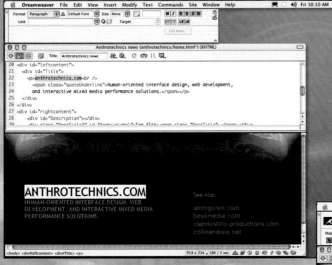

9.12b Dreamweaver Web authoring software enables you to create, view, and edit your pages using both a WYSIWG editor and a text editor that displays the actual HTML code.

9.12c You insert graphical elements, Flash animations, and other multimedia objects into each page. You test each page with various Web browsers to make sure they display everything properly.

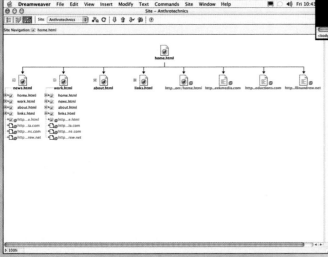

9.12d After testing the partially-completed site with various Web browsers, you compare this site map, created by Dreamweaver, with the original design. When the rest of the pages are completed and tested, you can load the site onto the Web so the world can view it.

- *Frames*—subdivisions of a Web browser's viewing area that enable visitors to scroll and view different parts of a page—or even multiple pages—simultaneously. Many users find frames confusing, and as the Web evolves frames are becoming less common.

- *Forms*—pages that visitors who want to order goods and services, respond to questionnaires, enter contests, express opinions, or add comments to ongoing discussions can fill in.

- *Animation*—moving pictures based on a variety of technologies, from simple repetitive GIF animations to complex interactive animations created with authoring tools such as Macromedia Flash.

- *Search engines*—tools for locating what you're looking for on a site. Most of these site-specific search engines are based on the same technology as Web-wide search engines. Many site builders license search engines from search engine companies.

- *Downloadable audio* clips—compressed sound files that you must download onto your computer's hard disk before the browser or some other application can play them. Some types of audio compression cause significant sound quality degradation. The MP3 compression format is popular because the compressed music files sound almost the same as the uncompressed originals.

- *Downloadable video* clips—compressed video files that you can download and view on a computer. Many are small, short, and jerky, but quality is rapidly improving as new video compression technologies mature.

- Streaming audio files—sounds that play without being completely downloaded to the local hard disk. Some streaming files play automatically while you view a page, providing background music and sound effects. Others, such as sound samples at music stores, play on request. Unlike downloaded media files, you can view or hear streaming media files within seconds, because they play while you're downloading them. For the same reason, streaming media files don't need to be limited to short clips. Concert-length streaming programs are common. High-quality streaming music requires a fast connection and can be interrupted by Internet traffic jams.

- Streaming video files—video clips that play while you're downloading them. Streaming video is even more dependent on high-bandwidth connection than streaming audio.

- *Real-time streaming audio* broadcasts, or *Webcasts*— streaming transmission of radio broadcasts, concerts, news feeds, speeches, and other sound events as they happen. Many Internet radio stations stream around the clock.

9.13 Streaming and downloadable media are available from a variety of Web sites. MSN Radio, shown at top, offers music streams on request. Apple's iTunes Music Store, below, offers hundreds of thousands of downloadable songs.

■ *Real-time streaming video* Webcasts—similar to streaming audio Webcasts, but with video.

■ *3-D environments*—drawn or photographed virtual spaces you can explore with mouse clicks.

■ *Personalization*—customization of content made possible because sites can remember information about guests from visit to visit. Some sites use login names and passwords to remember visitors. Others track and remember using cookies—small files deposited on the visitor's hard disk. Cookies can make online shopping and other activities more efficient and rewarding, but they can also pose a threat to personal privacy.

Today new Web ideas appear at an astounding rate—so fast that browser makers have trouble keeping up. Fortunately, the most popular browsers can be enhanced with plug-ins—software extensions that add new features. When a company introduces a Web innovation—say, a new type of animation—it typically makes a free browser plug-in available to users. Once you download the plug-in and install it in your browser, you can take advantage of any Web pages that include the innovation. Popular plug-ins become standard features in future browser versions, so you don't need to download and install them. Even if a browser can't play or display a particular type of graphics, animation, audio, or video by itself, it might be able to offload the task to a *helper application*—a separate program designed to present that particular media type.

The most popular free cross-platform plug-ins and helper applications include the following:

■ *RealONE* (Real) is one of the most popular programs for playing streaming audio and video, including live Webcasts. RealONE movies and sound files are encoded in proprietary formats so they can't be played with other media players.

■ *Windows Media Player* (Microsoft) is a direct competitor to RealPlayer, delivering streaming media in proprietary formats that are compatible with other players because Microsoft licenses the technology to other companies.

■ *QuickTime* (Apple) also delivers cross-platform streaming media in proprietary formats. QuickTime movies are generally very high quality, at the expense of being larger than the lower-quality media typically associated with RealONE and Windows Media Player.

■ *Shockwave/Flash* (Macromedia) plug-ins enable Web browsers to present compressed interactive multimedia documents and animations created with Flash MX, Director MX, and other authoring tools.

■ *Adobe Reader* and *Acrobat* (Adobe) display documents in *Portable Document Format (PDF)* so they look the same on the screen as on paper, even if the documents are viewed on computers that don't have the same fonts installed. Adobe Reader is a free application that can only display PDF documents, while the Acrobat products allow you to edit and create PDF documents.

9.14 This 3-D pool game is just one of many interactive games available from the Web. Like many online games, this one uses a Shockwave/Flash plugin to display animation and interactive elements.

HTML was originally designed to share scientific research documents—not to deliver media-rich documents in which design is as important as content. By popular demand, the HTML standard has been revised several times to incorporate new features. Newer versions of HTML, sometimes called *dynamic HTML*, allow HTML code to modify itself automatically under certain circumstances. Dynamic HTML supports *cascading style sheets* that can define formatting and layout features that aren't recognized in older versions of HTML.

Dynamic HTML also recognizes *scripts*—short programs—that can add interactivity, animation, and other dynamic features to Web pages. One common use of scripts is to add *rollovers* to onscreen buttons, so they visibly change when the pointer rolls over them. Scripts are typically written in a scripting language called JavaScript. Web pages that take advantage of the latest dynamic HTML features can be more interesting and interactive, but only if they are viewed with newer full-featured browsers. Unscrupulous Web programmers can use scripts to embed viruses and other unwanted elements into your computer. We'll explore these risks in the next chapter.

Dynamic Web Sites: Beyond HTML

HTML is flexible, but it's designed for page layout, not programming. By itself, it can't support online shopping, financial transaction processing, library catalogs, daily newspapers, search engines, and other applications with masses of

> If you thought a Web site consisted of **HTML** pages organized as a directory, **go back to the 20th century**. A successful Web site today consists primarily of **XML** code and a **database**.
>
> —Dana Blankenhorn, coauthor of *Web Commerce: Building a Digital Business*

rapidly changing data. This kind of dynamic Web site requires two things that HTML can't easily deliver: a database to store the constantly changing content of the site, and custom programming to make the appropriate data available to visitors through the Web site.

A **data-driven Web site** can display dynamic, changeable content without having constantly redesigned pages, thanks to a constantly evolving database that separates the content of the site from its design. For example, an online store's Web site doesn't have a separate HTML page for each catalog item. Instead, it has pages that are coded to display product information drawn from a database that can be continually updated. The Web site is a front end for the database; it serves as the visitor's window into the database. Likewise, the database is a data back end for the Web site.

9.15 Amazon.com is the world's largest online retailer, and the site uses massive databases to store items, inventory information, customer data, and transaction information. The dynamic Web site displays data that is personalized for each customer.

It's easy to create a Web site—just about anybody with an Internet connection can do it. It's not so easy to create an effective Web site—one that communicates clearly, attracts visitors, and achieves its goals. Here are a few pointers for making your Web publications work.

➡ **Start with a plan.** The Web is littered with Web sites that seem pointless. Many of those sites were probably constructed without a clear plan or purpose. Start with clear goals and design your entire site with those goals in mind.

➡ **Write for the Web.** Most people won't read long, scrolling documents on computer screens. Limit each page to a couple of screens worth of text. Provide clearly marked links to pages with more details for people who need them. And don't forget to check your spelling and grammar.

➡ **Keep it simple.** Web pages that are cluttered with blinking text, busy backgrounds, repetitive animations, and garish graphics tend to lose their visitors quickly. Stick with clean lines and clear design if you want people to stick around.

➡ **Keep it consistent.** Every page in your site should look like it's related to the other pages in your site. Fonts, graphical elements, colors, buttons, and menus should be consistent from page to page.

➡ **Make it obvious.** Your visitors should be able to tell within a few seconds how your site works. Unless you're building a puzzle palace, make sure the buttons and structure of your site are intuitive.

➡ **Keep it small.** Large photographs, complex animations, video clips, and sounds can make your Web site big and slow to load. People with standard modem connections won't want to wait two minutes for your graphically heavy Web page to load. If you need lots of pictures, use an image-editing program to optimize them for the Web.

➡ **Keep it honest.** Anybody can publish a Web site, without the benefit of an editor. Check your facts before you share your pages with the world.

➡ **Offer contact information.** Web communication shouldn't be one-way. Provide an email address or a form to enable your visitors to contact you. But if you include your email address, expect to receive lots of spam—software Web crawlers are always searching for new addresses on the Web.

➡ **Think like a publisher and a multimedia designer.** The rules of publishing and design, discussed in earlier chapters, apply to Web publishing, too.

➡ **Test before you publish.** Show your work to others—preferably people in your target audience—and watch their reactions carefully. If they get lost, confused, bored, or upset, you probably have more work to do before launching the final site.

➡ **Think before you publish.** It's easy to publish Web pages for the world—at least that part of the world that uses the Web. Don't put anything on your Web pages that you don't want the world to see; you may, for example, be asking for trouble if you publish your home address, your work schedule, and a photo of the expensive computer system in your study.

➡ **Keep it current.** It's easy to build a Web site, and it's even easier to forget to keep it up-to-date. If your Web site is worth visiting, it's worth revising. If the contents of your site are constantly in need of revision, consider using a database to house the data so you can automatically update the site when the data changes.

Programmers use a variety of programming languages for creating dynamic Web sites. The *Perl* scripting language is particularly popular for programming Web servers. Microsoft's Active Server Pages (ASP) and ASP .NET technologies allow programmers to work in their choice of programming languages.

Java, an object-oriented programming language developed by Sun Microsystems, is probably the best-known language for Web programming. (Java and JavaScript have little in common except their names. JavaScript is a simple scripting language for enhancing HTML Web pages; Java is a full-featured cross-platform programming language.) Small Java programs are called *applets* because they're like tiny applications. Java applets can be automatically downloaded onto your client computer through almost any modern Web browser. A Java applet is platform independent; it runs on a Windows PC, a Mac, a UNIX workstation, or anything else as long as the client machine has Java Virtual Machine (JVM) software installed. This JVM software is built into most modern browsers and is available for free download.

Microsoft offers several alternatives to Java. The oldest is *ActiveX*, a collection of programming technologies and tools for creating controls or components—programs that are similar in many ways to Java applets. ActiveX components require a compatible browser, such as Internet Explorer, to run properly.

Experts expect XML (extensible markup language), which includes all of HTML's features plus many additional programming extensions, to replace HTML. XML enables Web developers to control and display data the way they now control text and graphics. Forms, database queries, and other data-intensive operations that can't be completely constructed with standard HTML are much easier with XML. In effect, XML combines a programming language with a page layout language. XML is at the heart of Microsoft's .NET and other competing strategies for developing Web services.

XML isn't the only markup language that's emerging to go beyond the capabilities of HTML. XHTML, a sort of cross between HTML and XML, is backward compatible with HTML, making it easier to upgrade older sites. A subset of XHTML called XHTML basic is especially designed to work with phones, PDAs, and other small-screen wireless devices. XHTML and XHTML basic are designed to work together, so that sites designed with XHTML automatically work on handheld devices. XHTML isn't yet widely used, but it has strong support from the wireless industry and from the World Wide Web Consortium (W3C), an organization that sets standards for the Web. W3C is also developing a standard for SMIL (synchronized multimedia integration language), an HTML-like language designed to make it possible to link time-based streaming media so, for example, sounds, video, and animation can be tightly integrated with each other.

Inside Web Applications

The Web today is far more than a simple hypertext publishing medium. We'll now survey a variety of Web applications, from search engines and portals to peer-to-peer technologies and e-commerce applications.

> For **time** is the **longest distance** between two points.
> —Tennessee Williams

Search Engines

With its vast storehouses of information, the Web is like a huge library. Unfortunately, the Web is a poorly organized library; you might find information on a particular topic almost anywhere. (What can you expect from a library where nobody's in charge?) That's why search engines are among the Web's most popular tools.

All search engines are designed to make it easier to find information on the Web, but they don't all function the same way. A typical search engine uses *web crawlers* or *spiders*—software robots that systematically explore the Web, retrieve information about pages, and index the retrieved information in a database. Different search engines use different search and indexing strategies. For example, one search engine might record detailed information about key words in documents, while another might pay more attention to links to and from other documents. For some search engines, researchers organize and evaluate Web sites in databases; other search engines are almost completely automated.

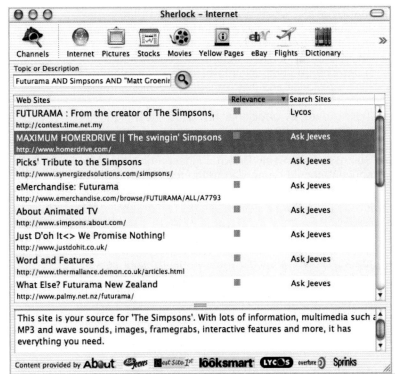

9.16 Apple's Sherlock is a meta-search engine built into Mac OS X that coordinates the results from multiple online search engines.

The Web is so easy to navigate that it's tempting to just dive in. But like a large library, the Web has more to offer if you learn a few tricks and techniques. Your goals should dictate your Web strategy.

➡ **Get to know your search engines.** Try several, choose your favorites, and learn the more advanced search features so you can minimize the time it takes to find what you're looking for. Search Engine Watch (**www.searchenginewatch.com**) is a good source of information about search engines.

➡ **Be specific when you search.** A search engine is more likely to give you the answer you're looking for if you search for "Epson USB scanner" than if you just type "scanner". An even better search would specify the scanner's model number.

➡ **Know your plusses and minuses.** In most search engines you can use a plus sign to signify that you want pages that contain all words. For example, "+Alaska +oil +wildlife" searches pages that contain all three words. On the other hand, a minus sign usually means "not". For example, "cancer −astrology" locates pages that contain "cancer" but not "astrology." When you use these symbols, you're using basic Boolean algebra—the logical basis of database queries.

➡ **Be selective.** As Robert P. Lipshutz wrote in *Mobile Computing*, "A few tidbits of accurate, timely and useful information are worth much more than a ream of random data, and bad information is worse than no information at all." When you're assessing a Web page's credibility, consider the author, the writing, the references, and the page sponsor's objectivity and reliability. Be aware that many of the most popular search engines charge companies to be listed prominently in their directories and that some give top billing to their own services and partners.

➡ **Triangulate.** A traditional navigation technique for sailors, triangulation involves using two points, other than yourself, to establish location. Xerox Chief Scientist John Seely Brown suggests that the same concept should be applied to the turbulent waters of the Web. Don't assume something is true because one Web source tells you so, unless you're sure the source is rock solid.

➡ **Organize your favorites.** When you find a page worth revisiting, record it on your list of favorites or bookmarks. Browsers enable you to organize your lists by category—a strategy that's far more effective than just throwing them all in a digital shoebox.

➡ **Protect your privacy.** Many Web servers keep track of all kinds of data about you: what site you visited before you came, where you clicked, and more. When you fill out forms to enter contests, order goods, or leave messages, you're providing more data for your hosts. Don't divulge any private information about yourself. And make sure you don't leave tracks that you're ashamed of as you hip-hop around the Web.

➡ **Be conscious of cookies and bugs.** Many Web servers send cookies to your browser when you visit them or perform other actions. Cookies are tidbits of information about your session that can be read later; they enable Web sites to remember what they know about you between sessions. Cookies make personalized portals and customized shopping experiences possible. Unfortunately, cookies can also provide all kinds of possibilities for snoopers who want to know how you spend your time online. By default, most browsers don't tell you when they leave a cookie. It's easy to change browser settings so your browser will refuse all cookies; accept cookies from the current site but not so-called third-party sites, such as those sent by advertisements that appear on many Web pages; accept cookies only from selected sites; or ask you, on a cookie-by-cookie basis, whether to accept or refuse cookies. Unfortunately, you can't easily turn off *Web bugs*—one-pixel graphic images that are programmed to send information about your Web use back to their creators.

➡ **Online shopping isn't always better.** In increasing numbers shoppers are abandoning brick-and-mortar stores for click-and-mortar Web stores. Online shops and auctions can save you money, especially if you comparison shop. But when a product doesn't work as advertised, or when you have after-sale questions, a Web merchant might not be as helpful as a local shopkeeper. Some don't even accept phone queries. If your purchase will require person-to-person communication before or after the sale, you're probably better off patronizing a local merchant. But if you must shop online, be sure to frequent reputable sites.

➡ **Shop with bots.** Bots are software robots, or agents, that can explore the Web and report back their findings. Several bots (such as mySimon at **www.mySimon.com**) are designed to help you find low prices by searching the databases of hundreds of merchants.

➡ **Shop with care.** The Web, like the nondigital world, has its share of less-than-honest merchants. Use services such as bizrate (**www.bizrate.com**) to evaluate questionable merchants before you lay your digital money down. If you're dealing with a private party or an unknown merchant, consider using a transaction service such as Paypal (**www.paypal.com**) to serve as a safe temporary depository for funds until the purchased product reaches you.

➡ **Remember why you're there.** The Web's extensive hyperlinks make it all too easy to wander off course when you're searching for important information. If you're using the Web to save time, stay focused or you may find that the Web costs more time than it saves.

Most search engines enable you to type queries using key words, just as you might locate information in other types of databases. You can construct complex queries using *Boolean logic* (for example, American AND Indian BUT NOT Cleveland), quotations, and other tools for refining queries. Some search engines enable you to narrow your search repeatedly by choosing subcategories from a hierarchical *directory* or *subject tree*. Whatever search technique you use, you're eventually presented with a rank-ordered list of Web pages. A page might go undetected by one search engine and appear at the top of a list on another. That's why some researchers still use *meta-search engines* such as MetaCrawler, OneSeek, and Apple's Sherlock—software tools that conduct parallel searches using several different search engines and directories. Of course, getting more hits isn't necessarily better. The best search engines provide you with relatively few high-quality results rather than overwhelming you with marginally relevant links.

Some popular search engines are designed to search for specific types of information. Specialized search engines can help you locate email addresses and phone numbers; others can help you find the lowest prices on the Web. These specialized search engines generally use technology similar to general search engine technology.

Most search engines have access to less than 1 percent of the pages on the Web. The rest are out of reach of the public or stored in databases that can't be searched by conventional search engines. Some search engines, including **invisibleweb.com**, can provide access to information in those databases. Web search technology continues to evolve with the Web.

Portals

Many Web sites that started out as search engines have evolved into portals—Web entry stations that offer quick and easy access to a variety of services. Popular general-interest portals include Yahoo!, MSN, and Netscape Netcenter. *Consumer portals* feature search engines, email services, chat rooms, references, news and sports headlines, shopping malls, other services, and advertisements—many of the same things found in online services such as AOL. You can personalize many of the portals so they automatically display local weather and sports scores, personalized TV and movie listings, news headlines related to particular subjects, horoscopes, and ads to meet your interests. Most browsers enable users to choose a home page that opens by default when the browser is launched; portals are designed with this feature in mind.

In addition to these general-interest portals, the Web has a growing population of specialized portals. *Corporate portals* on intranets serve the employees of particular corporations. *Vertical portals*, or *vortals*, like vertical market software (Chapter 4) target members of a particular industry or economic sector. For example, **webmd.com** is a portal for medically minded consumers and health-care professionals. A growing number of specialized portals are competing to be your browser's home page.

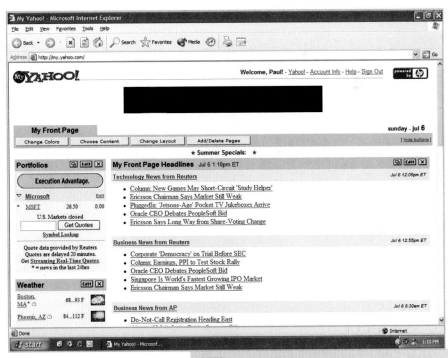

9.17 Like other Web portals, the popular Yahoo! site can be personalized to highlight news, weather, sports, and other information specified by the user.

Push Technology: Notifications and Alerts

> **We think we "surf"** the Web now, but what we really do is hopscotch across fragile stepping-stones of texts, or worse, spelunk in a vast unmapped cave of documents. Only when **waves of media** begin to cascade behind our screens—huge swells of unbrowsable stuff—will we truly surf.
>
> —Kevin Kelly and Gary Wolf, former *Wired* editors

The Web was built with pull technology—browsers on client computers pull information from server machines. With pull technology the browser needs to initiate a request before any information is delivered. But for some applications, it makes more sense to have information delivered automatically to the client computer. That's the way push technology works.

With push technology you subscribe to a service or specify the kinds of information you want to receive and the server delivers that information periodically and unobtrusively. Maybe you want up-to-the-minute weather maps displayed in a small window in the corner of your screen. You might prefer to see news headlines (on subjects of your choice) scroll across the top of your screen. You may want to automatically receive new product descriptions from selected companies. Or you might like to have the software on your hard disk automatically upgraded when upgrades are posted on the Web. All of this is possible with push technology.

Technically speaking, today's push technology is really pull technology in disguise. Your computer quietly and automatically pulls information from selected Web servers based on your earlier requests or subscriptions. As convenient as they are, push programs have the same basic problem as Web search engines: They give you what they think you want, but they may not be very smart. Their ability to deliver what you really need—without bombarding you with unwanted data—will get better as artificial intelligence technology improves.

In the meantime, push technology is used mostly for in-house delivery of information on intranets. Outside of the corporate enterprise, most push technology takes the form of *notifications* and *alerts*, services to which you've subscribed. Some notifications and alerts are free. For example, free MSN Alerts services include stock price changes, breaking news from MSNBC, and online auction statuses from eBay.com. Other alerts include fees. For example, MSN subscribers can get scheduling and to-do alerts. Email continues to be the single form of push technology that has been embraced by almost all Internet users.

Peer-to-Peer and Grid Computing

> The **genie** does not **go back** in the bottle—**period**.
>
> —Tom Peters, business guru and best-selling author

Of all the companies that came out of nowhere during the dot-com boom of the late '90s, Napster generated the most conversation—and controversy. When 19-year-old college student Shawn Fanning put a friendly user interface and a fresh spin on decades-old file-sharing technology, he created a virtual swap meet for students and others who wanted to share MP3 music files. Almost overnight Napster became one of the hottest Internet destinations, with millions of users downloading and sharing MP3s daily using Napster's software. In May of 2000, a tech company hired by the rock band Metallica revealed that 322,000 Napster users were illegally distributing their music. The Recording Industry Association of America sued the company because its software enabled users to download copyrighted recordings without paying the record companies or artists.

The Napster servers didn't contain those illegal recordings—it just displayed links to recordings scattered all over the Net. People who used Napster practiced peer-to-peer (P2P) computing—or, more specifically, *peer-to-peer file sharing*—by making music files on their hard drives available to others rather than posting them on central servers. In

April of 2001, a U.S. District Court judge ruled that Napster was violating federal copyright law and forced the company to change its software so that users no longer had free access to copyrighted recordings. Napster changed its software and its business model, but the peer-to-peer music exchange lived on through other programs and Web sites. The Gnutella file-sharing system, used by several different file-sharing programs, avoids Napster's legal problems by allowing users to share music, movies, and other files without going through a central directory. According to some experts, Gnutella's rapid growth suggests that it may become a Web standard.

Technologies like Gnutella make it difficult—or impossible—for laws to contain the peer-to-peer file-sharing phenomenon. Recording artists are divided on the issue; some encourage fans to share their music, while others fear that sharing will make it difficult for musicians to support themselves. A growing collection of legitimate music downloading services, such as the Apple iTunes Music Store—which let consumers inexpensively purchase songs and albums digitally online—provide consumers with a legal way to download music. (Copyright and intellectual property issues are discussed in more detail in the next chapter.)

Music sharing is just one application of peer-to-peer computing. The technology is being applied to a growing number of diverse applications. Books, movies, and computer software are shared using peer-to-peer technology—and with the same legal and ethical concerns. Businesses use P2P for group collaboration, for Web searches, and for sharing updates to virus-control software, among other things.

A related technology—grid computing—is, like P2P, a form of *distributed computing*. But grid computing isn't about sharing files; it's about sharing processing power. The best-known example is SETI@Home (**setiathome .ssl.berkeley.edu/**), a program that puts PCs all over the Internet together into a sort of virtual supercomputer that analyzes space telescope data in the search for extraterrestrial life. The SETI@Home program, when installed on a PC, uses the computer's idle time to do calculations and send the

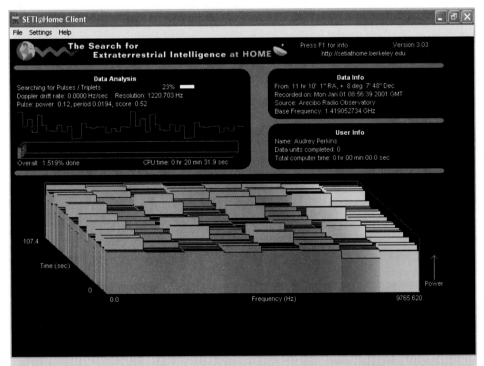

9.18 The SETI@Home project synchronizes the processing power of various connected computers from around the world. Anyone can donate their unused PC time to SETI@Home; the freely downloadable application starts up whenever your PC is not being used.

results back to SETI headquarters. Millions of PCs around the world can do the work of a million-dollar supercomputer in much less time. A similar program called FightAIDS@home (**fightaidsathome.com**) enables PCs to contribute spare processing cycles to the fight against AIDS.

Grid computing may soon extend far beyond these processor-sharing programs to a new Internet model that resembles a utility grid. IBM and other companies are supporting initiatives to build a grid-computing environment where anyone can plug in from anywhere and rent processing power and software from anywhere on the Net. Grid-computing applications are currently being used by the U.S. Department of Defense, the U.S. Depart-ment of Energy, NASA, the U.K National Grid, and a variety of academic and scientific communities.

Intranets, Extranets, and Electronic Commerce

> Our customers are **moving at Internet speed**. They need us to **respond** at Internet speed.
>
> —Laurie Tucker, Federal Express vice president

For many businesses, Internet protocols and software are almost as important as the Net itself. Members of these organizations communicate through intranets—self-contained intraorganizational networks that are designed using the same technology as the Internet. A typical intranet offers email, newsgroups, file transfer, Web publishing, and other Internet-like services, but not all of these services are available to people outside the organization. For example, an intranet Web document might be accessible only to company employees—not to the entire Internet community. If an intranet has a gateway connection to the Internet, the gateway probably has some kind of *firewall* to prevent unauthorized communication and to secure sensitive internal data.

Some private TCP/IP networks are designed for outside use by customers, clients, and business partners of the organization. These networks, often called extranets, are typically for electronic commerce (e-commerce)—business transactions through electronic networks. Most use *electronic data interchange (EDI)*—a decade-old set of specifications for ordering, billing, and paying for parts and services over private networks.

Some extranets are virtual private networks that use encryption software (described in the next chapter) to create secure "tunnels" through the public Internet. Others use their own lines or lease lines that aren't subject to the traffic and security problems of the public Internet. Extranets are especially useful for business-to-business (B2B) e-commerce—transactions that involve businesses providing goods or services to other businesses.

Business-to-consumer (B2C) e-commerce generally involves transactions that take place on the Internet, rather than an extranet, because consumers don't have access to private extranets. The Internet has spawned a wide variety of B2C businesses, including

- *Online catalog sales.* Online catalogs save paper, and they offer other advantages for consumers, including search engines, immediate availability reports, custom orders, and instant updates. But some types of merchandise don't lend themselves to online sales, and online customers can be frustrated by confusing user interfaces and minimal customer support.
- *Auctions.* The Internet makes long-distance auctions practical, allowing people to bid on all kinds of items. Some retail outlets use auctions to move clearance merchandise; some sites sell everything through auctions.
- *Reverse auctions.* Some sites allow customers to request goods or services and have merchants bid on prices. Everything from airline tickets to legal services is offered through reverse auctions.
- *Comparison shopping.* Specialized search engines search the Web for the lowest prices.
- *Financial services.* Checks, credit cards, and stocks are all available online.

B-to-C sites can offer a high degree of personalization—for example, suggesting products similar to the ones already ordered by a customer, or remembering a customer's personal preferences and sizes between visits. But personalization raises privacy and security concerns in many customers. (Security issues are discussed in detail in the next chapter.)

E-commerce is changing the way many companies do business. But e-commerce isn't cheap or easy. Profits have proven to be elusive for many online companies. Like the brick-and-mortar world, the Internet presents challenges along with opportunities for enterprising business people.

Web Services

Software costs can be daunting for companies that have to build e-commerce sites from the ground up. Several of the computer industry's biggest companies, including IBM, Hewlett Packard, Microsoft, Oracle, and Sun, are developing software tools to make e-commerce solutions easier to build and maintain. These systems have different names and features, but they all fall into a software category called *Web services*. Web services involve new kinds of Web-based applications that can be assembled quickly using existing *software components*. Component technology can, for example, make it easy to plug a shopping-cart component into an existing Web site or to design applications that can be accessed through a variety of Web-enabled devices. XML plays an important role in most Web services systems currently under development.

Unfortunately, the industry hasn't agreed on the details of this emerging technology. Sun, Hewlett Packard, and IBM are using Java to build their cross-platform service tools. Microsoft's .NET uses a wider variety of languages, including C#, which runs only on Windows platforms today, but is being ported to other platforms, including Linux. The open source community is working to port even more of .NET to Linux, hoping to keep .NET from being a proprietary system, and they're getting help from Microsoft. Meanwhile, the W3C is attempting to create Web services standards that the entire industry can embrace.

Pervasive Web services systems are still many years away. But they offer great hope for companies struggling with the challenges of creating successful e-commerce sites. Hints of the future are all over the Web. The popular online store Amazon.com pioneered Web services by letting developers freely access their back-end databases using .NET technology. And *Passport*, a .NET-based user authentication service, is used by hundreds of millions of Hotmail and MSN users to provide secure logons to the system from any PC on the planet. In the future, Web services will be as prevalent on the Web as actual Web sites. We just won't realize they're working silently in the background, like the electricity we take for granted today.

The Evolving Internet

The Internet started as a small community of scientists, engineers, and other researchers who staunchly defended the noncommercial, cooperative charter of the network. Today, the Net has swollen into a community of millions, including everybody from children to corporate executives. The rate of growth is so great that it raises questions about the Internet's ability to keep up; the amount of information transmitted may eventually be more than the Net can handle.

In the short term, the **impact** of new technologies like the Internet will be **less than the hype** would suggest. But in the long term, it will be vastly **larger than we can imagine** today.
—Paul Saffo, director of the Institute for the Future

The U.S. government no longer assumes primary responsibility for Internet expansion. Many funding and administrative duties have been passed on to private companies, allowing businesses to commercialize the Net. In 1995, for the first time, the number of commercial host sites on the Net exceeded the number of noncommercial sites. In the three-year period that followed, the Net experienced a hundredfold increase in monthly traffic.

Internet2 and the Next Generation Internet

As the Internet evolves into the network of the masses, congestion becomes more problematic for the scientists and researchers who made up the original Internet community. The U.S. government, working in conjunction with several large corporations, launched Internet2 in 1998 to provide faster network communications for universities and research institutions. A related effort from DARPA, the *Next Generation Internet (NGI)*, will consist of a nationwide web of optical fiber integrated with intelligent management software to maintain high-speed connections.

Internet2 will eventually be capable of transmitting data at 9.6 billion bits per second—enough to send all 30 volumes of the Encyclopedia Britannica in 1 second. Internet2 isn't available for commercial or recreational use; it is reserved for research and academic work. Participating universities are building virtual laboratories, digital libraries, telemedicine research facilities, and distance learning applications that take advantage of its tremendous bandwidth. The rest of us will undoubtedly inherit the technologies developed for Internet2.

Internet Issues: Ethical and Political Dilemmas

> **The Internet** still hasn't figured out how to **conduct itself in public**. . . . Everybody is trying to **develop the rules** by which they can conduct themselves in order to keep a **civil operation** going and not **self-destruct**.
>
> —George Lucas, filmmaker

The commercialization of the Internet has opened a floodgate of new services to users. People are logging into the Internet to view weather patterns, book flights, buy stocks, sell cars, track deliveries, listen to radio broadcasts from around the world, conduct videoconferences, coordinate disaster recovery programs, and do countless other private and public transactions. The Internet saves time, money, and lives, but it brings problems, too.

Computer Addiction

One growing problem is *computer addiction*. For a few hard-core networkers the world on the other side of the modem is more real and more interesting than the everyday physical world. One Alaskan reader wrote to advice columnist Ann Landers: "Computer chat lines can become every bit as addictive as cocaine. I have been hooked on both, and it was easier to get off coke." While this may seem strange, it's not unique. Many people feel the same way about television, spectator sports, or romance novels. Internet addiction, like any addiction, can be a serious problem—for individuals and for society. The problem is growing as more people go online, and no quick fixes are in sight.

Freedom's Abuses

Other problems relate more to greed than need. Commercialization has brought capitalism's dark side to the Internet. Spam scams, get-rich-quick hoaxes, online credit card thefts, email forgery, child pornography hustling, illegal gambling, Web site sabotage, online stalking, and other sleazy activities abound. The Internet has clearly lost its innocence.

Some of these problems have at least partial technological solutions. Concerned parents and teachers can now install filtering software that, for the most part, keeps children out of Web sites that contain inappropriate content. Commercial Web sites routinely use encryption so customers can purchase goods and services without fear of having credit card numbers stolen by electronic eavesdroppers. Several software companies and banks are developing systems for circulating digital cash on the Internet to make online transactions easier and safer. To protect against email forgery, many software companies are working together to hammer out standards for *digital signatures* using encryption techniques described in the next chapter.

Many problems associated with the rapid growth and commercialization of the Internet are social problems that raise important political questions. Online hucksterism and pornography have prompted government controls on Internet content, including the 1996 Communications Decency Act. Opponents to this law and other proposed controls argue that it's important to preserve the free flow of information; they stress the need to protect our rights to free speech and privacy on the Net. In 1996 the U.S. Supreme Court declared the Communications Decency Act unconstitutional, arguing that "the interest in encouraging freedom of expression in a democratic society outweighs any theoretical but unproven benefit of censorship." Nevertheless, the legal battle is certain to continue.

9.19 As part of the nonprofit Tech Corps program, these computer professionals volunteer their time and skills to help students and teachers put technology to good use.

In December of 2000, Congress passed the Children's Internet Protection Act. The act requires public libraries and schools that receive certain types of federal funding install content filters on computers with Internet access. Like the Communications Decency Act, the Children's Internet Protection Act faces legal challenges based on the First Amendment to the Constitution.

Questions about human rights online probably won't be resolved by legislators and judges, though. The Internet's global reach makes it nearly impossible for a single government to regulate it. Even if the governments of the world agree to try to restrict information flow, the Net seems to have developed a mind of its own. The same decentralized, packet-switching technology that was designed to protect government messages from enemy attack today protects civilian messages from government or corporate control. In the words of Internet pioneer John Gilmore, "The Net interprets censorship as damage and routes around it."

Universal Access Issues

During the 1990s the U.S. government pushed for the development of a National Information Infrastructure (NII)—an affordable, secure, high-speed network to provide "universal service" for all Americans. Probably the biggest roadblock to realizing the dream of NII is the digital divide that separates computer haves from have-nots.

Today more than half of the U.S. population has easy access to the Internet—a subset of America that excludes many poor people and minorities. Government programs to wire schools, libraries, and other public facilities have increased access for disadvantaged populations. But many Internet services that used to be free for all are now available only to paying customers. Families can't buy computers or Internet service if they're having trouble paying the rent. The problem of equal access isn't likely to go away without combined efforts of governments, businesses, and individuals.

Even if America achieves a universal-access NII, access issues still confront the rest of the world. The Internet is a global infrastructure, but huge populations all over the world are locked out. Many experts fear that we'll leave those populations behind as we move further into the information age. This kind of information stratification could be harmful to all of us unless we find ways to unlock the Internet for everybody who wants it.

Cyberspace: The Electronic Frontier

Cyberspace. **A consensual hallucination** experienced daily by billions of legitimate operators, **in every nation**, by children being taught mathematical concepts. . . . A graphic representation of data abstracted from the banks of **every computer in the human system. Unthinkable complexity**. Lines of light ranged in the nonspace of the mind, clusters and constellations of data. Like city lights, receding. . . .

—William Gibson, in *Neuromancer*

Science fiction writers suggest that tomorrow's networks will take us beyond the Internet into an artificial reality that has come to be known as cyberspace, a term coined by William Gibson in his visionary novel *Neuromancer*.

In *Neuromancer*, as in earlier works by Vernor Vinge and others, travelers experience the universal computer network as if it were a physical place, a shared virtual reality, complete with sights, sounds, and other sensations. Gibson's cyberspace is an abstract, cold landscape in a dark and dangerous future world. Vinge's novella *True Names* takes place in a network hideaway where adventurous computer wizards never reveal their true names or identities to each other. Instead, they take on mythical identities with supernatural abilities.

Today's computer networks are still light-years from the futuristic visions of Vinge and Gibson. But the Net today *is* a primitive cyberspace—a world where messages, mathematics, and money can cross continents in seconds. People from all over the planet meet, develop friendships, and share their innermost thoughts and feelings in cyberspace.

John Perry Barlow, cofounder of the Electronic Frontier Foundation, has called the online world an "electronic frontier," suggesting parallels to America's Old West. Until recently, the electronic frontier was populated mostly by free-spirited souls willing to forgo creature comforts. These digital pioneers built the roads and towns that are used today by less adventurous settlers and business interests.

9.20 Cindy Price and Josh Marquis met on an AOL message board devoted to the O. J. Simpson trial in 1995. They were married in 1996.

In spite of its rapid commercialization, the electronic frontier is far from tame. Network nomads pick digital locks and ignore electronic fences. Some explore nooks and crannies out of a spirit of adventure. Others steal and tamper with private information for profit or revenge. Charlatans and hustlers operate outside the law. Law enforcement agencies and lawmakers occasionally overreact.

There's a strong sentiment on the Net toward keeping controls to a minimum. Netizens commonly argue that the Web will always be free of control because of the way it's constructed. It's true that governments have so far had trouble regulating many Internet activities. But there's no guarantee that the free-spirited Internet will always remain that way.

In *The Code and Other Laws of Cyberspace*, Lawrence Lessig claims that, because of commerce and other forces, an architecture of control is being built into the Net—control by government and by businesses intent on maximizing Net profits. Lessig argues that the code—the way the Net is programmed—will determine how much freedom we have in the future Internet. "We can build, or architect, or code cyberspace to protect values we believe are fundamental, or we can build, or architect, or code cyberspace to allow those values to disappear. There is no middle ground. There is no choice that does not include some kind of *building*."

There are parallels in the nondigital world. Many city planning experts argue that industrialized nations have systematically (if not consciously) rebuilt their cities so that, in many places, it's just about impossible to live without a car. These car-centered cities have generated revenue for businesses and governments, and they've brought a new sense of freedom to many citizens. But for the poor, the disabled, the young, the old, and others who can't drive, these cities are anything but free. At the same time, other cities have thriving masses of car-free people. Design choices (and nonchoices) made decades ago determine the livability of our cities today.

In the same way, the design decisions being made today by software architects, corporate managers, government officials, and concerned citizens will determine the nature of our Internet experiences in the future. Will portals guide us to corporate-approved information sources? Will Netizens feel free to express controversial opinions and criticize powerful institutions without fear of lawsuits and prosecution? Will paths through cyberspace be accessible to everyone? As Mark Stefik says in *Internet Dreams: Archetypes, Myths, and Metaphors*, "Different versions of [cyberspace] support different kinds of dreams. We choose, wisely or not."

In the future, **everything with a digital heartbeat** will be connected to the Internet.

—Scott McNealy, CEO
of Sun Microsystems

Where is the Internet heading? Vint Cerf, one of the Internet's founders, thinks it's headed for space. He's putting much of his time and energy into a project called InterPlaNet, which he hopes will extend the Internet to the other planets in our solar system. According to the plan, electronic "post offices" will orbit other planets, routing messages between space explorers, both human and robot. The obstacles are significant—a message from Mars to Earth can take 20 minutes or more to reach Earth, an intolerably long time for Internet servers that "time out" if they don't receive messages quickly. According to Cerf, "the interplanetary network is an example of a much more general concept we call delay-tolerant networks." Even if you aren't expecting email from the red planet, the research being done on InterPlaNet may result in more reliable Internet for you here on Earth.

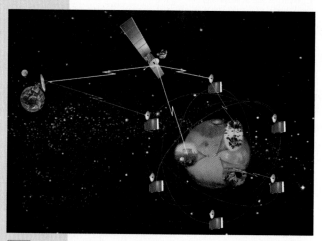

9.21 A visualization of the Marsnet proposed by Vint Cerf.

Whatever happens with InterPlaNet, tomorrow's Net surfers will find it easier to locate what they're looking for on the Web. Tim Berners-Lee, the inventor of the Web, is planning a *Semantic Web*—a Web full of data that's meaningful to computers as well as humans. With a Semantic Web, search engines will be able to deliver exactly what you're looking for instead of bombarding you with hundreds of possibility pages. Here's how Berners-Lee described it to the *Boston Globe*: "You'll tell a search engine, 'find me someplace where the weather is currently rainy and it's within a hundred miles of such and such a city.'…. A search engine… will come back and say, 'Look, I found

this place and I can prove to you why I know that it's raining and why I know it's within a hundred miles of this place.' So you'll be dealing with much firmer information."

Technology forecaster Paul Saffo suggests a blurring of the boundaries between the Web and interpersonal communication applications. When we visit a Web site that's being explored by hundreds of other people, we'll actually be able to experience their presence and interact with them in ways that go beyond today's simple chat rooms. In Saffo's words, "We're going to shift away from a model of people accessing information to a model of people accessing other people in an information-rich environment. The information will become the wallpaper surrounding conversational space."

We may be sharing Web space with more people in the future, but we'll also be sharing it with all kinds of gadgets. Today we think of the Web as a network of computers, but the Web isn't just for PCs, mainframes, and servers anymore. A variety of Internet appliances,

9.22 A smart refrigerator with Internet connectivity.

network computers, set-top boxes, PDAs, mobile phones, and other devices are being connected to the Internet in offices and homes. Everything from coffee makers to traffic lights may be routinely connected to the Web soon. Consider the possibilities:

You tell your alarm clock to wake you in time to catch the 8:00 A.M. flight to Washington. At 5:00 A.M. the clock checks the airline's Web site and determines that the flight has been delayed an hour. It also checks online traffic reports and finds that traffic is light. The clock resets your wakeup time accordingly, giving you an extra hour of sleep. As usual, it turns on the heat and the coffee maker 10 minutes before it wakes you. On the way to the airport, your car routes you around a congested construction spot. When you arrive at the airport, it tells you where to find a vacant parking spot close to the terminal.

Whether you consider this future fantasy appealing or appalling, the technology is on the horizon. One thing is clear: The Web is changing so fast it's impossible for anybody to predict exactly what it will look like even a few months from today.

Info With a Ball and Chain Steven Levy

Steven Levy has eloquently written for years about the human is-sues raised by the Internet. In this article, first published in the June 23, 2003 issue of Newsweek, *Levy looks at the hard ques-tions raised by online music distribution.*

When Steve Jobs introduced the iTunes music store a few weeks ago, the acclaim was nearly universal. Nonetheless, a small but vocal minority viewed the online emporium as a menace—because the iTunes program somewhat limits a consumer's ability to copy and share songs.

Even though Apple had broken ground by getting the record labels to accept fairly liberal terms of use—Apple-oids could listen to purchased songs on three computers and burn CDs—this bunch objected to any restrictions at all. They saw the iTunes store as a sugar-coated induce-ment for consumers to accept a new reality: some stuff on your computer isn't really under your control. And as far as that goes, the critics are right. Say goodbye to the "Information Wants to Be Free" era. We're entering the age of digital ankle bracelets.

The key to this shift is the technology that protects in-formation from unauthorized or illegal use. It's called digi-tal-rights-management software, or DRM. Like it or not, rights management is increasingly going to be a fact of your life. Not only will music, books and movies be steeped in it, but soon such mundane artifacts as docu-ments, spreadsheet files and e-mail will be joining the do-main of restricted information. In fact, the next version of Microsoft Office will enable creators of certain documents to issue restrictions that dictate who, if anyone, can read them, copy them or forward them. In addition, you can specify that the files and mail you send may "sunset" after a specified period of time, evaporating like the little tapes dead-dropped to Peter Graves in "Mission: Impossible."

On the one hand, it seems that digital-rights manage-ment is a no-brainer. What's wrong with media compa-nies' building in antitheft devices to protect their property? And shouldn't the creator of a document or e-mail be able to determine who can read or copy it? Surely, piracy is to be condemned and privacy to be cherished: DRM can go a long way toward implementing both those sentiments.

But certain critics consider the very concept anath-ema. "I don't think that DRM is in and of itself evil," says David Weinberger, who recently published an essay in *Wired* titled "Copy Protection Is a Crime Against Humanity." "But in the real world, it is evil. There's no user demand for it. It's being forced upon us by people with vested interests."

Edward Felten, a Princeton computer scientist, be-lieves that DRM perverts the basic deal of the Internet: the free flow of information benefits all. "The basic prob-lem is that DRM is trying to turn information into some-thing other than information so you can't pass it on," he says. "People want to control their technology, and the more the technology is eroded, the harder it is to use."

DRM's defenders say that the technology actually em-powers users. Without protections, entertainment compa-nies would never release their products in the digital market-place. Microsoft's Erin Cullen says that DRM software is flexible enough to limit illegal uses (like shar-ing a song with millions of "friends" on the Net) while allowing consumers to enjoy music and films in ways they always have.

In practice, though, DRM can stifle legal activity, too. For instance, copy protection on DVDs blocks not only il-legal copying, but the "fair use" ability to copy a frame or short scene into a home movie or school project. (To do this, you have to break the copy-protection scheme—an act that is specifically outlawed by the anticonsumer Digital Millennium Copyright Act.)

Critics like Weinberger also complain that computers enforcing DRM systems lack "the essential leeway by which ideas circulate." Sure, Microsoft rights manage-ment will allow creators to set the rules. But will corpora-tions dictate that every e-mail message and document be fitted with a virtual ball and chain: *no copying . . . no forwarding . . . no amending . . . no archiving*? Whistle-blowers won't be able to do what they do," says Joe Kraus of DigitalConsumer.org.

Even Congress, which has so far ignored consumers and coddled rights holders on copy protection, is waking up. Sen. Sam Brownback, a Kansas Republican, is about to introduce a bill "to ensure that our nation's media pro-ducers and distributors do not clamp down on the ways in which [consumers] traditionally and legally use media products."

We do need legislative help in keeping DRM under control. But ultimately, its fate will be determined by our own actions. As we have with the iTunes store, we'll vote with our dollars when we're satisfied that restrictions on our music and movies allow us the access we need. And corporations may well come to understand that it's bad policy to strictly hobble the flow of information. Will we suf-fer the worst-case DRM scenario: a world so constricted that we can't cut or paste a line from a poem, or forward the latest sick Internet joke to our buddies? I doubt it. But I do think that the files that arrive in our in boxes and juke-boxes will be on tighter leashes. And while I understand the reasoning for this, the prospect doesn't gladden my heart.

DISCUSSION QUESTIONS

1. Do you agree with David Weinberger's statement that, in the real world, DRM is evil? Why or why not?

2. Do you agree with the provision in the Digital Millennium Copyright Act that makes it illegal to copy a frame or short scene into a home movie or school project? Explain your answer.

SUMMARY

The Internet is a network of networks that connects all kinds of computers around the globe. It grew out of a military research network designed to provide reliable communication even if part of the network failed. The Internet uses standard protocols to allow internet communication to occur. No single organization owns or controls the Internet.

You can connect to the Internet in any of several ways; these ways provide different degrees of access to Internet services. A direct connection provides the most complete and fastest service, but users can also access most Internet information through modem connections. Broadband connections approach direct connection speeds, but they aren't universally available. Several online services have gateways to the Internet; these gateways enable users to access Internet information resources and send and receive Internet mail.

Most Internet applications are based on the client/server model. The user interface for these applications varies depending on the type of connection and the type of client software used by the user. A user might type UNIX commands to a host computer or use point-and-click tools on a personal computer. Different types of servers provide different kinds of Internet services, ranging from mail to the Web.

The earliest Web pages were simple hypertext pages; today the World Wide Web contains thousands of complex, media-rich structures that offer visitors a wealth of choices. The Web uses a set of protocols to make a variety of Internet services and multimedia documents available to users through a simple point-and-click interface. Web pages are generally constructed using a language called HTML. Many Web authoring tools automate the coding of HTML pages, making it easy for nonprogrammers to write and publish their own pages. Other languages and techniques are being

developed to extend the power of the Web in ways that go beyond the capabilities of HTML. Today, most large interactive Web sites are database-driven, so content can be updated automatically.

In addition to Web sites, a variety of applications are built on the protocols of the Internet and the Web. For example, people who use the Web depend on search engines to find the information they need. Search engines use a combination of automated searching and indexed databases to catalog Web resources.

Peer-to-peer computing was popularized by music sharing services, but its applications go beyond music sharing. Many businesses are exploring ways to apply P2P technology. Grid computing goes beyond P2P computing by enabling people to share processor power with others. Some organizations are working to build a grid-computing model that would make the Internet work like a shared utility.

E-commerce is built on Internet technology. Businesses use the Internet and the Web for business-to-business and business-to-customer communication. Many businesses have private networks, called intranets, based on Internet technology. Extranets are also private networks based on the same technology; extranets enable businesses to connect with their partners and customers without going through public Internet channels.

As the Internet grows and changes, issues of privacy, security, censorship, criminal activity, universal access, and appropriate Net behavior are surfacing. Even more questions will arise when all kinds of electronic devices are attached to the Web, communicating with each other from our homes, our offices, and our vehicles. We have many questions to answer as the Internet evolves from an electronic frontier into a futuristic cyberspace.

KEY TERMS

application server (ASP) (p. 318)
application service provider (ASP)
  (p. 318)
blog (p. 321)
broadband connections (p. 313)
business-to-business (B2B) (p. 332)
business-to-consumer (B2C) (p. 332)
cable modems (p. 315)
compression (p. 317)
cookie (p. 324)
cyberspace (p. 336)
data-driven Web site (p. 325)
dial-up connection (p. 313)

digital cash (p. 334)
digital divide (p. 335)
direct (dedicated) connection (p. 313)
download (p. 317)
DSL (digital subscriber line)
  (p. 313)
electronic commerce (e-commerce)
  (p. 332)
email server (p. 317)
extranets (p. 332)
file transfer protocol (FTP) (p. 317)
filtering software (p. 334)
grid computing (p. 331)

HTML (hypertext markup language)
  (p. 318)
Internet2 (p. 334)
Internet service providers (p. 315)
internetworking (p. 309)
intranets (p. 332)
Java (p. 326)
JavaScript (p. 325)
narrowband connections (p. 313)
open standards (p. 309)
packet-switching (p. 311)
peer-to-peer (P2P) computing (p. 330)
plug-in (p. 324)

portal (p. 329)
pull technology (p. 330)
push technology (p. 330)
satellite Internet connections (p. 315)
SMIL (synchronized multimedia
 integration language) (p. 327)
streaming audio (p. 323)
streaming video (p. 323)

TCP/IP (Transmission Control
 Protocol/Internet Protocol)
 (p. 309)
uniform resource locator (URL)
 (p. 318)
upload (p. 317)
virtual private networks (p. 332)
Web authoring software (p. 321)

Weblog (or blog) (p. 321)
Web server (p. 318)
Web services (p. 333)
Wi–Fi (p. 315)
World Wide Web (WWW) (p. 318)
XHTML (p. 327)
XML (extensible markup language)
 (p. 327)

INTERACTIVE QUIZ QUESTIONS

1. The *Computer Confluence* CD-ROM contains self-test quiz questions related to this chapter, including multiple-choice, true or false, and matching questions.

2. The *Computer Confluence* Web site, http://www.prenhall.com/beekman, contains self-test exercises related to this chapter. Follow the instructions for taking a quiz. After you've completed your quiz, you can email the results to your instructor.

3. The Web site also contains open-ended discussion questions called Internet Explorations. Discuss one or more of the Internet Exploration questions at the section for this chapter.

TRUE OR FALSE

1. The Internet was originally built on the assumption that all computers on the network would be equal in their ability to communicate with each other.

2. Because of its strongly centralized design, the Internet can withstand most attacks.

3. When a digital video file is sent on the Internet, it is broken into packets that travel independently to the designated destination.

4. The TCP/IP protocols at the heart of the Internet were published as open standards, not owned by any company.

5. The words in a domain name, like the lines in a post office address, are arranged hierarchically from little to big.

6. Technically, every Web URL begins with http://, although most browsers don't require you to type it.

7. Streaming video is distinguished from downloadable video by the fact that it is always real time—that is, it presents events as they happen.

8. Many Internet shopping sites use cookies to keep track of customer orders and preferences.

9. Peer-to-peer file sharing is almost always illegal, but many people do it anyway.

10. Internet2 is designed to replace the current Internet for most commercial applications within the decade.

MULTIPLE CHOICE

1. The Internet was originally a
   a. LAN at MIT.
   b. code-cracking network during World War II by the US Defense Department.
   c. network cooperatively created by several large hardware and software companies.
   d. small experimental research network called ARPANET.
   e. Microsoft product that quickly became too big for the company to control.

2. The Internet's central hub and control center is strategically located
   a. near Washington D.C.
   b. near the Microsoft campus in Redmond, Washington.
   c. in a top-secret location.
   d. in Silicon Valley.
   e. Nowhere; the Internet has no central hub.

3. Which of these domains is restricted to qualified organizations?
   a. .com
   b. .org
   c. .net
   d. .edu
   e. None are restricted; anyone can have a URL in any of these domains.

4. Which of these types of Internet connections is typically the slowest?
   a. direct connection through T1 lines.
   b. dial-up modem connections through phone lines.
   c. DSL connections through phone lines.
   d. cable modem connections through cable TV lines.
   e. satellite connections through satellite dishes.

5. Specialized servers are used on the Internet to
   a. function like email post offices.
   b. accept FTP requests to upload and download files.
   c. store applications that are rented or leased by large corporations.
   d. store and send Web pages.
   e. All of the above.

6. The first Web pages were
   a. strictly hypertext with no multimedia content.
   b. designed to simulate printed pages using HTML's table tools.
   c. the first true multimedia documents to be published on the Internet.
   d. viewable only with proprietary Microsoft software.
   e. sent via email from Doug Engelbart's office on the Stanford campus.

7. Quicktime, RealOne, and Shockwave are among the most popular Web browser
   a. plug-ins.
   b. cookies.
   c. cascading style sheets.
   d. search engines.
   e. security tools.

8. An online shopping catalog for a large outdoor outfitter is almost certainly
   a. a data-driven Web site that separates site content from design.
   b. carefully hand-coded in pure HTML to minimize errors.
   c. designed to work without cookies.
   d. limited to work with a single type of Web browser for consistency.
   e. All of the above.

9. The Internet will change drastically in the next decade, but the one thing that is likely to remain relatively unchanged is
   a. the dominance of HTML as a Web page creation language.
   b. the metaphor of the page as the container of Internet information.
   c. the TCP/IP protocol that's used to send and receive Internet messages.
   d. the ownership of the Internet by Microsoft.
   e. the percentage of non-U.S. Internet users.

10. The form of push technology that has been embraced by most Internet users is
    a. peer-to-peer sharing.
    b. Web searching.
    c. FTP.
    d. email.
    e. grid computing.

REVIEW QUESTIONS

1. Define or describe each of the key terms listed in the Key Terms section. Check your answers using the glossary.

2. Why is it hard to determine how big the Internet is today? Give several reasons.

3. Why are TCP/IP protocols so important to the functioning of the Internet? What do they do?

4. How does the type of Internet connection influence the things you can do on the Internet?

5. Explain the relationship between the client/server model and the fact that different users might experience different interfaces while accessing the same data.

6. What do email addresses and URLs have in common?

7. Briefly describe several software tools that can be used to develop Web pages.

8. How might you use remote login while visiting another school? What about file transfer? How might the Web make remote login unnecessary?

9. Why is file compression important on the Internet?

10. Briefly describe several software tools that can be used to develop Web pages.

11. How does push technology differ from standard Web page delivery techniques? How is it used?

12. What new services are available as a result of the commercialization of the Internet? What new problems are arising as a result of that commercialization?

DISCUSSION QUESTIONS

1. How did the Internet's Cold War origin influence its basic decentralized, packet-switching design? How does that design affect the way we use the Net today? What are the political implications of that design today?

2. Why is the World Wide Web important as a publishing medium? In what ways is the Web different from any publishing medium that's ever existed before?

3. As scientists, engineers, and government officials develop plans for the future of the Internet, they wrestle with questions about who should have access and what kinds of services to plan for. Do you have any ideas about the kinds of things they might want to consider?

4. Do you know anyone who has experienced Internet addiction? If so, can you describe the experience?

5. How do you think online user interfaces will evolve as bandwidth and processing power increase? Describe what cyberspace will feel like in the year 2010, in the year 2050, and beyond.

PROJECTS

1. Search the Web for articles related to the history and evolution of the Internet. Create a summary report on paper or on the Web.

2. Create a Web site on a subject of interest to you and link it to other Web sites. (When you're trying to decide what information to include in your home page, remember that it will be accessible to millions of people all over the world.)

3. Research peer-to-peer and grid-computing applications to determine how they're used. Write a report summarizing your findings.

4. Read several books and articles about cyberspace and write a paper comparing them. Better yet, write a hypertext document and publish it on the Web.

SOURCES AND RESOURCES

Books

There are thousands of books on the Internet. Many of them promise to simplify and demystify the Net, but they don't all deliver. The Internet is complex and ever-changing. The following list contains a few particularly good titles, but you should also look for more current books released since this book went to press.

When Wizards Stay Up Late: The Origins of the Internet, by Katie Hafner and Matthew Lyon (New York: Simon and Schuster, 1998). If you want to learn more about the birth of the Internet, this book is a great place to start. The authors describe the people, challenges, and technical issues in clear, entertaining prose.

How the Internet Works, Sixth Edition, by Preston Gralla (Indianapolis: Que, 2001). If you like the style of *How Computers Work*, you'll appreciate *How the Internet Works*. You won't learn how to use the Net, but you'll get a colorful tour of what goes on behind the scenes when you connect. There's a surprising amount of technical information in this graphically rich, approachable book.

The Unusually Useful Web Book, by June Cohen (Indianapolis: New Riders, 2003). Some Web books are written for programmers; some are written for designers; some are written for business people. This book, by a former VP of HotWired (the Web site that spun off *Wired* magazine) has something for all three audiences—and more. If you want to build a Web site that people will actually use, this book is a good investment.

HTML for the World Wide Web with XHTML and CSS Visual QuickStart Guide, Fifth Edition, by Elizabeth Castro (Berkeley, CA: Peachpit Press, 2003). There are dozens of books on HTML, but few offer the clear, concise, comprehensive coverage of this bestseller. The latest edition emphasizes the Web's gradual transition to XHTML, which makes the first couple of chapters a little more daunting for beginners. Still, if you want to build your own Web pages, this is a great place to start. Even if you know the basics of HTML, you'll appreciate the coverage of "advanced" topics like DHTML and CGI. Once you've read it, you'll almost certainly want to keep it as a reference.

Perl and CGI for the World Wide Web Visual QuickStart Guide, Second Edition, by Elizabeth Castro (Berkeley, CA: Peachpit Press, 2001). When you fill out a form on a Web page, it's likely that your input is processed by a script that's written in PERL following the CGI protocol. Castro's book takes up where her popular HTML book leaves off, introducing the basics of PERL and CGI for first-time scripters.

JavaScript for the World Wide Web Visual QuickStart Guide, Third Edition, by Tom Negrino and Dori Smith (Berkeley, CA: Peachpit Press, 1999). JavaScript is the most popular cross-platform scripting language for Web pages. A little bit of JavaScript can turn a static Web page into a dynamic interactive page. This book provides a quick introduction to the language, including applications involving forms, frames, files, graphics, and cookies. If you're ready to move beyond basic HTML, this book can help.

Web Style Guide: Basic Design Principles for Creating Web Sites, Second Edition, by Patrick J. Lynch and Sarah Horton (New Haven, CT: Yale University Press, 2002). Yale University was one of the first institutions to publish a Web style guide on the Web. This book, like that site, offers a clear, thoughtful discussion of techniques for designing effective Web sites.

The Non-Designer's Web Book, Second Edition, by Robin Williams and John Tollett (Berkeley, CA: Peachpit Press, 2000). Web publishing, like desktop publishing, can be hazardous if you don't have a background in design. Robin Williams and John Tollett provide a crash course in design for first-time Web authors. They assume you're using an authoring tool that hides the nuts and bolts of HTML; if you're not, you'll need to learn HTML elsewhere.

Return on Design: Smarter Web Design That Works, by Ani Phyo (Indianapolis, IN: New Riders, 2003). Web pro Ani Phyo clearly outlines seven necessary steps for creating usable Web sites. Her user-centered methodology satisfies a wide variety of clients, and this book explains how.

Train of Thought: Designing the Effective Web Experience, by John C. Lenker, Jr. (Indianapolis, IN: New Riders, 2002). This book focuses on the psychology of Web design, emphasizing the creation of Web *experiences*. It's packed with ideas, interviews, and images that just might inspire you to create great Web experiences for others.

From Anarchy to Power: The Net Comes of Age, by Wendy M. Grossman (New York: New York University Press, 2001). The Internet has gone through a radical transition in just a few years. This book chronicles the changes and comments on the profound social and political impact of those changes.

Harley Hahn's Internet and Web Yellow Pages, 2003 Edition, by Harley Hahn (Berkeley, CA: Osborne/McGraw Hill, 2002). Many books attempt to catalog the contents of the Web, but most of them can't compete with the currency and convenience of online Web search tools. Harley Hahn's popular directory combines solid research and a careful selection process with useful tips, clever insights, and amusing asides. The result is a book that's both fun and informative. The built-in CD-ROM contains the text in clickable hypertext format.

Peer-to-Peer: Harnessing the Power of Disruptive Technologies, edited by Andy Oram (Sebastopol, CA: O'Reilly and Associates, 2001). This collection of essays discusses the philosophy, applications, and implications of peer-to-peer technology, from music sharing to CPU sharing and beyond.

The Code and Other Laws of Cyberspace, by Lawrence Lessig (New York: Basic Books, 2000). This important book presents a strong argument that we might lose our liberty on the Internet unless we consciously work to preserve it. The way we build the Net today will determine what's possible in cyberspace tomorrow. Lessig, a lawyer, is an excellent writer with something important to say.

Crypto Anarchy, Cyberstates, and Pirate Utopias, edited by Peter Ludlow (Cambridge, MA: MIT Press, 2001). This lively, thought-provoking collection of essays presents a cyberspace made up of virtual communities that are outside of the circles of corporate and political power.

True Names: And the Opening of the Cyberspace Frontier, by Vernor Vinge and James Frenkel (New York: Tor Books, 2001). In 1981 (three years before the original publication of *Neuromancer*) Vernor Vinge's critically acclaimed novella, *True Names,* described a virtual world inside a computer network. Vinge didn't use the term *cyberspace*, but his visionary story effectively invented the concept. This book includes the wonderful original *True Names* novella and a collection of articles by cyberspace pioneers about the past, present, and future of cyberspace.

Neuromancer, Reissue Edition, by William Gibson (New York: Ace Books, 2003). Gibson's 1984 cyberpunk classic spawned several sequels, dozens of imitations, and a new vocabulary for describing a high-tech future. Gibson's future is gloomy and foreboding, and his futuristic slang isn't always easy to follow. Still, there's plenty to think about here.

Snow Crash, by Neal Stephenson (New York: Bantam, 2000). This early 1990s science fiction novel lightens the dark, violent cyberpunk future vision a little with Douglas Adams–style humor. Characters regularly jack into the Metaverse, a shared virtual reality network that is in many ways more real than the physical world where they live. The descriptions of this alternate reality heavily influenced the design of many VR-like Web sites today.

Web Pages

The World Wide Web is especially good at providing information about itself. Whether you want to learn HTML, see the latest Web traffic reports, or explore the technological underpinnings of the Net, you'll find Web links at the *Computer Confluence* Web site (**http://www.computerconfluence.com**) that can help.

AFTER YOU READ THIS CHAPTER YOU SHOULD BE ABLE TO:

■ Describe several types of computer crime and discuss possible crime-prevention techniques

■ Describe the major security issues facing computer users, computer system administrators, and law enforcement officials

■ Describe how computer security relates to personal privacy issues

■ Explain how security and computer reliability are related.

 Multimedia extras on the CD-ROM and the Web:

■ Inside the **hacker's world**

■ Computer security and **terrorism**

■ **Video** of nanotechnologist Ralph Merkle

■ **Animated illustrations** of how computer viruses and cryptography work

■ **Instant access** to glossary and key word references

■ Interactive **self-study quizzes**

   . . . *and more.*

 **computerconfluence.com**

COMPUTER SECURITY AND RISKS

KEMPELEN'S AMAZING CHESS-PLAYING MACHINE

In 1760 Wolfgang Kempelen, a 49-year-old Hungarian inventor, engineer, and advisor to the court of Austrian Empress Maria Theresa, built a mechanical chess player. This amazing contraption defeated internationally renowned players and earned its inventor almost legendary fame.

A Turkish-looking automaton sat behind a big box that sup-ported a chessboard and chess pieces. The operator of the machine could open the box to "prove" there was nothing inside but a network of cogwheels, gears, and revolving cylinders. After every 12 moves, Kempelen wound the machine up with a huge key.

> **Check.**
>
> —The only word ever spoken by Kempelen's chess-playing machine

Of course, the chess-playing machine was actually a clever hoax. The real chess player was a dwarf-sized person, who controlled the mechanism from inside and was concealed by mirrors when the box was opened. The tiny player couldn't see the board, but he could tell what pieces were moved by watching magnets below the chessboard.

Kempelen had no intention of keeping the deception going for long; he thought of it as a joke and dismantled it after its first tour. But he became a slave to his own fraud, as the public and the scientific community showered him with praise for creating the first "machine-man." In 1780 the Emperor Joseph II ordered another court demonstration of the mechanical chess player, and Kempelen had to rebuild it. The chess player toured the courts of Europe, and the public became more curious and fascinated than ever.

After Kempelen died in 1804, the machine was purchased by the impresario Maelzel, who showed it far and wide. In 1809 it challenged Napoleon Bonaparte to play. When Napoleon repeatedly made illegal moves, the machine-man brushed the pieces

10.1 Kempelen's chess-playing machine.

from the table. Napoleon was delighted to have un-nerved the machine. When he played the next game fairly, Napoleon was badly beaten.

The chess-playing machine came to America in 1826, where it attracted large, paying crowds. In 1834 two different articles—one by Edgar Allen Poe—revealed the secrets of the automated chess player. Poe's investigative article was insightful but not com-pletely accurate; one of his 17 arguments was that a true automatic player would invariably win.

After Maelzel's death in 1837, the machine passed from hand to hand until it was destroyed by fire in Philadelphia in 1854. During the 70 years that the automaton was publicly exhibited, its "brain" was supplied by 15 different chess players, who won 294 of 300 games.

With his elaborate and elegant deception, Kempelen might be considered the forerunner of the modern computer criminal. Kempelen was trapped in his fraud because the public wanted to believe that the automated chess player was real. Desire overtook judgment in thousands of people, who were captivated by the idea of an intelligent machine.

More than two centuries later, we're still fascinated by intelligent machines. In 1997 people all over the world watched (many via the Web) as IBM's Deep Blue computer trounced Garry Kasparov, the reigning international chess champion. But modern comput-ers don't just play games; they manage our money, our medicine, and our missiles. We're expected to trust information technology with our wealth, our health, and even our lives. The many benefits of our partnership with machines are clear. But blind faith in modern technology can be foolish and, in many cases, dangerous. In this chapter we examine some of the dark corners of our computerized society: legal dilemmas, ethical issues, and relia-bility risks. These issues are tied to a larger question: How can we make computers more secure so that we can feel more secure in our daily dealings with them? We'll look for an-swers to this question, and then ask several more difficult questions about our relationship to computer technology and our future.

Online Outlaws: Computer Crime

> Computers are **power**, and **direct contact** with power can bring out the **best** or **worst** in a person.
> —Former computer criminal turned corporate computer programmer

Like other professions, law enforce-ment is being transformed by in-formation technology. The FBI's National Crime Information Center provides police with almost instant information on crimes and crimi-nals nationwide. Investigators use PC databases to store and cross-reference clues in com-plex cases. Using pattern recognition technology, automated fingerprint identification sys-tems locate matches in minutes rather than months. Computers routinely scan the New York and London stock exchanges for connections that might indicate insider trading or fraud. Texas police use an intranet to cross-reference databases of photographs, finger-prints, and other crime-fighting information. *Computer forensics* experts use special soft-ware to scan criminal suspects' hard disks for digital "fingerprints"—traces of deleted files containing evidence of illegal activities. All of these tools help law enforcement officials ferret out criminals and stop criminal activities.

Like guns, people use computers to break laws as well as uphold them. Computers are powerful tools in the hands of criminals, and computer crime is a rapidly growing problem.

The Computer Crime Dossier

> Some will rob you with a **six gun**, and some with a **fountain pen**.
> —Woody Guthrie, in "Pretty Boy Floyd"

Today the computer has replaced both the gun and the pen as the weapon of choice for many crimi-nals. **Computer crime** is often defined as any crime accomplished through knowledge or use of computer technology.

Nobody knows the true extent of computer crime. Many computer crimes go undetected. Those that are detected often go unreported because businesses fear that they can lose more from negative publicity than from the actual crimes.

According to a 2001 survey of more than 500 companies and government agencies by the FBI and the Computer Security Institute, 85 percent detected computer security breaches in the preceding 12 months. These breaches included system penetration by outsiders, theft of information, changing data, financial fraud, vandalism, stealing of passwords, and preventing legitimate users from gaining access to systems. According to the survey, financial losses due to security breaches topped $377 million. By conservative estimates, businesses and government institutions lose billions of dollars every year to computer criminals.

10.2 A police officer uses his mobile computer to check records in a central law enforcement database.

The majority of computer crimes are committed by company insiders who aren't reported to authorities, even when they are caught in the act. To avoid embarrassment, many companies cover up computer crimes committed by their own employees and managers. These crimes are typically committed by clerks, cashiers, programmers, computer operators, and managers who have no extraordinary technical ingenuity. The typical computer criminal is a trusted employee with no criminal record who is tempted by an opportunity such as the discovery of a loophole in system security. Greed, financial worries, and personal problems motivate this person to give in to temptation.

Of course, not all computer criminals fit this profile. Some are former employees seeking revenge on their former bosses. Some are high-tech pranksters looking for a challenge. A few are corporate or international spies seeking classified information. Organized crime syndicates are turning to computer technology to practice their trades. Sometimes entire companies are found guilty of computer fraud.

The 2001 survey suggests that the explosive growth of Internet commerce is changing the demographics of computer crime: 70 percent reported that Internet connections were frequent points of attack; only 31 percent said that internal systems were frequent points of attack.

Comparing this survey with previous annual surveys shows unmistakable trends: Internet security breaches are on the rise, internal security breaches are on the rise, and computer crime in general is on the rise. All of these increases are happening in spite of increased security and law enforcement efforts.

Theft by Computer

Theft is the most common form of computer crime. Computers are used to steal money, goods, information, and computer resources. Here are a few examples:

> Every system has **vulnerabilities**. Every system **can be compromised**.
>
> —Peter G. Neumann, in *Computer Related Risks*

■ A part-time college student used his touch-tone phone and personal computer to fool Pacific Telephone's computer into ordering phone equipment to be delivered to him. He started a business, hired several employees, and pilfered about a million dollars' worth of equipment before he was turned in by a disgruntled employee. (After serving two months in jail, he became a computer security consultant.)

■ A former automated teller machine repairman illegally obtained $86,000 out of ATMs by spying on customers while they typed in passwords and then creating bogus cards to use with the passwords.

■ In 1988 several million dollars of assets at a major U.S. bank were illegally transferred to a private Swiss bank account. The transfer was noticed because a computer glitch on that particular day forced employees to check transactions manually; the automated procedure normally used wouldn't have noticed the suspicious transaction.

■ In 1999 the *London Times* revealed that several London banks had paid millions of pounds in ransoms to hackers who threatened to cripple their computer systems if they didn't pay. The banks paid rather than admitting publicly that their systems weren't secure against attack.

■ In 1999 two brothers in China were sentenced to death for using computers to redirect about $30,000 to bank accounts they controlled.

■ In 1999 an employee of PairGain, a maker of high-speed Internet products, posted an anonymous announcement on a Yahoo stock board; the message claimed that PairGain was about to be purchased by another company for nearly twice its current market value. Investors drove the stock price up about 40 percent before they learned they had been bilked out of thousands of dollars by a bogus message. An FBI task force retraced the perpetrator's electronic footprints and arrested him for stock manipulation a week later. This kind of pump-and-dump stock manipulation has been committed dozens of times since the PairGain crime.

■ In 2000 intruders broke into Creditcards.com, stole 55,000 credit card numbers, and held them for ransom. When their extortion attempt failed, they posted the numbers on the Web. The company has since created a more secure Web site.

■ In 2001 two young Russian men were arrested for breaking into several U.S. company networks, stealing sensitive information, and demanding ransom for it. The FBI captured the pair by using a fake computer security company as bait. When they demanded payment from the bogus company, FBI agents agreed. The two men were arrested when they landed in the United States to collect their bounty.

■ In May of 2001 Operation Cyber Loss, the FBI's crackdown on Internet fraud, netted 88 people in 10 days. According to the FBI, 56,000 people were defrauded of more than $117 million during the scams.

Some types of computer crime are so common that they've been given names. A common student scam uses a process called spoofing to steal passwords. The typical spoofer launches a program that mimics the mainframe computer's login screen on an unattended terminal in a public lab. When an unsuspecting student types an ID and password, the program responds with an error message and remembers the secret codes.

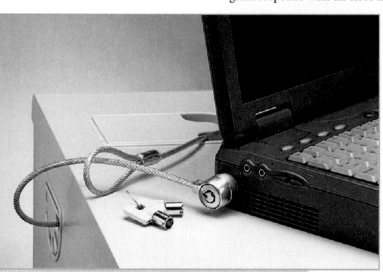

10.3 A portable computer is easy prey for thieves unless it is locked to something stationary and solid.

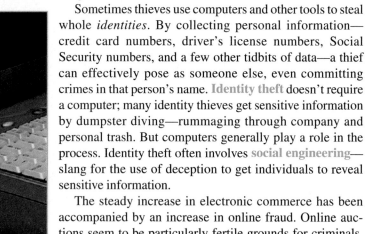

Sometimes thieves use computers and other tools to steal whole *identities*. By collecting personal information—credit card numbers, driver's license numbers, Social Security numbers, and a few other tidbits of data—a thief can effectively pose as someone else, even committing crimes in that person's name. Identity theft doesn't require a computer; many identity thieves get sensitive information by dumpster diving—rummaging through company and personal trash. But computers generally play a role in the process. Identity theft often involves social engineering—slang for the use of deception to get individuals to reveal sensitive information.

The steady increase in electronic commerce has been accompanied by an increase in online fraud. Online auctions seem to be particularly fertile grounds for criminals. "The ePrivacy and Security Report" from market research company eMarketer.com estimated that 87 percent of online fraud cases in 2000 were related to online auctions, with the average cost per victim being around $600.

One common type of computer theft today is the actual theft of computers. Notebook and handheld computers make particularly easy prey for crooks—especially in airports and other high-traffic, high-stress locations. Notebooks and PDAs are expensive items, but the information stored on a computer can be far more valuable than the computer itself.

All of these crimes are expensive—for businesses, law enforcement agencies, and taxpayers and consumers who ultimately must pay the bills. But as crimes go, the types of theft described so far are relatively uncommon. The same can't be said of the most widely practiced type of computer-related theft: software piracy.

Software Piracy and Intellectual Property Laws

Software piracy—the illegal duplication of copyrighted software—is rampant. Millions of computer users have made copies of programs they don't legally own and distributed them to family members, friends, and, sometimes, total strangers. Because so few software companies use physical copy pro-

> Information wants to be free. Information also wants to be expensive. **Information wants to be free** because it has become so cheap to distribute, copy, and recombine—**too cheap to meter. It wants to be expensive** because it can be **immeasurably valuable** to the recipient. **That tension will not go away**.
>
> —Stewart Brand, in *The Media Lab*

tection methods such as dongles to protect their products, copying software is as easy as duplicating an audio CD or photocopying a chapter of a book. Unfortunately, many people aren't aware that copying software, recorded music, and books can violate federal laws protecting intellectual property. Many others simply look the other way, convinced that software companies, music companies, and publishers already make enough money.

The Piracy Problem

The software industry, with a world market of more than $50 billion a year, loses billions of dollars every year to software pirates. The Business Software Alliance (BSA) estimates that more than one-third of all software in use is illegally copied, costing the software industry tens of thousands of jobs. Piracy can be particularly hard on small software companies. Developing software is just as difficult for them as it is for big companies like Microsoft and Oracle, but they often lack the financial and legal resources to cover their losses to piracy.

Software industry organizations, including the BSA and SPA Anti-Piracy (a division of the Software & Information Industry Association), work with law enforcement agencies to crack down on piracy. At the same time they sponsor educational programs to make computer users aware that piracy is theft, because laws can't work without citizen understanding and support.

Software piracy is a worldwide problem, with piracy rates highest in developing nations. In China approximately 95 percent of all new software installations are pirated; in Vietnam the piracy rate is 97 percent. A few Third World nations refuse to abide by international copyright laws. They argue that the laws protect rich countries at the expense of underdeveloped nations. In 1998 the Argentine Supreme Court ruled that the country's copyright laws don't apply to computer software.

10.4 In 1999 Moscow police attempted to make a dent in the illegal software market by destroying mountains of pirated software. Their efforts were largely unsuccessful, however. At this time, Russia has one of the highest software piracy rates in the world, second only to China's.

Intellectual Property and the Law

Legally, the definition of intellectual property includes the results of intellectual activities in the arts, science, and industry. Copyright laws have traditionally protected forms of literary expression, patent law has protected mechanical inventions, and contract law has covered trade secrets. Software doesn't fit neatly into any of these categories under the law. Copyright laws protect most commercial software programs, but a few companies have successfully used patent laws to protect software products.

The purpose of intellectual property laws is to ensure that mental labor is justly rewarded and to encourage innovation. Programmers, inventors, scientists, writers, editors, filmmakers, and musicians depend on ideas and the expression of those ideas for their incomes. Ideas are information, and information is easy to copy—especially in this electronic age. Intellectual property laws are designed to protect these professionals and encourage them to continue their creative efforts so society can benefit from their future work.

Most of the time, these laws help them to achieve their goals. A novelist can devote two or three years of her life to writing a masterpiece, confident that she won't find bootleg copies for sale on street corners when she finishes it. A movie studio can invest millions of dollars in a film, knowing that the investment will be returned, a little at a time, through ticket sales and video rentals. An inventor can work long hours to create a better mousetrap and know that MegaMousetrap City won't steal her idea.

But sometimes intellectual property laws are applied in such a way that they may stifle the innovation and creativity they're designed to protect. In 1999 Amazon.com was awarded a controversial patent for "one-click shopping," preventing other e-commerce sites from giving their customers a similar, simple shopping experience. Similarly, SightSound patented all paid downloads of "desired digital video or digital audio signals," RealNetworks patented streaming audio and video, and British Telecom claims to hold a 1976 patent that covers every Web hyperlink! Most experts agree that these ideas are too simple and broad to be owned by one company. And in many cases, the patent owner isn't the inventor of the concept—Douglas Engelbart demonstrated hyperlinking as early as 1967 at Stanford Research Institute. Such broad patents generally end up in court, where legal experts and technology experts debate the merits and scope of the ideas and the laws designed to protect them. Meanwhile, legislators attempt to update the laws to address ever-changing technological advances.

Most existing copyright and patent laws, which evolved during the age of print and mechanical inventions, are outdated, contradictory, and inadequate for today's information technology. Many laws, including the Computer Fraud and Abuse Act of 1984, clearly treat software piracy as a crime. The NET (No Electronic Theft) Act of 1997 closed a narrow loophole in the law that allowed people to give away software on the Internet.

The Digital Millennium Copyright Act (DMCA) of 1998 represents the most comprehensive reform of U.S. copyright law in a generation. The DCMA includes several controversial provisions that need to be clarified by the courts. According to the law, it is illegal to write a program that circumvents copy protection schemes, whether or not that program is used to copy DVDs, electronic books, or other protected material illegally. The DMCA also makes it a crime to share information about how to crack copy protection. Critics argue that the law suppresses freedom of speech, academic freedom, and the principle of *fair use*—the time-honored right to make copies of copyrighted material for personal and academic use and for other noncompetitive purposes. In 2001 the Recording Industry Association of America (RIAA) used the DMCA to shutdown the Napster music-sharing service; by 2003 the RIAA was using the DMCA to force Internet service providers to reveal the identities of individual song pirates, leading to serious questions about the scope and reach of this law.

In matters of software, the legal system is sailing in uncharted waters. Whether dealing with issues of piracy or monopoly, lawmakers and judges must struggle with difficult questions about innovation, property, freedom, and progress. The questions are likely to be with us for quite a while.

Software Sabotage: Viruses and Other Malware

Another type of computer crime is sabotage of hardware or software. The word sabotage comes from the early days of the Industrial Revolution, when rebellious workers shut down new machines by kicking wooden shoes, called sabots, into the gears. Modern computer saboteurs commonly use malware—malicious software—rather than footwear to do destructive deeds. The names given to the saboteurs' destructive programs—viruses, worms, and Trojan horses—sound more like biology than technology, and many of the programs even mimic the behavior of living organisms.

> The American government can stop me from going to the U.S., but **they can't stop my virus**.
>
> —Virus creator

Trojan Horses

A Trojan horse is a program that performs a useful task while at the same time carrying out some secret destructive act. As in the ancient story of the wooden horse that carried Greek soldiers through the gates of Troy, Trojan horse software hides an enemy in an attractive package. Trojan horse programs are often posted on shareware Web sites with names that make them sound like games or utilities. When an unsuspecting bargain hunter downloads and runs such a program, it might erase files, change data, or cause some other kind of damage. Some network saboteurs use Trojan horses to pass secret data to other unauthorized users.

One type of Trojan horse, a logic bomb, is programmed to attack in response to a particular event or sequence of events. For example, a programmer might plant a logic bomb that is designed to destroy data files if the programmer is ever listed as terminated in the company's personnel file. A logic bomb might be triggered when a certain user logs in, a special code is entered in a database field, or a particular sequence of actions is performed by the user. If the logic bomb is triggered by a time-related event, it is called a *time bomb*. A widely publicized virus included a logic bomb that was programmed to destroy PC data files on Michelangelo's birthday.

Trojan horses can cause serious problems in computer systems of all sizes. To make matters worse, many Trojan horses carry software viruses.

Viruses

A biological virus is unable to reproduce by itself, but it can invade the cells of another organism and use the reproductive machinery of each host cell to make copies of itself; the new copies leave the host and seek out new hosts to repeat the process. A software virus works in the same way: It spreads from program to program, or from disk to disk, and uses each infected program or disk to make more copies of itself. Virus software is usually hidden in the operating system of a computer or in an application program. Some viruses do nothing but reproduce; others display messages on the computer's screen; still others destroy data or erase disks.

Like most software code, a virus is usually operating-system specific. Windows viruses invade only Windows disks, Macintosh viruses invade only Macintosh disks, and so on. There are exceptions: *Macro viruses* attach themselves to documents that contain *macros*—embedded programs to automate tasks. Macro viruses can be spread across computer platforms if the documents are created and spread using cross-platform applications—most commonly the applications in Microsoft Office. Macro viruses can be spread through innocent-looking email attachments. Viruses spread through email are sometimes called *email viruses*.

One of the most widely publicized email viruses was 1999's Melissa virus. Melissa's method of operation is typical of email viruses: An unsuspecting computer user received an "Important message" from a friend: "Here is that document you asked for . . . don't show it to anyone else ;-)." The attached Microsoft Word document contained a list of passwords for Internet pornography sites. It contained something else: a macro virus written in Microsoft Office's built-in Visual Basic scripting language.

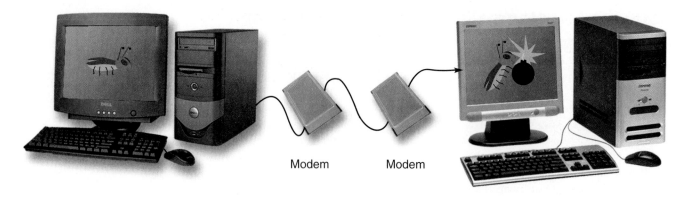

Modem   Modem

A programmer writes a tiny program—the virus—that has destructive power and can reproduce itself.

Most often, the virus is attached to a normal program; unknown to the user, the virus spreads to other software.

The virus is passed by disk or network to other users who use other computers. The virus remains dormant as it is passed on.

Depending on how it is programmed, a virus may display an unexpected message, gobble up memory, destroy data files or cause serious system errors.

10.5 How a virus works.

Once the document was opened, the macro virus went to work, sending a copy of the email message and infected document to the first 50 names on the user's Outlook address book. Within minutes, 50 more potential Melissa victims received messages apparently from someone they know—the user of the newly infected computer. Melissa spread like wildfire among Windows systems, infecting 100,000 systems in just a few days. Melissa wasn't designed to do damage to systems, but the sudden flurry of messages brought down some email servers. A nationwide search located the probable author of the Melissa virus, a 30-year-old New Jersey resident with a fondness for a topless dancer named Melissa.

Shortly after Melissa faded from the headlines, a similar, but more destructive, virus named Chernobyl infected more than 600,000 computers worldwide. South Korea alone suffered 300,000 attacks; about 15 percent of its PCs were damaged by the virus, at a cost of $250 million. In May of 2000, a Melissa-like virus called Love Bug spread from a PC in the Philippines around the world through innocent-looking "I Love You" email message attachments. In a matter of hours, the Love Bug caused billions of dollars in lost productivity and damage to computer systems.

In the summer of 2003, a rash of viruses plagued PC users, culminating in a massive epidemic caused by a virus called Sobig.f. Sobig was the fastest-spreading network virus ever. One message-filtering service intercepted more than a million copies of the virus in a single day. The Windows virus deposited a Trojan horse that could scan an infected PC's hard disk for email addresses in documents and address books and send copies of itself to those addresses. Sobig didn't destroy files or damage PCs, but it clogged networks and mailboxes worldwide.

Worms

Like viruses, worms (named for tapeworms) use computer hosts to reproduce themselves. But unlike viruses, worm programs travel independently over computer networks, seeking out uninfected workstations in which to reproduce. A worm can reproduce until the computer freezes from lack of free memory or disk space. A typical worm segment resides in memory rather than on disk, so the worm can be eliminated by shutting down all of the workstations on the network.

The first headline-making worm was created as an experiment by a Cornell graduate student in 1988. The worm was accidentally released onto the Internet, clogging 6,000 computers all over the United States, almost bringing them to a complete standstill and forcing operators to shut them all down so every worm segment could be purged from memory.

The total cost, in terms of work time lost at research institutions, was staggering. The student was suspended from school and was the first person convicted of violating the Computer Fraud and Abuse Act.

In the summer of 2001, a worm called Code Red made worldwide headlines. Code Red didn't attack PCs; its target was Internet servers running Microsoft server software. The U.S. government and Microsoft issued warnings about the worm and made free software patches available to protect servers. Even so, many servers were crippled by the repeated attacks from the worm, including servers owned and operated by Microsoft.

Virus Wars

The popular press usually doesn't distinguish among Trojan horses, viruses, and worms; they're all called computer viruses. Whatever they're called, these rogue programs make life more complicated and expensive for people who depend on computers. Researchers have identified more than 18,000 virus strains, with 200 new ones appearing each month. At any given time, about 250 virus strains exist in the wild—in circulation.

Modern viruses can spread faster and do more damage than viruses of a few years ago for several reasons. The Internet, which speeds communication all over the planet, also speeds virus transmission. Web pages, macros, and other technologies give virus writers new places to hide their creations. And increased standardization on Microsoft applications and operating systems has made it easier for viruses to spread. Just as natural mixed forests are more resistant to disease than are single-species tree farms, mixed computing environments are less susceptible to crippling attacks than is an organization in which everyone uses the same hardware and software.

When computers are used in life-or-death situations, as they are in many medical and military applications, invading programs can even threaten human lives. The U.S. government and several states now have laws against introducing these programs into computer systems.

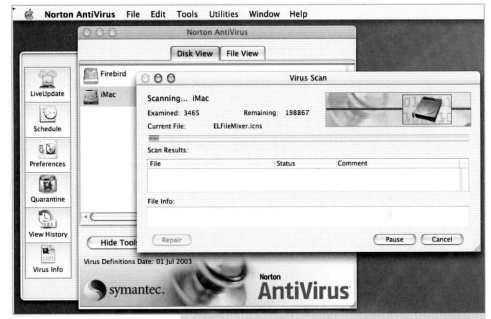

10.6 Antivirus software scans files for viruses, worms, and other software invaders. New versions of the software definition files should be downloaded regularly to ensure the software is up-to-date.

Antivirus programs (sometimes simply referred to as AV software) are designed to search for viruses, notify users when they're found, and remove them from infected disks or files. Most antivirus programs continually monitor system activity, watching for and reporting suspicious viruslike actions. But no antivirus program can detect every virus, and these programs need to be frequently revised to combat new viruses as they appear. Most antivirus programs can automatically download new virus-fighting code from the Web as new virus strains appear. But it can take several days for companies to develop and distribute patches for new viruses—and destructive viruses can do a lot of damage in that time.

The virus wars continue to escalate as virus writers develop new ways to spread their works. After a rash of 1999 email viruses, most users learned not to open unidentified email attachments, and software vendors started modifying their email applications to prevent this sort of attack. But before the year was over, a worm called BubbleBoy (named for an episode of TV's Seinfeld) demonstrated that a system could be infected by email even if the mail wasn't opened. Some viruses have even been developed to infect HTML code in Web pages or HTML email messages. HTML viruses can't (so far) infect your computer if you're viewing an infected Web page on another computer; the infected HTML code must be downloaded onto your machine.

Software companies continually test their products for security holes and try to make them more resistant to viruses, worms, and other security breaches. Because Microsoft Windows is the target of the great majority of malware, the company periodically releases security patches—software programs that plug potential security breaches in the operating system. These patches are provided as free downloads or automatic updates to all owners of the OS. But preventive security measures like these can sometimes backfire. In the summer of 2003, a worm called MS Slammer made worldwide headlines, shutting down hundreds of thousands of PCs as it moved from computer to computer looking for vulnerable targets. The worm was deployed more than a month after Microsoft had issued a security patch to fix the very problem that MS Slammer exploited. By publicizing the vulnerability, Microsoft inadvertently inspired malicious programmers to create the worm. These system saboteurs took advantage of the fact that many computer users fail to install security patches, leaving their systems ripe for attack. In response to MS Slammer, a well-intentioned programmer released a helper worm designed to search the Internet for machines that had been infected by MS Slammer and apply the Microsoft security patch to those machines. But this worm caused its own problems, slowing many systems to a crawl by repeatedly checking them for security problems.

Stories like this one happen more often than the information technology industry would like to admit. These stories serve as reminders that the virus wars are far from over. There will always be new ways to compromise connected systems.

Hacking and Electronic Trespassing

The Hacker Ethic: Access to computers—and anything which might teach you something about the way the world works—should be **unlimited** and **total**. Always yield to the **Hands-on Imperative**. All information should be **free**.
Mistrust Authority—Promote Decentralization.
Hackers should be judged by their **hacking**, not bogus criteria such as degrees, age, race, or position.
You can create **art and beauty** on a computer.
Computers can **change your life** for the better.

—Steven Levy, in *Hackers: Heroes of the Computer Revolution*

I don't drink, smoke, or take drugs. I don't steal, assault people, or vandalize property. **The only way** in which I am **really different** from most people is in **my fascination** with the ways and means of learning about **computers that don't belong to me**.

—Bill "The Cracker" Landreth, in *Out of the Inner Circle*

In the late 1970s, timesharing computers at Stanford and MIT attracted informal communities of computer fanatics who called themselves *hackers*. In those days a hacker was a person who enjoyed learning the details of computer systems and writing clever programs, referred to as hacks. Hackers were, for the most part, curious, enthusiastic, intelligent, idealistic, eccentric, and harmless. Many of those early hackers were, in fact, architects of the microcomputer revolution.

Over the years the idealism of the early hacker communities was at least partly overshadowed by cynicism, as big-money interests took over the young personal computer industry. At the same time the term hacking took on a new, more ominous connotation in the media. Although many people still use the term to describe software wizardry, it more commonly refers to unauthorized access to computer systems. Old-time hackers insist that this electronic trespassing is really *cracking*, or criminal hacking, but the general public and popular media don't recognize the distinction between hackers and crackers. Today's stereotypical hacker, like his early counterparts, is a young, bright, technically savvy, white, middle-class male who, in addition to programming his own computer, may break into others.

Of course, not all young computer wizards break into systems, and not all electronic trespassers fit the media stereotype. Still, hackers aren't just a media myth; they're real, and there are lots of them. Electronic trespassers enter corporate and government computers using stolen passwords and security holes in operating system software. Sometimes they use modems to dial up the target computers directly; in other cases they "travel" to their destinations through the Internet and other networks.

Many hackers are merely motivated by curiosity and intellectual challenge; once they've cracked a system, they look around and move on without leaving any electronic footprints. Some hackers claim to be acting in the public good by pointing out security problems in commercial software products. Some malicious hackers use Trojan horses, logic bombs, and other tricks of the trade to wreak havoc on corporate and government systems. A growing number of computer trespassers are part of electronic crime rings intent on stealing credit card numbers and other sensitive, valuable information. This kind of theft is difficult to detect and track because the original information is left unchanged when the copy is stolen.

According to the FBI, an Internet hack happens every 30 seconds. Hackers have defaced the Web sites of the White House, the U.S. Senate, the Department of the Interior, presidential candidates, countless online businesses, and even a hacker's conference. Sometimes Web sites are simply defaced with obscene or threatening messages; sometimes they're replaced with satirical substitutes; sometimes they're vandalized so they don't work properly. *Webjackers* hijack legitimate Web pages and redirect users to other sites—anywhere from pornographic sites to fraudulent businesses.

Denial of service (DoS) attacks bombard servers and Web sites with so much bogus traffic that they're effectively shut down, denying service to legitimate customers and clients. In a *distributed denial of service (DDoS) attack* the flood of messages comes from many compromised systems distributed across the Net. In a single week in February 2000, Yahoo, E*TRADE, eBay, and Amazon Web sites were crippled by denial of service attacks, costing their owners millions of dollars in business. Two months later a 15-year-old Canadian boy nicknamed "Mafia Boy" was arrested after he bragged online about causing the breakdowns. His expensive pranks didn't require any special expertise; he reportedly downloaded all of the software he used from the Internet. In August 2003, computers affected by the MS Slammer worm launched a DDoS attack on Microsoft's Windows Update Web site; this time bomb attack ironically prevented users from downloading the software patch that would have rendered MS Slammer impotent.

One famous case of electronic trespassing was documented in Cliff Stoll's bestselling book, *The Cuckoo's Egg*. While working as a system administrator for a university computer lab in 1986, Stoll noticed a 75-cent accounting error. Rather than letting it go, Stoll investigated the error. He uncovered a system intruder who was searching government, corporate, and university computers across the Internet for sensitive military information. It took a year and some help from the FBI, but Stoll eventually located the hacker—a German computer science student and part of a ring of hackers working for the KGB. Ironically, Stoll captured the thief by using standard hacker tricks, including a Trojan horse program that contained information on a fake SDI Net (Strategic Defense Initiative Network).

This kind of online espionage is becoming commonplace as the Internet becomes a mainstream communication medium. A more recent front-page-story-turned-book involved the 1995 capture of Kevin Mitnick, the hacker who had stolen millions of dollars' worth of software and credit card information on the Net. By repeatedly manufacturing new identities and cleverly concealing his location, Mitnick successfully evaded the FBI for years. But when he broke into the computer of computational physicist Tsutomu Shimomura, he inadvertently started an electronic cat-and-mouse game that ended with his capture and conviction. Shimomura was able to defeat Mitnick because of his expertise in computer security—the protection of computer systems and, indirectly, the people who depend on them.

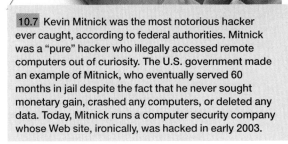

10.7 Kevin Mitnick was the most notorious hacker ever caught, according to federal authorities. Mitnick was a "pure" hacker who illegally accessed remote computers out of curiosity. The U.S. government made an example of Mitnick, who eventually served 60 months in jail despite the fact that he never sought monetary gain, crashed any computers, or deleted any data. Today, Mitnick runs a computer security company whose Web site, ironically, was hacked in early 2003.

Computer Security: Reducing Risks

In the **old world**, if I wanted to attack something physical, there was **one way to get there**. You could put guards and guns around it, **you could protect it**. But a database—or a control system—usually has multiple pathways, **unpredictable routes to it**, and seems intrinsically **impossible to protect**. That's why most efforts at computer security **have been defeated**.

—Andrew Marshall, military analyst

With computer crime on the rise, computer security has become an important concern for system administrators and computer users alike. Computer security refers to protecting computer systems and the information they contain against unwanted access, damage, modification, or destruction. According to a 1991 report of the Congressional Research Service, computers have two inherent characteristics that leave them open to attack or operating error:

1. A computer does exactly what it is programmed to do, including reveal sensitive information. Any system that can be programmed can be reprogrammed by anyone with sufficient knowledge.
2. Any computer can do only what it is programmed to do. "[I]t cannot protect itself from either malfunctions or deliberate attacks unless such events have been specifically anticipated, thought through, and countered with appropriate programming."

Computer owners and administrators use a variety of security techniques to protect their systems, ranging from everyday low-tech locks to high-tech software scrambling.

Physical Access Restrictions

One way to reduce the risk of security breaches is to make sure that only authorized personnel have access to computer equipment. Organizations use a number of tools and techniques to identify authorized personnel. Computers can perform some security checks; human security guards perform others. Depending on the security system, you might be granted access to a computer based on

- *Something you have*—a key, an ID card with a photo, or a *smart card* containing digitally encoded identification in a built-in memory chip
- *Something you know*—a password, an ID number, a lock combination, or a piece of personal history, such as your mother's maiden name
- *Something you do*—your signature or your typing speed and error patterns
- *Something about you*—a voice print, fingerprint, retinal scan, facial feature scan, or other measurement of individual body characteristics; these measurements are collectively called biometrics.

10.8 Biometeric devices provide high levels of computer and network security because they monitor human body characteristics that can't be stolen. IriScan's PC Iris (above) can compare the patterns in the iris of the user against a database of employees and other legitimate users. The U-Match Bio-Link Mouse (right) checks the thumbprint of the user against a database of prints approved for access.

Because most of these security controls can be compromised—keys can be stolen, signatures can be forged, and so on—many systems use a combination of controls. For example, an employee might be required to show a badge, unlock a door with a key, and type a password to use a secured computer.

In the days when corporate computers were isolated in basements, physical restrictions were sufficient for keeping out intruders. But in the modern office, computers and data are almost everywhere, and networks connect computers to the outside world. In a distributed, networked environment, security is much more problematic. It's not enough to restrict physical access to mainframes when personal computers and network connections aren't restricted. Additional security techniques—most notably passwords—are needed to restrict access to remote computers.

Passwords

Passwords are the most common tool used to restrict access to computer systems. Passwords are effective, however, only if they're chosen carefully. Most computer users choose passwords that are easy to guess: names of partners, children, or pets; words related to jobs or hobbies; and consecutive characters on keyboards. One survey found that the two favorite passwords in Britain were "Fred" and "God"; in America they were "love" and "sex." Hackers know and exploit these clichés; cautious users avoid them. Many security systems refuse to enable users to choose any real words or names as passwords so hackers can't use dictionary software to guess them systematically. Even the best passwords should be changed frequently.

Access-control software doesn't need to treat all users identically. Many systems use passwords to restrict users so they can open only files related to their work. In many cases, users are given read-only access to files that they can see but not change.

To prevent unauthorized use of stolen passwords by outsiders, many companies use call-back systems. When a user logs in and types a password, the system hangs up, looks up the user's phone number, and calls back before providing access.

Firewalls, Encryption, and Audits

Many data thieves do their work without breaking into computer systems; instead, they intercept messages as they travel between computers on networks. Passwords are of little use for hiding email messages when they're traveling through phone lines or Internet gateways. Still, Internet communication is far too important to sacrifice in the name of security. Many organizations use firewalls to keep their internal networks secure while enabling communication with the rest of the Internet. The technical details of firewalls vary considerably, but they're all designed to serve the same function: to guard against unauthorized access to an internal network. In effect, a firewall is a gateway with a lock—the locked gate opens only for information packets that pass one or more security inspections.

Firewalls aren't just for large corporations anymore. Without firewall hardware or software installed, a home computer with an always-on DSL or cable modem connection can be easy prey for Internet snoopers. Windows XP and Mac OS X include basic software firewalls, but these firewalls must be activated before they can provide protection.

Of course, the firewall's digital drawbridge has to let some messages pass through; otherwise there could be no communication with the rest of the Internet. How can those messages be secured in transit? To protect transmitted information, many organizations and individuals use encryption software to scramble their transmissions. When a

10.9 Hardware firewall products come in all shapes and sizes. These hardware devices are used to protect large businesses from attack.

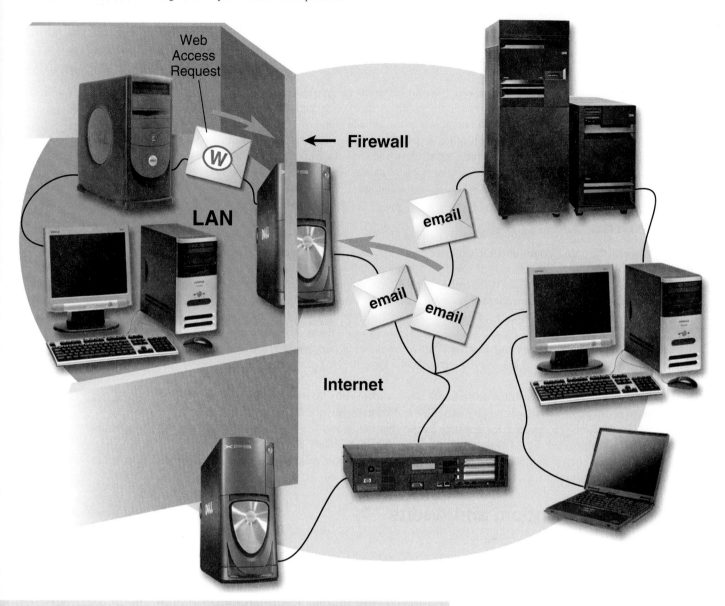

10.10 On a home or small business network, a PC can serve as a firewall by scaning every message for security risks before allowing it to pass out of a LAN.

user encrypts a message by applying a secret numerical code, called an *encryption key*, the message can be transmitted or stored as an indecipherable garble of characters. The message can be read only after it's been reconstructed with a matching key.

For the most sensitive information, passwords, firewalls, and encryption aren't enough. A diligent spy can "listen to" the electromagnetic signals that emanate from the computer hardware and, in some cases, read sensitive information. To prevent spies from using these spurious broadcasts, the Pentagon has spent hundreds of millions of dollars on a program called Tempest to develop specially shielded machines.

Audit-control software is used to monitor and record computer transactions as they happen so auditors can trace and identify suspicious computer activity after the fact. Effective audit-control software forces every user, legitimate or otherwise, to leave a trail of electronic footprints. Of course, this kind of software is of little value unless someone in the organization monitors and interprets the output.

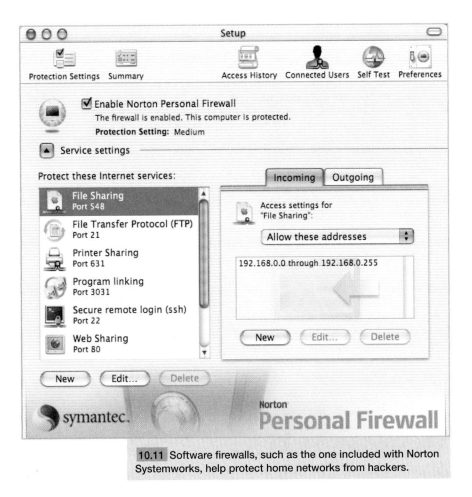

10.11 Software firewalls, such as the one included with Norton Systemworks, help protect home networks from hackers.

Backups and Other Precautions

Even the tightest security system can't guarantee absolute protection of data. A power surge or a power failure can wipe out even the most carefully guarded data in an instant. An **uninterruptible power supply (UPS)** can protect computers from data loss during power failures; inexpensive ones can protect home computers from short power dropouts. *Surge protectors* don't help during power failures, but they can shield electronic equipment from dangerous power spikes, preventing expensive hardware failures.

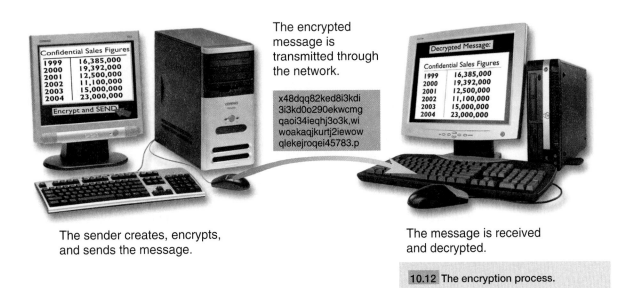

The encrypted message is transmitted through the network.

The sender creates, encrypts, and sends the message.

The message is received and decrypted.

10.12 The encryption process.

Cryptography

If you want to be sure that an email message can be read only by the intended recipient, you must either use a secure communication channel or secure the message.

Mail within many organizations is sent over secure communication channels—channels that can't be accessed by outsiders. But you can't secure the channels used by the Internet and other worldwide mail networks; there's no way to shield messages sent through public telephone lines and airwaves. In the words of Mark Rotenberg, director of the Electronic Privacy Information Center, "Email is more like a postcard than a sealed letter."

If you can't secure the communication channel, the alternative is to secure the message. You secure a message by using a cryptosystem to encrypt it—scramble it so it can be decrypted (unscrambled) only by the intended recipient.

Almost all cryptosystems depend on a key—a password-like number or phrase that can be used to encrypt or decrypt a message. Eavesdroppers who don't know the key have to try to decrypt it by brute force—by trying all possible keys until the right one is guessed.

Some cryptosystems afford only modest security: A message can be broken after only a day or week of brute force cryptanalysis on a supercomputer. More effective systems would take a supercomputer billions of years to break the message.

The traditional kind of cryptosystem used on computer networks is called a symmetric secret key system. With this approach the sender and recipient use the same key, and they have to keep the shared key secret from everyone else.

Secret Key System

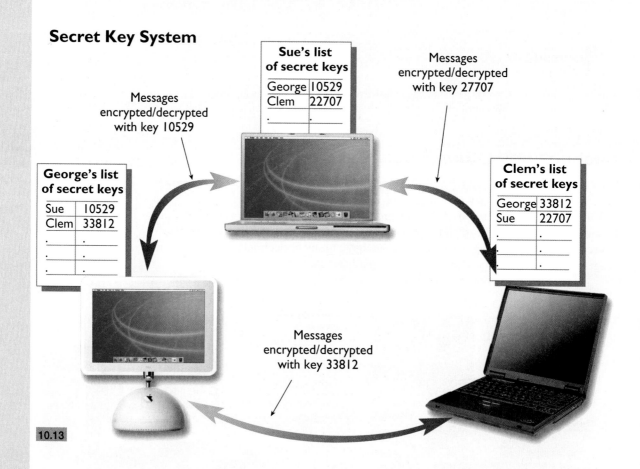

Sue's list of secret keys

George	10529
Clem	22707
.	.

Messages encrypted/decrypted with key 10529

Messages encrypted/decrypted with key 27707

George's list of secret keys

Sue	10529
Clem	33812
.	.
.	.
.	.

Clem's list of secret keys

George	33812
Sue	22707
.	.
.	.
.	.

Messages encrypted/decrypted with key 33812

10.13

The biggest problem with symmetric secret key systems is key management. If you want to communicate with several people and ensure that each person can't read messages intended for the others, then you'll need a different secret key for each person. When you want to communicate with new people, you have the problem of letting them know what the key is. If you send it over the ordinary communication channel, it can be intercepted.

In the 1970s, cryptographers developed public key cryptography to get around the key management problems. The most popular kind of public key cryptosystem, RSA, is being incorporated into most new network-enabled software. Phillip Zimmerman's popular shareware utility called PGP (for Pretty Good Privacy) uses RSA technology.

Public Key System

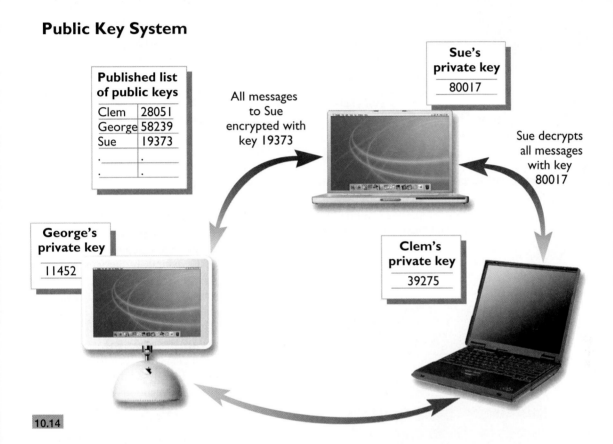

Published list of public keys

Clem	28051
George	58239
Sue	19373
.	.
.	.

All messages to Sue encrypted with key 19373

Sue's private key 80017

Sue decrypts all messages with key 80017

George's private key 11452

Clem's private key 39275

10.14

Each person using a public key cryptosystem has two keys: a private key known only to the user and a public key that is freely available to anyone who wants it. Thus a public key system is asymmetric: A different key is used to encrypt than to decrypt. Public keys can be published in phone directories, Web pages, and advertisements; some users include them in their email signatures.

If you want to send a secure message over the Internet to your friend Sue in St. Louis, you use her public key to encrypt the message. Sue's public key can't decrypt the message; only her private key can do that. The private key is specifically designed to decrypt messages that were encrypted with the corresponding public key. Since public/private key pairs can be generated by individual users, the key distribution problem is solved. The only keys being sent over an insecure network are publicly available keys.

You can use the same technology in reverse (encrypt with the private key, decrypt with the public key) for message authentication: When you decrypt a message, you can be sure that it was sent from a particular person on the network. In the future, legal and commercial documents will routinely have digital signatures that will be as valid as handwritten ones.

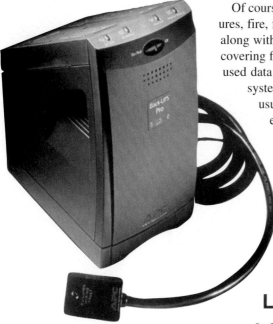

Of course, disasters come in many forms. Sabotage, human errors, machine failures, fire, flood, lightning, and earthquakes can damage or destroy computer data along with hardware. Any complete security system should include a plan for recovering from disasters. For mainframes and PCs alike, the best and most widely used data recovery insurance is a system of making regular backups. For many systems, data and software are backed up automatically onto disks or tapes, usually at the end of each workday. Most data processing shops keep several *generations* of backups so they can, if necessary, go back several days, weeks, or years to reconstruct data files. For maximum security, many computer users keep copies of sensitive data in several different locations. Storage technology called *RAID (redundant array of independent disk)* enables multiple hard disks to operate as a single logical unit. RAID systems can, among other things, automatically *mirror* data on multiple disks, effectively creating instant redundancy.

10.15 An uninterruptible power supply (UPS) protects a computer against power surges and momentary power loss.

Human Security Controls: Law, Management, and Ethics

In 2003 the supplier of the world's most used software products launched a "Trustworthy Computing" initiative. Microsoft's long-term goal was to make the software it develops as secure as possible when released, lessening the need for expensive and time-consuming security patches. Security experts throughout the computer industry are constantly developing new technologies and techniques for protecting computer systems from computer criminals. But at the same time, criminals continue to refine their craft. In the ongoing competition between the law and the lawless, computer security generally lags behind. In the words of Tom Forester and Perry Morrison in *Computer Ethics,* "Computer security experts are forever trying to shut the stable door after the horse has bolted."

Ultimately, computer security is a human problem that can't be solved by technology alone. Security is a management issue, and a manager's actions and policies are critical to the success of a security program. An alarming number of companies are lax about computer security. Many managers don't understand the problems and don't think they are at risk. It's important for managers to understand the practical, ethical, and legal issues surrounding security. Managers must make their employees aware of security issues and security risks. If managers don't defend against security threats, information can't be secure.

10.16 A RAID storage device combines hard drives to create a redundant data store that can withstand hardware failures.

Security, Privacy, Freedom, and Ethics: The Delicate Balance

In this age of advanced technology, **thick walls** and **locked doors** cannot guard our **privacy** or safeguard our **personal freedom**.
—Lyndon B. Johnson, 36th president of the United States, February 23, 1974

It's hard to overstate the importance of computer security in our networked world. Destructive viruses, illegal interlopers, crooked co-workers, software pirates, and cyber-vandals can erode trust, threaten jobs, and make life difficult for everyone. But sometimes computer security measures can create problems of their own. Complex access procedures, virus-protection programs, intellectual property laws, and other security measures can, if carried too far, interfere with people getting their work done. In the extreme, security can threaten individual human rights.

When Security Threatens Privacy

As we've seen in other chapters, computers threaten our personal privacy on several fronts. Corporate and government databases accumulate and share massive amounts of information about us against our will and without our knowledge. Internet-monitoring programs and software snoopers track our Web explorations and read our electronic mail. Corporate managers use monitoring software to measure worker productivity and observe their on-screen activities. Government security agencies secretly monitor telephone calls and data transmissions.

When security measures are used to prevent computer crime, they usually help protect privacy rights at the same time. When a hacker invades a computer system, legitimate users of the system might have their private communications monitored by the intruder. When an outsider breaks into the database of a bank, the privacy of every bank customer is at risk. The same applies to government computers, credit bureau computers, and any other computer containing data on private citizens. The security of these systems is important for protecting people's privacy.

But in some cases security and law enforcement can pose threats to personal privacy. Here are some examples:

■ In 1990 Alana Shoar, email coordinator for Epson America, Inc., found stacks of printouts of employee email messages in her boss's office—messages that employees believed were private. Shortly after confronting her boss, she was fired for "gross misconduct and insubordination." She filed a class-action suit, claiming that Epson routinely monitored all email messages. Company officials denied the charges but took a firm stand on their right to any information stored on, sent to, or taken from their business computers. The courts ruled in Epson's favor. Since then, many other U.S. court decisions have reinforced a company's right to read employee email stored on company computers.

■ In 1995 the U.S. government passed legislation requiring new digital phone systems to include additional switches that allow for electronic surveillance. This legislation protects the FBI's ability to wiretap at the expense of individual privacy. Detractors have pointed out that this digital "back door" could be abused by government agencies and could also be used by savvy criminals to perform illegal wiretaps. Government officials argue that wiretapping is a critical tool in the fight against organized crime.

■ The digital manhunt that led to the arrest of the programmer charged with authoring the Melissa virus was made as a direct result of information provided by America Online Inc. A controversial Microsoft document identification technology—the Global Unique Identifier, or GUID—may also have played a role. While virtually everyone was happy when the virus's perpetrator was apprehended, many legal experts feared that the same techniques will be used for less lofty purposes.

■ In 2000 the U.S. government found Microsoft guilty of gross abuses of its monopolistic position in the software industry. The government's case included hundreds of private email messages between Microsoft employees—messages that often contradicted Microsoft's public testimony.

■ A 2001 U.S. law required that mobile phones include GPS technology for transmitting the phone's location to a 911 operator in the case of an emergency call. Privacy activists fear that government agents and criminals will use this E911 technology to track the movements of phone owners.

■ In response to the terrorist attacks of September 11, 2001, the U.S. Congress quickly drafted and passed the USA Patriot Act, a sweeping act that redefined terrorism and the government's authority to combat it. The act defined "cyberterrorism" to include computer crimes that cause at least $5,000 in damage or destroy medical equipment. It increased the FBI's latitude to use wiretap technology to monitor suspects' Web browsing and email without a judge's order. Critics argued that this controversial law could easily be used to restrict the freedom and threaten the privacy of law-abiding citizens.

Even if you're not building a software system for the DOJ or the FBI, computer security is important. Viruses, disk crashes, system bombs, and miscellaneous disasters can destroy your work, your peace of mind, and possibly your system. Fortunately, you can protect your computer, your software, and your data from most hazards.

➡ *Share with care.* A computer virus is a contagious disease that spreads when it comes in contact with a compatible file or disk. Viruses spread rapidly in environments where disks and files are passed around freely, as they are in many student computer labs. To protect your data, keep your disks to yourself, and don't borrow disks from others.

➡ *Beware of email bearing gifts.* Many viruses hide in attachments to email messages that say something like "Here's the document you asked for. Please don't show anyone else." Don't open unsolicited email attachments, especially from senders you don't recognize; just throw them away.

➡ *Handle email with care.* Cunning thieves send email that looks like it comes from a legitimate company like PayPal or Amazon.com, asking you to update your personal information, including your credit card number and expiration date. But when you click on the link in the email, the Web site that loads isn't really from the legitimate company, opening unsuspecting users up to credit card theft. Regard all such emails with suspicion and be careful any time you enter a credit card number or other personal information online.

➡ *Handle shareware and freeware with care.* Some viruses enter systems in Trojan horse shareware and freeware programs. Treat public domain programs and shareware with care; test them with a disinfectant program before you install them on your hard disk. Viruses can be embedded in an email message or attachment, so scan attached files before opening them and use AV software regularly.

➡ *Don't pirate software.* Even commercial programs can be infected with viruses. Shrink-wrapped, virgin software is much less likely to be infected than pirated copies. Besides, software piracy is theft, and the legal penalties can be severe.

➡ *Disinfect regularly.* Virus protection programs are available for all kinds of systems, often for free. Use up-to-date virus protection software regularly.

➡ *Treat your removable disks as if they contained something important.* Keep them away from liquids, dust, pets, and (especially) magnets. Don't put your disks close to phones, speakers, and other electronic devices that contain hidden magnets. (Magnets won't harm CD-ROMs or DVD-ROMs, but scratches can make them unusable.)

➡ *Take your passwords seriously.* Choose a password that's not easily guessable, not in any dictionary, and not easy for others to remember. Don't post it by your computer, and don't type it when you're being watched. Change your password occasionally—immediately if you have reason to suspect it has been discovered.

➡ *If it's sensitive, lock it up.* If your computer is accessible to others, protect your private files with passwords and/or encryption. Many operating systems and utilities include options for adding password protection and encrypting files. If others need to see the files, lock them so they can be read but not changed or deleted. If secrecy is critical, don't store the data on your hard disk at all. Store it on removable disks and lock it away in a safe place.

➡ *If it's important, back it up.* Regularly make backup copies of every important file on different disks than the original. Keep copies of critical disks in different locations so that you have backups in case disaster strikes.

➡ *If you're sending sensitive information through the Internet, consider encryption.* Use a utility or a program like freeware PGP (Pretty Good Privacy) to turn your message into code that's almost impossible to crack.

➡ *Don't open your system to interlopers.* If you've got an always-on Internet connection—T1, DSL, or cable modem—consider using firewall hardware or software to detect and lock out snoopers. Set your file-sharing controls so access is limited to authorized visitors.

➡ *Prepare for the worst.* Even if you take every precaution, things can still go wrong. Make sure you aren't completely dependent on the computer for really important things.

One of the best examples of a new technology that can simultaneously improve security and threaten privacy is the active badge (sometimes called the *smart badge*). Researchers at the University of Cambridge and nearby Olivetti Research Center are developing and wearing microprocessor-controlled badges that broadcast infrared identification codes every 15 seconds. Each badge's code is picked up by a nearby network receiver and transmitted back to a badge-location database that is constantly being updated. Active badges are used for identifying, finding, and remembering:

■ *Identifying.* When an authorized employee approaches a door, the door recognizes the person's badge code and opens. Whenever anyone logs into a computer system, the badge code identifies the person as an authorized or unauthorized user.
■ *Finding.* An employee can check a computer screen to locate another employee and find out with whom that person is talking. With active badges there's no need for a paging system, and "while you were away" notes are less common.
■ *Remembering.* At the end of the day, an active-badge wearer can get a minute-by-minute printout listing exactly where he's been and whom he's been with.

Is the active badge a primitive version of the communicator on TV's *Star Trek* or a surveillance tool for Big Brother? The technology has the potential to be either or both; it all depends on how people use it. Active badges, like other security devices and techniques, raise important legal and ethical questions about privacy—questions that we, as a society, must resolve sooner or later.

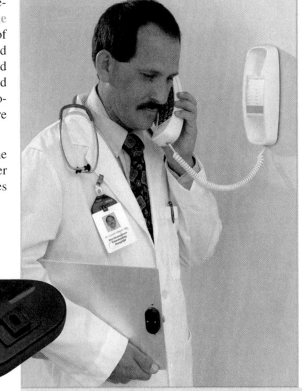

10.17 An administrator in a corporate network can temporarily log on to networked PCs and terminals with his elevated access privileges, perform some management tasks, and then walk away, leaving the system in its normal state. This active badge from Versus Technology also includes a button that can be programmed to send a message to a pager, open a locked door, or perform another task.

Justice on the Electronic Frontier

Federal and state governments have responded to the growing computer crime problem by creating new laws against electronic trespassing and by escalating enforcement efforts. Hackers have become targets for nationwide anticrime operations. Dozens of hackers have been

> Through our scientific genius, we have **made this world a neighborhood**; now through our moral and spiritual development, we must **make of it a brotherhood**.
>
> —The Rev. Martin Luther King, Jr.

arrested for unauthorized entry into computer systems and for the release of destructive viruses and worms. Many have been convicted under federal or state laws. Others have had their computers confiscated with no formal charges filed.

Some of the victims of these sting operations claim that they broke no laws. In one case a student was arrested because he published an electronic magazine that carried a description of an emergency 911 system allegedly stolen by hackers. Charges were eventually dropped when it was revealed that the "stolen" document was, in fact, available to the public.

Cases like this raise questions about how civil rights apply in the "electronic frontier." How does the Bill of Rights apply to computer communications? Does freedom of the press apply to online magazines in the same way it applies to paper periodicals? Can an electronic bulletin board operator or Internet service provider be held responsible for information others post on a server? Can online pornography be served from a house located in a neighborhood with antiporn laws? Are Internet service providers responsible when their users illegally trade music online?

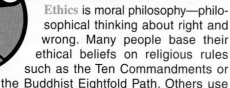

Ethics is moral philosophy—philosophical thinking about right and wrong. Many people base their ethical beliefs on religious rules such as the Ten Commandments or the Buddhist Eightfold Path. Others use professional codes such as the doctor's Hippocratic oath, which includes the often quoted "First do no harm." Still others use personal philosophies with principles such as "It's okay if a jury of observers would approve." But in today's changing world, deciding how to apply the rules isn't always easy. Sometimes the rules don't seem to apply directly, and sometimes they contradict each other. (How should you "Honor thy father" if you learn that he's using the home computer to embezzle money from his employer? Is it okay to allow a friend who's broke to borrow your Microsoft Office CD for a required class project?) These kinds of *moral dilemmas* are central questions in discussions of ethics. Information technology poses moral dilemmas related to everything from copying software to reporting a co-worker's sexually explicit screen saver or racist email.

Computer ethics can't be reduced to a handful of rules—the gray areas are always going to require thought and judgment. But principles and guidelines can help to focus thinking and refine judgments when dealing with technology-related moral dilemmas. The Association for Computing Machinery (ACM) **Code of Ethics**, reprinted in the Appendix of this book, is the most widely known code of conduct specifically for computer professionals. The ACM Code is worth understanding and applying even if you don't plan to be a "computer professional." Who shouldn't "Contribute to Society and Human Well-Being" or "Honor Confidentiality"? But these principles take on new meaning in an age of email and databases.

Here are some other guidelines that might help you to decide how to "do the right thing" when faced with ethical dilemmas at school, at work, or at home:

➡ **Know the rules and the law.** Many laws, and many organizational rules, are reflections of moral principles. For example, almost everyone agrees that *plagiarism*—presenting somebody else's work as your own—is wrong. It's also a serious violation of rules in most schools. And if the work is copied without permission, plagiarism can become copyright infringement, a serious legal offense … whether or not the work explicitly says that it is copyrighted.

➡ **Don't assume that it's okay if it's legal.** Our legal system doesn't define what's right and wrong. How can it, when we don't all agree on morality? The law is especially lax in areas related to information technology, because the technology changes too fast for lawmakers to keep up. It's ultimately up to each individual to act with conscience.

➡ **Think scenarios.** If you're debating between different actions, think about what might happen as a result of your actions. If you suspect your employer is falsifying spreadsheets to get around environmental regulations, what's likely to happen if you snoop around on his computer and blow the whistle on him? What's likely to happen if you don't? What are your other alternatives?

➡ **When in doubt, talk it out.** Discuss your concerns with people you trust—ideally, people with wisdom and experience dealing with similar situations. For example, if you're unsure about the line between getting computer help from a friend and cheating on homework, ask an instructor.

➡ **Make yourself proud.** How would you feel if you saw your actions on the front page of the *New York Times*, your company newsletter, or your family's hometown newspaper? If you'd be embarrassed or ashamed, you probably should choose another course of action.

➡ **Remember the golden rule: Do unto others as you would have them do unto you.** This universal principle is central to every major spiritual tradition, and it is amazingly versatile. One example: Before you download that bootleg MP3 file of that up-and-coming singer, think about how you'd feel about bootleggers if you were the singer.

➡ **Take the long view.** It's all too easy to be blinded by the rapid-fire rewards of the Internet and computer technology. Consider this guiding principle from a Native American tradition: In every deliberation, consider the impact of your decision on the next seven generations.

Laws like the Telecommunications Act of 1996 attempt to deal with these questions by outlining exactly what kinds of communications are legal online. Unfortunately, these laws generally raise as many questions as they answer. Shortly after passage a major section of the Telecommunications Act, called the Communications Decency Act, was declared unconstitutional by the Supreme Court. The debates continue inside and outside of the courts.

The Digital Millennium Copyright Act of 1998 (discussed earlier in this chapter) hasn't (so far) been found unconstitutional, but it has resulted in several lawsuits that raise serious human rights questions. In the summer of 2001, a Russian programmer and graduate student named Dmitry Sklyarov was arrested by the FBI after he spoke at a computer security conference in Las Vegas. His alleged crime was writing—not using—a program that cracks Adobe's copy protection scheme for e-books. After a Webwide demonstration against the arrest, Adobe publicly came out in favor of freeing Sklyarov.

The same law was used to silence Professor Edward Felton in 2001. The Princeton University computer scientist was threatened with a lawsuit from the Recording Industry Association of America if he presented a paper analyzing the system that encodes digital music; he withdrew the paper. Several months later Felton published the paper and the RIAA recanted its threat—but not its right to threaten similar suits in the future.

The DMCA was even used to file a suit against *2600* magazine because of a single Web site link. A Norwegian 15-year-old had written code allowing DVD movies to be played on Linux computers—code that broke the DVD copy protection scheme. *2600*'s Web site included a link to another site containing the program. (The *New York Times* Web site contained a link to the same site, but was not sued by the recording industry.)

When Congress passed the Telecommunications Act of 1996 and the Digital Millennium Copyright Act of 1998, it was attempting to make U.S. law more responsive to the issues of the digital age. But each of these laws introduced new problems by threatening rights of citizens—problems that have to be solved by courts and by future lawmakers. These laws illustrate the difficulty lawmakers face when protecting rights in a world of rapid technological change.

Security and Reliability

So far our discussion of security has focused mainly on protecting computer systems from trespassing, sabotage, and other crimes. But security involves more than criminal activity. Some of the most important security issues have to do with creating systems that can withstand software errors and hardware glitches.

> If the automobile had followed the same development cycle as the computer, a **Rolls Royce would today cost $100**, get a million miles per gallon, and **explode once a year**, killing everyone inside.
>
> —Robert X. Cringely, PBS computer curmudgeon

Bugs and Breakdowns

Computer systems, like all machines, are vulnerable to fires, floods, and other natural disasters, as well as breakdowns caused by failure of hardware components. But in modern computers, hardware problems are relatively rare when compared with software failures. By any measure bugs do more damage than viruses and computer burglars put together. Here are a few horror stories:

■ On November 20, 1985, the Bank of New York's computer system started corrupting government securities transactions. By the end of the day, the bank was $32 billion overdrawn with the Federal Reserve. Before the system error was corrected, it cost the bank $5 million in interest.

■ In September 1999, the Mars Climate Orbiter burned up as it approached Mars because controllers had mixed up British and metric units. Three months later, the Mars Polar Lander went silent 12 minutes before touchdown. Investigators suspect software errors are at least partly responsible for this spectacular mission failure.

- Programs on NASA observation satellites in the 1970s and 1980s rejected ozone readings because the programmers had assumed when they wrote the programs that such low numbers could not be correct. It wasn't until British scientists reported ozone-level declines that NASA scientists reprocessed the data and confirmed the British findings that the Earth's ozone layer was in danger.

- The Therac 25 radiation machine for tracking cancers was thoroughly tested and successfully used on thousands of patients before a software bug caused massive radiation overdoses, resulting in the partial paralysis of one patient and the death of another.

- On January 15, 1990, AT&T's 30-year-old signaling system software failed, bringing the long-distance carrier's network to its knees. Twenty million calls failed to go through during the next 18 hours before technicians found the problem: a single incorrect instruction hiding among a million lines of code.

- On February 25, 1991, 28 American soldiers were killed and 98 others wounded when an Iraqi Scud missile hit a barracks near Dhahran, Saudi Arabia. A tiny bug in a Patriot missile's software threw off its timing just enough to prevent it from intercepting the Scud. Programmers had already fixed the bug, and a new version of the software was being shipped to Dhahran when the attack occurred.

10.18 These South Koreans, like many people around the globe, stocked up on food and cooking gas cans to prepare for possible emergency shortages as a result of Y2K computer failures. Those failures, of course, never happened.

Every year brings new stories of breakdowns and bugs with catastrophic consequences. But it wasn't until 1999 that a computer bug—the Y2K (year 2000) bug, or millennium bug—became an international sensation. For decades programmers commonly built two-digit date fields into programs to save storage space, thinking "Why allow space for the first two digits when they never change?" But when 1999 ended, those digits did change, making many of those ancient programs unstable or unusable. Programmers knowledgeable in COBOL, FORTRAN, and other ancient computer languages repaired many of the programs. But others couldn't be repaired and had to be completely rewritten.

Businesses and governments spent more than 100 billion dollars trying to head off Y2K disasters. Many individuals bought generators and guns, stockpiled food and water, and prepared for a collapse of the computer-controlled utility grids that keep our economy running. When the fateful day arrived, the Y2K bug caused scattered problems, ranging from credit card refusals to malfunctioning spy satellites. But for most people, January 1, 2000, was business as usual. It's debatable whether disasters were averted by billions of dollars worth of preventive maintenance, or whether the Y2K scare stories were overblown. The truth is undoubtedly somewhere between these two extremes. In any event, Y2K raised the public's consciousness about its dependence on fickle, fragile technology.

Given the state of the art of programming today, three facts are clear:

1. It's impossible to eliminate all bugs. Today's programs are constructed of thousands of tiny pieces, any one of which can cause a failure if it's incorrectly coded.

2. Even programs that appear to work can contain dangerous bugs. Some bugs are easy to detect and correct because they're obvious. The most dangerous bugs are difficult to detect and may go unnoticed by users for months or years.

3. The bigger the system, the bigger the problem. Large programs are far more complex and difficult to debug than small programs, and the trend today is clearly toward large programs. For example, Microsoft Windows 95 has 11 million lines of code and was considered huge at the time; Windows XP has over 30 million!

As we entrust complex computerized systems to do everything from financial transaction processing to air traffic control, the potential cost of computer failure goes up. In the last decade, researchers have identified hundreds of cases in which disruptions to computer system operations posed some risk to the public, and the number of incidents has doubled every two years.

Computers at War

Nowhere are the issues surrounding security and reliability more critical than in military applications. To carry out its mission effectively, the military must be sure its systems are secure against enemy surveillance and attack. At the same time, many modern military applications push the limits of information technology farther than they've ever been before.

> Massive networking makes the U.S. the **world's most vulnerable target**.
>
> —John McConnell, former NSA director

Smart Weapons

The United States has invested billions of dollars in the development of smart weapons—missiles that use computerized guidance systems to locate their targets. A command-guidance system enables a human operator to control the missile's path while watching a missile's-eye view of the target on a television screen. A missile with a homing guidance system can track a moving target without human help, using infrared heat-seeking devices or visual pattern recognition technology. Weapons that use "smart" guidance systems can be extremely accurate in pinpointing enemy targets under most circumstances. In theory, smart weapons can greatly reduce the amount of civilian destruction in war if everything is working properly.

One problem with high-tech weapons is that they reduce the amount of time people have to make life-and-death decisions. As decision-making time goes down, the chance of errors goes up. In one tragic example, an American guided missile cruiser on a peacetime mission in the Persian Gulf used a computerized Aegis fleet defense system to shoot down an Iranian Airbus containing 290 civilians. The decision to fire was made by well-intentioned humans, but those humans had little time—and used ambiguous data—to make the decision.

10.19 In modern weapons systems, like those used by the North America Aerospace Defense Control (NORAD) in its Cheyenne Mountain Complex in Colorado Springs, Colorado, computers are critical components in the command and control process.

Autonomous Systems

Even more controversial is the possibility of people being left out of the decision-making loop altogether. Yet the trend in military research is clearly toward weapons that demand almost instantaneous responses—the kind that only computers can make. An autonomous system is a complex system that can assume almost complete responsibility for a task without human input, verification, or decision making.

The most famous and controversial autonomous system is the Strategic Defense Initiative (SDI)—former President Ronald Reagan's proposed "Star Wars" system for shielding the United States from nuclear attack. Recently resuscitated by President George W. Bush, the SDI system, as planned, will use a network of laser-equipped satellites and ground-based stations to detect and destroy attacking missiles shortly after launch, before they have time to reach their targets. SDI weapons will have to be able to react almost instantaneously, without human intervention. If they sense an attack, these system computers will have no time to wait for the president to declare war, and no time for human experts to analyze the perceived attack.

The automated missile defense system generates intense public debates about false alarms, hardware feasibility, constitutional issues, and the ethics of autonomous weapons. But for many who understand the limitations of computers, the biggest issue is software reliability. The system will require 10s of millions of lines of code. The system can't be completely tested in advance because there's no way to simulate accurately the unpredictable conditions of a global war. Yet to work effectively, the system will have to be absolutely reliable. In a tightly coupled worldwide network, a single bug could multiply and expand like a speed-of-light cancer. A small error could result in a major disaster. Many software engineers have pointed out that absolute reliability simply isn't possible now or in the foreseeable future.

In spite of years of political haggling, system failures, and cost overruns, the missile defense system is still in the works, and systems reliability issues remain. Supporters of automated missile defense systems argue that the technical difficulties can be overcome in time, and the U.S. government continues to invest billions in research toward that end. Whether or not a "smart shield" is ever completed, it has focused public attention on critical issues related to security and reliability.

Warfare in the Digital Domain

Even as the U.S. government spends billions of dollars on smart missiles and missile defense systems, many military experts suggest that future wars may not be fought in the air, on land, or at sea. The front lines of the future may, instead, be in cyberspace. By attacking through vast interconnected computer networks, an enemy could conceivably cripple telecommunications systems, power grids, banking and financial systems, hospitals and medical systems, water and gas supplies, oil pipelines, and emergency government services without firing a shot.

Several recent examples highlight our vulnerability:

- In 1994 Swedish hackers broke into telecommunications systems in central Florida and blocked several 911 systems by automatically dialing their numbers repeatedly. Anyone who called 911 with a legitimate emergency during the cyberattack was greeted with a busy signal.
- In 1996 a juvenile hacker disabled a key phone computer servicing a Massachusetts airport, paralyzing the airport control tower for six hours.
- In 1998 Israeli police working with the FBI, the U.S. Air Force, and NASA arrested three Israeli teens who successfully hacked into Department of Defense computers in both countries.
- During the 2000 U.S. election, dozens of politically motivated Web attacks occurred for various causes, parties, and countries. The attacks included Web site vandalism, denial of service attacks, and system snooping.

Thankfully, none of these crimes resulted in serious damage or injury. But terrorists, spies, or criminals might use the same techniques to trigger major disasters.

Recognizing the growing threat of system sabotage, then-Attorney General Janet Reno created the *National Infrastructure Protection Center* in early 1998. The NIPC's state-of-the-art command center is housed at FBI headquarters. The center includes representatives of various intelligence agencies (the departments of defense, transportation, energy, and treasury) and representatives of several major corporations.

Corporate participation is critical because private companies own many of the infrastructure systems that are most vulnerable to attack. Unfortunately, many businesses are slow to recognize the potential threat to their systems. They embrace the efficiency that networks bring, but they don't adequately prepare for attack through those networks.

In the wake of the terrorist attacks of September 2001, George W. Bush formed The President's Critical Infrastructure Board consisting of cabinet members and top presidential aides; this board was later transformed into the U.S. Department of Homeland Security. The cyberterrorism panel was designed to protect utilities and critical public services that depend on information networks.

Network attacks are all but inevitable, and such attacks can have disastrous consequences for all of us. In a world where computers control everything from money to missiles, computer security and reliability are too important to ignore.

Is Security Possible?

Computer thieves. Hackers. Software pirates. Computer snoopers. Viruses. Worms. Trojan horses. Wiretaps. Hardware failures. Software bugs. When we live and work with computers, we're exposed to all kinds of risks that didn't exist in the precomputer era. These risks make computer security especially important and challenging.

Because computers do so many amazing things so well, it's easy to overlook the problems they bring with them and to believe that they're invincible. But like Kempelen's chess-playing machine, today's computers hide the potential for errors and deception under an impressive user interface. This doesn't mean we should avoid using computers, only that we should remain skeptical, cautious, and realistic as we use them. Security procedures can reduce but not eliminate risks. In today's fast-moving world absolute security simply isn't possible.

Human Questions for a Computer Age

In earlier chapters we examined many social and ethical issues related to computer technology, including privacy, security, reliability, and intellectual property. These aren't the only critical issues before us. Before closing we'll briefly raise some other important, and as yet unanswered, questions of the information age.

The **important thing** to forecast is not the automobile but the **parking problem**; not the television but the **soap opera**.
—Isaac Asimov

It's the **end of the world** as we know it and **I feel fine.**
—R.E.M.

Will Computers Be Democratic?

In 1990 a spontaneous protest exploded across computer networks in reaction to the threat to privacy posed by Marketplace, a new CD-ROM product containing consumer information on millions of Americans. The firestorm of protest forced Lotus Development Corporation to cancel distribution of the product. In Santa Monica, California, homeless people used public-access terminals in the library to lobby successfully for more access to public showers. In France, student organizations used computer networks to rapidly mobilize opposition to tuition increases. In 1999 environmentalists, labor organizations, human rights groups, and a handful of anarchists used the Internet to mobilize massive protests at the World Trade Organization's Seattle meeting. The protests brought many issues surrounding the secretive WTO into the global spotlight for the first time.

The higher the technology, the **higher the freedom**. Technology enforces certain solutions: satellite dishes, computers, videos, international telephone lines force pluralism and freedom onto a society.
—Lech Walesa

When machines and computers, profit motives, and property rights are considered **more important than people**, the giant triplets of **racism**, **materialism**, and **militarism** are incapable of being conquered.
—Martin Luther King, Jr.

Computers are often used to promote the democratic ideals and causes of common people. Many analysts argue that modern computer technology is, by its very nature, a force for equality and democracy. On the other hand, many powerful people and organizations use information technology to increase their wealth and influence.

Will personal computers and the Internet empower ordinary citizens to make better lives for themselves? Or will computer technology produce a society of technocrats and technopeasants? Will computerized polls help elected officials better serve the needs of their constituents? Or will they just give the powerful another tool for staying in power? Will networks revitalize participatory democracy through electronic town meetings? Or will they give tyrants the tools to monitor and control citizens?

Will the Global Village Be a Community?

> Progress in commercial information technologies will improve productivity, bring the world closer together, and **enhance the quality of life**.
>
> —Stan Davis and Bill Davidson, in *2020 Vision*

> The **real question** before us lies here: do these instruments further **life and its values** or not?
>
> —Lewis Mumford in 1934

A typical computer today contains components from dozens of countries. The modern corporation uses computer networks for instant communication among offices scattered around the world. Information doesn't stop at international borders as it flows through networks that span the globe. Information technology enables organizations to overcome the age-old barriers of space and time, but questions remain.

In the post–Cold War era, will information technology be used to further peace, harmony, and understanding? Or will the intense competition of the global marketplace simply create new kinds of wars—information wars? Will electronic interconnections provide new opportunities for economically depressed countries? Or will they simply make it easier for information-rich countries to exploit developing nations from a distance? Will information technology be used to promote and preserve diverse communities, cultures, and ecosystems? Or will it undercut traditions, cultures, and roots?

Will We Become Information Slaves?

> Our inventions are wont to be **pretty toys** which distract our attention from serious things. They are but improved means to an **unimproved end**.
>
> —Henry David Thoreau

> **Computers are useless**. They can only give you answers.
>
> —Pablo Picasso

The information age has redefined our environment; it's almost as if the human species has been transplanted into a different world. Even though the change has happened almost overnight, most of us can't imagine going back to a world without computers. Still, the rapid changes raise questions.

Can human bodies and minds adapt to the higher stimulation, faster pace, and constant change of the information age? Will our information-heavy environment cause us to lose touch with the more fundamental human needs? Will we become so dependent on our "pretty toys" that we can't get by without them? Will we lose our sense of purpose and identity as our machines become more intelligent? Or will we learn to balance the demands of the technology with our biological and spiritual needs?

Standing on the Shoulders of Giants

When we use computers, we're standing on the shoulders of Charles Babbage, Ada King, Alan Turing, Grace Hopper, Doug Engelbart, Alan Kay, and hundreds of others who invented the future for us. Because of their foresight and effort we can see farther than those who came before us.

> If I have seen farther than other men, it is because **I stood on the shoulders of giants**.
>
> —Isaac Newton

In Greek mythology Prometheus (whose name means "forethought") stole fire from Zeus and gave it to humanity, along with all arts and civilization. Zeus was furious when he discovered what Prometheus had done. He feared that fire would make mortals think they were as great as the gods and that they would abuse its power. Like fire, the computer is a powerful and malleable tool. It can be used to empower or imprison, to explore or exploit, to create or destroy. We can choose. We've been given the tools. It's up to all of us to invent the future.

10.20 Prometheus brings fire from the heavens to humanity.

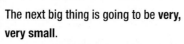

Microtechnology and Nanotechnology

The next big thing is going to be **very, very small**.

—Sarah Graham in *Scientific American*

We've seen how microcomputers have a gigantic impact on our lives, presenting us every day with great opportunities and risks. Scientists and engineers are working on machines that make today's microprocessors look massive. It's hard to imagine the impact these machines might have on our future.

MICROTECHNOLOGY

The miniaturization achieved in the computer industry is now producing *micromachines*—machines on the scale of a millionth of a meter. Microscopic moving parts are etched in silicon using a process similar to that of manufacturing computer chips. Universities, corporations, government labs, and start-up companies are doing research in *microelectromechanical systems (MEMS)*. For example, Japanese researchers have constructed a microcar not much bigger than a grain of rice.

So far most applications of microtechnology have been microsensors—tiny devices that can detect pressure, temperature, and other environmental qualities. Microsensors are used in cars, planes, and spacecraft, but they show promise in medicine, too. BioMEMS—MEMS that apply chip technology to biological applications—may soon cure some forms of deafness and blindness, stimulate paralyzed limbs, and deliver drugs precisely where they're needed. Researchers have developed a smart pill that combines a thermometer with a transmitter so it can broadcast temperatures as it travels through a human digestive tract. This pill is a first step toward other pills that might play more active roles inside our bodies. Tiny machines may someday be able to roam through bodies, locating and destroying cancer cells and invading organisms!

NANOTECHNOLOGY

If microtechnology is carried to its extreme, it becomes *nanotechnology*—the manufacture of machines on a scale of a few billionths of a meter. Nanomachines would have to be constructed atom by atom using processes drawn from particle physics, biophysics, and molecular biology. Researchers are working on molecular-scale electronics (moletronics) that might eventually produce computers that perform *billions* of times faster than today's fastest machines. Others are working on technology that may allow wires and switches to chemically assemble themselves at the molecular level, eliminating the need to etch circuits onto chips.

In 2001 IBM researchers built the first computer circuit contained within a single molecule. That same year scientists at Bell Labs—the birthplace of the first transistor in 1947—created a transistor from a single molecule. These breakthroughs could help carry the computing industry past the silicon dead end that's threatening to overturn Moore's Law within a few years. They may be stepping stones on the road to *quantum computers*—computers based on the properties of atoms and their nuclei and the laws of quantum mechanics.

Quantum computers are still decades away. But computers based on microtechnology and nanotechnology may be just a few years in the future. Many researchers think that molecular circuits could be produced at a fraction of the cost of today's microprocessors, because they're built through a purely chemical, or "self-assembly," process, similar to growing a crystal. "If we can truly make this kind of technology manufacturable . . . we'll have computing that's cheap enough to throw away," says Yale scientist Mark Reed.

Meanwhile, geneticists are gradually unlocking the secrets of DNA—biology's self-replicating molecular memory devices. These and other research threads may someday lead to atomic assembler devices that can construct nanomachines. Submicron computers, germ-sized robots, self-assembling machines, intelligent clothes, alchemy . . . the possibilities are staggering—and the possible risks grave. This technology of the tiny, like today's computer technology, raises difficult questions. It's our responsibility to ask those questions—and do our best to provide answers—as we build our future.

techtv

10.21 These tiny mirrors can rotate up and down to switch data in an optical network. More than 500 mirrors are fabricated on less than a square inch of silicon.

50um

10.22 This micromachine isn't much larger than red blood cells (lower right and top left) or a grain of pollen (top right).

Idiocy Imperils the Web

Jim Rapoza

We normally think of computer virus writers as villains and the people whose machines are infected as victims. Jim Rapoza suggests another way to assign blame for the virus problem in this column from the June 13 issue of Eweek. *Rapoza uses humor to make his point on a very serious matter.*

You people are such idiots!

Not *you*, of course. I mean those *other* people, the ones who make it so easy for every simple, standard virus to propagate across the Web. Twice in the last few weeks, I've had the same experience. I receive a security notice on a new virus, first Fizzer and then Palyh. I then find out that they infect Windows-based systems when a user opens an attachment from an unsolicited e-mail message. I then think to myself, "This won't be big; everyone knows you don't open attachments in unexpected e-mails." Then the virus spreads across tens of thousands of systems.

What's up with these people? Over the last few years, there have been hundreds of new viruses that spread in this manner. Most people figure out that if they keep grabbing the electric fence, they'll get a shock every time. So why do they continue to stupidly open attachments they aren't expecting?

To some degree, the fault for this lies with the technology press. We tend to take each new virus too seriously while not taking the time to shame the morons who are making it possible for the viruses to succeed.

Imagine if there were a rash of car thefts where thieves stole a bunch of cars that were left running with the doors open. Reporters wouldn't focus on the cleverness of the car thieves; they would point out the stupidity of the car owners. Or imagine thousands of cases of food poisoning from people eating completely raw chicken. I'm sure we would be reading plenty about the cluelessness of the "victims."

It's time for us to stop admiring virus writers and start dishing out heaping spoonfuls of shame to stupid users.

Instead of a headline like "Dangerous Fizzer Worm Attacks the Internet," how about "Thousands of Morons Open Obviously Virus-Laden E-mail Attachments"? I kind of like it. It has a light, comedic feel similar to headlines found at The Onion. But as Homer Simpson would say, it's funny because it's true. Stories like that should embolden smart users so that, instead of accepting their co-workers' incompetence, they will feel free to mock and ridicule these Typhoid Marys of the computer world.

The shaming wouldn't have to stop there. IT staff could put up posters identifying the stupidest virus-spreaders in the company. Rank-and-file employees could videotape their co-workers opening attachments with obvious virus subjects such as "Cool screensaver." We could have a new TV show, "America's Most Idiotic E-mail Users!" Webcams could be set up peering over the shoulders of those most likely to open an attachment. Watching a virus spread in real time could become a spectator sport.

But seriously, folks. It's very easy to teach even a kid how to avoid infecting most systems with viruses in e-mail attachments. So why isn't this message getting out? Because getting hit with a virus is considered acceptable. Too many people have taken the attitude that viruses are going to happen, and there's nothing you can do to stop them. This isn't true, but many people use it as a convenient excuse for their mistakes.

Obviously, we need to do a better job educating users, but we also need to remove the mystique that surrounds viruses. Virus victims need to realize that many viruses wouldn't exist without them and their careless use of their e-mail accounts.

It doesn't take a whole lot of effort to change. First, users need to be suspicious of the e-mail they receive. If you don't know who it's from and the subject is generic, delete it. If there are multiple versions of the same e-mail, it's most likely a virus or spam. And never, ever, open attachments that you weren't expecting. If you think it's something important, double-check with the sender.

When coupled with a good virus scanner, these simple efforts can keep most users from becoming victims of viruses that are doing little more than taking advantage of their stupidity. I follow these basic procedures, and I haven't had an e-mail-born virus infect one of my systems in more than five years.

So let's change our attitudes and our tactics. Let's get out the word that most of the time, when people get viruses, it's their own fault. Stupidity is nothing to be proud of.

DISCUSSION QUESTIONS

1. The author seems to be arguing that being the victim of a computer virus is something to be ashamed of. Do you agree? Explain your answer.

2. The author compares virus victims to careless car owners when he says, "Imagine if there were a rash of car thefts where thieves stole a bunch of cars that were left running with the doors open." A reader responded by asking what the reaction would be if the car companies gave us cars that could easily be stolen by 10-year-old thieves. Do you think this analogy makes sense? What does it suggest concerning solutions to the virus problem?

SUMMARY

Computers play an ever-increasing role in fighting crime. At the same time, law enforcement organizations are facing an increase in computer crime—crimes accomplished through special knowledge of computer technology. Most computer crimes go undetected, and those that are detected often go unreported. But by any estimate computer crime costs billions of dollars every year.

Some computer criminals use computers, modems, and other equipment to steal goods, money, information, software, and services. Others use Trojan horses, viruses, worms, logic bombs, and other software tricks to sabotage systems. According to the media, computer crimes are committed by young, bright computer wizards called hackers. Research suggests, however, that hackers are responsible for only a small fraction of computer crimes. The typical computer criminal is a trusted employee with personal or financial problems and knowledge of the computer system. The most common computer crime, software piracy, is committed by millions of people, often unknowingly. Piracy is a violation of intellectual property laws, which, in many cases, lag far behind the technology.

Because of rising computer crime and other risks, organizations have developed a number of computer security techniques to protect their systems and data. Some security devices, such as keys and badges, are designed to restrict physical access to computers. But these tools are becoming less effective in an age of personal computers and networks. Passwords, encryption, shielding, and audit-control software are all used to protect sensitive data in various organizations. When all else fails, backups of important data are used to reconstruct systems after damage occurs. The most effective security solutions depend on people at least as much as on technology.

Normally, security measures serve to protect our privacy and other individual rights. But occasionally, security procedures threaten those rights. The trade-offs between computer security and freedom raise important legal and ethical questions.

Computer systems aren't just threatened by people; they're also threatened by software bugs and hardware glitches. An important part of security is protecting systems—and the people affected by those systems—from the consequences of those bugs and glitches. Since our society uses computers for many applications that put lives at stake, reliability issues are especially important. In modern military applications, security and reliability are critical. As the speed, power, and complexity of weapons systems increase, many fear that humans are being squeezed out of the decision-making loop. The debate over high-tech weaponry is bringing many important security issues to the public's attention for the first time.

KEY TERMS

access-control software (p. 359)
active badge (p. 367)
antivirus (p. 355)
autonomous systems
   (p. 371)
backup (p. 364)
biometrics (p. 358)
Code of Ethics (p. 368)
computer crime (p. 348)
computer security (p. 358)
contract (p. 352)
copyright (p. 352)

denial of service (DoS) attack
   (p. 357)
encryption (p. 359)
ethics (p. 368)
firewall (p. 359)
hacking (p. 356)
identity theft (p. 350)
intellectual property (p. 352)
logic bomb (p. 353)
malware (p. 353)
nanotechnology (p. 376)
passwords (p. 359)

patent (p. 352)
sabotage (p. 353)
security patch (p. 356)
smart weapons (p. 371)
social engineering (p. 350)
software piracy (p. 351)
spoofing (p. 350)
Trojan horse (p. 353)
uninterruptible power supply (UPS)
   (p. 361)
virus (p. 353)
worms (p. 354)

INTERACTIVE QUIZ QUESTIONS

 1. The *Computer Confluence* CD-ROM contains self-test quiz questions related to this chapter, including multiple-choice, true or false, and matching questions.

 2. The *Computer Confluence* Web site, http://www.prenhall.com/beekman, contains self-test exercises related to this chapter. Follow the instructions for taking a quiz. After you've completed your quiz, you can email the results to your instructor.

The Web site also contains open-ended discussion questions called Internet Explorations. Discuss one or more of the Internet Exploration questions at the section for this chapter.

TRUE OR FALSE

1. Computer crimes often go unreported because businesses fear that they can lose more from negative publicity than from the actual crimes.

2. The majority of computer crimes are committed by hackers and vandals with no ties to the victim companies.

3. The software industry loses billions of dollars each year to piracy.

4. The owner of a patent must be the original inventor of the patented idea.

5. In general, computer viruses don't discriminate among operating systems; a typical virus can infect any system, regardless of platform.

6. Access-control software treats all users the same, in the same way a lock provides equal access to everyone with a key that fits the lock.

7. Computer security is ultimately a technological problem with technological solutions.

8. U.S. courts have ruled that your email is not private if you send and receive it on a computer at your workplace.

9. Computer ethics is defined as a collection of clear, unambiguous rules for dealing with computers.

10. While many questions remain about the viability of an automated missile defense system, computer scientists are confident that the software for the system will be reliable.

MULTIPLE CHOICE

1. According to a recent survey cited in the chapter,
   a. Internet security breaches are on the rise.
   b. internal security breaches are on the rise.
   c. computer crime in general is on the rise.
   d. All of the above are true.
   e. None of the above are true.

2. Which type of intellectual property law has traditionally applied to forms of literary expression?
   a. patents.
   b. copyrights.
   c. contract law.
   d. common law.
   e. None of the above.

3. Intellectual property laws
   a. have no significant relationship to patents and copyrights.
   b. are designed to prevent identity theft and similar crimes.
   c. were responsible for the rise of Napster and other music-sharing systems in the late 1990s.
   d. are intended to ensure that mental labor is justly rewarded and to encourage innovation.
   e. All of the above are true.

4. Most copyright and patent laws
   a. have been made obsolete by the Digital Millennium Copyright Act, a 1998 law widely praised for its effectiveness.
   b. were written during the PC era to deal with the intellectual property issues raised by digital technology.
   c. explicitly excluded works transmitted over computer networks.
   d. evolved during the age of print and mechanical inventions.
   e. None of the above.

5. A program that performs a useful task while at the same time carrying out some secret destructive act is called a
   a. virus.
   b. worm.
   c. Trojan horse.
   d. macro virus.
   e. None of the above.

6. Biometrics are often used
   a. to measure virus strength.
   b. to measure the speed of a spreading worm.
   c. to assess the power of a Trojan horse to bring down a computer system.
   d. to identify authorized personnel before allowing them to have access to computer systems.
   e. None of the above.

7. A surge protector can protect a system from
   a. firewalls.
   b. denial of service (DoS) attacks.
   c. power spikes.
   d. Trojan horses and worms.
   e. All of the above.

8. Which of these statements is true about bugs in computer software today?
   a. It's impossible to eliminate all bugs in a large program.
   b. Even a program that appears to work can contain dangerous bugs.
   c. The bigger the system, the bigger the number of bugs.
   d. All of the above are true.
   e. None of the above are true.

9. In our culture, people commonly base their ethical beliefs on all of these except
   a. religious rules.
   b. professional codes.
   c. personal philosophies.
   d. autonomous systems.
   e. personal principles.

10. Computer viruses can spread rapidly
    a. in environments where disks and files are passed around freely.
    b. in documents as email attachments.
    c. when infected shareware and freeware programs are downloaded onto PCs.
    d. All of the above.
    e. None of the above.

REVIEW QUESTIONS

1. Define or describe each of the key terms listed in the Key Terms section. Check your answers using the glossary.

2. Why is it hard to estimate the extent of computer crime?

3. Describe the typical computer criminal. How does he or she differ from the media stereotype?

4. What is the most common computer crime? Who commits it? What is being done to stop it?

5. What are intellectual property laws, and how do they apply to software?

6. Describe several different types of programs that can be used for software sabotage.

7. What are the two inherent characteristics of computers that make security so difficult?

8. Describe several different computer security techniques, and explain the purpose of each.

9. Every afternoon at closing time, the First Taxpayer's Bank copies all the day's accumulated transaction information from disk to tape. Why?

10. In what ways can computer security protect the privacy of individuals? In what ways can computer security threaten the privacy of individuals?

11. What are smart weapons? How do they differ from conventional weapons? What are the advantages and risks of smart weapons?

DISCUSSION QUESTIONS

1. Are computers morally neutral? Explain your answer.

2. Suppose Whizzo Software Company produces a program that looks, from the user's point of view, exactly like the immensely popular BozoWorks from Bozo, Inc. Whizzo insists that it didn't copy any of the code in BozoWorks; it just tried to design a program that would appeal to BozoWorks users. Bozo cries foul and sues Whizzo for violation of intellectual property laws. Do you think the laws should favor Bozo's arguments or Whizzo's? Why?

3. What do you suppose motivates people to create computer viruses and other destructive software? What do you think motivates hackers to break into computer systems? Are the two types of behavior related?

4. Some people think all mail messages on the Internet should be encrypted. They argue that if everything is encrypted, the encrypted message won't stand out, so everybody's right to privacy will be better protected. Others suggest that this would just improve the cover of criminals with something to hide from the government. What do you think, and why?

5. Would you like to work in a business where all employees were required to wear active badges? Explain your answer.

6. How do the issues raised in the debate over the missile defense system apply to other large software systems? How do you feel about the different issues raised in the debate?

PROJECTS

1. Talk to employees at your campus computer labs and computer centers about security issues and techniques. What are the major security threats according to these employees? What security techniques are used to protect the equipment and data in each facility? Are these techniques adequate? Report on your findings.

2. Perform the same kind of interviews at local businesses. Do businesses view security differently than your campus personnel?

SOURCES AND RESOURCES

Books

A Gift of Fire: Social, Legal, and Ethical Issues in Computing, Second Edition, by Sara Baase (Upper Saddle River, NJ: Prentice-Hall, 2003). This book offers a thorough, easy-to-read overview of the human questions facing us as a result of the computer revolution: privacy, security, reliability, accountability, and the rest.

Cyberethics: Morality and Law in Cyberspace, by Richard Spinello (Sudbury, MA: Jones and Bartlett, 2000). This book surveys most of the big issues of computer ethics: intellectual property, privacy, security, free speech, and others. Case studies help make theoretical concepts concrete.

Readings in CyberEthics, edited by Richard A. Spinello and Herman T. Tavani (Sudbury, MA: Jones and Bartlett, 2001). This collection of papers and articles includes sections on freedom of expression, property, privacy, and other critical subjects related to information technology.

Computer Network Security and CyberEthics, by Joseph Migga Kizza (Jefferson, NC: McFarland & Co., 2001). This book clearly analyzes the causes, cost, and consequences of computer crime and cracking.

Secrets and Lies: Digital Security in a Networked World, by Bruce Schneier (New York: Wiley, 2000). Mathematician and computer security expert Schneier tells you in clear, lively prose how to think like a computer thief so you can protect yourself and your organization from that thief.

The Hundredth Window: Protecting Your Privacy and Security in the Age of the Internet, by Charles Jennings and Lori Fena (New York: Free Press, 2000). The Internet is only as secure as its weakest link. This practical book can help you to understand where the weakest links are and how to protect your privacy online.

Identity Theft, by John R. Vacca (Upper Saddle River, NJ: Prentice Hall, 2003). This thorough book is written for professionals, but it's accessible enough that any technologically aware person should be able to learn how to safeguard personal information.

Cyberwars: Espionage on the Internet, by Jean Guisnel (New York: Plenum, 1997). If you need proof that the Internet has graduated from its role as a research assistant, read *Cyberwars*. Guisnel, a respected French journalist, exposes the emerging online battle zones where spies, saboteurs, government agents, drug traffickers, and others wage virtual wars. Even though we can't see them happening, we're all victims of the fallout from these dangerous battles.

Hackers: Heroes of the Computer Revolution, by Steven Levy (New York: Delta, 1994). This book helped bring the word *hackers* into the public's vocabulary. Levy's entertaining account of the golden age of hacking gives a historical perspective to today's anti-hacker mania.

The Cuckoo's Egg, by Cliff Stoll (New York: Pocket Books, 1989, 1995). This best-selling book documents the stalking of an interloper on the Internet. International espionage mixes with computer technology in this entertaining, engaging, and eye-opening book.

Takedown: The Pursuit and Capture of Kevin Mitnick, America's Most Wanted Computer Outlaw—by the Man Who Did It, by Tsutomu Shimomura with John Markoff (New York: Hyperion Books, 1996) and **The Fugitive Game**, by Jonathon Littman (New York: Little, Brown and Co., 1997). These two books chronicle the events leading up to and including the capture of Kevin Mitnick, America's number-one criminal hacker. *Takedown* presents the story from the point of view of the security expert who captured Mitnick. *The Fugitive Game* is written from a more objective, journalistic point of view.

Cyberpunk—Outlaws and Hackers on the Computer Frontier, Updated Edition, by Katie Hafner and John Markoff (New York: Simon & Schuster, 1995). This book profiles three hackers whose exploits caught the public's attention: Kevin Mitnick, a California cracker who vandalized corporate systems; Pengo, who penetrated U.S. systems for East German espionage purposes; and Robert Morris, Jr., whose Internet worm brought down 6,000 computers in a matter of hours.

The Hacker Crackdown: Law and Disorder on the Electronic Frontier, by Bruce Sterling (New York: Bantam Books, 1992). Famed cyberpunk author Sterling turns to nonfiction to tell both sides of the story of the war between hackers and federal law enforcement agencies. The complete text is available online along with rest-of-the-story updates.

Ender's Game, by Orson Scott Card (New York: Tor Books, 1999). This award-winning, entertaining science fiction opus has become a favorite of the cryptography crowd because of its emphasis on encryption to protect privacy.

The Blue Nowhere, by Jeffery Deaver (New York: Simon & Schuster, 2001). This suspenseful thriller involves a sadistic hacker who invades his victims' computers, meddles with their lives, and lures them to their deaths. Though fictional, the novel presents a terrifyingly accurate analysis of the lack of privacy and security on the Internet.

The Postman, by David Brin (New York: Bantam, 1990). This entertaining science fiction novel weaves a tale of the future that raises many of the same issues raised by Kempelen's chess-playing machine. The disappointing 1997 movie bears little resemblance to the novel.

Periodicals

Many popular magazines, from *Newsweek* to *Wired*, provide regular coverage of issues related to privacy and security of digital systems. Most of the periodicals listed here are newsletters of professional organizations that focus on these issues.

Information Security (www.infosecuritymag.com). This magazine focuses on security problems and solutions. Some of the articles are technical, but most are accessible to anyone with an interest in security issues.

The CPSR Newsletter, published by Computer Professionals for Social Responsibility (P.O. Box 717, Palo Alto, CA 94302, 415/322-3778, fax: 415/322-3798, email: cpsr@csli.stanford.edu). An alliance of computer scientists and others interested in the impact of computer technology on society, CPSR works to influence public policies to ensure that computers are used wisely in the public interest. Their newsletter has intelligent articles and discussions of risk, reliability, privacy, security, human rights, work, war, education, the environment, democracy, and other subjects that bring together computers and people.

EFFector, published by the Electronic Frontier Foundation (155 Second St., Cambridge, MA 02141, 617/864-0665, fax: 617/864-0866, email: effnews-request@eff.org). This electronic newsletter is distributed by EFF, an organization "established to help civilize the electronic frontier." EFF was founded by Mitch Kapor (see Chapter 6) and John Perry Barlow to protect civil rights and encourage responsible citizenship on the electronic frontier of computer networks.

Ethix: The Bulletin of the Institute for Business, Technology, and Ethics (www.ethix.org, email: contact@ethix.org). The IBTE is a relatively new nonprofit corporation working to transform business through appropriate technology and ethical values.

Web Pages

As you might suspect, the Net is the best source of up-to-the-minute information on computer security and related issues. Public and commercial organizations maintain Web pages devoted to these issues, and dozens of newsgroups contain lively ongoing discussions on controversial topics. Check the *Computer Confluence* Web site for the latest links.

AFTER YOU READ THIS CHAPTER YOU SHOULD BE ABLE TO:

- Describe how computers have changed the way people work in factories, offices, homes, and a variety of industries

- Describe several ways in which computers have changed the quality of jobs, both positively and negatively

- Speculate on how our society will adjust as more and more jobs are automated

- Explain how the information age places new demands on our educational system

- Describe several ways computers are used in classrooms today

- Discuss the advantages and limitations of computers as instructional tools

- Describe the role of computers in our homes and leisure activities in the next decade

Multimedia extras on the CD-ROM and the Web:

- **Food** technology on video

- A **PlayStation** Supercomputer

- A degree in **game design**

- **Instant access** to glossary and key word references

- Interactive **self-study quizzes**

    . . . *and more.*

www computerconfluence.com

COMPUTERS AT WORK, SCHOOL, AND HOME

ALAN KAY INVENTS THE FUTURE

Alan Kay has been inventing the future for most of his life. Kay was a child prodigy who composed original music, built a harpsichord, and appeared on NBC as a "Quiz Kid." Kay's genius wasn't reflected in his grades; he had trouble conforming to the rigid structure of the schools he attended. After high school he worked as a jazz guitarist and an Air Force programmer before attending college.

His Ph.D. project was one of the first microcomputers, one of several that Kay would eventually develop. In 1968 Kay was in the audience when Douglas Engelbart stunned the computer science world with a futuristic demonstration of interactive computing. Inspired by Engelbart's demonstration, Kay led a team of researchers at Xerox PARC (Palo Alto Research Center in California) in building the computer of the future—a computer that put the user in charge.

Working on a back-room computer called the Alto, Kay developed a bit-mapped screen display with icons and overlapping windows—the kind of display that became the standard two decades later. Kay also championed the idea of a friendly user interface. To test user-friendliness, Kay frequently brought his children into the lab, "because they have no strong motivation for patience." With feedback from children, Kay developed the first painting program and Smalltalk, the groundbreaking object-oriented programming language.

In essence, Kay's team developed the first personal computer—a single-user desktop machine designed for interactive use. But Kay, who coined the term "personal computer," didn't see the Alto as one.

> The best way to **predict the future** is to **invent it.**
>
> —Alan Kay

In his mind a true personal computer could go everywhere with its owner, serving as a calculator, a calendar, a word processor, a graphics machine, a communication device, and a reference tool. Kay's vision of what he called the Dynabook is only now, three decades later, appearing on the horizon.

Xerox failed to turn the Alto into a commercial success. But when he visited PARC, Apple's Steve Jobs was inspired by what he saw. Under Jobs a team of engineers and programmers built on the Xerox ideas, added many of their own, and developed the Macintosh—the

11.1 Alan Kay

first inexpensive computer to incorporate many of Kay's far-reaching ideas. Kay became a research fellow at Apple, where he called the Macintosh "the first personal computer good enough to criticize." Today, virtually all PCs have user interfaces based on Kay's groundbreaking work.

After 12 years at Apple, Kay became a research fellow at Disney, where he developed Squeak, a graphical programming tool for children. Kay describes his MO (modus operandi) as "start with end users, usually children, and try to think about the kinds of experiences that would help them to grow in different ways." In 2002 Kay joined Hewlett Packard's research lab, while continuing his work with Viewpoints Research Institute, a nonprofit organization that works to improve general education and the understanding of complex systems.

Kay continues his crusade for users, especially small users. He says, as with pencil and paper, "it's not a medium if children can't use it." In a recent collaborative research project, Kay and MIT researchers worked with schoolchildren to design artificial life

11.2 Alan Kay's Dynabook was the early prototype for the modern personal computer.

forms in artificial environments inside the computer. Like many of Kay's research projects, the Vivarium project had little relationship to today's computer market. This kind of blue-sky research doesn't always lead to products or profits. But for Alan Kay it's the way to invent the future.

Alan Kay is one of a small group of people whose work has had a profound effect on our workplaces, our schools, and our homes. In this chapter we'll look at the impact computer technology has had on these three facets of our lives. In later chapters we'll delve deeper into the practical business applications of information technology; in this chapter we'll pay more attention to the big picture.

Where Computers Work

All those ones and zeros we've been passing around—the **fuel that fans the digital fire**—have reached critical mass and ignited, **big time.**

—Steven Levy

It's becoming harder all the time to find jobs that haven't been changed in some way by computers. Consider these examples:

- *Entertainment.* The production of television programs and movies involves computer technology at every stage of the process. Videographers capture clips on digital video cameras and pipe them through FireWire cables into Powerbooks for in-the-field editing. Scriptwriters use specialized word processors to write and revise scripts, and they use the Internet to beam the scripts between Hollywood and New York. Artists and technicians use graphics workstations to create special effects, from simple scene fadeouts and rolling credits to giant creatures and intergalactic battles. Musicians compose sound tracks using synthesizers and sequencers. Sound editors use computer-controlled mixers to blend music with digital sound effects and live-action sound. Even commercials—especially commercials—use state-of-the-art computer graphics, animation, and sound to keep you watching the images instead of changing the channel with your remote control.

- *Publishing.* The newspaper industry has been radically transformed by computer technology. Reporters scan the Internet for facts, write and edit stories on location using notebook computers, and transmit those stories by modem to central offices. Artists design charts and drawings with graphics software. Photo retouchers use computers instead of brushes and magnifying glasses to edit photographs. Production crews

11.3 Computer games such as Otto Matic, a cartoon-style science fiction game, use 3D graphics to create compelling characters and environments.

assemble pages with computers instead of typesetting machines and paste-up boards. Many newspapers produce Web editions in addition to traditional paper publications. A few publications have abandoned paper altogether.

- *Medicine*. High-tech equipment plays a critical role in the healing arts, too. Hospital information systems store patient medical data, insurance records, and even X rays. Local area networks enable doctors, nurses, technicians, dietitians, and office staff to view and update information throughout the hospital. Doctors use wireless handheld devices to browse databases for drug interactions, order prescriptions, and have those prescriptions transmitted to pharmacies for fulfillment. For patients who are outside the hospital walls in remote locations, doctors use the Web to practice *telemedicine*. Computers monitor patient vital signs in intensive care units in hospitals, at home, and on the street with portable units that analyze signals and transmit warnings when problems arise. Databases alert doctors and pharmacists to the problems and possibilities of prescribed drugs. A variety of digital devices enable doctors to see inside our bodies. Every day computers provide medical researchers with new ways to save lives and reduce suffering.

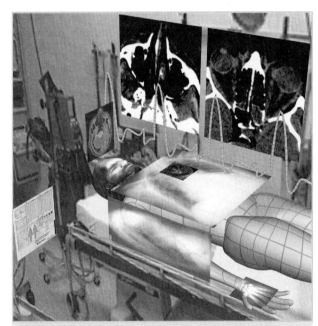

11.4 Medical students and professionals use this virtual emergency room to simulate processes of collecting vital signs and other patient data.

- *Airlines*. Without computers, today's airline industry simply wouldn't fly. Designers use CAD (computer-aided design) software to design aircraft. Engineers conduct extensive computer simulations to test them. Pilots use computer-controlled instruments to navigate their planes, monitor aircraft systems, and control autopilots. Air traffic controllers on the ground use computerized air traffic control systems to keep track of incoming and outgoing flights. And, of course, computerized reservation systems make it possible for all those planes to carry passengers.

11.5 Computers make data recording and analysis much easier for botanists and other scientists.

■ *Science.* From biology to physics, the computer has changed every branch of science. Scientists collect and analyze data using remote sensing devices, notebook computers, and statistical analysis programs. They catalog and organize information in massive databases, many of which are accessible through the Web. They use supercomputers, workstations, and processor-sharing grids to create computer models of objects or environments that would otherwise be out of reach. They communicate with colleagues all over the world through the Internet. It's hard to find a scientist today who doesn't work with computers.

Clearly, computers are part of the workplace. To get a perspective on how computers affect the way we work, we consider the three computerized workplaces that have attracted the most attention: the automated factory, the automated office, and the electronic cottage.

The Automated Factory

Businessmen go down with their businesses because they like the **old way** so well they cannot **bring themselves to change.**

—Henry Ford

In Chapter 13 we discuss the use of robots. In the modern automated factory *robots*—computer-controlled machines designed to perform specific manual tasks—are used for painting, welding, and other repetitive assembly-line jobs. (Robots are discussed in more detail in Chapter 15.) But robots alone don't make an automated factory. Computers also help track inventory, time the delivery of parts, control the quality of the production, monitor wear and tear on machines, and schedule maintenance. As described in Chapter 6, engineers use CAD (computer-aided design) and CAM (computer-aided manufacturing) technologies to design new products and the machines that build those products. Web cameras and Web displays built into assembly-line equipment enable workers and managers to monitor production and inventory from across the factory floor or across the continent.

An automated factory is more efficient than a traditional factory for two reasons:

■ Automation allows for tighter integration of planning with manufacturing, reducing the time that materials and machines sit idle.
■ Automation reduces waste in facilities, raw materials, and labor.

IBM's highly automated computer chip plant in East Fishkill, New York, produces tens of millions of chips each year using a fraction of the workforce used in other chip factories. When a fierce storm sent the employees home during the plant's first winter online, the computers and robotic machines continued to crank out chips through the night. This automated factory has greatly increased IBM's chip-making productivity.

If automation is good news for factory owners, it poses a threat to blue-collar workers who keep traditional factories running. In a typical high-tech manufacturing firm today, approximately half of the staff are engineers, accountants, marketing specialists, and other white-collar workers.

11.6 The assembly line for manufacturing computer chips is highly automated.

The Automated Office

As the number of factory jobs declines, office work plays a more important role in our economy. Modern offices, like modern factories, have been transformed by computers. Many automated offices have evolved along with their computers.

> We now **mass produce information** the way we used to **mass produce cars.**
>
> —John Naisbitt, in *Megatrends*

Office Automation Evolution

Office automation goes back to the mainframe era, when banks, insurance companies, and other large institutions used computers for behind-the-scenes jobs such as accounting and payroll. Early computer systems were faster and more accurate than the manual systems they replaced but were rigid and difficult to use. The machines and the technicians who worked with them were hidden away in basement offices, isolated from their organizations. The introduction of timesharing operating systems and database management systems enabled workers throughout organizations to access computer data. This kind of centralized computing placed computer-related decisions in the hands of central data processing managers.

Personal computers changed all that. Early Apple and Tandy computers were carried into offices on the sly by employees who wanted to use their own computers instead of company mainframes. But as managers recognized the power of word processors, spreadsheets, and other applications, they incorporated PCs into organizational plans. Jobs migrated from mainframes to desktops, and people used PCs to do things that the mainframes weren't programmed to do. In many organizations power struggles erupted between mainframe advocates and PC enthusiasts.

Enterprise Computing

Today, PCs are essential parts of the overall computing structure for most business enterprises. Workers use word processing software to generate memos and reports, marketing teams create promotional pieces using desktop publishing tools, and financial departments analyze budgets using spreadsheets. They communicate with each other and with the outside world through email, instant messaging, and the Web.

Chief information officers (CIOs) and chief technology officers (CTOs)—the chief decision makers concerning enterprise computer systems and technology—recognize the value of the PC, although some raise questions about its cost. Research suggests that the *total cost of ownership (TCO)* of a typical PC is many times more than the cost of hardware and software. Training, support, maintenance, troubleshooting, and other expenses push the TCO up to anywhere from $6,000 to $13,000 per PC per year! To reduce costs, a few companies are replacing PCs with *thin clients*—network computers, Internet appliances, and similar devices. These low-cost, low-maintenance machines enable workers to access critical network information without the overhead of a PC or workstation.

11.7 The CIO and CTO are responsible for managing the information systems and information technology in an organization.

Some companies have abandoned mainframes altogether; others still use them for their biggest data processing tasks. In the age of networks the challenge for the IS manager is to integrate all kinds of computers, from mainframes to PCs, into a single, seamless system. This approach, often called distributed computing, enables PCs, workstations, and mainframes to coexist peacefully and complement each other.

Workgroup Computing

Groupware enables groups of users to share calendars, send messages, access data, and work on documents simultaneously. The best groupware applications enable workgroups to do things that would be difficult otherwise; they actually change the way people work in groups. Many of these applications focus on the concept of *workflow*—the path of information as it flows through a workgroup. With groupware and telecommunication, workgroups don't need to be in the same room, or even the same time zone. During much of the 1990s, Lotus Notes dominated this market, offering a complete, if expensive, workgroup solution for corporations.

But the advent of the Web changed the workgroup landscape. Many of the functions of a groupware program like Notes—email, teleconferencing, shared databases, electronic publishing, and others—were available for little or no cost through freely available Internet technologies. Corporations started installing intranets using HTML, Web browsers, and other Internet technologies. And because these intranets were built on standardized protocols like TCP/IP, corporations could open their intranets to strategic partners and customers, creating extranets. Lotus and other groupware manufacturers have responded by rebuilding their applications using standard Internet technologies and protocols, so their customers could have the best of both worlds: computer systems built on universal public standards, and customer support and customization from a groupware specialist.

Whether they're built from off-the-shelf Internet software or commercially customized packages, workgroup systems have the potential to transform radically the way businesses operate. Ted Lewis, author of *The Friction Free Economy*, suggests that modern information technology makes an organization

- Flatter, so it's easier for workers at any level to communicate with workers at other levels
- More integrated, so different business units communicate more openly with each other
- More flexible, so businesses can react more quickly to changes in their environments
- Less concerned with managing people and more concerned with managing processes.

The Paperless Office

Experts have also predicted the paperless office—an office of the future in which magnetic and optical archives will replace reference books and file cabinets, electronic communication will replace letters and memos, and Web publications will replace newspapers and other periodicals. In the paperless office people will read computer screens, not paper documents.

All of these trends are real: Digital storage media are replacing many paper depositories, computers now deliver more mail messages than postal carriers do, and the Web has accelerated a trend toward online publishing. But so far, computers haven't reduced the flow of paper-based information. What has changed is the way people tend to use paper in the office. According to Paul Saffo of the Institute for the Future, "We've shifted from paper as storage to paper as interface. It is an ever more volatile, disposable, and temporary display medium."

HTML, XML, Adobe's popular *PDF (portable document format)* and other technologies make it easier for documents to be transmitted and stored electronically without loss of formatting. But none of these technologies has made a significant dent in the wall of paper that surrounds most office workers. In the near future we may see a less-paper office, but a paperless office seems unlikely.

Electronic Commerce

The paperless office may be years away, but paperless money is already here for many organizations. Electronic commerce (e-commerce) has been around for years in its most basic form—buying and selling products through the Internet or a smaller computer network. But today, there's more to electronic commerce than handling purchase transactions and funds transfers on the Internet. E-commerce also includes marketing, sales, support, customer service, and communication with business partners.

Early electronic commerce involved transactions between corporations. Even today, *business-to-business (B2B)* transactions account for far more online sales than do *business-to-consumer (B2C)* transactions. But consumer commerce on the Web is growing fast. Some businesses, including computer manufacturers Dell and Apple, allow customers to electronically order customized goods and services; this kind of customization-on-demand wasn't practical or possible for most businesses before the Internet took hold. The Web is also fertile ground for person-to-person auctions, reverse auctions, and other types of sales that aren't practical outside the Web.

During the economic boom of the nineties, thousands of start-up dot-com companies experimented with a variety of new ways to do business on the Internet. Many of those dot-coms turned into dot-bombs, while others survived and prospered into the new decade. "Pure play" Internet companies—companies whose businesses are entirely built on the Internet—have, for the most part, been absorbed or displaced by traditional companies. Many successful business leaders have recognized that the Internet is more of a medium than a separate industry and that success depends on taking advantage of multiple sales and communication channels rather than depending exclusively on the Net.

The Electronic Cottage

Before the industrial revolution, most people worked in or near their homes. Today's telecommunications technology opens up new possibilities for modern workers to return home for their livelihood. For hundreds of thousands of writers, programmers, accountants, data-entry clerks, and other information workers, telecommuting by modem replaces hours of commuting by car in rush hour traffic. Others use their own computers when they work at home rather than connecting by modem to company computers. The term *telecommuter* typically refers to *all* home information workers, whether they "commute" by modem or not.

> **Telecommuting** may allow us to **redefine the issues** so that we're not simply moving people to work but also **moving work to people.**
>
> —Booth Gardner, former Washington governor

Futurist Alvin Toffler popularized the term electronic cottage to describe a home where technology enables a person to work at home. Toffler and others predict that the number of telecommuters will skyrocket in the coming decades. So far, the predictions have held. The International Teleworkers Association estimates that the number of American telecommuters almost tripled between 1995 and 2000. According to market research company Cahners, roughly 5 million workers in the largest corporations—10 percent of the enterprise workforce—telecommute via the Internet.

- Telecommuting makes sense—it's easier to move information than people. There are many strong arguments for telecommuting:
- Telecommuting reduces the number of automobile commuters, thus saving energy, reducing pollution, and decreasing congestion and accidents on highways, streets, and parking lots.
- Telecommuting saves time. If an information worker spends two hours each day commuting, that's two hours that could be spent working, resting, or relaxing with the family.
- Telecommuting allows for a more flexible schedule. People who prefer to work early in the morning or late at night don't need to conform to standard office hours if they telecommute. For many people, including parents of small children, telecommuting may be the only viable way to maintain a job.

11.8 Novelist Richie Swanson, winner of the Peace Writing award, works at home . . . in his houseboat.

Considering Computer Careers

Until recently, people who wanted to work with computers were forced to choose among a few careers, most of which required highly specialized training. But when computers are used by everybody from fast-food salesclerks to graphic artists, just about anybody can have some kind of "computer career." Still, many rewarding and high-paying computer-related careers require a fair amount of specialized education. If you're interested in a computer-related job, consider the following tips:

➡ **Learn touch-typing.** Computers that can read handwriting and understand spoken English are probably in your future—but not your immediate future. Several low-cost typing tutorial programs can help you to teach your fingers how to type. The time you invest will pay you back quickly. The sooner you learn, the sooner you'll start reaping the rewards.

➡ **Use computers regularly to help you accomplish your immediate goals.** Word process your term papers. Use spreadsheets and other math software as calculation aids. Use the Web for research work. Computers are part of your future. If you use them regularly, they'll become second nature, like telephones and pencils. If you don't own a computer, find a way to buy one if you can.

➡ **Don't forsake the basics.** If you want to become a programmer, a systems analyst, a computer scientist, a computer engineer, or some other kind of computer professional, don't focus all your attention on computers. A few young technical wizards become successful programmers without college degrees; Bill Gates is probably the best-known example. But if you're not gifted and lucky, you'll need a solid education to land a good job. Math and communication skills (written and oral) are extremely important. Opportunities abound for people who can understand computers and communicate clearly.

➡ **Combine your passions.** If you like art and computers, explore computer art, graphic design, or multimedia. If you love ecology and computers, find out how computers are used by ecologists. People who can speak the language of computers and the language of a specialized field have opportunities to build bridges.

➡ **Ask questions.** The best way to find out more about computer careers is to ask the people who have computer careers. Most people are happy to talk about their jobs if you're willing to listen.

➡ **Cultivate community.** Computer networks are changing our lives, but people networks are still more important for finding and landing that dream job. Get to know the people in the professional community. Take an active part in that community. Join professional organizations. Give your time and energy to public service projects related to your field. Even if it doesn't pay off with a job offer, you'll be doing good work.

➡ **If you can't find your dream job, build it yourself.** Inexpensive computer systems provide all kinds of entrepreneurial opportunities for creative self-starters: publishing service bureaus, Web-site design, multimedia video production, custom programming, commercial art and design, freelance writing, consulting—the jobs are there for the making, if you have the imagination and initiative.

➡ **When you're ready to look, don't forget the Web.** There are plenty of job bulletin boards, online career-hunting centers, Internet headhunters, and e-cruiters offering jobs that might be just right for you.

➡ **Prepare for change.** In a rapidly changing world, lifelong careers are rare. Be prepared to change jobs several times. Think of education as a lifelong process. In Marshall McLuhan's words, "The future of work consists of learning a living."

■ Telecommuting can increase productivity. Studies suggest that telecommuting can result in a 10 percent to 50 percent increase in worker productivity, depending on the job and the worker.

Of course, telecommuting isn't for everybody. Jobs that require constant interaction with co-workers, customers, or clients aren't conducive to telecommuting. Working at home requires self-discipline. Some people find they can't concentrate on work when they're at home—beds, refrigerators, neighbors, children, and errands are simply too distracting. Others have the opposite problem: Workaholism cuts into family and relaxation time. Some workers who've tried full-time telecommuting complain that they miss the informal office social life and that their low visibility caused bosses to pass them over for promotions. In the words of one telecommuter, "When you're telecommuting you're far more productive than you can ever hope to be in the office, but you don't really have your finger on the pulse of the company." Most telecommuters report that the ideal work situation involves commuting to the office one or two days each week and working at home on the others.

Today, thousands of companies offer home-based work arrangements to millions of employees. Many firms encourage "boundaryless" employees to work in virtual teams when and where they can best get their jobs done. Other companies have strict policies against working at home. They cite resentment among office-bound colleagues, weakened corporate loyalty, and the difficulties of holding meetings as reasons for their policies. Some analysts suggest that as multimedia teleconferencing systems become affordable, telecommuting will become more popular with both workers and management. Workers and managers will be able to have a telepresence in the workplace when they aren't physically present.

In the meantime, several variations on the electronic cottage are taking hold. Many enterprising families use home computers to help them run small businesses from their home offices. A growing number of corporations and government organizations are establishing satellite offices and shared regional work centers outside of major urban centers that allow workers to commute to smaller offices closer to their neighborhoods. High-powered PCs and wireless handheld devices enable salespeople, executives, consultants, engineers, and others to take their offices with them wherever they travel. These mobile workers don't travel to the office; they travel with the office. Many experts predict that *m-commerce*—mobile commerce—will spread into dozens of other professions in the coming decade.

Computers and Jobs

When we think about automated factories, automated offices, and electronic cottages, it's easy to imagine utopian visions of computers in the workplace of tomorrow. But the real world isn't always picture-perfect, and many workers

> **John Henry told his captain** "A man ain't nothin' but a man. But before I let your steam drill beat me down **I'd die with a hammer in my hand. . . .**"
>
> —From the folk song "John Henry"

today are experiencing computers in less positive ways. In this section we look at some of the controversies and issues surrounding the automation of the workplace.

Computers and Job Quality

For many workers, computers have caused more problems than they have solved. Workers complain of stress, depersonalization, fatigue, boredom, and a variety of health problems attributed to computers. Some of these complaints are directly related to technology; others relate to human decisions about how technology is implemented.

De-Skilling and Up-Skilling

When a job is automated, it may be de-skilled; that is, it may be transformed so that it requires less skill. For example, computerized cash registers in many fast-food restaurants replace numbered buttons with buttons labeled "large fries" or "chocolate shake." Clerks who use these machines don't need to know math or think about prices. They simply push buttons for the food items ordered and take the money; computers do the rest.

Some of the most visible examples of de-skilling occur when offices automate clerical jobs. When word processors and databases replace typewriters and file cabinets, traditional typing-and-filing jobs disappear. Many secretaries are repositioned in data-entry jobs—mindless, repetitive jobs where the only measure of success is the number of keystrokes typed into a terminal each hour. When a clerical job—or any job—is de-skilled, the worker's control, responsibility, and job satisfaction are likely to go down. De-skilled jobs typically offer less status and less pay.

11.9 Specialized terminals like this one make it easy to log restaurant orders. How is this person's job different as a result of this technology?

In sharp contrast to those whose jobs are de-skilled into electronic drudgery, many workers find their jobs **up-skilled** by automation. For example, many clerical jobs become more technical as offices adopt databases, spreadsheets, email systems, Internet connections, fax modems, and other computer technology. In some cases, clerical workers use computer systems to do jobs formerly done by high-paid professionals and technicians. While many clerical people enjoy the added challenge and responsibility, others may be frustrated doing highly technical work with inadequate training. Clerical workers are seldom consulted before their jobs are computerized. And even though their work is more technically demanding than before, few clerical workers see this up-skilling reflected in their paychecks or level of responsibility.

Productivity and People

According to one study of 2,000 U.S. companies that implemented new office systems, at least 40 percent failed to achieve their intended results. Most of the failures were attributed to human or organizational factors rather than technical problems.

A computer system doesn't work in a vacuum. All too often computers are introduced into the workplace without any consideration of the way people work and interact. Workers are expected to adjust their work patterns to systems that are difficult and uncompromising. User training and support are often inadequate. It's hardly surprising that these computer-centered systems fail to spark productivity.

Many analysts argue that the most successful computer systems are **human-centered systems**. Such systems are designed to retain and enhance human skills rather than take them away. These analysts suggest that computer systems aren't likely to pay off unless they're accompanied by changes in the structure of work responsibilities, relationships with co-workers, and rewards for accomplishing job goals.

To create a human-centered system, systems analysts and designers must understand the work practices of the people who'll be using the system. It helps if users of the systems are involved in designing the system and the system-related jobs. In Norway, laws require that unionized workers be included in the planning and design of new computer systems. As a result, workers have greater control over their jobs and greater job satisfaction. Similar worker-centered approaches have been applied in Sweden, Britain, and, more recently, the United States.

Many experts believe that this human-centered approach is a key to increasing overall productivity. Productivity will almost certainly increase as organizations adjust to computer technology and computer technology becomes more adaptable to the needs of users.

Monitoring and Surveillance

Another controversial aspect of office automation is **computer monitoring**—using computer technology to track, record, and evaluate worker performance, often without the knowledge of the worker. Monitoring systems can provide a manager with instant, on-screen reports showing the number of keystrokes for each clerk, the length of each phone call placed by an employee, details of Web wanderings, and the total amount of idle time for each computer. Some network software even enables a manager to view a copy of any worker's screen secretly at any time.

For a manager worried about worker productivity, computer monitoring can serve as a valuable source of information. But computer monitoring brings with it several problems:

- *Privacy.* In Chapters 7, 9, and 10, we saw how the misuse of database and network technology can threaten personal privacy. Computer monitoring compounds that threat by providing employers with unprecedented data on workers. Some employers monitor personal email messages and punish or fire employees who send "unacceptable" messages.
- *Morale.* Privacy issues aside, computer monitoring can have a powerful negative impact on morale. Because employees can't tell when they're being monitored, many workers experience a great deal of stress and anxiety. The boss can be seen as an invisible eavesdropper rather than as a team leader.

- *Devalued skills*. In the traditional office, workers were evaluated based on a variety of skills. A slow-typing secretary could be valued for her ability to anticipate when a job needed to be done or her willingness to help others with problems. Computer monitoring tends to reduce a worker's worth to simple quantities like "number of keystrokes per hour." In such systems a worker might be penalized for repairing a sticky chair, showing a neighbor how to reboot a terminal, or helping a co-worker overcome an emotional crisis.

- *Loss of quality*. Monitored workers tend to assume that "if it's not being counted, it doesn't count." The result of this assumption is that quantity may become more important than quality.

Millions of workers are monitored by computer, including factory workers, telephone operators, truck drivers, and, in some cases, managers. Cyber-snooping goes far beyond counting keystrokes and idle time. According to a 2001 study by the American Management Association, three out of four U.S. companies engage in some kind of electronic surveillance of their employees, including reviewing email, monitoring phone use, videotaping, and checking computer files. In the words of the director of the study, "Workplace privacy is a contradiction in terms. It's an oxymoron. I know the illusion of privacy is there, but you are not using your own stuff. The phone, the keyboard, the connections, the job itself—they don't belong to you; they belong to the company, legally."

Electronic Sweatshops and Offshore Outsourcing

Computer monitoring is common practice in data-entry offices. A data-entry clerk has a single job: to read information from a printed source—a check, a hand-printed form, or something else—and type it into a computer's database. A typical data-entry shop might contain hundreds of clerks sitting at terminals in a massive, windowless room. Workers—often minorities and almost always female—are paid minimum wage to do mindless keyboarding. Many experience headaches, backaches, serious wrist injuries, stress, anxiety, and other health problems. And all the while, keystrokes and breaks are monitored electronically. Writer Barbara Garson calls these worker warehouses **electronic sweatshops**, because working conditions bring to mind the oppressive factory sweatshops of the nineteenth century.

A growing number of electronic sweatshops are located across national borders from corporate headquarters in countries with lax labor laws and low wage scales. The electronic immigrants in these offshore shops don't need green cards to telecommute across borders, and they work for a fraction of what workers in developed countries cost. A data-entry clerk in the Philippines, for example, earns about $6 per day. With wages that low, many companies find it cost-effective to have data entered twice and use software to compare both versions and correct errors.

Data-entry clerk jobs aren't the only ones that are being moved across national borders. When you call a technical support or customer support line for a U.S. corporation, there's a good chance the call will be answered by an operator in India, Mexico, or another country with lower wages than those earned in the United States. The global telecommunications network makes it easy for corporations to move telephone and Internet support to cheaper job markets. Offshore operators are often given American-sounding names and trained not to reveal their locations to callers. Forrester Research predicts that 3.3 million service jobs will move offshore within the next 15 years.

11.10 Many data-entry workers spend their days in warehouse-sized buildings filled with computers.

Even highly educated programmers and system designers in the United States are being replaced by offshore workers by the thousands. The computer software industry in India, for example, employs tens of thousands of workers at a fraction of the cost of similarly skilled U.S. workers. The globalization of job markets makes it easy for corporations to shop for the cheapest labor forces with little or no regard for national boundaries, labor laws, and community impact.

Employment and Unemployment

My father had worked for the same firm for 12 years. They fired him. They **replaced him with a tiny gadget** this big that does everything that my father does only it **does it much better**. The depressing thing is **my mother** ran out and bought one.

—Woody Allen

When Woody Allen told this joke more than three decades ago, automation was generating a great deal of public controversy. Computer technology was new to the workplace, and people were reacting with both awe and fear. Many analysts predicted that automation would lead to massive unemployment and economic disaster. Others said that computers would generate countless new job opportunities. Today, most people are used to seeing computers where they work, and the computers-versus-jobs debate has cooled down. Job automation may not be a hot topic in comedy clubs today, but it's still an important issue for millions of workers whose jobs are threatened by machines.

Workers Against Machines

Automation has threatened workers since the earliest days of the industrial revolution. In the early nineteenth century an English labor group called the Luddites smashed new textile machinery; they feared that the machines would take jobs away from skilled craftsmen. The Luddites and similar groups in other parts of Europe failed to stop the wheels of automation. Modern workers have been no more successful than their nineteenth-century counterparts in keeping computers and robots out of the workplace. Every year brings new technological breakthroughs that allow robots and computers to do jobs formerly reserved for humans. And telecommunications technology has helped globalize job markets, making it easy for multinational corporations to move millions of information jobs to countries with low wages and lax labor laws.

Of course, computer technology creates new jobs, too. Somebody has to design, build, program, sell, run, and repair the computers, robots, and networks. But many displaced workers don't have the education or skills to program computers, design robots, install networks, or even read printouts. Those workers are often forced to take low-tech, low-paying service jobs as cashiers or custodians, if they can find jobs at all. Because of automation the unskilled, uneducated worker may face a lifetime of minimum-wage jobs or welfare. Technology may be helping to create an unbalanced society with two classes: a growing mass of poor, uneducated people and a shrinking class of affluent, educated people.

11.11 Robots do almost all of the assembly-line work in this factory.

Cautiously Optimistic Forecasts

Nobody knows for sure how computer technology will affect employment in the coming decades; it's impossible to anticipate what might happen in 10 or 20 years. And experts are far from unanimous in their predictions—especially since the economic downturn of 2001.

Most experts agree that information technology will result in painful periods of adjustment for many factory workers, clerical workers, and other semiskilled and unskilled laborers whose jobs are automated or moved to Third World countries. But many also believe that the demand for professionals—especially engineers, teachers, and health care professionals—is likely to rise as a result of shifts in the information economy.

Will we have enough skilled workers to fill those jobs? Economic growth may depend on whether we have a suitably trained workforce. The single most important key to a positive economic future may be education. But will we, as a society, be able to provide people with the kind of education they'll need? We'll deal with that question, and the critical issues surrounding education in the information age, later in this chapter.

Will We Need a New Economy?

In the long run, education may not be enough. It seems likely that at some time in the future, machines will be able to do most of the jobs people do today. We may face a future of *jobless growth*—a time when productivity increases not because of the work people do but because of the work of machines. We're already seeing signs of increased growth and productivity without a corresponding increase in jobs. If productivity isn't tied to employment, we'll have to ask some hard questions about our political, economic, and social system:

- Do governments have an obligation to provide permanent public assistance to the chronically unemployed?
- Should large companies be required to give several months' notice to workers whose jobs are being eliminated? Should they be required to retrain workers for other jobs?
- Should large companies be required to file "employment impact statements" before replacing people with machines in the same way they're required to file environmental impact statements before implementing policies that might harm the environment?
- If robots and computers are producing most of society's goods and services, should all of the profits from those goods go to a few people who own the machines?
- If a worker is replaced by a robot, should the worker receive a share of the robot's "earnings" through stocks or profit sharing?
- The average workweek 150 years ago was 70 hours; for the last 50 years it has been steady at about 40. Should governments and businesses encourage job sharing and other systems that allow for less-than-40-hour jobs?
- What will people do with their time if machines do most of the work? What new leisure activities should be made available?
- How will people define their identities if work becomes less central to their lives?

These questions force us to confront deep-seated cultural beliefs and economic traditions, and they don't come with easy answers. They suggest that we may be heading into a difficult period when many old rules don't apply anymore. But if we're successful at navigating the troubled waters of transition, we may find that automation fulfills the dream expressed by Aristotle more than 2,000 years ago:

> *If every instrument could accomplish its own work, obeying or anticipating the will of others . . . if the shuttle could weave, and the pick touch the lyre, without a hand to guide them, chief workmen would not need servants, nor masters slaves.*

Education in the Information Age

The **future is a race** between **education** and **catastrophe**.
—H. G. Wells

The information age is not just affecting the workplace. Its influences are felt in our educational system, too. Before it's over, the information revolution will have a profound and permanent effect on the way we learn.

The Roots of Our Educational System

The American educational system was developed more than a century ago to teach students the basic facts and survival skills they would need for jobs in industry and agriculture—jobs they would probably hold for their entire adult lives. This industrial age system has been described as a factory model for three reasons:

- It assumes that all students learn the same way and that all students should learn the same things.
- The teacher's job is to "pour" facts into students, occasionally checking the level of knowledge in each student.
- Students are expected to work individually, absorb facts, and spend most of their time sitting quietly in straight rows.

Despite its faults, the factory model of public education helped the United States to dominate world markets for most of the twentieth century. But the world has changed drastically since the system was founded. Schools have changed, too, but not fast enough to keep pace with the information revolution. Most experts today agree that we need to rebuild our educational system to meet the demands of the information age.

Information Age Education

Education is the **kindling of a flame**, not the filling of a vessel.
—Socrates

What should education provide for students in the information age? Research and experience suggest several answers:

- *Technological familiarity.* Many of today's older workers are having trouble adjusting to the information age because of technophobia—the fear of technology. These people grew up in a world without computers, and they experience anxiety when they're forced to deal with them. To prepare for the future, students need to learn how to work comfortably with all kinds of knowledge tools, including pencils, books, calculators, computers, and the Internet. But technological familiarity shouldn't stop with learning how to work with tools. Students need to have a clear understanding of the *limitations* of the technology and the ability to assess the benefits and risks of applying technology to a problem. They need to be able to *question* technology.
- *Literacy.* In the information age, it's more important than ever that students graduate with the ability to read and write. Many jobs that did not require reading or writing skills a generation ago now use high-tech equipment that demands literacy. A factory worker who can't read computer screens isn't likely to survive the transition to an automated factory.
- *Mathematics.* In the age of the five-dollar calculator, many students think learning math is a waste of time. In fact, some educators argue that we spend too much time teaching students how to do things like long division and calculating square roots—skills that adults seldom, if ever, do by hand. These arithmetic skills have little to do with being able to think mathematically. To survive in a high-tech world, students need to be able to see the mathematical systems in the world around them and apply math concepts to solve problems. No calculator can do that.

■ *Culture.* An education isn't complete without a strong cultural component. Liberal arts and social studies help us recognize the interconnections that turn information into knowledge. Culture gives us roots when the sands of time shift. It gives us historical perspective that allows us to see trends and prepare for the future. Culture provides a human framework with which to view the impact of technology. It also gives us the global perspective to live in a world where communication is determined more by technology than by geography.

■ *Communication.* In the information age communication is a survival skill. Isolated factory workers and desk-bound pencil pushers are vanishing from the workplace. Modern jobs involve interactions—between people and machines and between people and people. The fast-paced, information-based society depends on our human ability to communicate, negotiate, cooperate, and collaborate, both locally and globally.

■ *Learning how to learn.* Experts predict that most of the jobs that will exist in 10 years do not exist today and that most of those new jobs will require education past the high school level. With this rapidly changing job market, it's unreasonable to assume that workers can be trained once for lifelong jobs. Instead of holding a single job for 40 years, today's high school or college graduate is likely to change jobs several times. Those people who do keep the same jobs will have to deal with unprecedented change. The half-life of an engineer's specialized knowledge—the time it takes for half of that knowledge to be replaced by more current knowledge—is just over three years.

These facts suggest that we can no longer afford to think of education as a one-time vaccination against illiteracy. In the information age, learning must be a lifelong process. To prepare students for a lifetime of learning, schools must teach students more than facts; they must make sure students learn how to think and learn.

Computers Go to School

The information age is making new demands on our educational system, requiring radical changes in what and how people learn. Many educators believe that computers are essential parts of those changes. Ninety-nine percent of all elementary and secondary schools in the United States have installed computers. Students and teachers are using those computers in a variety of ways.

> The only thing we know about **the future** is that it will be **inhabited by our children**. Its quality, in other words, is **directly proportional** to **world education**.
>
> —Nicholas Negroponte, Director of the MIT Media Lab

Computer-Aided Instruction

In 1953, B. F. Skinner visited his daughter's fourth-grade class and watched the teacher try to teach arithmetic to everyone in the class at the same speed. The experience inspired him to build a teaching machine—a wooden box that used cards, lights, and levers to quiz and reward a student. His machine was based on the principles of behaviorist psychology: Allow the student to learn in small steps at an individualized pace and reward correct answers with immediate positive feedback. When PCs appeared in classrooms, students started using drill-and-practice software based on those same principles: individualized rate, small steps, and positive feedback.

> The ordinary classroom **holds the bright kids back** and makes the kids that need more time **go too fast**. They fall further and further behind until they can't keep up—**it's a terrible system**.
>
> —B. F. Skinner, father of behaviorist psychology and inventor of the first "teaching machine"

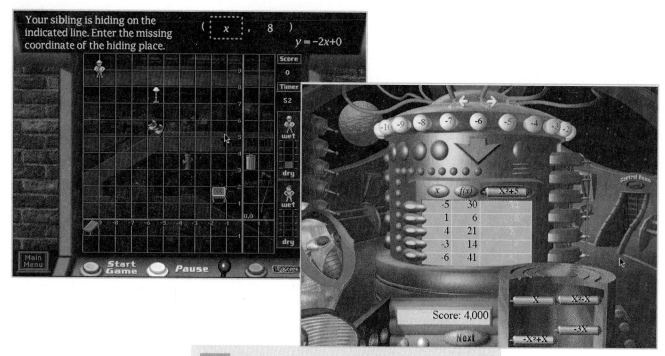

11.12 Students practice basic math skills with programs like *Grade Builder: Algebra I*, and *Math Workshop Deluxe*.

A traditional drill-and-practice program presents the student with a question and compares the student's answer with the correct answer. If the answers match, the program offers rewards or praise. If the answers don't match, the program offers an explanation and presents a similar problem. The program may keep track of student responses and tailor questions based on error patterns; it might also provide reports on student progress to the teacher. Today, most drill-and-practice programs embed the lesson in animated games, but the underlying principles remain the same.

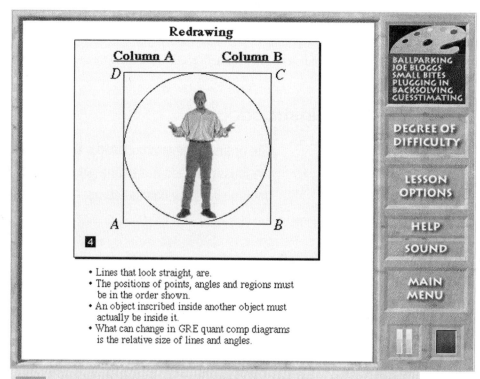

11.13 Students can prepare for standardized tests using *Inside the SAT and ACT.*

Computer-aided instruction (CAI) software is one of the most common types of courseware (educational software) for three reasons: It's relatively easy to produce, it can be easily combined with more traditional educational techniques, and it produces clear, demonstrable results. CAI offers many advantages over workbooks and worksheets:

- *Individualized learning.* The individual student can learn at his or her own pace. Teachers can spend their time working one-on-one with students—an important activity that's all but impossible in typical presentation-and-discussion classrooms.
- *Motivation.* CAI can turn practice into a game. It motivates students to practice arithmetic, spelling, touch-typing, piano playing, and other skills that might otherwise be tedious to learn.
- *Confidence.* CAI can help children become comfortable with computers as well as with the subject matter being taught. A well-designed program is infinitely patient, and it enables students to make mistakes in private. Research has shown that younger children, disadvantaged children, and in particular students with learning disabilities tend to respond positively to CAI.

11.14 CAI is useful for strengthening basic motor skills such as typing. In *Typing Tutor 10*, onscreen tutorials guide the student through a complete set of typing lessons, with the computer monitoring every keystroke for accuracy.

Not all CAI software deserves praise. Much CAI software is flawed because it gives inappropriate feedback, enables students to practice mistakes, and discourages students from moving into new material. Even the best CAI can work only with tightly defined subjects in which every question can have a single, clear, unambiguous answer. CAI presents information in the form of facts, leaving no room for questioning, creativity, or cooperation. In a sense, CAI programs students.

Programming Tools

In the 1960s, with colleagues at MIT, Seymour Papert developed a computer language called LOGO so children could program computers rather than the other way around. Children can write LOGO programs as soon as they're old enough to read and write a few simple words.

Rather than teaching through lessons and tests, LOGO creates environments for learning. The most famous of these LOGO environments enables children to draw pictures using a technique called turtle graphics. With turtle graphics a child uses LOGO commands to make a "turtle" move, dragging a "pen" to draw lines as it moves. The "turtle" can be a small robot that moves around on the floor or a graphical creature that lives on a computer screen.

In many schools today, the phrase "computer-aided instruction" means **making the computer teach the child**. One might say the computer is being used to **program the child**. In my vision, **the child programs the computer** and, in doing so, both acquires a **sense of mastery** over a piece of the most modern and powerful technology and establishes an **intimate contact** with some of the **deepest ideas** from science, from mathematics, and from the art of intellectual model building.

—Seymour Papert, in *Mindstorms*

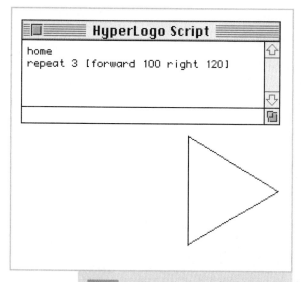

HyperLogo Script

```
home
repeat 3 [forward 100 right 120]
```

11.15 This sequence of LOGO commands tells the turtle to go home, move forward 100 steps, turn right 120 degrees, and then repeat these steps two more times, creating a triangle.

LOGO helps children learn advanced computer science concepts such as recursion—the ability of a program or procedure to call, or refer to, itself, as in this example:

```
TO CIRCLE
FORWARD 1 RIGHT 1
CIRCLE
END
```

This LOGO program tells the computer "to draw a circle, go 1 step forward, turn 1 degree to the right, and repeat all of these instructions." Of course, there's a bug here: This procedure doesn't know when to stop. But debugging is part of programming, and students who learn LOGO learn that making mistakes is part of the process.

LOGO has other environments that go beyond geometry and graphics. LEGO LOGO enables children to use LOGO commands to control motorized machines and robots built out of LEGO building blocks.

Papert and many educators predicted that LOGO would help children become better at general problem solving and logical thinking. Research suggests that LOGO enhances creativity and originality in children, but there's no conclusive evidence that it improves their general thinking skills more than other teaching tools. Like a chalkboard, LOGO can be an effective tool in the hands of a good teacher.

LOGO—like Pascal and Basic, two other programming languages designed for students—is less popular in schools today than it was a decade ago. Today's computer applications make programming seem irrelevant to the average student. Children don't need to learn how to write TV programs before they watch TV, and in most schools they don't learn to program computers before they use them.

11.16 Students in this class build LEGO robots and write LOGO programs to control them.

Simulations and Games

When Papert developed LOGO, he based his educational psychology on the work of renowned Swiss developmental psychologist Jean Piaget. According to Piaget, children have a natural gift for learning on their own; they learn to talk, get around, and think without formal training. A child growing up in France learns French effortlessly because the child's environment has the necessary materials. In Papert's vision the computer can provide an environment that makes learning mathematics, science, and the arts as effortless as learning French in France.

> No compulsory learning can remain **in the soul**. . . . In teaching children, **train them by a kind of game**, and you will be able to **see more clearly** the natural bent of each.
>
> —Plato, in *The Republic, Book VII*

Many **educational simulations** today are based on the same idea: Children learn best through exploration and invention. These simulations allow students to explore artificial environments, whether imaginary or based on reality. Educational simulations are metaphors designed to focus student attention on the most important concepts. Most educational simulations have the look and feel of a game, but they challenge students to learn through exploration, experimentation, and interaction with other students.

With a simulation, the students are in control of the learning environment. It's up to them to find and use information to draw conclusions. Students can experience the consequences of their actions without taking real-world risks. Simulations enable students to have experiences that wouldn't be possible otherwise. Instead of simply spewing facts, simulations provide a context for knowledge.

Students love playing well-designed simulation games, but many schools don't use simulations because there's no room for them in the formal curriculum. In spite of our culture's age-old tradition of learning through games, many educators question the educational value of games in the classroom. Of course, educational simulations, like all simulations, come up short as substitutes for reality. Many students can play with simulation games for hours without learning anything concrete. The risks of simulations, outlined in Chapter 5, apply to educational simulations, too. But when field trips aren't possible, computer simulations can offer affordable alternatives.

11.17 *Star Wars Droid Works* combines entertainment with education by simulating a robot factory. Given specifications and parts, players must apply principles of science and engineering to successfully construct a variety of robots.

Productivity Tools

Today the trend in schools is clearly toward teaching children to use computers as tools. Word processors, spreadsheets, graphics programs, Web browsers, email programs—the software tools used by adults—are the tools students learn most often in schools. Once students learn to use these general-purpose tools, they can put them to work in and out of school.

> For me, the phrase **"computer as pencil"** evokes the kind of uses I imagine **children of the future** making of computers. Pencils are used for **scribbling** as well as writing, **doodling** as well as drawing, for **illicit notes** as well as for official assignments.
>
> —Seymour Papert, in *Mindstorms*

Some schools also provide special-purpose tools for classroom use, including these:

■ Laboratory sensing hardware and software that can be used to collect scientific data (such as temperature) and convert it into computer data to be analyzed by students
■ Collaborative writing groupware that enables students to work collectively on creative writing and editing projects
■ Music synthesizers with sequencing and notation software for teaching music composition.

Digital Media

> I hear and I **forget**, I see and I **remember**, I do and I **understand**.
> —Ancient Chinese proverb

Many teachers use computers and multimedia tools to create in-class presentations. Presentations can range from simple PowerPoint slide shows to elaborate graphical simulations or multimedia demonstrations. Unlike videos and other linear technologies, computer-based presentations can be customized to meet the needs of each class.

To get students more involved in the learning process, many teachers use interactive multimedia software that puts students in control. Sometimes these interactive lessons are created by teachers; more often they're purchased on CDs or explored through the Web.

11.18 Professionally produced multimedia programs like Steven Hawking's *Life in the Universe* can make abstract concepts and facts more accessible and exciting.

In many classrooms, students use authoring tools to create their own multimedia presentations. Students create CD-ROMs, videos, interactive kiosks, and (especially) Web pages about their classes, schools, student organizations, and special projects. The Web makes it possible for these students to reach worldwide audiences with their presentations.

This kind of student involvement promotes learning, but it has drawbacks. One problem is economic: Few schools can afford the hardware, software, and floor space for multiple student media workstations. Another problem is both social and political: When students are creating or using interactive media, they aren't conforming to the traditional factory model. Instead of sitting quietly listening to the teacher, they're taking control of the machinery and the learning process. The teacher becomes a supervisor and a mentor rather than a conveyor of information.

This kind of restructuring of the educational process is threatening to many administrators, teachers, parents, and community members who are used to the old ways.

Distance Education: Virtual Schools

> Very soon now, it might not matter where **your body** happens to be . . . as long as you maintain a **presence in the networks**.
> —Steven K. Roberts, technomad

For some students the most important application of computers in schools is distance education—using technology to extend the educational process beyond the walls of the school. Grade-school students can network with kids in other parts of the world through the Internet. Middle-school classes can use electron microscopes, telescopes, and other powerful tools around the world through real-time Internet connections. High-school correspondence courses can be completed by modem rather than by mail. Students with handicaps can do coursework without traveling to central sites. Two-way video links allow "visiting" experts to talk to students in outlying classrooms and answer their questions in real time. Networked school districts can offer multischool videoconference courses in Chinese, college-level calculus, and other subjects that might have tiny enrollments if offered only at a single school. Teachers can receive additional education without leaving their districts.

Telecommunication technology is particularly important for students in remote locations. If a child in a small town develops an interest in a narrow subject, whether it's aboriginal anthropology or classical Russian ballet, that student may find pursuing that interest a discouraging process. But through an Internet connection, reference materials, special-interest newsgroups, long-distance mentors, and like-minded modem pals are all within reach. In many areas rural interactive television networks keep remote schools and towns from fading away.

Distance education is particularly attractive to women with children. Two-thirds of the adult distance learners are female, and 80 percent of them have children. Distance education also offers promise for workers whose jobs are changed or eliminated by a shifting economy. Many displaced and dissatisfied workers can't afford to relocate their families to college towns so they can learn new skills. But if colleges and universities offer electronic outreach programs, these people can update their skills while remaining in their communities.

Since 1990 online degree programs have appeared at dozens of universities and colleges. Students use PCs and modems to do everything from ordering books to taking final exams. Many online students see their professors in person for the first time at graduation ceremonies.

The demand for distance education is growing rapidly. In some countries distance education students compose 40 percent of the total undergraduate population. Some experts predict that the majority of college students will be off-campus students in a decade or two.

Of course, a college education is more than a collection of information. Students learn and grow as a result of all kinds of experiences in and out of the classroom. Many significant learning experiences can't be transmitted through phone lines and TV cables. The *Chronicle of Higher Education* reported in 2000 that distance learning dropout rates ranged from 20 to 50 percent—10 to 20 percent higher than those for classroom students. Still, online schools are an important step toward an educational system that encourages lifelong learning.

Computers at School: Midterm Grades

Many schools have been using computers in classrooms for more than a decade. In these days of shrinking budgets, taxpayers are asking whether classroom computer technology pays off. Has it lived up to its promise as an educational tool

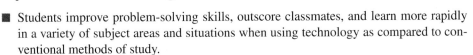

The business of education is to give the student both **useful information** and **life-enhancing experience,** one largely measurable, the other not. . . .

—John Gardner, in *The Art of Fiction*

in the schools? According to most experts, the answer is mixed but optimistic.

High Marks

A number of independent studies in the 1990s confirm that information technology can improve education. Some findings:

- Students improve problem-solving skills, outscore classmates, and learn more rapidly in a variety of subject areas and situations when using technology as compared to conventional methods of study.
- Students find computer-based instruction to be more motivational, less intimidating, and easier to persist with than traditional instruction.
- In many cases students' self-esteem is increased when they use computers. This change is most dramatic in cases of at-risk youngsters and students with handicaps.

- Using technology encourages cooperative learning, turn taking among young children, peer tutoring, and other valuable social skills.
- Computer technology can make learning more student-centered and stimulate increased teacher/student interaction.
- Well-designed interactive multimedia systems can encourage active processing and higher-order thinking.
- Students who create interactive multimedia reports often learn better than those who learn with more traditional methods.
- Students can become more productive, more fluid writers with computers.
- Computers can help students master the basic skills needed to participate and succeed in the workforce.
- Positive changes occur gradually as teachers gain experience with the technology.
- Technology can facilitate educational reform.

Room for Improvement

> This stuff is **so bad**, it must be **educational**.
>
> —Aunt Selma on *The Simpsons*

Other findings temper—and sometimes contradict—these positive conclusions. Researchers have also found that:

- If the only thing that changes is the delivery medium (from traditional media to computer media), the advantages of technology are small—or nonexistent.
- Kids and teachers forget advanced computer skills if they don't use them.
- Students have unequal access to technology; economically disadvantaged students have less computer access at school and at home. Sadly, these are the students who can benefit most when given access to technology.
- Technology doesn't reduce teacher workloads; if anything, it seems to make their jobs harder (of course, many teachers welcome the extra work because they believe it brings results).
- There's a gender gap that typically puts the computer room in the boys' domain; the gap can be reduced by stressing computer activities that involve collaboration.
- Many of the outcomes of technology-based education don't show up with traditional educational assessment methods.
- Sending students to a computer lab for 30 minutes a week has little or no value; computers are more effective when they're in classrooms where students can use them regularly.

11.19 Research shows that writing improves when students use word processors. Every student in Henrico County, Virginia has been supplied with Apple iBooks for writing, research, and other assignments. Research suggests that the program has produced positive results.

■ Younger students may be better served by art, music, and shop classes than by computer classes; unfortunately, these important parts of the curriculum are often eliminated to make room for computers.

Stories abound of reduced dropout rates and attitudinal changes among at-risk students; improved math, reading, and language scores; and overall academic improvement among students in high-tech schools. But computer technology doesn't always bring happy head-lines. In some schools, computers are little more than ex-pensive, time-consuming distractions. What makes tech-nology work for some schools and not for others? A closer look at the success stories reveals that they didn't achieve results with technology alone. When we compare these schools with less fortunate schools, several issues emerge:

■ *Money*. Most American schools have found funds to purchase computers. Unfortunately, many of those com-puters are technologically outdated. Most classrooms don't even have phone lines, let alone Internet connec-tions. Not surprisingly, computers tend to be concen-trated in affluent school districts, so economically disad-vantaged students have the least access to them.

■ *Planning and support*. When school districts spend money on technology without thoughtful long-term planning and sustained support, their investments are not likely to pay off.

■ *Teacher training*. Unfortunately, teacher training is often missing from schools' high-tech formulas. Teachers need training, support, and time to integrate technology into their curricula.

11.20 Technology can have a positive impact on education if it's part of a program that includes teacher training, ongoing support, and radical restructuring of the traditional "factory model" curriculum.

■ *Restructuring*. Just as businesses need to rethink their organizational structures to automate successfully, schools need to be restructured to make effective use of computer technology. The goal is education, and technology is just one tool for achiev-ing that goal. Interactive media, individualized instruction, telecommunication, and co-operative learning simply don't fit well into the factory school. To meet the educational challenges of the information age, we'll need to invest in research and planning involv-ing teachers, students, administrators, parents, businesses, and community leaders.

The Classroom of Tomorrow

To give us a head start in building the schools of the future, Apple, IBM, Microsoft, Toshiba, and other companies, along with some state

> The further one pursues knowledge, **the less one knows**.
> —Lao Tse, 500 B.C.

and local governments, have helped create model technology classrooms and schools in communities around the United States and Canada. Most of these pilot projects suggest that technology can, in the proper context, have a dramatic effect on education. For exam-ple, here's a quote from Apple's Web site summarizing the results of the Apple Classroom of Tomorrow (ACOT) project:

After more than a decade of research, ACOT's research demonstrated that the intro-duction of technology into classrooms can significantly increase the potential for learning, especially when it is used to support collaboration, information access, and the expression and representation of students' thoughts and ideas. Realizing this opportunity for all students, however, required a broadly conceived approach to ed-ucational change that integrated new technologies and curricula with new ideas about learning and teaching, as well as with authentic forms of assessment.

Information technology, then, can be a powerful change agent, but not by itself. In an interview for online magazine *ZineZone*, educational computing pioneer Seymour Papert was asked whether technology is a Trojan horse for systematic and lasting change. His reply: "I think the technology serves as a Trojan horse all right, but in the real story of the Trojan horse, it wasn't the horse that was effective, it was the soldiers inside the horse. And the technology is only going to be effective in changing education if you put an army inside it which is determined to make that change once it gets through the barrier."

Computers Come Home

There is **no reason** for any individual to have a **computer in their home**.
—Ken Olson, president of Digital Equipment Corporation, 1977

The same year Ken Olson made this statement, Apple Computer introduced the Apple II computer. In the years that followed Apple, Commodore, Tandy, Atari, IBM, and dozens of other companies managed to sell computers to millions of individuals who had "no reason" to buy them.

Today there are more computers in homes than in schools. Most American homes contain at least one computer. The small office, home office market—dubbed *SOHO* by the industry—is one of the fastest-growing computer markets today. While many home computers gather dust, others are being put to work, and play, in a variety of ways.

11.21 A home office like this one can be used for taking care of family business or running a family business.

Household Business

Frank Gilbreth, a turn-of-the-century pioneer of motion study in industry, applied "scientific management" techniques to his home. He required his 12 children to keep records on bathroom "work-and-process charts" of each hair combing, tooth brushing, and bathing. He gave them demonstrations on efficient bathing techniques to minimize "unavoidable delays." While it may have worked for Gilbreth, this "scientific management" approach to home life is not likely to catch on today. Still, certain aspects of family life are unavoidably businesslike, and a growing number of people are turning to computers to help them take care of business.

Not everyone is convinced that computers are useful or practical at home. But those people who do use home computers generally find that they can put the same applications to work at home that they use in their offices: Web browsers for entertainment, research, shopping, and other applications; email programs for connecting with others; word processors for writing; personal information managers for tracking calendars and contacts; and accounting programs for managing income and expenses.

Few home computer users type *every* financial transaction into the computer. Some people type in only "important" transactions. Others download transaction summary statements from their bank Web sites. But for most people computerized money management won't happen until there's an effortless way to record transactions—perhaps a device that, when inserted into the computer, can tell the software about each purchase and paid bill.

That device may turn out to be a smart card. A smart card looks like a standard credit card, but instead of a magnetic strip it contains an embedded microprocessor and memory. (Memory cards, which contain memory but no micro-processors, are occasionally called smart cards even though they aren't really "smart.") Some smart cards even contain touch-sensitive keypads for entering numbers. Whether it has a keypad or not, a smart card receives most of its input when it's slipped into a special slot on a computer. Data stored in smart cards can be password protected. There are hundreds of millions of smart cards in Europe, and they're rapidly infiltrating America.

Smart cards are obvious candidates to replace magnetic-strip credit cards. In addition to storing critical ID information, a smart card can automatically record each transaction for later retrieval. But smart cards have other applications, too. College students use smart cards as meal tickets. Office workers use smart cards as keys to access sensitive data on computers. Smart cards have replaced food stamps and drivers' licenses in some states. Many Europeans use smart cards to pay highway tolls and unscramble cable TV broadcasts. The Chinese government plans to replace citizen ID cards with smart cards, raising new questions about protection of personal privacy. You might soon use one card to buy groceries, check out library books, and store personal medical information in case of an emergency. Future smart cards will use pattern recognition techniques to verify signatures on checks or credit slips and help prevent millions of dollars in fraud and forgery.

11.22 A smart card contains a tiny microprocessor and digital memory.

Education and Information

Millions of people use home computers for education and information. Many educational software programs are used by children and adults in homes. Edutainment programs specifically geared toward home markets combine education with entertainment so they can compete with television and electronic games. Encyclopedias, dictionaries, atlases, almanacs, medical references, and other specialized references now come in low-cost CD-ROM or DVD-ROM versions—often with multimedia capability. Many CD-ROM references have been eclipsed by Web references that offer more up-to-the-minute information—often for free. Of course, Internet connections also provide email, discussion groups, and other communication options for home users.

> **Newspapers** as we know them **won't exist**. They will be printed for a **readership of one**. **Television** won't simply have sharper pictures. You'll have one button that says **tell me more**, and another button that says **tell me less**.
>
> —Nicholas Negroponte, director of the MIT Media Lab

As computer technology and communication technology converge on the home market, they're producing services that may soon threaten television and newspapers as our main sources of information. Television is a broadcast medium—it transmits news and information to broad audiences. Computer technology enables narrowcasting services—custom newscasts and entertainment features aimed at narrow groups or at individuals. (Individualized broadcasting is sometimes called *pointcasting*.) With a narrowcasting service, you might create a personalized news program that includes a piece on the latest Middle Eastern crisis, highlights of last night's Blazers vs. Lakers game, this weekend's weather forecast at the coast, announcements of upcoming local jazz concerts, and a reminder that there are only five more shopping days until your mother's birthday. Personalized news services can flag particular subjects ("I'm especially interested in articles on the Amazon rain forest") and ignore others ("No Hollywood gossip, please").

Several Web portals, including Netscape and Yahoo, enable users to personalize their "front pages" with customized headlines, stock quotes, weather information, television and movie schedules, and other features. Avant Go and other wireless portals can automatically download customized content into PDAs and other handheld devices. These Web-based products hint at the kinds of customization we might see when television adds interactivity.

Personalized Web portals enable people to control what they see on their home pages, but not what they see on other sites. Some families depend on filtering software to block their browsers so children can't visit sites that contain pornography and other "inappropriate" content. Filtering programs can be customized, but they're not 100 percent accurate. They're also subject to the biases of their authors and corporate owners. In early 2000, extensive tests of America Online's filtering revealed that kids had free access to Web sites of the conservative Republican and Libertarian parties but were blocked from viewing the Democratic and Green party sites. Young teens could access sites promoting gun use, including the National Rifle Association, but not the Coalition to Stop Gun Violence and other gun safety organizations. Both AOL and The Learning Company, who designed the filtering software, denied bias. But the findings show how censorship can squelch the free flow of ideas that's a critical part of the educational process.

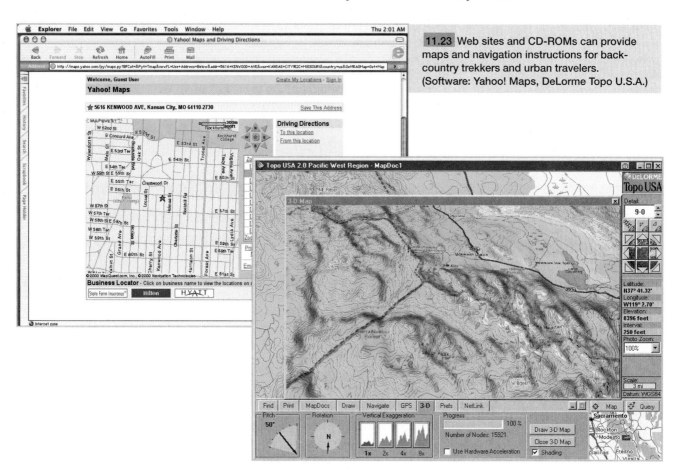

11.23 Web sites and CD-ROMs can provide maps and navigation instructions for backcountry trekkers and urban travelers. (Software: Yahoo! Maps, DeLorme Topo U.S.A.)

Home Entertainment Redefined

Television has a **"brightness"** knob, but it **doesn't seem to work**.

—Gallagher, stand-up comic

You don't want a television with knobs marked **"volume"** and **"brightness"** and **"contrast."** You want a television with knobs marked **"sex"** and **"violence"** and **"political bias."**

—Nicholas Negroponte, director of the MIT Media Lab

Regardless of how people say they use home computers, surveys suggest that many people use them mostly to play games. Computer games and video game machines (which are just special-purpose computers) represent a huge industry—one that is likely to evolve rapidly in the coming years.

Most computer games are simulations. Computer games can simulate board games, card games, sporting events, intergalactic battles, street fights, corporate takeovers, or something else, real or imaginary. Many require strategy and puzzle solving; others depend only on eye–hand coordination. Many of the most popular games require some of each. With dazzling graphics, digitized sound, and sophisticated effects, many of today's computer games represent state-of-the-art software. But in a few years these computer games are likely to look as primitive as early Pong games look today.

Enhanced realism of computer games may not be completely beneficial for society. In the years before the 1999 Columbine High School mass murder, the killers spent hundreds of hours blasting virtual people in graphic first-person games like Doom. In the aftermath of the tragedy, many people suggested that the violent games were partially responsible for the horrific killings. A year later, published research confirmed a link between violent video games and real-world violence. Two studies suggested that even brief exposure to violent video games can temporarily increase aggressive behavior and that children who play violent games tend to have lower grades and more aggressive tendencies in later years. Further research may confirm or clarify these results. In the meantime, pressure grows for game manufacturers to consider the impact of their products on young minds.

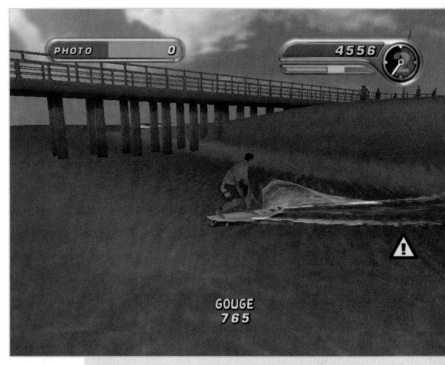

11.24 Kelly Slater's Pro Surfer, like many computer games, simulates a real-world sport using 3-D graphic technology.

Sometimes the impact of video games on young minds is measurably positive. In a recent study researchers at East Virginia Medical School in Norfolk, working with NASA scientists, used PlayStation games to successfully treat children diagnosed with attention deficit disorder (ADD). Using basic biofeedback technology and off-the-shelf video games, children were able to quickly learn to control their brain waves so they could improve concentration. The fast-action games provided strong motivation for the young learners. A commercial product based on this project may soon be available to help the 5 to 7 percent of U.S. elementary-school students with ADD.

The entertainment industry is exploring a variety of ways of adding interactivity to entertainment products. A few years ago, one of the most popular types of games was *interactive fiction*—stories with primitive natural language interfaces that gave players some control over plot. Today, arcade-style games, puzzle-based adventure games, and other multimedia-rich genres capture most of the attention of computer gamers. But interactivity is finding its way into other entertainment technology—most notably on the Web and on DVDs.

Many DVD movies allow for customized movie viewing—language, subtitles, commentary, soundtracks, and sometimes even camera angle are under viewer control. A few DVDs allow actual branching within a film. We may soon see truly *interactive movies*—features in which one or more of the characters or plot lines are controlled by the viewers.

11.25 Researchers are using video game technology in biofeedback experiments on children with attention deficit disorder.

11.26 Sarah McLachlan's *Freedom Sessions* was one of the first enhanced audio CDs that included video and animation along with standard audio tracks. Today many musicians use the Web and DVDs to deliver multimedia material to their fans.

We're also likely to see a growth in interactive TV—broadcast television with options for interactivity built in. In 1999 two popular game shows, *Wheel of Fortune* and *Jeopardy*, began broadcasting interactive versions that enabled viewers to play along with contestants. Some experts think this kind of programming is likely to increase sharply as more TV viewers buy set-top boxes with keyboards and other input devices. Interactive TV has been popular for years in Europe, where digital TV had an early audience.

Interactive TV and DVDs are, for the most part, solitary activities. But the Internet opens up new possibilities for social entertainment, as well. We're already seeing multiplayer multimedia games on the Web. How long will it be until these games have the richness of plot and cinematography of today's films? When will today's chat rooms and virtual communities evolve into rich environments for interaction and exploration? As technology improves and the multimedia market grows, we can expect all kinds of hybrid forms of entertainment.

Creativity and Leisure

If you can talk, **you can sing**. If you can walk, **you can dance**.
—A saying from Zimbabwe

A 2000 report by the Childhood Alliance, a group of education experts, raises serious questions about computer use, especially by young children. "Intense use of computers can distract children and adults from . . . essential experiences." Specifically, the time children spend in front of a computer screen is time they aren't involved in physical activities and self-generated, imaginative play. "A heavy diet of ready-made computer images and programmed toys appears to stunt imaginative thinking." The report also argues that computers expose kids to adult hazards, including repetitive-stress injury and social isolation.

Many people worry that television, computer games, and other media are replacing too many real-world activities. Instead of making up stories to share, we watch sitcoms on TV. Instead of playing music on guitars, we play music on boom boxes. Instead of playing one-on-one basketball, we play one-on-one video games.

Is electronic technology turning us into a mindless couch-potato culture? Perhaps. But there's another possibility. The same technology that mesmerizes us can also unlock our creativity. Word processors help many of us to become writers, graphics software brings out the artists among us, Web authoring tools provide us with worldwide publishing platforms, electronic music systems enable us to compose music even if we never mastered an instrument, and digital video and multimedia systems open doors to cable-access TV channels.

Will computers drain our creativity or amplify it? In the end it's up to us. . . .

High Score Education

By James Paul Gee

We commonly hear complaints from educators that kids spend too much time playing computer games and not enough time learning. In his book, What Video Games Have to Teach Us About Learning and Literacy, *Professor James Paul Gee of the University of Wisconsin-Madison suggests that video games may have quite a bit to teach us about the learning process. This October, 2002,* Wired *essay outlines some of his ideas on the subject.*

The US spends almost $50 billion each year on education, so why aren't kids learning? Forty percent of students lack basic reading skills, and their academic performance is dismal compared with that of their foreign counterparts. In response to this crisis, schools are skilling-and-drilling their way "back to basics," moving toward mechanical instruction methods that rely on line-by-line scripting for teachers and endless multiple-choice testing. Consequently, kids aren't learning how to think anymore—they're learning how to memorize. This might be an ideal recipe for the future Babbitts of the world, but it won't produce the kind of agile, analytical minds that will lead the high tech global age. Fortunately, we've got *Grand Theft Auto: Vice City* and *Deus X* for that.

After school, kids are devouring new information, concepts, and skills every day, and, like it or not, they're doing it controller in hand, plastered to the TV. The fact is, when kids play videogames they can experience a much more powerful form of learning than when they're in the classroom. Learning isn't about memorizing isolated facts. It's about connecting and manipulating them. Doubt it? Just ask anyone who's beaten *Legend of Zelda* or solved *Morrowind*.

The phenomenon of the videogame as an agent of mental training is largely unstudied; more often, games are denigrated for being violent or they're just plain ignored. They shouldn't be. Young gamers today aren't training to be gun-toting carjackers. They're learning how to learn. In *Pikmin*, children manage an army of plantlike aliens and strategize to solve problems. In *Metal Gear Solid 2*, players move stealthily through virtual environments and carry out intricate missions. Even in the notorious *Vice City*, players craft a persona, build a history, and shape a virtual world. In strategy games like *WarCraft III* and *Age of Mythology*, they learn to micromanage an array of elements while simultaneously balancing short- and long-term goals. That sounds like something for their résumés.

The secret of a videogame as a teaching machine isn't its immersive 3-D graphics, but its underlying architecture. Each level dances around the outer limits of the player's abilities, seeking at every point to be hard enough to be just doable. In cognitive science, this is referred to as the regime of competence principle, which results in a feeling of simultaneous pleasure and frustration—a sensation as familiar to gamers as sore thumbs. Cognitive scientist Andy diSessa has argued that the best instruction hovers at the boundary of a student's competence. Most schools, however, seek to avoid invoking feelings of both pleasure and frustration, blind to the fact that these emotions can be extremely useful when it comes to teaching kids.

Also, good videogames incorporate the principle of expertise. They tend to encourage players to achieve total mastery of one level, only to challenge and undo that mastery in the next, forcing kids to adapt and evolve. This carefully choreographed dialectic has been identified by learning theorists as the best way to achieve expertise in any field. This doesn't happen much in our routine-driven schools, where "good" students are often just good at "doing school."

How did videogames become such successful models of effective learning? Game coders aren't trained as cognitive scientists. It's a simple case of free-market economics: If a title doesn't teach players how to play it well, it won't sell well. Game companies don't rake in $6.9 billion a year by dumbing down the material—aficionados condemn short and easy games like *Half Life: Blue Shift* and *Devil May Cry 2*. Designers respond by making harder and more complex games that require mastery of sophisticated worlds and as many as 50 to 100 hours to complete. Schools, meanwhile, respond with more tests, more drills, and more rigidity. They're in the cognitive-science dark ages.

We don't often think about videogames as relevant to education reform, but maybe we should. Game designers don't often think of themselves as learning theorists. Maybe they should. Kids often say it doesn't feel like learning when they're gaming—they're much too focused on playing. If kids were to say that about a science lesson, our country's education problems would be solved.

DISCUSSION QUESTIONS

1. Do you agree with the author's suggestion that videogames do a better job of teaching than many of our schools do? Why or why not?

2. Do you think the benefits of video games outweigh the potential problems they create? Explain your answer.

SUMMARY

Information technology is having a profound influence on the way we live and work, and it is likely to challenge many of our beliefs, assumptions, and traditions.

Factory work is steadily declining as we enter the information age, but factories still provide us with hard goods. The modern, automated factory uses computers at every level of operation. Computer-aided design, computer-aided manufacturing, robots, automated assembly lines, and automated warehouses all combine to produce factories that need very few laborers.

Far more people work in offices than in factories, and computers are critically important in the modern office. Early office automation centered on mainframes that were run by highly trained technicians; today's office is more likely to emphasize networked PCs and workstations for decentralized enterprise computing. So far, predictions for widespread computer-supported cooperative work and paperless offices haven't come true.

A growing number of workers use computers to work at home part- or full-time, staying in contact with their offices through the Internet. Telecommuting has many benefits for information workers, their bosses, and society as a whole. Still, telecommuting from home is not for everybody. Satellite offices, cottage industries, and portable offices offer alternatives that may be more practical for some workers.

The impact of computers varies from job to job. Some jobs are de-skilled—transformed so they require less skill—while others are up-skilled into more technologically complex jobs. Experts speculate that productivity will rise as organizations adjust to the new technology and develop human-centered systems that are adapted to the needs and work habits of employees.

Computer monitoring is a controversial procedure that raises issues of privacy and, in many cases, lowers worker morale. De-skilling, monitoring, and health risks are particularly evident in electronic sweatshops—data-entry warehouses packed with low-paid keyboard operators. Many of these sweatshops—as well as millions of other jobs—have been relocated in countries with low wages and lax labor laws.

The biggest problem of automation may be the elimination of jobs. Automation will almost certainly produce unemployment and pain for millions of people unless society is able to provide them with the education they'll need to take the new jobs created by technology. Automation may ultimately force us to make fundamental changes in our economic system.

Our educational system was developed a century ago to train workers for lifelong jobs. In the information age, when students can expect to change jobs several times, we need schools that teach technological familiarity, literacy, mathematics, culture, communication, problem solving, and, most importantly, the ability to learn and adapt to an ever-changing world.

Students use a variety of instructional tools in schools today, including these:

- Computer-aided instruction (CAI). Tutorials and/or drill-and-practice software covering concrete facts in specific subject areas
- Programming tools. Languages such as LOGO, Pascal, BASIC, and HTML that enable students to design their own software and Web pages
- Simulations and games. Artificial environments that enable students to learn through exploration, experimentation, and interaction with other students
- Productivity tools. Word processors, spreadsheets, and other real-world tools
- Computer-controlled media. Presentation graphics, hypermedia, interactive multimedia, and authoring tools that enable varying degrees of student control
- Distance education tools. Telecommunication tools, including the Internet, that enable students and teachers to communicate electronically without having to be in the same physical location

Clearly, computer technology can have a positive educational impact, but computers alone can't guarantee improvement. Research, planning, teacher training, community involvement, and classroom restructuring should accompany new technology.

A small but growing number of families use home computers for basic business applications, education, information access, communication, entertainment, and creative pursuits. All of these applications will radically change as the technology evolves over the next decade.

KEY TERMS

authoring tools (p. 404)
automated factory (p. 388)
automated offices (p. 389)
chief information officers (CIOs) (p. 389)
chief technology officers (CTOs) (p. 389)

computer-aided instruction (CAI) (p. 401)
computer monitoring (p. 394)
courseware (p. 401)
de-skilled (p. 393)
distance education (p. 404)
distributed computing (p. 389)

drill-and-practice software (p. 399)
educational simulations (p. 403)
edutainment (p. 409)
electronic commerce (e-commerce) (p. 390)
electronic cottage (p. 391)
electronic sweatshops (p. 395)

INTERACTIVE QUIZ QUESTIONS

1. The *Computer Confluence* CD-ROM contains self-test quiz questions related to this chapter, including multiple-choice, true or false, and matching questions.

2. The *Computer Confluence* Web site, **www.computerconfluence.com**, contains self-test exercises related to this chapter. Follow the instructions for taking a quiz. After you've completed your quiz, you can email the results to your instructor.

3. The Web site also contains open-ended discussion questions called Internet Explorations. Discuss one or more of the Internet Exploration questions at the section for this chapter.

TRUE OR FALSE

1. Engineers use CAD (computer-aided design) and CAM (computer-aided manufacturing) to design new products and the machines that build those products.

2. Office automation began in the personal computer era.

3. Research suggests that the total cost of ownership (TCO) of a typical PC in an organization is not much more than the cost of the hardware and software.

4. Business-to-business (B2B) transactions account for more online sales than business-to-consumer (B2C) transactions.

5. Clerical workers typically see up-skilling to more technologically demanding work reflected in their paychecks or level of responsibility.

6. To create a human-centered system, systems analysts and designers must understand the work practices of the people who'll be using the system.

7. Offshore workers are replacing highly educated programmers and system designers in the United States by the thousands.

8. Half of the specialized knowledge of a typical engineer becomes obsolete in just a few years.

9. In most cases, student self-esteem decreases when using computers.

10. Research has proven that there is no link between violent video games and real-world violence.

MULTIPLE CHOICE

1. The graphical user interface that's common on virtually all modern computers was pioneered decades ago by Alan Kay and others in a research group at
   a. Apple.
   b. Dell.
   c. IBM.
   d. Microsoft.
   e. Xerox.

2. Which of these statements about telecommuting is not true?
   a. Telecommuting saves energy and reduces pollution.
   b. Roughly 5 million workers in the largest corporations telecommute via the Internet.
   c. Studies show a 10–50% reduction in productivity for telecommuters.
   d. Telecommuting allows for more flexible work schedules.
   e. Telecommuters prefer to commute to the office one or two days per week.

3. Computer monitoring in offices as discussed in this chapter does not include
   a. on-screen reports showing the number of keystrokes for each clerk.
   b. viewing a copy of any worker's screen secretly at any time.
   c. legally reading employees' personal email messages.
   d. tracking Web sites visited by employees.
   e. using heat sensors to record when an employee leaves a workstation.

4. Which of these is a negative aspect of computer monitoring in the workplace?
   a. The boss can be seen as an invisible eavesdropper rather than as a team leader.
   b. Computer monitoring creates stress in employees.
   c. Quantity may become more important than quality.
   d. Valuable qualities and unmeasured work may be overlooked and not valued.
   e. These are all negative aspects.

5. Computer-aided instruction (CAI)
   a. leaves room for questioning, creativity, and cooperation.
   b. presents information in the form of facts.
   c. requires students to work at the same pace.
   d. works well when there are multiple answers to questions.
   e. is inappropriate for young or disadvantaged children.

6. Educational simulations
   a. are generally accepted in formal school curricula.
   b. have little in common with computer games.
   c. generally don't allow students to be in control of the learning environment.
   d. are based on the concept of learning through exploration and invention.
   e. typically require students to have basic programming skills.

7. Which of these is not part of distance education?
   a. grade-school students networking with kids in other parts of the world.
   b. sharing electron microscopes through real-time Internet connections.
   c. taking courses via the Internet without traveling to central sites.
   d. live videoconferences involving students and faculty at remote campuses.
   e. required face-to-face meetings with professors throughout a degree program.

8. Which of these statements have researchers found not to be true?
   a. Technology reduces teacher workloads.
   b. If the only thing that changes is the delivery medium, advantages of using new technology are small.
   c. The students who can benefit most from technology have the least access.
   d. Computers are more effective for learning when located in the classroom.
   e. Art, music, and shop classes may serve young students better than computer classes.

9. In order for computer technology to be successful in schools,
   a. money is necessary to keep technology up-to-date and to pay for Internet access.
   b. thoughtful long-term planning and sustained support is required.
   c. teachers need training and support to integrate technology into curricula.
   d. schools should be restructured.
   e. All of the above.

10. Which of these cannot result from children playing computer games?
    a. invoking feelings of both pleasure and frustration.
    b. learning how to learn.
    c. stretching the outer limits of abilities, the regime of competence.
    d. intense computer use distracting children from essential experiences.
    e. All of these are possible results of children playing computer games.

REVIEW QUESTIONS

1. Define or describe each of the key terms listed in the "Key Terms" section. Check your answers using the glossary.

2. What are the major components of the modern automated factory?

3. How has the evolution of the automated office paralleled the evolution of the computer?

4. What are the advantages and disadvantages of telecommuting from the point of view of the worker? Management? Society?

5. Describe several software tools used by managers, and explain how they help them do their jobs.

6. What is de-skilling? What is up-skilling? Give examples of each.

7. Describe several of the controversies surrounding the electronic sweatshop.

8. Why is education critical to our future as we automate more jobs?

9. What were the goals of education in the industrial age? Which are still appropriate in the information age? Which are not?

10. What kind of an education does a student need to prepare for living and working in the information age?

11. How do educational simulation games differ from traditional computer-aided instruction? What are the advantages and disadvantages of each?

12. Describe how multimedia can be used by teachers and students in the classroom. Give several examples.

13. Give several examples of ways that distance learning can enhance education.

14. Technology alone is no guarantee that students will learn better or faster. What else is necessary to ensure success?

15. Describe several ways people use home computers.

16. What are smart cards, and how are they used?

17. How is home entertainment being changed by computer technology and telecommunication?

DISCUSSION QUESTIONS

1. What evidence do we have that our society is going through a paradigm shift?

2. What will have to happen before the paperless office (or the less-paper office) becomes a reality?

3. Many cities are enacting legislation to encourage telecommuting. If you were drafting such legislation, what would you include?

4. People who work in electronic sweatshops run the risk of being replaced by technology. Discuss the trade-offs of this dilemma from the point of view of the worker and society at large.

5. What do you think are the answers to the questions raised at the end of the section on automation and unemployment? How do you think most people would feel about these questions?

6. Socrates was illiterate and avoided the written word because he felt it weakened the mind. Similarly, many people today fear that we're weakening our children's minds by making them too dependent on computers and calculators. What do you think?

7. In many schools students spend two years of math education learning long division—a skill that's almost never used in the age of the five-dollar calculator. Some educators argue that students' time could be better spent learning other things. What do you think? What about calculating square roots by hand?

8. Do you think it's important for students to learn to program in LOGO, Pascal, Basic, or some other language? Why or why not?

9. Do you think educational games are good ways for students to learn in schools? Give examples that support your arguments.

10. Think about educational goals in relation to technology. What should people be able to do with no tools? What should people be able to do if they have access to pencils, papers, and books? What should people be able to do if they have access to computer technology?

11. Describe your past school experience in terms of technology. How did it measure up? What has been missing from your education so far?

12. Do you think home computers strengthen families and communities? Explain.

13. Do you think home computers in the future will make people more or less creative? Why?

PROJECTS

1. Interview several people whose jobs have been changed by computers and the Internet. Report on your findings.

2. Think about how computers have affected the jobs you've held. Report on your experiences.

3. Try several different types of educational software. If possible, observe students using the software. Prepare a report comparing the strengths and weaknesses of each.

4. Observe how computers are used in local schools or on your campus. Report on your findings.

5. Survey the Web for educational resources on a particular subject. Report on your findings.

6. Using a multimedia authoring tool or HTML, design a simple courseware lesson. Make sure you set clear goals before you start. When your project is completed, try it with several students.

7. Plan a model technology school. Describe how it would differ from conventional schools and why.

SOURCES AND RESOURCES

Books

Making the Information Society: Experiences, Consequences, and Possibilities, by James W. Cortada (Upper Saddle River, NJ: Prentice Hall, 2002). Why is the information revolution so strongly identified with America? This book examines the cultural and social context of the information revolution in America, past, present, and future.

The Dilbert Principle, by Scott Adams (New York: HarperBusiness, 1997) and **The Dilbert Future,** by Scott Adams (New York: HarperBusiness, 1998). These books, like the Dilbert comic strip, contain irreverent insights into the inner workings of the information-age workplace. Adams understands the world he satirizes—he has an MBA from Berkeley and 17 years of experience in a cubicle working for Pacific Bell. *The Dilbert Principle* targets managers who are clueless about the human needs of their staff; *The Dilbert Future* lampoons our high-tech future. Dilbert has been criticized because it paints a cynical picture of hopelessness in the workplace rather than encouraging workers to organize and solve problems. Still, the satire in these books allows us to laugh at ourselves, and that can't be all bad.

Utopian Entrepreneur, by Brenda Laurel (Cambridge, MA: MIT Press, 2001). Brenda Laurel, a pioneer in user interface design and PC software development, wrote this book as a guide for those seeking socially positive work in the information age. Human values meet electronic commerce in this refreshing book.

The Hacker Ethic and the Spirit of the Information Age, by Pekka Himanen (New York: Random House, 2001). This book argues that Linus Tovalds, Steve Wozniak, and other pioneers of the information revolution are defining a new work ethic based on curiosity, passion, and sharing rather than duty and guilt. Whether or not you agree with the arguments, you'll probably find the presentation worthwhile.

White Collar Sweatshop: The Deterioration of Work and Its Rewards in Corporate America, by Jill Andresky Fraser (New York: Norton, 2000). This book stretches the sweatshop metaphor beyond data-entry warehouses, arguing that modern management techniques are oppressive to all but the top executives in many high-tech companies.

Dot Calm: The Search for Sanity in a Wired World, by Debra A. Dinnocenzo and Richard B. Swegan (San Francisco: Berrett-Koehler, 2001). This is a guide for coping with the pace and pressure of a high-tech work environment. It provides practical tips and techniques that apply to a variety of work situations.

The End of Work, by Jeremy Rifkin (New York: Putnam, 1994). This book discusses the changing nature of work and the disappearance of jobs as we know them. Information technology isn't the only cause, but it plays a critical role in these changes.

Future Courses: A Compendium of Thought about Education, Technology, and the Future, edited by Jason Ohler (Bloomington, IN: Technos Press, 2001). This collection of articles by Esther Dyson, Ray Kurzweil, Neil Postman, Bill Gates, and other visionaries, speculates about the future of technology in education. There's plenty to think about here.

Mindstorms: Children, Computers, and Powerful Ideas, Second Edition, by Seymour Papert (New York: Basic Books, 1999) and **The Children's Machine,** by Seymour Papert (New York: Basic Books, 1994). These two books outline the views of one widely respected theorist and researcher on technology in education: Seymour Papert, the inventor of LOGO. *Mindstorms* was written during the period when Papert was doing pioneering work with LOGO. In *The Children's Machine*, Papert discusses why the computer revolution failed to revolutionize education.

Multimedia Learning, by Richard E. Mayer (New York: Cambridge University Press, 2001). The theory and practice of multimedia education are explored in this book based on a survey of research in the field.

Information Technology in Schools: Creating Practical Knowledge to Improve Student Performance, edited by Bena Kallick and James W. Wilson (New York: Jossey-Bass, 2000). This book provides a road map for putting technology to work to achieve educational goals in schools.

High-Tech Heretic: Reflections of a Computer Contrarian, by Clifford Stoll (New York: Anchor Books, 2000). Stoll first caught the public's eye when he cracked an international hacker ring, as described in Chapter 12. In this book, Stoll argues that computers have been oversold as tools for schools and may do more harm than good.

Oversold and Underused: Computers in Classrooms, by Larry Cuban (Cambridge, MA: Harvard University Press, 2001). This book offers another critical look at the impact of computers on education. Cuban's approach is more academic and less rambling than Stoll's.

What Video Games Have to Teach Us about Learning and Literacy, by James Paul Gee (New York: Macmillan, 2003). Gee, a respected education professor, finds the good in video games. He argues that we can learn a lot about learning and thinking by looking at interactive games.

Amusing Ourselves to Death: Public Discourse in the Age of Show Business, by Neil Postman (New York: Viking Press, 1986), **Technopoly: The Surrender of Culture to Technology** (New York: Vintage Books, 1993), and **The End of Education: Redefining the Value of School,** by Neil Postman (New York, Knopf, 1995). In these books, noted social critic Neil Postman takes on schools and technology, two powerful forces that are shaping our lives. In *Amusing Ourselves to Death*, Postman argues that television has injured, and is injuring, our ability to think, by reducing every public discourse to just another form of entertainment. In *Technopoly* he argues that the our tools, especially computers, no longer play supporting roles; instead, they radically shape our culture, our families, and our world views. In *The End of Education*, he presents a picture of modern education in which economic utility has become the defining principle. Postman presents compelling problems and suggests possible solutions in these important books.

High Tech, High Teach: Technology and Our Search for Meaning, John Naisbitt with Nana Naisbitt and Douglas Philips (New York: Broadway Books, 1999). In this book, the author of *Megatrends* examines a future in which technology saturates every aspect of American society. What impact will this "Technologically Intoxicated Zone" have on our lives and consciousness? How will our relationship with technology evolve? These are the kinds of questions *High Tech, High Teach* tackles.

Trigger Happy: Videogames and the Entertainment Revolution, by Steven Poole (New York: Arcade Publishing, 2000). Poole surveys the video game landscape and argues that this new entertainment form deserves the same kind of critical analysis we apply to other entertainment arts.

Digital Illusion: Entertaining the Future with High Technology, edited by Clark Dodsworth, Jr. (Reading, MA: Addison-Wesley Publishing Company, 1998). The entertainment industry is the driving force behind many of the technological breakthroughs of the information age. This fascinating collection of papers explores the future of entertainment, including video games, digital video and film, virtual reality, networked games, and immersive amusement park rides. Big fun!

Game Creation and Careers: Insider Secrets from Industry Experts, by Marc Saltzman (Indianapolis: New Riders, 2004). If you think you'd like to design your own video games for fun or profit, this book is worth your time. You'll read war stories and advice by many of the biggest players in the industry.

Periodicals

eWeek. This weekly magazine includes news and commentary on the changing face of electronic technology in business.

Infoworld. This weekly magazine is aimed at IT professionals, but it's not too technical for interested observers from outside the industry.

Information Week. This weekly news magazine focuses on business and the technology that drives it.

Syllabus. This magazine focuses on higher education and technology. Themes of issues range from multimedia tools to distance education on the Web.

T.H.E. Journal. (Technological Horizons in Education). This magazine covers both K–12 and higher education with a mixture of product announcements and articles.

Technos: Quarterly for Education and Technology. This publication by the *Journal of the Agency for Instructional Technology* bills itself as "a forum for the discussion of ideas about the use of technology in education, with a focus on reform." Most of the articles are clearly protechnology, but many deal with controversial issues, for example, a roundtable discussion called "Violence, Games, and Art."

Technology & Learning. This magazine, aimed at K–12 educators, focuses on uses of technology to enhance education.

Learning and Leading with Technology, from ISTE (480 Charnelton St., Eugene, OR 97401-2626, 800/336-5191). ISTE (International Society for Technology in Education) is an important and influential organization whose focus is the effective use of computer technology in the classroom. *Learning and Leading with Technology* is their most accessible and widely read publication.

Popular Science. This tinkerer's magazine is a good source of information on the latest computerized gadgets for consumers.

Web Pages

Check the *Computer Confluence* Web site for links to Internet sources on information-age jobs, technology in the workplace, and the evolving information economy.

The Web is bursting with exciting educational material, much of it created by students. Check the *Computer Confluence* Web site for links to many sites devoted to learning and teaching. You'll also find a sampling of Web links related to entertainment, family life, and home applications.

AFTER READING THIS CHAPTER, YOU SHOULD BE ABLE TO:

- Describe the components of a system and the characteristics of an information system

- Discuss a business organization as a system by using the value chain model

- Explain how transaction processing systems are used to support business processes

- Discuss how computers are used to support automated manufacturing and design

- Describe several ways computers support the work of managers

- Describe how a business organization can use information technologies to compete effectively by improving efficiency and by improving its products and services

 Multimedia extras on the CD-ROM and the Web:

- **Dilbert's Dad** talks tech

- Instant access to glossary and key word references

- Interactive self-study quizzes

    . . . and more.

 computerconfluence.com

INFORMATION SYSTEMS IN BUSINESS

ANDY GROVE, THE PARANOID CHIP MERCHANT

The competition in the computer industry is fierce. Andy Grove, cofounder and now chairperson of the board of Intel, is always worrying about big issues affecting the computer industry: Why do people watch so much TV? Why are people so enthralled with PCs if they are frustrating to use? Why were he and Microsoft's Bill Gates and other industry hotshots surprised by the sudden popularity of the Internet?

Grove worries, but he has faith in three principles he uses to manage Intel: Moore's Law, the Cannibal Principle, and his own Grove's Law. Gordon Moore, another cofounder of Intel, observed that the performance of chip technology, as measured against its price, doubles every 18 months or so. This observation, dubbed Moore's Law, explains why computer hardware often seems outdated within months of purchase. The Cannibal Principle, also stated by Moore, says that semiconductor technology absorbs the functions of what previously were discrete electronic components onto a single new chip. That's why computer components can be packed with more and more features at lower and lower cost. Moore's Law and the Cannibal Principle guarantee a wide-open future for the semiconductor industry. But Andy Grove likes to worry about the competition, so he follows a third principle of his own: Only the paranoid survive.

Observing these principles, Grove led Intel to become the world's largest maker of computer chips. He helped start Intel in 1968 and as CEO led Intel from tenth place to the top of the heap in the semi-

> Only the **paranoid survive**.
>
> —Andrew Grove

conductor industry. He now serves as Intel's chairperson of the board. Intel has built microprocessors that power more than 80 percent of the world's personal computers and has become one of the most profitable companies in America doing it.

But is Grove satisfied? No! (Remember Grove's Law.) Grove's goal for Intel is to be the global standard for consumer computers. He envisions computers that will incorporate all the features and capabilities of today's best multimedia PCs but as standard equipment and at much lower cost. Grove says that the typical PC doesn't come close to

12.1 Andy Grove

pushing the limits of Intel's microprocessor, primarily because Microsoft's software hasn't kept pace with Intel's designs. Using Moore's Law and the Cannibal Principle, Grove assumes that Intel's processors will improve continuously in performance and take over many functions that now require extra chips, add-on hardware, and extra software. Grove envisions microprocessors of the future subsuming today's game players, TVs, and VCRs and becoming the basis for superb digital entertainment and communication machines.

Grove is always worrying about the issues that face Intel. For example, when Intel introduced the Pentium chip in 1994, customers found a flaw in the chip. After initially downplaying the problem, the company was forced by competitive necessity to replace the flawed chips for free and modify its marketing and

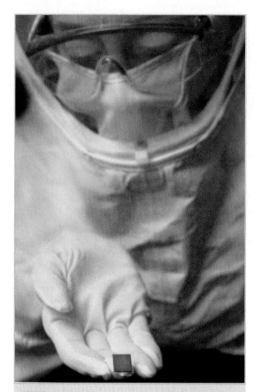

12.2 Intel has built a massive financial empire on tiny silicon chips.

customer support practices. Grove managed to sell some of the arithmetically challenged chips to jewelry makers for use in cufflinks and earrings. Also, he dreamed up the phenomenally successful "Intel Inside" advertising campaign that helped dampen sales of clones of Intel microprocessors made by competitors.

He has no doubt that he and his employees must be paranoid about the industry's competitive forces and be afraid of competitors. But he also believes that fear inside the company is harmful. Although Grove's management style is straightforward and results oriented, he believes a leader must be sure that no one in an organization is afraid to express an opinion. He attributes much of the success of Intel to having created a healthy work environment in which motivated people can flourish. But Grove's Law probably keeps him awake nights, wondering how to push his competitors to the limit.

The phenomenal success of Andy Grove and Intel isn't accidental. Grove's victories in the microprocessor wars are due in large part to his ability to think strategically and to harness information technology to manage Intel well to support his business strategies.

In this chapter, we'll explore the information technologies that support managerial work in an organization. First we'll see how managers use information technology to get the right information, at the right time, in the right form. Then we'll look at various types of information systems managers use to communicate and make decisions. We'll see how managers use information technology strategically to compete effectively with other companies. And we'll look at the process managers use to plan for new information systems.

Systems and Organizations

I firmly believe that any organization, in order to **survive** and **achieve success**, must have a **sound set of beliefs** on which it premises all its policies and actions . . . the basic **philosophy, spirit, and drive** of an organization have far more to do with its relative achievements than do technological or economic resources. . . .

—Thomas Watson, Jr.

Information technology is at the center of the information revolution. But the role and impact of information technology in business can be complex and confusing without the help of clearly defined concepts. The relationships between computers, networks, and organizations are easier to understand if we consider them as systems.

Earlier in the book, we discussed computer systems, operating systems, simulation systems, and other systems without paying much attention to the nature of a system. We now explore the concepts that define systems in general and business information systems in particular.

Anatomy of a System

A system is a set of interrelated parts that work together to accomplish a purpose. To accomplish its purpose, a system performs three basic functions: *input*, *processing*, and *output*. During input, needed materials are gathered and organized. During processing, the input materials are manipulated to produce the desired output, such as a product or service. During output, the result is transferred or delivered to customers, clients, or other systems.

Does this definition sound familiar? The description of a basic computer in Chapter 2 included each of these functions along with a storage function for saving and retrieving data for processing. By this definition, then, a computer is a system.

A system has two additional functions: *feedback* and *control*. Feedback measures the performance of the input, processing, and output functions of the system and provides the measurement data to the control function. Control evaluates the feedback data and adjusts the system's input and processing functions to ensure the desired output is produced.

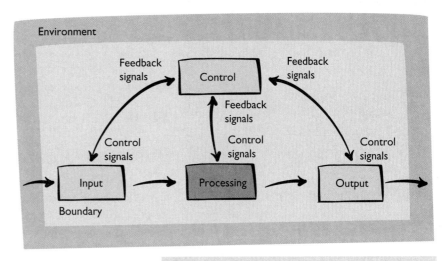

12.3 A system is a group of interrelated or interacting elements working together toward a common goal.

Every system has a *boundary* that defines its limits; anything outside the system's boundary is part of the system's *environment*. The system's environment provides input resources to the system and uses the output from the system.

A system can be a part, or a *subsystem*, of a larger system. For example, a personal computer can be a subsystem of a LAN, which might be a subsystem of a larger WAN, which could be a subsystem of the Internet. When the output of one subsystem is used as

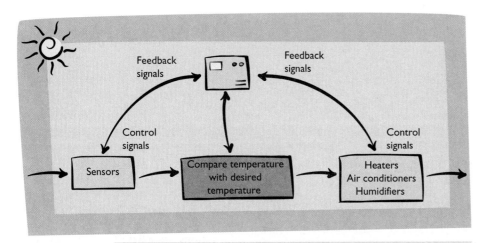

12.4 A building's climate control system uses feedback from the environment to determine how to adjust temperature and humidity controls.

12.5 A ski resort uses sensors on the slopes that monitor weather to help employees know when and how long to operate snow-making equipment.

In every business, however large or small, every person must have a **broad vision** and a **sense of place** in that vision.

—Sir David Scholey

input for another subsystem, the two systems have a shared boundary, or interface. A large system (like the Internet or a corporation) can have many interfacing subsystems.

Let's bring these abstract definitions down to earth with concrete examples. A computerized climate control system in a modern office building is designed by engineers to continually maintain a comfortable temperature and humidity for the office workers—that's the purpose of the system. The system accepts input from human operators that tell it what ideal temperature and humidity to maintain. The system also accepts regularly timed input from sensors that tell it what the actual temperature and humidity are in the building. If temperature or humidity is significantly different than the target value, the system sends output signals to heaters, air conditioners, or humidifiers to adjust conditions accordingly. The monitoring sensors provide feedback from the environment; the system controller processes the feedback and responds by adjusting output signals.

Similarly, a ski resort might use a computer system to maintain an adequate snow level on its ski slopes. Sensors gather temperature and other weather data at several locations around the slopes. The computer processes this information, and the ski resort staff uses the information to decide when to turn the snow-making equipment on or off.

Business Organizations as Systems

While the concept of a system can be (and often is) used to describe biological and other natural phenomena, the systems we're discussing here are designed and used by people. A business organization (commonly referred to also as a company or a firm) is a system designed for the purpose of creating products and services for customers. When we view a company as a system within an environment, each of the basic system concepts takes on a specific meaning.

The firm's environment is made up of customers, stockholders, and other organizations such as competitors, suppliers,

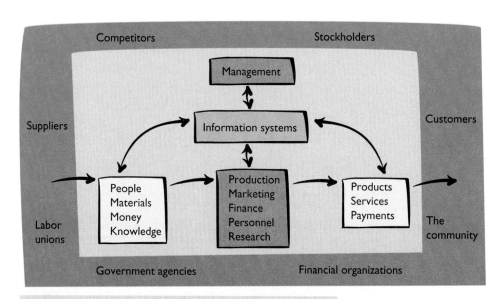

12.6 A business organization is a system that uses a variety of resources to produce goods and services for customers.

banks, and government agencies. From the environment, a company acquires people, materials, money, knowledge, and other resources as input. These resources are used in work processes such as manufacturing, marketing and sales, accounting and finance, all of which are needed to produce desired outputs for customers. These outputs include products and services as well as dividends, taxes, and information that are transferred to entities in the environment. The firm's managers perform the control function to ensure that the input, processing, and output functions perform properly. Information systems play a key role in the feedback and control functions, collecting data from each of the primary activities and processing the data into information needed by managers.

The Value Chain Model of a Business Organization

One way to understand a business organization as a system is to use the value chain model, developed by Harvard professor Michael E. Porter. According to the value chain model, an organization performs a series of activities to provide products and services for customers. Each activity adds something valuable to the production of the product or service. The value chain model divides the activities of an organization into two types—primary activities and support activities.

> Art is the **beautiful** way of doing things.
> Science is the **effective** way of doing things.
> Business is the **economic** way of doing things.
> —Elbert Hubbard, U.S. author

There are five primary activities in an organization's value chain:

- Inbound logistics receives and stores supplies and materials from the firm's environment and distributes them when and where they are needed in the organization.
- Operations uses the supplies and materials to create or manufacture the organization's products and services.
- Outbound logistics delivers the products and services when and where needed by customers.
- Marketing and sales investigates customer needs and promotes the value of and sells the products and services in the environment (marketplace).
- Service maintains and enhances the usefulness of the product or service to customers through, for example, training and maintenance.

The value chain model includes four support activities of an organization to ensure that the primary activities can function efficiently and effectively:

- Management and other administrative services (for example, accounting, finance, and legal) comprise the general management structure of the organization that deals with banks, government agencies, and other organizations in the firm's environment.

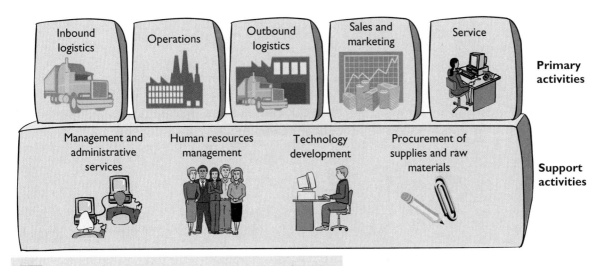

12.7 The value chain model shows the activities in an organization that make a product or service more desirable to customers.

- Human resources recruits, hires, trains, and develops the people in the firm.
- Research and technology development creates new products and services and looks for ways to improve the efficiency and effectiveness of the company's primary activities.
- Procurement interacts with the organization's suppliers and vendors to ensure high-quality supplies and materials are available to the organization.

Each of the primary and support activities can be viewed as a subsystem of the organization. The activities interact by exchanging their inputs and outputs, the output of one activity being the input to another activity. The specific combination of primary and support activities an organization uses to accomplish a specific objective is often referred to as a *business process*. More specifically, a business process is a related set of primary and support activities that uses people, information, and other resources (such as information technology) to create valuable products and/or services for customers. For example, a typical business process is a sale-purchase transaction with customers—the people in marketing and sales take an order from a customer and give the order to the operations employees; the operations people may order supplies to produce the product to fill the order; the outbound logistics people receive the filled order and ship the requested product. The accounting and finance support people receive the filled customer order and send a bill or invoice to the customer.

Generally speaking, we can think of three major types of business processes in organizations—transaction-oriented, communications, and decision-making processes. In today's business world, information and information technology play important key roles in each of these three types of business processes of an organization. We next examine the concept of *information systems* and how information systems are used in transaction-oriented business processes. Later in the chapter we consider how information systems are used in communications and decision making.

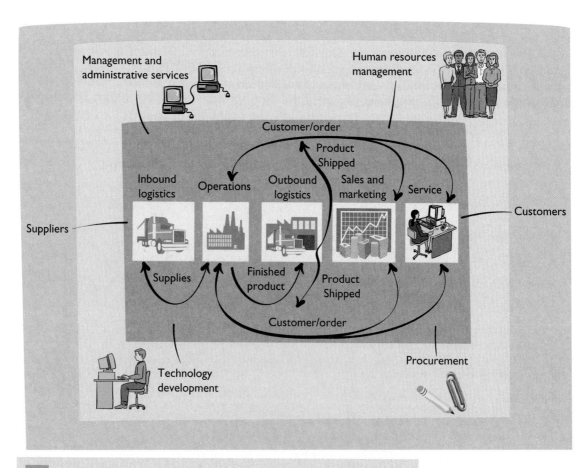

12.8 A business process, such as a sale-purchase transaction with customers, is the interaction of primary and support activities in the organization's value chain.

Information Systems

We can think of an information system as a subsystem that supports the information needs of other business processes within an organization. The overall purpose of an information system is to help people in the organization gather and use information, communicate with other people within and outside the organization, and make effective decisions.

> We are moving very rapidly in all forms of production and services to a **knowledge-based economy** in which what you earn depends on what you can learn. Not only what you know today, but **what you are capable of learning tomorrow**.
>
> —Tracy LaQuey, in *The Internet Companion*

Like other systems, an information system performs input, processing, and output functions, and contains feedback and control functions. The output of an information system is an information product of some kind—for example, a report or other document. The input of an information system is data, or raw facts, about other subsystems in the business or other systems in the environment, such as descriptions of customer needs, materials purchased, and sales transactions. The processing function organizes and arranges the data in ways that people can understand and use. An information system also has a storage function to save data and information products for future use. The control function assures that the information product outputs are of high quality and are useful to the information users for problem solving and decision making.

An information system involves people using information and information technologies to perform business processes, or tasks, that are important for the mission and objectives of the organization within a business environment. Let's examine some of the important terms in that sentence.

People

All members of an organization use information to perform their jobs—they're end users. Think of employees in an organization as forming a hierarchical management structure of users: clerical and production workers at the basic level; operational managers who supervise production, clerical, and other nonmanagement workers at the next level; middle managers who are responsible for programs and facilities on another level; and managers who are responsible for the organization performance as a whole at the top. Another set of end users is people in the organization's environment who use the firm's information products and services, such as suppliers and customers.

The structure and design of an information system is defined by another group of people—the system designers. Managers decide how money, time, and other resources should be allocated to design, implement, and maintain the organization's information systems. These three groups of people—users, designers, and managers—are all important for the successful use of information technology in an organization.

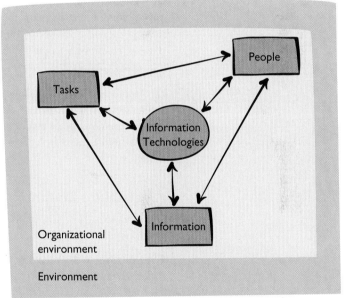

12.9 An information system is a set of information technologies that enable people in an organization to accomplish tasks effectively by providing access to data.

Tasks

When you think about a particular business process, you can describe it as a sequence of tasks. For example, when you go shopping you usually perform certain tasks in sequence, such as entering the store, locating items in the store, selecting the items you'd like to buy, purchasing the items, and then carrying your purchases to your car. Similarly, many tasks are simple and straightforward, such as typing a memo to a colleague. Other tasks are complex—creating an advertising campaign for a product, for example.

Information

Information has two dimensions: physical or digital representation and human cognition. As a commodity, information refers to facts, statistics, or other data that are valuable or useful to a person for accomplishing a task. These valuable pieces of information are organized and represented in some physical or digital form—a newspaper, email message, or report, for example. You can also think of information as the cognitive state of a person who understands the tasks to be performed. From a cognitive point of view, people need information to be able to answer questions such as what, when, where, who, how, and why.

Organization

An organization can be defined by its purpose, the tasks or activities that it performs, and its structure. The purpose of an organization is usually to provide or sell a product or service to its clients or customers. An organization that produces physical products, such as automobiles or computers, is called a manufacturing organization. A firm that provides a service, such as legal or medical advice, is called a service organization. Although business organizations operate for a profit, not-for-profit organizations, such as charitable organizations and government agencies, provide goods and services without the intent of making a profit. Both profit and not-for-profit organizations usually comprise several departments, such as accounting, finance, and marketing, to accomplish the tasks in the organization's value chain. Often, the people within one or several departments are organized into workgroups to accomplish a specific task.

Environment

The global, competitive business environment presents problems and opportunities that a business organization must cope with to thrive. Today, many firms need to conduct trade and coordinate with their suppliers and distributors on a global scale. Customers can shop in a worldwide marketplace, so firms must do business in open, unprotected worldwide markets.

Information Technology in Information Systems

In the context of business information systems, information technology performs five functions: acquisition, processing, storage and retrieval, presentation, and transmission.

- **Acquisition** is a process of capturing data about an event that is important to the organization. Managers, clerks, or other users expect the data to be useful later. An example of acquisition is the identification of each grocery item captured by a scanning device during checkout at a grocery store.
- **Processing** is an activity that manipulates and organizes information in ways that adds value to the information so it is useful to users. For example, one function of data processing in a grocery store is to calculate the total grocery bill during checkout.
- **Storage and retrieval** is an activity that systematically accumulates information for later use and then locates the stored information when needed. For example, a grocery information system would use a database to store revised information about inventory levels of grocery items after each customer has checked out.
- **Presentation** is the process of showing information in a format and medium useful to the user. A grocery receipt given to a customer is one example; a summary report displayed on a manager's screen is another.
- **Transmission** is the process of sending and distributing data and information to various locations. For example, a grocery store may send information about inventory levels and sales to headquarters frequently.

Information Systems for Business Transactions

A transaction is an event that occurs in any of the primary activities
of the company: manufacturing,
marketing, sales, and accounting. A

> Being good in business is the **most fascinating kind of art**. . . .
> —Andy Warhol

transaction might be a sale to a customer, a purchase from a supplier or vendor, or a payroll payment to an employee. An organization can use an information system to track
transactions in order to operate efficiently.

A transaction processing system (TPS) is a basic accounting and record-keeping system
that keeps track of routine daily transactions necessary to conduct business. Examples of
transaction processing systems include sales-order entry, ticket and hotel reservations, payroll, accounts receivable, and inventory. Transaction processing systems are important because they make it possible to control business processes intelligently based on accurate information. For example, by tracking the number of cars a dealership sells a week, a manager
can make a fairly accurate assessment of the number of cars to order from the manufacturer.
Similarly, by tracking the number of students that enroll in an introduction to computers
course each fall semester, a university can determine the number of books it needs to order.

Transaction processing systems typically require high processing speeds to manipulate
large volumes of data stored in databases. These systems capture data users and managers
use to produce documents and reports. Many systems enable people to retrieve information
interactively through database query systems, groupware applications, and intranet Web
pages. A transaction processing system must ensure a high level of accuracy and security
of the data.

Transaction processing is a cyclical process with five steps:

1. *Data entry.* The first step in TPS is to enter
   the transaction data into machine-readable
   form. This involves online data entry (typing at a terminal, scanning bar codes, or
   other direct input into the computer) or
   transcribing paper source documents into
   an electronic format acceptable to a computer. Data entry can also use Electronic
   Data Interchange (EDI) to electronically
   exchange business transactions between
   companies using standard document formats for purchase orders, invoices, and
   shipping notices. (EDI is discussed in more
   detail later in the chapter.)

2. *Processing the data.* A typical transaction
   processing system organizes and sorts the
   data and performs calculations. Data can
   be processed in two ways: Batch process-
   ing involves gathering and manipulating all the data to be
   processed for a particular time period; real-time processing involves processing each transaction as it occurs. Batch processing
   is used when processing is needed periodically, such as monthly
   payroll or checking account statements. Real-time processing is appropriate when
   users need the data immediately, as with bank ATM machines.

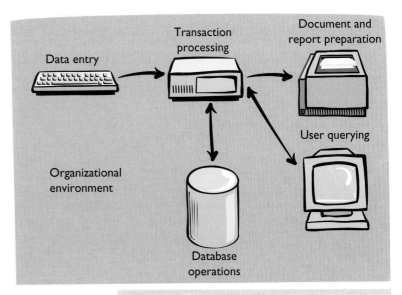

12.10 A transaction processing cycle consists of the
same steps as in other systems: input, processing,
storage, and output.

3. *Storing and updating the data.* This step involves storing the transaction data in database files so it can be retrieved later in processing some future transaction. For example, the amount you paid on this month's phone bill is used in calculating the amount
   you're billed next month. Many large organizations use data warehousing software to
   create and maintain large databases containing data on all aspects of the company.

4. *Document and report preparation.* A transaction processing system produces several
   types of action documents and reports. An action document initiates an action by the

12.1 The Information Flow Through a Transaction Processing System

Running a nursery business involves selling to customers, keeping track of inventory and ordering from vendors, paying employees, and keeping track of income and expenses.

1. Sales transaction processing system. When a customer buys a plant, the clerk enters the information into a cash register, and the customer receives a receipt.

12.11a

2. Inventory control transaction processing system. The sale of the plant is recorded for inventory control by reading the UPC code on the price tag. This allows the buyers for the nursery to know how much stock for any plant is available and when to order more.

SKU 274878
RETAIL $6.00

12.11b

12.11c

3. Accounts receivable transaction processing system. The nursery keeps records of amounts owed by customers. The clerk prepares invoices to credit customers.

12.11d

12.11f

6. General ledger transaction processing system. The income and expenses are organized in reports so that the nursery's owners know the health of the company.

4. Accounts payable transaction processing system. When an account needs to be paid, the clerk can print the check. In accounts payable, the nursery knows how much to pay each vendor and when to send the check.

12.11e

12.11g

7. Payroll transaction processing system. The nursery keeps track of the time each employee works and produces paychecks and other payroll statements.

5. Purchasing transaction processing system. When new stock needs to be purchased, the vendors' bills for the new inventory moves to accounts payable.

431

recipient or verifies for the recipient that a transaction has occurred. For example, a billing statement produced by your phone company is intended to trigger an action on your part, namely to make a payment. A sales receipt verifies the details of a purchase you make. Other examples of action documents are payroll checks, invoices, warehouse packing lists, and sales receipts. Reports are used by management to monitor the transactions that occur over a period of time. Reports can contain detailed information about specific transactions or summary information about a group of transactions, such as totals and averages. These reports are customized for specific users.

5. *User inquiry.* Managers and other workers can ask questions and retrieve information about any transaction activity when it's needed. The responses can be presented on the screen or in hardcopy form.

The transaction processing cycle repeats regularly, with output from one cycle serving as input to the next cycle. Each transaction system is a subsystem of the business as a whole, and these subsystems can interact in a variety of ways.

Enterprise Resource Planning

Transaction processing systems exist in all functional areas of a business's value chain. Most early computer applications in business were designed to maintain accurate and up-to-date records of business transactions; today's accounting systems perform the same function. Typically, an accounting system is made up of a number of subsystems that keep track of the revenues, expenditures, and cash requirements of a business. Typical subsystems include order processing, inventory control, accounts receivable, accounts payable, payroll, and general ledger. Each subsystem is itself a transaction processing system. The subsystems exchange information; the output of one subsystem is the input to another subsystem.

Many managers look for ways to create cross-functional information systems by reengineering, or combining and integrating two or more transaction processing systems. Careful reengineering can increase the efficiency and effectiveness of a business process by reducing wasted time, paperwork, and unnecessary work procedures. Work practices can also be restructured to minimize costs and maximize worker effectiveness.

This approach of creating information systems to support an organization's operational business processes is referred to as **enterprise resource planning (ERP)**. An ERP system links, simplifies, and speeds up a company's entire transaction processing cycle. The primary focus is to improve customer service, and the ultimate goal is to make it easier for both suppliers and customers to do business with the company. A typical ERP system collects transaction data from various business processes and stores the data in a unified database or data warehouse. Once stored in the database, the data can be shared automatically between business processes and retrieved by managers in all parts of the organization.

ERP can improve the free flow of information between different parts of the firm. A company can also use ERP to improve the coordination of its value chain logistics activities and the logistics activities of its suppliers and customers, a concept called **supply chain management**. ERP software is evolving quickly to support the growing need of organizations to conduct their business transactions over the Internet.

ERP systems are usually large and complex and take a lot of time and money to implement. In a recent survey of 63 companies—including small, medium, and large companies in a range of industries—the average total cost of an ERP was $15 million (the highest was $300 million and the lowest was $400,000). The largest ERP software vendor is SAP, a German-based multinational company with sales in 50 countries. Other vendors include Peoplesoft, Baan, Oracle, and J. D. Edwards.

Because of the complexity involved in planning and implementing ERP systems, many companies have had difficulty implementing the systems successfully the first time they tried. For example, Whirlpool's initial ERP implementation crippled the shipping system, leaving appliances stacked on loading docks—and therefore not delivered to paying customers—for a full eight weeks. Hershey Foods had a 19 percent drop in earnings caused by an incompetent ERP implementation that wreaked distribution havoc during one Halloween season. And a new ERP system at Volkswagen resulted in significant delays in parts shipments, causing product inventories to build up to costly levels.

Automated Information Systems for Design and Manufacturing

Computer-aided design (CAD) and computer-aided manufacturing (CAM), introduced in Chapter 6, are used to support design and manufacturing business

Automation does not make **optimism** obsolete.
—George Keith Funston, president, New York Stock Exchange

processes within the organization's value chain. Manufacturing transforms raw materials into a finished product. Design refers to creating and developing both new products and new ways of manufacturing those products. The objective of automation systems is to increase the productivity of the manufacturing and design processes to increase product quality and customer satisfaction.

12.12 CAD enables product designers to "build" product prototypes and "test" them as computer objects.

12.13 The assembly line for manufacturing computer chips is highly automated.

Product designers and engineers use computer-aided design (CAD) to draw product or process designs on the screen. All the design files are stored in a CAD database containing detailed product and process specifications and other information.

Computer-aided manufacturing (CAM) software retrieves the design specifications of the product from the CAD database, controls machines on the factory floor to manufacture the product, and monitors the overall physical process of manufacturing the product. CAM improves the efficiency of the manufacturing process by reducing the time needed to set up machines or robots for the next production run. CAM makes it possible for a company to respond to a customer's unique needs by making the product to order and delivering it in a short time, rather than making a large number of the products and storing them in inventory. For example, Panasonic uses CAD to take a customer's order for a custom-made bicycle; it then faxes the design file to the manufacturing plant, where CAM sets up the production run and produces the bicycle, all in just a few hours.

Computer-integrated manufacturing (CIM) is the concept of integrating CAD and CAM systems with other information systems in the company. CIM automates the information flow between design, manufacturing, and other functional areas in a company, and it simplifies and automates as many manufacturing processes as possible. CIM can improve product consistency, reduce waste, increase report accuracy, and improve the overall quality and flexibility of the manufacturing process.

Interorganizational Information Systems

Without **communications** there would be no **life**.

—Norbert Wiener

In Chapter 11 we explored the automated office and saw how information systems can be used to automate communications and reduce paper flow within an organization. **Interorganizational information systems (IOS)** use networking technology to facilitate communication between an organization and its suppliers, customers, and other organizations. With an IOS, a company can share business data and exchange transactions with other companies electronically. There are two forms of IOS—electronic data interchange and business alliances.

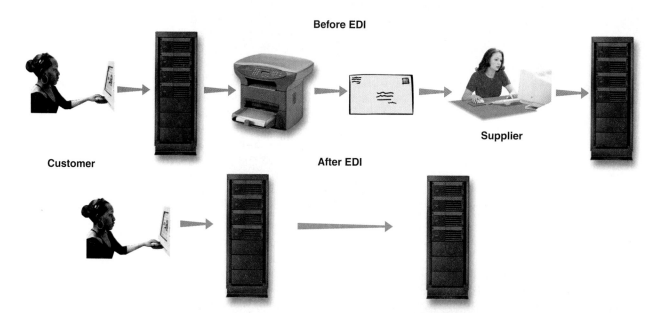

Before EDI

Customer

Supplier

After EDI

12.14 EDI can integrate the order-entry activity of a customer and the order-filling activity of a supplier. In this case, Dillard's, the customer, orders clothing from Haggar, the supplier. Integration is possible because EDI enables the customer and the supplier to use consistent technical standards and share information about each other's activities. Integration increases efficiency for both the customer and the supplier by eliminating delays and increasing accuracy.

Electronic Data Interchange (EDI) is the direct, computer-to-computer exchange of standardized, common business transaction documents, such as purchase orders and invoices, between business partners, suppliers, and customers. EDI uses international standards for data formatting that enable companies to exchange large amounts of information in real time around the world.

EDI systems have been developed for particular business partners for decades. In the retail clothing industry, Dillard's department store uses EDI to send purchase orders electronically to Haggar, one of its apparel manufacturers. If Haggar doesn't have the cloth to manufacture a needed item of clothing, it uses EDI to place an order electronically with the textile manufacturer Burlington Industries. In the automotive industry, Ford, General Motors, and other car manufacturers use EDI to order parts from their suppliers; in turn, the suppliers must agree to implement EDI and use it for transactions with the car manufacturer. In terms of the federal government, all contractors wanting government contracts are required to link into the government's EDI systems.

A business alliance is a cooperative arrangement between two or more businesses with complementary capabilities. A good example is Calyx & Corolla, a direct-mail flower company. Calyx & Corolla maintains customer databases, a Web site, and an online catalog, and it does all its own marketing. But rather than create its own distribution system, Calyx & Corolla has an agreement with FedEx, which handles the logistics of delivering the flowers from the growers to the customers. Similarly, Calyx & Corolla has an agreement with MasterCard and American Express, which handle all the credit authorization and payment activities. Calyx & Corolla also created alliances with independent flower growers worldwide. When a customer order is entered on Calyx & Corolla's Web site, the customer's credit is verified electronically with MasterCard or American Express; the order is sent electronically to the appropriate flower grower and to FedEx; and MasterCard or American Express charges the bill to the customer's account and transmits electronically payments to FedEx, Calyx & Corolla, and the flower grower.

Another example of a business alliance is an *information partnership* in which the companies, usually in different industries, share information for their mutual benefit. For example, United Airlines and MCI WorldCom have an arrangement in which customers receive United Airlines frequent flyer miles for MCI WorldCom services. By sharing information, these types of partnerships help companies gain new customers and subsequently new opportunities for cross-selling and targeting products.

A type of business alliance that is becoming more popular because of the Internet is the *industrial network,* in which the systems of several companies in an industry are linked. Procter & Gamble has developed a system to coordinate its manufacturing facilities and suppliers with grocery store point-of-sale systems, warehouses, and shippers. The system enables Procter & Gamble and its business partners to monitor all its products from raw materials to customer purchase.

International Information Systems

Information technology makes it economically feasible for a company to do business internationally and conduct its business processes virtually any time and anywhere. Using the global telecommunications network, a company can communicate with suppliers and customers located anywhere in the world, employ engineers and designers in a number of different countries, and have production facilities located at cost-effective geographic sites worldwide. Any information system that supports international business activities is called an international information system.

The international business environment poses several challenges when compared to a purely domestic business environment. An international environment is multilingual and multicultural, has multiple governments, has many different regulations regarding privacy and intellectual property protection, has varying standards for telecommunications and other technologies, and has multiple geographic conditions, time zones, and monetary currencies. All of these factors affect the flow of data between countries, commonly called transborder data flow.

Even though good business practices make sense around the world, many issues are unique to a particular country. Some countries do not allow personal data about employees to leave the country. Many countries have weak, nonexistent, or poorly enforced software copyright laws. Inexpensive labor costs in one country may be the result of what another country considers unethical labor practices. Some countries have poorly maintained and aging telecommunication infrastructures.

Information Technology and Management

> The most **important quality in a leader** is that of being acknowledged as such.
>
> —André Maurois, French author

Every organization has limited time, money, and people. To stay in business, an organization must use these resources wisely. **Management** is a set of activities that helps people efficiently use resources to accomplish an organization's goals. A small business might have only one person designated as a manager. Large multinational organizations may have hundreds of managers. Whatever the size of the organization, managers plan, organize, direct, and control the various processes in the company. In all of these roles, managers make decisions.

A manager makes a *structured decision* when he or she understands the situation clearly and uses established procedures and information to resolve the problem. Structured decisions, such as deciding how many inventory items to reorder in a university cafeteria, are usually relatively simple and routine and can sometimes be made by a computer. Some structured decisions, such as deciding a university's department course schedule for the semester, can be very complex, because they involve many established procedures and large quantities of information.

A manager makes a *semistructured decision* when there's some uncertainty about a problem and the manager must use his or her judgment. For example, a car dealership manager may need to decide how many of a new-model automobile to order for delivery three months in the future when uncertain about the actual demand for the model.

Decision type	Problem type	Methodology
Structured	Repetitive, routine	Procedures, rules
Semistructured	Partial structure, Partial "fuzzy"	Judgment, procedure
Unstructured	"Fuzzy," complex	Judgment, intuition

12.15 Managers use several methods to solve different types of problems in various decision-making situations.

12.16 An organization usually has a hierarchy of managers responsible for work at several levels.

Sometimes a manager faces unique circumstances or must anticipate events over a relatively long period of time. In these situations, a manager must make an *unstructured decision* requiring many quantitative and ethical judgments that have no clear answers. For example, a manager may need to decide how the company should respond to a competitor that has introduced an entirely new product line with excellent customer services.

In a large organization there are typically three management levels: operational, tactical, and strategic. Managers have different functions and roles and face different types of decisions at each level.

A manager at the *operational level* is responsible for supervising the day-to-day activities in the organization's value chain. Operational-level managers are also referred to as lower-level managers, supervisors, and group leaders.

A manager at the *tactical level*—a middle manager—may be responsible for a large organizational unit, such as a sales region or a production plant. Typically, a middle manager develops short-term plans for the next year or so and then makes sure his or her employees perform according to the plans. Tactical-level managers responsible for the development and use of information systems in an organization are called information systems managers.

A manager at the *strategic level* is called a top manager and is responsible for the long-range issues related to the business's growth and development. Top managers include the board of directors, chief executive officers, and vice presidents. The top manager responsible for the overall planning of information systems in an organization is called the chief information officer (CIO).

It is important for managers at all levels to get the right information at the right time in the right form. Managers depend on communication for the information they need. Managers spend up to 90 percent of their time communicating with other people in the

12.17 Communication involves a person expressing an idea (using text, voice, pictures, or other media) and sending it through a channel to another person who interprets the message. Feedback helps to clarify a garbled or unclear message.

12.18 Managers find that video teleconferencing with people in different places at the same time can be effective.

organization and in the company's external environment. We've already seen (in this chapter and earlier chapters) several tools that managers can use to facilitate communication. Email, instant messaging, teleconferencing, blogging, and other "standard" Internet communication tools and techniques can be used to grease the management communication wheels in an organization. Groupware programs, intranets, and virtual private networks can extend the communication capabilities of managers beyond their local offices. And interorganizational information systems can extend those capabilities to business partners, customers, and others outside their companies.

But facilitating communication isn't the only way information technology helps managers get the information they need. A variety of software tools are available to make managers more effective and efficient. We'll now survey those tools and see how managers use information technology strategically to compete effectively with other companies.

Information Technology and Decision Making

Business is a **good game**—lots of competition and a minimum of rules. **You keep score with money**.

—Nolan Bushnell, founder of Atari

In many ways, it is more difficult to make decisions in today's business environment than it has been in the past. How can a manager choose among a large number of alternative solutions made possible by modern technology? Because many modern organizations use large, complex, interconnected systems, the risk—and cost—of making a wrong decision can be massive, especially when you consider the international nature of business today. On the other hand, the benefits can be immense when wise decisions ripple rapidly through a tightly linked organization.

Management Information Systems

A management information system (MIS) gives a manager the information he or she needs to make decisions, typically structured decisions, regarding the operational activities of the company. These decisions require the manager to measure performance and compare that measurement information with predetermined standards of performance. Transaction processing systems provide the MIS with data on the performance of the primary activities of the company. The MIS extracts the relevant data from databases of the transaction processing systems, organizes and summarizes the data in useful ways, and provides the information to the manager in various reports. The manager can use the reports in the intelligence phase of decision making to identify any operational problems.

Management information systems are also referred to as management reporting systems because their main output is a variety of reports for managers. An MIS provides three types of reports: detailed reports, summary reports, and exception reports. Each type of report typically shows both actual and planned performance measures for certain transactions that allow a manager to compare actual performance with planned performance.

MIS reports are usually distributed to managers routinely as scheduled reports. A manager can also use the query language and report-generation capabilities of a newer MIS to retrieve ad hoc, on-demand reports. Many organizations now have intranet infrastructures that enable managers to use Web browsers to retrieve and view MIS reports.

Typically, an MIS provides access to an organization's internal transaction data but not to information external to the organization. An MIS doesn't provide analytic capabilities other than straightforward statistical operations for summary and exceptions reports. As a result, an MIS can supply performance information to managers about the primary activities of the company but is not particularly useful in helping managers decide how to actually improve performance.

Decision Support Systems

A **decision support system (DSS)** helps a manager make semistructured decisions, such as budget planning and sales forecasting, and unstructured decisions, such as new product development and contract negotiating. The term *decision support system* also refers to a way of thinking about how information systems should be designed to support managerial decision making. The DSS design philosophy is to provide managers with the tools they need to analyze information they deem relevant for a particular decision or class of decisions. A DSS is designed with the decision style of the managers in mind and provides powerful information access, processing, and reporting capabilities the managers can use in a flexible manner whenever needed.

A DSS has three major components that a manager uses interactively to retrieve and manipulate relevant data. The *data management* component is a database of relevant internal and external information of the organization. Current and historical information is extracted from the company's MIS and transaction processing applications. External information, such as stock prices, research data, and company information about customers, competitors, and vendors, is accessed through publicly available databases. Database management software enables the manager to query the database and retrieve relevant information, much like an MIS.

The *model management* component enables the manager to evaluate alternative problem solutions and identify the best solution using appropriate software.

> You can lead a **horse to water**, but you can't make him enter **regional distribution codes** in data field 92 to **facilitate regression analysis** on the back end.
>
> —John Cleese, corporate consultant and former member of *Monty Python's Flying Circus*

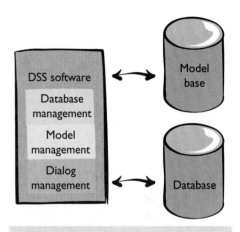

12.20 The components of a decision support system. Managers can use the system interactively to analyze information for decision making.

12.21 Group decision support systems can enhance the dynamics of face-to-face contact in group meetings.

A retail chain processes a tremendous amount of data daily. Depending on how it is handled, this information can be either overwhelming or enlightening. To make the best use of the information, many chains use management information systems to aid in decision making. This example follows the many paths of information through the Frostbyte Outdoor Outfitters Corporation.

12.19d Top-level managers use reports that summarize long-term trends to analyze overall business strategies.

12.19a When a new shipment arrives, a clerk records it using a terminal; inventory and accounting files are updated automatically.

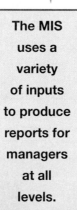

The MIS uses a variety of inputs to produce reports for managers at all levels.

12.19c

12.19e Mid-level managers use summary and exception reports to spot trends and unusual circumstances.

12.19b When a clerk punches a sale into the terminal, a database records changes in financial and inventory files.

12.19f Low-level managers use detailed reports to keep tabs on day-to-day operations.

Sales Volume vs. Average Temperature as of 6/30/02

	Jan.	Feb.	Mar.	Apr.	May	June
Sales Volume	1798	1700	1609	1532	1302	1216
Sales	$24,398	$24,673	$22,468	$21,003	$18,068	$16,328
Average temperature	24	32	41	48	58	71

12.19g On-demand reports integrate information and show relationships. Example: impact of cold weather on ski sales.

Year-End Sales by Item: Top 20 as of 12/31/02

ITEM	SOLD UNITS	RETURNED UNITS	TOTAL UNITS	TOTAL SALES
Beaver Kayaks	58	3	55	$12,375
Possum Packs	1240	212	1028	$20,046
Possum Parkas	1003	323	680	$17,000
Rhinoceros Hiking Boots	1162	429	733	$47,645
Snoreswell Sleeping Bags	923	62	861	$39,175

12.19h Summary reports show departmental totals or trends. Example: most popular footwear.

Items Temporarily Out of Stock as of 12/31/02

ITEM	OUT SINCE	DATE AVAILABLE
Fancy Flashlights	10/31/02	1/4/03
Foxy Flannels	10/31/02	1/2/03
Snappy Tents	10/02/02	1/2/03

12.19i Exception reports reflect unusual relationships. Example: out-of-stock gear.

Daily Sales Register by Type: 7/31/02

ITEM	UNITS	SALES
Parkas	62	$1209
Flashlights	154	$1540
Tents	2	$500
Hiking Boots	78	$65

12.19j Detail reports give complete, detailed information on routine operations. Example: daily orders.

For example, a manager could use a spreadsheet model to learn how product sales correlate with differences in income, age, and other characteristics of consumers; based on this analysis, the manager could use the model to then forecast future sales. The model management component also contains other model-building tools, such as graphics software, that a manager can use to design and implement customized graphs and charts.

The third DSS component is the user interface, or *dialog management*. Most DSS user interfaces are graphical interfaces that enable the manager to view information in a variety of forms, including graphs, charts, lists, tables, and reports.

Many decisions are made by a team or group of managers. **Group decision support systems (GDSS)** are designed to improve the productivity of decision-making meetings by enhancing the dynamics of collaborative work. Physically, the GDSS usually takes the form of a room equipped with computers, DSS database and modeling software, LAN connections, and a large-screen projection of computer output for viewing by the group. The GDSS also includes specific communication-oriented software tools that support the development and sharing of ideas.

During a decision-making meeting, managers can use the GDSS capabilities as if they were using their own DSS to perform an analysis or some other management activity. A manager can show his or her work to the group using the large-screen projection system or keep it confidential. The managers as a group can use the GDSS software tools to brainstorm and organize their ideas, comments, suggestions, criticisms, and other information. A GDSS enables the group members to share information anonymously, encouraging them to participate without risking the counterproductive dynamics of group meetings.

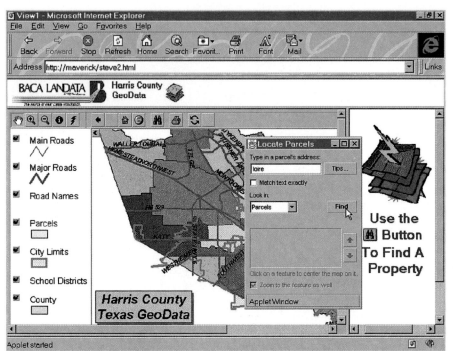

12.22 Real estate agents can use a GIS to view property data at various layers, such as proximity to schools and shopping, city limits, and owner information.

A **geographic information system (GIS)** is a special type of DSS designed to work with map and other spatial information. A GIS is made up of mapping and analytic modeling software, databases that contain map images, geographic and demographic data, and a user interface enabling a manager to query the database interactively and see the results shown on a map. Government agencies and more than 100 commercial companies produce spatial information databases containing demographic, employment, and consumer-habit information that can be incorporated into a business-oriented GIS. A manager might use a GIS to identify the best location for a new retail store or branch office, analyze customer buying preferences in a geographical area, or plan delivery and service routes.

Executive Information Systems

An **executive information system (EIS)** combines features of MIS and DSS to support unstructured decision-making by top managers. A top manager can use an EIS to monitor key indicators of the company's performance, such as profitability, finance and marketing, and human and technology resources. An EIS also makes it easy for a manager to access economic, consumer, and environmental trends affecting the company.

An EIS has design components similar to a DSS. The EIS data management component provides interactive access to the company's important information, and the model management component provides access to data on the company's critical success factors. The *dialog management component* is the set of human–computer interactive features that enables the executive to select the necessary data and display it in a variety of formats, including summary and exception reports, lists, charts, tables, and graphs.

An EIS enables the executive to *drill down* through the available information to the level of detail needed. For example, an executive may view a summary report and notice that sales in a particular region have declined over the past month. The executive can retrieve the detailed sales information for that particular sales region. Examining this data, the executive might decide to retrieve information about product sales at a particular store or by a particular salesperson.

Using the database management capability of an EIS, an executive has access to up-to-the-minute data on internal operations of the company and a wide variety of external online information, including news services, financial market databases, economic information, and other publicly

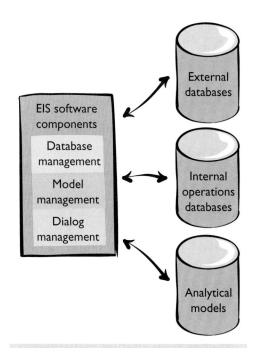

12.24 The components of an executive information system. Managers can use the system to monitor the important economic and social trends affecting the organization, as well as the important performance measures of the company.

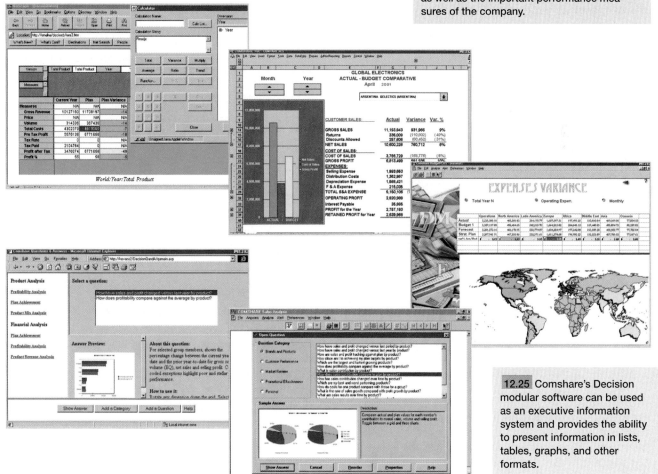

12.25 Comshare's Decision modular software can be used as an executive information system and provides the ability to present information in lists, tables, graphs, and other formats.

A decision support system can provide a manager with powerful tools for analysis of information. Different management decisions call for different types of analysis. A DSS handles these four types of analysis:

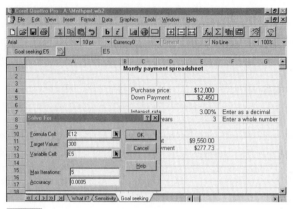

12.23a

What if? analysis. DSSs have been designed to support many types of decision-making applications, including corporate planning and forecasting, product pricing, flight scheduling, transportation routing, and investment analysis. Even though each DSS is designed to solve a specific problem, managers can use any DSS to ask and answer what-if? questions. For example, a manager may want to know what the monthly payment for a product will be for a certain purchase price, loan length, and interest rate. By using an analytic model, a manager can change the value of one or more key input variables or parameters and immediately see the effect on the output variables or proposed solution.

12.23b

Sensitivity analysis. By varying the value of key input variables systematically, or by asking a sequence of what-if? questions, the manager performs a sensitivity analysis. A sensitivity analysis shows the manager the degree of change in the results or output of a model as the value of a key variable or assumption changes incrementally. With a

well-designed user interface, a manager can evaluate any number of what-if? questions to do a sensitivity analysis easily and quickly.

12.23c

Goal-seeking analysis. A variation of sensitivity analysis is goal-seeking analysis, which attempts to find the value of one or more key input variables of a model that will result in a desired level of output. For example, a manager might wish to know what down payment would be necessary to obtain a particular monthly payment. The manager could enter a value for the down payment variable and observe the resulting monthly payment calculation and then reiterate this process until the desired monthly payment level is found. Some DSSs enable managers to perform goal seeking automatically.

12.23d

Optimization analysis. Another variation of sensitivity analysis is optimization analysis. All decisions are made under certain constraints and limitations, such as a limited budget. Optimization analysis attempts to find the highest or lowest value of one or more variables, given certain limits or constraints. For example, a manager could use an analytic model to calculate the optimal monthly payment for a product, given that the purchase price, the interest rate of the loan, and the down payment cannot exceed certain limits. Spreadsheet software has the ability to perform optimization analysis.

available information. This ability to access both internal and external information makes an EIS a powerful tool during the intelligence phase of decision making.

Information Systems in Perspective

MIS, EIS, and DSS support decision making by providing managers easy access to relevant information and by providing analytic tools for manipulating the information. But they aren't the only software tools used by executives.

> Anyone who believes that the **competitive spirit in America** is dead has never been in a **supermarket** when the cashier opens another **checkout line**.
>
> —Ann Landers, advice columnist

Expert systems (ES) supports decision making by providing managers with access to computerized expert knowledge. An expert is someone who has mastery of an extraordinary amount of knowledge within a narrow domain. An ES is designed to replicate the decision-making process of a human expert. Today's expert systems are based on years of artificial intelligence research devoted to replicating elusive human cognitive abilities in machines. Expert systems are discussed in Chapter 15, "Is Artificial Intelligence Real?"

Decision support features	MIS	DSS	EIS	ES
Type of decision maker	Many operational managers	Individual and small groups of tactical managers	Individual strategic manager	Individual strategic, tactical, or operational manager
Type of problem	Structured	Semistructured	Unstructured	Structured
Type of information	Predesigned reports on internal operations	Interactive queries and responses for specific problems	On-line access to internal and external information on many issues	Conclusions and recommendation for a particular complex problem
Type of use	Indirect	Direct	Direct	Direct
Phase of decision making	Intelligence	Design, choice	Intelligence	Implementation

12.26 Comparison of design features for MIS, DSS, EIS, and ES.

Information systems provide critical information and advice, but they aren't without risks. Poorly designed information systems can hamper a manager's ability to make quality decisions. Systems notwithstanding, the human manager always has the responsibility for the quality of every decision. Some managers complain that these systems provide too much information—too many reports, too many printouts, too many summaries, too many details. This malady is known as information overload. Managers who are bombarded with computer output may not be able to separate the best from the rest. What's worse, managers who rely too heavily on computer output run the risk of overlooking more conventional, nondigital sources of insight. Although user training is essential, the best managers know that no computer or information system can replace the human communication and decision-making skills necessary for successful management.

Information Technology to Support Business Strategy

All **strategy** depends on **competition**.

—Bruce D. Henderson, American educator

A business competes with other companies based primarily on the cost and value of products and services. An information system that is crucial to the company's competitive success is called a strategic information system. Such a system could be a management information system or a decision support system or any of the other types of information systems we've discussed.

How can organizations use information technology strategically? Let's consider three examples of how top managers use the competitive forces model to help answer that general question.

■ An *entry barrier* is usually an innovative new product or service that is difficult for a competitor to emulate. A classic example is Merrill Lynch, a large financial services firm that developed a system called Cash Management Account that provided customers many new financial, banking, and investment services. The system was costly and difficult to implement, and it took several years for competing brokerage firms and banking institutions to develop similar products. In the meantime, Merrill Lynch continued to innovate and enhance the product, making it all the harder for competitors to catch up.

12.27 Small businesses, like this bistro, compete successfully by using information technology to provide new services for their customers.

- *Switching costs* are the time, effort, and money a customer or supplier would have to expend changing to a competitor's product or service. For example, Baxter Healthcare International, Inc., the supplier of nearly two-thirds of all products used by U.S. hospitals, developed an inventory and ordering system that enables hospitals to order online from the Baxter supply catalog using Baxter computer terminals installed in the hospitals. Participating hospitals became unwilling to switch to another supplier because of the convenience of the system.
- Sometimes businesses can add value to a product to differentiate it from the competition. For example, with the iPod music player, iTunes software, and the online iTunes music store, Apple computer was able to create a unique niche in the digital music industry; competitors had trouble matching Apple's products on all three fronts.

Managers use IT strategically to improve the efficiency and effectiveness of the organization. Efficiency is how primary and support activities produce desired output with less work or lower costs. Effectiveness is how customers evaluate the quality of the output—products and services—of the value chain.

There are several ways to use information technology to improve efficiency: empowering people, eliminating waste, using the best-known way to do the work, automating work, and integrating value chain activities within the company and with other organizations.

- *Empowering people.* A company can improve employees' abilities to use information technologies for competitive advantage. For example, the competitiveness of CitySoft, a Web development and site management company, has everything to do with the skills

12.28 Information workers are empowered to do their work well by having access to the right information, the right tools, and the right training.

of its employees. The company works with neighborhood-based training centers in New York City's Harlem and East Harlem that teach practical courses such as advanced HTML and Web design. The training centers have the goal of creating job opportunities in the tech sector for local residents. CitySoft has primarily hired Web developers who were trained at the centers. A recipient of the MIT Sloan eBusiness Award for social responsibility, CitySoft has landed Web site design work from companies very much in the economic mainstream—companies such as Accenture, Houghton Mifflin, and Reebok.

■ *Eliminating waste.* It is estimated that 20 to 30 percent of the work done in business organizations is simply waste—a waste of time, a waste of paper or other physical resources, or a waste of effort. IT can cut waste by making it easier to access, duplicate, transmit, and display information in a variety of formats. For example, many insurance sales representatives use laptop computers to evaluate different insurance plans directly with customers, eliminating the unnecessary steps of going back to the office to do the calculations and then getting back with the customer at a later date.

■ *Using the best-known way to do the work.* IT can be used to perform the best repeatable, structured procedures that consistently result in high work productivity. For example, point-of-sale scanners record transaction data automatically and thus minimize repetitive record keeping and data handling involved in many jobs.

■ *Automating work.* Work requiring repetition, endurance, and speed is usually highly structured; automating this work results in significant productivity gains. Automated factories and computer-controlled robots are good examples.

■ *Integrating across functions and organizations.* Information technologies can be used to transmit information between a company's value chain activities. The tight integration of sales and production activities is common in many companies because the more integrated those activities are, the faster the production activity can respond to new orders from sales. For example, Motorola coordinated its production and sales activities so that production of a customized electronic pager can begin 17 minutes after an order is placed in the field and be sent to the customer within two to three hours.

A company can improve its effectiveness by using information technology to improve how customers interact directly with the company. Some of these interactions include purchasing the product, ensuring that the product fits the customer's requirements, using the product, and maintaining the product.

■ *Purchasing the product.* Companies use information technology to help customers purchase products through increasing product awareness, improving the availability of a product, and making it easier to pay. For example, many organizations get information about consumer buying patterns contained in marketing databases and then target their advertising at individuals who are likely to buy their products. Also, many companies use online order-entry systems to replenish items in the store quickly so that items are always available.

■ *Fitting the product to customer requirements.* IT can be used to match products to customer needs and to customize products based on customer needs. For example, customers at a Home Depot store can meet with a salesperson and lay out the redesign of a kitchen or bathroom on a computer screen; the salesperson can use the results to make sure the customer purchases the correctly sized cabinets and other fixtures.

■ *Using the product.* Information technology is used to add features so that the product is more useful to the customer. For example, embedding computer semiconductor technology adds data processing and programmability to everyday products, such as kitchen appliances, VCRs, and automobiles.

■ *Making the product easier to maintain.* Businesses with effective field service operations use IT as an essential component of their service and repair activities. For example, Otis Elevator manufactures each of its elevators with a modem and microprocessor to report any malfunctions automatically to a dispatching office. Pagers and other communication devices are used to contact a service technician immediately whenever an elevator problem occurs. Each technician uses a handheld computer to communicate instantly with a central office for technical assistance and job-dispatching information. A complete history of service calls for each elevator is stored in a centralized database that can be used by technicians to diagnose an elevator malfunction easily and by designers to redesign the elevator to eliminate recurring malfunctions.

Planning for Information Systems

We've seen how information systems can play critical roles throughout a business, from the highest
levels of management to the factory
floor. But information systems

A **complex system that works** is invariably found to have evolved from a **simple system that worked.**

—John Gall

don't happen automatically; they need to be designed, developed, and debugged before
they can be put to work. To ensure successful systems development, managers must first
plan how information technology will be used within the context of the overall mission and
goals of their organization. We'll examine the process of systems design and development
in Chapter 14. In this section we'll look at the steps involved in planning for information
systems.

Planning is a process of identifying a desired goal or objective and then deciding what
will be done to achieve the objective, when it will be done, who will do it, and how it will
be done. Since information technology plays an important role at all levels of an organization, IT planning is a major concern of top management. Information technology planning
involves four phases:

- Aligning the information technology plan with the overall business plan of the organization
- Describing the firm's IT infrastructure
- Allocating resources to specific information systems and projects
- Planning specific information system projects.

Aligning the Information Technology Plan with the Overall Business Plan

This first phase of IT planning is called strategic planning. The strategic plan defines the
mission of the company, identifies the company's environment and internal strengths and
weaknesses, and defines the competitive strategy of the company. A component of an organization's strategic plan is an IT plan that describes the IT mission within the company,
reviews the company's current IT capa-
bilities and applications, and describes
the IT strategies and policies to support
the organization's overall strategy.

Organizations use several strategic
planning approaches to make sure IT
plans truly reflect business needs. The
critical success factors (CSF) approach identifies the variables that are
crucial for the success of the business
from the top managers' point of view
and identifies IT plans for systems that
provide access to information about
those critical success factors. A CSF
typically relates to the major competitive forces faced by the company and to
operational problems and opportunities. Examples of CSFs include quality

Information Technology Planning Phases	
Major IT Planning Activity	**Description**
Strategic planning	Align the overall business organization plan with the information technology plan
Information technology infrastructure analysis	Conduct an organizational information infrastructure analysis to identify the desirable features for the information technology infrastructure
Resource allocation	Select the information system projects to invest in
Project planning	Develop the plan schedule and budget for specific information system projects

12.29

customer service, correct pricing of products and services, tight control of manufacturing
costs, and the efficient and effective use of employees.

Describing the Information Technology Infrastructure

The second phase in IT planning is to describe the desirable features for the organization's IT infrastructure. The IT infrastructure comprises all the organization's information systems hardware, software, and telecommunications equipment; the information system department's staff and other personnel; and the organizational structure and procedures that affect accessing, processing, and using information in the company. The IT infrastructure should be designed to support the business operations, communications, decision making, and competitive strategy of the company.

An approach many companies use to define their IT infrastructure is organizational information requirements analysis, also called enterprise modeling. This approach is used to summarize the company's current IT infrastructure, to identify the practical range of business and product strategies based on the current infrastructure, and to identify information system projects that offer the most benefits to the organization.

Allocating Resources

The third phase of information technology planning is resource allocation, a process of selecting the information system projects in which to invest. Every organization has a limited budget, a limited number of people, and limited time. The information system department must decide how to allocate these limited resources. Typically, resources must be allocated for maintaining or enhancing existing systems; developing new systems for supporting managerial, clerical, and other users; and developing new ideas and techniques for incorporating IT into improving business operations, products, and services.

Many managers use cost-benefit analysis to decide whether an information system project is worthwhile on its own merits and also in comparison with other proposed information system projects. Costs usually relate to hardware and software, salaries of the information system staff, and the ongoing operation and maintenance of a system. Tangible benefits, such as the reduction in the number of customer complaints and the increase in the number of sales orders, can be measured relatively easily. Intangible benefits, such as better employee morale and better supervision, are harder to measure. A top manager might find it difficult to make an honest comparison of proposed information system projects based solely on anticipated costs and benefits.

Project Planning

The fourth phase of IT planning is project planning. The purpose of project planning is to organize a sequence of steps to accomplish a particular project's goals and to keep the project on schedule and within budget. A project plan includes a description of the measurable project goals that are used to evaluate the success of the project. A project goal can relate to the process of building the information system—completing the project by a certain date, for example. The project goal might also relate to business operations after the system is installed—for example, decreasing the time to place an order by a certain amount.

A project plan describes what needs to be done to accomplish each step in the system's life cycle. (The systems development life cycle is discussed in Chapter 14.) The plan specifies what deliverable output is to be produced at the completion of each step in the project. A deliverable can be a report, a computer program, a progress report, or any other tangible output. The plan specifies a schedule identifying how long certain steps are forecasted to take to complete and the forecasted date of completion. The project plan also specifies milestones, or checkpoints, to allow managers to review the project's progress when certain deliverables are produced, after a certain amount of the budget is used, or on a time basis, such as weekly or monthly.

Managers use *project management software* to help coordinate, schedule, and track complex projects. Many project plans use a Gantt chart to represent a project schedule visually. A Gantt chart shows each step or category of steps in a plan, along with their planned and actual start and completion times.

Project managers use the **critical path method (CPM)** to keep track of a project's schedule. CPM is a mathematical model of a project's schedule used to calculate when particular activities will be completed. A project manager first estimates the time needed to complete each activity and then determines the total time required to finish a project by locating the longest path, called the critical path, through the interconnected activities of the project. A critical path chart shows visually the interconnection of steps in a project. Project managers sometimes use a variation of CPM called the program evaluation and review technique *(PERT)*. With PERT, a manager uses three time estimates: an optimistic, a pessimistic, and a most likely time to complete each activity. The appearance of PERT and CPM diagrams is the same—both reflect single times for each activity. In the case of a PERT diagram, the single times are computed from the three estimates.

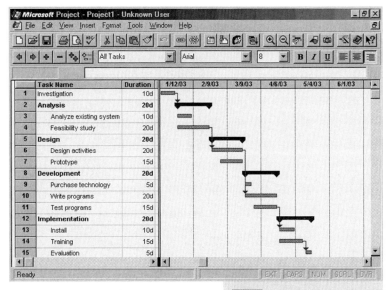

12.30 A manager can view a Gantt chart and see at a glance the overall schedule of an information system project.

Managers use Gantt charts and CPM or PERT diagrams to identify bottlenecks in a project and anticipate the impact problems and delays will have on project completion times.

Social Responsibility in the Information Age

Socially responsible computing is a key concern in business today because of the many ways an information worker's actions can affect other people. **Social responsibility** refers to both legal and ethical behavior. Laws define a society's proper, or legal, behavior and out-

In the 20th century B.C. the Code of Hammurabi declared that if a house collapsed and killed its owner, the **builder of the house was to be put to death**. In the 20th century A.D. many builders of computer software would **deny responsibility** and pass the entire risk to the user.

—Helen Nissenbaum

line the actions a government can take in response to improper behavior. Ethics are sets of principles or moral standards that help guide behavior, actions, and choices. Ethical dilemmas are difficult choices involving conflicting goals, responsibilities, and loyalties that may or may not be covered by laws. Information workers face many situations in which they must make decisions about ethical and legal behavior. Here are a few examples:

- Viewing email files of project team members or subordinates
- Making a recommendation to sell mailing lists of customers to other businesses
- Using a browser during working hours to shop
- Helping to implement a system that will result in five people losing their jobs.

Social responsibility applies to a company as a whole as well as to individuals. A company that is socially responsible attempts to balance the interests of its various stakeholder groups—including employees, suppliers, customers, stockholders, and the local community. In essence, a company has a social contract with the community to enhance the material well-being of all the community's members, even if it means lower than maximized profits for its stockholders or higher than the lowest prices for its customers. A socially responsible company might donate money to local charities or the arts, give employees time off to do volunteer work, avoid any fraud or deception of the public, or play an active role in establishing and supporting community programs.

Regarding its own employees, a company is obliged to treat them with personal respect, healthy working conditions, fair wages, and employment continuity. Within this context, a socially responsible company can provide a stable and predictable ethical working environment by establishing policies and procedures, called a code of ethics, to guide the behavior of its information workers. Companies have developed codes of ethics covering issues such as email privacy, software licenses and copyrights, access to hardware and files, and data and intellectual property ownership. Many professional organizations develop ethical codes that apply to their members; the ACM Code of Ethics in this book's appendix is a prime example for computer professionals.

The Rules of Thumb box in Chapter 10 offered several ethical guidelines. Here are some additional guidelines for information professionals that were developed by Donn B. Parker, a leading expert on computer ethics:

- *Informed consent.* If you are in doubt about the ethics or laws of a particular action, inform those whom your action will affect of your intentions and obtain their consent before proceeding.
- *The higher ethic.* You should take the action that achieves the greater good for everyone involved.
- *Most restrictive action.* When you are deciding to take or avoid taking an action, assume that the most severe damage that could happen will happen.

The Case for Rest   Peter Coffee

People in the business world often speak of moving at Internet time—a pace that allows products to be developed in months, as opposed to years. In this article, which first appeared in the May 26, 2003 issue of Eweek, *Peter Coffee discusses the dark side of our always-connected work culture.*

As I looped around the east edge of Phoenix, heading home from the GigaWorld IT Forum, I heard NPR's salute to National Night Shift Workers Day conclude with a poem by Karen Jane Glenn. "Let us now praise the night shift," she began. "Those on the 8-to-4, the 10-to-6 . . . the sleep-deprived . . . the wired." I could relate. It seems as if every week brings me more e-mail messages that are time-stamped during the interval that Navy men call the mid-watch, from midnight to four in the morning. And I have to admit that I'm also sending more of those midwatch messages myself.

As it happened, the theme of the conference I'd just attended was "Deliver more with less." I don't remember seeing "less sleep" as a formal part of the agenda—but as I listened to Glenn's poem, it seemed as if that topic should have been addressed. After all, National Science Foundation statistics estimate U.S. adults averaging less than 7 hours' sleep at night; other studies point to sleep-deprivation effects that include difficulty following discussions; poor judgment in complex situations; difficulty in devising a new approach to a stubborn problem; and failure to notice changes in situations.

In practical terms, this means that people aren't functioning as well as they should in everyday situations such as planning a project, responding to a cyber-attack, debugging an application or monitoring network operations.

Spread thin by staff reductions, and losing formerly productive time to diversions such as extra security delays in airports, people are putting in 10-hour and even 20-hour days for what used to be considered 8 hours' pay. That may not be as good a deal for the employer as it first seems, if the extra hours represent neutral or even negative contributions. Yes, it's great that people can work at any time, from anywhere, but sleep-deprived zombies aren't the shock troops of enterprise success—whether they're "the wired" of Glenn's poem or not.

International operations can approach the 24-hour day as a relay race, rather than a marathon. IBM, for example, has adopted a two-shift approach to some of its software development efforts, with teams in Seattle setting daily work specifications for offshore teams in India, China, Latvia and Belarus. Overnight offshore development returns product to Seattle the next day for review, and the cycle continues.

The company says this process reduces development cycles by 35 percent, yielding time-to-market benefits that are worth even more than the reductions in development cost. Note well that this is not about stretching a given number of people across a greater number of hours: It's about taking advantage of the 24-hour day in operations that circle the globe.

The problem with success stories like this is that smaller companies may feel that they must do likewise. I'm reminded of former Avis CEO Robert Townsend's warning that some corporate behaviors don't scale well from large to small organizations. The smaller company that decides to open an office in Bangalore, or outsource some of its operations to a contractor in Tel Aviv, may find that it has blunted its competitive edge of being able to get close to its customers and thoroughly understand their needs. Being just like IBM, only a hundred times smaller, is like being a miniature elephant in an ecological niche that's better suited to a fox.

In organizations of every size, managers need to avoid letting IT push their people across the line that separates anytime/anywhere flexibility from all-the-time/everywhere expectation. When intermediate deadlines start being regarded as purely pro forma, and everyone knows that the real schedule squeezes three days on the timetable into a 24-hour all-nighter at the end of every product cycle, that's a cultural problem that has to be solved by cultural forces. When managers treat crash-and-burn schedules as a sign of commitment and not as a problem to be fixed, that's a cultural force that pushes in the wrong direction.

C. Northcote Parkinson was right: Work does expand to fill the time available. IT can make that available time appear to be "all the time." I'm not saying that our e-mail systems need a curfew. I am saying that the human side of management includes making it clear that you want good hours, not just more of them.

DISCUSSION QUESTIONS

1. Do you agree that our technology and culture promote an unhealthy pace of life? Explain your answer.

2. What do you think can be done to promote healthier lifestyles in the modern information workplace?

SUMMARY

A system is a set of interrelated parts that work together to accomplish a goal by performing three basic functions: input, processing, and output. A system has two additional functions: feedback, which provides measurements of the system's input, processing, and output; and control, which evaluates the feedback data and adjusts the system's input and processing functions to ensure the desired output is produced. Everything outside the system's boundary is called the environment. A system can be a subsystem of another system and may interact with other systems in its environment. Users, designers, and managers all play a role in defining the system's purpose, its boundaries, and its subsystems. Computers are systems. Business organizations can also be viewed as systems.

The value chain model defines a business organization as a system. According to the value chain model, the organization is a sequence, or chain, of activities, each adding something valuable to the production of a product or service. The value chain model divides the activities of an organization into five primary activities and four support activities. Each of the primary and support activities is a subsystem with inputs and outputs; these subsystems interact with each other to create the overall performance of the organization.

As a subsystem of a larger business organization, an information system is a set of interrelated parts that work together to produce, distribute, and use information products. One purpose of an information system is to provide information in the feedback and control functions of a larger system. An information system involves people using information and information technologies to perform tasks that are important for the mission and objectives of the organization within a business environment. Information systems provide many benefits to an organization including higher-quality information used to improve workflow, communication, decision making, and products and services.

Information systems that support transaction-based business processes of a firm are called transaction processing systems. The transaction processing cycle might be based on income, expenditures, production, or cash management, but in every case transaction processing goes through a series of five steps repeatedly: data entry, processing the data, storing and updating the data, document and report preparation, and user inquiry. Integrated operations management uses software to automate many transaction processing applications of a company. CAD, CAM, and CIM systems are also well suited for manufacturing environments.

Communications between organizations is improved with Electronic Data Interchange, enabling companies to send each other standard business documents electronically, and cooperative arrangements called business alliances.

Managers have complicated jobs that involve functions and roles that require communication and decision making. A number of information system configurations have been developed to support managerial needs for information.

Managers perform planning, organizing, directing, and controlling functions. An organization has three levels of management: operational, tactical, and strategic. Typically, operational managers need to make structured decisions; tactical, or middle, managers need to make semistructured decisions; and strategic, or top, managers, need to make unstructured decisions. An organizational goal is to provide the right information (content) to a manager at the right time and in the right form so it is the most valuable for the situation at hand.

A manager uses a management information system (MIS) to make structured decisions at the operational level in an organization. A manager uses a decision support system (DSS) to make semistructured decisions at the tactical level in an organization. Group decision support systems (GDSSs) are used to enhance collaborative decision making in teams. Geographic information systems (GIS) support decision making with map and other spatial information. A manager uses an executive information system (EIS) to make unstructured decisions at the strategic level in an organization. A manager can use an EIS to access internal and external information about key indicators of the company's performance and about business and other environmental trends affecting the company.

A strategic information system is any information system that is crucial to the company's competitive success. Top managers can focus information systems strategically on improving the efficiency or the effectiveness of the organization's value chain.

Information systems are tools that should be designed to meet the information needs of the people using them. Poorly designed information systems can result in information overload and hamper a manager's ability to communicate effectively or make quality decisions. A company's information code of ethics should address the privacy, intellectual ownership, and the information quality and access policies to guide its managers and information workers and foster an ethical information culture.

An organization typically creates an overall IT plan before developing particular systems. The IT plan describes intended overall use of information technology to meet the company's needs. The organization then follows the plan, using cost-benefit analysis to select specific projects to develop and project planning techniques to track system development schedules.

KEY TERMS

acquisition (p. 428)
action document (p. 429)
batch processing (p. 429)
business alliance (p. 435)
business organization (p. 424)
business process (p. 426)
chief information officer (CIO) (p. 437)
code of ethics (p. 452)
computer-aided design (CAD) (p. 433)
computer-aided manufacturing (CAM) (p. 433)
computer-integrated manufacturing (CIM) (p. 434)
cost-benefit analysis (p. 450)
critical path method (CPM) (p. 451)
critical success factors (CSF) (p. 449)
data warehousing (p. 429)

decision support system (DSS) (p. 439)
effectiveness (p. 447)
efficiency (p. 447)
Electronic Data Interchange (EDI) (p. 429)
Enterprise Resource Planning (ERP) (p. 432)
executive information system (EIS) (p. 442)
expert system (ES) (p. 445)
Gantt chart (p. 450)
geographic information system (GIS) (p. 442)
group decision support system (GDSS) (p. 442)
information overload (p. 445)
information system (p. 427)
infrastructure (p. 450)
international information system (p. 435)

interorganizational information systems (IOS) (p. 434)
management (p. 436)
management information system (MIS) (p. 438)
management levels (p. 437)
management reporting system (p. 438)
organizational information requirements analysis (p. 450)
real-time processing (p. 429)
social responsibility (p. 451)
strategic information system (p. 446)
strategic planning (p. 449)
supply chain management (p. 432)
system (p. 423)
transaction (p. 429)
transaction processing system (TPS) (p. 429)
transborder data flow (p. 435)
value chain model (p. 425)

INTERACTIVE QUIZ QUESTIONS

1. The *Computer Confluence* CD-ROM contains self-test quiz questions related to this chapter, including multiple-choice, true or false, and matching questions.

2. The *Computer Confluence* Web site, www.computerconfluence.com, contains self-test exercises related to this chapter. Follow the instructions for taking a quiz. After you've completed your quiz, you can email the results to your instructor.

TRUE OR FALSE

1. The Cannibal Principle says that semiconductor technology absorbs the functions of what previously were discrete electronic components onto a single new chip.

2. To accomplish its purpose, a system performs three basic functions: input, processing, and output.

3. Everything inside a system's boundary is called the system's environment.

4. An information system is a subsystem that supports the information needs of other business processes within an organization.

5. In business information systems, information technology performs five functions: acquisition, processing, storage and retrieval, presentation, and transmission.

6. Transaction processing is linear, rather than cyclical, by nature.

7. A business alliance is a cooperative arrangement between two or more businesses with complementary capabilities, such as marketing and distribution.

8. Industrial networks may link the systems of several companies in an industry.

9. Managers spend up to 90 percent of their time communicating with other people in the organization and in the company's external environment.

10. Information overload makes it easier for managers to separate the best from the rest.

MULTIPLE-CHOICE

1. Which of these is not a value chain activity in an organization?
   a. inbound logistics.
   b. operations.
   c. cognition.
   d. outbound logistics.
   e. marketing.

2. Factors affecting the international business environment and transborder data flow include
   a. multiple languages and cultural differences.
   b. the laws and regulations of governments, including copyright and privacy issues.
   c. varying telecommunications standards and technologies.
   d. different monetary systems.
   e. All of these factors affect international business environments.

3. Which is true? A transaction processing system (TPS)
   a. would not be useful for tracking course enrollment.
   b. is an organization's basic accounting and record-keeping system.
   c. does not require high processing speeds.
   d. is not searchable using database queries.
   e. All of these are true.

4. Which is not one of the four major phases in information technology (IT) planning?
   a. aligning the IT plan with the overall business plan.
   b. describing the firm's IT infrastructure.
   c. allocating resources to specific information systems and projects.
   d. planning specific information system projects.
   e. critical path method (CPM).

5. Which of the following is not typically performed by management information systems (MIS)?
   a. providing detailed reports, summary reports, and exception reports.
   b. extracting relevant data from databases of the transaction processing systems.
   c. providing managers with information needed to make decisions.
   d. making recommendations on how to improve performance.
   e. organizing and summarizing data in useful ways.

6. Which is not a kind of system used to support decision making?
   a. executive information system (EIS).
   b. geographic information system (GIS).
   c. group decision support system (GDSS).
   d. transaction processing system (TPS).
   e. expert system (ES).

7. Group decision support systems (GDSS)
   a. are designed to enhance collaborative decision making.
   b. are usually in the form of a meeting room equipped with hardware and software tools.
   c. allow individuals to use the GDSS as a private DSS to work out ideas during meetings.
   d. enables group members to share information anonymously if desired.
   e. Group decision support systems do all of these.

8. Which is correct? A geographic information system (GIS) is
   a. a type of DSS designed to work with maps and other spatial information.
   b. typically used with the critical path method in system design.
   c. a type of expert system used to provide expertise in geology.
   d. a form of transaction processing system used for geographical simulations.
   e. impractical with today's technology.

9. When writing an organization's information code of ethics, which topic would you not include?
   a. privacy.
   b. access to information.
   c. information quality.
   d. encryption algorithms for security.
   e. intellectual property.

10. Which is not true? Socially responsible companies
    a. attempt to balance the interests of stakeholders.
    b. always optimize profits regardless of human consequences.
    c. have a social contract with the community to enhance the material well-being of all community members.
    d. may allow time off to employees for volunteer work.
    e. avoid any fraud or deception of the public.

REVIEW QUESTIONS

1. Define or describe each of the key terms in the "Key Terms" section. Check your answers using the glossary.

2. What are the types of information workers in our information economy?

3. What are the major components of a system? What is the difference between a system and a subsystem?

4. What are the components of the value chain model?

5. What are the basic systems components of an information system?

6. How would you describe the conceptual context within which information systems exist in an organization?

7. What are the five information activities that information technologies perform in a system?

8. What is the purpose of a transaction processing system?

9. What are the steps in a transaction processing cycle?

10. What are the functions and roles of a manager in an organization?

11. Describe three types of decisions. Which types of decisions are made by different management levels in an organization?

12. Describe the characteristics of a MIS. What kinds of reports does it produce?

13. Describe the characteristics of a DSS. What types of information tools does it provide?

14. Describe the characteristics of a GIS. Why would a GIS be useful in a business organization?

15. What are the design features and uses of an EIS?

16. Describe three basic strategies organizations use to compete successfully.

17. How can a strategic information system be used to improve an organization's efficiency? Effectiveness?

DISCUSSION QUESTIONS

1. Use systems terminology to describe a real-world situation, such as organizing a sporting event or looking for a job. Does the systems model increase your understanding of the situation or make it more confusing?

2. Many companies are trying to improve the quality of their products and services for customers. How can you use the value chain model to identify what business processes to change so as to improve quality?

3. How could you evaluate whether decisions are made effectively in an organization? What factors or variables would you need to consider in your analysis?

4. Identify and discuss some of the ethical dilemmas and issues involved with a MIS. A DSS. An ES.

5. How could you evaluate whether an information system could be used strategically to help an organization compete more successfully?

6. Describe some of the social responsibilities of information workers in an organization with which you are familiar, such as a bank, police station, retail store, or a government office.

PROJECTS

1. Scan through a newspaper or magazine and pick a situation that is interesting to you. Describe the situation as a system and identify the information activities in the situation. Think about how the situation could be improved. Write a report describing your analysis and recommendations.

2. Use the value chain model to describe the primary and support activities of a business organization you are familiar with, such as a student group, church or volunteer organization, a family-owned business, your favorite restaurant or clothing store, or any other business. Use a predesigned template available with your word processor to write a memo describing your analysis and recommendations. Attach the memo document to an email message and send it to your professor.

3. Interview the owner of a small business, such as a photo shop, stationary store, or coffee shop. Describe the important transactions and the five-step transaction processing cycle for the organization. Identify some relevant information ethics issues for the organization. Create a presentation of your findings using a presentation software package such as Microsoft PowerPoint.

4. With a class partner, interview a manager in a large company. Use the information systems in context model (people, tasks, information, organization, environment, and information technology) to guide your interview. Prepare a report describing the company as a system. Exchange reports with another class group; then read and comment on each other's reports.

5. With a class colleague, interview a manager of an organizational unit at your school. Ask the manager to describe the activities he or she performed during the previous workday and the information needed to perform those activities. Discuss the results of the interview with your class colleague and compose a memo to the manager, thanking him or her, and summarizing what you learned.

6. Identify the various kinds of information systems that are used by your favorite professional sports team. Prepare a report on your findings.

7. With a group, visit a service organization in your community, such as a hospital, fire department, church, or restaurant. Interview a manager to identify the information systems he or she uses to support decision-making responsibilities. Present a report to your class describing your findings.

CASE STUDIES

United Colors of Benetton

Benetton is one of the world's largest garment companies. Starting from a shop in Venice, Italy, Benetton now operates over 5,000 shops in 75 countries and works with over 200 suppliers worldwide. Located in Castrette (Italy), Benetton's design and manufacturing facility produces over 90 million garments yearly, along with sportswear and sports equipment, footwear, bags, and accessories. Benetton emphasizes quick response, flexibility, low prices to customers, and excellent service.

Benetton uses a variety of technologies to accomplish its goals. For example, it uses proprietary cloth cutting and dyeing equipment that makes it possible to respond quickly to changes in garment color preferences. Benetton uses computer networks and computer-aided design systems to plan and coordinate activities among its suppliers and outlets. It also uses a computerized warehouse that services the company's seven factories in Italy.

Its manufacturing system is based on technical innovation and flexibility in manufacturing processes. The plant consists of twin units (one producing cotton garments and shirts, the other tailored garments, skirts, and jeans), an au-

tomated distribution center, and a unit dedicated to the production of woolen garments. One of Benetton's most innovative systems is Robostore 2000, an automated packaging and distribution system. Nineteen staff persons manage the system, which handles over 30,000 packages a day, organizing deliveries according to geographical area and individual client. The system, and other automated systems at Benetton, has considerably improved the efficiency and speed of customer service while reducing transport costs.

Benetton is well known for its research into new composite materials and innovative product design. This research has been applied successfully to its sports clothing and sports equipment products of tennis rackets, skis, and snowboards.

The company maintains an efficient transaction processing system. When a customer purchases a sweater, for example, in Boston, Massachusetts, the details of the sale (product color, size, quantity, and so on) are captured with a point-of-sale bar code scanner and transmitted electronically to a computer system in Italy. The sale's details are combined with other transactions from outlets worldwide to determine the daily production schedule at each of the seven factories. The company does not dye its sweaters until it receives information on which retail stores need colors. This manufacturing process allows Benetton to rapidly adjust the product mix to changes in customer demand. After the sweaters are dyed, they are shipped directly from the centralized warehouse to the retail outlets, with quantities of different products determined by the recent sales transactions. Similarly, items that are not selling in each retail outlet are monitored closely and removed on a regular basis.

Benetton maintains so much detailed information in its database that it can fine-tune products to the demographics and tastes of the customers of each store. Colors, styles, and sizes can be adjusted to the specific characteristics of customers for stores only a few blocks apart.

Adapted from the Benetton Web site at **http://www.benetton.it**

Discussion Questions

1. Use the system model to describe Benetton as a system. Discuss the purpose of Benetton; its environment, inputs, processes, and outputs; and how it handles feedback.

2. Discuss the primary and support activities in Benetton's value chain.

3. Describe the types of transactions Benetton handles on a day-to-day basis.

4. Discuss the challenges to Benetton's information systems due to its large global presence.

L'Oréal's Data Warehouse

The main distribution facility for cosmetic giant L'Oréal's retail division in Cranbury, N.J., ships over 200 million haircare and cosmetic products every year to mass-volume retailers and food and drug chains around the country. L'Oréal used to keep shipping and point-of-sale (POS) information locked up in a number of separate databases, making it difficult for employees to retrieve the figures necessary for determining sales, identifying hot products, and determining candidates for advertising campaigns. But now, L'Oréal is developing a data warehousing system to incorporate all sales information under one roof. The system is expected to eliminate inefficiency in data management, improve internal communications, upgrade salesforce automation, and pave the way for the information systems department to redefine its role from data processing to strategic leadership.

Prior to the data warehousing system, L'Oréal recorded tremendous amounts of sales and marketing information, but the data was so disorganized that few employees outside the information systems department knew how to find it. Net sales figures were in one set of files, while data on returns was somewhere else. If a marketing executive wanted information about shipments and returns on a particular product, he or she had to ask a programmer to produce a custom report. Sometimes, when programmers were preoccupied with other work, such requests would take as long as two weeks

to fill. Once employees received their reports, it could take them days to interpret them. Most reports were 32 columns wide and contained more than 50 pages, making it difficult for employees to locate the information they needed.

The new data warehousing system is being implemented on a state-of-the-art NT SQL 7.0 server. The system enables L'Oréal employees to view the data through a Web browser and reduces the wait time on some queries to three seconds.

During the system's development, several users and administrators served as a core team to support the project from a business perspective, and L'Oréal's senior management team formed a governance committee to resolve business issues. These users established procedures to move data from the old shipping systems into the data warehouse so that the data conformed to the new, standard definitions for the data. For example, the term "net sales" used to mean something different to everyone, but now everyone knows the same way to calculate net sales. Having standard definitions of data enables L'Oréal's managers to focus more on understanding the numbers rather than struggling with their meanings. One of the most important aspects of the data warehousing project was to improve interdepartmental communication.

The data warehouse has already come in handy in preparing for the next fiscal year. How many bottles of L'Oréal for Kids shampoo were delivered to Wal-Mart this summer? Of those, how many were sold? Marketing employees can use answers to questions like these to determine advertising and promotional strategies for the new millennium. Users report that the new system is quicker and more efficient than the old one. They also say they appreciate how the system enables them to retrieve data themselves, without calling on the information systems department.

It will take another year to complete the data warehouse system project. L'Oréal expects the system to result in speedy delivery of other business applications, faster and better salesforce automation, and the ability to get at data in ways the old system did not allow. L'Oréal employees will be able to use the warehouse not only to see how its products are selling but also to see how L'Oréal products compete with products from other companies.

Adapted from Matt Villano, "Data Gets a Makeover," CIO *Magazine, October 1, 1999,* **http://www.cio.com/archive/ 100199 inprintcio.html***; and L'Oréal's Web sites, 2001:* **www.loreal.com** *and* **http://www.lorealpro.net/**

Discussion Questions

1. Identify some of the primary and support activities in L'Oréal's value chain.

2. Discuss how L'Oréal's data warehouse system supports the company's transaction processing.

3. Discuss the benefits of L'Oréal's data warehousing system.

4. Identify the roles people play in designing and using L'Oréal's data warehousing system.

Venetian Wireless Guest Check-in

The Venetian Hotel in Las Vegas is launching a pilot system that's aimed at using wireless devices to ensure that rooms are ready for arriving guests. Guests will meet hotel clerks at any of several entrances, including the car drop-off area, and be able to show a credit card to check reservations via a wireless LAN connection to a server in real time. Once the reservation has been confirmed, the clerk will be able to encode a room-key card for the guest.

The goal is to eliminate check-in lines at the 3,000-room hotel, which is connected to a casino and conference center. The pilot is expected to cost less than $100,000 and will be deemed a success if it helps business flow and is not a disruption for clerks to handle the devices. Venetian Hotel officials are hoping the system will facilitate guest needs and serve them faster.

Clerks will use rugged handheld computers running the Palm OS operating system, with attached magnetic strip readers for gathering credit card information. The handheld will be secured with a strap to a clerk's hand, and it will be connected to a separate device on the belt to encode the room-key cards. A short-range radio connection from the handheld to the device on the belt will be used instead of a coiled phone-type cord or an infrared connection, which were considered too awkward in previous trials.

The Venetian Hotel was designed with wireless innovations in mind, including cell towers that permit a variety of cell phones to function. Eventually, guests will be able to check in with their personal cell phones using a password. The hotel's wireless communications network is similar to many that are now being installed by businesses around the world in places such as in Capetown, South Africa, and Helsinki, Finland.

Adapted from Matt Hamblen, "Las Vegas Hotel to Try Wireless Check-In," Computerworld, *May 28, 2001; and* http://www.computerworld.com/cwi/story/0,1199,NAV47_STO60898,00.html

Discussion Questions

1. Discuss the communication concepts involved in the Venetian Hotel's wireless system.

2. Discuss how the Venetian Hotel's wireless applications provide more timely and effective communication between the hotel staff and customers.

3. Are there ethical issues related to the Venetian Hotel's use of wireless technologies?

The Knowledge Crunch

It takes more than good flavor and a hearty crunch to sell the salty snacks churned out at Frito-Lay. Corporate executives knew that using corporate information would give employees something they could sink their teeth into. But information was scattered around the company in disparate systems, and there was no easy way for the geographically dispersed salesforce to get at it. For example, multiple salespeople would ask the corporate sales, marketing, and operations staff for the same types of information and data, such as current private-label trends in their snack category or research on people's shopping behavior. The result was Frito-Lay's support staff ended up performing the same tasks over and over. If that information lived in a central, easily accessible spot, the salespeople could access it as needed.

Additionally, much valuable knowledge was squirreled away on each salesperson's system. There were many idiosyncratic, inefficient methods of capturing information. The sales team also lacked a place for brainstorming and collaboration online. If somebody got a piece of research and wanted to get input from account executives in Baltimore and Los Angeles, the ability to collaborate [online] just wasn't there.

To address these information issues, Frito-Lay designed an information system to be implemented on their corporate intranet. The goals of the system were to streamline knowledge, exploit customer-specific data, and foster team collaboration. The system is a single point of access to multiple sources of information and provides personalized access. The system was designed to give the sales department a central location for all sales-related customer and corporate information and cut down on the time it takes to find and share research. In addition to different types of information about customers—including sales, analysis, and the latest news—the system contains profiles on who's who in the corporation, making finding an internal expert a snap.

Frito-Lay used a consultancy company that built the system in about three months using technologies previously approved by Frito-Lay's IS department, including Lotus Domino, BusinessObjects' WebIntelligence, Java, IBM's DB2 database, and Autonomy, a natural language search engine that enables users to search information in different repositories. The system, known as the Customer Community Portal (CCP), went live in January 2000. Users access the system through a Netscape Navigator browser and enter their name and password on the Frito-Lay intranet.

CCP paid off with increased sales. For example, the growth rate of the customer's business in the salty snack category doubled within a year. It also made the sales teams happier. For example, the members of one of the sales teams reside in 10 different cities, so the system became extremely valuable for communication and helped cut down on travel. A year after implementing the system, the sales teams were able to share documents concurrently instead of having to send faxes around the country to different offices. They can now manipulate large amounts of data and can look at it online versus having to have somebody physically travel to the retail customer. It's almost a distance-learning tool as much as anything else.

The CCP helped foster a sense of camaraderie and relationship building. For example, the system lists the team members' birthdays. People can also share best practices—on anything under the sun. If someone developed an effective sales presentation for a potential customer in Boston, a salesperson in San Francisco could co-opt the information. Salespeople can also find the latest news about their customers, and there's an automatic messaging feature that informs team members who is online.

Managers use the system for helping them assess employee skill sets, because each salesperson is required to catalog his or her strengths and areas of expertise. It helps managers analyze where people's gaps might be without having to travel to another member's location.

The system has also helped boost employee retention rates. Turnover used to be terrible because salespeople felt pressured to find vital information and communicate with the rest of the sales team. Salespeople felt frustrated and disconnected because there was no way to collaborate efficiently with the rest of their group unless they flew into a central location.

Adapted from Esther Shein, "The Knowledge Crunch," CIO Magazine, *May 1, 2001;* **http://www.cio.com/archive/050101/crunch.html**

Discussion Questions

1. Discuss how the CCP system supports communications and decision making at Frito-Lay.

2. Discuss the information needs of the salespersons and managers at Frito-Lay.

3. Discuss the various decision support features of the CCP system.

4. Discuss any ethical information issues related to using the CCP system. What are your suggestions for resolving those issues?

5. Discuss features you would suggest for improving the CCP system.

Weyerhaeuser's Roots

Weyerhaeuser Co. is an $11 million forest products company that uses Internet technology to empower its employees, eliminate waste, and improve the efficiency of its internal business processes. The company operates 28 high-tech sawmills that use laser scanners to position logs to guarantee the best cut. Information about each day's cutting is entered into a database and linked to daily reports, which are published on the home page of Weyerhaeuser's intranet, named Roots. The intranet is also used to share real-time production, environmental, personnel, and safety information with workers at locations all over the Northwest.

Roots supports 16,000 workers with email, 6,500 employees with Netscape Navigator and Microsoft Internet Explorer browsers, and intranet-based applications. Roots is implemented using 40 Web servers that publish 8,000 Web pages that are designed using Microsoft FrontPage. Roots receives about 3,600 hits per day.

Roots is continuously modified and improved to meet corporate goals. Initially, the hierarchical organization of Root's content mirrored that of Weyerhaeuser. The information content is being redesigned based on how subjects and topics relate to one another. Management is still debating whether Weyerhaeuser should give open access to every employee or restrict access in several ways. Weyerhaeuser's CIO has moved quickly to implement a companywide process for standardizing on new Internet technology.

Adapted from Alex Frankel, "New Growth," CIO Web Business, *11(3), 11/1/97, pp. 37–41; David Bovet and Joseph Martha,* Value Nets: Breaking the Supply Chain to Unlock Hidden Profits. *New York, John Wiley & Sons, 2000; and from Weyerhaeuser's Web site at* **http://www.Weyerhaeuser.com/**

Discussion Questions

1. Which of the three basic strategies—cost leadership, differentiation, or innovation—do you think Weyerhaeuser is following?

2. What competitive advantages does Weyerhaeuser gain by developing and using Internet technologies to improve communications and other business processes?

3. Discuss how Weyerhaeuser's decision-making processes may be improved through its use of Internet technologies.

4. Discuss any ethical issues related to Weyerhaeuser's intranet use by employees.

SOURCES AND RESOURCES

Books

Only the Paranoid Survive: How to Exploit the Crisis Points That Challenge Every Company, by Andrew S. Grove (New York: Bantam Books, 1999). In this widely publicized book, now in paperback, the founder and previous CEO of Intel shares his business philosophy and lots of stories from the front lines of the microprocessor wars.

Competitive Advantage: Creating and Sustaining Superior Performance, by Michael Porter (New York: Simon & Shuster, 1998). In this updated classic text, the author describes the competitive forces affecting how a business organization can survive and thrive in the global competitive business environment.

Harvard Business Review on Managing the Value Chain (Boston: Harvard Business School Press, 2000). This collection of eight essays examines the changing relationship between suppliers, customers, and competitors in the age of technology and globalization, outlining key ideas and providing guidance for incorporating shifts in the value chain into a firm's strategic outlook.

Competing for the Future, by Gary Hamel and C. K. Prahalad (Boston: Harvard Business School Press, 1994). This worldwide bestseller written by a couple of academics is surprisingly readable. The authors claim that to compete successfully, managers must develop an independent point of view about tomorrow's opportunities and build capabilities to take advantage of them. The book is full of examples of how information technology is used strategically in organizations.

A Better Way to Think About Business: How Personal Integrity Leads to Corporate Success, by Robert C. Solomon (Oxford: Oxford University Press, 1999). Have you ever thought that business ethics is a contradiction in terms? Solomon doesn't think so. He writes that corporations are members of the larger community and that without a base of shared values and trust, today's national and international business world would fall apart.

Evolve! Succeeding in the Digital Culture of Tomorrow, by Rosabeth Moss Kanter (Boston: Harvard Business School Press, 2001). The book challenges the new economy with having had a "lobotomy" about basic business fundamentals. Using examples from both private and public sector companies, Kanter shows how digital innovation can be achieved within a company. She skewers the cliches and uses them to expose the shallow thinking that has led to disaster. She gets beyond the technical whizbang to look at the human possibilities of a global community.

Mission Critical: Realizing the Promise of Enterprise Systems, by Thomas H. Davenport (Boston: Harvard Business School Press, 2000). As information-dependent companies of all types continually expand and globalize, the need to share critical data between far-flung sites increases dramatically. This text is an introduction to Enterprise Resource Planning systems and how they are useful for organizations. The text is easy to understand, gives real-world examples of benefits and pitfalls of different implementation methods, and gives you a good idea of the magnitude of an ERP project.

The Cluetrain Manifesto: The End of Business as Usual, by Christopher Locke, Rick Levine, Doc Searls, David Weinberger (New York: Perseus Books, 2000). *The Cluetrain Manifesto* began as a Web site (www.cluetrain.com) in 1999 when the authors posted 95 theses pronouncing what they felt was the new reality of the networked marketplace. For example, thesis 2: "Markets consist of human beings, not demographic sectors," and thesis 20: "Companies need to realize their markets are often laughing. At them," and thesis 62: "Markets do not want to talk to flacks and hucksters. They want to participate in the conversations going on behind the corporate firewall." The book enlarges on these themes through seven essays filled with dozens of stories and observations about how business gets done in America and how the Internet will change it all.

Cyberethics: Social & Moral Issues in the Computer Age, by Robert M. Baird, Reagan Mays Ramsower, and Stuart E. Rosenbaum (Editors) (New York: Prometheus Books, 2000). This very readable book explores the moral dilemmas that are arising as computer technology penetrates further into our professional, private, and social lives. The book is an anthology of 26 essays exploring issues such as anonymity, personal identity, and the moral dimensions of creating new personalities; privacy; ownership of intellectual property and copyright law; and the impact of computers on democracy and community.

The New Science of Management Decision, by Herbert A. Simon (Englewood Cliffs, NJ: Prentice-Hall, 1977). This book is a business classic. Simon describes the process of problem solving in a variety of business and personal settings.

The Nature of Managerial Work, by Henry Mintzberg (New York: Harper & Row, 1973). Another business classic. Mintzberg's description of the various roles of managers in organizations has been the basis of subsequent research and insights into how information systems can be applied to management.

Speed Is Life: Street Smart Lessons from the Front Lines of Business, by Robert Davis (New York: Doubleday & Company, 2001). Bob Davis was the founder and CEO of Lycos. He discusses how quickly companies must act in order to seize new opportunities; explains why size is important in a global economy; and highlights the critical importance of creating and extending a company's brand.

Common Knowledge: How Companies Thrive by Sharing What They Know, by Nancy M. Dixon (Boston: Harvard Business School Press, 2000). The author describes insights into how organizational knowledge is created and how information systems can effectively communicate that knowledge within the organization. The book provides in-depth studies of several organizations—including Ernst & Young, Bechtel, Ford, Chevron, British Petroleum, Texas Instruments, and the U.S. Army—that are leading the field in successful knowledge transfer.

Periodicals

Computerworld. This weekly newspaper for computer professionals has a section called "Computer Careers" with advice and information on information technology professions.

Business Week. Besides national and international business news, this magazine publishes interesting articles about the information industry and the use of information technologies in companies.

Information Week. This magazine is laid out much like *Business Week* and contains interesting articles covering the information industry. It's a good source for business-related Web sites.

Upside. This magazine is aimed at managers, entrepreneurs, and others who want to track the business side, rather than the technological side, of the computer industry.

Darwin. This magazine's theme is showing how business is evolving in the information age and the individual and social impacts of this evolution.

Business Geographics covers the geographic technology revolution in business and is written for managers and the general business reader.

Journals like the **MIS Quarterly, Journal of Management Information Systems, Harvard Business Review**, and **Journal of Organizational Computing and Electronic Commerce** are written primarily for researchers and academics who want to keep up with current research in the field.

Professional Organizations for Information Workers

Association for Computing Machinery (ACM)
http://www.acm.org (You'll find the complete text of the ACM's Code of Ethics in the Appendix of this book.)

Association of Information Technology Professionals (AITP)
http://www.aitp.org

Association of Information Systems (AIS)
http://www.aisnet.org/

Institute for Certification of Computer Professionals (ICCP)
http://www.iccp.org/

Institute of Electrical and Electronics Engineers (IEEE)
http://www.ieee.org

International Federation for Information Processing (IFIP)
http://www.ifip.or.at/

Society of Information Management (SIM)
http://www.simnet.org/

The American Society for Information Science
http://www.asis.org

Web Pages

The Web has become a hotbed of business activity in recent years; .com is the fastest-growing domain on the Web. Look for links to the best .com sites on the *Computer Confluence* Web site, **http://www.computerconfluence.com**

AFTER YOU READ THIS CHAPTER YOU SHOULD BE ABLE TO:

- Describe the phases a company goes through using the Internet for business

- Describe the forms of electronic commerce

- Describe the purpose, characteristics, and uses of intranets and extranets

- Describe the design and use of public Web sites for supporting business–customer transactions

- Describe some of the technical requirements of electronic commerce

- Describe some of the ethical issues of electronic commerce

 Multimedia extras on the CD-ROM and the Web:

- John Gage: Sun Microsystems Chief Researcher on Tomorrow's Networks

- Interactive self-study quizzes

   . . . and more.

 computerconfluence.com

13

ELECTRONIC COMMERCE AND E-BUSINESS

JEFF BEZOS: THE VIRTUAL BOOKSELLER

Jeff Bezos was always interested in anything that could be revolutionized by computers. As a child, he wanted to be an astronaut. As an adult intrigued by the amazing growth in use of the Internet, Jeff created a business model that leveraged the Internet's unique ability to deliver huge amounts of information rapidly and efficiently.

He founded Amazon.com, Inc. with high ambitions in 1994. He initially named the company Cadabra.com before changing it to Amazon.com, after the most voluminous river in the world. Amazon opened its virtual doors in July 1995 with a mission to use the Internet to transform book buying into the fastest, easiest, and most enjoyable shopping experience possible. His mantra, imitated by hundreds of other Internet companies as well, was "get big fast." Amazon did just that, expanding beyond books to become a general store selling music, electronics, household goods, and a myriad of other products. Its growth seemed phenomenal—20 million customers in more than 160 countries bought $2.8 billion worth of merchandise in 2000. Bezos is proud of that performance, which is better than any start-up company in history. Unfortunately, Amazon also lost $1.4 billion in the process.

Fueled by big dreams and seemingly endless cash from investors, Amazon created an unprecedented offering for consumers to use a Web site to purchase merchandise at a low price, with responsive

> Most people never have the opportunity, **even in a small way**, to make history, which Amazon.com is trying to do.
> It's **work hard, have fun, make history**. That's what we're trying to do.
>
> —Jeff Bezos, founder and CEO of Amazon.com

service and quick shipment. When you visit the Amazon.com Web site, you can browse virtual aisles in hundreds of product categories, get instant personalized recommendations based on your prior purchases the moment you log on, receive via email the latest reviews of exceptional new titles in categories that interest you, use other shopping services by linking to other retail Internet sites, and purchase your selections easily using online ordering features.

13.1 Jeff Bezos.

13.2 Amazon.com's automated warehouse streamlines order processing.

But the big dreams and investors' cash shriveled quickly during the economic slowdown of 2000. Amazon had formed business alliances with many other Internet retailers (such as Pets.com and Living.com, at the time the largest pet supply and home furnishings companies on the Internet) and other established retailers (such as Borders and Toys 'R' Us). Bezos promised investors big returns from agreements to promote these companies on Amazon's Web site. Most of the Internet companies paid Amazon in stock, not cash. During the economic slowdown, many of the Internet companies went out of business, leaving Amazon with worthless stocks. The other retailers suffered their own difficulties, leaving Amazon with greatly reduced revenues.

Bezos acknowledges he underestimated the impact of the economic slowdown on the Internet industry generally and on Amazon's sales in particular. To survive, he analyzed why Amazon lost money. He found, like many of his critics, that Amazon's business model was too complicated, expensive, and inefficient. His new mantra, copied from any number of successful companies, is "march to profitability." Instead of designing flashy new features for its Web site or developing grandiose business strategies, Bezos focused on cutting costs and raising revenues. Amazon undertook an efficiency drive that included using a new accounting system that calculated how much money Amazon made or lost on each product it sold. Amazon got rid of unprofitable products, reduced the number of errors in its packing and shipping process, moved its call center operations to India, and converted its international warehouses into regional hubs to cut down on inventory levels and delivery times. These measures worked—in 2003 Amazon was a profitable company.

Still, Bezos wants Amazon to be the online equivalent of Wal-Mart, with so much sales volume that it has the buying power and efficiency to sell the same products available everywhere, but at low prices, and still make money.

Jeff Bezos's Amazon.com is a major player in the global electronic marketplace. Adam Smith, the founding father of economics, described the market concept in his book *The Wealth of Nations* in 1776, theorizing that "if every buyer knew every seller's price, and if every seller knew what every buyer is willing to pay, everyone in the market would be able to make fully informed decisions and society's resources would be distributed efficiently." The information technologies we describe throughout this book are making a global electronic marketplace possible, coming close to Smith's ideal. The confluence of traditional commerce and networks are revolutionizing the world of business. This confluence is electronic commerce.

Electronic Commerce in Perspective

Firms are increasingly **organized in networks**, both **internally** and in their **relationships**.

—Manuel Castells, *The Rise of the Network Society*

Electronic commerce (e-commerce) is the process of sharing business information, maintaining business relationships, and conducting business transactions through the use of telecommunications networks. The term *e-commerce* is relatively new, but the ideas underlying e-commerce have been evolving since computers were first developed for business applications 50 years ago. Some go back as far as 1845, when Samuel Morse invented the telegraph. Most businesses use one or more traditional e-commerce tools, including bar coding, fax communication, Electronic Data Interchange, enterprisewide messaging system, and other private LAN and WAN systems. Since the development of the World Wide Web and the beginning of the commercial use of the Internet in the early 1990s, e-commerce has become Internet based.

Internet-based e-commerce is much more than a set of Internet technologies. E-commerce also involves reorganizing internal business processes, fostering external business alliances, and creating new consumer-oriented products and services. With e-commerce, companies need to be able to share internal business information and conduct electronic transactions with customers, partners, suppliers, and sometimes even their competitors via the Internet. The term *e-business* is sometimes used interchangeably with the term *e-commerce* to refer to this broader concept. In this book, *e-commerce* is used in its broadest scope and *e-business* is used to refer to the e-commerce activities of a particular company or organization.

○	1,000,000
○	100,000
○	10,000
○	1,000
○	100
•	10
·	1

Internet Hosts

13.3 The e-commerce infrastructure is concentrated in, but not limited to, North America and Europe.

How E-Commerce Is Transforming Business

Internet-based electronic commerce continues to develop at a rapid rate despite the economic slowdown of the early 2000s. It's estimated that e-commerce will account for over 8 percent of worldwide sales of goods and services within just a few years.

E-commerce is all about cycle time, speed, globalization, enhanced productivity, **reaching new customers** and **sharing knowledge** across institutions for **competitive advantage**.

—Lou Gerstner, IBM's CEO

Recent surveys indicate that there are several thousand Internet-based companies—dot coms—that make up only 10 to 15 percent of Internet economy revenue and jobs. But the Internet economy has evolved to include the millions of traditional, so-called brick-and-mortar, companies. Fortune 1000 and Global 2000 companies, especially in industries such as chemicals, energy, financial services, manufacturing, retail, and utilities are pushing ahead aggressively with entire portfolios of e-business projects.

E-commerce in the United States and Europe is particularly strong—in the trillions of U.S. dollars. E-commerce currently accounts for about 5 percent of the total U.S. economy. A study by the University of Texas indicates that Internet-related revenue growth is about 20 times the growth rate for the U.S. economy. Companies engaging in e-commerce generate nearly one in five dollars of their revenues from the Internet and directly support millions of workers, including thousands of jobs that wouldn't exist without the Internet.

Most business executives believe the Internet is either essential or important to their company's success. In one survey a majority of CEOs said that e-commerce has changed the way they do business by, for example, improving relationships with customers and suppliers, boosting online sales, and bringing efficiency to their supply chain.

The expected benefits of e-commerce for a company are enormous. Another University of Texas study indicates that a company selling goods and services over the Internet is three times more likely to see expense reductions, two and a half times more likely to see productivity gains, and more than two and a half times more likely to see market share growth and penetration of new markets as a result of its Internet applications compared with U.S. businesses overall. Such a company can create a competitive advantage by dramatically expanding its market from local to national, to international, and to global. The company can substantially increase the speed and efficiency of business transaction processes, such as order processing, by automating tasks previously performed manually. The company can gather valuable customer information, enabling it to form closer interactive relationships with its customers and more accurately anticipate their future purchasing needs. And there is the promise of significant cost savings in conducting business transactions.

One of the fastest-growing types of e-commerce is mobile commerce (m-commerce). M-commerce, sometimes also called *m-business*, typically involves connecting to the Internet and intranets using handheld computers, cellular phones, PDAs, and laptop PCs. Wireless technologies hold tremendous potential for helping workers—doctors, home-care nurses, real estate agents, sales managers, utility representatives, and others—conduct business more effectively outside the office. M-commerce applications generate billions of dollars of revenue each year, and the total m-commerce revenue grows each year.

E-Commerce Models

Cyberspace has spawned a **more resilient type of business**. Sans physical plant and inventory, a Web-based business can **reinvent itself** in a matter of weeks.

—David Raths, Inc. Technology

The basic idea of e-commerce is that at least two parties—a seller and a buyer—exchange information, products, or services using network technology The exchange, or transaction, can occur between individuals, businesses, or organizations.

There are several e-commerce models based on who is involved in the transaction:

13.4 Many real estate agencies list available properties on their public Web sites. Links are provided for customers to explore specific properties, find information about the community, and communicate via email with the real estate agent.

- *Business-to-business (B2B).* The business-to-business (B2B) model represents inter-organizational information systems in which a company handles transactions within its own value chain and with other businesses and organizations, such as its suppliers, distributors, and bank. For example, Wal-Mart purchases the products it sells in its stores from its vendors over the Internet. B2B is sometimes referred to as business-to-employee (B2E) when the focus is primarily on handling the activities that take place within the organization. Most employees in midsized and large companies have access to internal Web intranet sites. B2B is the dominant form of e-commerce, and it is growing at a phenomenal rate. Companies worldwide are spending billions of dollars each year to develop their B2B capabilities. As a result of this investment in B2B infrastructure, B2B transactions are increasing all over the world. The United States alone does hundreds of billions of dollars in B2B transactions each year.

■ *Business-to-consumer (B2C).* The **business-to-consumer (B2C)** model represents retail transactions between a company and individual customers. Examples of B2C are dot-com companies, such as Amazon.com and E*Trade.com, and traditional companies, such as Lands' End and United Airlines, that use the Internet to sell to customers via a Web site. B2C is the most visible aspect of e-commerce from a consumer's point of view. According to the Boston Consulting Group, the Web is the fastest-growing retail channel, even though dot coms declined during the recession of the early 2000s. Much of the retail online sales activity is in the categories of gifts and flowers, entertainment, and computer software and hardware. Worldwide revenues of B2C are in the hundreds of billions of U.S. dollars, but still far less than B2C revenues.

■ *Consumer-to-consumer (C2C).* The **consumer-to-consumer (C2C)** model represents individuals, organizations, or companies that are selling and buying directly with each other via the Internet. The best-known example of C2C is eBay, the phenomenally successful Web auction that enables individuals and businesses to offer items for sale and bid on items to buy. Millions of people use eBay every year; many entrepeneurs have built their own small businesses on the eBay infrastructure.

These e-commerce models apply as well to non-business institutions, such as religious organizations, academic institutions, government agencies, and not-for-profit and social organizations.

In the following sections, we'll describe intranets, extranets, and public Web sites that support e-commerce transactions in more detail.

Intranets: E-Commerce to Support Internal Business Processes

In business-to-employee (B2E) e-commerce, an organization uses Internet technology, organized as an intranet, to support its internal value chain activities as efficiently as possible. Intranets based on Internet technology offer several advantages over customized, proprietary networks: cross-platform capability, open standards, reduced hardware and software costs, easy installation, and minimal user training. Most important is that intranets can dramatically improve communications within the organization—any employee with security authorization can access the organization's intranet from any geographic location using a Web browser.

13.5 Consumers can search for products and purchase them easily online using the catalog display feature of Web sites designed for B2C e-commerce, such as the REI Web site.

13.6 A consumer can use a C2C Web auction site, such as eBay.com, to buy, sell, or trade just about any type of product with other people.

My bottom line is that **intranets** are about **people empowerment**, not technology.

—Randy J. Hinrichs, Microsoft Corp.

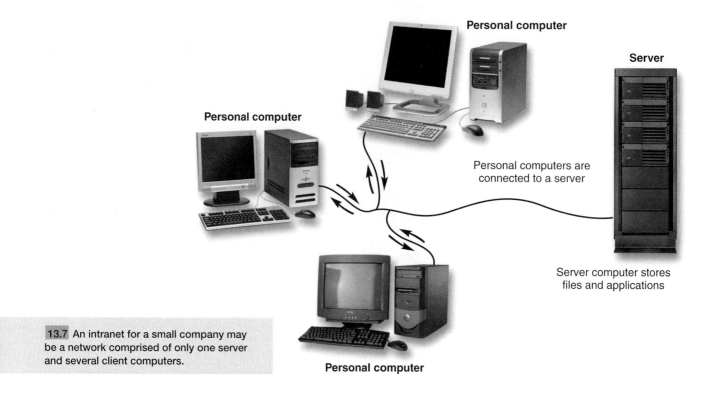

Personal computer

Personal computer

Server

Personal computers are
connected to a server

Server computer stores
files and applications

13.7 An intranet for a small company may
be a network comprised of only one server
and several client computers.

Personal computer

Characteristics of a B2E Intranet

An intranet is made up of physical technology and information content. The physical elements of an intranet are a network, at least one computer with server software installed (including TCP/IP), and other computers with client software installed (including TCP/IP and Web browsers). The physical network can be a LAN or WAN. Most intranets use Ethernet topology to physically connect the computers, printers, and other hardware on the network.

The communication software for an intranet includes middleware and TCP/IP. *Middleware* is software that handles the actual physical communications connections between the computers, scanners, printers, and other devices on the network. The TCP/IP software handles the intranet communication protocols for messages transferred between the server and client computers. (See Chapter 9 for more on Internet technology.)

An intranet also includes firewall software for security; the firewall keeps unauthorized Internet users out of the intranet. Other software used to protect the intranet include user identification and authentication, data encryption, and virus protection. (See Chapter 10 for more on security.)

An intranet should provide users within an organization easy access to information. The information content of an intranet is designed in the same way public Web sites are designed. An intranet home page typically presents information about what's available on the network and navigational tools—buttons, menus, and maps—to find the information easily. A company usually establishes guidelines for the design of individual Web pages, and then each department in the organization is responsible for the information it wants to publish on the intranet.

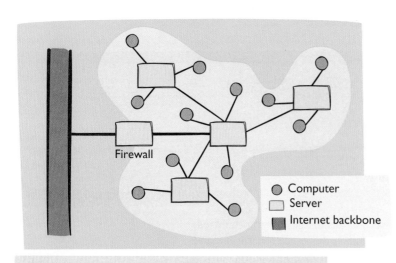

Firewall

○ Computer
□ Server
▮ Internet backbone

13.8 A large company's intranet may be a network comprised
of several servers and many client computers. Firewall security
guards against unauthorized access to the intranet.

How Organizations Use B2E Intranets

Businesses use intranets to support their internal business processes in three basic ways: to provide employees access to important information for their jobs; to facilitate employees' teamwork and collaboration within and between departments; and to process internal company transactions online.

> Stop thinking about the **technology** and start thinking about **what people are doing**. That's the secret to good design.
>
> —Donald A. Norman, interface design expert

Information Access for Employees

Many large companies have massive amounts of information stored in databases on their intranets. Any employee with a connection to the intranet can have access to the information using a Web browser. For example:

- Children's Healthcare of Atlanta (CHA) has 4,500 employees who use the company's intranet, Careforce Connection, to access current employee data, medical research, and health care rules and regulations. The intranet has reduced CHA's administrative claims denials and administrative costs and improved customer service.
- Los Alamos National Laboratory publishes several million internal classified, technical, and administrative documents on its intranet. By making this information available electronically, the Los Alamos scientists and managers can access the information quickly and easily and the organization is saving an estimated $500,000 per year in printing and distribution costs.
- Deere & Co. has employees in 10 countries who use Deere's intranet to read the latest information about the company's pension and benefit plans, review the company's financial position, and work on projects.
- General Motors' intranet, named Socrates, lets 100,000 GM employees worldwide search more than 500 internal GM sites, providing news, information, and services related to GM as a whole and their divisions in particular. The site serves up hundreds of thousands of page views a day.
- Newaygo, Michigan, School District's intranet is used by students, teachers, and parents to access school-related information, including lunch menus, sports schedules, daily announcements, attendance records, and much more.
- Delta Airlines' DeltaNet houses aircraft maintenance manuals online. The FAA requires airlines to make sure their manuals are accurate and timely and levies significant fines if they fail. DeltaNet has reduced the labor needed to update the manuals and avoid hefty fines.

Collaboration and Teamwork

Teamwork and collaboration are becoming the expected way for people to do work in many organizations. Intranets make possible the easy access and distribution of information in an organization, no matter where employees are located geographically. For example:

- Chrysler's Dashboard intranet provides collaborative workgroup support for its 40,000 employees; employees can access competitive intelligence information, financial modeling tools, and many other work-related information resources.
- Engineers at Ford use its intranet to collaborate on car design; the engineers can view computer-generated models of cars to ensure that all the parts fit together correctly.
- Camp Fire Boys & Girls use their intranet, The Camp Fire Café, as the communication link between the national Camp Fire office and more than 125 independent local councils throughout the United States.

Internal Business Transactions

Employees in many organizations can use Web browsers to conduct actual internal business transactions on the organization's intranet. Having employees work electronically on an intranet increases efficiency, reduces paperwork costs, and increases the speed of updating information. For example:

- Lucent Technologies, Inc.'s, intranet, named Benefits Central, automates benefit enrollment transactions of nearly 100,000 employees; individual employees are able to use their Web browser to make changes in their health, retirement, and other benefits programs.
- The U.S. Department of Health and Human Services' intranet, named Medical Program, is used to do all the agency's health insurance services.
- Millipore Corp., a manufacturer of scientific and chemical purification products, uses its intranet, named @Millipore, to support employee self-service pages, including expense reporting, travel booking, and business-card ordering, and uses push technology to distribute to employees information from 120 subscription-based corporate databases.
- Rainforest Café, an international theme restaurant and retail chain, uses its intranet to send daily sales reports from its stores to its Houston headquarters.
- PricewaterhouseCoopers, a large accounting and management consulting firm, provides employees an intranet named KnowledgeCurve. Formerly paper-based processes, such as filling out health care reimbursement forms, accessing corporate credit card statements, booking travel, and registering for courses, are now are taken care of online. It's available in 34 countries and has more than 100,000 users.

Extranets to Connect Business Alliances

> In the future, **all companies** will be **Internet companies**.
> —Andy Grove

As an organization uses the Internet and develops its intranet, it may find that its business partners are developing their own intranets. Some organizations recognize that they could work together more easily and efficiently if they could link their intranets directly, creating an extranet. Extranets play an important role in the global business strategy of many companies, enabling them to build alliances with vendors, suppliers, and other organizations internationally. These alliances are sometimes referred to as *e-marketplaces*.

An extranet, or extended intranet, is a private interorganizational information system connecting the intranets of two or more companies in an e-marketplace. An extranet extends the cross-functional activities between trusted business partners and facilitates their working relationships. Companies using an extranet can place orders with each other, check each other's inventory level, confirm the status of an invoice, and exchange many other types of business information. For example, Hilton Hotels operates a business-to-business extranet to communicate with companies that have contractual agreements to use Hilton's facilities for business travel. Hilton's corporate customers install links to the Hilton Web site on their own intranets, and those links call up customized Web pages with contractual prices and travel limitations.

Characteristics of a B2B Extranet

Organizations can set up an extranet in one of three ways:

- A *secure private network* physically attaches the intranets with private leased telephone lines. These types of intranets are relatively expensive because monthly leased-line charges can become very costly, especially as additional business partner intranets are added to the network. On the other hand, each business partner can operate inside the system to the full extent of its access and security privileges. Security is relatively high for business transactions because only a limited number of partners have access to the system.

■ A *public network* uses a public communications network, such as a public utility telecommunication network or the Internet. These types of intranets are relatively inexpensive to set up and maintain, but security is low. Intranets within a public network extranet are protected only by firewalls and user logon procedures, which are not guarantees that unauthorized users will be blocked from accessing the system.

■ A **virtual private network (VPN)** uses a public network with special protocols that provide a secure, private "tunnel" across the network between the business partners' intranets. An extranet is called an *Internet VPN* when the public network used is the Internet. VPNs are becoming the preferred method for extranets for a variety of reasons. VPN-based extranets are relatively economical, because companies pay only a flat fee per month plus a fee for the time used for transactions. Privacy and security are good, because data are specially coded—a process called *encapsulation*—for sending transactions over the Internet; essentially, transactions are conducted via an encrypted channel, or tunnel, between the intranet firewalls of the extranet.

Ensuring secure transactions is a major concern of companies conducting B2B transactions over the Internet, regardless of the type of extranet used. (See Chapter 10 to review the many computer security issues with which an organization must cope.)

Public network

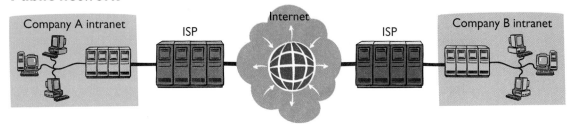

Virtual private network

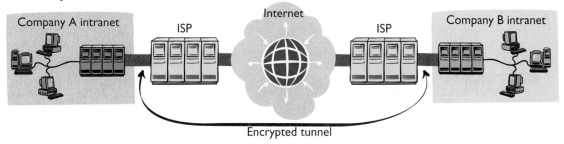

Secure private network

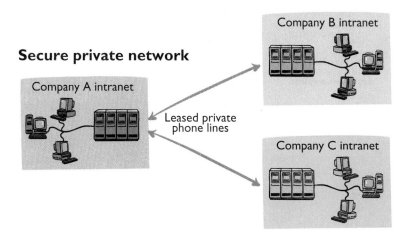

13.9 These three types of extranets enable organizations to connect their intranets to facilitate business transactions, communications, and other shared activities.

How Business Alliances Use B2B Extranets

Companies constituting a business alliance can use an extranet to achieve certain strategic benefits, such as:

- Increasing the speed of business-to-business transactions
- Reducing errors on intercompany transactions
- Reducing costs of telecommunications
- Increasing the volume of business with partners
- Exchanging business-to-business documents
- Checking on inventory and order status from suppliers
- Collaborating with business partners on joint projects.

Wal-Mart and its suppliers use a B2B extranet. Wal-Mart built direct software linkages between its suppliers' factories and the cash registers at its stores. One major supplier, Procter & Gamble, can monitor the shelves at Wal-Mart stores through real-time satellite linkups that send messages to the factory whenever a checkout clerk swipes a Proctor & Gamble item past a scanner at the register. With this kind of minute-to-minute information, Protor & Gamble knows when to make, ship, and display more products at the Wal-Mart stores. The system saves Proctor & Gamble so much in time, reduced inventory, and lower order-processing costs that it can afford to give Wal-Mart "low, everyday prices" without putting itself out of business. As a result, Wal-Mart moves products through its stores more quickly and with less overhead.

Another example of a B2B extranet is Caterpillar Inc., a multinational heavy machinery manufacturer. Caterpillar developed extranet applications to reduce the time needed to develop and redesign its vehicle products. The company connected its engineering and manufacturing divisions with its suppliers, distributors, overseas factories, and corporate customers, all in a global extranet. Caterpillar customers, for example, can use the extranet to modify order information while the vehicle is still on the assembly line. This ability to collaborate remotely between the customer and the product developers decreases time delays in redesign work.

The trade association of automotive manufacturers and suppliers has developed an extranet named Automotive Network Exchange (ANX). The extranet was designed as an Internet VPN to provide a global infrastructure for trading partners within the industry, including DaimlerChrysler Corp., Ford Motor Co., General Motors Corp., and several dozen major suppliers. ANX reduces telecommunication costs significantly by eliminating the need for manufacturers to have T1 lines to connect with their suppliers. ANX also reduces the time it takes a supplier to fill an order. Ford, for example, expects to compress some work-order communications from three weeks to five minutes.

A company can use an extranet successfully through proper planning and collaboration with its business partners. Many companies have problems implementing extranets because employees don't trust the network as the main method for sharing information. As with intranets, extranets work well only if the business partners are willing to share information openly and consistently. In an effort to enhance a climate of trust, several corporations from the United States, Europe, and Asia have formed the Global Trading Web Council, a multi-industry

13.10 FedEx provides services required for shipping and tracking packages worldwide. The shipping status of packages and other critical information is stored on the FedEx extranet, which is integrated with the customer's order and warehousing systems.

corporate alliance that aims to be the world's first international B2B network. Sponsored by CommerceOne, an e-commerce software and services company, the council is intended to integrate various extranets into the Global Trading Web, where organizations can have marketplace-to-marketplace communication.

B2C: The Customer Connection

Intranets support an organization's internal business processes; extranets support business-to-business processes of two or more organiza-

> **Wow!** They've got the Internet **on computers** now!
>
> —Homer Simpson, on *The Simpsons*

tions. E-commerce also facilitates business transactions with consumers. To conduct B2C transactions on the Internet, a company provides customers with a public Web site where they can search product catalogs, retrieve product information, order and pay for a product, and look up customer service information. For example, Dell Computer Corporation has unique Web sites for customers in more than 80 countries and 23 languages. These sites generate close to half of Dell's revenue. Many companies in and out of the computer business have used Dell's B2C Web site as a model for their own businesses.

Customer-centered Web Design

A company must develop a well-designed Web site to conduct business effectively with consumers on the Internet. A good design can keep customers coming back; a bad design can drive them away. Features of a well-designed Web site include:

- *Speed of transactions.* As with any business transaction, speed of service is critical for attracting and keeping customers. If a company's Web site is too slow, customers will find and use a competitor's faster Web site.
- *Large, up-to-date product selection.* Electronic catalogs can hold thousands of pages of product information at a fraction of the cost of printed catalogs. In fact, many companies, such as Prentice Hall, this book's publisher, have developed entirely new electronic content products that are available only on the Web.
- *Ease of use.* The customer should be able to move easily through a business transaction without getting lost or confused. A Web site should be well organized, providing navigation tools and a search engine to find and evaluate product information and well-designed online forms so that the customer can complete a transaction quickly. Amazon.com sells a variety of products exclusively through the Web. Regular customers can search for products, read reviews from other customers, compare prices, and complete purchases with just a few mouse clicks. Amazon recently added a revolutionary content-search feature that allows customers to search the *contents* of thousands of books for key words and phrases, streamlining the research process in ways that were out of the question only a few years ago.
- *Secure transactions.* Currently, there are two obstacles to expanding B2C e-commerce: ensuring safe and private transactions technically and consumer perception of whether the Internet is safe or unsafe for credit card usage. Both obstacles are gradually being overcome. Message encryption standards use software for authenticating the parties involved in a credit card purchase on the Internet, and transmitting credit card numbers over the Internet using encryption is safer now than many people think.
- *After-sale features.* After a customer completes a purchase transaction, the Web site should provide the customer after-sale information, including confirmation of the order and online support for customer questions regarding delivery, repairs and maintenance, and warranty. Examples of these after-sales features are common on travel, car, and hotel reservation Web sites.

Several managerial questions concern the effectiveness of an organization's B2C Web site. What is it doing for us? Is it helping us compete? Is the site helping us meet corporate goals and improve the bottom line? How can we manage it better?

13.1
Online Shopping

1. Most online shopping sites are dynamic, database-backed sites whose pages are automatically generated and updated. When you visit a large online store you are using your Web browser to search site databases.

2. When you decide to place an item in your shopping cart, your request is sent to the store's Web server, which sends a cookie to your computer—a small file containing information on the desired item. Cookies are used by the Web site to keep track of your potential purchases. Cookies might also be used to track the different pages you visit on the site and customize the display to match your preferences. For example, if you view several MP3 players, the site might show you more display ads related to portable audio.

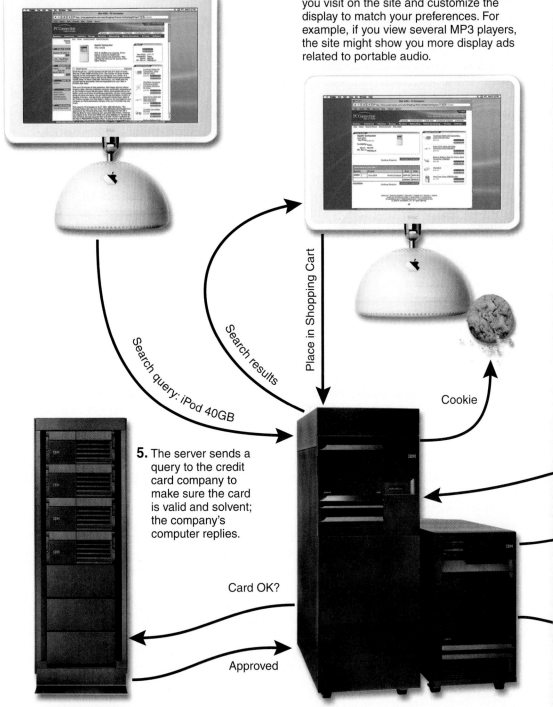

Search query: iPod 40GB

Search results

Place in Shopping Cart

Cookie

5. The server sends a query to the credit card company to make sure the card is valid and solvent; the company's computer replies.

Card OK?

Approved

13.11

**Credit Card
Company Computer**

3. When you "proceed to checkout," the site displays all the items in your shopping cart, using the cookies on your hard disk to determine what you've put there.

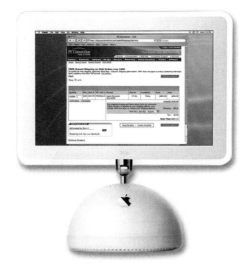

4. When you continue the checkout process, you're routed to a secure part of the Web site so you can enter personal information and credit card numbers and know that they'll be encrypted before being sent through the Internet.

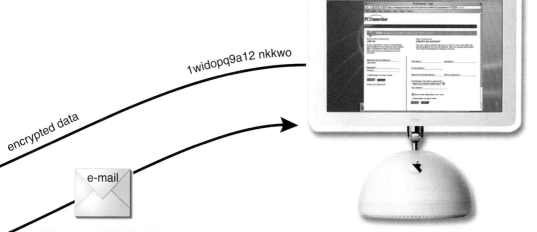

1widopq9a12 nkkwo

encrypted data

e-mail

...Your order will ship today...

6. Once the transaction has been approved, the server sends a message to the warehouse where the order is filled. It also sends a confirmation email to you.

13.12 Apple's iTunes music store allows consumers to buy downloadable songs that can be burned to CDs, played on a Mac or PC, or moved to an iPod portable music player. Apple's iTunes software is free, and song sales aren't highly profitable because royalties and fees must be paid to music publishers. But the popularity of the music store has helped make the iPod into a big revenue generator for the company.

When a company develops a public Web site, it should be in response to a business need, although many firms have developed sites without knowing why. The best Internet sites have well-articulated goals and target specific markets, and their success is measured against specific objectives. Depending on the objectives, there are many ways to measure the effectiveness of a Web site, and the number of hits a site gets is not necessarily one of them.

Content, structure, and design elements can make a huge difference in the site's success. It makes sense for a company to publish catalogs, brochures, and annual reports electronically. The multimedia and hypertext capabilities of the Web allow for richer and more varied content than customers could find in the paper versions of these documents. A well-designed Web site should give visitors essential information organized in such a way that they can find the information they need quickly. Web sites are usually organized in some combination of hierarchical and sequential structures wherein the most important information can be accessed in just a few mouse clicks. A well-designed site has a consistent look and feel on every page.

One way to foster customer loyalty is to include interactive features that enable users to provide feedback and comments about their needs, how well the site is filling those needs, and suggestions for improvement. Three interactive features are often included on public Web sites: email, discussion groups, and chat rooms.

Customer Relationship Management

In any kind of business, a company's relationship with its customers is important. In e-businesses, where customers rarely, if ever, see or speak to company representatives,

customer relationship management, or **CRM**, can be the difference between success and failure. In the information industry, CRM usually refers to methodologies, software, and Internet capabilities for managing customer relationships in an organized way. A typical CRM system is a customer database that can provide information for managers, salespeople, marketing departments, and sometimes even the customers themselves. The database might include past purchases, customer preferences, service schedules, and customer communications, among other things. A well-designed CRM system can benefit company and customers alike.

Some Technical Requirements of E-Commerce

A company, organization, or individual who wants to engage in e-commerce must have a *Web server*, including both hardware and software. The server must have the capacity to handle the initial traffic on the site, and it should have adequate scalability—the ability to expand as

> If we want our institutions to be more productive, then **we must learn to focus** the power of **information technology** not on the **institutions** themselves but on the **individuals** inside the institutions.
>
> —John Sculley, in *Odyssey*

Web site traffic increases. Large organizations frequently have the technical know-how and capacity to run their Web sites on their own servers. However, many small- and medium-sized companies opt for Web hosting, or contracting with another company, usually an ISP, to run the site on that company's servers. A third-party host provider can help choose the best server hardware/software combination and provide management and staffing services for the site. The Web Host Guild, a consortium of Web hosting companies, is developing industry standards for all hosting companies and tries to protect consumers from unscrupulous host providers to help identify honest, legitimate host companies.

E-commerce software on a Web server provides the commercial services to consumers and business partners on the Web site. Most servers run on either Windows computers or on Unix- or Linux-based operating systems. Besides the operating system, there are other important Web server software features. Web server software includes basic capabilities of security, FTP, search engines, and data analysis of visitor information to the site. Web server software also includes site-management capabilities that check for problems and errors, especially link checking. Other Web server software includes tools to develop Web sites and Web pages, especially pages with dynamic content, or information that changes in response to a Web client's request.

13.13 A company that engages in e-commerce must maintain a stable, secure, environmentally sound computer room for its Web site servers and other equipment.

13.14 The Yahoo! shopping site arranges product information as a catalog and provides links to specific merchants' Web sites.

E-commerce software must provide access to business information, usually as searchable directories and catalogs. E-commerce software should also provide on-demand customer service. Of course, e-commerce software must support transaction processing. The software must be able to do all the typical calculations for a transaction, including computing taxes and shipping costs. The software must also be able to collect payments from customers accurately and securely.

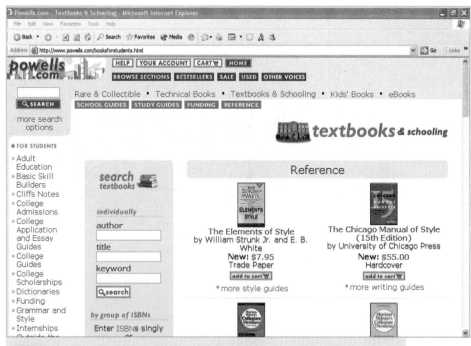

13.15 Powell's bookstore is one of the largest bookstores in the world; its online site is a valuable resource for people looking for new and used books.

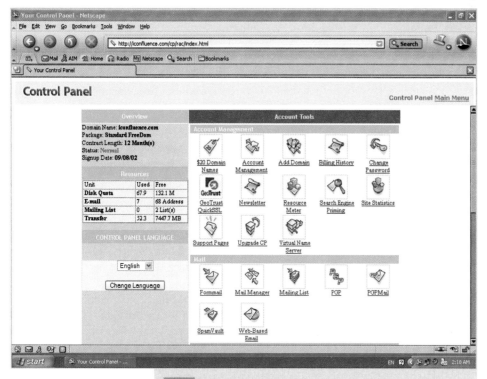

13.16 OneWorldHosting is a Web hosting service that provides inexpensive and easy-to-use tools to individuals and small companies for building and maintaining an e-commerce site.

Many large companies in B2B develop their own e-commerce software, but small and midsize businesses in both B2B and B2C use a **Web hosting service**. Similar to a server host provider, a Web hosting service provides the e-commerce software and expertise to run an online business. Some services provide free space on their servers and easy-to-use templates to set up business Web pages. A drawback of these free host sites is that customer purchases are handled via email between the hosting service and the merchants, who must handle all the transaction steps, including processing the payment from the customer. A full-service Web hosting service provides comprehensive customer transaction processing along with shopping cart software and better software tools to build and maintain a business Web site, all for a monthly fee and usually some percentage of each customer transaction.

Ethical Issues of E-Commerce

One of the main challenges of e-commerce is to maintain trust between the people engaging in transactions. If that trust is lost, it is difficult to reestablish, and the po-

> We have **profoundly forgotten** everywhere that cash-payment is **not the sole relation** of human beings.
>
> —Thomas Carlyle

tential benefits for the company, and for society as a whole, are diminished. Publishing the company's information code of ethics on the company's Web site ensures that users—both the company's information workers and customers—are aware of the company's e-commerce policies. The code of ethics should include:

- A statement of the organization's privacy policy
- A statement that a person's permission must be secured before his or her ID, photo, ideas, or communications are used or transmitted

■ A statement on how the company will inform customers of the intended uses of personal information gathered during an online transaction and how to secure permission from customers for those uses

■ A statement that addresses issues of ownership with respect to network postings and communications

■ A statement of how the company monitors, or tracks, user behaviors on the Web site.

Even though voluntary ethical policies are important, poor practices for handling personal information are a big problem for American businesses and government.

Consumers are becoming increasingly impatient with companies and organizations that abuse their personal information. Here are some recent well-publicized examples:

■ Online auction house ReverseAuction.com allegedly collected consumers' personal information from competitor eBay and sent emails to those consumers soliciting their business. According to the U.S. Federal Trade Commission (FTC), ReverseAuctions.com signed up at eBay, disregarded the privacy agreement posted on the rival auction site, and copied the information from bidders to send them solicitations that were later deemed deceptive by the FTC. ReverseAuctions consented to a settlement but said it did not gather any confidential information from the eBay site.

■ Interloc, an online bookseller and ISP, was accused of intercepting email messages directed by online bookseller Amazon.com to Interloc's bookseller clients with Interloc's email addresses. The company was accused of trying to steal business strategies from its industry competitor. Alibris, the new owner of Interloc, settled the case.

■ The FTC brought suit against Liberty Financial Companies for violating the privacy rights of children who frequented its Young Investor Web site. The FTC alleged that the company had used prizes and contests to encourage children to disclose their names and addresses as well as information such as stock holdings and the amount of weekly allowances that could be used to market to their parents.

Unlike Canada, Europe, Australia, and even Hong Kong, Americans lack both the legislation that would establish overall privacy standards and a regulatory agency that could advise businesses on acceptable privacy practices. In the United States, businesses and trade organizations tend to favor self-regulation, fearing that government rules would quash the growth of e-commerce. IBM and Disney are good examples of self-regulation—both do a great deal of advertising on other Web sites and have a policy that any site they advertise on must have an ironclad privacy policy.

The United States has many laws relating to the issue of privacy, but they affect only certain industries and consumer segments. For example, Americans have the legal right to see their credit records. Another law prohibits video rental stores from releasing the names of the movies that you rent. The Health Insurance Portability and Accountability Act requires health care providers and hospitals to protect the confidentiality of an individual's health information. The Children's Online Privacy Protection Act of 1998 (COPPA) requires certain commercial Web sites to obtain parental consent before collecting, using, or disclosing personal information about children under 13. However, a report from the Annenberg Public Policy Center of the University of Pennsylvania revealed that many sites with the highest percentage of child visitors under age of 13 often did not follow the COPPA rules.

The United States does not have an overall scheme for dealing with the issues of data privacy. In contrast, the European Union adopted the European Union's Data Protection Directive in October 1998. The directive establishes a high level of legal protection for the privacy of individuals and personal data within the EU. The directive also prohibits companies from transferring personally identifiable information from EU member countries to jurisdictions where that information is not treated with respect by law. Because the United States does not have an umbrella privacy policy, the EU could choose to stop the transfer of all data to it. Clearly, there's much work to be done to protect personal privacy in the age of global e-commerce.

Service Matters
Jim Rapoza

The Internet has been called a global marketplace because it brings together buyers and sellers on a worldwide scale. But when you shop at a local market, you can talk face-to-face with sellers when you buy or return an item. As he explains in this article, first published in the May 19, 2003 issue of eWeek, writer Jim Rapoza discovered that the human connection has been sacrificed by some Internet merchants.

Is there anything more indefensible—both technically and morally—than poor customer service on e-commerce Web sites? I don't think so.

An e-commerce site can have the best interfaces, great underlying technology and complete interactivity, but if it doesn't treat customers well and isn't forthcoming with information and support, nothing else will matter.

Conversely, a site can have a primitive interface, but if it provides excellent support and treats its customers in an honest and straightforward manner, those customers will probably come back, even though the site isn't the flashiest.

Like any person who regularly shops on the Internet, I have had both types of experience. I regularly return to the sites that treat me right while blacklisting those that don't have the time to deal with me.

Few companies can get away with providing customers with almost no support or updated information. One of the only ones that can is Amazon.com, which regularly fares poorly on consumer rating sites such as www.planetfeedback.com but somehow still manages to remain among the top Media Metrix e-commerce sites.

Here's an example of Amazon.com's idea of customer service: I decided to use an Amazon gift certificate to buy a big-ticket item from Amazon in March. I wasn't in any hurry for delivery, so I decided to choose the free delivery.

A month went by. I received a notice that the delivery would be delayed. The item was marked on the notice as in stock, but there was no information on why the shipment would be delayed.

Another month went by. I received another notice saying the product would be delayed, again without any reason provided. This time, I decided some customer support was in order.

How to find customer support on Amazon.com? Clicking on the Help link brought me to a page full of marginally useful FAQ items. So I then clicked on the link labeled "Still Need Help? Contact Customer Service."

But again, no customer service was apparent, simply more information directing me to past FAQs. I then clicked on a link for General Questions. This brought me to yet another page with FAQ information. Buried at the bottom was a button labeled "E-mail us."

So here I am, four links deep in the Web site, and all I get is a 1995-style HTML e-mail form. A day after filling this out, I got a very polite e-mail response with apologies for the delay and a $5 gift certificate. But I still received no reasons for the delay of an item still listed as in stock.

Compare this with another experience at about the same time. Sick of buying new batteries for her Panasonic portable CD player, my wife asked if I could get her rechargeable batteries and a power adapter for it.

Heading to Panasonic's Web site, I was happy to find both support and part-ordering links right on the home page. From these pages, there were a number of useful links for calling, e-mailing or finding information on my own.

Heading into the part-ordering area, I was stunned by the primitive interface. It wasn't altogether easy finding things, but I was able to locate both the batteries and the charger for my wife's player.

A couple of days after placing the order, I received an e-mail, clearly produced by an automated system, informing me that one of the items was unavailable. But the notice did state the item was out of stock and listed the date it was expected to be back in stock. It also gave me the option to cancel the purchase.

Not needing the item immediately, I did not cancel; it was delivered on the day it was supposed to be back in stock.

Now, there was no magic here, just straightforward information. If Amazon provided the same, I would feel a lot more comfortable about ever getting my purchase. And don't tell me Amazon can't implement similar automated technology to make its customer support more friendly. Postponement must be a cornerstone of Amazon.com's business strategy: in profitability, order shipments and customer satisfaction.

The bottom line: It's not good business to keep your customers in the dark. Before implementing flashy technology, give your customers the information they need.

DISCUSSION QUESTIONS

1. Have you had experiences similar to the ones described by the author? What was your reaction?

2. Do you agree that customer service is the thing that brings people back to a Web site? Why or why not?

SUMMARY

E-commerce is the sharing of business information, maintaining of business relationships, and conducting of business transactions through the use of telecommunications networks, especially the Internet. E-commerce is also about reorganizing internal business processes and external business alliances and creating new consumer-oriented products globally.

There are three main e-commerce configurations using the Internet: intranet, extranet, and public Web sites. An intranet is an internal information system based on Internet technology, including TCP/IP protocols and Web tools, to support the value chain activities between individuals and departments within an organization. An extranet is a private interorganizational information system connecting the intranets of two or more companies in a business alliance. A company can connect its intranet to the Internet and operate a publicly accessible Web site to support business-to-customer transactions.

An intranet comprises physical technology and information content. The physical elements of an intranet are a network, a computer with server software installed including TCP/IP, and other computers with client software including TCP/IP and a Web browser. A firewall protects the intranet against unauthorized access by users on a network external to the organization. The company establishes guidelines for the design of individual Web pages, and then each department in the organization is responsible for the information it wants to publish on the intranet. Companies use intranets to provide employees access to important information for their jobs, to facilitate teamwork and collaboration within and between departments, and to process internal company transactions online.

An extranet extends the cross-functional activities between trusted business partners and facilitates their working relationships. Extranets play an important role in the global business strategy of many companies, large and small, enabling them to build alliances with vendors, suppliers, and other organizations internationally. An extranet can be set up either as a secure private network, as a public network, or as a virtual private network (VPN). Each configuration uses a different type of telecommunications technology to connect the intranets comprising the extranet. A major concern of companies conducting business-to-business transactions over an extranet is the guarantee of secure transactions.

A third aspect of e-commerce is to conduct business transactions with customers. A company can connect its intranet to the Internet and operate a publicly accessible Web site. A customer can use a Web browser to connect to the company's Internet site and conduct transactions online—browsing through product catalogs, retrieving specific product information, using online forms to order and pay for products, or to conduct other transactions. A company's Web site should be easy to use, support speedy and secure transactions, and provide up-to-date product selections.

Although e-commerce has many technical requirements, Web server and e-commerce software requirements are particularly important. The Web server must have the capacity to handle the volume of e-commerce transactions on a company's Web site. Also, appropriate server software must include capabilities of security, FTP, search engines, site management, and tools to develop Web sites and Web pages, especially pages with dynamic content. The e-commerce software requirements include the capability of information search and retrieval, providing on-demand customer service, and supporting customer transaction processing.

A company conducting business on the Internet should develop an information code of ethics that ensures that users of the Web site—both the company's information workers and customers—will be aware of the company's e-commerce policies, especially consumer information privacy.

KEY TERMS

business-to-business (B2B) (p. 468)
business-to-consumer (B2C) (p. 469)
business-to-employee (B2E) (p. 468)
consumer-to-consumer (C2C) (p. 469)
customer relationship management
    (CRM) (p. 479)

dot com (p. 467)
electronic commerce (e-commerce)
    (p. 466)
e-commerce software (p. 479)
extranet (p. 472)
firewall (p. 470)

intranet (p. 470)
mobile commerce (m-commerce)
    (p. 468)
virtual private network (VPN)
    (p. 473)
Web hosting service (p. 481)

INTERACTIVE QUIZ QUESTIONS

 1. The *Computer Confluence* CD-ROM contains self-test quiz questions related to this chapter, including multiple-choice, true or false, and matching questions.

 2. The *Computer Confluence* Web site, *www.prenhall.com/beekman*, contains self-test exercises related to this chapter. Follow the instructions for taking a quiz. After you've completed your quiz, you can email the results to your instructor.

TRUE OR FALSE

1. The e-commerce infrastructure is concentrated in, but not limited to, North America and Europe.

2. M-commerce is particularly useful in conducting business in traditional offices.

3. Amazon.com is primarily a business-to-business (B2B) e-commerce firm.

4. The linked intranets between two or more companies in a business alliance for sharing business information are called an extranet.

5. In a virtual private network (VPN), data is transmitted through the Internet via a secure "tunnel" between intranets.

6. Security of transactions is a major concern of companies conducting B2B transactions over the Internet, regardless of the type of extranet.

7. The number of hits on a Web site is the best indication of the site's effectiveness.

8. Many small and medium-sized companies contract with a Web hosting company to run their sites on the Web-hosting company's servers.

9. The business-to-consumer (B2C) model is the predominant form of e-commerce.

10. Most experts believe that self-regulation and compliance with Internet privacy codes of ethics by American companies make regulatory privacy laws unnecessary in the United States.

MULTIPLE CHOICE

1. Which is not an e-commerce model mentioned in the chapter?
   a. business-to-business (B2B).
   b. business-to-government (B2G).
   c. business-to-consumer (B2C).
   d. consumer-to-consumer (C2C).
   e. business-to-employee (B2E).

2. Using Internet technology for intranets is advantageous because of
   a. open standards.
   b. the cross-platform environment.
   c. geographic independence.
   d. reduced hardware and software costs.
   e. All of these are benefits of using Internet technology for intranets.

3. Which is not a use of a business intranet?
   a. business-to-consumer transactions.
   b. providing access to important information.
   c. facilitating teamwork and collaboration.
   d. conducting internal business transactions.
   e. None of these are business intranet uses.

4. The capabilities of e-commerce software include all but
   a. finding and delivering information.
   b. on-demand customer service.
   c. providing the site content.
   d. processing transactions.
   e. computing taxes and shipping costs.

5. An extranet may not be set up as
   a. a secure private network.
   b. a public network.
   c. a virtual private network (VPN).
   d. a local area network.
   e. a wireless network.

6. Which is not part of a typical Internet technology-based intranet?
   a. a computer with server software, and computers with client software.
   b. middleware software for handling communication between hardware devices.
   c. an extranet.
   d. TCP/IP software for handling messages between server and clients.
   e. firewall software for security.

7. Strategic benefits of extranet use in business alliances include
   a. increasing the speed of business-to-business transactions.
   b. reducing errors on intercompany transactions.
   c. reducing costs of telecommunications.
   d. increasing the volume of business with partners.
   e. All of these are strategic benefits of business alliances.

8. E-marketplaces use business extranets except to
   a. place orders with each other.
   b. check each other's inventory level.
   c. confirm the status of invoices.
   d. exchange other types of business information.
   e. All of these are uses of business extranets.

9. Which of these is false?
   a. The most successful e-businesses avoid the use of firewalls.
   b. Business-to-business e-commerce generally doesn't work across national boundaries.
   c. eBay is an example of the consumer-to-consumer (C2C) e-commerce model.
   d. In business-to-employee (B2E) e-commerce, an organization uses an intranet to support its internal value chain activities.
   e. Business-to-consumer (B2C) e-commerce is the range of retail transactions between a company and individual customers.

10. Which is not a critical feature of a business-to-consumer (B2C) Web site?
    a. speedy transactions.
    b. large and up-to-date product selection.
    c. flashy technology.
    d. user-friendly interface and customer service.
    e. secure transactions.

REVIEW QUESTIONS

1. Define or describe each of the key terms in the "Key Terms" section. Check your answers using the glossary.

2. Is e-commerce possible without the Internet? Explain your answer.

3. Describe the three forms of e-commerce.

4. What are the purposes of an intranet? What are the main characteristics of an intranet?

5. What are three important ways companies use intranets?

6. What is the purpose of an extranet? What are the main characteristics of an extranet?

7. Describe some of the issues a company must deal with to conduct business with consumers over the Internet successfully.

8. List the capabilities e-commerce software should provide.

9. Describe some ethical issues involved in electronic commerce.

DISCUSSION QUESTIONS

1. Discuss why you believe e-commerce is important in today's business world. What impacts do you think e-commerce is having on consumers?

2. Can you identify examples of e-commerce applications within your college or university? Discuss how your school could use an intranet to improve its internal operations, such as class registration. How could such an intranet be used to competitive advantage for your school?

3. Can you identify opportunities for using an extranet at your college or university? Discuss how your school could form a business alliance with its suppliers (such as book publishers and office suppliers) and use an extranet to conduct its B2B transactions more efficiently? How could such an extranet be used to competitive advantage for your school?

4. Discuss the issues you would need to consider if you were to create a B2C Web site for a small company.

PROJECTS

1. Find an example of a business organization that is using the Internet to increase its competitive advantage in its industry. What competitive strategy is the organization following? Is the Internet being used to decrease costs? Increase value to the customers? Use a word processor to compose a report describing your findings to your teacher.

2. Form a team and visit a local company that has a Web site. Interview the manager and others about the company's Internet philosophy. What is the purpose of the company's Web site? Who designed the site? Who maintains the site? Does the company advertise on the Internet? Does the company use an intranet or extranet? What are the company's plans for its future use of the Internet? Summarize your findings.

3. Create a list of characteristics of a well-designed B2C Web site. Locate the public Web sites of several competitors in the same industry. Then use your list to evaluate the effectiveness of each of the Web sites. Summarize your findings.

4. Visit two Web sites that offer a similar shopping experience—for example, two clothing sites or two bookstore sites. Evaluate how each company handles your security and privacy concerns.

5. Form a team and create a storefront business. When you finish building your store, visit it as a customer and print several of your store's Web pages.

CASE STUDIES

Kroger Online

Kroger Co., the nation's largest grocery chain, has a two-pronged Internet strategy: moving full-force on its e-marketplace to streamline its supply chain, while taking a patient approach on the still unproven business of online grocery sales.

Kroger Chairman and CEO Joseph Pichler wants to find a profitable online shopping formula. "We're not waiting for somebody else to be successful and then jumping on the bandwagon. We are aggressively testing models, but so far we have not found one that meets the test for ROI (return on investment)."

But other Kroger executives like the success of Kroger's B2B strategy. For example, Kroger participated in four GlobalNetXchange auctions, which were used to procure supplies for stores. Kroger became a partner in GNX, joining founders Carrefour Corp. (France), J Sainsbury (U.K.), METRO AG (Germany), Oracle Corp., and Sears, Roebuck & Co.

Kroger execs think the best is yet to come. GNX is now identifying a supply-chain software provider—likely to be Oracle—to provide CPFR (Collaborative Planning, Forecasting and Replenishment) and other supply-chain applications. Kroger expects the exchange's links to suppliers to increase distribution efficiencies and reduce the cost of purchasing food products.

With more than 2,300 supermarkets in 31 states, Kroger is king of the U.S. food-retailing hill. Its $13 billion merger with Fred Meyer stores helped push annual sales to over $43 billion. And while competitors Albertson's and A&P have had disappointing earnings, Kroger's performance only solidified its position.

Like many of its brick-and-mortar competitors, Kroger has just dipped a toe in e-retailing, with only its King Soopers unit in Colorado offering online grocery shopping. Similarly, Albertson's has pilot online programs in the Dallas and Seattle areas.

Adapted from David Lewis, "Kroger Takes Separate Roads to the Internet," September 18, 2000.

Discussion Questions

1. Describe the type of e-commerce model represented by Kroger. How would you describe Kroger's e-commerce strategy?

2. As a food vendor, what advantages or disadvantages are there to being a supplier to Kroger? What are the advantages or disadvantages to Kroger's customers?

3. What competitive advantages or disadvantages does Kroger have compared to its competitors because of its e-commerce strategy?

Foreign Laws Trip Up Another Net Company

Internet companies based in the United States are running into trouble with international laws. A German court ruled that America Online (AOL) is liable for allowing customers to trade pirated music on its service. A similar case in the United States is the recording industry's crusade against music piracy. In a landmark case for the online music industry, Napster is being sued by the Recording Industry Association of America for alleged piracy. Napster's software enables users to share MP3 libraries with others, and RIAA say

Napster is building a business on the backs of artists and copyright owners. The case may help settle whether product manufacturers are liable for the ways in which their products are used.

Although phone companies are protected from liability, if someone uses a phone to harass someone, ISPs are not as well protected against their users' infractions. Under the Digital Millennium Copyright Act, ISPs can be liable if they are notified of copyright infringements but fail to take action. The ruling in Germany against AOL means that online services may have to take more seriously the threat of copyright infringements beyond U.S. borders.

The AOL case isn't the only instance of an Internet company butting heads with international laws. A Bavarian court ruled recently that the former top executive of Compuserve's German subsidiary was not guilty of distributing pornography, because he couldn't have done anything to block access to a number of sites effectively. The executive had been convicted, because customers could use the online service to download child pornography from Internet sites in the United States.

"With the global nature of the Web, when you're doing business on the Internet, you are subject to those laws internationally," commented a Washington, D.C., attorney who specializes in e-commerce and intellectual property law. "The lesson is, make sure you comply."

Based on Kathleen Murphy, "Foreign Laws Trip up Another Net Company," Internet World News, 2(72), April 13, 2000.

Discussion Questions

1. Discuss the information ethics issues in the case.

2. Discuss how you believe information ethics issues differ between the United States and other areas of the world.

3. Discuss the responsibilities, if any, of an ISP to its customers.

Dr Pepper

Dr Pepper Bottling Co. celebrated its 110th anniversary as the oldest operational bottling plant. Dr Pepper/Seven Up Inc., a $1.5 billion division of $7 billion Cadbury Schweppes, is moving away from a classic, if not chaotic, approach to the way its bottlers send data to retailers. It has developed an extranet, named Bottler Hub/Extranet, that automates the communication of pricing data to Dr Pepper's 1,400 independent and franchise bottlers. Dr Pepper's hopes also the extranet will help it keep, if not increase, its 10.6 percent share of the $58 billion soft drink market that is dominated by Coca-Cola Co. and Pepsi Co.

Before deploying Bottler Hub, Dr Pepper/Seven Up bottlers sent voluminous faxes to the main office with pricing,

confirmation updates, and profitability reports. A small platoon of workers fielded the faxes—up to 70,000 per year—and directed them to the intended recipients. Although the bottlers set the pricing, retailers such as Wal-Mart had complained about their approach to faxing weekly price changes. Because many bottlers were mom-and-pop organizations and didn't have the resources to modernize the process, Dr Pepper/Seven Up decided to put in a centralized system that would make the information available online to retail outlets.

Now, a bottler logs into the system with a Web browser, inputs personalized information, such as price changes negotiated with retailers, and sends the information to Dr Pepper/Seven Up. Dr Pepper/Seven Up collects the pricing information from all the bottlers, because large retailers, such as Wal-Mart, don't want 1,400 bottlers coming to them.

Given the limited resources of independent bottlers and Dr Pepper's need to accommodate its retail customers, the extranet is having immediate benefits for all parties. The extranet is also more efficient at handling pricing data for large retailers as well.

The Bottler Hub/Extranet was developed in Java using IBM's VisualAge developer tools. The Java 2 Enterprise Edition components link to Dr Pepper's SAP financial, manufacturing, and enterprise resource planning applications. The applications connect to Unix-based IBM WebSphere application servers.

Dr Pepper/Seven Up has other plans for the extranet too. The company will begin collecting case sales data online, enabling merchants to report how many cases of soda they sell. The data will be used to measure sales growth and to analyze brands and packages that are sold by a bottler within a territory to the major retail chains.

Dr Pepper/Seven Up plans to give its field salespeople Palm-based devices to get real-time information from them. The salespeople will use Handspring Visors to gather data for surveys while they are in the field. The sales data can be used for collaborative planning and demand forecasting.

Adapted from Mike Koller, "Bottler Extranet: Just What Dr Ordered," InternetWeek, May 28, 2001, pp. 49–50.

Discussion Questions

1. Discuss the ways Dr Pepper is using its extranet to compete with other bottlers. How does the extranet give Dr Pepper a strategic advantage, if any?

2. What kinds of business alliances does Dr Pepper's extranet make possible?

3. Discuss some of the problems and risks Dr Pepper faces in further developing its extranet.

4. How would you evaluate the effectiveness of Dr Pepper's extranet?

SOURCES AND RESOURCES

Books

B2B Basics: How to Build a Profitable E-Commerce Strategy, by Michael J. Cunningham (New York: Perseus Publishing, 2001) This book is packed with explanations and a history of the Internet and e-commerce. A good reference to use as a base for building a B2B strategy.

Radical Simplicity: Transforming Computers into Me-Centric Appiances, by Dr. Frederick Hayes-Roth and Daniel Amor (Upper Saddle River, NJ: Prentice Hall, 2003). In this little book Hewlett-Packard alumni discuss the evolution of computer technology, the Internet, and related technologies. They describe many opportunities for e-commerce as a result of this evolution.

Designing Web Usability, by Jakob Nielsen ((Indianapolis, IN: New Riders Publishing, 1999). Creating Web sites that truly meet the needs and expectations of the wide range of online users is not all that simple. The author is a renowned Web-usability guru and he shares his insightful thoughts on Web site design in this highly regarded paperback. The book is packed with annotated examples of actual Web sites and describes many of the design precepts all Web developers should follow.

Bum Rate: How I Survived the Gold Rush Years on the Internet, by Michael Wolff (New York: Simon & Schuster, 1998). The author is the founder of Wolff New Media, a major Internet content provider. He tells his own rags-to-riches tale and shares insights on several Internet pioneers, including AOL head Steve Case and *Wired* magazine founders Louis Rossetto and Jane Metcalfe.

e-Business 2.0: Roadmap for Success, by Ravi Kalakota and Marcia Robinson (Reading, MA: Addison-Wesley, 2001). The authors present a survey of how the processes of business have changed as a result of Internet technologies. The emphasis is on companies that sell things to large numbers of consumers. The authors argue convincingly that information technology isn't an end in itself, but a tool that can facilitate valuable changes in business processes.

Electronic Commerce: A Managerial Perspective, by Efraim Turban, Jae Lee, David King, and H. Michael Chung (Upper Saddle River, NJ: Prentice Hall, 2000). This textbook covers the rapidly changing field of e-commerce, including intranets, extranets, marketing, business-to-business transactions, electronic payment, and more. Case studies and examples supplement the theoretical material.

E-business and E-commerce for Managers, by H. M. Deitel, P. J. Deitel, and K. Steinbuhler (Upper Saddle River, NJ: Prentice Hall, 2001). Deitel and Deitel specialize in textbooks on a wide range of programming topics. This book is aimed at managers rather than programmers. It has lots of useful information about making the Internet into a business tool. Topics range from technical to legal and ethical in nature.

The Essential Guide to Internet Business Technology, by Gail Honda and Kipp Martin (Upper Saddle River, NJ: Prentice Hall, 2002). This book, part of Prentice Hall's popular Essential Guide series, focuses on putting the Internet to work in a business environment. Starting with the basics, this book covers all the important topics in enough depth to provide answers for most business users.

Electronic Commerce, by Gary Schneider and James Perry (Cambridge, MA: Course Technology, 2000). A popular textbook that covers all the important aspects of e-commerce with plenty of actual real-world examples.

Evolve: Succeeding in the Digital Culture of Tomorrow, by Rosabeth Moss Kanter (Cambridge, MA: Harvard Business School Press, 2001). Much has been written about "e-culture," the unique corporate culture created around the Internet. This book aims to help companies successfully incorporate the principles of this new culture, which include nurturing networks of partners, making connections between online and offline employees, and attracting top talent.

Periodicals

There are several periodicals devoted either in whole or in part to electronic commerce topics. Many of these periodicals are available in print and on the Web.

CIO Web Business focuses on management-level information of the Internet economy, e-business strategies, and up-to-date statistics on Web usage. Available on the Web at **www.webbusiness.cio.com**.

Business 2.0 provides practical, interesting, and in-depth information on how to succeed in the Internet age. Available on the Web at **www.business2.com**.

eWeek focuses specifically on issues related to building and maintaining dot com businesses. Available on the Web at **www.eweek.com**.

World Wide Web Pages

The Web has several sites that are valuable resources. The *Computer Confluence* Web site, **http://www.computerconfluence.com**, will help you find them.

AFTER YOU READ THIS CHAPTER YOU SHOULD BE ABLE TO:

- Describe the process of designing, programming, and debugging a computer program

- Explain why there are many different programming languages and give examples of several

- Explain why computer languages are built into applications, operating systems, and utilities

- Outline the steps in the life cycle of an information system and explain the purpose of program maintenance

- Explain the relationship between computer programming and computer science

- Describe the problems faced by software engineers in trying to produce reliable large systems

Multimedia extras on the CD-ROM and the Web:

- Computer Scientist David Gelernter Builds the Future

- **Instant access** to glossary and key word references

- Interactive **self-study quizzes**

    . . . *and more.*

 computerconfluence.com

14

SYSTEMS DESIGN AND DEVELOPMENT

GRACE MURRAY HOPPER SAILS ON SOFTWARE

Amazing Grace, the grand old lady of software, had little to apologize for when she died at the age of 85 in 1992. More than any other woman, Grace Murray Hopper helped chart the course of the computer industry from its earliest days.

Hopper earned a Ph.D. from Yale in 1928 and taught math for 10 years at Vassar before joining the U.S. Naval Reserve in 1943. The Navy assigned her to the Bureau of Ordnance Computation at Harvard, where she worked with Howard Aiken's Mark I, the first large-scale digital computer. She wrote programs and operating manuals for the Mark I, Mark II, and Mark III.

Aiken often asked his team, "Are you making any numbers?" When she wasn't "making numbers," Hopper replied that she was "debuggers/debugging" the computer. Today, that's what programmers call the process of finding and removing errors, or bugs, from programs. Scientists and engineers had referred to mechanical defects as bugs for decades; Thomas Edison wrote about bugs in his inventions in 1878. But when Hopper first used the term, she was referring to a real bug—a 2-inch moth that got caught in a relay, bringing the mighty Mark II to a standstill! That moth carcass is taped to a page in a log book, housed in a Navy museum in Virginia.

Hopper recognized early that businesses could make good use of computers. After World War II she left Harvard to work on the UNIVAC I, the first general-purpose commercial computer, and other commercial computers. She played central roles in the development of the first compiler (a type of computer language translator that makes most of today's software possible) and COBOL, the first computer language designed for developing business software.

Throughout most of her career Hopper remained anchored to the Navy. When she retired from the fleet with the rank of rear admiral at the age of 79, her list of accomplishments filled eight single-spaced pages in her Navy biography.

> The only phrase I've ever disliked is, **"Why, we've always done it that way."** I always tell young people, **"Go ahead and do it. You can always apologize later."**
>
> —Grace Murray Hopper

14.1 Grace Murray Hopper (1906–1992).

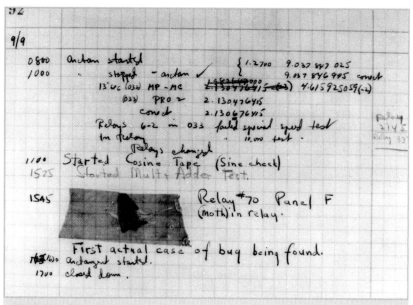

14.2 This moth was one of the first computer bugs—it was removed from a relay in the Mark I.

But Hopper's greatest impact was probably the result of her tireless crusade against the "We've always done it that way" mind-set. In the early days of computing, she worked to persuade businesses to embrace the new technology. In later years, she campaigned to shift the Pentagon and industry away from mainframes and toward networks of smaller computers. Her vigorous campaign against the status quo earned her a reputation as being controversial and contrary. That didn't bother Amazing Grace, whose favorite maxim was "A ship in port is safe, but that's not what ships are for."

Today's computer software is so sophisticated that it's almost invisible to the user. Just as a great motion picture can make you forget you're watching a movie, the best PC software enables you to do your creative work without ever thinking about the instructions and data flowing through the computer's processor as you work. But whether you're writing a paper, solving a calculus problem, flying a simulated space shuttle, or exploring the nooks and crannies of the Internet, your imaginary environment stands on an incredibly complex software substructure. The process of creating that software is one of the most intellectually challenging activities ever done by people.

In this chapter we look at the process of turning ideas into working computer programs and information systems. We'll start by looking at systems design and consider the life cycle of a typical program. We examine computer languages and the ways programmers use them to create software. In addition, we look at how computer users take advantage of the programming languages built into applications, operating systems, and utilities. We also confront the problems involved with producing reliable software and consider the implications of depending on unstable software. In the process of exploring software we'll see how the work of programmers, analysts, software engineers, and computer scientists affects our lives and our work.

How People Make Programs

> It's the only job I can think of where I get to be both an **engineer** and an **artist**. There's an incredible, rigorous, technical element to it, which **I like** because you have to do very **precise thinking**. On the other hand, it has a wildly creative side where **the boundaries of imagination are the only real limitation**.
>
> —Andy Hertzfeld, co-designer of the Macintosh

Most computer users depend on professionally programmed applications—spreadsheets, image-editing programs, Web browsers, and the like—as problem-solving tools. But in some cases it's necessary or desirable to write a program rather than use one written by somebody else. As a human activity, computer programming is a relative newcomer. But programming is a specialized form of the age-old process of problem solving. Problem solving typically involves four steps:

■ **Understanding the problem.** Defining the problem clearly is often the most important—and most overlooked—step in the problem-solving process.

- **Devising a plan for solving the problem.** What resources are available? People? Information? A computer? Software? Data? How might those resources be put to work to solve the problem?
- **Carrying out the plan.** This phase often overlaps with step 2, since many problem-solving schemes are developed on the fly.
- **Evaluating the solution.** Is the problem solved correctly? Is this solution applicable to other problems?

The programming process can also be described as a four-step process, although in practice these steps often overlap:

- Defining the problem
- Devising, refining, and testing the algorithm
- Writing the program
- Testing and debugging the program.

Most programming problems are far too complex to solve all at once. To turn a problem into a program, a programmer typically creates a list of smaller problems. Each of these smaller problems can be broken into subproblems that can be subdivided in the same way. This process, called stepwise refinement, is similar to the process of developing an outline before writing a paper or a book. Programmers sometimes refer to this type of design as top-down design because the design process starts at the top, with the main ideas, and works down to the details.

The result of stepwise refinement is an algorithm—a set of step-by-step instructions that, when completed, solves the original problem. (Recall Suzanne's French toast recipe in Chapter 4.) Programmers typically write algorithms in a form called pseudocode—a cross between a computer language and plain English. When the details of an algorithm are in place, a programmer can translate it from pseudocode into a computer language.

From Idea to Algorithm

Let's develop a simple algorithm to illustrate the process. Let's start with a statement of the problem:

A schoolteacher needs a program to play a number-guessing game so students can learn to develop logical strategies and practice their arithmetic. In this game the computer picks a number between 1 and 100 and gives the player seven turns to guess the number. After each incorrect try, the computer tells the player whether the guess is too high or too low.

> One programs, just as one writes, not because one understands, but **in order to come to understand**. Programming is an act of design. To write a program is to legislate the laws for **a world one first has to create in imagination**.
>
> —Joseph Weizenbaum, in *Computer Power and Human Reason*

In short, the problem is to write a program that can

```
play a guessing game
```

Stepwise Refinement

The first cut at the problem breaks it into three parts: a beginning, a middle, and an end. Each of these parts represents a smaller programming problem to solve.

```
begin game
repeat turn until number is guessed or seven turns are completed
end game
```

These three steps represent a bare-bones algorithm. In the completed algorithm, these three parts are carried out in sequence. The next refinement fills in a few details for each part:

```
begin game
    display instructions
    pick a number between 1 and 100
repeat turn until number is guessed or seven turns are completed
    input guess from user
    respond to guess
end repeat
end game
display end message
```

The middle part of our instructions includes a sequence of operations that repeats for each turn: everything between "repeat" and "end repeat." But these instructions lack crucial details. How, for example, does the computer respond to a guess? We can replace "respond to guess" with instructions that vary depending on the guessed number:

```
if guess = number, then say so and quit;
else if guess < number, then say guess is too small;
else say guess is too big
```

Finally, we need to give the computer a way of knowing when seven turns have passed. We can set a counter to 0 at the beginning and add 1 to the counter after each turn. When the counter reaches 7, the repetition stops, and the computer displays a message. That makes the algorithm look like this:

```
begin game
    display instructions
    pick a number between 1 and 100
    set counter to 0
repeat turn until number is guessed or counter = 7
    input guess from user
    if guess = number, then say so and quit;
    else if guess < number, then say guess is too small;
    else say guess is too big
    add 1 to counter
end repeat
end game
    display end message
```

14.3 Software development has become a global industry. These programmers in India write software for a company based in America.

Control Structures

A computer can't understand this algorithm, but the pseudocode is clear to any person familiar with **control structures**—logical structures that control the order in which instructions are carried out. This algorithm uses three basic control structures: sequence, selection, and repetition.

A sequence control structure is a group of instructions followed in order from the first through the last. In our algorithm example, as in most computer languages, the sequence is the default structure; that is, it applies unless a statement says otherwise:

```
display instructions
pick a number between 1 and 100
set counter to 0
```

A selection (or decision) control structure is used to make logical decisions—to choose between alternative courses of action depending on certain conditions. It typically takes the form of "If (some condition is true), then (do something) else (do something else)":

```
if guess < number, then say guess is too small;
else say guess is too big
```

A repetition control structure is a looping mechanism. It allows a group of steps to be repeated several times, usually until some condition is satisfied. In this algorithm the indented statements between "repeat" and "end repeat" repeat until the number is guessed correctly or the counter is equal to 7:

```
repeat turn until number is guessed or counter = 7
input guess from user
...
add 1 to counter
end repeat
```

As our example illustrates, these simple control structures can be combined to produce more complex algorithms. In fact, any computer program can be constructed from these three control structures.

Testing the Algorithm

The next step is **testing** the algorithm. Testing of the completed program comes later; this round of testing is designed to check the logic of the algorithm. We can test it by following the instructions using different sets of numbers. We might, for example, use a target number of 35 and guesses of 15, 72, 52, and 35. Those numbers test all three possibilities in the if–then–else structure (guess is less than target, guess is greater than target, and guess equals target), and they show what happens if the player chooses the correct number. We should also test the algorithm with seven wrong guesses in a row to make sure it correctly ends a losing game.

From Algorithm to Program

When testing is complete, the algorithm is ready to become a program. Because the algorithm has the logical structure of a program, the process of coding—writing a program from the algorithm—is simple and straightforward. Statements in the algorithm translate directly into lines of code in whichever programming language best fits the programmer's needs.

> You know, computer science **inverts the normal**. In normal science you're given a world and **your job is to find out the rules**. In computer science, you give the computer the rules and **it creates the world**.
>
> —Alan Kay

A Simple Program

Let's look at the algorithm rewritten in C++, a popular variation of the C programming language. (The name C doesn't stand for anything; the language grew out of a less successful language called B.) This program, like most well-written C++ programs, is organized into three parts, similar to a recipe in a cookbook:

1. The program heading, containing the name of the program and data files (equivalent to the name and description of the dish to be cooked)
2. The declarations and definitions of variables and other programmer-defined items (equivalent to the list of ingredients used in the recipe)
3. The body of the program, containing the instructions, sandwiched between curly braces, { } (equivalent to the cooking steps).

The program listing looks a little like a detailed version of the original algorithm, but there's an important difference: Because it's a computer program, every word, symbol, and punctuation mark has an exact, unambiguous meaning.

The words highlighted with italics in this listing are key words with predefined meanings in C++. These key words, along with special symbols like 1 and 5, are part of the stan-

High-level language program statement

Machine-language program translation of statement

Interpreter

14.4 An interpreter translates the source code of a program to machine language one statement at a time. It must repeat this process every time the program is run.

dard vocabulary of C++. The programmer defines the words *number, guess,* and *counter,* so they become part of the program's vocabulary when it runs. Each of these words represents a *variable*—a named portion of the computer's memory whose contents the program can examine and change.

As programs go, this C++ program is fairly easy to understand. But C++ isn't English, and some statements occasionally need clarification or further documentation. For the sake of readability, most programs include comments—the programmer's equivalent of Post-it notes. In C++, lines that begin with double slashes (//) contain comments. The computer ignores comments; they're included to help human readers understand (or remember) something about the program.

Into the Computer

The program still needs to be entered into the computer's memory, saved as a disk file, and translated into the computer's native machine language before it can be executed, or run. To enter and save the program, we can use a text editor. A *text editor* is like a word processor without the formatting features that writers and publishers require. Some text editors, designed with programming in mind, provide automatic program indenting and limited error checking while the program is being typed.

To translate the program into machine language, we need translation software. The translation program might be an **interpreter** (a program that translates and transmits each statement individually, the way a United Nations interpreter translates a Russian speech into English) or a **compiler** (a program that translates an entire program before passing it on to the computer, as a scholar might translate the novel *War and Peace* from Russian to English). Most C++ translators are compilers because compiled programs tend to run faster than interpreted programs.

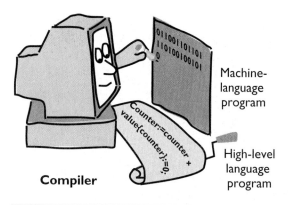

Machine-language program

Counter:=counter + value(counter):=0;

High-level language program

Compiler

14.5 A compiler translates all of the source code of a program to machine language once, before executing the program.

A typical compiler software package today is more than just a compiler. It's an integrated *programming environment,* including a text editor, a compiler, a *debugger* to simplify the process of locating and correcting errors, and a variety of other programming utilities. **Syntax errors**—violations of the grammar rules of the programming language—are often flagged automatically as soon as they're typed into the editor. **Logic errors**—problems with the logical structure that cause differences between what the program is supposed to do and what it actually does—aren't always as easy to detect. That's why debugging and testing can take a large percentage of program development time.

Programming Languages and Methodologies

C++ is one of hundreds of computer languages in use today. Some are tools for professional programmers who write the software the rest of us use. Others are intended to help students learn the fundamentals of programming. Still others enable computer users to automate repetitive tasks and customize software applications. Since the earliest days of computing, programming languages have continued to evolve toward providing easier communication between people and computers.

Programming in C++

SCREEN TEST

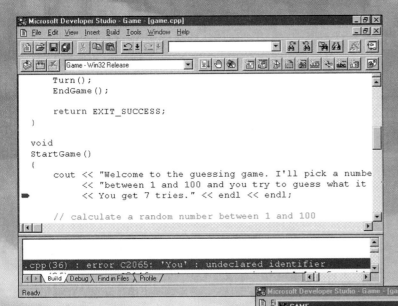

14.6a You decide to convert the algorithm on page 495 into a working program. Once your game program is written, you can type it into the editor window. The editor automatically indents statements as you type, so it's easy to see the logical structure of the program. The editor also points out a syntax error.

14.6b You run the program to test for logic errors. When you test it with a series of incorrect guesses, it fails to stop after seven guesses. And when you correctly guess the answer, it fails to stop but asks you again for a guess.

14.6c You see the logic error in the statement "Counter—", which decrements the counter by 1. It should say "Counter++" to increment the counter by 1. You correct the error and rerun the program to test it again for more errors. Like most programs, this one could go through several rounds of testing, debugging, and refining before the programmer is satisfied.

497

Machine Language and Assembly Language

Every computer has a native language—a **machine language**. Similarities exist between different brands of machine languages: They all have instructions for the four basic arithmetic operations, for comparing pairs of numbers, for repeating instructions, and so on. But like English and French, different brands of machine languages are different languages, and machines based on one machine language can't understand programs written in another.

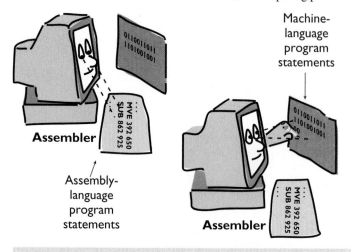

From the machine's point of view, machine language is all binary. Instructions, memory locations, numbers, and characters are all represented by strings of 0s and 1s. Because binary numbers are difficult for people to read, machine-language programs are usually displayed with the binary numbers translated into decimal (base 10), *hexadecimal* (base 16), or some other number system. Even so, machine-language programs have always been hard to write, read, and debug.

The programming process became easier with the invention of **assembly language**—a language that's functionally equivalent to machine language but is easier for people to read, write, and understand. In assembly language, programmers use alphabetic codes that correspond to the machine's numeric instructions. An assembly-language instruction for subtract, for example, might be SUB. Of course, SUB means nothing to the computer, which only responds to commands like 10110111. To bridge the communication gap between programmer and computer, a program called an **assembler** translates each assembly-language instruction into a machine-language instruction. Without knowing any better, the computer acts as its own translator.

14.7 An assembler translates each statement of assembly language source code into the corresponding machine-language statement.

Because of the obvious advantages of assembly language, few programmers write in machine language anymore. But assembly-language programming is still considered low-level programming; that is, it requires the programmer to think on the machine's level and to include an enormous amount of detail in every program. Assembly language and machine language are *low-level languages*. Low-level programming is a repetitive, tedious, and error-prone process. To make matters worse, a program written in one assembly language or machine language must be completely rewritten before it can be run on computers with different machine languages. Many programmers still use assembly language to write parts of video games and other applications for which speed and direct communication with hardware are critical. But most programmers today think and write on a higher level.

High-Level Languages

Computer programming is an art form, like the creation of **poetry** or **music**.
—Donald E. Knuth, author of *The Art of Computer Programming*

High-level languages, which fall somewhere between natural human languages and precise machine languages, were developed during the early 1950s to simplify and streamline the programming process. Languages such as FORTRAN and COBOL made it possible for scientists, engineers, and businesspeople to write programs using familiar terminology and notation rather than cryptic machine instructions. Today, programmers can choose from hundreds of other high-level languages.

Interpreters and compilers translate high-level programs into machine language. Whether interpreted or compiled, a single statement from a high-level program turns into several machine-language statements. A high-level language hides most of the nitty-gritty details of the machine operations from the programmer. As a result, it's easier for the programmer to think about the overall logic of the program—the big ideas.

Besides being easier to write and debug, high-level programs have the advantage of being transportable between machines. A program written in standard C can be compiled and run on any computer with a standard C compiler. The same applies for programs written in Java, Basic, FORTRAN, COBOL, and other standardized languages.

Transporting a program to a new machine isn't always that easy. Most high-level programs need to be partially rewritten to adjust to differences among hardware, compilers, operating systems, and user interfaces. For example, programmers might need to rewrite 20 percent of the code when translating the Windows version of an application program into a Macintosh version, or vice versa. Still, high-level programs are far more portable than programs written in assembly and machine languages.

Of the hundreds of high-level languages that have been developed, a few have become well known because of their widespread use:

- *FORTRAN* (Formula Translation), the first commercial high-level programming language, was designed at IBM in the 1950s to solve scientific and engineering problems. Many scientists and engineers still use modern versions of FORTRAN today.
- *COBOL* (Common Business Oriented Language) was developed when the U.S. government in 1960 demanded a new language oriented toward business data processing problems. COBOL programmers still work in many data processing shops around the world.
- *LISP* (List Processing) was developed at MIT in the late 1950s to process nonnumeric data like characters, words, and other symbols. LISP is widely used in artificial intelligence research, in part because it's easy to write LISP programs that can write other programs.
- *Basic* (Beginner's All-purpose Symbolic Instruction Code; sometimes spelled with all caps: BASIC) was developed in the mid-1960s as an easy-to-learn, interactive alternative to FORTRAN for beginning programmers. Before Basic, a student typically had to submit a program, wait hours for output from a compiler, and repeat the process until every error was corrected. Because Basic was interpreted line-by-line rather than compiled as a whole, it could provide instant feedback as students typed statements and commands into their terminals. When personal computers appeared, Basic enjoyed unprecedented popularity among students, hobbyists, and programmers. Over the years Basic has evolved into a powerful, modern programming tool for amateur and professional programmers. True Basic is a modern version of Basic developed by the original inventors of Basic. The most popular Windows version of Basic today—in fact, the most popular programming language ever created—is Microsoft's *Visual Basic*. REALBasic is a Macintosh-based Basic similar to Visual Basic.
- *Pascal* (named for the seventeenth-century French mathematician, inventor, philosopher, and mystic) was developed in the early 1970s as an alternative to BASIC for student programmers. Pascal was designed to encourage structured programming, a technique described in the next section. Pascal is seldom used by professional programmers.
- *C* was invented at Bell Labs in the early 1970s as a tool for programming operating systems such as UNIX. C is a complex language that's difficult to learn. But its power, flexibility, and efficiency have made it—along with its variants—the language of choice for professionals who program personal computers.
- *C++* is the language we used in our Screen Test example. C++ is a variation of C that takes advantage of a modern programming methodology called object-oriented programming, described later in this chapter.
- *C#* is a popular Windows-only language that's similar to C++.
- *Java* is a modern programming language developed by Sun Microsystems. Java is similar to C++, but simpler to learn and to use. Java excels at producing Web-based applets that run on multiple platforms.
- *J++* is a Java-like language from Microsoft for programming on the Windows platform.
- *ActiveX* is a Microsoft language designed specifically for creating Web components similar to Java applets.
- *Python* is a Java-like language popular with Linux open-source programmers.
- *Ada* (named for Ada King, the programming pioneer profiled in Chapter 1) is a massive language based on Pascal. It was developed in the late 1970s for the U.S. Defense Department. Ada never caught on outside the walls of the military establishment.
- *PROLOG* (Programming Logic) is a popular language for artificial intelligence programming. As the name implies, PROLOG is designed for working with logical relationships between facts.
- *LOGO* is a dialect of LISP specially designed for children.

Structured Programming

We but teach **bloody instructions**, which being taught, return **to plague the inventor**.

—Shakespeare, *Macbeth*

A programming language can be a powerful tool in the hands of a skilled programmer. But tools alone don't guarantee quality; the best programmers have specific techniques for getting the most out of their software tools. In the short history of computer programming, computer scientists have developed several new methodologies that have made programmers more productive and programs more reliable.

For example, computer scientists in the late 1960s recognized that most FORTRAN and BASIC programs were riddled with GoTo statements—statements used to transfer control to other parts of the program. (Remember "Go to Jail. Do not pass Go. Do not collect $200"?) The logical structure of a program with GoTo statements can resemble a tangled spider's web. The bigger the program, the bigger the logical maze and the more possibility for error. Every branch of a program represents a loose end that a programmer might overlook.

Raw data

Processed data

Unstructured programming

14.8 Computer software contains two kinds of information algorithms that correspond to the program code that performs some task, and data, upon which the algorithms operate. The algorithms are the gears and levers in this figure, the machinery that transforms the raw material of data. An unstructured program is like a huge, complicated machine that can't easily be broken down into sections.

In an attempt to overcome these problems, computer scientists developed structured programming—a technique to make the programming process easier and more productive. A structured program doesn't depend on the GoTo statement to control the logical flow. Instead, it's built from smaller programs called modules, or subprograms, which are in turn made of even smaller modules. The programmer combines modules using the three basic control structures: sequence, repetition, and selection. A program is well structured if the following are true:

- ■ It's made up of logically cohesive modules.
- ■ The modules are arranged in a hierarchy.
- ■ It's straightforward and readable.

The Pascal and Ada languages were designed to encourage structured programming and discourage "spaghetti code." The success of these languages prompted computer scientists to develop versions of Basic and FORTRAN that were conducive to structured programming.

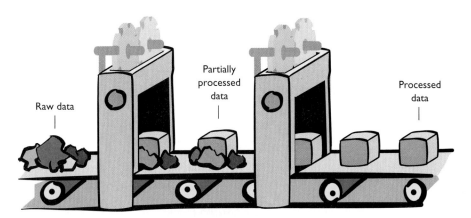

Structured programming

14.9 Structured programming breaks the big complicated machine into more manageable modules, each of which has a clearly defined task. Structured programs are easier to understand and debug because they are logically structured.

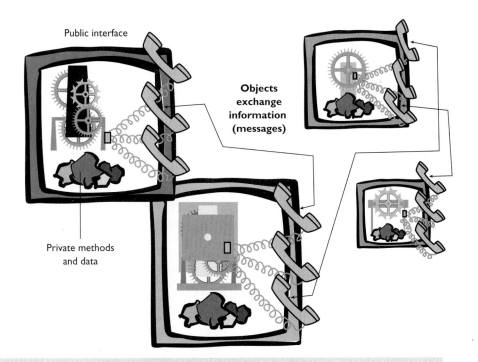

14.10 Object-oriented programming (OOP) binds data with the methods and properties which will act on that data. In OOP, each object contains a small storehouse of data that is appropriate for the object.

HOW IT WORKS

14.1
The Evolution of Basic

The Basic programming language has evolved through three major phases. These examples show how the programming process has changed during the last three decades. The first two Basic examples shown here are complete listings of programs to play the number-guessing game; the third example is a glimpse of a program to play a slot machine game.

1. Early Basic. The program with numbered lines is written in a simple version of Basic—the only kind that was available in the early days of the language. Statements are executed in numerical order unless control is transferred to another statement with a GoTo statement.

```
10 REM INITIALIZE
20 RANDOMIZE
30 PRINT "THE GUESSING GAME"
40 PRINT "I WILL THINK OF A NUMBER BETWEEN 1 AND 100."
50 PRINT "TRY TO GUESS WHAT IT IS"
60 LET C = 0
70 LET N = INT(RND(1) * 100)
80 INPUT "WHAT IS YOUR GUESS?";G
90 IF G = N THEN PRINT "THAT IS CORRECT!"
100 IF G < N THEN PRINT "TOO SMALL--TRY AGAIN"
110 IF G > N THEN PRINT "TOO BIG--TRY AGAIN"
120 LET C = C + 1
130 IF C = 7 THEN GOTO 180
140 IF G <> N THEN GOTO 80
150 IF G <> N THEN PRINT "I FOOLED YOU 7 TIMES! THE ANSWER WAS ";N
160 END
```

14.11a

```
REM Guessing Game
REM written by Rajeev Pandey

DECLARE SUB StartGame (Counter!, Number!)
DECLARE SUB Turn (Counter!, Guess!, Number!)
DECLARE SUB EndGame (Number!)

CALL StartGame(Counter, Number)
DO
     CALL Turn(Counter, Guess, Number)
LOOP UNTIL (Guess = Number) OR (Counter = 7)
IF Guess <> Number THEN
     CALL EndGame(Number)
END IF

SUB EndGame (Number)
PRINT "I fooled you 7 times!"
PRINT "The answer was "; Number
END SUB

SUB StartGame (Counter, Number)
PRINT "Welcome to the guessing game. I'll think of a
number"
PRINT "between 1 and 100 and you will guess what it
is."
Counter = 0
RANDOMIZE TIMER
Number = INT(RND(1) * 100)
END SUB

SUB Turn (Counter, Guess, Number)
INPUT "What's your guess?"; Guess
IF Guess = Number THEN
     PRINT "You got it!"
ELSE
     IF Guess < Number THEN
          PRINT "Too small, try again."
     ELSE
          PRINT "Too big, try again."
     END IF
END IF
Counter = Counter + 1
END SUB
```

14.11b

2. Structured Basic. The modular program on the bottom is written in QuickBASIC, a newer version of the language with many structured programming features. The main program has been reduced to a handful of statements at the top of the listing (after the DECLARE statement); these statements display the overall logic of the program. As it's running, the main program uses CALL statements to transfer control to each of the three subprograms, which take care of the game's beginning, each turn, and the game's end.

3. Visual Basic. The screen shows an example of Microsoft's popular Visual Basic, a modern programming environment that includes many of the ideas and tools of object-oriented programming and visual programming.

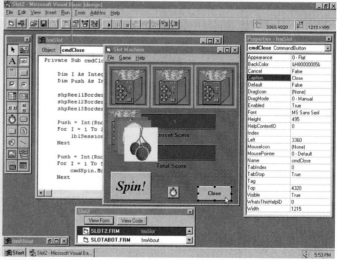

14.11c

Object-Oriented Programming

Structured programming represented a big step forward for programmers; it enabled them to produce better, more reliable programs in less time. But structured pro-

Programmers work the way medieval craftsmen built cathedrals— **one stone at a time**.

—Mitch Kapor

gramming wasn't the last word in programming; today, object-oriented programming (OOP) has captured the attention of the software development community. Object-oriented programming was first used in the 1970s, most notably in a language called Smalltalk. In object-oriented programming, a program is not just a collection of step-by-step instructions or procedures; it's a collection of objects. Objects contain both data and instructions and can

send and receive messages. For example, an onscreen button in a multimedia program might be an object, containing both a physical description of the button's appearance and a script telling it what to do if it receives a mouse-click message from the operating system. This button object can be easily reused in different programs because it carries with it everything it needs to operate.

With OOP technology, programmers can build programs from prefabricated objects in the same way builders construct houses from prefabricated walls. OOP also makes it easy to use features from one program in other programs, so programmers don't have to start from scratch with every new program. The object that sorts addresses in alphabetical order in a mailing list database can also be used in a program that sorts hotel reservations alphabetically.

Smalltalk is still used for object-oriented programming, but today many other languages include object technology. C++, used in our example earlier, is a popular dialect of C that supports object-oriented programming. C++ doesn't contain *visual* objects like icons. On the surface it looks like just another language. But the object-oriented nature of the language enables programmers to write programs built around logical objects rather than procedures. Java has more of an object-oriented design than C++.

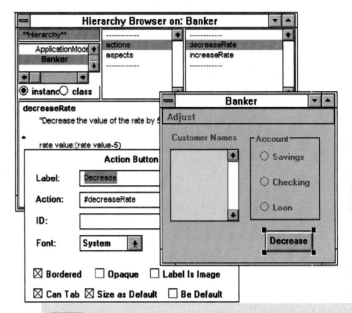

14.12 SmallTalk is the original OOP programming language. The name SmallTalk was used because it was tested on the children at Xerox PARC laboratories.

Object-oriented tools and techniques are becoming common in databases, multimedia authoring tools, and other software environments. Object-oriented programming is particularly well suited for highly interactive programs (such as graphical operating systems, games, and customer transaction stations) and programs that imitate or reflect some dynamic part of the real world (such as simulations and air traffic control systems). Most experts believe that OOP is the wave of the future.

Visual Programming

Many people find it easier to work with pictures instead of words. Visual programming tools enable programmers to create large portions of their programs by drawing pictures and pointing to onscreen objects, eliminating much of the tedious coding of traditional programming. Apple's HyperCard was probably the first popular example of a visual programming environment. HyperCard includes a programming language called HyperTalk, but a HyperCard programmer doesn't need to speak HyperTalk to create working applications.

Today, Microsoft's Visual Basic is widely used by professionals and hobbyists alike because of its visual approach to programming. Visual J++ applies a similar visual approach to Microsoft's Java-like language. Today's visual programming tools haven't completely

14.2
Object-Oriented Programming

The paradigm of structured programming follows the classic view of data as raw material being processed on an assembly line. At some level, all computer programs process data in a mechanistic fashion. But at a higher level, object-oriented programming rejects the assembly line metaphor for another approach.

The fundamental tenet of OOP is that software should be designed using the same techniques that people use to understand and categorize the world around them.

In OOP, a program is designed to consist of a group of objects—each with its own characteristics or attributes (called properties) and actions that it can do (called methods).

Every object has a "public" face: the properties and methods that other objects can see and interact with. Objects also have private methods for their internal use.

In OOP, data is bound together, or encapsulated, with the methods and properties of an object. Each object can maintain its own storehouse of data appropriate for that object.

OOP also relies on the idea of hierarchical categorization of objects to enable programmers to create new objects that are derived from objects that are already defined. The new object can inherit the properties and methods of the object it descends from and add new properties and methods as needed. People have used such hierarchies for centuries in understanding the physical and biological world.

How might all of this work in practice, say, for a graphical operating system? For example, there could be a generic "window" object whose properties included its size, position, color, and so on and whose methods included things like closing and resizing. A more specialized window could be derived from this, for example, a window with scroll bars attached.

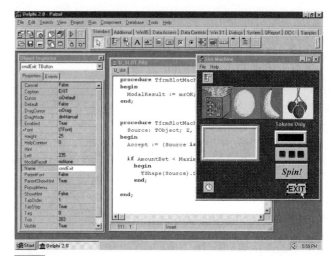

14.13 Delphi is a popular object-oriented development tool based on Pascal.

transformed programming into a visual process; programmers must still understand how to read and write code to create complex programs. But visual programming can save hours of coding time, especially when creating user interfaces—the graphical shells that interact with users. Because they can simplify many of the most difficult parts of the programming process, visual languages make programming more accessible to nonprogrammers.

Languages for Users

Some computer languages are designed with nonprogrammers in mind. They aren't as powerful and versatile as professional programming languages, but they meet the modest needs of specific users.

Macro Languages

Many user-oriented languages are intended to enable users to create programs, called *macros*, that automate repetitive tasks. User-oriented macro languages (also called scripting languages) are built into many applications, utilities, and operating systems. Using a macro language, a spreadsheet user can build a program (a macro) to automatically create end-of-month reports each month by locating data in other worksheets, inserting values into a new worksheet, and calculating results using formulas carried over from previous months. Using an operating system's scripting language, a user might automate the process of making backup copies of all documents created during the last seven days.

Some macro languages require you to design and type each macro by hand, just as you would if you were writing a Basic program. In fact, Microsoft Office includes a scripting variation of Visual Basic called Visual Basic for Applications (VBA). Another type of macro maker "watches" while the user performs a sequence of commands and actions; it then memorizes the sequence and turns it into a macro automatically. The user can then examine and edit the macro so that it performs the desired actions under any circumstances.

Fourth-Generation Languages

Many experts suggest that languages have evolved through four generations: machine language, assembly language, high-level languages, and fourth-generation languages, sometimes called 4GLs. Each generation of languages is easier to use and more like natural language than its predecessors. There's no consensus on exactly what constitutes a fourth-generation language, but these characteristics are most commonly mentioned:

■ 4GLs use English-like phrases and sentences to issue instructions.
■ 4GLs are nonprocedural. Pascal, C, and Basic are procedural languages—tools for constructing procedures that tell the computer how to accomplish tasks. Nonprocedural languages enable users to focus on what needs to be done, not on how to do it.
■ 4GLs increase productivity. Because a 4GL takes care of many of the how-to details, programmers can often get results by typing a few lines of code rather than a few pages.

One type of 4GL is the query language that enables a user to request information from a database with carefully worded English-like questions. A query language serves as a database user interface, hiding the intricacies of the database from the user. SQL (see Chapter 7) is the standard query language for most database applications today. Like most query languages, SQL requires the user to master a few rules of syntax and logic. Still, a query language is easier to master than FORTRAN or COBOL.

Component Software

Recent developments in the software industry may soon result in software that provides users with the kind of power formerly reserved

> When we make a **new tool**, we see a **new cosmos**.
> —Freeman Dyson, physicist

for programmers—and at the same time reverse a long-standing trend toward bloated computer applications. Throughout most of the short history of the personal computer, applications have steadily grown in size as developers add more and more features to their products. Even though no single user needs all of the features in a modern spreadsheet program, every user who buys that program must buy all of the code that provides those features. Many modern applications are so bloated with features that they make huge demands on memory and hard disk space.

Component software tools may reverse the trend toward mega-applications by enabling users to construct small custom applications from software components. Component software isn't completely new; users have been able to add custom components to applications and operating systems for years. Many programs support skins— components designed to customize the way the program looks on the screen. But components aren't just for cosmetic purposes. Dozens of plug-in extensions add features and capabilities to Microsoft Internet Explorer, Adobe Photoshop, QuarkXPress, Macromedia Director, and other popular applications. This customizability is possible only if applications are programmed to allow it. More and more software programs, including operating systems, are designed with extensibility in mind.

Component software is the logical extension of object-oriented programming; it may soon reach a level where users and managers can build their own applications. Instead of buying an everything-but-the-kitchen-sink word processor, you might be able to buy word processor components—spelling checkers, outliners, formatters—based on your individual needs. Components can be distributed through the Internet as well as traditional software channels, so you can quickly download features when you need them. Web services (described in Chapter 10 and 15) are based on the idea of using components to create Web-centered systems and applications.

Extreme Programming

> The best part is to work **side by side** with someone else. It's a very **stimulating environment**, and you don't run into **roadblocks** or **mental blocks**.
>
> —Doug Watt, senior engineer

Extreme programming (XP) is a relatively new programming methodology that focuses more on the culture of programming than on technology. The traditional approach to programming is for a project to be divided among programmers, each of whom is responsible for particular programs or modules. Extreme takes a collaborative approach to application development. The entire programming team "owns" the code; each member of the team has a right to improve it and the responsibility for making it work properly. Extreme programmers work in pairs on projects rather than write code alone. Pair programming reduces the number of individual errors and ensures that more team members are familiar with all aspects of the code. Extreme programming involves close communication with customers and clients; they're considered part of the team. And in spite of its name, extreme programming doesn't involve marathon coding sessions to make deadlines for major releases. Instead, extreme programming emphasizes frequent releases of smaller updates and reasonable (40-hour) work weeks for programmers.

Extreme programming is still outside the norm; its nonhierarchical approach runs counter to many corporate cultures, and it's still too new to have a long history of success stories. But the approach is growing in popularity—especially in organizations that embrace collaboration.

Programming for the Web

Many experts see a future in which PC applications will take a back seat to Web-based applications. Web-based personal information managers, reference tools, and games are steadily growing in popularity. Because of the distributed nature of the Web and the limited bandwidth of many Internet connections, Web-based applications present several challenges for users. Programmers can, and do, use a variety of languages, including C and C++, to write Web applications. But some programming tools are particularly useful for developing Web applications:

- *HTML* is, technically, a page-description language rather than a programming language. HTML commands tell Web browsers how to arrange text, graphics, and multimedia elements on Web pages and how to link those pages. But there are many similarities between HTML coding and program writing, and many popular extensions to HTML take it far beyond the basics of page layout.
- *JavaScript* is an interpreted scripting language that enables Web page designers to add scripts to HTML code. Interpreted JavaScript scripts can add animation, interactivity, and other dynamic content to otherwise static Web pages.
- *VBScript* is Microsoft's answer to JavaScript based on Visual Basic.
- *Java* is a full-featured object-oriented language that's especially popular for creating Web applets—small compiled programs that run inside other applications—typically Web browsers. Java also excels at creating cross-platform applications that run on many different kinds of computers, regardless of operating systems.

- *ActiveX* is a Microsoft language similar in some ways to Java, but without support on all platforms and browsers.
- *Perl* (Practical Extraction and Reporting Language) is an interpreted scripting language that is particularly well suited for writing scripts to process text—for example, complex Web forms. Perl runs on Web servers, not inside a Web browser.
- *XML* is a powerful markup language that overcomes many of the limitations of HTML. XML separates Web page content from layout, so Web pages can be designed to display different ways on different devices. XML is also particularly well suited for creating database-backed Web sites. Many experts expect a combination of XML and HTML to replace HTML as the dominant Web document development tool.

```java
//guessing game program written by Keith Vertanen
import java.util.*;                        // needed for Random class
import java.io.*;                          // needed for BufferedReader class

class guessing_game {

        public static void main(String[] args) throws IOException {

                int number, guess, counter = 0;

                // we need a stdin object to receive input from the user
                BufferedReader stdin = new BufferedReader (new
                        InputStreamReader(System.in));

                System.out.println("Welcome to the guessing game. I'll pick a number");
                System.out.println("between 1 and 100 and you try to guess what it is.");
                System.out.println("You get 7 tries.");
                System.out.println("");

                // create a new random number object
                Random rand = new Random();

                // calculate a random number between 1 and 100
                number = Math.abs(rand.nextInt() % 100) + 1;

                // do this loop for each guess. Leave the loop when the guess is
                // correct or when 7 incorrect guesses have been made
                do {
                        System.out.println("What's your guess?");

                        // allow the user to enter a line of text, convert to an integer
                        guess = Integer.parseInt(stdin.readLine());

                        if (guess == number)
                                System.out.println("You guessed it!");
                        else
                                if (guess < number)
                                else
                                        System.out.println("Too small, try again.");
                                else
                                        System.out.println("Too big, guess again.");
                        ++counter;
                } while ((counter < 7) && (guess!= number));
                if (guess !=number))
                                        System.out.println("I fooled you 7 times - the number
                                                was " + number + "!");
        } // method main
        }
```

14.14 This listing shows the guessing-game program rewritten in Java, a C-like language that runs on a variety of platforms including Windows, Mac OS X, and Linux.

Programs in Perspective: Systems Analysis and the Systems Life Cycle

It has often been observed that we more frequently fail **to face the right problem** than fail **to solve the problem we face.**

—Russell Ackoff, American systems scientist

Programs don't exist in a vacuum. Programs are part of larger information systems—collections of people, machines, data, and methods organized to accomplish specific functions and to solve specific problems. Programming is only part of the larger process of designing, implementing, and managing information systems. In this section we examine that larger process.

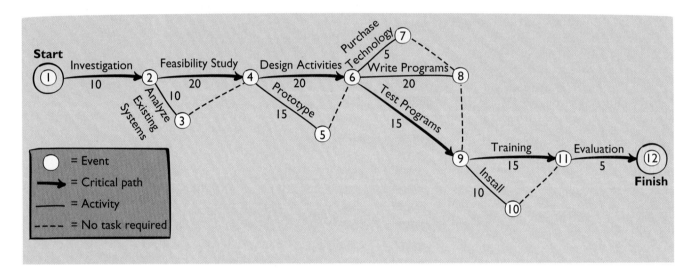

14.15 The critical path through the interconnected activities of a project shows the activities that must be completed on time to finish the whole project on time.

Systems Development

Systems development is a problem-solving process of investigating a situation, designing a system solution to improve the situation, acquiring the human, financial, and technological resources to implement the solution, and finally evaluating the success of the solution.

The systems development process begins when someone recognizes that a problem needs to be solved or an opportunity exists that can be taken advantage of. A typical situation might resemble one of these:

- A mom-and-pop music store needs a way to keep track of instrument rentals and purchases so that billing and accounting don't take so much time.
- A college's antiquated, labor-intensive registration system forces students to endure long lines and frequent scheduling errors.
- A catalog garden-supply company is outgrowing its small, slow, PC-based software system, resulting in shipping delays, billing errors, and customer complaints. At the same time, the company is losing business because competitors now sell on the Web.
- The success of an upcoming oceanographic investigation hinges on the ability of scientists to collect and analyze data instantaneously so the results can be fed into remote-control navigation devices.
- A software manufacturer determines that its PC graphics program is rapidly losing market share to a competitor with more features and a friendlier user interface.
- A small retail store doing business on the Web realizes it can modify its Web site to market to customers internationally.

An organization may face several problems and opportunities, each of which may require the company to develop new IT applications. Each new project requires people, money, and other organizational resources, so a *steering committee* may be formed to decide which projects should be considered first. The steering committee comprises people from each of the a functional areas of the organization.

After the steering committee decides to go ahead with a proposed project, a project team is formed to develop the system. The project team typically includes one or more end users and systems analysts. An **end user** is a person who uses the information system directly or uses the information produced by the system. A **systems analyst** is an IT professional primarily responsible for developing and managing the system.

The systems analyst is usually part of the organization's information systems department. But the business organization may choose to contract, or outsource, the systems analyst from an outside consulting firm. **Outsourcing** avoids the need for permanent in-house staff by allowing the organization to hire talent for selected activities on a contract basis. A growing industry provides outsourced services for specific applications via the Internet. Many U.S. companies outsource across national borders, taking advantage of lower wages in India, China, and other countries.

A project team comprising only end users can develop many small-scale systems without the direct involvement of a professional systems analyst. This systems development approach, called **end-user development**, is popular in organizations where end users have access to and training in the use of Web site development tools, spreadsheet and database management packages, and fourth-generation languages.

The Systems Development Life Cycle

Whether it's a simple, single-user accounting system for a small business or a Web-based, multiuser management information system for a large organization, a system has a life cycle. The **systems development life cycle (SDLC)** is a sequence of seven steps or phases the system passes through between the time it is conceived and the time it is phased out. The phases of the system development life cycle are investigation, analysis, design, development, implementation, maintenance, and retirement.

> The first 90 percent of the task **takes 90 percent** of the time. The last 10 percent **takes the other 90 percent**.
>
> —A systems development proverb

Investigation

The purpose of the *investigation* phase is to study the existing business problem or opportunity and determine whether it is feasible to develop a new system or redesign the existing system if one exists. The project team conducts a feasibility study to identify the nature of the problem or opportunity, to examine the current system to determine how well it meets the needs of the users and the organization, and to assess whether a new or improved information system is a feasible solution.

The project team tries to answer several feasibility questions:

- *Technical feasibility.* Can the required hardware and software be purchased or developed? Is the technology reliable? Does the system have sufficient information-processing capacity to handle the number of individuals who will use the system? Does the system provide for accurate, reliable, and secure data?
- *Economic feasibility.* Will the costs of developing and operating the proposed system be offset by the benefits of using the system? Is the system a good investment? Can sufficient money and personnel resources be committed to complete the system's development on time?
- *Operational feasibility.* Does the proposed system meet the needs of the organization? Are the changes in work procedures required by the proposed system acceptable? Can the proposed system be developed on a timely schedule?
- *Organizational feasibility.* Does the proposed system support the goals and strategy of the organization? Are there any legal implications of the system, such as copyrights, patents, or federal regulations?

Based on its investigation, the project team makes one of three recommendations: leave the current system as is, improve or enhance the current system, or develop an entirely new system. The systems analyst documents the findings of the investigation in a written feasibility report that is presented to the steering committee. Based on the feasibility study, the steering committee decides whether to continue with the analysis phase of the SDLC.

Analysis

During the *analysis* phase, the systems analyst gathers documents, interviews users of the current system (if one exists), observes the system in action, and gathers and analyzes data to understand the current system and identify new requirements—features or capabilities that must be included in the system to meet the needs of the users. The systems analyst identifies the requirements related to each subsystem of the proposed system:

- *Input/output requirements.* The characteristics of the user interface, including the content, format, and timing requirements for data-entry screens and managerial reports
- *Processing requirements.* The calculations, decision rules, data processing capacity, and response time needed
- *Storage requirements.* The content of records and of databases and procedures for data retrieval
- *Control requirements.* The desired accuracy, validity, and security of the system; for example, to prevent data-entry errors and guarantee an easy-to-use, user-friendly system.

The systems analyst documents the work done in the analysis phase in a written functional requirements report. The report explains the current business procedures and how the current system works, identifies the problems with the current procedures and system, and describes the requirements for the new or modified system. The steering committee reviews the requirements report and decides whether to proceed with the design phase of the SDLC.

Design

The investigation phase focuses on why; the analysis phase focuses on what, and the *design* phase focuses on how. In the design phase, the systems analyst develops the system specifications that describe how exactly the system requirements, identified in the analysis phase, will be met. The systems analyst considers important how-to questions in three categories:

- *User interface design.* How will the various outputs of the system be designed? Where will input data come from, and how will it be entered into the system? How will the various windows, menus, and other user–computer dialogue characteristics be designed?
- *Database design.* How will the data elements and structure of the files that compose the database be designed?
- *Process design.* How will the programs and the procedures for the proposed system be designed? Should the system be centralized in a single computer or distributed through a network of desktop computers?

The systems analyst answers these questions, sometimes proposing alternative solutions through a design approach called prototyping. A **prototype** is a limited working system that gives users and management an idea of how the completed system will work. **Prototyping** is an iterative process in which the systems analyst can modify the prototype until it meets the needs and expectations of the

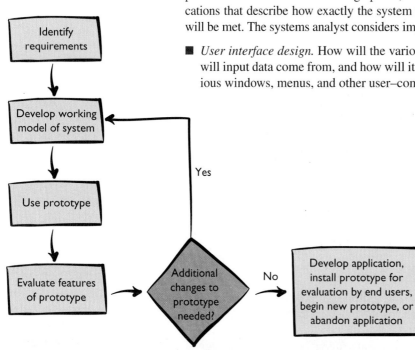

14.16 Prototyping is an interactive methodology in which the prototype is continually modified and improved until it meets the needs of the end users.

organization. Prototyping makes the design phase faster and easier for the systems analyst, especially for systems where the users' requirements are difficult to define. Once the design is acceptable, the systems analyst can fill in the details of the output, input, data files, processing, and system controls.

Prototyping is used widely by companies to develop e-commerce applications quickly, especially for designing the human interface components such as data-entry screens and Web pages. By encouraging end-user involvement in the design phase, prototyping increases the probability the system will satisfy the users' needs.

Development

After the design phase is completed, the actual system development can begin. The *development* phase is a process of turning the design specifications into a real working system. Development includes a complex mix of scheduling; hardware, software, and communications purchasing; documentation; and programming. For most large projects, the development phase involves a team of programmers, technical writers, and clerical people under the supervision of a systems analyst. A large part of the development schedule is devoted to testing the system. Members of the system development team perform early testing to locate and eliminate bugs. This initial testing is known as **alpha testing**. Later potential end users who are willing to work with almost-finished software perform **beta testing** and report bugs to the developers.

Implementation

The *implementation* phase occurs when the testing phase is completed and the new system is ready to replace the old one. For commercial software packages, this phase typically involves extensive training and technical user support to supplement sales and marketing efforts. For large custom systems, implementation includes end-user education and training, equipment replacement, file conversion, and careful monitoring of the new system for problems.

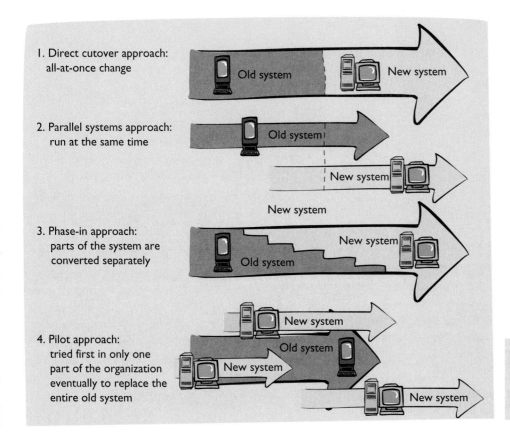

1. Direct cutover approach: all-at-once change
   Old system / New system

2. Parallel systems approach: run at the same time
   Old system
   New system

3. Phase-in approach: parts of the system are converted separately
   New system
   Old system / New system

4. Pilot approach: tried first in only one part of the organization eventually to replace the entire old system
   New system
   Old system / New system
   New system

14.17 The systems analyst must choose carefully the system conversion approach that is best for the organization and the end users.

College registration is a complex system involving hundreds of people and masses of information. A registration system must be solidly designed, carefully maintained, and eventually replaced as the needs of the college change. In this example, we follow systems analysts at Chintimini College as they guide a registration system through a system life cycle.

1. Investigation. Analysts at the college's Information Processing Center identify several problems with the antiquated manual registration system: long lines, frequent scheduling errors, and expensive labor costs. After studying registration systems at other schools, they determine that a registration-by-phone system might be the best solution to these problems.

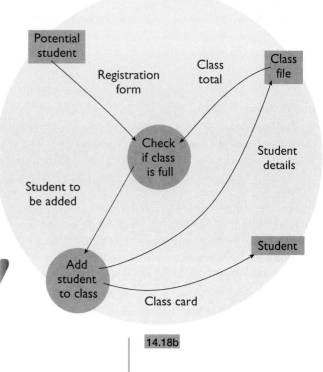

14.18b

14.18a

2. Analysis. Analysts use a *data flow diagram* to illustrate the flow of data through the old registration system. They'll use the information in this diagram to help them develop the new system.

14.18g

7. Retirement. After a few years, the phone registration system has developed problems of its own. The college begins developing a new system that will allow students to register through the Web. When the new Web registration system reaches the implementation phase of its life cycle, the phone-in system is retired.

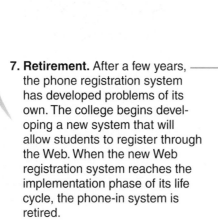

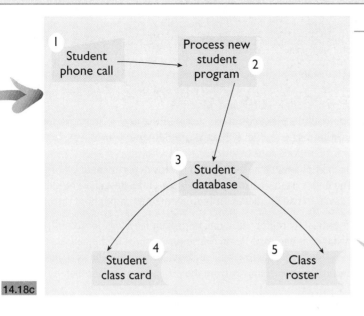

3. Design. Analysts use standard symbols to create a *system flowchart* to show the relationship among programs, files, input, and output in the new system.

1 Student phone call

2 Process new student program

3 Student database

4 Student class card

5 Class roster

14.18c

4. Development. Analysts use a *Gantt chart* to plan the schedule deadlines and milestones for creating the new system.

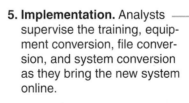

Program specifications
Programming
Unit testing
Documentation
System testing
File conversion
Training

0 1 2 3 4 5 6 7 8 9 10 11 12 13 14 15 16
Weeks

14.18d

5. Implementation. Analysts supervise the training, equipment conversion, file conversion, and system conversion as they bring the new system online.

6. Maintenance. Analysts monitor and evaluate the new system, eliminating problems and correcting bugs as they uncover them.

14.18f

14.18e

The systems analyst can choose one of four approaches for converting to the new system:

- The direct cutover approach simply replaces the old system with the new system. The organization relies fully on the new system with the risk that parts of the new system might not work correctly.
- The parallel systems approach operates the old system along with the new system for a period of time. The old system is gradually phased out as users gain skills and confidence that the new system is stable and reliable.
- The phase-in approach implements subsystems of the new system gradually over a period of time or, alternatively, the system is implemented in only a few departments, branch offices, or plant locations at a time.
- The pilot approach implements the new system in one department or other work site in the organization. The new system is used and modified at this test site until the systems analyst believes the system can be successfully implemented throughout the organization.

End-user training is critical to implementing an information system successfully. During training, clerical and managerial end users learn to use the features of the new system effectively. They learn how to handle problems that may arise when they use the system. The training is often handled by end-user representatives from the project team rather than by technicians.

Maintenance

The *maintenance* phase involves monitoring, evaluating, repairing, and enhancing the system throughout the lifetime of the system. Some software problems don't surface until the system has been operational for a while or the organization's needs change. Systems often need to be adjusted to keep up-to date with new products, services, customers, industry standards, and government regulations. Ongoing maintenance enables organizations to deal with those problems and opportunities for improvement when they arise.

Evaluation is an important aspect of maintenance. The system is evaluated periodically to determine whether it is providing the anticipated benefits and meeting organizational needs. Also, evaluation provides the feedback necessary for management to assess whether the system was developed on schedule and within budget and to identify what adjustments to make in the system development process in the future.

Retirement

At some point in the life of a system, ongoing maintenance isn't enough. Because of changes in organizational needs, user expectations, available technology, increasing maintenance costs, and other factors, the system may no longer meet the needs of the users or the organization and is ready for *retirement*. At that point it's time to phase it out and launch an investigation for a newer system, which begins another round of the systems development life cycle.

Systems Development Tools and Techniques

You can observe a lot by just watching.

—Yogi Berra

Systems analysts use a variety of tools and techniques throughout the systems development life cycle. Some are used to gather data; some are used to describe or design the system's features, procedures, and processes; and others are used to document the system in reports.

Data Collection Techniques

Data collection techniques include document review, interviews, questionnaires, observation, and sampling. These techniques can be used during any phase of the systems development life cycle.

- *Document review.* Typically, a great deal of information about the current system can be found in company documents such as business plans, reports, manuals, correspondence, and systems documentation. The systems analyst can review these documents in the investigation and analysis phases to find out how the current system is designed and how it is supposed to operate.

- *Interview.* Systems analysts interview managers, employees, customers, suppliers, and other people to gather information about business processes and problems and to collect ideas and suggestions for improvement. In a structured interview the systems analyst asks the same questions of each person. In an unstructured interview the systems analyst might vary the questions from person to person.

- *Questionnaire.* The systems analyst can collect information from a large group of people using a questionnaire. Questionnaires are convenient, and respondents can remain anonymous if desired.

- *Observation.* The systems analyst can watch an employee perform a task, or see how people interact with one another, or observe whether procedures work as expected.

- *Sampling.* If the system is large or has many users, the systems analyst can collect data at prescribed time intervals or from a subset of the users. For example, the systems analyst could interview a sample of 10 percent of the users or observe 5 percent of the transactions of a business to get a sense of how well the current system is working.

Modeling Tools

Modeling tools are graphic representations of a system. Many such tools are available, but the modeling tools most widely used by systems analysts are system flowcharts, data flow diagrams, data dictionaries, and decision tables.

- A system flowchart is a graphical depiction of the physical system that exists or is proposed. A system flowchart uses standard symbols to show the overall structure of a system, the sequence of activities that take place in the system, and the type of media or technology used at each step. System flowcharts are used both in the analysis and design phases of the SDLC to show the current system and the design for the proposed system.

- A data flow diagram (DFD) is a simple graphical depiction of the movement of data through a system. A data flow diagram uses symbols to show the movement of data, the processes that use and produce data, the storage of data, and the people or other entities that originate input or receive output from the system. A system-level DFD depicts the entire system in summary form; a level-one DFD expands the processes in the system-level DFD to show more detail. Processes in the level-one DFD can in turn be expanded to show more detail, and so on to an appropriate level of detail.

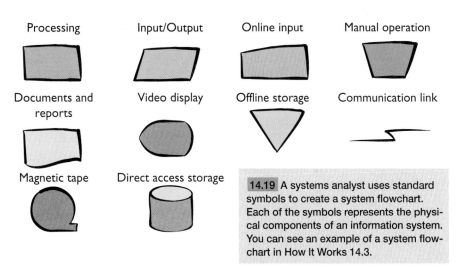

14.19 A systems analyst uses standard symbols to create a system flowchart. Each of the symbols represents the physical components of an information system. You can see an example of a system flowchart in How It Works 14.3.

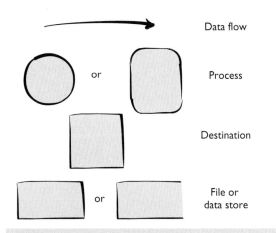

14.20 A systems analyst needs to use only four symbols to create a data flow diagram. You can see how a DFD graphically shows the underlying logical flow of data in a system in How It Works 14.3.

■ A **data dictionary** is a catalog, or directory, that describes all the data flowing through a system. Systems analysts use a data dictionary to keep track of all the system's data elements and data structures. Data elements are the fields stored in the system's databases. A **data structure** refers to a set of data elements used together, such as an invoice or other paper or electronic document.

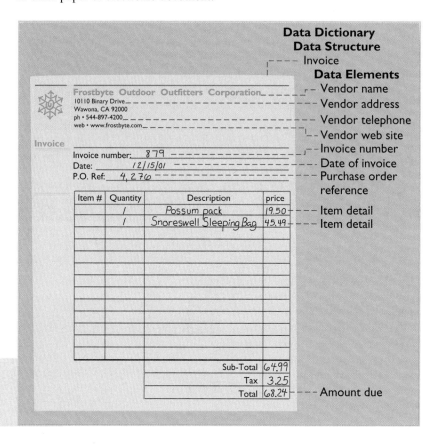

14.21 Data fields in a document can be grouped and represented as data elements and data structures in the data dictionary.

■ A **decision table** shows, in a row–column format, the decision rules that apply and what actions to take when certain conditions occur. A systems analyst can describe and analyze a complex procedure more effectively by constructing a decision table of if–then statements than by writing a complicated narrative of all the possible combinations of conditions and actions.

	Decision rules				
	1	**2**	**3**	**4**	**5**
Conditions If...	No	Yes	Yes	Yes	No
And if...	Yes	Yes	No	Yes	No
And if...	Yes	Yes	No	No	Yes
Actions Then do...	✓				
Then do...			✓		✓
Then do...		✓		✓	

14.22 A decision table shows if–then rules in a tabular format. The upper half of the table includes the if conditions, and the lower half shows the then actions. Each numbered column is a decision rule that shows the action(s) to be taken when certain conditions occur. In a real decision table, the leader dots in the left column would be filled in with information specific to the system.

Computer-Aided Systems Engineering (CASE)

Today, many systems development tools and techniques are included in commercially available software packages referred to as computer-aided systems engineering (CASE). Most CASE tools software packages include

- Charting and diagramming tools to draw system flowcharts and data flow diagrams
- A centralized data dictionary containing detailed information about all the system components
- A user interface generator to create and evaluate many different interface designs
- Code generators that automate much of the computer programming to create a new system or application.

Some CASE software packages contain tools that apply primarily to the analysis and design phases of the systems development life cycle; others contain tools that automate the later phases of systems development, implementation, and maintenance. Integrated CASE tools incorporate the whole spectrum of tools to support the entire systems development life cycle.

The trend today is to run on Internet time with short system development schedules. CASE has an essential niche in the design of large systems. But over the last decade, the tools that worked well migrated out from under the CASE umbrella into other programming tools and suites such as Microsoft's Visual Studio, a development tool suite for building Windows and Web applications, and Microsoft's Visio, an easy-to-use yet powerful charting and diagramming tool. We take a closer look at computer programming in the next section.

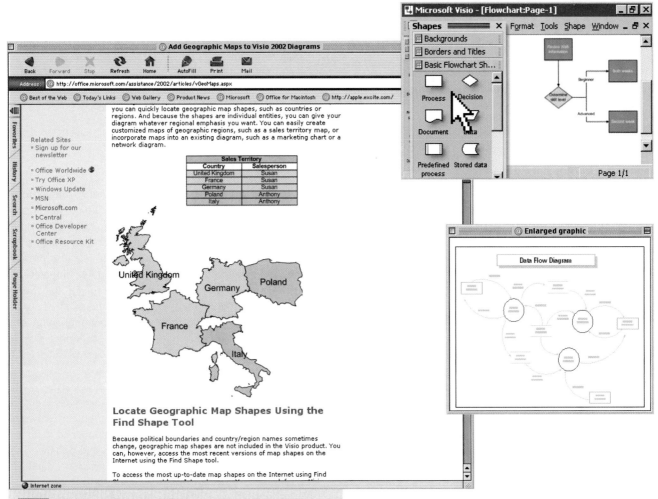

14.23 Systems analysts can use Microsoft Visio® to create data flow diagrams, Gantt charts, and many other types of diagrams useful in systems development work.

Avoiding Information Technology Project Failures

Less than a third of IT projects are completed on time, on budget, and with the promised functionality. The major components of an IT failure are time wasted working on the wrong solution and the potential competitive advantage lost by not working on the right solution. Here are a few tips for information workers to avoid six ways IT projects can fail.

➡ IT projects need executive sponsorship. Many IT projects tend to cut across departments and force a lot of people to change the way they work every day. Such change, if not sold by senior management, can create fear, and every fearful middle manager in every department can create bureaucratic roadblocks that reduce the project's chance to succeed. Make sure the IT projects you are working on have an executive of the company supporting that project.

➡ IT projects need user input. Lack of user input is the most likely factor to characterize a bad IT project. It's important to discuss projects up front with everybody who has a stake in the outcome, including users and customers, business partners, and internal departments on whose cooperation a project's success depends.

➡ IT projects need specifications. If the project requirements aren't well specified up front and the project begins anyway, you have no consensus among stakeholders. A series of meetings and discussions at the beginning of the project will help build consensus on what an IT project can and cannot do.

➡ IT projects need realistic expectations. Undefined expectations frequently lead to dreaded scope creep—in which an initially straightforward technology project is asked to solve more and more problems until it grows bloated and unmanageable. Scope creep, in turn, tends to destroy schedules and eat up resources. Make sure a project management process is in place that explicitly sets expectations and budgets resources.

➡ IT projects need cooperative business partners. Many IT projects involve a vendor of some sort—a software company, a system integrator, or a consultant. When they're wooing you, those companies say they're your partners. But no matter how much they want your project to succeed or how honorable their intentions, they have pressures of their own that may lead to disagreements during the project. Make sure your company negotiates a reasonable and fair contract with the vendor.

➡ IT projects need open and honest communication. Workers don't want to be the bearers of bad news, and senior managers contrive not to hear that news if it is ever delivered. As a result, nobody sounds the alarm on IT projects that have disaster written all over them until it's too late. Make sure you participate in building a culture in your company that values open and honest communication.

The Science of Computing

Telescopes are to astronomy as **computers** are to computer science.

—Edgar Dykstra, computer scientist

We've seen how programmers and systems analysts create and maintain computer programs used by scientists, businesspeople, artists, writers, and others. But just as the rest of us take advantage of the programmer's handiwork, the programmer depends on tools and ideas developed by computer scientists—professionals who work in the academic discipline called computer science. What is computer science, and why is it important in the world of computers?

Because most introductory computer science courses focus on programming, many students equate computer science with computer programming. But programming is little more than a tool in the computer scientist's intellectual toolbox; it has about as much to do with computer science as English grammar has to do with writing novels.

Computer science is a relatively new discipline with ties to electrical engineering, mathematics, and business. Many computer scientists prefer to call the field *computing science* because it focuses on the process of computing rather than on computer hardware. Computing takes a variety of forms, and computer science includes a number of focus areas, ranging from the rarefied world of computer theory to practical nuts-and-bolts work in software engineering. Some areas of specialization within computer science—database management, graphics, artificial intelligence, and networks, for example—provide academic underpinnings for specific categories of computer applications. Other branches of computer science deal with concepts that can apply to almost any type of computer application. These include the following:

- *Computer theory.* The most mathematical branch of computer science, computer theory applies the concepts of theoretical mathematics to computational problems. Theoreticians often work not with real computers but with theoretical computers that exist only in the minds of the theoreticians. As in most fields, many theoretical concepts eventually find their way into practical applications.

- *Algorithms.* Many computer scientists focus on algorithms—the logical underpinnings of computer programs. The design of algorithms can determine whether software succeeds or fails. A well-designed algorithm is not only reliable and free of logical errors but also efficient, so it can accomplish its goals with a minimum of computer resources and time. Computers spend most of their time doing mundane tasks like sorting lists, searching for names, and calculating geometric coordinates. These frequently performed operations must be built on rock-solid, efficient algorithms if a computer system is to be responsive and reliable.

- *Data structures.* If algorithms describe the logical structure of programs, data structures determine the logical structure of data. Data structures range from simple numeric lists and tables (called arrays) to complex relations at the core of massive databases. Computer scientists continue to develop improved techniques for representing and combining different forms of data, and these techniques find their way into all kinds of software.

- *Programming concepts and languages.* As we've seen, programming languages have evolved through several generations in the short history of computers. Thanks to computer scientists in the tradition of Grace Hopper, each new wave of languages is easier to use and more powerful than the one that came before. Programming language specialists strive to design better programming languages to make it easier for programmers to turn algorithms into working software. Computer scientists are also responsible for the development of techniques like structured programming and object-oriented programming—techniques that make programmers more productive and programs more reliable.

- *Computer architecture.* Straddling the boundary between the software world of computer science and the hardware world of computer engineering, computer architecture deals with the way hardware and software work together. How can multiple processors cooperate? How does the bandwidth of a bus affect performance? What are the trade-offs for different storage media? These are the types of questions that concern computer architecture specialists.

- *Management information systems.* Management information systems (MIS) is part computer science, part business. In fact, MIS studies are done in computer science departments at some institutions, in business departments at others, and in MIS departments at others. MIS specialists focus on developing systems that can provide timely, reliable, and useful information to managers in business, industry, and government. MIS specialists apply the theoretical concepts of computer science to real-world, practical business problems.

- *Software engineering.* When an engineer designs a bridge or a building, tried-and-true engineering principles and techniques ensure that the structure won't collapse unexpectedly. Unfortunately, we can't trust software the way we trust buildings; software designers simply don't have the time-honored techniques to ensure quality. Software engineering is a relatively new branch of computer science that attempts to apply engineering principles and techniques to the less-than-concrete world of computer software. We conclude this chapter with a brief look at the problems faced by software engineers—problems that affect all of us.

The State of Software

It's impossible to make anything foolproof, because **fools are so ingenious**.

—Roger Berg, inventor

In spite of advances in computer science, the state of software development is less than ideal. Software developers and software users are confronted with two giant problems: cost and unreliability.

Software Problems

We build our computers the way we build our cities—**over time, without a plan, on top of ruins**.

—Ellen Ullman, software engineer and author of *Close to the Machine*

As computers have evolved through the decades, the cost of computer hardware has steadily gone down. Every year brings more powerful, reliable machines and lower prices. At the same time, the cost of developing computer software has gone up. The software industry abounds with stories of computer systems that cost millions of dollars more and took years longer to develop than expected. Many systems become so costly to develop that their developers are forced to abandon them before completion. Twenty-five percent of commercial software projects are canceled before they are completed. In 2000 these cancellations cots the U.S. economy $60 billion.

But while prices rise, there's no corresponding increase in the reliability of software. Ever since Grace Hopper pulled a moth from the Mark II's relay, bugs have plagued computers, often with disastrous consequences, as you saw in the previous chapter. A recent study found that programmers average 100 to 150 mistakes per 1000 lines of code!

Software errors can take a variety of forms, including errors of omission, syntax errors, logic errors, clerical errors, capacity errors, and judgment errors. But whatever its form, a software error can be devilishly difficult to locate and even more difficult to remove. According to one study 15 to 20 percent of attempts to remove program errors actually introduce new errors!

Software Solutions

The major difference between a thing that might go wrong and a thing that **cannot possibly go wrong** is that when a thing that cannot possibly go wrong goes wrong it usually turns out to be **impossible to get at or repair**.

—Douglas Adams, in *Mostly Harmless*

Computer scientists and software engineers are responding to reliability and cost problems on five main fronts:

■ *Programming techniques.* So far, structured programming and object-oriented programming are the best-known and most successful techniques for increasing programmer productivity and program reliability. Programmers who use these techniques can concentrate on the overall logic of their creations without getting distracted by minute details. The result is less expensive, more reliable software. But these are small steps on a long road toward more dependable programming methodologies. It's too early to tell whether extreme programming and other more modern techniques will take us much farther down that road.

■ *Programming environments.* Today's best programming tools include sophisticated text editors, debuggers, record-keeping programs, and translators, all interwoven into a seamless graphic work environment. A high-quality programming environment can help a programmer manage the complexities of a large project. During the past two decades, CASE tools have emerged, enabling analysts and programmers to automate many of the tedious and error-prone steps involved in turning design specifications into programs. In spite of early promise, CASE tools haven't been widely adopted. Today, the industry is more focused on environments built around component technology that makes it easier to reuse reliable code. In any case, programming environments have a long way to go before they can guarantee reliable software, if that's even possible.

14.24 Thousands of lives depend on reliable functioning of the computers and software used by air traffic controllers.

- *Program verification.* Software engineers would like to be able to prove the correctness of their programs in the same way mathematicians prove the correctness of theorems. Computer scientists have developed program verification techniques that work well for small programs. Unfortunately, these techniques have achieved only limited success with the complex commercial programs people depend on today. There's little hope for automated program verification either. Computer scientists have proven that some problems can't be solved with algorithms, and program verification is one such problem.

- *Clean-room programming.* One new experimental approach to software development is modeled after microchip manufacturing techniques. Clean-room programming combines formal notation, proofs of correctness, and statistical quality control with an evolutionary approach to programming. Programmers grow systems individually, certifying the quality of each before integrating it with the others. It's too early to tell whether this rigorous, engineering-like approach will achieve widespread quality gains, but early tests show some promise.

- *Human management.* Project management techniques from business and engineering have been applied successfully to many software engineering projects. These human management techniques have more to do with person-to-person communication than with programmer-to-machine communication. Because many information system failures result from human communication errors, successful human management can improve a system's overall reliability. But again the benefits of human management methodologies aren't great enough to offset the massive problems facing software engineers today.

Computer scientists have accomplished a great deal in the short history of the field. Software development is easier than it used to be, and computers today can accomplish far more than anyone dreamed a few decades ago. But software engineers have failed to keep up with the fast-paced evolution in computer hardware, and it's still incredibly difficult to produce reliable, cost-effective software. More than a decade ago, computer scientist Ted Lewis summed up the problem in one of his laws of computing. Today, when we're routinely asked to entrust our money, our health, our legal rights, and our lives to software, it's important for all of us to remember that law: "Hardware is soft; software is hard."

The Future of Programming

It could well be that by the close of the twenty-first century, a new form of **truly accessible programming** will be the province of everyone, and will be viewed **like writing**, which was once the province of the ancient scribes but eventually became **universally accessible**.

—Michael Dertouzos, in *What Will Be*

Object-oriented programming. Visual programming. Component software. Distributed Web applications. With these trends gaining momentum, what can we say about the future of programming? It's not clear what programming languages will look like in the future, but three trends seem likely:

➡ *Programming languages will continue to evolve in the direction of natural languages like English.* Today's programming languages, even the best of them, are far too limited and unintelligent. Tomorrow's programming tools should be able to understand what we want even if we don't specify every detail. When we consider artificial intelligence in the next chapter, we deal with the problems and promise of natural language computer communication.

➡ *The line between programmer and user is likely to grow hazy.* As programming becomes easier, there's every reason to believe that computer users will have tools that enable them to construct applications without mastering the intricacies of a technical programming language.

➡ *Computers will play an ever-increasing role in programming themselves.* Today's visual programming environments can create programs in response to user clicks and commands. Tomorrow's programming tools may be able to write entire programs with only a description of the problem supplied by users. The day after tomorrow we may see computers anticipating problems and programming solutions without human intervention!

These three trends come together in the work of some of the pioneers of modern programming. In the 1970s Charles Simonyi developed the first WYSIWYG word processor at Xerox PARC and went on to pilot the development of Word, Excel, and other products as Microsoft's chief architect. Recently, he left Microsoft and started a new company dedicated to creating tools that will make it possible for everyday computer users to write complex software. The goal is to make the code look like the design, so that by simply creating the design a user can write software. According to Simonyi, "Software should be as easy to edit as a PowerPoint presentation."

Simonyi envisions a process called *intentional programming,* which allows programmers to focus on the intention of their programs rather than the technical details of coding. The programmer, who might be an expert in health care, or oceanography, or marketing, might be able to use a modeling language to describe a design to solve a problem; a software generator would then write the actual code automatically based on the design description. The user interface for the modeling language might resemble a PowerPoint palette for some users; it might have a more mathematical look for others.

Another software pioneer, IBM's Grady Booch, is attempting to make it possible for modeling languages to weave security functions into software modeling tools, and to make modeling tools that can build entire systems of programs. Meanwhile, the inventor of Java, James Gosling, is working on a modeling tool at Sun that might accept older programs and make it easier to find logical problems embedded in them.

14.25 Charles Simonyi recently founded Intentional Software to change the way people create software.

14.26 Jet engine turbines wouldn't work if they were hand-crafted because of the inevitable variations introduced during hand work. Turbines are made by precision machines, which in turn are created and maintained by people. Charles Simonyi says software would be more reliable if we could create it with machines called "modeling languages" instead of writing code by hand.

Whatever happens, one thing seems likely: Future programming tools will have little in common with today's languages. When computer historians look back, they'll marvel at how difficult it was for us to instruct computers to perform even the simplest actions. Simonyi is optimistic about the future of software: "Look at what the hardware people have managed to do with Moore's Law. Now it's gong to be software's turn."

Kill the Operating System! Simson Garfinkel

When we think of computer software, we think of Windows, Linux, the Mac OS, and the applications they support. But in this September 2003 column from Technology Review, *Simson Garfinkel argues that we need to start thinking about software like they do in the movies.*

You use Windows, I use a Mac, and we both know people who use GNU/Linux. But for all the differences between these three families of computer operating systems, they implement the same fundamental design; all are equally powerful, and equally limiting.

Virtually every operating system in use today is based on a single computer system architecture developed in the 1960s and '70s. This architecture divides code running on computers into a "kernel," responsible for controlling the computer's hardware, and so-called application programs, which are loaded into the computer's memory to perform individual tasks. Applications, in turn, operate on named files arranged in a tree of folders. True, there are a few niche operating systems that don't adhere to this tripartite structure, but they are but bit players on the digital stage. Even PalmOS has a kernel, apps, and files (which PalmOS mistakenly calls "databases"). It's almost inconceivable that this approach won't be the dominant paradigm for many years to come. And that's a deep problem for the future of computing.

Hollywood, though, has a better idea. When computers show up in good science fiction movies, they rarely have interfaces with windows, icons, applications, and files. Instead, Hollywood's systems let people rapidly navigate through a sea of information and quickly address their needs. Some technical folks scoff at this representation as unrealistic. But why is that so?

Computing's standard model owes its success to the economics of the computer industry. The first computer programs were monolithic systems that talked to the hardware, communicated with users, and got the job done. But soon it became clear that organizations were spending far more money on software, custom software development, and training then they would ever spend on hardware alone. These businesses wanted guarantees that the programs they were creating would run on next year's computer. The only way to assure this was to take all of the hardware-specific code and put it into some kind of "supervisor" program—what we now call the kernel. The supervisor evolved into a kind of traffic cop that could allow multiple programs to run on the same computer at the same time without interfering with one another. That was vital back in the day when a single computer might have dozens of simultaneous users. It's equally important today for people who run dozens of programs simultaneously on their desktop systems.

But you could imagine building computers differently. Movie directors have pointed the way, showing interfaces that appear to make all of the computer's data and power always instantly available. Achieving such flexibility, however, would require us to rethink operating-system dogma. For example, instead of isolating applications from each other—where transferring data between them requires cutting, pasting, and usually reformatting—a hypothetical computer might run all programs at the same time and in the same workspace. Programs might not display information in their own distinct windows, the way they do now; instead, they would work behind the scenes, contributing as needed to a common display.

Most people can't imagine how such a system would work. The idea of editing an Adobe Illustrator document with Microsoft Word seems nonsensical: one program is designed for drawings, the other for words—and besides, they're made by different companies! Yet many Illustrator documents contain blocks of text: why not use Word's superior text-editing capabilities? In our imagined new computer, the boundaries between applications would melt away.

Computer scientists periodically experiment with systems that do away with the software barriers on which today's computers are based, but these systems are rarely successful in the marketplace. Both the Lisp Machine and the Canon Cat encouraged developers to create programs that ran in the same workspace, rather than dividing the computer up into different applications. The Apple Newton stored information not in files but in "soups"—little object-oriented databases that could be accessed by many different programs, even at the same time. The commercial failure of these systems does not vindicate today's way of computing but rather is testimony to just how dangerous the dominant-paradigm trap actually is. Consider files and directories. The hierarchical directory system used by Windows, Mac OS, and Unix made sense to computer pioneers who grew up using paper and filing cabinets. But why limit today's computers with 40-year-old metaphors? Computers have fantastic search capabilities. Some documents logically belong in multiple places; why not eliminate the folders and store all of the computer's information in one massive data warehouse? That's the way computers in the movies seem to work.

It's not such a far-fetched notion. It wouldn't take much to enable today's computers to store every version of every document they have ever been used to modify: most people perform fewer than a million keystrokes and mouse clicks each day; a paltry four gigabytes could hold a decade's worth of typing and revisions if we stored those keystrokes directly, rather than using the inefficient Microsoft Word document format. Alas, the convenient abstractions of directories and files make it difficult for designers to create something different. With a little thought, though, we could do far better. Hollywood has dreamed it; now Silicon Valley needs to make it real

DISCUSSION QUESTIONS

1. What do you think of the author's suggestions about rethinking the fundamental ways computers organize and process our information?

2. Do you have other suggestions for solving the problems outlined here?

SUMMARY

Computer programming is a specialized form of problem solving that involves developing an algorithm for solving a problem. Most programmers use stepwise refinement to repeatedly break a problem into smaller, more easily solvable problems. An algorithm typically is developed in pseudocode, which describes the logic of the program before being translated into a programming language. A translator program—either a compiler or an interpreter—checks for syntax errors (language errors) and, if it finds none, translates the program into machine language so the computer can execute the instructions. Logic errors might not surface until the translated program is run, and maybe not even then. The programming process isn't completed until the program is thoroughly tested for errors.

Computer languages have evolved through several generations, with each generation being easier to use and more powerful than the one that came before. Machine language—the original computer language of 0s and 1s—is primitive and difficult to program. Assembly language uses a translator called an assembler to turn alphabetic codes into the binary numbers of machine language, but in every other way it is identical to machine language.

High-level languages, such as FORTRAN, COBOL, Basic, and C++, are more like English and therefore easier to work with than either machine or assembly language. What's more, they generally can be transported between computers with a minimum of rewriting. Most modern languages encourage structured programming, a technique that involves combining subprograms using only the three fundamental control structures: sequence, selection, and repetition. Structured programming produces programs with fewer logic errors. Still, when program efficiency is critical, many programmers use languages such as C that enable them to work at a lower level of machine logic.

Many applications contain built-in macro languages, scripting languages, and query languages that put programming power in the hands of users. Query languages are representative of fourth-generation languages (4GLs), which are nonprocedural; that is, they enable the programmer to focus on defining the task rather than outlining the steps involved in accomplishing the task. Visual programming tools enable the programmer to use icons, drawing tools, menus, and dialog boxes to construct programs without writing code. Object-oriented programming (OOP) tools enable programmers to construct programs from objects with properties and provide the ability to send messages to each other; many believe that OOP represents the future of programming.

Programs are part of larger information systems. An information system has a life cycle that starts with the initial investigation of the problem; proceeds through analysis, design, development, and implementation phases; and lingers in an ongoing maintenance phase until the system is retired. A systems analyst manages a typical information system with the help of a team of programmers and other computer professionals. Systems analysts use a variety of tools and techniques to help them develop and manage systems, including data collection techniques, modeling tools, and CASE technology.

Computer scientists are responsible for the software tools and concepts that make all other software development possible. Computer science focuses on the process of computing through several areas of specialization, including theory, algorithms, data structures, programming concepts and languages, computer architecture, management information systems, artificial intelligence, and software engineering.

One of the most challenging problems facing computer science is the problem of software reliability. Current software development techniques provide no assurance that a software system will function without failure under all circumstances. As more and more human institutions rely on computer systems, it becomes increasingly important for computer scientists to find ways to make software that people can trust.

KEY TERMS

algorithm (p. 493)
alpha testing (p. 511)
applets (p. 506)
assembler (p. 498)
assembly language (p. 498)
beta testing (p. 511)
C (p. 499)

C++ (p. 499)
coding (p. 495)
compiler (p. 496)
component software (p. 505)
computer-aided system engineering
    (CASE) (p. 517)
computer architecture (p. 519)

computer science (p. 518)
control structures (p. 494)
data dictionary (p. 516)
data flow diagram (p. 512)
data structures (p. 516)
decision table (p. 516)
end user (p. 509)

INTERACTIVE QUIZ QUESTIONS

 1. The *Computer Confluence* CD-ROM contains self-test quiz questions related to this chapter, including multiple-choice, true or false, and matching questions.

 2. The *Computer Confluence* Web site, **www.computerconfluence.com**, contains self-test exercises related to this chapter. Follow the instructions for taking a quiz. After you've completed your quiz, you can email the results to your instructor.

TRUE OR FALSE

1. Programming is a form of problem solving.

2. The final step in programming is the creation of an algorithm.

3. Assembly language and machine language are high-level languages.

4. Visual languages enable the programmer to use icons, drawing tools, menus, and dialog boxes to construct programs without writing code.

5. Managers often find it difficult to make an honest comparison of proposed projects based solely on costs and benefits because of hard-to-measure intangible benefits.

6. The phases of the systems development life cycle (SDLC) are investigation, analysis, design, development, implementation, maintenance, and retirement.

7. Prototyping is a noninteractive methodology in which the prototype is continually modified and improved until it meets the needs of the end users.

8. Computer-aided systems engineering (CASE) software packages are used to automate many routine systems development tasks, create clear documentation, and coordinate efforts, especially in large system projects.

9. Software reliability has increased as the cost of developing computer software has increased.

10. So far, structured programming is the most successful technique for increasing programmer productivity and program reliability.

MULTIPLE CHOICE

1. Which is not a typical part of programming today?
   a. understanding and defining the problem.
   b. writing the computer language.
   c. devising, refining, and testing the algorithm.
   d. writing the program.
   e. testing and debugging the program.

2. To turn a problem into an executable program, the programmer
   a. uses stepwise refinement to repeatedly break the problem into smaller steps.
   b. creates and tests an algorithm—a set of step-by-step instructions.
   c. typically writes algorithms in pseudocode.
   d. translates pseudocode into a computer language.
   e. All of the above are part of programming.

3. Machine language is not
   a. the native language of the computer.
   b. based on binary—strings of 0s and 1s.
   c. commonly used today to write computer programs.
   d. difficult to read and debug errors.
   e. usually displayed in decimal, hexadecimal, or another number system.

4. High-level languages
   a. require considerable rewriting to transport between machines.
   b. are inappropriate for concentrating on the overall logic of programs.
   c. reveal most details of machine operations to the programmer.
   d. use familiar terminology and notation rather than cryptic machine instructions.
   e. are more difficult to work with than either machine or assembly language.

5. In object-oriented programming (OOP),
   a. objects can send and receive messages.
   b. objects can be easily reused in different programs.
   c. objects have everything they need to operate.
   d. programmers can build programs from prefabricated objects.
   e. All of the above are true.

6. Which of the following is not true about software component tools?
   a. Users construct small custom applications from software components.
   b. They can be used only if applications are programmed to allow it.
   c. They may reverse the trend toward mega-applications.
   d. They are the logical extension of object-oriented programming.
   e. All of these statements are true.

7. Which is not a process in systems development?
   a. outsourcing end users and systems analysts.
   b. investigating a situation.
   c. designing a system solution to improve the situation.
   d. acquiring resources to implement the solution.
   e. evaluating the success of the solution.

8. Which is not an implementation approach used when converting to a new system?
   a. direct cutover—replacing the old system with the new system at one time.
   b. parallel—gradually phasing out the old system while running both systems.
   c. RAD—rapid application development.
   d. phase in—partial implementation of parts of the new system.
   e. pilot—implementing the new system at one site and modifying until satisfactory.

9. Modeling tools create graphic representations of a system, and include the
   a. system flowchart—a graphical depiction of the physical system.
   b. data flow diagram (DFD) illustrating the movement of data.
   c. data dictionary—a directory describing all the data flowing through a system.
   d. decision tables showing if–then rules that apply when conditions occur.
   e. All of these are system modeling tools.

10. Software project cancellation in the United States
    a. happens occasionally, but is not particularly costly to the economy.
    b. happens to about one-fourth of all projects and costs billions of dollars a year.
    c. used to be a major problem, but has been almost completely eliminated.
    d. is most often due to security breaches.
    e. none of the above.

REVIEW QUESTIONS

1. Define or describe each of the key terms listed in the "Key Terms" section. Check your Answers using the glossary.

2. Here's an algorithm for directions to a university bookstore from a downtown location:

   - Go south on 4th Street to Jefferson Street.
   - Turn left on Jefferson Street.
   - Proceed on Jefferson past the stoplight to the booth at the campus entrance.
   - If there's somebody in the booth, ask for a permit to park in the bookstore parking lot; otherwise, just keep going.
   - When you reach the bookstore parking lot, keep circling the lot until you find an empty space.
   - Park in the empty space.

   Find examples of sequence, selection, and repetition control structures in this algorithm.

3. Find examples of ambiguous statements that might keep the algorithm in Question 2 from working properly.

4. Assume that Robert, a driver, is going to do the driving in Question 2. Use stepwise refinement to add more detail to Question 2's algorithm so Robert has a better chance of understanding the instructions.

5. Design an algorithm to play the part of the guesser in the number-guessing game featured in this chapter. If you base your algorithm on the right strategy, it will always be able to guess the correct number in seven or fewer tries. (*Hint*: Computer scientists call the right strategy *binary search*.)

6. When does it make sense to design a custom program rather than use off-the-shelf commercial software? Give some examples.

7. Why is structured programming so widely practiced today by software developers?

8. Why are so many computer languages in use today?

9. Assemblers, compilers, and interpreters are all language trRQlators. How do they differ?

10. What is the difference between writing a program and designing an information system? How are they related?

11. What is the relationship between computer science and computer programming?

12. Give examples of several different kinds of computer errors, and describe how these errors affect people.

13. What techniques do software engineers use to improve software reliability?

DISCUSSION QUESTIONS

1. Is programming a useful skill for a computer user? Why or why not?

2. Should programmers be licensed? Is programming a craft, a trade, or a profession?

3. Suppose you want to computerize a small business for a nonprofit organization. What questions might a systems analyst ask when determining what kind of system you need?

4. What do you think programming will be like in 10 years? 20 years? 50 years?

5. Computer science is in the college of science at some universities and in the college of engineering at others. Is computer science a science, a branch of engineering, or both?

6. Why is it so difficult to produce error-free software?

PROJECTS

1. The computer is often blamed for human errors. Find some examples of "the computer did it" errors in newspapers, magazines, or conversations with others. For each example, try to determine whether the computer is, in fact, to blame.

2. Try to determine what safeguards are used to ensure that automated teller machines don't malfunction and that they can't be violated.

3. Find out what safeguards are used to ensure the security of computer systems in your local elections.

SOURCES AND RESOURCES

Books

As you might expect, there are hundreds of books on programming and computer science, most of which are specifically written about particular programming languages and platforms. Most of the books listed here are more general.

Karel++: A Gentle Introduction to the Art of Object-Oriented Programming, by Joseph Bergin, Mark Stehlik, Jim Roberts, and Richard Pattis (New York: Wiley, 1997). This book provides a refreshingly different approach to learning how to program. Instead of immersing yourself in the many details of a full-blown programming language, you can guide Karel the robot through an object-filled robot world. Karel's language is similar to C++ and Java, but simpler and friendlier. The emphasis here is on logic and reasoning rather than calculation. A software simulator is available to accompany the book.

C by Dissection: The Essentials of C Programming, Fourth Edition, by Al Kelley and Ira Pohl (Reading, MA: AddisonWesley, 2000). This text introduces beginners to the C language with lots of "dissected" examples.

Understanding Object-Oriented Programming with Java, by Timothy Budd (Reading, MA: Addison Wesley, 1998). There are dozens of how-to Java books on the market. This text explains the whys as well as the hows of this important new language. Budd uses Java examples to clearly illustrate the concepts of object-oriented programming.

Extreme Programming Explained, by Kent Beck (Reading, MA: Addison Wesley, 1999). This book, written by the owner of a software company, was largely responsible for the extreme programming movement.

The Analytical Engine: An Introduction to Computer Science Using the Internet, by Rick Decker and Stuart Hirshfield (Belmont, CA: ITP, 1998). This well-written, innovative text illustrates many of the concepts of computer science using a Web site to add interactivity.

Computer Science: An Overview, Sixth Edition, by J. Glenn Brookshear (Reading, MA: Addison Wesley, 2000). This excellent survey covers algorithms, data structures, operating systems, and software engineering from a current computer science perspective.

Algorithmics: The Spirit of Computing, by David Harel (Reading, MA: Addison Wesley, 1992). This book explores the central ideas of computer science from basic algorithms and data structures to more advanced concepts.

The New Touring Omnibus: 66 Excursions in Computer Science, by A. K. Dewdney (New York: Computer Science Press, 1993). This unusual book contains 66 short chapters covering a wide range of computer science topics, from algorithms to VLSI computers. Much of the material is technical and mathematical, but the writing is clear and engaging.

Dynamics of Software Development, by Jim McCarthy (Redmond, WA: Microsoft Press, 1995). A lifelong software developer offers advice in the form of rules (like "Don't flip the bozo bit") for shipping software on time. The book is filled with anecdotes and war stories from the front lines of software development.

The Mythical Man-Month: Essays on Software Engineering, Anniversary Edition, by Frederick P. Brooks, Jr. (Reading, MA: Addison Wesley, 1995). This classic, often-quoted book outlines clearly the problems of managing large software projects. This twentieth-anniversary edition includes four new chapters that provide an up-to-date perspective.

Computers Ltd: What They Really Can't Do, by David Harel (Oxford: Oxford University Press, 2000). As the title suggests, this book explores the limits of computer power in particular and human knowledge in general.

Rescuing Prometheus: Four Monumental Projects That Changed Our World, by Thomas P. Hughes (New York: Vantage Books, 1999). This book profiles four of the biggest technological projects of the last century. These projects forced their developers to push the limits of systems design.

Out of Their Minds: The Lives and Discoveries of 15 Great Computer Scientists, by Dennis Shasha and Cathy Lazere (New York: Copernicus, 1998). The people profiled in this book were responsible for many of the most important ideas in computer science today. The profiles illuminate their achievements through interviews and explanations; technical details are confined to boxes so they don't interrupt the flow of the human stories. Closing sections explore two questions: What do these people have in common, and where is the field of computer science heading in the next quarter century?

Web Pages

Check the *Computer Confluence* Web site at **www.computer confluence.com** for links to the Association for Computing Machinery (ACM) and other sites that cover material related to this chapter.

AFTER YOU READ THIS CHAPTER YOU SHOULD BE ABLE TO:

- Explain the two basic approaches of artificial intelligence research

- Describe several hard problems that artificial intelligence research has not yet been able to solve

- Describe several practical applications of artificial intelligence

- Explain what robots are and give several examples illustrating what they can—and can't—do.

 Multimedia extras on the CD-ROM and the Web:

- Daniel Dennett on **Minds and machines**

- **Instant access** to glossary and key word references

- Interactive **self-study quizzes**

    . . . *and more.*

 computerconfluence.com

15

IS ARTIFICIAL INTELLIGENCE REAL?

ALAN TURING, MILITARY INTELLIGENCE, AND INTELLIGENT MACHINES

Alan M. Turing, the British mathematician who designed the world's first operational electronic digital computer during the 1940s, may have been the most important thinker in the history of computing. While a graduate student at Princeton in 1936, Turing published "On Computable Numbers," a paper that laid the theoretical groundwork for all of modern computer science. In that paper, he described a theoretical *Turing machine* that could read instructions from punched paper tape and perform all the critical operations of a computer. The paper also established the limits of computer science by mathematically demonstrating that some problems simply cannot be solved by any kind of computer.

After receiving his doctorate in 1938, Turing had an opportunity to translate theory into reality. Anticipating an invasion by Hitler's forces, the British government assembled a team of mathematicians and engineers with the top secret mission of cracking the German military code. Under the leadership of Turing and others, the group built Colossus, a single-purpose machine regarded by many today as the first electronic digital computer. From the time Colossus was completed in 1943 until the end of the war, it successfully cracked Nazi codes—a fact concealed by the British government until long after the war ended.

Many experts believe that Colossus was ultimately responsible for the defeat of the Nazis.

Turing effectively launched the field of artificial intelligence (AI) with a 1950 paper called "Computing Machinery and Intelligence." In this paper, he pro-

> The extent to which we regard something as **behaving in an intelligent manner** is determined as much by **our own state of mind and training** as by the properties of the object under consideration.
>
> —Alan Turing

posed a concrete test for determining whether a machine was intelligent. In later years, Turing championed the possibility of emulating human thought through computation. He even co-wrote the first chess-playing program.

Turing was an unconventional and extremely sensitive person. In 1952 he was professionally and socially devastated when he was arrested and injected with hormones for violation of British anti-homosexuality laws.

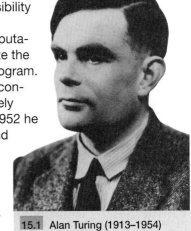

15.1 Alan Turing (1913–1954)

The 41-year-old genius apparently committed suicide in 1954, years before the government made his wartime heroics public. Four decades after his death, Turing's work still has relevance to computer scien-

15.2 Colossus, 1945.

tists, mathematicians, and philosophers. The architecture of today's computers is built on Turing's ideas. The highest award in computer science, the Turing Award, bears his name. It's impossible to know what he might have contributed had he lived through those decades.

Alan Turing spent much of his short life trying to answer the question "Can machines think?" That's still a central question of **artificial intelligence (AI)**, the field of computer science devoted to making computers perceive, reason, and act in ways that have, until now, been reserved for human beings. But today even those who believe that computers can't "think" have to admit that AI research has produced impressive results: computers that can communicate in human languages; systems that can provide instant expertise in medicine, science, and other fields; world-class electronic chess players; and robots that can outperform humans in a variety of tasks. In this chapter we explore the technology, applications, and implications of artificial intelligence.

Thinking About Thinking Machines

What is intelligence, anyway? It is only a word that people use to name those **unknown processes** with which our brains **solve problems we call hard**. But whenever you learn a skill yourself, you're **less impressed or mystified** when other people do the same. This is why the meaning of "intelligence" **seems so elusive**: It describes not some definite thing but only the momentary **horizon of our ignorance** about how minds might work.

—Marvin Minsky, AI pioneer

If you ask 10 people to define intelligence, you're likely to get 10 different answers, including some of these:

- The ability to learn from experience
- The power of thought
- The ability to reason
- The ability to perceive relations
- The power of insight
- The ability to use tools
- Intuition.

Intelligence is difficult to define and understand, even for philosophers and psychologists who spend their lives studying it. But this elusive quality is, to many people, the characteristic that sets humans apart from other species. So it's not surprising that controversy has continually swirled around the questions "Can a machine be intelligent?" and "Can a machine think?"

Can Machines Think?

A **machine** may be deemed **intelligent** when it can **pass for a human being** in a blind test.

—Alan Turing

In his landmark 1950 paper, Alan Turing suggested that the question "Can machines think?" was too vague and philosophical to be of any value. To make it more concrete, he proposed an "imitation game." The **Turing test**, as it came to be known, involves two people and a computer. One person, the interrogator, sits alone in a room and types questions into a computer terminal. The questions can be about anything—math, science, politics, sports, entertainment, art, human relationships, emotions— anything. As answers to questions appear on the terminal, the interrogator attempts to guess whether those answers were typed by the other person or generated by the computer. By repeatedly fooling interrogators into thinking it is a person, a computer can demonstrate intelligent behavior. If it acts intelligent, according to Turing, it is intelligent.

Turing did not intend this test to be the only way to demonstrate machine intelligence; he pointed out that a machine could fail and still be intelligent. Even so, Turing believed that machines would be able to pass his test by the turn of the century. So far, no computer has come close, in spite of 40 years of AI research. While some people still cling to the Turing test to define artificial intelligence, most AI researchers favor less stringent definitions.

> Hello, Earth person!

> Hello there judge, are you ready to have some fun?

Interrogator

15.3 In the Turing test, a human interpreter types statements and questions into a terminal and tries to guess which contestant is human, based on the answers given.

What Is Artificial Intelligence?

This definition from a 1977 edition of a textbook is similar to definitions that commonly appear in today's popular press. This type of definition captures the general idea of artificial intelligence, but it breaks down

> **Artificial intelligence** is the study of ideas which enable computers to do the **things that make people seem intelligent**.
> —Patrick Henry Winston, in *Artificial Intelligence*

when applied to specific examples. Does AI include doing lightning-fast calculations? Finding a word in a dictionary as fast as a person can type it? Remembering hundreds of telephone numbers at a time? If a person could do all of these things, that person would "seem intelligent." But these activities aren't good examples of artificial intelligence because they're trivial for computers. In fact, many computer scientists believe that if it's easy to do with a computer, it can't be artificial intelligence. Here's a more recent textbook definition that reflects that point of view:

According to this definition, artificial intelligence is a moving frontier. The short history of the field bears this out. In the 1950s, many AI researchers struggled to create

> **Artificial intelligence** is the study of how to make computers do things at which, **at the moment, people are better**.
> —Elaine Rich, in *Artificial Intelligence*

computers that could play checkers and chess. Today, computers can beat the best human players, and relatively few AI researchers study these games. In the words of one researcher, artificial intelligence is "whatever hasn't been done yet." Moving-frontier definitions of AI tend to be accurate, but they're short on specifics. A more concrete and complete definition might combine Rich's definition with this one from the *latest* edition of Winston's popular textbook:

> **Artificial intelligence** is the study of the computations that make it possible to **perceive, reason,** and **act**.
> —Patrick Henry Winston, in *Artificial Intelligence*

Perceive, *reason*, and *act* are words used more commonly in psychology, the science of human behavior, than in computer science. In fact, psychologists work alongside computer scientists on many AI research projects. Computer scientists tend to be motivated by the challenge of producing machine intelligence for its own sake. Psychologists, on the other hand, are interested in AI because it provides new insights into natural intelligence and the workings of the human brain.

These points of view symbolize two common approaches to AI. One approach attempts to use computers to simulate human mental processes. For example, an AI expert might ask people to describe how they solve a problem and attempt to capture their answers in a software model.

The simulation approach has three inherent problems:

- Most people have trouble knowing and describing how they do things. Human intelligence includes unconscious thoughts, instantaneous insights, and other mental processes that are difficult or impossible to understand and describe.
- There are vast differences between the structure and capabilities of the human brain and those of the computer. Even the most powerful supercomputers can't approach the brain's ability to perform **parallel processing**—breaking a complex job into many smaller, simpler jobs and completing those jobs simultaneously.
- The best way to do something with a machine is often very different from the way people would do it. Before the Wright brothers, dozens of inventors failed to produce flying machines because they tried to make their inventions imitate birds. Similarly, many early AI attempts failed because they were designed to mimic human intelligence rather than to take advantage of the computer's unique capabilities.

The second, more common, approach to AI involves designing intelligent machines independent of the way people think. According to this approach, human intelligence is just one possible kind of intelligence. A machine's method of solving a problem might be different from the human method but no less intelligent.

Whichever approach they take, scientists face problems that are difficult and far too complex to solve all at once. Most AI researchers choose to break those problems into smaller problems that are easier to solve—to create programs that can function intelligently when confined to limited *domains*.

15.4 Many early flying machines that imitated birds never got off the ground.

Opening Games

One of the first popular domains for AI research was the checkerboard. Much early AI work focused on games like checkers and chess because they were easy to represent in the computer's digital memory, they had clearly defined rules, and the goals were unmistakable. Instead of struggling with nebulous issues surrounding thought and intelligence, game researchers could focus on the concrete question "How can I create a program that wins consistently?" Their answers included many AI techniques that are still used today in a variety of applications:

- *Searching*. One way to win a game is through *searching*—looking ahead at the possibilities generated by each potential move: "I have four possible moves—A, B, C, and D. If I do A, then my opponent might do X, Y, or Z. If my opponent responds by doing X, then I can do E, F, G, or H . . . and so on." Obviously, high-speed computers are better at this kind of repetitive processing than people. Early AI programs could not check all possible decision points in a complicated game like checkers, which has approximately

10^{21} choices. Today's powerful computers can perform massive database searches quickly, making this kind of look-ahead searching practical for some game-playing programs. Researcher Jonathan Schaeffer's checker-playing program uses an enormous database of board positions to evaluate every move. The program plays as well as the best human players in the world. It uses what's known as a *brute-force* technique—rapidly repeating a simple operation until an answer is found. This kind of exhaustive searching doesn't fit many definitions of intelligence. For more complex games like chess, and for most domains outside of the world of games, the staggering number of decision points makes brute-force searching impractical. So searching is generally guided by a planned strategy and by rules known as heuristics.

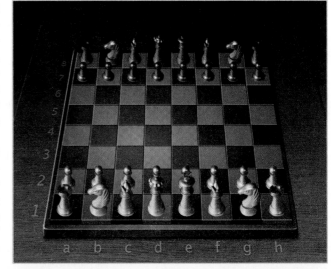

■ *Heuristics.* A **heuristic** is a rule of thumb. Unlike hard-and-fast algorithms, heuristics guide us toward judgments that experience tells us are likely to be true. In everyday life we apply heuristics such as "To loosen a stuck jar lid, run warm water over it." A checker-playing program might employ a heuristic that says, "Keep checkers in the king's row as long as possible."

■ *Pattern recognition.* The best human chess and checkers players remember thousands of critical board patterns and know the best strategies for playing when those or similar patterns appear. Game-playing programs recognize recurring patterns, too, but not nearly as well as people do. Computer players often have trouble identifying situations that are similar but not identical. Pattern recognition is probably the single biggest advantage a human game player has over a computer opponent; it helps compensate for the computer's speed and thoroughness at searching ahead.

■ *Machine learning.* The best game-playing programs learn from experience using **machine learning** techniques. If a move pays off, a learning program is more likely to use that move (or similar moves) in future games. If a move results in a loss, the program will remember to avoid similar moves.

15.5 Home computer programs like Chess for Mac OS X (top) use many of the same techniques employed by Deep Blue, the IBM supercomputer that beat world chess champion Garry Kasparov (bottom).

Today a $40 program can turn a personal computer into a chess wizard. Computer systems can hold their own against the best human chess players by examining hundreds of thousands of moves per second. When IBM's Deep Blue, a customized RS/6000 SP supercomputer, beat grand master Garry Kasparov in a 1997 rematch, people all around the world watched with a level of interest that's seldom given to scientific work.

Still, most AI researchers have moved on to more interesting and practical applications. But whether working on vision, speech, problem solving, or expert decision making, researchers still use the successful strategy of game researchers—to restrict the domain of their programs so that problems are small enough to understand and solve. We'll see how this strategy has paid off in several important areas of AI, starting with natural language communication.

Natural Language Communication

Language is **no less complex or subtle** a phenomenon than the **knowledge** it seeks to transmit.

—Raymond Kurzweil, in *The Age of Intelligent Machines*

In Turing's classic test of machine intelligence, the computer is considered to be intelligent if it can successfully pose as a person in a typed conversation. Since the earliest days of computing, scientists have dreamed of machines that could communicate in natural languages like English, Russian, and Japanese. Over the years natural language communication has continually challenged researchers. Many problems relate to recognizing and reproducing human speech—issues we deal with later in the chapter. But even when it's typed directly into the machine, natural language text poses significant software challenges.

Machine Translation Traps

One early project attempted to create a program that could translate scientific papers from Russian to English and from English to Russian. Automatic translation offered hope for increased communication between scientists during the tense Cold War years. The method seemed straightforward and foolproof: A parsing program (or parser) would analyze sentence structure and identify each word according to whether it was a subject, verb, or other part of speech; another program would look up each word in a translation dictionary and substitute the appropriate word.

After spending 15 years and millions of dollars on research, scientists abandoned the project. Even with the help of human editors, machine translators couldn't compete with humans in speed and accuracy. A typical translation correctly processed only about 80 percent of the desired text.

The automatic translation project became the target of jokes that, if not strictly factual, were effective at pointing out the problems of machine translation. In one famous story, scientists asked the computer to translate English into Russian and then translate the results back into English. As the story goes, "The spirit is willing, but the flesh is weak" came back as "The wine is agreeable, but the meat is rotten" and "out of sight, out of mind" became "blind and insane" or "invisible idiot."

This early translation project may not have lived up to its promoters' expectations, but it taught them a valuable lesson: Translation without understanding is impossible. To translate a sentence accurately, the translator must know what the sentence means.

Conversation without Communication

Similar lessons emerged from Joseph Weizenbaum's work with ELIZA, one of the first software programs to converse in a limited form of natural language. Weizenbaum, an MIT professor, designed ELIZA in the 1960s to simulate the role of a therapist in a typed conversation with a patient. A sample ELIZA session follows on page 535 (the computer's responses are capitalized).

As impressive as this dialog seems, there's no understanding here. ELIZA uses a few simple tricks to *simulate* understanding, including recognizing a few key words (like *mother*), identifying categories for some of those words (*family*), and repeating phrases from earlier in the conversation. But ELIZA's tricks are far from foolproof. In response to "Necessity is the mother of invention," ELIZA might say, "Tell me more about your family." An ELIZA session can easily deteriorate into nonsense dialog laced with grammatical errors and inappropriate responses. Clearly, ELIZA lacks the understanding to pass as a human in a Turing test.

Men are all alike.
IN WHAT WAY
They're always bugging us about something or other.
CAN YOU THINK OF A SPECIFIC EXAMPLE
Well, my boyfriend made me come here.
YOUR BOYFRIEND MADE YOU COME HERE
He says I'm depressed much of the time.
I AM SORRY TO HEAR YOU ARE DEPRESSED
It's true. I am unhappy.
DO YOU THINK COMING HERE WILL HELP YOU NOT TO BE UNHAPPY
I need some help, that much seems certain.
WHAT WOULD IT MEAN TO YOU IF YOU GOT SOME HELP
Perhaps I could learn to get along with my mother.
TELL ME MORE ABOUT YOUR FAMILY
My mother takes care of me.
WHO ELSE IN YOUR FAMILY TAKES CARE OF YOU
My father.
YOUR FATHER
You are like my father in some ways.
WHAT RESEMBLANCE DO YOU SEE
You are not very aggressive but I think you don't want me to notice that.
WHAT MAKES YOU THINK I AM NOT VERY AGGRESSIVE
You don't argue with me.
WHY DO YOU THINK I DON'T ARGUE WITH YOU
You are afraid of me.
DOES IT PLEASE YOU TO BELIEVE I AM AFRAID OF YOU
My father is afraid of everybody.
WHAT ELSE COMES TO MIND WHEN YOU THINK OF YOUR FATHER
Bullies.
DOES THAT HAVE ANYTHING TO DO WITH THE FACT THAT YOUR BOYFRIEND MADE YOU COME HERE

From *Computer Power and Human Reason*, by Joseph Weizenbaum.

15.6 A conversation with ELIZA.

Nonsense and Common Sense

Years after ELIZA's creation this poetry appeared in *The Policeman's Beard Is Half Constructed*, the first book ever written by a computer. RACTER, like ELIZA, produced English language output without really understanding it. Why do machines that flawlessly follow

> Bill sings to Sarah, Sarah sings to Bill. Perhaps they will do **other dangerous things** together. They may eat lamb or stroke each other. They may chant of **their difficulties and their happiness**. They have **love** but they also have **typewriters. That is interesting**.
>
> —A poem by RACTER, in *The Policeman's Beard Is Half Constructed*,
> programmed by William Chamberlain and Thomas Etter

instructions written in Basic, C++, and other computer languages have so much trouble with *natural language* communications?

Part of the problem is the massive vocabulary of natural languages. A typical computer language has less than a hundred key words, each with a precise, unambiguous meaning. English, in contrast, contains hundreds of thousands of words, many of which have multiple meanings. Of course, a person or a machine doesn't need to understand every word in the dictionary to communicate successfully in English. Most natural language processors work with a *subset* of the language. But as the early scientific translation efforts showed, restricting vocabulary isn't enough.

Every language has a syntax—a set of rules for constructing sentences from words. In a programming language, the syntax rules are exact and unambiguous. Natural language parsing programs have to deal with rules that are vague, ambiguous, and occasionally contradictory. One early parser, when asked to analyze the sentence "Time flies like an arrow," replied with several possible interpretations, including one statement with time as the subject, another statement with flies as the subject, and two commands in which the reader was the subject!

Still, computers are far more successful dealing with natural language syntax than with semantics—the underlying meaning of words and phrases. In natural language, the meaning of a sentence is ambiguous unless it's considered in context. "The hens were ready to eat" means one thing if it follows "The farmer approached the hen house" and something else if it follows "The chef approached the oven." To make matters worse, human conversations are filled with idiomatic expressions ("Susan had a cow when she heard the news") and unspoken assumptions about the world or specific subject matter ("Catch the T at Harvard Square and take it to MIT"). In short, the computer lacks what we call *common sense*—the wealth of knowledge and understanding about the world that people share.

The most successful natural language applications limit the *domain* so that virtually all relevant information can be fed to the system. If the domain—the "world"—is small enough and the rules of that world are clear and unambiguous, a computer can have "common sense" that makes natural language communication possible. For example, many database query languages accept and understand English commands but only within a narrow range. The biggest market for natural language processing today is language translation—the same market that produced AI's first major failure. Several Web sites offer on-the-fly translation of text files or Web pages. (One of the most popular is Alta Vista's Babel Fish, named for the universal translator fish in Douglas Adams's *Hitchhiker's Guide to the Galaxy*.) Translation programs still can't translate books or conversations flawlessly, but they can greatly increase the productivity of people who translate technical manuals and other works that focus on narrow domains.

Natural language processing has come a long way since ELIZA's early conversations. Computers still can't pass the Turing test, but they can at least fool some of the people some of the time. Or so it seems, based on the results of the Loebner Prize Competition, devoted to finding a winner of the Turing test. In the first of these annual competitions, held in 1991, 10 untrained judges tried to determine which of the eight entries were human by carrying on typed conversations via terminals. Because the contest organizers believed that any computer would be trounced in an open-ended Turing test, they included rules to protect the entrants from unrestricted questioning. Here's a short sample of a dialog between a judge and the winning entry, a program called PC Therapist. The PC-based program, which took three years to write, played the role of a jester and made occasional typing errors so it would appear more human. It worked: 5 of the 10 judges thought PC Therapist was a person.

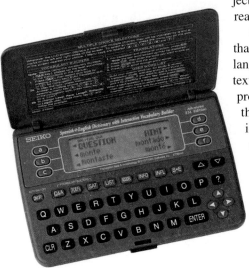

15.7 Inexpensive pocket electonic translators serve world travelers by providing instant access to common words but not whole sentences.

01:32:25	Judge 6	Hello, earth person!
01:33:03	Terminal 5	Hello there judge, are you ready to have some fun? How ya doin, judge? Hello—how's the weather up there today?
01:33:35	Judge 6	Dark clouds with occasional bursts of sunshine (or rather camera flashes).
01:34:45	Terminal 5	The trouble with the rat race is that even if you win you're still a rat. Whimsy can be flimsy, right? How important is that to you?
01:35:26	Judge 6	Can't say I understand the question . . . but the whimsy of a poet is one thing and the whimsy of most of us is another.
01:36:51	Terminal 5	How do you know you can't say you understand the question . . . but the whimsy of a poet is one thing and the whimsy of most of us is another.
01:37:37	Judge 6	Are you repeating me just for laughs?
01:38:04	Terminal 5	I'm sorry, I do sometimes repeat myself . . . perhaps it's because I can't find my electronic organizer!

Reprinted from *AI Magazine*, Summer 1992.

15.8 A conversation with PC Therapist.

Natural language processing relates to other AI technologies discussed later in the chapter. Speech recognition and optical character recognition provide input to natural language systems, freeing the human communicator from the keyboard. On the output side, speech synthesis allows the computer to talk back in English or another language. But natural language input and output are meaningless without a knowledge base that allows the computer to understand the ideas behind the words.

Knowledge Bases and Expert Systems

A preschool child can take you on a tour of the neighborhood, explaining how people use every building, describing the interconnected lives of every person you meet, and an-

> The computer can't tell you the **emotional story**. It can give you the exact mathematical design, but **what's missing is the eyebrows**.
> —Frank Zappa

swering questions about anything you see along the way. A computer at city hall can give you facts and figures about building materials and assessed values of houses, but it can't provide you with a fraction of the knowledge conveyed in the child's tour. The human brain, which isn't particularly good at storing and recalling facts, excels at manipulating *knowledge*—information that incorporates the *relationships* among facts. Computers, on the other hand, are better at handling data than knowledge. Nobody knows exactly how the brain stores and manipulates knowledge. But AI researchers have developed, and continue to develop, techniques for representing knowledge in computers.

Knowledge Bases

While a database contains only facts, a knowledge base also contains a system of rules for determining and changing the relationship among those facts. Facts stored in a database are rigidly organized in categories; ideas stored in a knowledge base can be reorganized as new information changes their relationships.

Computer scientists so far have had little success in developing a knowledge base that can understand the world the way a child does. Even before they start school, children know these things:

- If you put something in water, it will get wet.
- If Susan is Mark's sister, Mark is Susan's brother.
- You can't build a tower from the top down.
- Dogs commonly live in houses, but cows seldom do.
- People can't walk through walls.
- If you eat dinner in a restaurant, you're expected to pay for the food and leave a tip.
- If you travel from Dallas to Phoenix, time passes during the trip.

These statements are part of the mass of common-sense knowledge that children acquire from living in the world. Because computers can't draw on years of human experience to construct mental models of the world, they don't automatically develop common sense. Much AI research centers on providing computers with ways to acquire and store real-world, common-sense knowledge. Researchers have had little success at developing computer systems with the kinds of broad, shallow knowledge found in children. But when knowledge bases are restricted to narrow, deep domains—the domains of experts—they can be effective, practical, intelligent tools. For example, knowledge bases lie at the heart of hundreds of expert systems used in business, science, and industry.

Artificial Experts

An **expert** is one who knows **more and more** about **less and less**.

—Nicholas Murray Butler

As the quote suggests, an expert is someone who has an extraordinary amount of knowledge within a narrow domain. By confining activities to that domain, the expert achieves mastery. An **expert system** is a software program designed to replicate the decision-making process of a human expert. At the foundation of every expert system is a knowledge base representing ideas from a specific field of expertise. Because it's a collection of specialized knowledge, an expert system's knowledge base must be constructed by a user, an expert, or a knowledge engineer—a specialist who interviews and observes experts and painstakingly converts their words and actions into a knowledge base. Some new expert systems can grow their own knowledge bases while observing human decision makers doing their jobs. But for most expert systems the process is still human-intensive.

Strictly speaking, expert systems derive their knowledge from experts; systems that draw on other sources, such as government regulations, company guidelines, and statistical databases, are called knowledge-based systems. But in practice, the terms *expert system* and *knowledge-based system* are often used interchangeably.

A knowledge base commonly represents knowledge in the form of if-then rules like these:

- If the engine will not turn over and the lights do not work, then check the battery.
- If checking the battery shows it is not dead, then check the battery connectors.

Most human decision making involves uncertainty, so many modern expert systems are based on fuzzy logic. *Fuzzy logic* allows conclusions to be stated as probabilities (e.g., "There's a 70 percent chance . . .") rather than certainties. Here's an example from MYCIN, one of the first expert systems designed to capture a doctor's expertise:

```
If (1) the infection is primary bacteremia, and
   (2) the site of the culture is one of the sterile sites, and
   (3) the suspected portal of entry of the organism is the gas-
   trointestinal tract, then there is suggestive evidence (0.7) that
   the identity of the organism is bacteriodes.
```

Along with the knowledge base, a complete expert system also includes a human interface, which enables the user to interact with the system, and an inference engine, which puts the user input together with the knowledge base, applies logical principles, and produces the requested expert advice.

Sometimes expert systems aid experts by providing automated data analysis and informed second opinions. In other cases, expert systems support nonexperts by providing advice based on judgments of one or more experts. Whatever their role, expert systems work because they function within narrow, carefully defined domains.

Expert Systems in Action

Some of the first successful expert systems were developed around medical knowledge bases. Because medical knowledge is orderly and well documented, researchers believed it could be captured successfully in knowledge bases. They were right. The MYCIN medical expert system outperformed many human experts in diagnosing diseases. Dozens of other working medical expert systems exist, although few are actually used in medical practice.

The business community has been more enthusiastic than the medical community in its acceptance and use of expert systems. Here are a few examples of expert systems in action:

15.9 This expert system leads the user through the process of diagnosing problems with malfunctioning cameras.

■ XCON, one of the most successful expert systems in commercial use today, has been configuring complex computer systems since it was developed at Digital Equipment Corporation in 1980. The system's knowledge base consists of more than 10,000 rules describing the relationship of various computer parts. It reportedly does the work of more than 300 human experts, and it makes fewer mistakes than humans do. (In 1998 Digital was purchased by PC manufacturer Compaq, in large part because of Digital's strong track record in configuring, maintaining, and troubleshooting complex systems. In 2002 Compaq merged with Hewlett Packard, a former rival of Digital.)

■ American Express uses an expert system to automate the process of checking for fraud and misuses of its no-limit credit card. Credit checks must be completed within 90 seconds while the customer waits, and the cost of an error can be high. The company spent 13 months developing a system modeled on the decision-making expertise of its best credit clerks.

■ At Blue Cross/Blue Shield of Virginia an expert system automates insurance claim processing. The expert system handles up to 200 routine claims each day, allowing human clerks to spend more time on tough situations that require human judgment. The developers of the system extracted diagnostic rules from manuals and watched human claims processors apply those rules.

■ Boeing Company factory workers use an expert system to locate the right parts, tools, and techniques for assembling airplane electrical connectors. The system replaces 20,000 pages of documentation and reduces the average search time from 42 to 5 minutes.

There are hundreds of other examples of expert system applications: pinpointing likely sites for new oil explorations, aiding in automobile and appliance repairs, providing financial management advice, targeting direct-mail marketing campaigns, detecting problems in computer-controlled machinery, predicting weather, advising air traffic controllers, suggesting basic page layouts for publishers, controlling military machinery, providing assistance to musical composers. . . . The list is growing at an astounding rate. You can even think of the grammar checkers built into many word processors as expert systems, because they apply style and syntax rules developed by language experts. Expert systems are available on the Web for doing everything from classifying whales and insects to conducting sophisticated Web searches.

One of the most unusual expert systems is AARON, an automated artist programmed by Harold Cohen, artist and professor at the University of California at San Diego. AARON uses more than 1,000 rules of human anatomy and behavior to create drawings of people, plants, and abstract objects with a robotic drawing machine. The drawings, which are unique works in a style similar to Cohen's, are widely acclaimed in the art community. A version of AARON is now available as a PC screen saver; it fills idle time on the PC by drawing original art on the screen.

When AARON creates a drawing, an interesting question arises: Who is the artist, Cohen or AARON? Cohen claims he is; he sees AARON as a dynamic work of art. The question may seem frivolous, but it's related to a larger question with profound implications: When expert systems make decisions, who's responsible? If a doctor uses an expert system to decide

15.10 Harold Cohen's AARON produces drawings like the image above. In the photo below, Cohen demonstrates AARON to curious onlookers.

to perform surgery and the surgery fails, who's liable—the doctor, the programmer, the software company, or somebody else? If you're denied medical benefits because of a bug in an expert system, do you sue a person, an organization, or a program? If a power plant explodes because an expert system fails to detect a fault, who's to blame? As expert systems proliferate, questions like these are certain to confront consumers, lawyers, lawmakers, and technicians.

Expert Systems in Perspective

From the following examples it should be clear that expert systems offer many advantages. An expert system can perform these tasks:

- Help train new employees
- Reduce the number of human errors
- Take care of routine tasks so workers can focus on more challenging jobs
- Provide expertise when no experts are available
- Preserve the knowledge of experts after those experts leave an organization
- Combine the knowledge of several experts
- Make knowledge available to more people.

But expert systems aren't without problems. For one, today's expert systems are difficult to build. To simplify the process, many software companies sell expert system shells—generic expert systems containing human interfaces and inference engines. These programs can save time and effort, but they don't include the part that is most difficult to build—the knowledge base.

Even with a knowledge base, an expert system isn't the machine equivalent of a human expert. Unlike human experts, automated expert systems are poor at planning strategies. Their lack of flexibility makes them less creative than human thinkers. Most importantly, expert systems are powerless outside of their narrow, deep domains of knowledge. While most expert system domains can be summarized with a few hundred tidy rules of thumb, the world of people is full of inconsistencies, special cases, and ambiguities that could overwhelm even the best expert systems. A simple rule like "birds can fly" isn't sufficient for a literal-minded computer, which would need something more like this tongue-in-cheek rule from Marvin Minsky's book, *Society of Mind*:

> *Birds can fly, unless they are penguins and ostriches, or if they happen to be dead, or have broken wings, or are confined to cages, or have their feet stuck in cement, or have undergone experiences so dreadful as to render them psychologically incapable of flight.*

Clearly, knowledge engineers can't use rules to teach computers all they need to know to perform useful, intelligent functions outside narrow domains. If they're ever going to exhibit the kind of broad-based intelligence found in children, AI systems need to acquire knowledge by reading, looking, listening, and drawing their own conclusions about the world. These skills all depend on techniques of pattern recognition.

Pattern Recognition: Making Sense of the World

Experience has shown that science frequently develops most fruitfully once we learn to examine the **things that seem the simplest**, instead of **those that seem the most mysterious**.
—Marvin Minsky

A baby can recognize a human face, especially its mother's, almost from birth. A mother can hear and recognize her child's cry even in a noisy room. Computers are notoriously inferior at both of these tasks, which fall into the general category of pattern recognition. Pattern recognition involves identifying recurring patterns in input data with the goal of understanding or categorizing that input.

Pattern recognition applications represent half of the AI industry. Applications include face identification, fingerprint identification, handwriting recognition, scientific data analysis, weather forecasting, biological slide analysis, surveillance satellite data analysis, robot vision, optical character recognition, automatic voice recognition, and expert systems. We next examine the problems and the promise of several types of pattern recognition, starting with the recognition of visual patterns.

Image Analysis

Image analysis is the process of identifying objects and shapes in a photograph, drawing, video, or other visual image. It's used for everything from colorizing classic motion pictures to piloting cruise missiles. An effortless process for people, image analysis is extremely demanding for computers. The simple process of identifying objects in a scene is complicated by all kinds of factors: masses of irrelevant data, objects that partially cover other objects, indistinct edges, changes in light sources and shadows, changes in the scene as objects move, and more. With all of these complications it's amazing that people are able to make any sense out of the images that constantly bombard their eyes.

Until recently, image analysis programs required massive amounts of memory and processing power. But today's PCs are capable of running image processing software with practical applications. For example, security programs enable PCs with video cameras to recognize faces of valid users with a high degree of reliability.

Still, today's software can't hold a candle to the human visual system when it comes to general image analysis. But AI researchers have had considerable success by restricting the domain of visual systems. One of the biggest success stories in AI work is a limited but practical form of computer vision: optical character recognition.

15.11 This Mars rover robot (left) is equipped with visual and tactile sensors that employ pattern recognition technology. Mei Mei (right) is a waiter robot at a Chinese restaurant in Japan. It uses infrared sensors to move to tables to deliver water and menus.

Optical Character Recognition

Optical character recognition (OCR), discussed in Chapter 3, is far from perfect. But it has progressed to the point that the U.S. Postal Service can use it to sort much of the mail sent every day. Similar technology is available for PC users who have typewritten or printed text that they want to process.

The first step in general OCR is to scan the image of the page into the computer's memory with a scanner, digital camera, or fax modem. The scanned image is nothing more than a pattern of bits in memory. It could just as easily be a poem by Robert Frost or a photograph

15.12 A child can easily sort these letters into A's and B's. This problem is difficult for computers, however. Why?

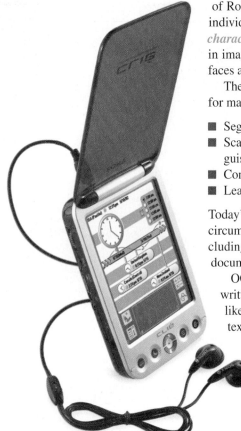

of Robert Frost. Before a computer can process the text on a page, it must recognize the individual characters and convert them to text codes (ASCII or the equivalent). *Optical character recognition (OCR) software* locates and identifies printed characters embedded in images—it "reads" text. This is no small task for a machine, given the variety of typefaces and styles in use today.

The process of recognizing text in a variety of fonts and styles is surprisingly difficult for machines. State-of-the-art OCR programs use several techniques, including these:

- Segmentation of the page into pictures, text blocks, and (eventually) individual characters
- Scaled-down expert system technology for recognizing the underlying rules that distinguish letters
- Context "experts" to help identify ambiguous letters by their context
- Learning from actual examples and feedback from a human trainer.

Today's best programs can achieve up to 99 percent accuracy—even better under optimal circumstances. It's reliable enough to be practical for many text-intensive applications, including reading aloud to the blind, converting typewritten documents and incoming fax documents to editable text, and processing transactions for database systems.

OCR technology also can be applied to handwritten text, but not as reliably. In typewritten and typeset text, character representation is consistent enough that one *a* looks like another *a*, at least when they're the same typeface. But because most handwritten text lacks consistency, software has more trouble recognizing individual characters reliably. Nonetheless, the technology is getting better all the time, making more applications practical for pen-based computers. Handwriting recognition is especially important in Japan, China, and other countries with languages that don't lend themselves to keyboarding. But it's also useful with Western languages in situations where keyboarding isn't practical. Some professionals use tablet PCs, which can recognize characters written directly on the screen with a stylus. Even the classic three-ring student notebook may eventually have an electronic counterpart that automatically turns handwritten notes into text that can be fed directly into a word processor.

15.13 The Palm OS used in popular handheld computers can't recognize handwriting but it can recognize characters written in block style. This capability allows Palm OS users to communicate with their handhelds using only a stylus.

Automatic Speech Recognition

Our ears process far less information than our eyes, but that information, especially human speech, is extremely important to our understanding of the world. In Chapters 3 and 7 we discussed audio digitizers—input devices that capture spoken words, music, and other sounds so they can be stored as digital data. But digitized voice input, like scanned text, must be processed by sophisticated software before a computer can interpret it as words. **Automatic speech recognition** systems, discussed in Chapters 3 and 5, use pattern recognition techniques similar to those used by vision and OCR systems, including these:

- Segmentation of input sound patterns into individual words and phonemes
- Expert rules for interpreting sounds
- Context "experts" for dealing with ambiguous sounds
- Learning from a human trainer.

Training is especially important in speech recognition because of the tremendous differences among human voices. But voice recognition systems with *speaker independence*— the ability to recognize speech without being trained to a speaker—are becoming more common, making speech recognition practical for more applications.

Speech recognition systems are used by factory workers and others whose hands are otherwise occupied while they use the computer. American Airlines' PEGASUS enables customers to make reservations automatically by speaking to a computer over the telephone. Similar systems allow automated banking, credit card verification, and other remote applications. Several companies offer Web browsers and plug-ins that enable Internet users to navigate Web pages by talking to them. Speech recognition systems empower many disabled users by enabling them to give verbal commands to computers and robotic devices. PC software companies have developed programs that enable standard word processors to accept spoken input—both text and formatting commands. IBM researchers have combined speech recognition with a camera for tracking gestures, so users can point while they speak commands like "Move this paragraph up to here." Many of today's researchers are working to combine speech recognition and natural language understanding in a single machine that can accept commands in everyday spoken English, *Star Trek* style.

Talking Computers

It's easier for machines to speak passable English than to recognize it. There are many applications for voice output, including preschool education, telephone communication, navigation guidance systems in cars, and reading machines for visually impaired computer users.

Many computer applications speak like humans by playing prerecorded *digitized speech* (along with other *digitized sounds*) stored in memory or on disk. For an application with a limited vocabulary (reciting telephone numbers for automated directory assistance) or limited choices (an interactive educational game with short prerecorded speeches), digitized speech is practical and reliable.

Recorded speech won't work for applications in which the text to be spoken is unpredictable, such as a talking word processor, because all the sounds must be prerecorded. These types of applications require *text-to-speech* conversion—the creation of *synthetic speech* by converting text files into phonetic sounds. With *speech synthesis* software or hardware, PCs can recite anything you can type, but with voices that sound artificial and robotic. Human spoken language is complex and difficult to duplicate with software, but researchers are making great strides in improving synthetic voice quality. In 2001 AT&T Labs introduced Natural

15.14 Voice recognition software can make PC applications accessible to people who can't use a keyboard as an input device.

Voices Text-to-Speech Engine, a speech synthesizer with a close-to-human voice. This product is unusual in that it can be customized to imitate any human "voice talent" (with only a slight robotic accent). This type of product could close the gap between recorded speech and synthetic speech. It may soon be possible, for example, to play interactive games that use celebrity voices to read text typed by players. As the technology improves, it will raise questions about legal rights—can a TV network use an actor's voice to say things the actor never really said? It will also raise questions about fraud and believability. One potential client for Natural Voices noted: "Just like you can't trust photography anymore, you won't be able to trust a voice either."

Neural Networks

Artificial intelligence research has produced many amazing success stories and some embarrassing failures. The successes—intelligent applications that outperform their human counterparts—tend to involve tasks that require sequential thinking, logical rules, and orderly relationships. AI has been less successful at competing with natural human intelligence in applications such as language, vision, speech, and movement—applications where massive amounts of data are processed in parallel.

The **human brain** uses a type of circuitry that is very slow . . . at least **10,000 times slower** than a digital computer. On the other hand, the **degree of parallelism vastly outstrips** any computer architecture we have yet to design. . . . For such tasks as vision, language, and motor control, the brain is **more powerful than 1,000 supercomputers**, yet for certain **simple tasks** such as multiplying digital numbers, it is less powerful than the 4-bit microprocessor found in a **ten-dollar calculator**.

—Raymond Kurzweil, in *The Age of Intelligent Machines*

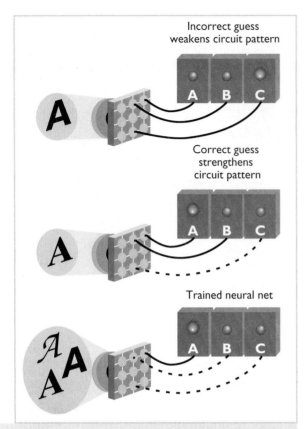

Incorrect guess
weakens circuit pattern

Correct guess
strengthens
circuit pattern

Trained neural net

15.15 For a neural net to learn to recognize the letter A, it must go through a series of trials in which circuit patterns that produce incorrect guesses are weakened and patterns that produce correct guesses are strengthened. The end result is a circuit pattern that can recognize the letter A in a variety of forms.

It's not surprising that computers excel at linear, logical processes; almost every computer that's ever been created is designed to process digital information sequentially through a single CPU. The human brain, on the other hand, consists of billions of neurons, each connected to thousands of others in a massively parallel, distributed structure. This kind of structure gives the brain an advantage at most perceptual, motor, and creative skills.

Much current work in AI is focused on neural networks (or neural nets)—distributed, parallel computing systems inspired by the structure of the human brain. Instead of a single, complex CPU, a neural network uses a network of a few thousand simpler processors called neurons. Neural networks aren't programmed in the usual way—they're trained. Instead of using a rule-based approach, a neural network learns patterns by trial and error, just as the brain does. When patterns are repeated often, neural networks, in effect, develop habits. This kind of learning can present problems for some kinds of applications because no rules are clearly defined. When a neural net makes a decision, you have no way to ask why.

Neural networks also store information differently than traditional computers. Concepts are represented as patterns of activity among many neurons, so they are less susceptible to machine failure. Because it distributes knowledge throughout the network, a neural net (like the human brain) can still function if some of its neurons are destroyed.

Many neural net algorithms are developed on parallel-processing supercomputers with thousands of processors. Intel Corporation and other hardware companies produce neural net chips containing thousands of neurons. A number of software companies have developed programs that simulate neural nets on PCs and other nonparallel machines. However, none of today's neural net hardware or software approaches the complexity or the capacity of the human brain.

Most researchers consider today's neural nets as, at best, baby steps in the direction of machines that can more closely emulate the workings of human "wetware." There's considerable debate in the AI community about the future of neural nets. Some see neural nets as playing only a limited role in AI; others expect them to eclipse the traditional rule-based approach.

Even so, neural nets are already being put to use in a variety of applications, ranging from artificial vision to expert systems. Neural nets are especially useful for recognizing patterns buried in huge quantities of numbers, such as in scientific research, loan processing, and stock market analysis. Some modems use neural nets to distinguish signals from random telephone-line noise. American Express uses neural net software to read millions of charge slips each day. Federico Faggin, co-designer of the first microprocessor, suggests that future neural nets will be used to verify signatures (on digital touch tablets) for electronic commerce on computer networks. Optimistic researchers hope that neural networks may someday provide hearing for the deaf and eyesight for the blind.

15.16 A member of the Merce Cunningham Dance Company dances with a score by David Tudor, composed in part by Intel's 80170 ETANN (Electronically Trainable Artificial Neural Network). The music for this particular performance is determined in part by dancer movements and audience noise.

The Robot Revolution

Nowhere are AI technologies more visible than in the field of robotics. Vision, hearing, pattern recognition, knowledge engineering, expert decision making, natural language understanding, speech—they all come together in today's robots.

> 1. A robot **may not injure a human being**, or, through inaction, allow a human being to come to harm.
> 2. A robot **must obey the orders** given it by human beings, except where such orders would conflict with the First Law.
> 3. A robot **must protect its own existence** as long as such protection does not conflict with the First or Second Law.
>
> —Isaac Asimov's *Three Laws of Robotics*

What Is a Robot?

The term *robot* (from the root word *robota*, the Czech word for "forced labor") first appeared in a 1923 play called *R.U.R.* (for Rossum's Universal Robots) by Czech playwright Karel Capek. Capek's robots were intelligent machines that could see, hear, touch, move, and exercise judgment based on common sense. But these powerful machines eventually rebelled against their human creators, just as hundreds of fictional robots have done in succeeding decades. Today, movies, TV, and books are full of imaginary robots, both good and evil.

As exotic as they might seem, robots are similar to other kinds of computer technology people use every day. While a typical computer performs *mental* tasks, a robot is a computer-controlled machine designed to perform specific *manual* tasks. A robot's central processor might be a microprocessor embedded in the robot's shell, or it might be a supervisory computer that controls the robot from a distance. In any case, the processor is functionally identical to the processor found in a PC, a workstation, or a mainframe computer.

The most important hardware differences between robots and other computers are the input and output peripherals. Instead of sending output to a screen or a printer, a robot sends commands to joints, arms, and other moving parts. The first robots had no corresponding input devices to monitor their movements and the surrounding environment. They were effectively deaf, blind, and in some cases dangerous—at least one Japanese worker was killed by an early sightless robot. Most modern robots include input *sensors*.

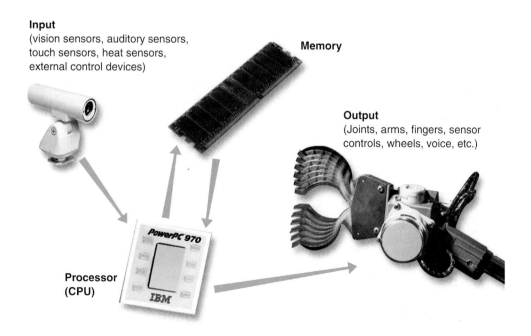

Input
(vision sensors, auditory sensors, touch sensors, heat sensors, external control devices)

Memory

Output
(Joints, arms, fingers, sensor controls, wheels, voice, etc.)

Processor (CPU)

PowerPC 970
IBM

15.17 A robot is, in effect, a computer with exotic peripherals.

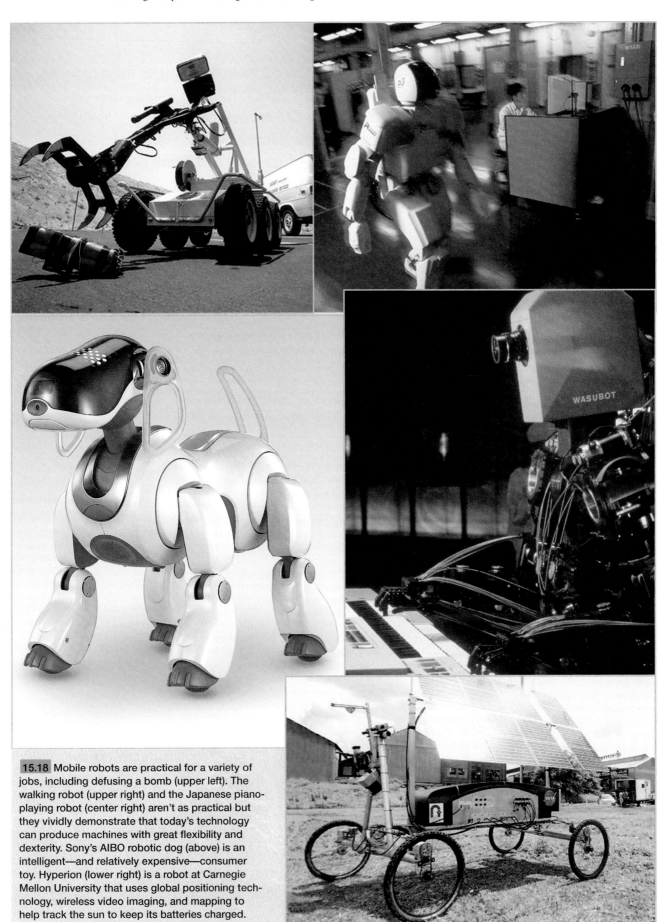

15.18 Mobile robots are practical for a variety of jobs, including defusing a bomb (upper left). The walking robot (upper right) and the Japanese piano-playing robot (center right) aren't as practical but they vividly demonstrate that today's technology can produce machines with great flexibility and dexterity. Sony's AIBO robotic dog (above) is an intelligent—and relatively expensive—consumer toy. Hyperion (lower right) is a robot at Carnegie Mellon University that uses global positioning technology, wireless video imaging, and mapping to help track the sun to keep its batteries charged.

These sensing devices enable robots to correct or modify their actions based on feedback from the outside world.

Industrial robots seldom have the human-inspired anatomy of Hollywood's science fiction robots. Instead, they're designed to accomplish particular tasks in the best possible way. Robots can be designed to see infrared light, rotate joints 360 degrees, and do other things that aren't possible for humans. On the other hand, robots are constrained by the limitations of AI software. The most sophisticated robot today can't tie a pair of shoelaces, understand the vocabulary of a 3-year-old child, or consistently tell the difference between a cat and a dog.

Steel-Collar Workers

From a management point of view robots offer several advantages:

- Obviously, many robots save labor costs. Robots are expensive to design, install, and program. But once they're operational, they can work 24 hours a day, 365 days a year, without vacations, strikes, sick leave, or coffee breaks.
- Robots can also improve quality and increase productivity. They're especially effective at doing repetitive jobs in which bored, tired people are prone to make errors and have accidents.
- Robots are ideal for jobs such as cleaning up hazardous waste and salvaging undersea wreckage from downed planes—jobs that are dangerous, uncomfortable, or impossible for human workers.

For all these reasons, the robot population is exploding. Today, hundreds of thousands of industrial robots do welding, part fitting, painting, and other repetitive tasks in factories all over the world. In most automated factories robots work alongside humans, but in some state-of-the-art factories the only function of human workers is to monitor and repair robots. Robots aren't used just in factories. Robots also shear sheep in Australia, paint ship hulls in France, disarm land mines in the Persian Gulf, and perform precision hip operations and other surgery.

Commercial robots still can't compete with people for jobs that require exceptional perceptual or fine-motor skills. But robots in research labs suggest that a new generation of more competitive robots is on the way. A robot developed at Bell Labs can defeat most human opponents at ping-pong. A human-sized Japanese robot named Wabot-2 can read sheet music and perform it on an organ or synthesizer using 10 fingers and 2 feet. Other researchers are taking a different approach, using fleets of insect-sized robots to do jobs that larger robots can't easily do. The technologies used in these experimental robots will undoubtedly show up in a variety of machines, from automated servants for people with disabilities to flying robots for the military. We may be within a few years of self-propelled robot housecleaners!

The robot revolution isn't necessarily good news for people who earn their living doing manual labor. While it's true that many of the jobs robots do are boring, dirty, or dangerous, they're still jobs. The issues surrounding automation and worker displacement are complex, and they aren't limited to factories.

AI Implications and Ethical Questions

From the earliest days of AI, research has been accompanied by questions about the implications of the work. The very idea of intelligent machines is at the same time confusing, exciting, and frightening to many people. Even when they don't work very well, AI programs generate emotional responses in the people who use them.

Earlier we met ELIZA, the therapy simulator developed to demonstrate natural language conversation. ELIZA's simple-minded approach wasn't intended to fool anyone in a

> We are **on the edge of change** comparable to **the rise of human life** on Earth. The precise cause of this change is the imminent creation by technology of **entities with greater-than-human intelligence**.
>
> —Vernor Vinge, mathematician and science fiction writer

Turing test, but it did have an impact on the people who used it. Many ELIZA users became emotionally attached to the program and attributed to it compassion and empathy. Weizenbaum's secretary asked him to leave the room so she could converse in private with ELIZA. Some therapists even saw ELIZA as the beginning of a new age of automated therapy. Weizenbaum was shocked by the way people attributed human capabilities to such an obviously flawed technology. He responded with *Computer Power and Human Reason*, a landmark book that presents the case for maintaining a distinction between computers and people. Weizenbaum argues that "[t]here are certain tasks which computers ought not to be made to do, independent of whether computers can be made to do them."

International political and economic leaders, many of whom are encouraging increased AI research and development, don't share Weizenbaum's caution. As it matures, AI technology finds its way out of the research lab and into the marketplace. A growing number of programs and products incorporate pattern recognition, expert systems, and other AI techniques. In the near future we're likely to see more products with embedded AI, including intelligent word processors that can help writers turn rough drafts into polished prose, smart appliances that can recognize and obey their owners' spoken commands, and vehicles that can perform their own diagnostics and, in many cases, repairs. We'll also see more *distributed intelligence*— AI concepts applied to networks rather than to individual computers.

Where will it all lead? Will intensive AI research result in computers capable of intelligent behavior outside narrow domains? Patrick Winston, director of MIT's Artificial Intelligence Laboratory, once said, "The interesting issue is not whether machines can be made smarter but if humans are smart enough to pull it off. A raccoon obviously can't make a machine as smart as a raccoon. I wonder if humans can."

Many AI researchers believe that sooner or later they will pull it off. Some think artificial intelligence is the natural culmination of the evolutionary process—that the next intelligent life-form on earth will be based on silicon rather than the carbon that is the basis of human life. Danny Hillis, supercomputer designer who now does research for Disney Corporation, exemplifies this point of view when he says, "We are not evolution's ultimate product. There's something coming after us, and I imagine it is something wonderful. But we may never be able to comprehend it, any more than a caterpillar can comprehend turning into a butterfly."

Computer mathematician and science fiction writer Vernor Vinge argues that the competitive nature of our society makes such a prospect almost inevitable. What business or government will voluntarily curtail research on AI, computer networks, and biotechnology, knowing that competing institutions will continue to pursue similar research? Vinge calls the moment of creation of greater-than-human intelligence a *singularity*—a point where our old models will have to be discarded and a new reality will rule.

If smarter-than-human beings come to pass, how will they relate to the less intelligent humans that surround them? This kind of thinking isn't easy—it goes to the heart of human values and forces us to look at our place in the universe.

Slaves to Our Machines   Clive Thompson

Do computers work for us, or do we work for them? Clive Thomas, a New York writer, wrote about this question in the October 2002 issue of Wired. *The article was provocatively subtitled "Welcome to your future as a PC plug-in."*

Computers are supposed to work for humans, right? PDAs help us remember things, instant messaging lets us chatter endlessly, TurboTax figures our deductions. We're the masters——they're the slaves. Or maybe not.

Consider this: Porn solicitations make up about 8 percent of the more than 2 billion spam messages sent annually. Last year, Yahoo! wanted to block porn spambots from obtaining free email accounts. It created a brilliant but simple reverse Turing test: To get an account, you have to identify a randomly generated word that's been slightly stretched and distorted. This proves you're a human, not a robot. Machines are terrible at visual recognition tasks—sure enough, the "picture test" blocked out the spambots.

Here's the weird thing: Some purveyors of porn developed a way to fight back. They rewrote the spambot code so that when the bots reach the visual recognition test, a human steps in to help out. The bots route the picture to a person who's agreed to sit at a computer and identify these images. Often, insiders say, it's a hormonal teen who's doing it in exchange for free porn. The kid identifies the picture, the spambot takes the answer, and—bingo—it's able to log in. "It's the only way we know for getting around the picture test," says Luis von Ahn, a grad student at Carnegie Mellon who helped develop the Yahoo! test. (Yahoo! claims it's never heard of the workaround.)

Now consider how deeply strange this is. Instead of a machine augmenting human ability, it's a *human* augmenting *machine* ability. In a system like this, humans are valuable for the specific bit of processing power we provide: visual recognition. We are acting as a kind of co-processor in much the same way a graphics chip works with a main Pentium processor—it's a manservant lurking in the background, rendering the pretty pictures onscreen so the Pentium can attend to more pressing tasks.

Of course, we humans have always had a symbiotic relationship with our machines. We're the perennial backup. When the *Apollo 13* computers crashed, NASA geeks whipped out their slide rules and went to work, relying on old-fashioned gray matter. But as a species, we've always assumed our role was the superior one in the man–machine universe. Techies from Nikola Tesla to Bill Gates are famous for cheerily prophesying the day when computers will do all the drudge work, leaving us humans to dedicate our magnificently supple brains to "creative" tasks.

Except, as our machines get smarter and faster, our much-vaunted creative powers may not be so valuable.

What's more useful, in man–machine systems, is our flexibility—our ability to deal with periodically messy, wrenching situations. We won't be doing the brain work; we'll be doing the scut work.

Sound crazy? Sure, but the service industry has been moving in this direction for years. Speech recognition systems from corporations like SpeechWorks have reached success levels of up to 95 percent, smoothly routing calls automatically—unless the voice print is slurred or heavily accented, in which case the call is sent to a human for special processing.

COMPUTERS HOG THE BEST GIGS, WHILE WE'RE STUCK WITH MCJOBS

This summer, Mitel was awarded a patent for a voice recognition system that has a "mood detector"—it can recognize "high stress or annoyance" in angry callers. If the system detects swearing, yelling, or keypad mashing, the computer will automatically route the caller to a human. That's because humans are superior to machines—when it comes to irrational outbursts.

It's a pretty cool system. Unless, of course, you're the poor phone attendant whose job it is to talk to *angry nutcases* all day long. Consider this a form of digital Taylorization—the creation of an entirely new class of McJob. The machines might ultimately hog all the interesting critical thinking—the crunching of patterns, the teasing of strategies from corporate data—while we humans serve as little more than neural sensors, sitting in a cold, dark server room, getting paid minimum wage to have chunks of fuzzy data hurled at us for disambiguation. Sign me up!

So maybe our old sci-fi dystopias were wrong. Movies like *The Terminator* and *2001* fret about machines becoming so smart that they get rid of us. It's unlikely to happen, because in the end, they'll always need us to do the cleanup. Welcome to your future: as a USB plug-in for your computer. It's a dirty job, but somebody's got to do it.

DISCUSSION QUESTIONS

1. Do you think computer creativity will evolve faster than machine vision and flexibility? Explain your answer.

2. Do you think in the future most human jobs will be in support of computers, as the author suggests? Why or why not?

SUMMARY

Artificial intelligence has many definitions. Most AI research focuses on making computers do things at which people generally are better. Some AI researchers try to simulate human intelligent behavior, but most try to design intelligent machines independent of the way people think. Successful AI research generally involves working on problems with limited domains rather than trying to tackle large, open-ended problems. AI programs employ a variety of techniques, including searching, heuristics, pattern recognition, and machine learning, to achieve their goals.

From a practical standpoint, natural language communication is one of the most important areas of AI study. Natural language programs that deal with a subset of the language are used in applications ranging from machine translation programs to natural language interfaces. But no program is capable of handling the kind of unrestricted natural language text people deal with every day. Natural language programs are confounded by the English language's large vocabulary, convoluted syntax, and ambiguous semantics—the meanings behind the words.

AI researchers have developed a variety of schemes for representing knowledge in computers. A knowledge base contains facts and a system for determining and changing the relationship between those facts. Today's knowledge bases are practical only for representing narrow domains of knowledge such as the knowledge of an expert on a particular subject. Expert systems are programs designed to replicate the decision-making process of human experts. An expert system includes a knowledge base, an inference engine for applying logical rules to the facts in a knowledge base, and a human interface for interacting with users. Once the

knowledge base is constructed (usually based on interviews and observations of human experts), an expert system can provide consultation that rivals human advice in many situations. People successfully use expert systems in a variety of scientific, business, and other applications.

Pattern recognition is an important area of AI research that involves identifying recurring patterns in input data. Pattern recognition technology is at the heart of computer vision, voice communication, and other important AI applications. These diverse applications all use similar techniques for isolating and recognizing patterns. People are better at pattern recognition than computers, in part because the human brain can process masses of data in parallel. Modern neural network computers are designed to process data in the same way the human brain does. Many researchers believe that neural nets, as they grow in size and sophistication, will help computers improve their performance at many difficult tasks.

A robot is a computer-controlled machine designed to perform specific manual tasks. Robots include output peripherals for manipulating their environments and input sensors that enable them to perform self-correcting actions based on feedback from outside. Robots perform a variety of dangerous and tedious tasks, in many cases outperforming human workers. As robot technology advances, artificial workers will do more traditional human jobs.

In spite of the numerous difficulties AI researchers encounter when trying to produce truly intelligent machines, many experts believe that people will eventually create artificial beings that are more intelligent than their creators—a prospect with staggering implications.

KEY TERMS

artificial intelligence (p. 532)
automatic speech recognition (p. 544)
automatic translation (p. 536)
digitized sound (p. 545)
digitized speech (p. 545)
expert system (p. 540)
expert system shell (p. 542)
heuristic (p. 535)

image analysis (p. 543)
knowledge base (p. 539)
machine learning (p. 535)
natural language (p. 536)
neural network (neural net) (p. 546)
optical character recognition (OCR) (p. 543)
parallel processing (p. 534)

parsing program (p. 536)
pattern recognition (p. 542)
robot (p. 547)
semantics (p. 538)
speech synthesis (p. 545)
syntax (p. 538)
synthetic speech (p. 545)
Turing test (p. 532)

INTERACTIVE QUIZ QUESTIONS

1. The *Computer Confluence* CD-ROM contains self-test multiple-choice quiz questions related to this chapter. You can email the results of your CD quiz to your instructor.

2. The *Computer Confluence* Web site, www.computerconfluence.com, contains self-test ex-

ercises related to this chapter. Follow the instructions for taking a quiz. After you've completed your quiz, you can email the results to your instructor.

TRUE FALSE QUESTIONS

1. Alan M. Turing maintained that if a computer acts intelligently, then it is intelligent.

2. For psychologists, artificial intelligence provides insights into natural intelligence and the workings of the human brain.

3. The most powerful supercomputers can match the human brain's ability to perform parallel processing.

4. Artificial intelligence researchers restrict the domain of their programs so that problems are small enough to understand and solve.

5. Natural language communication poses problems for AI programs because of its complexity.

6. A knowledge base commonly represents knowledge in the form of if-then rules.

7. It's easier for a computer to recognize printed English than to speak passable English.

8. The brain is the basis of neural network research.

9. Most modern robots have input sensors that enable them to modify their actions.

10. Some AI researchers think that humans will be able to make a machine that is smarter than humans.

MULTIPLE CHOICE

1. Some AI techniques used today in applications include
   a. searching—looking ahead at possibilities.
   b. heuristics—rules of thumb.
   c. pattern recognition—recognizing recurring patterns.
   d. machine learning—programs learning from experience.
   e. All of the above.

2. Semantics is
   a. the set of rules for constructing sentences from words.
   b. the underlying meaning of words and phrases.
   c. a set of idiomatic expressions.
   d. the study of knowledge bases.
   e. the translation of text files.

3. Natural language processing
   a. made it possible for computers to pass the Turing test.
   b. makes computers understand multiple meanings of words.
   c. cannot flawlessly translate books or conversations.
   d. utilizes all words in a language.
   e. All of the above.

4. A complete expert system includes
   a. a knowledge base.
   b. a way to produce the requested advice.
   c. an inference engine.
   d. a way for users to interact with the system.
   e. All of the above.

5. The downside of expert systems is that
   a. expert systems are not good at strategizing.
   b. it is very work-intensive to build the knowledge base.
   c. they are less flexible and creative than human thinkers.
   d. expert systems only handle a narrow domain of knowledge.
   e. All of the above.

6. Image analysis
   a. represents about half of the AI industry.
   b. is the process of identifying objects and shapes in visual images.
   c. is a simplified form of pattern recognition technology.
   d. is difficult for both computers and humans to perform.
   e. All of the above.

7. The field of pattern recognition includes
   a. image analysis.
   b. optical character recognition (OCR).
   c. automatic speech recognition.
   d. neural network research.
   e. All of the above.

8. Optical character recognition applications cannot yet
   a. read aloud to the blind.
   b. be trained by human feedback to recognize fonts and styles.
   c. locate and identify print characters embedded in images.
   d. be used with written Asian scripts.
   e. Actually, OCR applications can do all of these things.

9. Techniques used in pattern recognition include
   a. segmentation of input.
   b. expert rules.
   c. context experts.
   d. learning from a human trainer.
   e. All of the above.

10. Which of these is not true?
    a. Neural networks use thousands of processors called neurons.
    b. Neural networks are trained, not programmed in the usual way.
    c. Neural nets use a rule-based approach to recognize patterns.
    d. Neural networks learn by trial and error.
    e. Neural nets store information as patterns.

REVIEW QUESTIONS

1. In what sense is AI a "moving frontier"?

2. What are the disadvantages of the approach to AI that attempts to simulate human intelligence? What is the alternative?

3. Describe several techniques used in game-playing software, and explain how they can be applied to other AI applications.

4. Why did early machine translation programs fail to produce the desired results?

5. Why is the sentence "Time flies like an arrow" difficult for a computer to parse, translate, or understand? Can you find four possible meanings for the sentence?

6. What is the relationship between syntax and semantics? Can you construct a sentence that follows the rules of English syntax but has nonsense semantics?

7. What is a knowledge base? What is an expert system? How are the two related?

8. Give examples of successful expert system applications. Give examples of several tasks that can't be accomplished with today's expert system technology, and explain why they can't.

9. What are some of the problems that make machine vision so challenging?

10. In what ways are the techniques of optical character recognition similar to those of speech recognition programs?

11. What rules might a computer use to sort the characters shown on page 543 into A's and B's?

12. In what ways are neural networks designed to simulate the structure of the human brain? In what ways do neural nets perform differently than standard single-processor CPUs?

13. What kind of hardware is necessary for a robot to be self-correcting so it can modify its actions based on outside feedback?

14. What distinguishes a robot from a desktop computer?

DISCUSSION QUESTIONS

1. Is the Turing test a valid test of intelligence? Why or why not?

2. If you were the interrogator in the Turing test, what questions would you ask to try to discover whether you were communicating with a computer? What would you look for in the answers?

3. List several mental tasks that people do better than computers. List several mental tasks that computers do better than people. Can you find any general characteristics that distinguish the items on the two lists?

4. Computers can compose original music, produce original artwork, and create original mathematical proofs. Does this mean that Ada King was wrong when she said, in effect, that computers can do only what they're told to do?

5. The works of AARON, the expert system artist, are unique, original, and widely acclaimed as art. Who is the artist, AARON or Harold Cohen, AARON's creator? Is AARON a work of art, an artist, or both?

6. If an expert system gives you erroneous information, should you be able to sue it for malpractice? If it fails and causes major disruptions or injury, who's responsible? The programmer? The publisher? The owner? The computer?

7. Some expert systems and neural nets can't explain the reasons behind their decisions. What kinds of problems might this limitation cause? Under what circumstances, if any, should an expert system be required to produce an "audit trail" to explain how it reached conclusions?

8. What kinds of human jobs are most likely to be eliminated because of expert systems? What kinds of new jobs will be created because of expert systems?

9. What kinds of human jobs are most likely to be eliminated because of robots? What kinds of new jobs will be created as a result of factory automation?

10. Are Asimov's three laws of robotics adequate for smoothly integrating intelligent robots into tomorrow's society? If not, what laws would you add?

PROJECTS

1. Public domain versions of Weizenbaum's ELIZA program are available for most types of desktop computers. They're also available on the Web. Try conversing with one of these programs. Test the program on your friends and see how they react to it. Try to determine the rules and tricks that ELIZA uses to simulate conversation. If you're a programmer, try writing your own version of ELIZA.

2. When Turing first proposed the Turing test, he compared it to a similar test in which the interrogator tried to guess the sex of the people typing answers to questions. See if you can devise such a test. What, if anything, does it prove?

3. Try to find examples of working expert systems and robots in your school or community and present your findings.

4. Test OCR software, grammar-checking software, expert systems, and other types of consumer-oriented AI applications. How "intelligent" are these applications? In what ways could they be improved?

5. Survey people's attitudes and concerns about AI and robots. Present your findings.

SOURCES AND RESOURCES

Books

The Age of Intelligent Machines, by Raymond Kurzweil (Cambridge, MA: MIT Press, 1992). If you want to learn more about AI, this award-winning book is a great resource in spite of its age. With clear prose, beautiful illustrations, and intelligent articles by the masters of the field, Kurzweil explores the historical, philosophical, academic, aesthetic, practical, fanciful, and speculative sides of AI. Kurzweil knows the field from first-hand experience; he has successfully developed and marketed several "applied AI" products, from reading machines for people with visual impairments and electronic musical instruments to expert systems. A companion video is also available.

The Age of Spiritual Machines, by Raymond Kurzweil (New York: Penguin USA, 2000). While *The Age of Intelligent Machines* surveys the past and present of AI, *The Age of Spiritual Machines* boldly looks into a possible future. Will humans really be able to download themselves into machine bodies and brains? If this kind of question interests you, you'll enjoy this book.

Godel, Escher, Bach: An Eternal Golden Braid, 20th Anniversary Edition, by Douglas R. Hofstadter (Boulder, CO: Basic Books, 1999). This Pulitzer Prize winner is part mathematics, part philosophy, and part *Alice in Wonderland*. If you like to think deeply about questions like "What is thought?" you'll find plenty to think about here.

Artificial Minds, by Stan Franklin (Cambridge, MA: MIT Press, 1997). Franklin explores the fascinating territory between computer science, cognitive psychology, and philosophy. He makes a case that there's a continuum between "mind" and "nonmind" and that we're entering an era when it's possible to explore that continuum in ways never before possible. This book is challenging and thought-provoking.

Artificial Intelligence, Third Edition, by Patrick Henry Winston (Reading, MA: Addison-Wesley, 1992). This best-selling introductory text for computer science students is thorough and well written. Like most computer science texts, it's probably too technical and mathematical for most casual readers.

Lisp, by Patrick Henry Winston and Berthold K. P. Horn (Reading, MA: Addison-Wesley, 1989). A popular introduction to Common LISP, the widely used programming language of AI.

Kasparov Versus Deep Blue: Computer Chess Comes of Age, by Monty Newborn (New York: Springer, 1997). This book describes in graphic detail the historic computer match between Deep Blue and Garry Kasparov in 1996—the year before Deep Blue beat the world champion. It's worthwhile reading for any chess player who wants to understand how computers have invaded this turf that used to be uniquely human.

Emergence: The Connected Lives of Ants, Brains, Cities, and Software, by Steven Johnson (New York: Scribner, 2001). Neural networks clearly demonstrate that intelligent behavior can result from putting together many simple, dumb, devices. This book clearly explains how that principle applies to everything from ant colonies to robots.

Society of Mind, by Marvin Minsky (New York: Simon & Schuster, 1988). Another MIT AI pioneer presents his thoughts on the relationship between people and intelligent machines. A dense but thought-provoking book.

Robot: Mere Machine to Transcendent Mind, by Hans P. Moravec (New York: Oxford University Press, 1998). A pioneer designer of robots speculates about the future of robots and our relationship with them. Starting with Turing, Moravec traces an evolutionary path toward a future in which robots colonize space.

Robo Sapiens: Evolution of a New Species, by Peter Menzel and Faith D'Alusio (Cambridge, MA: MIT Press, 2000). This book combines photography and text to produce a portrait of today's robot culture and raise fascinating questions about the evolution of that culture.

Across Realtime, by Vernor Vinge (New York: Baen Books, 1991). Vinge's science fiction opus takes you into a future after the singularity that produced artificial superintelligence. Vinge is a master storyteller, and there's plenty to think about here. (For a nonfiction discussion of the singularity, see Vinge's "Technological Singularity," in *Whole Earth Review*, Winter 1993, page 88.)

Video

Fast, Cheap, and Out of Control. In this 1997 documentary, maverick filmmaker Errol Morris profiles four different men attempting to examine the relation between science and humanity, including a robot expert. This highly acclaimed film interweaves interviews, old movie clips, and a hypnotic score to create a fascinating mosaic.

AI. Stephen Spielberg's big-budget film isn't a masterpiece of art or scientific exposition, but it does a reasonable job of raising questions about life and technology that may loom large in our future.

Web Pages

Check the *Computer Confluence* Web site for links to Internet sources on expert systems, pattern recognition, and other AI topics.

ACM Appendix

ACM Code of Ethics and Professional Conduct (Adopted by ACM Council October 16, 1992)

Commitment to ethical professional conduct is expected of every member (voting members, associate members, and student members) of the Association for Computing Machinery (ACM).

This Code, consisting of 24 imperatives formulated as statements of personal responsibility, identifies the elements of such a commitment. It contains many, but not all, issues professionals are likely to face. Section 1 outlines fundamental ethical considerations, while Section 2 addresses additional, more specific considerations of professional conduct. Statements in Section 3 pertain more specifically to individuals who have a leadership role, whether in the workplace or in a volunteer capacity such as with organizations like ACM. Principles involving compliance with this Code are given in Section 4.

The Code shall be supplemented by a set of Guidelines, which provide explanation to assist members in dealing with the various issues contained in the Code. It is expected that the Guidelines will be changed more frequently than the Code.

The Code and its supplemented Guidelines are intended to serve as a basis for ethical decision making in the conduct of professional work. Secondarily, they may serve as a basis for judging the merit of a formal complaint pertaining to violation of professional ethical standards.

It should be noted that although computing is not mentioned in the imperatives of Section 1, the Code is concerned with how these fundamental imperatives apply to one's conduct as a computing professional. These imperatives are expressed in a general form to emphasize that ethical principles which apply to computer ethics are derived from more general ethical principles.

It is understood that some words and phrases in a code of ethics are subject to varying interpretations, and that any ethical principle may conflict with other ethical principles in specific situations. Questions related to ethical conflicts can best be answered by thoughtful consideration of fundamental principles, rather than reliance on detailed regulations.

1. General moral imperatives
2. More specific professional responsibilities
3. Organizational leadership imperatives
4. Compliance with the code

1. General Moral Imperatives

As an ACM member I will . . .

1.1 Contribute to Society and Human Well-Being

This principle concerning the quality of life of all people affirms an obligation to protect fundamental human rights and to respect the diversity of all cultures. An essential aim of computing professionals is to minimize negative consequences of computing systems, including threats to health and safety. When designing or implementing systems, computing professionals must attempt to ensure that the products of their efforts will be used in socially responsible ways, will meet social needs, and will avoid harmful effects to health and welfare.

In addition to a safe social environment, human well-being includes a safe natural environment. Therefore, computing professionals who design and develop systems must be alert to, and make others aware of, any potential damage to the local or global environment.

1.2 Avoid Harm to Others

"Harm" means injury or negative consequences, such as undesirable loss of information, loss of property, property damage, or unwanted environmental impacts. This principle prohibits use of computing technology in ways that result in harm to any of the following: users, the general public, employees, and employers. Harmful actions include intentional destruction or modification of files and programs leading to serious loss of resources or unnecessary expenditure of human resources such as the time and effort required to purge systems of "computer viruses."

Well-intended actions, including those that accomplish assigned duties, may lead to harm unexpectedly. In such an event the responsible person or persons are obligated to undo or mitigate the negative consequences as much as possible. One way to avoid unintentional harm is to carefully consider potential impacts on all those affected by decisions made during design and implementation.

To minimize the possibility of indirectly harming others, computing professionals must minimize malfunctions by following generally accepted standards for system design and testing. Furthermore, it is often necessary to assess the social consequences of systems to project the likelihood of any serious harm to others. If system features are misrepresented to users, coworkers, or supervisors, the individual computing professional is responsible for any resulting injury.

In the work environment the computing professional has the additional obligation to report any signs of system dangers that might result in serious personal or social damage. If one's superiors do not act to curtail or mitigate such dangers, it may be necessary to "blow the whistle" to help correct the problem or reduce the risk. However, capricious or misguided reporting of violations can, itself, be harmful. Before reporting violations, all relevant aspects of the incident must be thoroughly assessed. In particular, the assessment of risk and responsibility must be credible. It is suggested that advice be sought from other computing professionals. See principle 2.5 regarding thorough evaluations.

1.3 Be Honest and Trustworthy

Honesty is an essential component of trust. Without trust an organization cannot function effectively. The honest computing professional will not make deliberately false or deceptive claims about a system or system design, but will instead provide full disclosure of all pertinent system limitations and problems.

A computer professional has a duty to be honest about his or her own qualifications, and about any circumstances that might lead to conflicts of interest.

Membership in volunteer organizations such as ACM may at times place individuals in situations where their statements or actions could be interpreted as carrying the "weight" of a larger group of professionals. An ACM member will exercise care to not misrepresent ACM or positions and policies of ACM or any ACM units.

1.4 Be Fair and Take Action Not to Discriminate

The values of equality, tolerance, respect for others, and the principles of equal justice govern this imperative. Discrimination on the basis of race, sex, religion, age, disability, national origin, or other such factors is an explicit violation of ACM policy and will not be tolerated.

Inequities between different groups of people may result from the use or misuse of information and technology. In a fair society, all individuals would have equal opportunity to participate in, or benefit from, the use of computer resources regardless of race, sex, religion, age, disability, national origin or other such similar factors. However, these ideals do not justify unauthorized use of computer resources nor do they provide an adequate basis for violation of any other ethical imperatives of this code.

1.5 Honor Property Rights Including Copyrights and Patents

Violation of copyrights, patents, trade secrets and the terms of license agreements is prohibited by law in most circumstances. Even when software is not so protected, such violations are contrary to professional behavior. Copies of software should be made only with proper authorization. Unauthorized duplication of materials must not be condoned.

1.6 Give Proper Credit for Intellectual Property

Computing professionals are obligated to protect the integrity of intellectual property. Specifically, one must not take credit for other's ideas or work, even in cases where the work has not been explicitly protected by copyright, patent, etc.

1.7 Respect the Privacy of Others

Computing and communication technology enables the collection and exchange of personal information on a scale unprecedented in the history of civilization. Thus there is increased potential for violating the privacy of individuals and groups. It is the responsibility of professionals to maintain the privacy and integrity of data describing individuals. This includes taking precautions to ensure the accuracy of data, as well as protecting it from unauthorized access or accidental disclosure to inappropriate individuals. Furthermore, procedures must be established to allow individuals to review their records and correct inaccuracies.

This imperative implies that only the necessary amount of personal information be collected in a system, that retention and disposal periods for that information be clearly defined and enforced, and that personal information gathered for a specific purpose not be used for other purposes without consent of the individual(s). These principles apply to electronic communications, including electronic mail, and prohibit procedures that capture or monitor electronic user data, including messages, without the permission of users or bona fide authorization related to system operation and maintenance. User data observed during the normal duties of system operation and maintenance must be treated with strictest confidentiality, except in cases where it is evidence for the violation of law, organizational regulations, or this Code. In these cases, the nature or contents of that information must be disclosed only to proper authorities.

1.8 Honor Confidentiality

The principle of honesty extends to issues of confidentiality of information whenever one has made an explicit promise to honor confidentiality or, implicitly, when private information not directly related to the performance of one's duties becomes available. The ethical concern is to respect all obligations of confidentiality to employers, clients, and users unless discharged from such obligations by requirements of the law or other principles of this Code.

2. More Specific Professional Responsibilities

As an ACM computing professional I will . . .

2.1 Strive to Achieve the Highest Quality, Effectiveness and Dignity in Both the Process and Products of Professional Work

Excellence is perhaps the most important obligation of a professional. The computing professional must strive to achieve quality and to be cognizant of the serious negative consequences that may result from poor quality in a system.

2.2 Acquire and Maintain Professional Competence

Excellence depends on individuals who take responsibility for acquiring and maintaining professional competence. A professional must participate in setting standards for appropriate levels of competence, and strive to achieve those standards. Upgrading technical knowledge and competence can be achieved in several ways: doing independent study; attending seminars, conferences, or courses; and being involved in professional organizations.

2.3 Know and Respect Existing Laws Pertaining to Professional Work

ACM members must obey existing local, state, province, national, and international laws unless there is a compelling ethical basis not to do so. Policies and procedures of the organizations in which one participates must also be obeyed. But compliance must be balanced with the recognition that sometimes existing laws and rules may be immoral or inappropriate and, therefore, must be challenged. Violation of a law or regulation may be ethical when that law or rule has inadequate moral basis or when it conflicts with another law judged to be more important. If one decides to violate a law or rule because it is viewed as unethical, or for any other reason, one must fully accept responsibility for one's actions and for the consequences.

2.4 Accept and Provide Appropriate Professional Review

Quality professional work, especially in the computing profession, depends on professional reviewing and critiquing. Whenever appropriate, individual members should seek and utilize peer review as well as provide critical review of the work of others.

2.5 Give Comprehensive and Thorough Evaluations of Computer Systems and Their Impacts, Including Analysis of Possible Risks

Computer professionals must strive to be perceptive, thorough, and objective when evaluating, recommending, and presenting system descriptions and alternatives. Computer professionals are in a position of special trust, and therefore have a special responsibility to provide objective, credible evaluations to employers, clients, users, and the public. When providing evaluations the professional must also identify any relevant conflicts of interest, as stated in imperative 1.3.

As noted in the discussion of principle 1.2 on avoiding harm, any signs of danger from systems must be reported to those who have opportunity and/or responsibility to resolve them. See the guidelines for imperative 1.2 for more details concerning harm, including the reporting of professional violations.

2.6 Honor Contracts, Agreements, and Assigned Responsibilities

Honoring one's commitments is a matter of integrity and honesty. For the computer professional this includes ensuring that system elements perform as intended. Also, when one contracts for work with another party, one has an obligation to keep that party properly informed about progress toward completing that work.

A computing professional has a responsibility to request a change in any assignment that he or she feels cannot be completed as defined. Only after serious consideration and with full disclosure of risks and concerns to the employer or client, should one accept the assignment. The major underlying principle here is the obligation to accept personal accountability for professional work. On some occasions other ethical principles may take greater priority.

A judgment that a specific assignment should not be performed may not be accepted. Having clearly identified one's concerns and reasons for that judgment, but failing to procure a change in that assignment, one may yet be obligated, by contract or by law, to proceed as directed. The computing professional's ethical judgment should be the final guide in deciding whether or not to proceed. Regardless of the decision, one must accept the responsibility for the consequences.

However, performing assignments "against one's own judgment" does not relieve the professional of responsibility for any negative consequences.

2.7 Improve Public Understanding of Computing and Its Consequences

Computing professionals have a responsibility to share technical knowledge with the public by encouraging understanding of computing, including the impacts of computer systems and their limitations. This imperative implies an obligation to counter any false views related to computing.

2.8 Access Computing and Communication Resources Only When Authorized To Do So

Theft or destruction of tangible and electronic property is prohibited by imperative 1.2—"Avoid harm to others." Trespassing and unauthorized use of a computer or communication system is addressed by this imperative. Trespassing includes accessing communication networks and computer systems, or accounts and/or files associated with those systems, without explicit authorization to do so. Individuals and organizations have the right to restrict access to their systems so long as they do not violate the discrimination principle (see 1.4). No one should enter or use another's computer system, software, or data files without permission. One must always have appropriate approval before using system resources, including communication ports, file space, other system peripherals, and computer time.

3. Organizational Leadership Imperatives

Background Note: This section draws extensively from the draft IFIP Code of Ethics, especially its sections on organizational ethics and international concerns. The ethical obligations of organizations tend to be neglected in most codes of professional conduct, perhaps because these codes are written from the perspective of the individual member. This dilemma is addressed by stating these imperatives from the perspective of the organizational leader. In this context "leader" is viewed as any organizational member who has leadership or educational responsibilities. These imperatives generally may apply to organizations as well as their leaders. In this context "organizations" are corporations, government agencies, and other "employers" as well as volunteer professional organizations.

As an ACM member and an organizational leader, I will . . .

3.1 Articulate Social Responsibilities of Members of an Organizational Unit and Encourage Full Acceptance of those Responsibilities

Because organizations of all kinds have impacts on the public, they must accept responsibilities to society. Organizational procedures and attitudes oriented toward quality and the welfare of society will reduce harm to members of the public, thereby serving public interest and fulfilling social responsibility. Therefore, organizational leaders must encourage full participation in meeting social responsibilities as well as quality performance.

3.2 Manage Personnel and Resources to Design and Build Information Systems that Enhance the Quality of Working Life

Organizational leaders are responsible for ensuring that computer systems enhance, not degrade, the quality of working life. When implementing a computer system, organizations must consider the personal and professional development, physical safety, and human dignity of all workers. Appropriate human-computer ergonomic standards should be considered in system design and in the workplace.

3.3 Acknowledge and Support Proper and Authorized Uses of an Organization's Computing and Communication Resources

Because computer systems can become tools to harm as well as to benefit an organization, the leadership has the responsibility to clearly define appropriate and inappropriate uses of organizational computing resources. While the number and scope of such rules should be minimal, they should be fully enforced when established.

3.4 Ensure that Users and those Who Will Be Affected by a System Have Their Needs Clearly Articulated During the Assessment and Design of Requirements; Later the System Must Be Validated to Meet Requirements

Current system users, potential users and other persons whose lives may be affected by a system must have their needs assessed and incorporated in the statement of requirements. System validation should ensure compliance with those requirements.

3.5 Articulate and Support Policies that Protect the Dignity of Users and Others Affected by a Computing System

Designing or implementing systems that deliberately or inadvertently demean individuals or groups is ethically unacceptable. Computer professionals who are in decision making positions should verify that systems are designed and implemented to protect personal privacy and enhance personal dignity.

3.6 Create Opportunities for Members of the Organization to Learn the Principles and Limitations of Computer Systems

This complements the imperative on public understanding (2.7). Educational opportunities are essential to facilitate optimal participation of all organizational members. Opportunities must be available to all members to help them improve their knowledge and skills in computing, including courses that familiarize them with the consequences and limitations of particular types of systems. In particular, professionals must be made aware of the dangers of building systems around oversimplified models, the improbability of anticipating and designing for every possible operating condition, and other issues related to the complexity of this profession.

4. Compliance with the Code

As an ACM member I will . . .

4.1 Uphold and Promote the Principles of this Code

The future of the computing profession depends on both technical and ethical excellence. Not only is it important for ACM computing professionals to adhere to the principles expressed in this Code, each member should encourage and support adherence by other members.

4.2 Treat Violations of this Code as Inconsistent with Membership in the ACM

Adherence of professionals to a code of ethics is largely a voluntary matter. However, if a member does not follow this code by engaging in gross misconduct, membership in ACM may be terminated.

This Code and the supplemental Guidelines were developed by the Task Force for the Revision of the ACM Code of Ethics and Professional Conduct: Ronald E. Anderson, Chair, Gerald Engel, Donald Gotterbarn, Grace C. Hertlein, Alex Hoffman, Bruce Jawer, Deborah G. Johnson, Doris K. Lidtke, Joyce Currie Little, Dianne Martin, Donn B. Parker, Judith A. Perrolle, and Richard S. Rosenberg. The Task Force was organized by ACM/SIGCAS and funding was provided by the ACM SIG Discretionary Fund. This Code and the supplemental Guidelines were adopted by the ACM Council on October 16, 1992.

©1998 Association for Computing Machinery, Inc.

Glossary

3-D environments p. 324 Drawn or photographed virtual spaces you can explore with mouse clicks.

3-D modeling software p. 209 Software that enables the user to create 3-D objects. The objects can be rotated, stretched, and combined with other model objects to create complex 3-D scenes.

3G p. 284 The next generation of mobile wireless technology, which promises high-bandwidth connections that will support true multimedia, including real-time video.

802.11a p. 283 A newer, higher-bandwidth, longer-range version of Wi-Fi.

802.11b p. 283 See Wi-Fi.

802.11g p. 283 A newer, higher-bandwidth, longer-range version of Wi-Fi. Called Airport Extreme by Apple.

A

AAC p. 213 Advanced Audio Codec, one of a number of relatively new methods of audio compression than can squeeze music files to a fraction of their original CD-file sizes, often without perceptible loss of quality.

absolute references p. 178 References in a spreadsheet to a specific cell address.

access time p. 78 The amount of time, measured in nanoseconds, it takes for a CPU to retrieve a unit of data from memory. Also the amount of time, measured in milliseconds, it takes for a CPU to retrieve a unit of data from a disk drive.

access-control software p. 359 Software that only allows user access according to the user's needs. Some users can open only files that are related to their work. Some users are allowed read-only access to files they can see but not change.

account p. 184 Monetary category that represents various types of income, expenses, and liabilities.

accounting and financial management software p. 184 Software especially designed to set up accounts, keep track of money flow between accounts, record transactions, adjust balances in accounts, provide an audit trail, automate routine tasks such as check writing, and produce reports.

acquisition p. 428 The process of capturing data about an event that is important to the organization.

action document p. 429 In a transaction processing system, a document that initiates an action by the recipient or verifies for the recipient that a transaction has occurred.

active badge p. 367 A microprocessor-controlled ID badge that broadcasts infrared identification codes to a network receiver that updates a badge-location database.

ActiveX p. 326 A collection of programming technologies and tools that can be used to create programs that are similar in many ways to Java applets.

Ada p. 499 A massive programming language, named for programming pioneer Ada King and based on Pascal, that was developed in the late 1970s for the U.S. Defense Department.

adaptive radio p. 298 A technology that enables wireless devices to selectively transmit messages based on other wireless network traffic, thus avoiding the interference that plagues many other wireless technologies.

address p. 176 In a spreadsheet, the location of a cell, determined by row number and column number.

affective computers p. 192 Computers that use sensors to detect the emotional states of their users, and respond accordingly.

agents p. 148 Software programs that can ask questions, respond to commands, pay attention to users' work patterns, serve as a guide and a coach, take on owners' goals, and use reasoning to fabricate their own goals.

agricultural age p. 45 The era covering most of the past ten thousand years, during which humanity lived mainly by domesticating animals and growing food using plows and other agricultural tools.

alerts p. 330 Along with notifications a popular noncorporate type of push technology on the Web, mostly offered through services that alert subscribers to stock price changes, breaking news, and the like

algorithm p. 128 A set of step-by-step instructions that, when completed, solves a problem.

alias p. 21 See user name.**p. 291** An alternative name for a file, such as might be made for an email distribution list to save the trouble of typing or selecting many names if you send messages to the same group of people repeatedly.

all-in-one devices p. 102 See multifunction printer.

alpha testing p. 511 Initial testing of a system; also called "pre-beta testing."

analog signal p. 279 A continuous wave.

analysis p. 510 The phase of the systems development life cycle in which details are fleshed out before design begins.

Analytical Engine p. 31 The first computer, conceived by Charles Babbage. Programmed with punch cards, it included functions of input, output, processing, and storage.

animation p. 212 The process of simulating motion with a series of still pictures.

antivirus p. 355 A program designed to search for viruses, notify users when they're found, and remove them from infected files.

applet p. 147 A small compiled program designed to run inside another application—typically a Web browser.

application program (application) p. 9 Software tool that allows a computer to be used for specific purposes.

application service provider (ASP) p. 318 A company that manages and delivers application services on a contract basis.

application suite (office suite) p. 135 A collection of several related application programs that are also sold as separate programs.

architecture p. 76 Design that determines how individual components of the CPU are put together on the chip. More generally used to describe the way individual components are put together to create a complete computer system.

arithmetic logic unit (ALU) p. 74 The part of the CPU that performs data calculations and comparisons.

armature p. 108 The part of a disk drive that moves the read/write head across the disk surface.

artificial intelligence p. 532 The field of computer science devoted to making computers perceive, reason, and act in ways that have, until now, been reserved for human beings.

ASCII p. 69 American Standard Code for Information Interchange, a code that represents characters as 8-bit codes. Allows the binary computer to work with letters, digits, and special characters.

assembler p. 498 A program that translates each assembly-language instruction into a machine-language instruction.

assembly language p. 498 A language that is functionally equivalent to machine language but is easier for people to read, write, and understand. Programmers use alphabetic codes that correspond to the machine's numeric instructions.

asynchronous communication p. 291 Delayed communication, such as that used for newsgroups and mailing lists, where the sender and the recipients don't have to be logged in at the same time.

attachments p. 21 A way to send formatted word processor documents, pictures, and other multimedia files via email.

audio digitizers p. 97 Hardware devices or software programs that capture a sound and store it as a data file on a disk.

audit trail p. 184 In accounting, a set of records enabling you to retrace the history of transactions.

audit-control software p. 360 Monitors and records computer transactions as they happen so auditors can trace and identify suspicious computer activity after the fact.

authoring tools p. 404 Software used to create multimedia presentations.

automated factory p. 388 A factory that uses extensive computer systems, robots, and networks to streamline and automate many jobs.

automated offices p. 389 Offices that use extensive computer systems and networks to streamline information flow and automate many processes.

automated teller machine (ATM) p. 278 A device that enables users to remotely access and deposit money from their bank accounts through the use of a network.

automatic correction (autocorrect) p. 160 A word processing feature that catches and corrects common typing errors.

automatic footnoting p. 160 A word processing feature that places footnotes where they belong on the page.

automatic formatting p. 160 A word processing feature that applies formatting to the text.

automatic hyphenation p. 160 A word processing feature that divides long words that fall at the ends of lines.

automatic link p. 180 A link between worksheets in a spreadsheet that ensures that a change in one worksheet is reflected in the other.

automatic recalculation p. 178 A spreadsheet capability that allows for easy correction of errors and makes it easy to try out different values while searching for solutions.

automatic speech recognition p. 544 See speech recognition.

automatic translation p. 536 The process of using software to translate written or spoken communication from one natural language to another.

autonomous systems p. 371 Complex systems that can assume almost complete responsibility for a task without human input, verification, or decision making.

avatars p. 228 Graphical bodies used to represent a person in a virtual meeting place; can range from a simple cartoon sketch to an elaborate 3-D figure or an exotic abstract icon.

B

Back and Forward buttons p. 18 Browser buttons that allow you to retrace your steps while navigating the Web and return to previously visited sites.

backbone p. 277 A collection of common pathways used to transmit large quantities of data between networks in a wide-area network (WAN).

backup p. 364 The process of saving data—especially for data recovery. Many systems automatically back up data and software onto disks or tapes.

backward compatible p. 73 Able to run software written for older CPUs. Also, when referring to a software program, able to read and write files compatible with older versions of the program.

bandwidth p. 280 The quantity of information that can be transmitted through a communication medium in a given amount of time.

bar chart p. 182 A chart that shows relative values with bars, appropriate when data fall into a few categories.

bar code reader p. 94 A reading tool that uses light to read universal product codes, inventory codes, and other codes created out of patterns of variable-width bars.

Basic p. 499 Beginner's All-purpose Symbolic Instruction Code, a programming language developed in the 1960s as an easy-to-learn, interactive alternative to FORTRAN for beginning programmers; it is still widely used today in forms such as Microsoft's popular Visual Basic.

batch processing p. 253 Accumulating transactions and feeding them into a computer in large batches.

baud rate p. 279 An older measurement of modem speed; today bits per second (bps) is a more accurate term.

bay p. 78 An open area in the system box for disk drives and other peripheral devices.

beta testing p. 511 Testing of almost-finished software by potential end users.

binary p. 67 A choice of two values, such as yes and no or zero and one.

binary number system p. 69 A system that denotes all numbers with combinations of two digits.

biometrics p. 358 Measurements of individual body characteristics, such as a voice print or fingerprint; sometimes used in computer security.

BIOS (basic input/output system) p. 79 The firmware programs in read-only memory.

bit p. 67 Binary digit, the smallest unit of information. A bit can have two values—0 or 1.

bit depth p. 99 Color depth, the number of bits devoted to each pixel in a color display.

bitmapped graphics p. 203 Graphics in which images are stored and manipulated as organized collections of pixels rather than as shapes and lines. Contrast with object-oriented graphics.

bits per second (bps) p. 279 The standard unit of measure for modem speed.

blog p. 321 Short for Web log, a personal Web page that often carries diary-like entries or political commentaries. Blogs are fast proliferating as new software allows users to create Web pages without having to learn the technical details of HTML and Web authoring.

Bluetooth p. 283 A type of wireless technology that enables mobile phones, handheld computers, and PCs to communicate with each other regardless of operating system.

bookmarks p. 18 Personal lists kept on a browser of favorite or memorable Web sites that are often revisited. Also called favorites.

Boolean logic p. 329 A complex query structure supported by most search engines; one example is "American AND Indian BUT NOT Cleveland."

booting p. 140 Loading the non-ROM part of the operating system into memory.

bot p. 192 Software robots that crawl around the Web collecting information, helping consumers make decisions, answering email, and even playing games.

bounce p. 291 The automatic return of an undeliverable email message to its sender.

bridges p. 277 Hardware devices that can pass messages between networks.

broadband connection p. 281 An Internet connection such as DSL or cable modem that offers higher bandwidth, and therefore faster transmission speed, than standard modem connections.

browse p. 241 The process of finding information in a database or other data source, such as the World Wide Web.

brute-force p. 535 A computing technique of rapidly repeating a simple operation until an answer is found.

bug p. 127 An error in programming.

bullet charts p. 210 Graphical elements, such as drawings and tables, integrated into a series of charts that list the main points of a presentation.

burn p. 6 To record data onto CD-R and CD-RW disks.

bus p. 78 Group of wires on a circuit board. Information travels between components through a bus.

business alliance p. 435 A cooperative arrangement between two or more businesses with complementary capabilities.

business organization p. 424 A company or a firm; a system designed for the purpose of creating products and services for customers.

business process p. 426 A related set of primary and support activities that uses people, information, and other resources to create valuable products and/or services for customers.

business-to-business (B2B) p. 332 E-commerce transactions that involve businesses providing goods or services to other businesses.

business-to-consumer (B2C) p. 332 E-commerce transactions that involve businesses providing goods or services to consumers.

business-to-employee (B2E) p. 468 Another name for the B2B model when the focus is primarily on handling the activities that take place within the organization.

button p. 8 A hot spot on a screen that responds to mouse clicks. A button can be programmed to perform one of many tasks, such as opening a dialog box or launching an application.

byte pp. 67 Grouping of 8 bits.

C

C p. 499 A complex computer language invented at Bell Labs in the early 1970s as a tool for programming operating systems such as UNIX; now one of the most widely-used programming languages.

C# p. 499 A popular Windows-only programming language that's similar to C++.

C++ p. 499 A variation of the C programming language that takes advantage of a modern programming methodology called object-oriented programming.

cable modems p. 315 A type of broadband Internet connection that uses the same network of coaxial cables that delivers TV signals.

camera-ready p. 170 Typeset-quality pages, ready to be photographed and printed.

cards p. 78 See expansion card.

carpal tunnel syndrome p. 106 An affliction of the wrist and hand that results from repeating the same movements over long periods.

cascading style sheets p. 325 A feature of dynamic HTML that gives users more control over how a Web page is displayed. Cascading style sheets can define formatting and layout elements that aren't recognized in older versions of HTML.

CD-R p. 110 (compact disk–recordable) An optical disk you can write information on, but you cannot remove the information.

CD-ROM drive p. 6 A common optical drive in computers that can read data from CD-ROM disks.

CD-ROM p. 110 Compact disc—read-only memory, a type of optical disk that contains data that cannot be changed; CD-ROMs are commonly used to distribute commercial software programs.

CD-RW drive p. 6 A disk drive that can read and write on rewritable optical disks.

CD-RW p. 110 Compact disk–rewritable, an optical disk that allows writing, erasing, and rewriting.

cell p. 176 The intersection of a row and a column on the grid of a spreadsheet.

central processing unit (CPU) p. 5 Part of the computer that processes information, performs arithmetic calculations, and makes basic decisions based on information values.

centralized database p. 254 A database housed in a mainframe computer, accessible only to information-processing personnel.

character-based interface p. 141 A user interface based on text characters rather than graphics.

chat room p. 291 Public real-time teleconference.

chief information officers (CIOs) p. 389 Along with chief technology officers (CTOs), the chief decision makers concerning enterprise computer systems and technology in a business enterprise.

chief technology officers (CTOs) p. 389 Along with chief information officers (CIOs), the chief decision makers concerning enterprise computer systems and technology in a business enterprise.

click p. 8 The action of pressing a button on a mouse.

client/server p. 254 Client programs in desktop computers send information requests through a network to server databases on mainframes, minicomputers, or desktop computers; the servers process queries and send the requested data back to the client.

client/server model p. 285 For a local-area network, a hierarchical model in which one or more computers act as dedicated servers and all the remaining computers act as clients. The server fills requests from clients for data and other resources.

clip art p. 207 A collection of redrawn images that you can cut out and paste into your own documents.

Clipboard p. 159 A special portion of memory for temporarily holding information for later use.

clock p. 73 The timing device producing electrical pulses for synchronizing the computer's operations.

cluster p. 76 A grouping of multiple processors or servers to, for example, improve graphic rendering speeds or increase reliability.

CMOS p. 78 Complementary metal oxide semiconductor, a special low-energy kind of RAM that can store small amounts of data for long periods of time on battery power. CMOS RAM is used to store the date, time, and calendar in a PC. CMOS RAM is called parameter RAM in Macintoshes.

COBOL p. 499 Common Business Oriented Language, developed when the U.S. government in 1960 demanded a new language oriented toward business data processing problems.

code of ethics p. 368 Policies and procedures, such as those developed by companies and by organizations such as the ACM (Association for Computing Machinery), to guide the behavior of information workers.

coding p. 495 Writing a program from an algorithm.

color depth p. 99 Bit depth, the number of bits devoted to each pixel.

color monitor p. 101 A monitor with the capability of displaying a wide range of colors, with greater depth than a gray-scale monitor.

color-matching p. 170 Technology enabling desktop publishers to match colors on the screen with printed colors.

columns p. 176 Along with rows, comprise the grid of a spreadsheet.

command-line interface p. 141 User interface that requires the user to type text commands on a command-line to communicate with the operating system.

communication software p. 285 Software that enables computers to interact with each other over a phone line or other network.

compatible (compatibility) p. 73 The ability of a software program to run on a specific computer system. Also, the ability of a hardware device to function with a particular type of computer.

compiler p. 129 A translator program that translates an entire program from a high-level computer language before the program is run for the first time.

component software p. 505 Software designed in small, independent units (components) that can be plugged into applications and operating systems to add features as needed.

compression p. 216 Making files smaller using special encoding schemes. File compression saves storage space on disks and saves transmission time when files are transferred through networks.

computed field p. 241 In a database, a field containing formulas similar to spreadsheet formulas; they display values calculated from values in other numeric fields.

computer addiction p. 334 The condition in which networking and surfing the Net become more real and interesting than the everyday physical world.

computer architecture p. 519 The branch of computer science that deals with the way hardware and software work together.

computer crime p. 348 Any crime accomplished through knowledge or use of computer technology.

computer forensics p. 348 The use of computer technology and applications as tools to help law enforcement officials stop criminal activities.

computer monitoring p. 394 Using computer technology to track, record, and evaluate worker performance, often without the knowledge of the worker.

computer science p. 518 A relatively new discipline that focuses on the process of computing through several areas of specialization, including theory, algorithms, data structures, programming concepts and languages, computer architecture, management information systems, artificial intelligence, and software engineering.

computer security p. 358 Protecting computer systems and the information they contain against unwanted access, damage, modification, or destruction.

computer telephony integration (CTI) p. 293 The linking of computers and telephones to gain productivity, such as by allowing PCs to serve as speakerphones, answering machines, and complete voicemail systems.

computer-aided design (CAD) p. 209 The use of computers to design products.

computer-aided instruction (CAI) p. 401 Software programs for teaching that combine drill-and-practice software and tutorial software.

computer-aided manufacturing (CAM) p. 210 When the design of a product is completed, the numbers are fed to a program that controls the manufacturing of parts. For electronic parts the design translates directly into a template for etching circuits onto chips. Also called computer integrated manufacturing (CIM).

computer-aided systems engineering (CASE) p. 517 Commercially available software packages that typically include charting and diagramming tools, a centralized data dictionary, a user interface generator, and code generators.

computer-integrated manufacturing (CIM) p. 210 The combination of CAD and CAM.

concurrent processing p. 137 A large computer working on several jobs at the same time. The computer uses multiple CPUs to process jobs simultaneously.

consumer portals p. 329 Portals that include search engines, email services, chat rooms, references, news and sports headlines, shopping malls, other services, and advertisements—many of the same things found in online services such as AOL.

consumer-to-consumer (C2C) p. 469 The e-commerce model which represents individuals, organizations, or companies that are selling and buying directly with each other via the Internet.

contacts p. 20 The people with whom one corresponds regularly, kept as a list in an email program or service.

context-sensitive menus p. 143 Menus offering choices that depend on the context.

contract p. 352 A type of law that covers trade secrets.

control structures p. 494 Logical structures that control the order in which instructions are carried out.

cookie pp. 324 Small files deposited on a user's hard disk by Web sites, enabling sites to remember what they know about their visitors between sessions.

copy p. 159 An editing function in a word processing program that duplicates words and temporarily stores them in a clipboard, allowing them to be pasted into another part of the same document or a different document.

copy protected p. 133 Produced in a way that prevents any physical copying, such as is the case with software CDs and DVDs, especially some entertainment products.

copyright p. 352 A type of law that traditionally protects forms of literary expression.

copyrighted software p. 133 Software that prevents a disk from being copied.

corporate portals p. 329 Specialized portals on an intranet that serve the employees of a particular corporation.

cost-benefit analysis p. 450 A comparison of costs (such as salaries of the information system staff) to benefits (such as a reduction in the number of customer complaints), which managers use to decide whether an information system project is worthwhile on its own merits and also in comparison with other proposed information system projects.

courseware p. 401 Educational software.

CPU p. 5 See central processing unit.

cracking p. 356 Unauthorized access and/or vandalism of computer systems; short for criminal hacking.

critical path method (CPM) p. 451 A mathematical model of a project's schedule used to calculate when particular activities will be completed.

critical success factors (CSF) p. 449 A strategic planning approach that identifies the variables that are crucial for the success of the business from the top managers' point of view and identifies IT plans for systems that provide access to information about those critical success factors.

cross-platform applications p. 147 Programs, such as Adobe Photoshop, that are available in similar versions for multiple platforms.

CRT (cathode-ray tube) monitors p. 100 Television-style monitors used as the output device for many desktop computers.

cursor (arrow) key p. 7 A keyboard key that moves the cursor up or down, right or left, on the screen.

cursor p. 7 A line or rectangle, sometimes flashing, that indicates your location on the screen or in a document.

custom application p. 136 An application programmed for a specific purpose, typically for a specific client.

customer relationship management (CRM) p. 256 Software systems for organizing and tracking information on customers.

cut p. 159 An editing function in a word processing program that deletes words from a document and temporarily stores them in a clipboard, allowing them to be pasted into another part of the same document or a different document.

cut-and-paste p. 162 Copying or deleting text from one point and pasting it into another point in the document.

cyberspace p. 336 A term used to describe the Internet and other online networks, especially the artificial realities and virtual communities that form on them. First coined by William Gibson in his novel, *Neuromancer*.

D

data p. 34 Information in a form that can be read, used, and manipulated by a computer.

data dictionary p. 516 A catalog, or directory, that describes all the data flowing through a system.

data files p. 9 Documents that contain passive data rather than instructions.

data flow diagram p. 512 A simple graphical depiction of the movement of data through a system.

data management p. 439 A component of the decision support system, in which a manager queries and retrieves relevant information from a database of internal and external information of the organization.

data mining p. 255 The discovery and extraction of hidden predictive information from large databases.

data structure p. 516 A set of data elements used together, such as an invoice or other paper or electronic document.

data transfer rates p. 110 The speed at which a drive, for example, can read or write data.

data translation software p. 287 Software that enables users of different systems with incompatible file formats to read and modify each other's files.

data type p. 240 See field type.

data warehouse p. 254 An integrated collection of corporate data stored in one location.

database p. 240 A collection of information stored in an organized form in a computer.

database management system (DBMS) p. 250 A program or system of programs that can manipulate data in a large collection of files (the database), cross-referencing between files as needed.

database program p. 240 A software tool for organizing the storage and retrieval of the information in a database.

data-driven Web site p. 325 A Web site that uses database technology to present information dynamically based on current conditions and client requests.

date field p. 241 A field containing only dates.

debugger p. 496 A program use to simplify the process of locating and correcting errors during the program development process.

debugging p. 128 Finding and correcting errors—bugs—in computer software.

decision support system (DSS) p. 439 A computer system that provides managers with the tools they need to analyze information they deem relevant for a particular decision or class of decisions.

decision table p. 516 A table that shows, in a row–column format, the decision rules that apply and what actions to take when certain conditions occur.

decode unit p. 75 Takes the instruction read by the prefetcher and translates it into a form suitable for the CPU's internal processing.

Delete key p. 7 A keyboard key that acts as an eraser by, for example, removing highlighted text in a word document.

denial of service (DoS) attack p. 357 A type of computer vandalism that bombards servers and Web sites with so much bogus traffic that they're effectively shut down, denying service to legitimate customers and clients.

design p. 510 The phase of the systems development life cycle that focuses on how the problem will be solved.

de-skilled p. 393 Transformed in such a way that a job requires less skill.

desktop publishing (DTP) p. 169 Software used mainly to produce print publications. Also, the process of using desktop publishing software to produce publications.

desktop replacements p. 40 Heavy but powerful laptops that perform as well as desktop PCs.

development p. 511 The phase of the systems development life cycle in which the system is built and tested.

device drivers p. 140 Small programs that allow input/output devices to communicate with the computer.

dialog box p. 142 In a graphical user interface, a box that enables the user to communicate with the computer.

dialog management component p. 443 A component of the executive information system made up of the set of human–computer interactive features that enables the executive to select the necessary data and display it in a variety of formats, including summary and exception reports, lists, charts, tables, and graphs.

dial-up connection p. 313 A temporary connection to an Internet host that uses a modem and standard telephone lines.

digit p. 67 A discrete, countable unit.

digital p. 67 Information made up of discrete units that can be counted.

digital camera p. 96 A camera that captures images and stores them as bit patterns on disks or other digital storage media instead of using film.

digital cash p. 334 A system for purchasing goods and services on the Internet without using credit cards.

digital divide p. 335 A term that describes the divide between the people who do and do not have access to the Internet.

digital signal p. 279 A stream of bits.

digital signatures p. 334 A developing identity verification standard that uses encryption techniques to protect against email forgery.

digital video p. 214 Video reduced to a series of numbers, which can be edited, stored, and played back without loss of quality.

digital video camera p. 96 A video camera that captures footage in digital form so that clips can be transferred to and from a computer for editing with no loss of quality.

digitize p. 96 Converting information into a digital form that can be stored in the computer's memory.

digitized sound p. 545 Computerized sound output.

digitized speech p. 545 Computerized voice output that mimics human speech.

DIMMs p. 79 Dual in-line memory modules.

direct connection p. 15 A dedicated, direct connection to the Internet through a LAN, with the computer having its own IP address.

directories p. 256 See directory.

directory p. 19 A logical container used to group files and other directories. Also called a folder.

disk drive p. 107 See diskette drive.

diskette drive p. 6 Device used to retrieve information from a disk and, in some cases, to transfer data to it.

diskettes p. 6 Small, magnetically sensitive, flexible plastic wafers housed in a plastic case, used as a storage device.

display p. 7 See monitor.

distance education p. 404 Using computers, networks, and other technology to extend the educational process beyond the walls of a school, connecting students and faculty at remote locations.

distributed computing p. 331 Integrating all kinds of computers, from mainframes to PCs, into a single, seamless system.

distributed database p. 254 Data strewn out across networks on several different computers.

distributed denial of service (DDoS) attack p. 357 A denial of service attack in which the flood of messages comes from many compromised systems distributed across the Net.

distributed intelligence p. 548 Artificial intelligence concepts applied to networks rather than to individual computers.

docking station p. 40 A device for expanding a laptop computer so that it has the power and flexibility of a desktop.

document p. 9 A file, such as a term paper or chart created with applications.

documentation p. 132 Instructions for installing the software on a computer's hard disk.

domain name registry p. 321 A company that provides its customers with domain names that are easier to remember and use.

domain name system (DNS) p. 311 A system that translates a computer's numerical IP address into an easier-to-remember string of names separated by dots.

domains p. 311 A class of Internet addresses indicated by a suffix such as .com, .gov, or .net.

dot coms p. 467 Internet-based companies.

dot-matrix printer p. 102 A type of impact printer, which forms images by physically striking paper, ribbon, and print hammer together, the way a typewriter does.

dots per inch (dpi) p. 203 A measurement of the density of pixels, defining the resolution of a graphic.

double-click p. 8 To click a mouse button twice in rapid succession.

download p. 287 To copy software from an online source to a local computer.

downloadable audio p. 323 Compressed sound files that you must download onto your computer's hard disk before the browser or some other application can play them.

downloadable video p. 323 Compressed video files that can be downloaded and viewed on a computer.

downstream traffic p. 313 Information transmitted from the Internet to the subscriber.

drag p. 8 To move the mouse while holding the mouse button down. Used for moving objects, selecting text, drawing, and other tasks.

drag-and-drop p. 159 Editing feature that enables the user to move selected text or an object by dragging it (with the mouse) from one part of the screen to another.

drawing software p. 207 Stores a picture as a collection of lines and shapes. Also stores shapes as shape formulas and text as text.

drill-and-practice software p. 399 Teaching software based on the principles of individualized rate, small steps, and positive feedback.

drum scanners p. 96 Scanners used in publishing applications where image quality is critical.

DSL (digital subscriber line) p. 313 A type of broadband connection to the Internet offered by phone companies.

dual-boot PCs p. 147 PCs that can switch back and forth between two operating systems by rebooting.

DVD p. 111 Digital video disk or digital versatile disk, a popular type of high-capacity optical disk used in both consumer video playback machines and computers.

DVD drive p. 6 An optical disk drive that can read high-capacity DVD disks.

DVD/CD-RW drive p. 111 A disk drive that combines the capabilities of a DVD-ROM drive and a CD-RW drive in a single unit.

DVD+MRW p. 111 An emerging new standard, also called Mt. Rainier, for rewritable media.

DVD+R p. 111 Recordable DVD disk.

DVD+RW p. 111 DVD disk that allows writing, erasing, and rewriting.

DVD-RAM p. 111 A type of optical disk with multigigabyte capacity that can be read, written, and erased.

DVD-ROM drive p. 110 An optical disk drive that can read high-capacity DVD disks.

dynamic HTML p. 325 A relatively new version of HTML that supports formatting and layout features that aren't supported in standard HTML.

E

e-business p. 467 Though sometimes used interchangeably with the broader term e-commerce, here used to refer to the e-commerce activities of a particular company or organization.

e-commerce software p. 479 Programs on a Web server that provide the commercial services to consumers and business partners on the Web site.

educational simulations p. 403 Software that enables students to explore artificial environments that are imaginary or based on reality. Most have the look and feel of a game, but they challenge students to learn through exploration, experimentation, and interaction with other students.

edutainment p. 409 Programs geared toward home markets that combine education and entertainment.

effectiveness p. 447 How an organization's customers evaluate the quality of the output—products and services—of the value chain.

efficiency p. 447 How an organization's primary and support activities produce desired output with less work or lower costs.

electronic book (ebook) p. 175 A handheld device that displays digital representations of the contents of books.

electronic commerce (e-commerce) p. 332 Business transactions through electronic networks.

electronic cottage p. 391 A home in which modern technology enables a person to work at home.

electronic data interchange (EDI) p. 332 A set of specifications for conducting basic business transactions over private networks.

electronic mail (email) p. 19 Allows Internet users to send mail messages, data files, and software programs to other Internet users and to users of most commercial networks and online services.

electronic paper (epaper) p. 175 A flexible experimental output device that can be read like printed paper, erased, and reused.

electronic sweatshops p. 395 Worker warehouses where most of the work is mindless keyboarding, computer monitoring is a common practice, wages are low and working conditions poor, and repetitive stress injuries are common.

electronica p. 222 Sequenced music that is designed from the ground up with digital technology.

email server p. 317 A specialized server that acts like a local post office for a particular Internet host.

email viruses p. 353 Viruses spread via email.

e-marketplaces p. 472 International, extranet-based alliances between vendors, suppliers, and other organizations.

embedded computer p. 41 Computer that is embedded into a consumer product, such as a wristwatch or game machine, to enhance those products. Also used to control hardware devices.

emoticons p. 296 Text-based substitutes, such as the smiley face :-) , for body language and tone of voice, which have been developed by online communities.

emulation p. 147 A process that enables programs to run on a noncompatible operating system.

encryption p. 359 Protects transmitted information by scrambling the transmissions. When a user encrypts a message by applying a secret numerical code (encryption key), the message can be transmitted or stored as an indecipherable garble of characters. The message can be read only after it's been reconstructed with a matching key.

end user p. 509 A person who uses the information system directly or uses the information produced by the system.

end-user development p. 509 A systems development approach in which a project team comprising only end users develops many small-scale systems without the direct involvement of a professional systems analyst.

end-user license agreement (EULA) p. 133 An agreement typically including specifications for how a program may be used, warranty disclaimers, and rules concerning the copying of the software.

Enter key p. 7 A keyboard key with a number of special functions, such as moving the cursor to the beginning of the next line, or activating a selected option.

enterprise network systems p. 276 Large, complex networks with hundreds of computers that are tracked and maintained with network management system software.

enterprise resource planning (ERP) p. 432 Creating information systems to support an organization's operational business processes.

entry barrier p. 446 A market obstacle, usually an innovative new product or service that is difficult for a competitor to emulate.

equation solver p. 181 A feature of some spreadsheet programs that determines data values.

ergonomic keyboard p. 91 A keyboard that places the keys at angles that allow your wrists to assume a more natural position while you type, potentially reducing the risk of repetitive-stress injuries.

ergonomics p. 106 The science of designing work environments that enable people and things to interact efficiently and safely.

Ethernet p. 279 A popular networking architecture developed in 1976 at Xerox.

Ethernet port p. 279 A network interface port that is included on main circuit boards in most newer PCs for easy connection to Ethernet networks.

EULA p. 133 See end-user license agreement (EULA).

executable files p. 9 Files, such as applications, that contain instructions that can be executed by the computer.

executive information system (EIS) p. 442 A system that combines features of management information and decision support systems to support unstructured decision-making by top managers.

expansion cards p. 78 Special-purpose circuit boards that can be inserted in a computer's expansion slots.

expansion slot p. 78 An area inside the computer's housing that holds special-purpose circuit boards.

expert system shells p. 542 Generic expert systems containing human interfaces and inference engines.

expert systems (ES) p. 445 Information systems or software programs designed to replicate the decision-making process of a human expert.

export data p. 242 Transmitting records and fields from a database program to another program.

extension p. 15 A file name feature, usually three characters following a period at the end of the file name, that gives more information about the file's origin or use.

external drives p. 6 Disk drives, such as hard disks for additional storage, not included in a system unit but rather attached to it via cables.

external modem p. 279 A modem located in a box linked to a serial port or USB port, rather than being installed on a circuit board inside the computer's chassis.

extranets p. 332 Private TCP/IP networks designed for outside use by customers, clients, and business partners of an organization. These networks are typically for electronic commerce.

extreme programming (XP) p. 506 A relatively new programming methodology that focuses more on the culture of programming than on technology, in which the entire programming team "owns" the code; each member of the team has a right to improve it and the responsibility for making it work properly.

F

facsimile (fax) machine p. 103 An output device capable of sending, in effect, a photocopy through a telephone line, allowing for fast and convenient transmission of information stored on paper.

fair use p. 352 The time-honored right to make copies of copyrighted material for personal and academic use and for other noncompetitive purposes.

favorites p. 18 See bookmarks.

fax modem p. 103 Hardware peripheral that enables a computer to send onscreen documents to a receiving fax machine by translating the document into signals that can be sent over phone wires and decoded by the receiving fax machine.

feedback loop p. 189 In a computer simulation, the user and the computer responding to data from each other.

fiber-optic cable p. 281 High-capacity cable that uses light waves to carry information at blinding speeds.

field p. 240 Each discrete chunk of information in a database record.

field type p. 240 The characteristic of a field that determines the kind of information that can be stored in that field.

file p. 9 An organized collection of related information stored in a computer-readable form.

file manager p. 250 A program that enables users to manipulate files on their computers.

file server p. 287 In a LAN, a computer used as a storehouse for software and data that are shared by several users.

file transfer protocol (FTP) p. 317 A communications protocol that enables users to download files from remote servers to their computers and to upload files they want to share from their computers to these archives.

filtering software p. 334 Software that, for the most part, keeps offensive and otherwise inappropriate Web content from being viewed by children, on-duty workers, and others.

Find p. 15 A command used to locate a particular word, string of characters, or formatting in a document.

find-and-replace (search and replace) p. 159 Finding selected words or phrases throughout a document and replacing them with a different word or phrase.

firewall p. 332 A system used by intranets and other networks for preventing unauthorized communication and securing sensitive internal data.

FireWire (IEEE 1394) p. 278 See IEEE 1394.

FireWire (IEEE 1394, FireWire 400, FireWire 800) p. 116 See IEEE 1394.

firmware p. 41 A program, usually for special-purpose computers, stored on a ROM chip so it cannot be altered.

flash memory p. 78 A type of erasable memory chip used in cell phones, pagers, portable computers, and handheld computers, among other things.

flatbed scanners p. 96 Scanners that look and work like a photocopy machine, except that they create computer files instead of paper copies.

floppy disk drive p. 6 A drive found mostly on older computers that enables them to store small amounts of information on pocket-sized plastic-covered diskettes. Also called diskette drive.

folder p. 15 A container for files and other folders. Also called a directory.

font p. 159 A size and style of typeface.

footer p. 160 Block of information that appears at the bottom of every page in a document, displaying repetitive information such as an automatically calculated page number.

force feedback joystick p. 104 A joystick that receives signals from a computer and gives tactile feedback, such as jolts and bumps, matching the visual output of the game or simulation, an example of an enhanced input device that delivers output.

form p. 323 On the Web, a page (or part of a page) that enables visitors to enter information into fields.

form views p. 241 A view of the database that shows one record at a time.

format p. 159 How the words in a document will look on the page, including individual characters, paragraphs, and the complete document.

formatting p. 159 The function of software, such as word processing software, that enables users to change the appearance of a document by specifying the font, point size, and style of any character in the document, as well as the overall layout of text and graphical elements in the document.

formula p. 176 Step-by-step procedure for calculating a number on a spreadsheet.

FORTRAN p. 499 Formula Translation, the first commercial high-level programming language, designed at IBM in the 1950s to solve scientific and engineering problems.

fourth-generation languages (4GLs) p. 505 The fourth generation of programming languages (after machine, assembly, and high-level languages), which use Englishlike phrases and sentences to issue instructions, are nonprocedural, and increase productivity.

frame p. 212 In animation, one still picture in a video or animated sequence.

frames p. 323 Subdivisions of a Web browser's viewing area that enable visitors to scroll and view different parts of a page—or even multiple pages—simultaneously.

full-access dial-up connections p. 313 Enables a computer connected via modem and phone line to temporarily have full Internet access and a temporary IP address.

full-color p. 170 A desktop published document that uses a wide range of color. Contrast with spot color.

function p. 178 A predefined set of calculations, such as SUM and AVERAGE, in spreadsheet software.

function keys (f-keys) p. 7 Keyboard keys, often twelve lined along the top of the keyboard, that send special commands to the computer depending upon the program being run.

fuzzy logic p. 540 A type of logic that allows conclusions to be stated as probabilities rather than certainties.

G

Gantt chart p. 450 A type of chart capable of representing a project schedule visually, by showing each step or category of steps in a plan, along with their planned and actual start and completion times.

gateways p. 277 Computers connected to two networks that translate communication protocols and transfer information between the two.

GB (gigabyte) p. 72 Approximately 1000MB.

generation p. 364 One cycle of backups; many data-processing shops keep several generations of backups so they can, if necessary, go back several days, weeks, or years to reconstruct data files.

geographical information system (GIS) p. 245 A specialized database that combines tables of data with demographic information and displays geographic and demographic data on maps.

geostationary communications satellites p. 273 Satellites that match the Earth's rotation so they can hang in a stationary position relative to the spinning planet below, relaying wireless transmissions between locations.

gigahertz p. 73 Billions of clock cycles per second, a measurement of a computer's clock speed.

GIGO (garbage in, garbage out) p. 180 Valid output requires valid input.

Global Positioning System (GPS) p. 277 A defense department system with 24 satellites that can pinpoint any location on the Earth.

GPS receiver p. 277 A device that can use Global Positioning System signals to determine its location and communicate that information to a person or a computer.

grammar and style checker p. 166 Component of word processing software that analyzes each word in context, checking for content errors, common grammatical errors, and stylistic problems.

graphical user interface (GUI) p. 141 A user interface based on graphical displays. With a mouse, the user points to icons that represent files, folders, and disks. Documents are displayed in windows. The user selects commands from menus.

graphics tablet p. 92 A pressure-sensitive touch tablet used as a pointing device. The user presses on the tablet with a stylus.

gray-scale monitors p. 100 Monitor that displays black, white, and shades of gray but no other colors.

grid computing p. 331 A form of distributed computing in which not files but processing power is shared between networked computers.

group decision support systems (GDSS) p. 442 Systems designed to improve the productivity of decision-making meetings by enhancing the dynamics of collaborative work.

groupware p. 166 Software designed to be used by work groups rather than individuals.

H

hacker p. 22 Someone who uses computer skills to gain unauthorized access to computer systems. Also sometimes used to refer to a particularly talented, dedicated programmer.

hacking p. 356 Electronic trespassing and vandalism.

handheld computer p. 40 A portable computer small enough to be tucked into a jacket pocket.

handwriting recognition software p. 95 Software that translates the user's handwritten forms into ASCII characters.

hard disk p. 5 A rigid, magnetically sensitive disk that spins rapidly and continuously inside the computer chassis or in a separate box attached to the computer housing. Used as a storage device.

hardware p. 5 Physical parts of the computer system.

hardware compression p. 219 Compression using hardware rather than software.

header p. 160 Block that appears at the top of every page in a document, displaying repetitive information such as a chapter title.

help file p. 132 A documentation file that appears onscreen at the user's request.

helper application p. 324 A program designed to help users view particular types of graphics, animation, audio, or video that can't be played by the browser.

heuristic p. 535 A rule of thumb.

hexadecimal p. 498 Base 16 number system; often used to represent machine-language programs.

hierarchical menus p. 143 Menus that organize commands into compact, efficient submenus.

high-level language p. 129 A programming language that falls somewhere between natural human languages and precise machine languages, developed to streamline and simplify the programming process.

hits p. 19 Web pages containing requested key words, displayed in a list by a Web browser.

host name p. 21 The name of the host computer, network, or ISP address where the user receives email, contained in the part of an Internet email address that comes after the at sign (@).

host system p. 286 A computer that provides services to multiple users.

hot swap p. 114 To remove and replace peripheral devices without powering down the computer and peripherals. Some modern interface standards such as USB and FireWire allow hot-swapping.

hot-sync p. 246 Synchronizing of data, typically between a handheld computer and a desktop PC.

HTML (hypertext markup language) p. 160 An HTML document is a text file that includes codes that describe the format, layout, and logical structure of a hypermedia document. Most Web pages are created with HTML.

http (hypertext transfer protocol) p. 318 The internet protocol used to transfer Web pages.

human-centered systems p. 394 Computer systems designed to retain and enhance human skills rather than take them away.

hyperlink p. 18 A word, phrase, or picture that acts as a button, enabling the user to explore the Web or a multimedia document with mouse clicks.

hypermedia p. 223 The combination of text, numbers, graphics, animation, sound effects, music, and other media in hyperlinked documents.

hypertext link p. 44 A Web connection to another document or site, like the many that loosely tie together millions of Web pages.

hypertext p. 18 An interactive cross-referenced system that allows textual information to be linked in nonsequential ways. A hypertext document contains links that lead quickly to other parts of the document or to related documents.

I-beam p. 8 The I-beam shaped pointer used to highlight text and move the cursor within a text document.

icon p. 8 In a graphical user interface, a picture that represents a file, folder, or disk.

identity (ID) theft p. 22 The crime, committed by hackers or other unscrupulous individuals, of obtaining enough information about a person to assume his or her identity, often as a prelude to illegally using the victim's credit cards.

IEEE 1394 p. 116 An industry standard for relatively new, extremely fast serial communications protocol, especially well suited for multimedia applications such as digital video. Apple, which developed the standard, refers to IEEE 1394 as FireWire.

image analysis p. 543 The process of identifying objects and shapes in a photograph, drawing, video, or other visual image.

image processing software p. 204 Software that enables the user to manipulate photographs and other high-resolution images.

imagesetters p. 170 See phototypesetting machines.

impact printer p. 102 Printer that forms images by physically striking paper, ribbon, and print hammer together.

implementation p. 511 The phase of the systems development life cycle in which the system is put into use.

import data p. 241 To move data into a program from another program or source.

inbox p. 21 The place where email programs and services store recipients' incoming messages.

industrial age p. 45 The recent modern era, characterized by the shift from farms to factories.

information p. 66 Anything that can be communicated.

information age p. 46 The current era, characterized by the shift from an industrial economy to an information economy and the convergence of computer and communication technology.

information appliance p. 45 Network computer or other Internet-capable device used in offices and homes.

information overload p. 445 The state of being bombarded with too much computer output, a risk of poorly designed information systems.

information system p. 427 A collection of people, machines, data, and methods organized to accomplish specific functions and to solve specific

problems. Programming is part of the larger process of designing, implementing, and managing an information system.

infrared wireless p. 283 The use of invisible infrared radiation and infrared ports to send and receive digital information short distances, now possible on many laptops and handheld computers.

infrastructure p. 450 Information technology's basic framework, comprising all the organization's information systems hardware, software, and telecommunications equipment; the information system department's staff and other personnel; and the organizational structure and procedures that affect accessing, processing, and using information in the company.

inkjet printer p. 102 A nonimpact printer that sprays ink directly onto paper to produce printed text and graphic images.

input p. 34 Information taken in by the computer.

input device p. 65 Device for accepting input, such as a keyboard.

instant messaging p. 291 A technology that enables users to create buddy lists, check for buddies who are logged in, and exchange typed messages and files with those who are.

instructions p. 74 Computer codes telling the CPU to perform a specific action.

integrated circuit p. 36 A chip containing hundreds, thousands, or even millions of transistors.

integrated software p. 135 Software packages that include several applications designed to work well together.

intellectual property p. 352 The results of intellectual activities in the arts, science, and industry.

interactive fiction p. 411 Stories with natural-language interfaces that offer players some control over plot.

interactive movies p. 411 Video-based or animated features in which one or more characters are controlled by the viewers.

interactive multimedia p. 224 Multimedia that enables the user to take an active part in the experience.

interactive processing p. 253 Interacting with data through terminals, viewing and changing values online in real time.

interactive TV p. 412 Broadcast television with built-in options for game playing or other forms of interactivity.

interface standards p. 113 Standards for ports and other connective technology agreed upon by the hardware industry so that devices made by one manufacturer can be attached to systems made by other companies.

internal drives p. 6 Disk drives that are included in a system unit.

internal modem p. 279 A modem that is built into the system unit.

international information system p. 435 Any information system that supports international business activities.

Internet p. 15 A global interconnected network of thousands of networks linking academic, research, government, and commercial institutions, and other organizations and individuals. Also known as the Net.

Internet appliance p. 45 Non-PC devices such as set-top boxes that are connected to the Internet.

Internet service provider (ISP) p. 19 A business that provides its customers with connections to the Internet along with other services.

Internet telephony (IP telephony) p. 293 A combination of software and hardware technology that enables the Internet to, in effect, serve as a telephone network. Internet telephony systems can use standard telephones, computers, or both to send and receive voice messages.

Internet VPN p. 473 Internet virtual private network, what an extranet is called when the public network used is the Internet.

Internet2 p. 334 An alternative Internet-style network that provides faster network communications for universities and research institutions.

internetworking p. 309 Connecting different types of networks and computer systems.

interorganizational information systems (IOS) p. 434 Systems that use networking technology to facilitate communication between an organization and its suppliers, customers, and other organizations.

interpreter p. 496 A translation program that translates and transmits each source code statement individually into machine language.

intranet p. 44 A self-contained intraorganizational network that is designed using the same technology as the Internet.

investigation p. 509 Animated features in which one or more of the characters are controlled by the viewers; in the systems development life cycle, the phase to study the existing business problem or opportunity and determine whether it is feasible to develop a new system or redesign the existing system if one exists.

IP address p. 311 A unique string of four numbers separated by periods that serves as a unique address for a computer on the Internet. The IP address of the host computer and sending computer is included with every packet of information that traverses the Internet.

ISDN p. 313 A digital broadband service offered by phone companies. Because it is slower and more expensive than DSL and other broadband options, ISDN is not widely used today.

J

J++ p. 499 A Java-like language from Microsoft for programming on the Windows platform.

Java p. 147 A platform-neutral, object-oriented programming language developed by Sun Microsystems for use on multiplatform networks.

Java virtual machine p. 147 Software that gives a computer the capability to run Java programs.

JavaScript p. 325 A Web scripting language similar to, but otherwise unrelated to, Java.

jobless growth p. 397 A period of time when productivity increases not because of the work people do but because of the work of machines.

joystick p. 92 A gearshift-like device used as a controller for arcade-style computer games.

justification p. 160 The alignment of text on a line: left justification (smooth left margin and ragged right margin), right justification, (smooth right margin and ragged left margin).

K

KB (kilobyte) p. 72 About 1000 bytes of information.

kerning p. 169 The spacing between letter pairs in a document.

key field p. 251 A field that contains data that uniquely identifies the record.

keyboard p. 6 Input device, similar to a typewriter keyboard, for entering data and commands into the computer.

keyboard/mouse ports p. 113 Ports for attaching keyboard and mouse to most older PCs.

keychain USB flash memory devices p. 112 Tiny devices that plug directly into the computer's USB port and are becoming popular for storing and transporting data files.

knowledge p. 539 Information that incorporates the relationships among facts.

knowledge base p. 539 A database that contains both facts and a system of rules for determining and changing the relationship among those facts.

L

label p. 176 In a spreadsheet, a text entry that provides information on what a column or row represents.

laptop computer p. 40 A flat-screen, battery-powered portable computer that you can rest on your lap.

laser printer p. 102 A nonimpact printer that uses a laser beam to create patterns of electrical charges on a rotating drum. The charged patterns attract black toner and transfer it to paper as the drum rotates.

LCD (liquid crystal display) displays p. 101 See liquid crystal display (LCD) displays.

leading p. 169 The spacing between lines of text.

legacy-free PCs p. 116 PCs using USB ports.

Level 1 cache p. 75 Memory storage that can be quickly accessed by the CPU.

Level 2 cache (L2 cache) p. 75 Memory storage that is larger than a level 1 cache but not as quickly accessed by the CPU.

line chart p. 182 A chart that shows trends or relationships over time, or a relative distribution of one variable through another.

line printer p. 102 An impact printer used by mainframes to produce massive printouts. They print characters only, not graphics.

link p. 18 See hyperlink.

links p. 223 See hyperlink.

Linux p. 125 An operating system based on UNIX, maintained by volunteers, and distributed for free. Linux is used mostly in servers and embedded computers, but is growing in popularity as a PC operating system.

liquid crystal display (LCD) displays p. 100 Flat-panels displays, once primarily used for portable computers but now replacing bulkier CRT monitors for desktops.

LISP p. 499 List Processing, a high-level computer language developed at MIT in the late 1950s to process nonnumeric data like characters, words, and other symbols.

list views p. 241 Showing data by displaying several records in lists similar to a spreadsheet.

local area network (LAN) p. 42 A network in which the computers are close to each other, usually in the same building. Typically includes a collection of computers and peripherals; each computer and shared peripheral is an individual node on the network.

logged in p. 21 Connected to a computer system or network.

logic bomb p. 353 A program designed to attack in response to a particular logical event or sequence of events. A type of software sabotage.

logic errors p. 496 Errors in the logical structure of a program that cause differences between what the program is supposed to do and what it actually does.

login name p. 19 See user name.

LOGO p. 499 A computer language developed in the 1960s for children.

lossless compression p. 219 Systems allowing files to be compressed and later decompressed without a loss of data.

lossy compression p. 219 A type of compression in which some quality is lost in the process of compression and decompression.

low-level languages p. 498 Programming languages that require the programmer to think on the machine's level and to include an enormous amount of detail in every program, such as machine language and assembly language.

Luddites p. 396 A nineteenth century English labor group that smashed new textile machinery to protect their jobs; today the term is often used to describe someone who opposes new technology in general.

lurker p. 297 A person who silently monitors mailing lists and newsgroups without posting messages.

M

Mac OS p. 9 The operating system for the Apple Macintosh computer.

machine language p. 129 The language that computers use to process instructions. Machine language uses numeric codes to represent basic computer operations.

machine learning p. 535 Artificial intelligence techniques that make it possible for machine performance to improve based on feedback from past performance.

macro languages p. 504 User-oriented languages that enable users to create programs (macros) that automate repetitive tasks; also known as scripting languages.

macro p. 178 Custom-designed embedded procedure program that automates tasks in application programs.

macro viruses p. 353 Viruses that attach to and are transmitted through macros embedded in documents; usually spread via email.

magnetic disk p. 107 Storage medium with random-access capability, accessed by the computer's disk drive.

magnetic ink character reader p. 94 A device that reads numbers printed with magnetic ink on checks.

magnetic tape p. 105 A storage medium used with a tape drive to store large amounts of information in a small space at relatively low cost.

mail merge p. 166 A feature of a word processor or other program that enables it to merge names and addresses from a database mailing list into personalized form letters and mailings.

mailbox p. 21 A storage area for email messages.

mailing lists p. 289 Email discussion groups on special-interest topics. All subscribers receive messages sent to the group's mailing address.

mainframe computer p. 38 Expensive, room-size computer, used mostly for large computing jobs.

maintenance p. 514 The phase of the systems development life cycle

malware p. 353 Malicious software, especially destructive programs such as the viruses, worms, and Trojan horses devised and spread by computer saboteurs.

management p. 436 A set of activities that helps people efficiently use resources to accomplish an organization's goals.

management information system (MIS) p. 438 Also known as a management reporting system, a system that gives a manager the information he or she needs to make decisions, typically structured decisions, regarding the operational activities of the company.

management levels p. 437 The three management tiers (operational, tactical, and strategic) typically found in a large organization.

management reporting systems p. 438 Another name for management information systems, because their main output is a variety of detailed, summary, and exception reports for managers.

mathematics processing software p. 185 Software designed to deal with complex equations and calculations. A mathematics processor enables the user to create, manipulate, and solve equations easily.

MB (megabyte) p. 72 Approximately 1000K, or 1 million bytes.

m-commerce p. 468 Mobile commerce, in which workers use laptops and wireless handheld devices to take their offices with them wherever they travel.

megabits p. 72 Approximately 1000 bits.

memory p. 5 Stores programs and the data they need to be instantly accessible to the CPU.

menu p. 8 An onscreen list of command choices.

menu-driven interface p. 141 User interface that enables users to choose commands from onscreen lists called menus.

mesh networks p. 298 Decentralized alternatives to today's central-hub-based networks, allowing a message to hop from wireless device to wireless device until it finds its destination.

meta-search engines p. 329 A software tool that conducts parallel searches using several different search engines and directories.

metropolitan area network (MAN) p. 276 A service that links two or more LANs within a city.

microelectromechanical systems (MEMS) p. 376 Microscopic electricity-powered machines using a process similar to that of manufacturing computer chips.

micromachines p. 376 Miniature machines on the scale of a millionth of a meter, some made with microscopic moving parts etched in silicon using a process similar to that of manufacturing computer chips.

microphone, speaker, headphone, and MIDI p. 113 Sound equipment that can be connected to computer systems using special ports typically included on expansion boards.

microprocessor p. 5 Now known as a personal computer.

Microsoft Windows p. 9 The most popular and powerful PC operating system; uses a graphical user interface.

middleware p. 254 Connectivity software linking the client and server machines, providing easy access to information.

MIDI p. 221 Musical Instrument Digital Interface, a standard interface that allows electronic instruments and computers to communicate with each other and work together.

milliseconds (ms) p. 78 A thousandth of a second.

mirror p. 364 To automatically duplicate copies of data to multiple disks, effectively creating instant backups.

model management p. 439 A component of the decision support system, in which a manager evaluates alternative problem solutions and identifies the best solution using appropriate software.

modeling p. 188 The use of computers to create abstract models of objects, organisms, organizations, and processes.

modem p. 15 Modulator/demodulator. A hardware device that connects a computer to a telephone line.

moderated (mail or news) group p. 290 Monitored by a moderator who filters out inappropriate or off-topic messages so subscribers don't need to receive or read them.

modules p. 500 In structured programming, a program is built from smaller programs called modules.

monitor p. 7 An output device that displays text and graphics onscreen.

monochrome monitors p. 99 Monitors that display two colors, usually black and white.

monospaced font p. 159 A font in which all characters are equal width, like a typewriter's characters.

Moore's law p. 36 The prediction made in 1965 by Gordon Moore that the power of a silicon chip of the same price would double about every 18 months for at least two decades.

moral dilemma p. 368 A predicament for which rules and ethics don't seem to apply, or to contradict one another.

morph p. 215 Video clip in which one image metamorphoses into another.

motherboard p. 72 The circuit board that contains a computer's CPU. Also called a system board.

mouse p. 6 A handheld input device that, when moved around on a desktop or table, moves a pointer around the computer screen.

MP3 p. 217 A method of compression that can squeeze a music file to a fraction of its original CD file size with only slight loss of quality.

MS-DOS p. 141 Microsoft Disk Operating System, an operating system with character-based user interface; it was widely used in the 1980s and early 1990s but has been superceded by Windows.

multifunction printer (MFP) p. 102 An all-in-one output device that usually combines a scanner, a laser or inkjet printer, and a fax modem.

multimedia p. 224 Using some combination of text, graphics, animation, video, music, voice, and sound effects to communicate.

multimedia authoring software p. 225 Enables the creation and editing of multimedia documents.

multiprocessing p. 76 Employing two or more microprocessors in a computer in order to improve overall performance. Also known as symmetric multiprocessing.

multitasking p. 137 Concurrent processing for personal computers. The user can issue a command that initiates a process and continue working with other applications while the computer follows through on the command.

N

nanosecond (ns) p. 78 A billionth of a second; a common unit of measurement for read and write access time to RAM.

nanotechnology p. 376 The manufacture of machines on a scale of a few billionths of a meter.

narrowband connections p. 313 Dial-up Internet connections; named because they don't offer much bandwidth when compared to other types of connections.

narrowcasting p. 409 Providing custom newscasts and entertainment features aimed at narrow groups or individuals.

National Infrastructure Protection Center p. 372 A state-of-the-art command center created to fight the growing threat of system sabotage. The center includes representatives of various intelligence agencies (the departments of defense, transportation, energy, and treasury), and representatives of several major corporations.

natural language p. 129 Language that people speak and write every day.

Net p. 16 See Internet.

.NET p. 147 An operating system platform from Microsoft that blurs the line between the Web and Microsoft's operating systems and applications.

netiquette p. 296 Rules of etiquette that apply to Internet communication.

network p. 42 A computer system that links two or more computers.

network administrators p. 276 Workers who take care of the behind-the-scenes network details so others can focus on using the network.

network card p. 113 A network interface card that adds a LAN port to a PC.

network computer (NC) p. 44 A computer designed to function as part of a network rather than as a PC.

network interface card (NIC) p. 278 Card that adds an additional serial port to a computer. The port is especially designed for a direct network connection.

network license p. 287 License for multiple copies or removing restrictions on software copying and use at a network site.

network management system software p. 276 Software that helps network administrators maintain healthy networks, especially useful for managing large, complex networks with hundreds of computers.

network operating system (NOS) p. 285 Server operating system software for a local-area network.

neural networks (neural nets) p. 546 Distributed, parallel computing systems inspired by the structure of the human brain.

newsgroups p. 290 Ongoing public discussions on a particular subject consisting of notes written to a central Internet site and redistributed through a worldwide newsgroup network called Usenet. You can check into and out of them whenever you want; all messages are posted on virtual bulletin boards for anyone to read anytime.

Next Generation Internet (NGI) p. 334 A future nationwide web of optical fiber integrated with intelligent management software to maintain high-speed connections.

node p. 275 Each computer and shared peripheral on a local-area network.

nonimpact printer p. 102 A printer that produces characters without physically striking the page.

nonlinear editing p. 214 A type of video editing in which audio and video clips are stored in digital form on hard disks for immediate access via video editing software.

nonsequential p. 223 Nonvolatile memory; memory for permanent storage of information.

nonvolatile memory p. 77 Memory that is not lost when the computer is turned off. An example is the read-only memory that contains start-up instructions and other critical information.

notebook computer p. 40 Another term for laptop computer.

notifications p. 330 Along with alerts a popular noncorporate type of push technology on the Web, notifying users about online auction status, fees due, and the like.

numeric field p. 241 A field containing only numbers.

object-oriented database p. 256 Instead of storing records in tables and hierarchies, stores software objects that contain procedures (or instructions) with data.

object-oriented graphics p. 207 The storage of pictures as collections of lines, shapes, and other objects.

object-oriented programming (OOP) p. 503 Programming in which a program is not just a collection of step-by step instructions or procedures; it's a collection of objects. Objects contain both data and instructions and can send and receive messages.

online banking p. 184 Use of the Internet to conduct basic banking transactions.

online help p. 132 Documentation and help available through a software company's Web site.

online services p. 317 Internet access and a variety of other services in a privately controlled environment offered by gateway companies such as America Online (AOL).

Open p. 9 To load a file into an application program's workspace so it can be viewed and edited by the user.

open architecture p. 116 A design that allows expansion cards and peripherals to be added to a basic computer system.

open source software p. 125 Software that can be distributed and modified freely by users; Linux is the best-known example.

open standards p. 309 Standards not owned by any company.

operating system (OS) p. 9 A system of programs that performs a variety of technical operations, providing an additional layer of insulation between the user and the bits-and-bytes world of computer hardware.

operational level p. 437 The management level responsible for supervising the day-to-day activities in the organization's value chain.

optical character recognition (OCR) p. 94 Locating and identifying printed characters embedded in an image, allowing the text to be stored as an editable document. OCR can be performed by wand readers, pen scanners, and OCR software.

optical disk drive p. 107 A disk drive that uses laser beams to read and write bits of information on the surface of an optical disk.

optical mark reader p. 94 A reading device that uses reflected light to determine the location of pencil marks on standardized test answer sheets and similar forms.

organizational information requirements analysis p. 450 Also called enterprise modeling, an approach many companies use to summarize their current IT infrastructure, to identify the practical range of business and product strategies based on the current infrastructure, and to identify information system projects that offer the most benefits to the organization.

Outline View p. 163 The outliner option built into Microsoft Word, which enables you to examine and restructure the overall organization of a document, while showing each topic in as much detail as you need.

outliner p. 163 Software that facilitates the arrangement of information into hierarchies or levels of ideas. Some word processors include outline views that serve the same function as separate outliners.

output p. 34 Information given out by the computer.

output device p. 65 Device for sending information from the computer, such as a monitor or printer.

outsourcing p. 509 Hiring talent for selected activities on a contract basis.

overhead projection panels p. 100 Equipment using LCDs to project computer screen images.

P

P2P model p. 286 See peer-to-peer model.

packet p. 309 A collection of information that travels as a unit through the Internet. Internet messages are broken into packets that travel independently to their destinations.

packet-switching p. 311 The standard technique used to send information over the Internet. A message is broken into packets that travel independently from network to network toward their common destination, where they are reunited.

page-description language p. 208 A language used by many drawing programs that describes text fonts, illustrations, and other elements of the printed page.

page-layout software p. 169 In desktop publishing, software used to combine various source documents into a coherent, visually appealing publication.

painting software p. 203 Enables you to paint pixels on the screen with a pointing device.

palette p. 203 A collection of colors available in drawing software.

palm-sized computer p. 40 A portable computer often small enough to tuck into a shirt pocket. Also known as a handheld computer.

paperless office p. 390 An office of the future in which magnetic and optical archives will replace reference books and file cabinets, electronic communication will replace letters and memos, and digital publications provided through the Internet and on-line services will replace newspapers and other periodicals.

paradigm shift p. 45 A change in thinking that results in a new way of seeing the world.

parallel port p. 113 A standard port on most PCs for attaching a printer or other device that communicates by sending or receiving bits in groups, rather than sequentially.

parallel processing p. 76 Using multiple processors to divide jobs into pieces and work simultaneously on the pieces.

parameter RAM p. 78 CMOS RAM, a special low-energy kind of RAM used to store the date, time, and calendar in Macintoshes.

parsing program (parser) p. 536 In translation, a program that analyzes sentence structure and identifies each word according to its part of speech. Another program looks up each word in a translation dictionary and substitutes the appropriate word.

Pascal p. 499 A high-level computer language, named for the seventeenth-century French mathematician and inventor, developed in the early 1970s as an alternative to BASIC for student programmers.

Passport p. 333 A .NET-based user authentication service.

paste p. 159 An editing function in a word processing program that takes words temporarily stored in a clipboard and drops them into another part of the same document or a different document.

patent p. 352 A type of law that protects mechanical inventions.

path p. 318 The hierarchical nesting of directories (folders) that contain a Web resource, as described in the third part of the URL, following the dot address.

pattern recognition p. 542 Identifying recurring patterns in input data with the goal of understanding or categorizing that input.

PB (petabyte) p. 72 The equivalent of 1024 terabytes, or 1 quadrillion bytes.

PC card p. 81 A credit-card-size card that can be inserted into a slot to expand memory or add a peripheral to a computer; commonly used in portable computers. Sometimes called by its original name, PCMCIA.

PDF (portable document format) p. 174 Allows documents of all types to be stored, viewed, or modified on any Windows or Macintosh computer, making it possible for many organizations to reduce paper flow.

peer-to-peer (P2P) computing p. 330 See peer-to-peer model.

peer-to-peer (P2P) file sharing services p. 221 Services that enable networked users to make files on their hard drives available to others rather than posting them on central servers.

peer-to-peer model p. 286 A LAN model that allows every computer on the network to be both client and server.

pen scanners p. 94 Wireless pen-shaped scanners that can perform optical character recognition.

pen-based computer p. 95 A keyboardless machine that accepts input from a stylus applied directly to a flat-panel screen.

peripheral p. 5 An external device, such as a keyboard or monitor, connected via cables to the system central processing unit.

Perl p. 326 Practical extraction and reporting language, a Web scripting language that is particularly well-suited for writing scripts to process text—for example, complex Web forms.

personal area network (PAN) p. 286 A network that links a variety of personal electronic devices, such as mobile phones, handheld computers, and PCs, so they can communicate with each other.

personal computer p. 5 A small, powerful, relatively low-cost microcomputer.

personal digital assistant (PDA) p. 40 A pocket-sized computer used to organize appointments, tasks, notes, contacts, and other personal information. Sometimes called handheld computer or palmtop computer. Many PDAs include additional software and hardware for wireless communication.

personal information manager (PIM) p. 246 A specialized database program that automates an address/phone book, an appointment calendar, a to-do list, and miscellaneous notes. Also called an electronic organizer.

Personalization p. 324 Customization of a Web site's content, made possible because sites can use login names, passwords, and cookies to track and remember information about guests from visit to visit.

PERT p. 451 Program evaluation and review technique, a variation of the critical path method used to keep track of a project's schedule; PERT features optimistic, pessimistic, and most likely time estimates to complete each activity.

photo management software p. 206 Programs that simplify and automate common tasks associated with capturing, organizing, editing, and sharing digital images.

photo printer p. 102 A type of newer inkjet printer specially optimized to print high-quality photos captured with digital cameras and scanners.

phototypesetting machines p. 170 Machines enabling desktop publications to be printed at 12000dpi or higher.

pie chart p. 182 A round pie-shaped chart with slices that show the relative proportions of the parts to a whole.

pixel p. 203 A picture element (dot) on a computer screen or printout. Groups of pixels compose the images on the monitor and the output of a printout.

plagiarism p. 368 The act of presenting someone else's work as one's own.

Plain Old Telephone Service (POTS) p. 313 Used with a modem for narrowband dial-up Internet connections.

platform independent p. 116 The ability of a peripheral device to work on multiple platforms. For example, a USB disk drive could be used with both Macintosh and Windows computers.

platform p. 147 The combination of hardware and operating system software upon which application software is built.

platters p. 108 Flat discs that are the part of the hard disk that holds information.

plotter p. 103 An automated drawing tool that produces finely scaled drawings by moving pen and/or paper in response to computer commands.

plug-in p. 324 A software extension that adds new features.

point size p. 159 Measurement of characters, with one point equal to 1/72 inch.

pointing stick (TrackPoint) p. 92 A tiny joystick-like device embedded in the keyboard of a laptop computer.

point-of-sale (POS) terminal p. 94 A terminal with a wand reader, barcode scanner, or other device that captures information at the check-out counter of a store.

pop-up menus p. 143 Menus that can appear anywhere on the screen.

port p. 78 Socket that allows information to pass in and out.

port replicator p. 40 A device that duplicates a laptop's ports, for ease of connection to monitors, printers, and other peripherals.

portable computers p. 40 Small, battery-powered computers such as laptops.

portal p. 19 A Web site designed as a Web entry station, offering quick and easy access to a variety of services.

PostScript p. 208 A standard page-description language.

PPP (point-to-point protocol) p. 313 A protocol that enables a computer to connect to the Internet via modem and temporarily have full Internet access and IP address.

prefetch unit p. 74 Part of the CPU that fetches the next several instructions from memory.

presentation graphics software p. 210 Automates the creation of visual aids for lectures, training sessions, and other presentations. Can include everything from spreadsheet charting programs to animation editing software, but most commonly used for creating and displaying a series of on-screen slides to serve as visual aids for presentations.

print server p. 286 A server that accepts, prioritizes, and processes print jobs.

printer p. 7 Output device that produces a paper copy of any information that can be displayed on the screen.

processor p. 65 Part of the computer that processes information, performs arithmetic calculations, and makes basic decisions based on information values.

program p. 34 Instructions that tell the hardware what to do to transform input into output.

program verification p. 521 The process of proving the correctness of a program.

programming environment p. 496 An integrated compiler software package, including a text editor, a compiler, a debugger, and a variety of other programming utilities.

programming p. 492 A specialized form of problem solving, typically involving the four steps of defining the problem; devising, refining, and testing the algorithm; writing the program; and testing and debugging the program.

project management software p. 450 Programs that help coordinate, schedule, and track complex projects.

PROLOG p. 499 Programming Logic, a popular language for artificial intelligence programming.

proportionally spaced font p. 160 Fonts that allow more room for wide characters, such as W, than for narrow characters, such as I.

protocol p. 285 A set of rules for the exchange of data between a terminal and a computer or between two computers.

prototype p. 510 A limited working system or subsystem that is created to give users and managers an idea of how the complete system will work.

prototyping p. 510 An iterative process in which the systems analyst can modify the prototype until it meets the needs and expectations of the organization.

pseudocode p. 493 A cross between a computer language and plain English, a form that programmers typically use to write algorithms before translating them into computer language.

p-to-p model p. 286 See peer-to-peer model.

public domain software p. 134 Free software that is not copyrighted, offered through World Wide Web sites, electronic bulletin boards, user groups, and other sources.

public network p. 473 A network that uses a public communications network, such as a public utility telecommunication network or the Internet, a method an organization can use to set up an extranet.

pull technology p. 330 Technology in which browsers on client computers pull information from server machines. The browser needs to initiate a request before any information is delivered.

pull-down menus p. 142 In a graphical user interface, menus located at the top of the screen or window and accessed with a mouse or with keyboard shortcuts. Also called drop-down menus.

push technology p. 330 Technology in which information is delivered automatically to a client computer. The user subscribes to a service and the server delivers that information periodically and unobtrusively. Contrast with pull technology.

Python p. 499 A Java-like language popular with Linux open-source programmers.

Q

quantum computers p. 376 Computers based on the properties of atoms and their nuclei and the laws of quantum mechanics.

query p. 241 An information request.

query language p. 245 A special language for performing queries, more precise than the English language.

R

RAID (redundant array of independent disk) p. 364 A storage device that allows multiple hard disks to operate as a unit.

RAM (random access memory) p. 5 Memory that stores program instructions and data temporarily.

random access p. 107 Storage method that allows information retrieval without regard to the order in which it was recorded.

raster (bit-mapped) graphics p. 203 Painting programs create raster graphics that are, to the computer, simple maps showing how the pixels on the screen should be represented.

read/write head p. 108 The mechanism that reads information from, and writes information to, the spinning platter in a hard disk or disk drive.

real time p. 214 When a computer performs tasks immediately.

real-time communication p. 291 Internet communication that enables you to communicate with other users who are logged on at the same time.

real-time processing p. 429 Processing each transaction as it occurs, which is appropriate when users need the data immediately, as with bank ATM machines.

real-time streaming audio p. 323 Streaming transmission of radio broadcasts, concerts, news feeds, speeches, and other sound events as they happen.

real-time streaming video p. 324 Similar to streaming audio Webcasts, but with video.

record p. 240 In a database, the information relating to one person, product, or event.

record matching p. 261 Compiling profiles by combining information from different database files by looking for a shared unique field.

regional work centers p. 393 Shared offices established by corporations and government organizations in various locales to reduce commuting times.

register p. 74 Subdivision of the ALU in the CPU, usually 32 or 64 bits in size.

relational database p. 252 A program that allows files to be related to each other so that changes in one file are reflected in other files automatically.

relative references p. 178 References to a spreadsheet cell in relation to the current cell.

remote access p. 15 Network access via phone line, TV cable system, or wireless link.

removable cartridge media p. 107 See removable media.

removable media p. 6 Storage media designed to be removed and transported easily, including Zip, Jaz, and Orb disks.

repetitive-stress injuries p. 91 Conditions that result from repeating the same movements over long periods, such as keyboarding-induced carpal tunnel syndrome, a painful affliction of the wrist and hand.

replication p. 178 Automatic replication of values, labels, and formulas, a feature of spreadsheet software.

report p. 242 A database printout that is an ordered list of selected records and fields in an easy-to-read form.

resolution p. 99 Density of pixels, measured by the number of dots per inch.

retinal display p. 118 A device that works without a screen by drawing pixels directly on the user's retina with a focused beam of light.

retirement p. 514 The final phase of the systems development life cycle, in which a system is phased out.

right to privacy p. 261 Freedom from interference into the private sphere of a person's affairs.

right-click p. 8 Hitting the right-hand part of mouse button so that, for example, while pointing to an object the computer may display a menu of choices.

rip p. 213 Copy songs from a CD to a computer's hard drive.

robots p. 547 Computer-controlled machines designed to perform specific manual tasks.

rollover p. 325 A common use of Web scripting, used to make onscreen buttons visibly change when the pointer rolls over them.

ROM (read-only memory) p. 77 Memory that includes permanent information only. The computer can only read information from it; it can never write any new information on it.

routers p. 277 Programs or devices that decide how to route Internet transmissions.

S

sabotage p. 353 A malicious attack on work, tools, or business.

samplers p. 221 An electronic musical instrument that can sample digital sounds, turn them into notes, and play them back at any pitch.

sampling rate p. 217 The rate that a sound wave is sampled; the more samples per second, the more closely the digitized sound approximates the original.

sans-serif font p. 159 A font without fine lines at the ends of the main strokes of each character.

satellite Internet connections p. 315 A broadband technology available through many of the same satellite dishes that provide television channels to viewers. For many rural homes and businesses, satellite Internet connections provide the only high-speed Internet access options available.

satellite offices p. 393 Workplaces that enable workers to commute to smaller offices closer to their homes.

scanner pp. 94 An input device that makes a digital representation of any printed image. See flatbed scanners, slide scanners, drum scanners, and sheetfed scanners.

scatter chart p. 182 Discovers a relationship between two variables.

scientific visualization software p. 187 Uses shape, location in space, color, brightness, and motion to help you understand invisible relationships, providing graphical representation of numerical data.

scripting languages p. 504 User-oriented languages that enable users to create programs (macros) that automate repetitive tasks; also known as macro languages.

scripts p. 325 Short programs that can add interactivity, animation, and other dynamic features to a Web page or multimedia document.

SCSI p. 113 Small Computer Systems Interface, an interface design enabling several peripherals to be strung together and attached to a single port.

Search p. 15 Looking for a specific record.

search engine p. 18 A program for locating information on the Web.

secure private network p. 472 A network that physically attaches intranets with private leased telephone lines, a method an organization can use to set up an extranet.

security patch p. 356 Software programs that plug potential security breaches in an operating system, often provided as free downloads or automatic updates to all owners of the OS.

select (records) p. 241 Looking for all records that match a set of criteria.

selecting text p. 162 Highlighting text, usually by dragging the cursor across it.

selects p. 8 Chooses an object, as by moving the pointer to a picture of a tool or object on the screen and clicking the mouse.

Semantic Web p. 338 As conceived by World Wide Web inventor Tim Berners-Lee, a Web that will be full of data that's meaningful to computers as well as humans.

semantics p. 538 The underlying meaning of words and phrases.

semistructured decision p. 436 A type of management decision used when there's some uncertainty about a problem and the manager must use his or her judgment.

sensor p. 99 A device that enables digital machines to monitor a physical quantity of the analog world, such as temperature, humidity, or pressure, to provide data used in robotics, environmental climate control, and other applications.

sequencing software p. 221 Software that enables a computer to be used as a tool for musical composition, recording, and editing.

sequential p. 217 Linear in form, and designed to be read from beginning to end, as are conventional text media like books.

sequential access p. 107 Storage method that requires the user to retrieve information by zipping through it in the order in which it was recorded.

serial port p. 113 A standard port on most PCs for attaching a modem or other device that can send and receive messages one bit at a time.

serif font p. 159 A font, like those in the Times family, embellished with fine lines at the ends of the main strokes of each character.

server p. 39 A computer especially designed to provide software and other resources to other computers over a network.

service bureaus p. 170 Businesses used by desktop publishers to provide camera-ready pages.

set-top box p. 45 A special-purpose computer designed to provide Internet access and other services using a standard television set and (usually) a cable TV connection.

shareware p. 134 Software that is free for the trying, with a send-pay-ment-if-you-keep-it honor system.

sheetfed scanners p. 96 Small scanners that accept pages one at a time through a sheet feeder.

shell p. 143 A program layer that stands between the user and the operating system.

silicon chip p. 36 Hundreds of transistors packed into an integrated circuit on a piece of silicon.

Silicon Valley p. 37 The area around San Jose, California, that has become a hotbed of the computer industry since the 1970s, when dozens of microprocessor manufacturing companies sprouted and grew there.

SIMMs p. 79 Single in-line memory modules.

site license p. 287 License for multiple copies or removing restrictions on software copying and use at a network site.

slide scanners p. 96 Scanners for slides and negatives only.

slot p. 78 Area in the computer's housing for inserting special-purpose circuit boards.

smart badge p. 367 See active badge.

smart card p. 408 A card that looks like a standard credit card but features an embedded microprocessor and memory instead of a magnetic strip.

smart weapon p. 371 A missile that uses computerized guidance systems to locate its target.

SMIL (synchronized multimedia integration language) p. 327 An HTML-like language designed to make it possible to link time-based streaming media so that, for example, sounds, video, and animation can be tightly integrated with each other.

social engineering p. 350 Slang for the use of deception to get individuals to reveal sensitive information.

social responsibility p. 451 Legal and ethical computing behavior, a key concern in business today because of the many ways an information worker's actions can affect other people.

software p. 9 Instructions that tell the hardware what to do to transform input into output.

software components p. 333 Pieces of existing software that can be used to assemble Web services quickly. Component technology can, for example, make it easy to plug a shopping-cart component into an existing Web site.

software engineering p. 519 A branch of computer science that applies engineering principles and techniques to the world of computer software.

software license p. 133 An agreement allowing the use of a software program on a single machine.

software piracy p. 351 The illegal duplication of copyrighted software.

software-defined radio p. 298 A technology that allows a single wireless hardware device to be reprogrammed on the fly to serve a variety of functions.

SOHO p. 408 Small office home office, referring to one of today's fastest growing computer markets.

solid-state storage p. 112 Storage, such as flash memory, with no moving parts. Solid-state storage is likely to replace disk storage in the future.

sort p. 241 Arrange records in alphabetic or numeric order based on values in one or more fields.

sound card p. 104 A circuit board that allows the PC to accept microphone input, play music and other sound through speakers or headphones, and process sound in a variety of ways.

source document p. 169 In desktop publishing, the articles, chapters, drawings, maps, charts, and photographs that are to appear in the publication. Usually produced with standard word processors and graphics programs.

spam p. 21 Internet junk mail.

spam filters p. 21 Tools found in most email programs whose purpose is to limit or control Internet junk mail.

speaker independence p. 168 Speech recognition technology that works without having to be trained to an individual voice.

speech recognition p. 97 The identification of spoken words and sentences by a computer, making it possible for voice input to be converted into text files.

speech synthesis p. 545 The use of software or hardware to allow PCs to recite anything typed, though with voices that sound artificial and robotic.

speech-recognition software p. 167 See speech recognition, Chapter 3.

spelling checker (batch or interactive) p. 165 A built-in component of a word processor or a separate program that compares words in a document with words in a disk-based dictionary and flags words not found in the dictionary. May operate in batch mode, checking all the words at once, or interactive mode, checking one word at a time.

spiders p. 327 See web crawlers.

spoofing p. 350 A process used to steal passwords online.

spot color p. 170 The relatively easy use of a single color (or sometimes two) to add interest to a desktop publishing product.

spreadsheet software p. 176 Enables the user to control numbers, manipulating them in various ways. The software can manage budgeting, investment management, business projections, grade books, scientific simulations, checkbooks, financial planning and speculation, and other tasks involving numbers.

stack chart p. 182 Stacked bars to show how proportions of a whole change over time.

statistical analysis software p. 187 Specialized software that tests the strength of data relationships, produces graphs showing how two or more variables relate to each other, uncovers trends, and performs other statistical analyses.

statistics p. 185 The science of analyzing and collecting data.

steering committee p. 508 An organizational group that may be formed to decide which projects should be considered first.

stepwise refinement p. 493 Breaking programming problems into smaller problems, and breaking each smaller problem into a subproblem that can be subdivided in the same way.

storage device p. 65 Long-term repository for data. Disks and tape drives are examples.

stored query p. 241 A commonly used query recorded by a database so that it can be accessed quickly in the future. The ability to generate stored queries is a powerful feature that helps databases blur the line between application programs and development tools.

storyboard p. 214 The first step in a video project, a guide for shooting and editing scenes.

strategic information system p. 446 Any information system that is crucial to a company's competitive success.

strategic level p. 437 The management level responsible for long-range issues related to the business's growth and development.

strategic planning p. 449 The first phase of information technology planning, which involves developing a plan that defines the mission of the company, identifies the company's environment and internal strengths and weaknesses, and defines the competitive strategy of the company.

structured decision p. 436 A type of management decision used when the manager understands the situation clearly and uses established procedures and information to resolve the problem.

structured programming p. 500 A technique to make programming easier and more productive. Structured programs are built from smaller programs, called modules or subprograms, that are in turn made of even smaller modules.

Structured Query Language (SQL) p. 245 A query language available for many different database management systems. More than a query language, SQL also accesses databases from a wide variety of vendors.

style sheet p. 160 Custom styles for each of the common elements in a document.

stylus p. 92 An input device, with much the same point-and-click functions as a mouse, used to send signals to a pressure sensitive graphics tablet.

subject tree p. 19 A hierarchical catalog of Web sites compiled by researchers, like that found at Yahoo!

subnotebooks p. 40 Portable computers, smaller than a notebook or laptop, about the size of a hardbound book.

subprograms p. 500 In structured programming, a program is built from smaller programs called subprograms.

subsystem p. 423 A system that is a part of a larger system.

supercomputer p. 39 A super-fast, super-powerful, and super-expensive computer used for applications that demand maximum power.

supply chain management p. 432 The use of enterprise resource planning to improve the coordination of a company's value chain logistics activities and the logistics activities of its suppliers and customers.

surge protectors p. 361 Devices that protect electronic equipment from sudden power surges.

switches p. 311 Hardware that decides how to route Internet transmissions. Switches are similar to software routers, but faster and less flexible.

switching costs p. 447 The time, effort, and money a customer or supplier would have to expend changing to a competitor's product or service.

symmetric multiprocessing p. 76 See multiprocessing.

syntax p. 538 A set of rules for constructing sentences from words. Every language has a syntax.

syntax errors p. 496 Violations of a programming language's grammar rules.

synthesized sounds p. 217 Synthetically generated computer sounds.

synthesizer p. 104 A device that can produce—synthesize—music and other sounds electronically. A synthesizer might be a stand-alone musical instrument or part of the circuitry on a computer's sound card.

synthetic speech p. 545 Speech generated by computers by converting text into phonetic sounds.

system p. 423 A set of interrelated parts that work together to accomplish a purpose through the three basic functions of input, processing, and output.

system bus p. 78 A group of wires that transmits information between components on the motherboard.

system flowchart p. 515 A graphical depiction of the physical system that exists or is proposed, such as to show the relationship among programs, files, input, and output in a system.

system software p. 9 Software that handles the details of computing. Includes the operating system and utility programs.

systems analyst p. 509 An information technology professional primarily responsible for developing and managing the system.

systems development life cycle (SDLC) p. 509 A sequence of seven steps or phases through which an information system passes between the time the system is conceived and the time it is phased out.

systems development p. 508 A problem-solving process of investigating a situation, designing a system solution to improve the situation, acquiring the human, financial, and technological resources to implement the solution, and finally evaluating the success of the solution.

T

T1 p. 313 A direct connect digital line that can transmit voice, data, and video at roughly 1.5Mbps.

T3 p. 313 A direct connect digital line that transmits voice, data, and video even faster than a T1 connection.

table p. 240 A grid of rows and columns; on many Web pages tables with hidden grids are used to align graphical images.

tactical level p. 437 The management level responsible for a large organizational unit, such as a sales region or a production plant.

tape drive p. 106 Storage device that uses magnetic tape to store information.

task bar p. 143 A button bar that provides one-click access to open applications and tools, making it easy to switch back and forth between different tasks.

task panel p. 10 A list of options, like those found across the top of the screen when you open a Microsoft Word document, that represents frequently used commands and files.

tax preparation software p. 184 Provides a prefabricated worksheet where the user enters numbers into tax forms. Calculations are performed automatically, and the completed forms can be sent electronically to the IRS.

TB (terabyte) p. 72 Approximately 1 million megabytes.

TCP/IP (Transmission Control Protocol/Internet Protocol) p. 309 Protocols developed as an experiment in internetworking, now the language of the Internet, allowing cross-network communication for almost every type of computer and network.

technophobia p. 398 The fear of technology.

telecommunication p. 274 Long-distance electronic communication in a variety of forms.

telecommuting p. 391 Working from home by modem, as do many programmers, accountants, and other information workers.

telemedicine p. 387 The practice of doctors using the Web to work with patients who are outside the hospital walls in remote locations.

telephony p. 293 Technology that enables computers to serve as speakerphones, answering machines, and complete voice mail systems.

templates p. 169 In desktop publishing, professionally designed empty documents that can be adapted to specific user needs. In spreadsheet software, worksheets that contain labels and formulas but no data values. The template produces instant answers when you fill in the blanks.

terminal p. 38 Combination keyboard and screen that transfers information to and from a mainframe computer.

terminal emulation software p. 286 Software that allows a PC to act as a dumb terminal—an input/output device that enables the user to send commands to and view information on the host computer.

testing p. 495 The process of checking the logic of an algorithm and the performance of a program.

text editor p. 496 An application that is similar to a word processor without the formatting features required by writers and publishers; some provide specialized features to aid in writing programs.

text-to-speech p. 545 The creation of synthetic speech by converting text files into phonetic sounds.

thesaurus p. 164 A synonym finder; often included with a word processor.

thin clients p. 389 Network computers, Internet appliances, or other devices designed to connect to the Internet but not perform all the other tasks performed by a PC.

time bomb p. 353 A logic bomb that is triggered by a time-related event.

timesharing p. 39 Technique by which mainframe computers communicate with several users simultaneously.

top-down design p. 493 A design process that starts at the top, with main ideas, and works down to the details.

total cost of ownership (TCO) p. 389 The net cost of computer ownership, including hardware, software, training, support, maintenance, troubleshooting, and other expenses.

touch screen p. 92 Pointing device that responds when the user points to or touches different screen regions.

touchpad (trackpad) p. 92 A small flat-panel pointing device that is sensitive to light pressure. The user moves the pointer by dragging a finger across the pad.

trackball p. 92 Pointing device that remains stationary while the user moves a protruding ball to control the pointer on the screen.

trackpad p. 92 See touchpad.

transaction p. 184 An event that occurs in any of the primary activities of the company: manufacturing, marketing, sales, and accounting.

transaction processing system (TPS) p. 429 A basic accounting and record-keeping system that keeps track of routine daily transactions necessary to conduct business.

transborder data flow p. 435 The flow of data between countries.

transistor p. 36 An electronic device that performs the same function as the vacuum tube by transferring electricity across a tiny resistor.

Trojan horse p. 353 A program that performs a useful task while at the same time carrying out some secret destructive act. A form of software sabotage.

true color p. 99 Color that is 24-bit or greater, allowing more than 16 million color choices per pixel, creating photorealistic images.

Turing test p. 532 A way to test machine intelligence.

tweening p. 213 The automatic creation of in-between frames in an animation.

twisted pair p. 276 A type of LAN cable that resembles the copper wires in standard telephone cables.

typeface p. 159 A style of characters used for printing.

U

ultrawideband p. 298 A low-power, short-range, wireless technology that transmits ultra-high-speed signals over a wide spectrum of frequencies.

Unicode p. 69 A 65,000-character set for making letters, digits, and special characters fit into the computer's binary circuitry.

uninterruptible power supply (UPS) p. 361 A hardware device that protects computers from data loss during power failures.

universal product codes (UPCs) p. 94 Codes created from patterns of variable-width bars that send scanned information to a mainframe computer.

UNIX p. 144 An operating system that allows a timesharing computer to communicate with several other computers or terminals at once. UNIX is the most widely available multi-user operating system in use. It is also widely used on Internet hosts.

unstructured decision p. 437 A type of management decision requiring many quantitative and ethical judgments that have no clear answers.

upgrade p. 133 A new and improved version of a software program.

upload p. 287 To post software or documents to an online source so they're available for others.

up-skilled p. 394 Transformed in such a way that a job requires more skill.

upstream traffic p. 313 Information transmitted from the subscriber to the Internet.

URL (uniform resource locator) p. 17 The address of a Web site.

USB (universal serial bus) p. 116 A data path standard that theoretically allows up to 126 devices, such as keyboards, digital cameras, and scanners, to be chained together from a single port, allowing for data transmission that is much faster and more flexible than through traditional serial and parallel ports.

USB 2.0 p. 116 A new, high-speed version of USB that offers fast transfer rates of 480 megabits per second.

user interface p. 141 The look and feel of the computing experience from a human point of view.

user name p. 19 A one-word name that you type to identify yourself when connecting—logging in—to a secure computer system, network, or email account. Sometimes called login name or alias.

utility programs p. 140 Software that serves as tools for doing system maintenance and some repairs that are not automatically handled by the operating system.

V

validator p. 180 A spreadsheet feature for checking the validity of logic and calculations.

value chain model p. 425 A business organization model developed by Harvard professor Michael E. Porter that focuses on the value-adding activities of a company's primary and support activities.

value p. 176 The numbers that are the raw material used by spreadsheet software to perform calculations.

variable p. 496 In programming, a named portion of the computer's memory whose contents the program can examine and change.

VBScript p. 506 A Web scripting language that is Microsoft's answer to JavaScript based on Visual Basic.

vector graphics p. 205 The storage of pictures as collections of lines, shapes, and other objects.

vertical portals (vortal) p. 329 Specialized portals that, like vertical market software, are targeted at members of a particular industry or economic sector.

vertical-market application p. 136 A computer application designed specifically for a particular business or industry.

video adapter p. 100 A circuit board installed inside the main system unit connecting the monitor to the computer.

video digitizer p. 98 A device that converts analog video signals into digital data.

video display terminal (VDT) p. 99 Output device that displays text and graphics and receives messages from the computer.

video editing software p. 211 Software for editing digital video, including titles, sound, and special effects.

video port p. 113 A port for plugging a color monitor into a computer's video board.

video projector p. 100 A projector that can project computer screen images for meetings and classes.

video teleconference p. 292 Face-to-face communication over long distances using video and computer technology.

videoconferencing p. 97 Face-to-face communication over long distances using video and computer technology.

virtual memory p. 137 Use of part of a computer hard disk as a substitute for RAM.

virtual private network (VPN) p. 473 A network that uses encryption software to create secure "tunnels" through the public Internet or between intranets, a method an organization can use to set up an extranet.

virtual private networks p. 332 Networks that use encryption software to create secure "tunnels" through the public Internet.

virtual reality p. 148 Technology that creates the illusion that the user is immersed in a world that exists only inside the computer, an environment that contains both scenes and the controls to change those scenes.

virtual worlds p. 228 Computer-generated worlds that create the illusion of immersion.

viruses p. 21 Software that spreads from program to program, or from disk to disk, and uses each infected program or disk to make copies of itself. A form of software sabotage.

Visual Basic p. 499 Microsoft's very popular Windows version of Basic.

visual programming p. 503 Programming featuring tools that enable programmers to create large portions of their programs by drawing pictures and pointing to onscreen objects, eliminating much of the coding of traditional programming.

voice input p. 97 Use of a microphone to speak commands and text data to a computer, which uses speech recognition software to interpret the input.

voicemail p. 293 A telephone-based messaging system with many of the features of an email system.

volume licenses p. 133 Special license agreements for entire companies, schools, or government institutions to make use of a program.

VRAM p. 100 A special portion of RAM dedicated to holding video images.

W

waveform audio p. 217 Sound-editing software in which a visual image is manipulated using the sound's wave form.

wearable computers p. 264 Strap-on computer units for active information gatherers.

Web p. 17 See World Wide Web.

Web browser p. 17 An application program that enables you to explore the Web by clicking hyperlinks in Web pages stored on Web sites.

Web bug p. 288 An invisible piece of code embedded in HTML-formatted email that is programmed to send information about its receiver's Web use back to its creator.

web crawlers p. 327 Software robots that systematically explore the Web, retrieve information about pages, and index the retrieved information in a database.

Web hosting service p. 481 A service that provides the e-commerce software and expertise to run an online business.

Web page p. 17 A single document on the World Wide Web (WWW), made up of text and images and interlinked with other documents.

Web server p. 318 A server that stores Web pages and sends them to client programs—Web browsers—that request them.

Web services p. 333 New kinds of Web-based applications that can be assembled quickly using existing software components.

Web site p. 17 A collection of related Web pages stored on the same server.

WebDAV p. 317 A new file server technology that performs the functions of FTP using software with a graphical interface that makes remote servers appear like simple file folders.

Webjacker p. 357 Someone who hijacks legitimate Web sites, redirecting unsuspecting visitors to bogus or offensive alternate sites.

Weblog p. 321 A personal Web page typically carrying diary-like entries or political commentaries. Often shortened to blog.

"what if?" questions p. 181 A feature of spreadsheet software that allows speculation by providing instant answers to hypothetical questions.

wide area network (WAN) p. 43 A network that extends over a long distance. Each network site is a node on the network.

Wi-Fi p. 283 A popular wireless LAN technology that allows multiple computers to connect to a LAN through a base station up to 150 feet away. Often referred to as 802.11b.

window p. 142 In a graphical user interface, a framed area that can be opened, closed, and rearranged with the mouse. Documents are displayed in windows.

Windows p. 143 See Microsoft Windows.

wireless keyboard p. 91 A keyboard that uses infrared signals rather than wires to communicate with a computer.

wireless network p. 276 A network in which a node has a tiny radio or infrared transmitter connected to its network port so it can send and receive data through the air rather than through cables.

wizard p. 160 A software help agent that walks the user through a complex process.

WMA p. 217 Windows Media Audio, one of a number of relatively new methods of audio compression than can squeeze music files to a fraction of their original CD-file sizes, often without perceptible loss of quality.

word size p. 76 The number of bits a CPU can process at one time, typically 8, 16, 32, or 64.

word wrap p. 159 The process of automatically moving words that do not fit on the current line to the next line in a document.

workflow p. 390 The path of information as it flows through a workgroup.

worksheet p. 176 A spreadsheet document that appears on the screen as a grid of numbered rows and columns.

workstation p. 39 A high-end desktop computer with massive computing power, though less expensive than a minicomputer. Workstations are the most powerful of the desktop computers.

World Wide Web (WWW) p. 17 Part of the Internet, a collection of multimedia documents created by organizations and users worldwide. Documents are linked in a hypertext Web that allows users to explore them with simple mouse clicks.

worms p. 354 Programs that use computer hosts to reproduce themselves. Worm programs travel independently over computer networks, seeking out uninfected workstations to occupy. A form of software sabotage.

writeback p. 75 The final phase of execution, in which the bus unit writes the results of the instruction back into memory or some other device.

WYSIWYG p. 159 Short for "what you see is what you get," pronounced "wizzy-wig." With a word processor, the arrangement of the words on the screen represents a close approximation to the arrangement of words on the printed page.

X

XHTML p. 327 Markup language that combines features of HTML and XML; its advantage is its backward compatibility with HTML.

XML p. 256 Extensible markup language, a language that enables Web developers to control and display data the way they control text and graphics. Forms, database queries, and other data-intensive operations that can't be completely constructed with standard HTML are much easier with XML.

Z

Zip disk p. 107 A popular type of removable cartridge storage media, developed by Iomega, that looks like a thicker version of a standard diskette and can hold up to 750MB of data.

Photo credits

4.17   Screen shots courtesy of Microsoft Corporation
4.18   Motorola, Inc.
4.19   Apple Computers, Inc.
4.20   Screen shot courtesy of Microsoft Corporation
4.22   OpenOffice.org
4.24   Courtesy of Microsoft Corporation
4.25   top: Argonne National Library
       bottom: Bill Sherman/Paul J. Rajlich
5.1   AP/Wide World Photos
5.2   Bootstrap Institute
5.6   Screen shots courtesy of Microsoft Corporation
5.7   Screen shot courtesy of Microsoft Corporation
5.8   Screen shot courtesy of Microsoft Corporation
5.9   top: Bartleby.com
       bottom: Internet Public Library
5.10   Screen shot courtesy of Microsoft Corporation
5.11   Screen shot courtesy of Microsoft Corporation
5.12   Screen shot courtesy of Microsoft Corporation
5.13   ScanSoft
5.14   Lonnie Duka/ Getty Images Inc. – Stone Allstock
5.16   Screens courtesy of Adobe Systems, Inc.
5.17   Courtesy of Adobe Systems, Inc.
5.18   David Patryas/Index Stock Imagery, Inc.
5.19   Courtesy of Salon.com
5.21   E Ink Corporation
5.22   Screen shot courtesy of Microsoft Corporation
5.23   Screen shots courtesy of Microsoft Corporation
5.24   Screen shots courtesy of Microsoft Corporation
5.25   Screen shot courtesy of Microsoft Corporation
5.28   Courtesy of Intuit, Inc.
5.31a Argonne National Laboratory
5.31b University of California, Los Angeles
5.32   Courtesy of Microsoft Corporation
5.33   top: Courtesy of Microsoft Corporation
       bottom: Courtesy of Laminar Research
6.1   © Sam Ogden
6.2   © CORBIS
6.3   Wacom Technology Corporation
6.4   Courtesy of Microsoft Corporation
6.6   Sanjay Kothari
6.7   Apple Computers, Inc.
6.8   MicroMedia
6.11   AP/Wide World Photos
6.12   Photo Researchers, Inc.
6.13   Screen shot courtesy of Microsoft Corporation
6.14   Screen shots courtesy of Microsoft Corporation
6.15   Courtesy of Macromedia, Inc.
6.18   Apple Computers, Inc.

6.19   Courtesy of Simon and Schuster Interactive and Knowledge Adventure
6.21   Courtesy of RioPort
6.22d Courtesy of Glyph/Image
6.22e Courtesy of Glyph/Image
6.23   Apple Computers, Inc.
6.24   Comstock Royalty Free Division
6.25   Courtesy of Ableton
6.26   Courtesy of Propellerhead Software
6.27   Courtesy of Sienna Software
6.28   Courtesy of Macromedia, Inc.
6.29   Mark Richards/PhotoEdit
6.30   David Barry/ Corbis/Outline
7.2   Courtesy of Microsoft Corporation
7.3   COPYRIGHT © EBAY INC. ALL RIGHTS RESERVED
7.5   Courtesy of Microsoft Corporation
7.6   Courtesy of Microsoft Corporation
7.7   Courtesy of Microsoft Corporation
7.8   Courtesy of NorthernLight.com
7.9   top: Courtesy of Apple Computers, Inc.
       bottom: Handspring, Inc.
7.10a Courtesy of Apple Computers, Inc.
7.10b Courtesy of Microsoft Corporation
7.10c Courtesy of Palm, Inc.
7.11   from left to right: © Tecmap Corporation; Eric Curry/CORBIS, © Jan Butchofsky-Houser/CORBIS, © David Cumming; Eye Ubiquitous/ CORBIS, © Solstice Photography/ Brand X Pictures/ PictureQuest, © PhotoLink/ Photodisc/ PictureQuest , © Royalty-Free/ CORBIS, © Solstice Photography/ Brand X Pictures/ PictureQuest, © Patrick Sheandell O Carroll/ PhotoAlto/ PictureQuest, © DigitalVision/ PictureQuest, © Royalty-Free/CORBIS, © David Samuel Robbins/CORBIS
7.14   (all) James A. Folts Photography
7.16   Courtesy of freeanswers.com
7.17   Robert E. Daemmrich/Getty Images, Inc.
7.19   The Image Bank/Getty Images, Inc.
7.20   AP/Wide World Photos
7.21   Peter Menzel Photography
8.1   Jeff Greenwald
8.2   Photofest
8.7   AP/Wide World Photos
8.8   Jean Miele/CORBIS Stock Market
8.9   AP/Wide World Photos
8.11   Courtesy of Linksys
8.12   (top to bottom) Champlain Cable Corporation; Courtesy of Inmac; Optical Cable Corp.; Extended Systems; Proxim, Inc.
8.13   AP/Wide World Photos
8.14   Getty Images Inc. – Stone Allstock
8.15   Reprinted with permission from Microsoft Corporation.
8.17   Courtesy of International Business Machines Corporation. Unauthorized use not permitted.
8.18   Courtesy of Microsoft Corporation
8.19   middle: Courtesy of Microsoft Corporation

       bottom: Courtesy of Apple Computers, Inc.
8.21   Courtesy of Google
8.22   Courtesy of AOL.com
8.23   Courtesy of Apple Computers, Inc.
8.24   Motorola
8.25   Qualcomm
9.1   © Clark Quinn
9.2   AP/Wide World Photos
9.4   school building: Courtesy of Yale University
       office buildings: © Steve Allen/ Brand X Pictures/ PictureQuest
9.5   (top to bottom) U.S. Robotics Corporation; Belken Components; Cisco Systems; Eicon Networks Inc.; NETGEAR, Inc.; Courtesy of Linksys; © CORBIS; Reprinted with permission from Microsoft Corporation.
9.6   © CORBIS
9.10   Courtesy of Microsoft Corporation
9.12   Screenshots Courtesy of Macromedia
9.13   top: Microsoft Corporation
       bottom: Apple Computers, Inc.
9.14   Courtesy of Shockwave.com
9.15   Amazon.com
9.16   Apple Computers, Inc.
9.17   Reproduced with permission of Yahoo! Inc. © 2003 by Yahoo! Inc. YAHOO! and the YAHOO! logo are trademarks of Yahoo! Inc.
9.18   SETI@Home Project
9.19   Tech Corps.
9.20   TimePix
9.21   Courtesy of NASA/JPL/Caltech
9.22   © The Electrolux Group
10.2   © CORBIS
10.3   Kensington Microware
10.4   Ivan Sekretarev/ AP/Wide World Photos
10.6   Screen shots courtesy of Symantec Corporation
10.7   © MARK POWELL/CORBIS SYGMA
10.8   left CheckPoint Technologies Software, Inc.
10.8   right Courtesy of Network Associates
10.11 Screen shot courtesy of Symantec Corporation
10.15 American Power Conversion Corporation
10.16 Courtesy of Snap Appliances
10.17 © 2001Versus Technology, Inc.
10.18 © AFP/CORBIS
10.19 © Mark Leffingwell/ AFP/CORBIS
10.21 Lucent Technologies/Bell Labs
10.22 Courtesy Sandia National Laboratories
11.1   John Barr/Getty Images, Inc.
11.2   Xerox Palo Alto Research Center
11.4   Copyright 1998, Courtesy of the Human Interface Technologies Laboratory, University of Washington.
11.5   Bill Bachman/Photo Researchers, Inc.
11.6   George Haling/Science Source/Photo Researchers
11.8   AP/Wide World Photos

11.9   MicroTouch Systems, Inc.
11.10   David Graham/Black Star
11.11   Telegraph Colour Library/FPG International LLC
11.12   Courtesy of Mattel Interactive
11.13   Courtesy of Princeton Review/The Learning Center
11.16   AP/Wide World Photos
11.17   Courtesy of Lucas Learning
11.18   Courtesy of MetaTools, Inc.
11.19   Courtesy of Henrico County Public Schools
11.20   Getty Images, Inc.
11.22   Morgen-Walke Associates
11.23   left: Courtesy of Yahoo.com
11.23   right: Courtesy of Del Lorme TopoUSA 2.0 © 2000
11.25   Argonne National Laboratory
11.26   Photo by Crystal Heald, courtesy of Network Productions
12.2   Courtesy of Intel
12.5   Photodisc/Getty Images, Inc.
12.11a-g © Jenny Thomas/Benjamin Cummings
12.12   Ford Motor Company
12.13   Photo Researchers, Inc.
12.17   Photodisc/Getty Images, Inc.
12.18   © Superstock
12.19a Scott Barrow/Superstock, Inc.
12.19b Bruce Forster/Tony Stone Images
12.19d Network Production/Rainbow
12.19e Tim Brown/Tony Stone Images
12.19f Stone
12.21   Courtesy of Professor Dr. Helmut Krcmar
12.22   Courtesy of Business Geographics Magazine
12.23a-d Corel® Quattro® Pro is a registered trademark of Corel Corporation Limited in Canada, the United States and/or other countries.

12.25   Courtesy of ComShare, Inc.
12.27   Corbis/Sygma
12.28   Getty Images
13.1   Reuters NewMedia Inc./CORBIS
13.2   © Macduff Everton/CORBIS
13.3   Courtesy of Matrix.net
13.4   RealEstate Plus
13.5   www.rei.com
13.6   Copyright © EBAY Inc. All rights reserved
13.10   FedEX
13.11   Courtesy of Apple
13.12   step 2: (right) Photodisc/Getty Images, Inc.
13.12   step 6: © Macduff Everton/CORBIS
13.12   screen shots: PC Connection
13.14   Courtesy Yahoo.com
13.15   Powells.com
14.1   U.S Navy News Photo
14.2   Naval Historical Center
14.3   © LWA-Sharie Kennedy/CORBIS
14.6a-c Courtesy of Microsoft Corporation
14.18a Robert E. Daemmrich/Getty Images, Inc.
14.18e The Image Bank
14.18f Stephan Derr/The Image Bank
14.18g Jim Craigmyle/Masterfile Corporation
14.24   Chad Slattery/Tony Stone Images
14.25   © PHIL SCHOFIELD/Getty Images
14.26   © Michael Melford/Getty Images
15.1   National Portrait Gallery, London
15.2   Photo Courtesy of the Computer Museum
15.4   © Corbis Bettman
15.5   © Corbis Bettman/Agence France Presse
15.9   Courtesy of Sun Microsystems
15.10   Becky Cohen
15.11   left: Agence France Presse/CORBIS
15.11   right: Becky Cohen

15.13   Courtesy of Sony
15.14   Lernout & Hauspie
15.16   Copyright Lawrence Ivy for the Merce Cunningham Dance Company
15.17   (clockwise from left) Courtesy of Industrial Video Systems; © Roger Ressmeyer/CORBIS
15.18   top left: Spencer Grant/Index Stock Imagery, Inc.
15.18   bottom left: Courtesy of Sony
15.18   top right: Peter Menzel, Photography
15.18   center right: Peter Menzel, Photography
15.18   bottom right: AP/Wide World Photos

Some images used in the following figures appear courtesy of:

1.7	7.15	9.3	10.10
2.4	8.5	9.4	10.12
3.7	8.6	9.8	10.13
4.23	8.10	9.9	10.14
5.15	8.16	9.11	
6.17	8.23	10.5	

Apple Computers, Inc.
Dell
Hewlett-Packard Company
Gateway
IBM Corporation
Imation Corp.
Microsoft Corporation
3com Corporation
Crucial Technology
Yamaha Corporation of America

Index

D. Hyde
12 Gregory Rd.
West Haven, CT 06516-3903